THE OFFICIAL®
PRICE GUIDE
TO
WATCHES

By **Cooksey Shugart** and **Tom Engle**

Edited by **Walter Presswood**

NINTH EDITION

HOUSE OF COLLECTIBLES
NEW YORK, NEW YORK 10022

Copyright © 1989 by Cooksey Shugart

All rights reserved under International and Pan-American Copyright Conventions.

Published by: The House of Collectibles
201 East 50th Street
New York, New York 10022

Distributed by Ballantine Books, a division of Random House, Inc., New York and simultaneously in Canada by Random House of Canada Limited, Toronto.

Manufactured in the United States of America

ISBN 0-876-37779-7

10 9 8 7 6 5 4 3 2 1

TABLE OF CONTENTS

Introduction..1
Collectamania 2
How to Use This Book 4
Appraising Watches 6
Grading Watches 8
Collecting on a Limited Budget...10
1988 Market Report 11
Chronology of Watches 18
History...22
That Great American Railroad Pocket Watch 25
Railroad Grade Watch Adjustments...29
Railroad Watch Dials 31
Railroad Watch Cases 32
Railroad Grade or Railroad Approved Watches 33
Colonial Watchmakers 39
The Gruen 50th Anniversary Watch 43
Prestige Watches 46
Repeating Watches..47
Outstanding, High-Grade and Scarce Watches 48
Watch Cases 51
Watch Size Gauges..54
Case Prices 61
Movement Identification 62
Nomenclature of Watch Parts 63
Inspecting Open-Faced Watches 65
Damaskeening 65
Display Case Watches 66
Watch Case Production 66
Gold Case Weights by Size..66
Care of Watches...67
Examination and Inspection of a Watch Before Purchasing 67
Watch Movement Parts..69
How a Watch Works...70
Regulators Identification...73
Jewels & Pivots...85
Winding & Setting 89
Cottage Industry Watchmaking in Colonial America 94
Ebauches 95
Worm Gear Escapement 98
Dial Making 98
Pin Lever Escapement (Dollar Watches) 100
Low Cost Production Watches (Dollar Watches)...............................101
Personalized Watches 104
Swiss Imported Fakes 105

American Pocket Watches (Pricing) 107
Abbreviations Used in *The Official Price Guide to Watches* 109
Comic & Character Watches 394
European Pocket Watches 405
Early Antique Watches 406
Clues to Dating Your Watch 408
Early European Watchmakers 412
Protecting Antique Watch Movements 417
Hallmarks of London 418
European Watches Collected in America 420
Repeating Watches 431
Tourbillon 449
Musical Watches 449
Production Totals 450
European Pocket Watch Listings (Pricing) 451
American & European Wrist Watches 487
Romancing The Wrist Watch 488
A Short History of Wrist Watches 491
Automatic Winding 493
How to read the Tachy-Telemeter dial 494
Chronograph 497
Swiss Code Initials 500
Wrist Watch Listings (Pricing) 501
Watch Terminology 686

ACKNOWLEDGMENTS

The success of previous editions of **The Official® Price Guide to Watches,** first published in 1980 (originally entitled **The Complete Guide to American Pocket Watches**) has been indeed gratifying. It is a humbling experience for any author to see a work accepted so well by a market so diverse as the watch field. Numerous people have told me that the market was anxious for a book of this type, and it is my hope that this book has lived up to their expectations.

We will endeavor to improve future editions of this book by incorporating suggestions, ideas, and new information from people throughout the field. This, we feel, will result in a continually updated and helpful guide.

I am especially appreciative of Bob Overstreet, author of **The Official® Overstreet Comic Book Price Guide**, for his encouragement.

To Walter Presswood, who is the editor of **The Official® Price Guide to Watches.**

To my wife Martha, for her complete understanding and assistance in compiling this book;

To the NAWCC Museum, Hamilton Watch Co., and Bowman Technical School, for allowing us to photograph their watches;

To Christie's and Osvaldo Patrizzi for photographs of watches;

And to the following people whose help was invaluable and will be long remembered: Frank Irick, John Cubbins, Harold Harris, Paul Gibson, Robert L. Ravel, M.D., William C. Heilman Jr., M.D., Thomas McEntyre, Paul Morgan, Bill Selover, Oscar Laube, Ed Kieft, Charles Wallace, Bob Walters, Jack Warren, Howard Schroeder, Edward M. McGinnis, James Gardner, Paul Zuercher, Irving E. Roth, Don Bass, Stephen Polednak, Dick Stacy, Ernest J. Lewis, Herbert McDonald, David Steger, Fred Favour, Ralph Warner, Estus Harris, Charles Cleves, Tom McIntyre, Ralph Ferone, Arnold C. Varey, Jeffrey Ollswang, Tom Rohr, Leon Beard, Glenn Smith, Kenneth Vergin, Thomas Rumpf, Denford Jones Photographics; and a special thanks to Peter Kushnir, Dr. J. Mauss, Robert D. Gruen, Jeff Hess, Col. R. A. Mulholland, Dick Ziebell, Jack Warren, Ron Starnes, Dick Flaute, Ralph Vinge, Edward Fletcher, Richard Walker, Alex Wolanguk, Carl Goetz, Miles Sandler, Dave Mycko (comic characters), and Martin Cullen.

* * *

Send only corrections, additions, deletions and comments to Cooksey Shugart, 780 Church St. N.E., Cleveland, TN 37311. When corresponding, please send a self-addressed, stamped envelope.

Special pricing consultants:

Dan Crawley	David Searles	Paul A. Duggan	Geoff White
(Dollar Watches)	(Foreign Watches)	(Wrist Watches)	(Complicated Watches)

INTRODUCTION

This book is dedicated to all watch collectors who we hope will find it an enjoyable and valuable reference to carry on buying trips or to trace the lost history of that priceless family heirloom.

The origin of this book began when I was given a pocket watch which had been in our family for many years. After receiving the prized heirloom I wanted to know its complete history, and thus the search began. Because of the lack of a comprehensive reference on American pocket watches the venture took me through volume after volume. Over the course of ten years many hours were accumulated in running down the history of this one watch. But the research sparked my interest in the pocket watch field and pointed to the need for a book such as this one. We hope it will provide the information that you are looking for.
— The Authors

Watches are unique collectibles. Since the beginning of civilization when man scooped up a handful of sand and created the hourglass, portable timepieces have held a fascination that demanded the attention of the wealthy and poor alike. Man has sought constantly to improve his time-measuring instruments and has made them with the finest metals and jewels. The pocket watch, in particular, became an ornamentation and a source of pride, and this accounts for its value among families for generation after generation.

The watch has become precious and sentimental to so many because it is one of the true personal companions of the individual night and day. Mahatma Gandhi, the father of India and one of the rare people in history who was able to renounce worldly possessions, was obsessed with the proper use of his time. Each minute, he held, was to be used in the service of his fellowman. His own days were ordered by one of his few personal possessions, a sixteen-year-old, eight-shilling Ingersoll pocket watch that was always tied to his waist with a piece of string.

Another factor that has made watches unique collectibles is the intricate artisanship with which they are put together. Many of the watches of yesteryear, which were assembled with extreme accuracy and fine workmanship, continue to be reliable timepieces today. They stand out as unique because that type of watch is no longer manufactured. In today's world of mass production, the watch with individual craftmanship containing precious jewels and metals can rarely be found—and, if found, it is rarely affordable.

The well-made watch is a tribute to man's skills, artisanship and craftsmanship at their finest level. That is why the watch holds a special place in the collectible field.

In America, there are about 80,000 avid watch collectors. About 5 million people own two or more watches, and an untold number possess at least one of these precious heirlooms.

The Official®   Price Guide to Watches does not attempt to estabtablish or fix values or selling prices in the pocket watch trade market.

It does, however, *reflect* the trends of buying and selling in the collector market. Prices listed in this volume are based on data collected and analyzed from dealers and shops all over the country.

These prices should serve the collector as a guide only. The price you pay for any watch will be determined by the value it has to you. The intrinsic value of any particular watch can be measured only by you, the collector, and a fair price can be derived only after mutual agreement between both the buyer and the seller.

It is our hope that this volume can help make your watch collecting venture both pleasurable and profitable.

Information contained herein may not necessarily apply to every situation. Data is still being found, which may alter statements made in this book. These changes, however, will be reflected in future editions.

Hopefully, everyone interested in horology will research the American pocket watch and add to his library on the subject.

COLLECTAMÁNIA

Hobby — Business — Pastime — Entertainment

Just name it. More than likely someone will want to buy or sell it: books, coins, stamps, bottles, beer cans, gold, glassware, baseball cards, guns, clocks, pocket watches, comics, art, cars, and....the list goes on and on.

Most Americans seem to be caught up in *collectamania*. More and more Americans are spending hour after hour searching through antique shops, auctions, flea markets and yard sales for those rare treasures of delight that have been lying tucked away for generations just waiting to be found.

This sudden boom in the field of collecting may have been influenced by fears of inflation or disenchantment with other types of investments. But more people are coming into the field because they gain some degree of nostalgic satisfaction from these new tangible ties with yesteryear. Collecting provides great fun and excitement. The tales of collecting and the resultant "fabulous finds" could fill volumes and inspire even the non-collector to embark upon a treasure hunt.

Collecting for the primary purpose of investment may prove to have many pitfalls for the amateur. The lack of sufficient knowledge is the No. 1 cause for disappointment. The inability to spot fakes or flawed merchandise can turn excitement into disappointment. And, in many fields, high-class forgers are at work, doing good and faithful reproductions in large quantities that can sometimes fool even the experts the first time they see them.

Collecting for fun and profit can be just that if you observe a fair amount of caution. Always remember, amidst your enthusiasm, that an object may not be what it would first appear. Below are a few guidelines that may be helpful to you:

1. **Make up your mind** as to what you want to collect and concentrate in this area. Your field of collecting should be one that you have a genuine liking for, and it helps if you can use the objects. It may help also to narrow your field even further, for instance, in collecting watches, to choose only one company or one type of pocket watch.

2. **Gain all the knowledge you can** about the objects you collect. The more knowledge you have the more successful you will be in finding valuable, quality pieces. Amassing the knowledge required to be a good collector is easier if you have narrowed your scope of interest. Otherwise, it may take years to become an "expert." Don't try to learn everything there is to know about a variety of fields. This will end in frustration and disappointment. Specialize.

3. **Buy the best you can afford,** assuming the prices are fair. The advanced collector may want only mint articles; but the novice collector may be willing to accept something far less than mint condition due to caution and economics. Collectible items in better condition continue to rise in value at a steady rate.

4. **Deal with reputable dealers** whom you can trust. Talk with the dealer; get to know the seller; get a business card; know where you can contact the dealer if you have problems, or if you want the dealer to help you find something else you may be looking for.

HOROLOGICAL PUZZLE

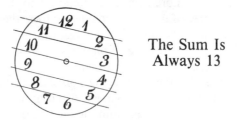

The Sum Is
Always 13

HOW TO USE THIS BOOK

The Official® Price Guide to Watches is a simple reference, with clear and carefully selected information. The first part of the book is devoted to history, general information, and a how-to section. The second part of the guide consists mainly of a listing of watch manufacturers, identification guides, and prices. This is a unique book because it is designed to be taken along as a handy pocket reference for identifying and pricing watches. With the aid of this book, the collector should be able to make on-the-spot judgments as to identification, age, quality, and value. This complete guide and a pocket magnifying glass will be all you need to take on your buying trips.

*   *   *

Watch collecting is fast growing as a hobby and business. Many people collect for the enjoyment and profit. The popularity of watches continues to rise because watches are a part of history. The American railroad brought about the greatest watch of that time—the railroad pocket watch. Since that time America has produced some of the best quality pocket watches that money could buy. The gold-filled cases made in America have never been surpassed in quality or price in the foreign market. With the quality of movement and cases being made with *guaranteed* high standards as well as beauty, the American pocket watch became very desirable. Because they are no longer being made in the U. S. A., pocket watches continue to rise in value.

The watch is collected for its beauty, quality in movement and case, and the value of metal content. Solid gold is the top of the line; platinum and silver are also very desirable. (Consider that some watches in the early 1900s sold between $700 and $1,000. This is equal to or greater than the price of a good car of the same period.)

As with limited edition prints, a watch of supreme excellence is also limited and will increase in value. There is universal appeal and excitement in owning a piece of history, and your heirloom is just that. At one time pocket watches were a status symbol. Everyone competed for beauty and quality in the movement and case. Solid gold cases were adorned with elaborate engravings, diamonds, and other precious jewels. The movements were beautiful and of high quality. Manufacturers went to great lengths to provide movements that were both accurate and lovely. Fancy damaskeening on the back plates of nickel with gold lettering, 26 jewels in gold settings, and a solid gold train (gears) were features of some of the more elaborate timepieces. The jewels were red rubies, or diamond-end stones, or sapphires for the pallet stones. There were gold timing screws, and more. The faces were made by the best artisans of the day— hand-painted, jewel-studded, with fancy hands and double-sunk dials made of enamel and precious metals.

*   *   *

HOW TO DETERMINE MANUFACTURER

When identifying a watch, look on the face or dial for the name of the company and then refer to the alphabetical list of watch companies in this book. If the face or dial does not reveal the company name you will have to seek information from the movement's back plate. The company name or the town where it was manufactured will likely be inscribed there. The name engraved on the back plate is referred to as the "signature." After locating the place of manufacture, see what companies manufactured in that town. This may require reading the histories of several companies to find the exact one. Use the process of elimination to narrow the list.

Note: Some of the hard-to-identify watches are extremely collectible and valuable. Therefore, it is important to learn to identify them.

HOW TO DETERMINE AGE

After establishing the name of the manufacturer, you may be interested in the age of the watch. This information can be obtained by using the serial number inscribed on the back movement plate and referring to the production table. It is often difficult to establish the exact age, but this method will put you within a two- or three-year period of the date of the manufacture.

The case that houses the movement is not necessarily a good clue to the origin of the movement. It was a common practice for manufacturers to ship the movements to the jewelers and watchmakers uncased. The customer then married the movement and case. That explains why an expensive movement can be found in a cheaper case or vice versa.

If the "manufacturer's" name and location are no help, the inscription could possibly be that of a jeweler and his location. Then it becomes obvious there is no quick and easy way to identify some American-made watches. However, the following steps may be helpful. Some watches can be identified by comparing the models of each company until the correct model is found. Start by sizing the watch and then comparing the varied plate shapes and styles. The cock or bridge for the balance may also be a clue. The general arrangement of the movement as to jeweling, whether it is an open face or hunting case, and style of regulators may help to find the correct identification of the manufacturer of the movement.

Numbers on a watch case should not be considered as clues to the age of the movement because cases were both American- and foreign-made, and many of the good watches were re-cased through the years.

APPRAISING WATCHES

Watch collecting is still young when compared to fields of the standard collectibles: coins and stamps. The watch collecting field is growing but information is still scarce, fragmented, and sometimes unreliable. To be knowledgeable in any field, one must spend the time required to study it.

The value of any collectible is determined first by demand. Without demand there is no market. In the watch trade, the law of supply and demand is also true. The supply of the American watches has stopped and the demand among collectors continues to rise. There are many factors that make a watch desired or in demand. Only time and study will tell a collector just which watches are most collectible. After the collector or investor finds out what is desirable, then a value must be placed on it before it is sold. If it is priced too high, the watch will not sell; but, on the other hand, if it is priced too low, it will be hard to replace at the selling price. The dealer must arrive at a fair market price that will move the watch.

There are no two watches alike. This makes the appraising more difficult and oftentimes arbitrary. But there are certain guidelines one can follow to arrive at a fair market price. When watches were manufactured, most companies sold the movements to a jeweler, and the buyer had a choice of dials and cases. Some high-grade movements were placed in a low-grade case and vice versa. Some had hand-painted multicolored dials; some were plain. The list of contrasts goes on. Conditions of watches will vary greatly, and this is a big factor in the value. The best movement in the best original case will bring the top price for any type of pocket watch.

Prices are constantly changing in the watch field. Gold and silver markets affect the price of the cases. Scarcity and age also affect the value. These prices will fluctuate regularly.

APPRAISING GUIDELINES

Demand, supply, condition, and **value** must be the prime factors in appraising an old watch.

Demand is the most important element. Demand can be determined by the number of buyers for the particular item. A simple but true axiom is that value is determined by the price someone is willing to pay.

In order to obtain a better knowledge in appraising and judging watches, the following guidelines are most useful. Consider all these factors before placing a value on the watch. (There is no rank or priority to the considerations listed.)

1. Demand: Is it high or low?
2. Availability: How rare or scarce is the watch?
   How many of the total production remain?
3. Condition of both the case and movement **(very important)**.
4. Low serial numbers: The first one made would be more valuable than later models.
5. Historical value.
6. Age.
7. Is it an early handmade watch?
8. Type of case: beauty and eye appeal; value of metal content.
9. Is it in its original case? **(very important)**.
10. Complications: Repeaters, for example.

11. Type of escapement.
12. Size, number of jewels, type of plates (¾, full and bridge), type of balance, type of winding (key-wind, lever-set, etc.), number of adjustments, gold jeweled settings, damaskeening, gold train.
13. What grade of condition is it? Pristine, Mint, Extra Fine, Average, Fair, or Scrap?
14. Identification ability.
15. Future potential as an investment.
16. Quality (high or low grade), or low cost production watches (dollar watch).
17. How much will this watch scrap out for?

GRADING WATCHES

Pricing in this book is based on the following grading system:

PRISTINE MINT (G-10): Absolutely factory new; sealed in factory box with wax paper still intact.

MINT PLUS (G-9): Still in factory box; has had paper removed for inspection only; has never been used.

MINT (G-8): Same as factory new but with very little use; no faint scratches; is original in every way—crystal, hands, dial, case, movement; used briefly and stored away; may be in box.

NEAR MINT (G-7): Completely original in every way; faint marks may be seen with a loop only; expertly repaired; movement may have been cleaned and oiled.

EXTRA FINE (G-6): May or may not be in factory box; looks as though watch was used very little; crystal may have been replaced; original case, hands, dial, and movement. If watch has been repaired, all original replacement parts have been used. Faint case scratches are evident but hard to detect with the eye. No dents and no hairline on dial are detectable.

FINE (G-5): May have new hands and new crystal, but original case, dial and movement; faint hairline in dial; no large scratches on case; slight stain on movement; movement must be sharp with only minor scratches.

AVERAGE (G-4): Original case, dial and movement; movement may have had a part replaced, but part was near to original; slight brass showing through on gold-filled case; no rust or chips in dial; may have hairlines in dial that are hard to see. All marks are hard to detect, but may be seen without a loop.

FAIR (G-3): Hairlines in dial and small chips; brass can be seen through worn spots on gold-filled case; rust marks in movement; a small dent in case; wear in case, dial, and movement; well used; may not have original dial or case.

POOR (G-2): Watch may not run; needs new dial; case well worn, with many dents; hands may be gone; replacement crystal may be needed.

SCRAP (G-1): Not running; bad dial; rusty movement; brass showing badly; may not have case; some parts not original; no crystal or hands. Good for parts.

Below is an example of how the price is affected by the different grades of the same watch:

Hamilton 992B

G-10	$290
G-9	$255
G-8	$225
G-7	$200
G-6	$175
G-5	$160
G-4	$150
G-3	$70
G-2	$45
G-1	$35

The value of a watch can only be assessed after the watch has been carefully inspected and graded. It may be difficult to evaluate a watch honestly and objectively, especially in the rare or scarce models.

If the watch has any defects, such as a small scratch on it, it can not be Pristine. It is important to realize that older watches in grades of Extra Fine or above are extremely rare and may never be found.

COLLECTING ON A LIMITED BUDGET

Most collectors are always looking for that sleeper, which *is* out there waiting to be found. One story goes that the collector went into a pawn shop and asked the owner if he had any gold pocket watches for sale. The pawn broker replied, "No, but I have a 23J silver cased pocket watch at a good price." Even though the pocket watch was in a cheaper case, the collector decided to further explore the movement. When he opened the back to look at the movement, there he saw engraved on the plates 24J Bunn Special and knew immediately he wanted to buy the pocket watch. The movement was running, and looked to be in first grade shape. The collector asked the price. The broker said he has been trying to get rid of the pocket watch, but had no luck and if he wanted it, he would sell it for $35. The collector took the pocket watch and replaced the bent-up silver case for a gold-filled J. Boss case, and sold it a month later for $400. He had a total of $100 invested when he sold it, netting a cool $300 profit.

Most collectors want a pocket watch that is in mint or near-mint condition and original in every way. But consider the railroad pocket watches such as the Bunn Special in a cheaper case. The railroad man was compelled to buy a watch with a quality movement, even though he may have only been able to afford a cheap case. The railroad man had to have a pocket watch that met certain standards set by the railroad company. A watch should always be judged on quality and performance and not just on its appearance. The American railroad pocket watch was unsurpassed in reliability. It was durable and accurate for its time, and that accounts for its continuing value today.

If you are a limited-budget collector, you would be well advised not to go beyond your means. But watch collecting can still be an interesting, adventurous, and profitable hobby. If you are to be successful in quadrupling your purchases that you believe to be sleepers, you must first be a hard worker, have perserverence and let shrewdness and skill of knowledge take the place of money. A good starting place is to get a working knowledge of how a pocket watch works. Learn the basic skills such as cleaning, mainspring and staff replacement. One does not have to be a watchmaker, but should learn the names of parts and what they do. If a watch that you are considering buying does not work, you should know how and what it takes to get it in good running order or pass it by. Stay away from pocket watches that do not wind and set. Also avoid "odd" movements that you hope to be able to find a case for. Old watches with broken or missing parts are expensive and all but impossible to have repaired. Some parts must be made by hand. The odd and low-cost production watches are fun to get but hard to repair. Start out on the more common basic-jeweled lever pocket watches. The older the watch, the harder it is to get parts. Buy an inexpensive pocket watch movement that runs and play with it. Get the one that is newer and for which parts can be bought; and get a book on watch repairing.

You will need to know the history and demand of a watch. Know what collectors are looking for in your area. If you cannot find a buyer, then, of course, someone else's stock has become yours.

1988 MARKET REPORT

Sales at Christie's, Sotheby's, and Habsburg-Feldman auction houses were very successful. Most of the fine timepieces purchased there have gone to the European collectors. American investors should take note of that fact. Habsburg-Feldman set a record with the Patek, Philippe & Co. minute repeating, platinum wrist watch, circa 1920s, bringing the outstanding price of 345,000 Swiss francs, or about $246,500 U.S. Patek, Philippe & Co. enameled, white gold "world time," with a 24-hour dial showing time in 41 cities, also brought a fine price at 195,500 Swiss francs, or about $139,640 U.S. A rectangular perpetual moon phase by Audemars Piguet, made for E. Gubelin, sold for about $105,000 U.S. The first pocket watch made by Elgin, Serial No. 101, was sold by Christie's and fetched a price of $12,000, which was a good buy for the bidder.

Patek, Philippe & Co. World Time with a 24-hour dial showing time in 41 cities. Sold for about $139,640 U.S. dollars.

Patek, Philippe & Co. face and movement. Sold by Habsburg-Feldman for a record price of about $246,500 U.S. dollars.

Railroad pocket watches remained as solid as a rock this year. As in past years, they seem to be as stable as ever in both the buying and selling markets. Wrist watches continue to be good sellers, with complicated timepieces leading the way. Wrist watches with time only must have unusual case design to have a strong appeal to the buyer. Wrist watches in all grades, having a poor finish on the dial or case, are not selling. The dial and hands must match, also. Such things affecting the condition and the overall beauty of a watch make a big difference to collectors.

SPECIAL AUCTION REPORT

Collectors and dealers from the United States and Europe gathered in New York City on Tuesday, June 21, 1988, for the sale at auction of the collection of the late Dr. Warner D. Bundens, past president of the N.A.W.C.C. The sale was held at Sotheby's on York Avenue.

Dr. Bundens, an orthopedic surgeon, was widely known and respected as a collector of American watches, although his interests extended to fine European watches as well. His collection was enhanced when Col. George E. Townsend, author of **Almost Everything You Wanted to Know About American Watches But Didn't Know Whom to Ask,** bequeathed his collection to his longtime friend.

The rarities offered were stunning by their sheer quantity alone: seven Albert Potter watches including a one minute tourbillon ($24,200) (prices include 10 percent buyer's premium); Serial No. 1 ($17,600); Chronometer No. 44 ($7,150); a superb gold calendar watch ($9,900); as well as a rare W. C. Potter chronometer ($8,800), and two Potter ebauches ($1,540). The fact that certain of the Potter watches were recased diminished the interest of some bidders, but enthusiasm was nevertheless strong, and the prices attained were reasonable, given the condition and state of originality.

The sale was not without surprises, the most notable being the Howard pocket watch with helical hairspring (Lot 57). The catalogue failed to note this important variation, as well as the distinctive plate layout that reminds one more of the Series II than any standard Series III. Although in an associated Howard Series III case of later period, the rarity of the piece is immense, with fewer than five examples known to exist from this important experimental period. The gallery, which had estimated the watch at $700-$900, collectively blushed as they announced the correction to the catalogue description, and blushed again as the price rocketed to a whopping $18,700.

Other Howards included a superb 18K Series VII hunter cased watch, with foliate engraving in a scallop shell pattern, in mint condition ($3,300); a Series I movement, No. 721, recased in a display case ($1,430); a massive 18K Series III keywind hunter cased watch in fine condition ($4,125); an Edward Howard movement in display case, No. 278 ($1,925); and a number of other 18K and 14K L and N size watches.

Of interest among the products of the American Waltham Watch Co. were: a Dennison, Howard & Davis Model 1857, No. 1540 ($990); a C. T. Parker pin-plate, No. 1024 ($1,045); a recased Chronodrometer ($1,100); a fine 18K hunting cased 16-size KW model with vibrating hairspring (the hairspring was not catalogued) ($1,650); and a recased Premier Maximus ($2,475).

A fine grouping of Waltham chronographs and repeaters was highlighted by the split-second chronograph five minute repeater No. 3793201. This watch was apparently the first in a run of 10 watches made with some participation from C. H. Meylan, which has yet to be documented. Of the lot of 10, the following watches have come to light: two perpetual calendar five minute repeaters, three one minute repeaters, two with chronograph, and rumours of a clockwatch, as yet unsubstantiated. No other split chronograph five minute repeater is known to this author at present. As this history is only known by a limited number of people and was not published in the catalogue, the watch slipped through at a very reasonable price of $7,700.

The Waltham collection sale reached its culmination with the offering of Warren No. 29, ostensibly the 12th American factory production timepiece of the Model 1857. One of only a handful of surviving examples, the watch is of extreme historic importance, and, although recased, fetched a price of $29,700. A fine Samuel Curtis, No. 418, was sold next, followed by two rare 4-size crystal plate Walthams ($8,250 each).

"Caveat emptor" is, of course, the necessary watchword at any auction or in any market, and this sale was no exception. Lot 50, a Grade 947 Hamilton, was a case in point: Serial No. 239126 is printed on the main plate, and the 947 and 23 Jewels markings are on the barrel plate, as well as the barrel arbor jewel. Consultation with the Hamilton serial number lists shows No. 239126 as being a Grade 943, 21 jewel, hunting movement. If the serial number list is correct, then the 947 barrel plate was simply added to the 943 movement. Was there a mistake in the serial list or was Lot 50 not what it appeared to be? The answer may only come with the disassembling of the watch to see if all plate ID numbers match. This risk cost $6,050.

Other rare watches included a Fasoldt, recased in a perfect gold copy of an original Fasoldt case ($8,250); a 21 jewel Pennsylvania Special ($880). A fine 20 jewel Lancaster No. 1415 ($3,300 with a Newark); a lot of three Dan Patch watches ($1,650); a gold hunting cased Otay ($3,575); a recased G. P. Reed ($3,575); an 18-size Rockford 21 jewel wind indicator ($2,475); a lovely and very rare G. P. Reed Monitor, running two days with calendar dial, 18K ($12,100); J. P. Stevens No. 54 ($2,750); and a Geneva Potter made for J. P. Stevens ($4,950).

Almost 200 railroad watches went off the block, singly or in lots, as well as 62 Waterbury watches in one lot ($5,225). There were a number of American clocks, carriage clocks, ship's chronometers and deck watches. Balance cocks and watch keys formed another delightful segment to the sale.

The remainder of the sale consisted of fine European watches of many varieties. Highlights included a fine gold openface Patek Philippe minute repeating split chronograph with register ($9,570); a large gold double dial world time watch with moon phases and calendar for Henry Lewis & Co. ($6,875.); a number of novelty watches: an attractive quarter repeating Adolf Lange hunting cased watch ($12,100); a recased Patek Philippe minute repeating, perpetual calendar chronograph with moon phases ($14,300); some fine enamel form watches and ladies' enamel watches; a superb platinum, diamond and enamel lapel watch and fob, Cartier ($8,250); and an attractive gold skeleton automaton repeater with concealed erotic automation ($9,075).

Breguet watches were a feature of the afternoon, including a montre-a-tact ($9,075); a gold key with moon phase calendar ($6,600);

and a fine gold subscription watch ($18,700). The sale ended with some handsome enamel watches, many of which were passed owing to excessive reserves, and finally, a J. R. Arnold pocket chronometer in later case ($4,400); a rare gold calendar pair case, ca. 1758, (18,700); and a gold pair case watch by Thomas Tompion ($4,675).

Prices in general reflected strong enthusiam for the material and the reputation of the source. It was a sale where dealer participation was largely incidental, while the collectors dominated the bidding. Buyers, upon questioning, were generally delighted with their purchases, and only disappointed that they could not buy more.

RECORD-SETTING PRICES

Two records were broken in 1986 when the hammer fell at Christie's, signaling a new era of watch collecting. Record-setting prices were paid for both a pocket watch and a wrist watch.

The pocket watch that commanded more than a million dollars was a rare mid-17th century superb blue enamel and diamond-decorated watch which brought 1,870,000 Swiss francs or about $1,038,889 US. A wristwatch, considered to be a newer field of collectibles, also set a record at 287,000 Swiss francs or about $158,899 US. The wristwatch was a rare gold-cased perpetual calendar bracelet watch with split seconds.

The pocket watch was a highly important rare French gold, enamel, and diamond-set watch, signed Jehan Cremsdorff, Paris, and made circa 1650. The case is considered to be one of the finest examples of enameling in the manner of the Blois school and incorporates the techniques of champleve, *en relief* and *peinture en camaieu* on enamel. The richness and variety of enamel techniques, used in the construction of the case of gold and turquoise blue enamel, are unrivaled. It has been encrusted with additional gold in high relief, which is partly chaised and partly enameled with flowers in a technique known as *l'emaillage sur ronde-bosse d'or*. The pendant is in the form of a ribbon tie, also in the turquoise blue enamel. The hinged cover is also decorated with a star pattern of baguette-cut diamonds flanked by diamond-set flowers. Turquoise blue enamel was used in many interiors of watch cases in the 17th Century but only four or five watches are known to exist with the case entirely decorated in the turquoise blue color. The case work was probably done by Henri Toutaia, a goldsmith in Chateaudun, France.

The Cremsdorff movement has circular gilt plates. The balance cock is held in place with a screw in the center. The ratchet-wheel set-up is elaborately hand-pierced, while the ratchet wheel is made of blued-steel with a locking spring. The pillars are of the pierced Egyptian style. The works has the short train of gears in which a three-wheel train lacks the center wheel. (The fusee now has a chain, and the verge type escapement now has a later type brass balance.) The size of the watch is about 60mm.

The owner prior to the sale had little idea as to the value of the watch. He reported it had been valued in 1978 for about 600 Swiss francs or $335 US. Christie's consultant, however, identified it as an important watch.

It is a watch of incomparable quality and beauty, extremely rare, and may not be seen for sale again for a great while.

The other record price, in the newer collectible field of wrist watches, was set with a rare gold cased gentleman's size perpetual calendar bracelet watch with split-second chronographs made by Patek, Philippe & Co. in 1955. The Patek Philippe firm was the successful bidder at 287,000 Swiss francs or about $158,899 US.

This high grade watch was commissioned to be made by E. Gubelin and is one of three examples thought to have been made. The gold bracelet of unusual reeded square panels was supplied by Gubelin. The movement is damaskeened with a nickel finish. The 25-jeweled movement has a gilt train. The movement was adjusted for eight positions. The dial is a matte silvered dial signed Patek Philippe Geneve and

Left: Patek Phillippe movement finished by E. Gubelin, minute repeater, which sold for about $55,000. **Center: Patek Phillippe** split-second chronograph with day-date & moon phases sold for about $48,000. **Right: Patek Phillippe** movement finished by E. Gubelin, split-second chronograph with day-date & moon phases, sold for about $158,899.

Gubelin. The perpetual calendar with apertures for the weekday and month are at 12 o'clock position, and the date can be seen at the 6 o'clock position with the moon phases. The fly back split center-seconds chronograph with 30-minute recording is at the 3 o'clock position and continuous seconds is at the 9 o'clock position, with an outer tachometric recording scale. The movement is 39mm in size.

Also two wrist watches by Patek Philippe in the mechanical watch period brought exciting prices. A minute repeating gold cased and bracelet finished by Gubelin in May 1956 fetched a price of 99,000 Swiss francs or about $55,000 US. Also, a watch presented to a member of King Hussein's family of Jordan brought a price of 88,000 Swiss francs or about $48,900 US. This was a gold-cased leather bracelet watch. The watch is a chronograph with fly-back center-seconds, and an outer tachometric recording scale and subsidiary 30-minute recording at 3 o'clock with continuous seconds at 6 o'clock. The watch also has a perpetual calendar with day, date, month, and moon phases.

Longines Aviator wrist watch in large gold case. Only eight are known to exist. This watch was manufactured March 6, 1937 and sold for about $27,000 in 1986.

    A large and very rare gold-cased aviator's watch by Longines was purchased by Longines for its museum. The price paid was 49,500 Swiss francs or about $27,500 US. This watch was manufactured by the Longines Wittnauer Co. from a design provided by Col. Charles A. Lindberg. The watch was supplied on March 6, 1937, through their Portuguese agents. The standard movements were either in silver or nickel cases and it is believed that no more than eight were made in gold. The massive case is 18K gold and about 47mm in diameter.

    Two pocket watches by Breguet, "souscripton" watches, brought $11,975 US and $10,890 US, respectively. A pocket watch by Louis Raby, watchmaker to Napoleon III, sold for about $12,100 US.

CHRONOLOGY
OF
WATCHES

1500   First watches being made.
1505   Stackfreed came into use.
1515   French watches appear.
1525   Fuzee being used.

1530	Brass plates used for the first time.
1550	Oval or egg-shaped watches in vogue.
1570	Octagon- and hexagonal-shaped watches in vogue.
1575	Mechanism for setting up the mainspring was developed (pre-wind up).
1585	Swiss watches first appear.
1590	Chain for the fuzee first used. (Became more popular about 1650.)
1595	Rock crystal cases made.
1600	English watches first appear.
1610	Most watches were being signed.
1620	Glass used on watches to help protect dial; tabs under glass were used.
1625	"Form watches"—bizzare-shaped skulls, books, crosses, etc. produced.
1630	Tortoise shell cases first used; these lasted until 1800.
1632	Enamel was being painted in colors.
1635	White enamel dials and worm gear were used.
1640	Pair cases appear.
1650	Repousse in both gold and silver was produced.
1660	Rim used on the outer edge of the balance cock.
1675	Spiral balance spring was being used.
1677	Repeating watch with rack form of striking was produced.
1678	Four-wheel train was developed.
1680	Serial numbers began to appear as well as hallmarks. Cottage industry or subdivision begins.
1685	Regulator first used with balance spring.
1687	Minute hand appears.
1695	Cylinder escapement (became more popular in the 1800s).
1700	Jewels used in Swiss watches (first used in 1750 by English; initially for end stones).

English watch produced about 1600. Note balance cock is pinned to back plate.

English watch produced about 1650. Note endless screw type regulator.

1710	Dust band.
1715	Oil sink used.
1725	Rach lever used.
1750	Compensation balance introduced; all white dials made of enamel; center second hand; dumb repeaters; duplex escapements.
1760	Chronometer escapement used seconds bit at 6 o'clock position.

1765   Lever escapement developed by Mudge.

1770   Separate bridges start on ebauches movements; fusee cutting engine being used.

1774   Dust cap seen.

1780   Thinner watches seen, helical hair spring developed, gong wires bells began to disappear.

1790   Watches with movable figures manufactured; overcoil used by Breguet.

1800   Club foot escapement devised, single case replaces pair case, tourbillon escapement invented by Breguet.

1810   Spherical balance spring was developed.

1820   Winding by using the button on the pendant.

1856   Screw-on bezel was invented.

1859   Gold-filled cases were patented.

TRANSFORMATION IN THE WATCH
1530-1965

1550

Foliot

1630

Ratchet wheel Click   Cock   Pallet
Upper plate   Winding arbor   Balance
Pillar   Fusee   Center wheel   Crown wheel   Verge   Potence
Catgut   Contrate wheel   Pallet
Lower pillar plate   Dial   Pinion   Hour wheel
Barrel and main spring   Hour hand
Fusee wheel

1800

Verge Escapement

1860

Cylinder Escapement

Lever Escapement

1900

CENTER WHEEL

THIRD WHEEL — PALLET

BARREL

BARREL ARBOR

MAINSPRING

ESCAPE WHEEL BALANCE WHEEL

FOURTH WHEEL

1930

1600

1650

1550

1880

1900 1920 1930

1935

21

HISTORY

With the settlement and development of America, the American Watch came into being. The American Watch was so well made the whole world demanded and used it. Because these watches were placed on the market reasonably priced, the common man could own them. For the first time watches were made with interchangeable parts; each part could be taken from one watch and placed in another without altering either in any way, and both watches would still give perfect time. In America, the term "watchmaker" did not necessarily apply to one who manufactured watches, but more generally to those engaged in repairing and cleaning watches or capable of "making" and fitting any part of a watch. Today a watchmaker simply orders replacement parts, due to the interchangeable parts system.

It would be hard to determine who was the first watchmaker in America. From the early 1800s, many of the movements were made in small quantities. Watches were made to order and were not carried in stock in a shop. These watches were hand-made, and the watchmaker depended upon Europe for supplies such as springs, jewels, balances, hands, etc. Therefore, watchmakers could not be regarded as total manufacturers, although the watchmaker did deliver watches of his own making for which he made some of the parts, such as the case and wheels, etc.

American watches should be divided into two periods; those made prior to 1850 (Colonial Watches) and those made after 1850 (Modern Watches). The colonial watchmakers made some of their parts and imported some parts from abroad, mainly England. The making of certain parts required an investment in equipment which most watchmakers were not able or willing to make, because the insufficient number of customers could not justify the outlay of capital. Colonial watchmakers imported blanks and then finished the wheels, often making them fit their own special designs and needs. Many of these personalized movements are signed by the watchmaker. This was not a new practice, as English watchmakers had been doing it for years. Watches from the Colonial Period are certainly collectible and should be considered to be of American origin.

By 1775 Thomas Harland was very prosperous as a tradesman, as well as a watchmaker. Harland probably produced about 200 watches that were plain and of the verge type. There are only a few Harland watches known to be in existence, although he worked in the watch trade until about 1806 and may have trained Luther

Goddard.

In 1809 Goddard (1762-1842) of Shrewbury, Mass., began to make watches of the verge type, and his company produced some 650. Goddard could not compete with the cheaper foreign watches, but produced the greatest number of watches made in America to that date. These were hand-made and did not have interchangeable parts. A cousin to the famous clockmaker Simon Willard, Goddard served as apprentice with Simon from 1778 to 1783. His watch movements were medium size and were English in general appearance. The watch was most often placed in open-faced, silver-type cases. The plates were highly engraved and fire-gilded. The plates, wheels, barrel, fusees, cock, and some other brass parts were also made by Goddard & Company. Some of the watch parts were made by other specialists. The first watch was made in about 1812, and movements were marked as follows: L Goddard, L Goddard & Co., Luther Goddard & Son, P Goddard, L & P Goddard, D P Goddard & Co., and P & D Goddard.

Example of a **Luther Goddard** movement. His basic watch consisted of 16-18 size, pair case, open face-thick bulls-eye type, and of high quality. Total production was about 600.

In 1838 the first machine-made watch, with interchangeable parts, was placed on the American market by Pitkin (Henry) & Brother (James F.). These watches were ¾ plate, 16 to 18 size, and had a slow train. The machines that were used to make these watches were made by the Pitkin Brothers and were very crude. The same fate fell to the Pitkins as it did to Goddard; the cost of manufacturing was too great to compete with the foreign market. The total Pitkin production was 900 watches. A few other attempts were made but none noteworthy. The first 50 watches were marked H & JF PITKIN. In 1841, they moved to New York City. These watches were marked Pitkin & Co., or Pitkin American Lever Watch. Some, with detached lever, were marked Pitkin & Co. (about 18's).

Jacob Custer produced 12 to 15 watches in about 1843, making all the parts except the hairspring and fusee chains.

In 1850 a small shop was built opposite Mr. Howard's Clock Co., and some English and Swiss watchmakers were put to work. A Mr. Dennison, in the spring of 1850, completed the first watch designed to run eight days, which was about 18 size. It was not until 1853 that the first watch was placed on the market for sale. It was marked "Warren" and sold for about $40. The company went on to become the Waltham Company.

Aaron L. Dennison.

Edward Howard.

Aaron L. Dennison and Edward Howard both had the grand idea of mass-producing watches. In 1849, financed by Samuel Curtis, they became partners. They started out as American Horologe Co., then later that same year became the Warren Mfg. Co. In the fall of 1852 some 17 watches were made. The first watches placed on the market were made in 1853, serial numbers 18 to 110, marked "Warren." Some 800 were made after that, and they were marked "Samuel Curtis." Some others were marked "Fellows & Schell." In September 1853, the name changed once again to The Boston Watch Co., and another factory was established in Waltham, Mass., which began operation on Oct. 5, 1854. These watches were marked C. T. Parker, Dennison & Davis P.S.B. (Nos. 1,001 to 5,000). In May 1857, the company was sold at a sheriff's auction to R. E. Robbins. The company was reorganized to form the Appleton, Tracy & Co. From the Boston Watch Co. came the E. Howard and Co. which remained at the old Boston Watch Co. factory in Roxbury, Mass. On Dec. 11, 1857, the E. Howard & Co. was formed. From the Appleton, Tracy & Co. came the Waltham Watch Company.

From this beginning all the watch factories in America sprang forth. By 1884 there were nine first-class factories making on the average of 3,650 watches a day. These American machine-made watches kept the foreign market in complete disarray until the early 1900s.

THAT GREAT AMERICAN
RAILROAD POCKET WATCH

It was the late nineteenth century in America. The automobile had not yet been discovered. The personal Kodak camera was still not on the market. Women wore long dresses, and the rub board was still the most common way to wash clothes. Few homes had electricity, and certainly the radio had not yet invaded their lives. Benjamin Harrison was president. To be sure, those days of yesteryear were not quite as nostalgically simple as most reminiscing would have them be. They were slower, yes, because it took longer to get things done and longer to get from one place to another. The U.S. mail was the chief form of communication linking this country together, as America was inching toward the Twentieth Century.

The tremendous impact of the railroad on the country during this era should not be underestimated. Most of the progress since the 1830s had chugged along on the back of the black giant locomotives that belched steam and fire, up and down the countryside. In fact, the trains brought much life and hope to the people all across the country, delivering their goods and food, bringing people from one city to another, carrying the U.S. mail, and bringing the democratic process to the people by enabling candidates for the U.S. Presidency to meet and talk with people in every state.

Truly the train station held memories for most everyone and had a link with every family.

In 1891, the country had just eased into the period that historians would later term the "Gay Nineties." It was on April 19 of that year that events occurred near Cleveland, Ohio, that clearly pointed out that the nation's chief form of transportation was running on timepieces that were not reliable. The time had come for strict standards for pocket watches used by the railroaders. From the ashes of this smoldering

Ohio disaster rose the phoenix in the form of the great American railroad pocket watch, a watch unrivaled in quality and reliability.

That April morning the fast mail train, known as No. 4, was going East. On the same track an accommodation train was going West. It was near Elyria, about 25 miles from Cleveland, Ohio, that the engineer and conductor of the accommodation train were given written orders to let the fast mail train pass them at Kipton, a small station west of Oberlin.

As the accommodation train was leaving the station at Elyria, the telegraph operator ran to the platform and verbally cautioned the engineer and conductor, "Be careful, No. 4 is on time." The conductor replied, "Go to thunder. I know my business."

The train left Elyria on time according to the engineer's watch. What was not known was that the engineer's watch had stopped for four minutes and then started up again. Had the conductor looked at his own watch, the impending disaster could have been avoided.

The two trains met their destiny at Kipton; the accommodation train was under full brakes, but the fast mail was full speed ahead. Both engineers were killed as well as nine other people. The railroad companies (Lake Shore Railroad and Michigan Southern Railway) sustained great losses in property as did the U.S. Post Office.

Following this disaster, a commission was appointed to come up with standards for timepieces that would be accepted and adopted by all railroads. The commission learned that, up to the time of the Kipton crash, conductors on freight trains were depending on cheap alarm clocks. The railroading industry had grown, fast new trains were now in service, and the same lines were used by several different railways. Very often, in only a short space of time, two trains would cover the same track. The industry now had to demand precision in its timekeeping.

By 1893 the General Railroad Timepiece Standards were adopted, and any watch being used in rail service—by railroaders responsible for schedules—was required to meet the following specifications:

> Be open faced, size 18 or 16, have a minimum of 17 jewels, adjusted to at least five positions, keep time accurately to within a gain or loss of only 30 seconds a week, adjusted to temperatures of 34 to 100 degrees Fahrenheit, have a double roller, steel escape wheel, lever set, micrometric regulator, winding stem at 12 o'clock, grade on back plate, use plain Arabic numbers printed bold and black on a white dial, and have bold black hands.
>
> Some also wanted a Breguet hairspring, adjusted to isochronism and 30 degrees Fahrenheit with a minimum of 19 jewels.

The railroad man was compelled to buy a timepiece more accurate than many scientific instruments of precision used in laboratories. The American pocket watch industry was compelled to produce just such an instrument—which it did. The railroad watch was a phenomenal timekeeper and durable in long life and service. It had the most minute adjustments, no small feat because watchmaking was rendered far more difficult than clockmaking, due to the fact that a clock is always in one position and watches must be accurate from several positions.

The 1893 railroad pocket watch standards were adopted by almost every railroad line. While each company had its individual standards, most all of them included the basic recommendations of the commission.

The key figure in developing the railroad watch standards was Webb C. Ball of Cleveland, Ohio, the general time inspector for over 125,000 miles of railroad in the U.S., Mexico, and Canada. Ball was authorized by railroad officials to establish the timepiece inspection system. After Ball presented his guidelines, most American manufacturers set out to meet those standards and a list of the different manufacturers producing watches of the grade that would pass inspection, was soon available.

According to the regulations, if a watch fell behind or gained 30 seconds in 7 to 14 days, it must be sent in for adjustment or repair. Small cards were given to the engineers and conductors—the railroad timekeepers—and a complete record of the watch's performance was written in ink. All repairs and adjustments were conducted by experienced and approved watchmakers; inspections were conducted by authorized inspectors.

Because this system was adopted universally and adhered to, and because American watch manufacturers produced a superior railroad watch, the traveling public was assured of increased safety and indeed the number of railroad accidents occurring as a result of faulty timepieces was minimized.

Prior to the 1891 collision, some railroad companies had already initiated standards and were issuing lists of those watches approved for railroad use. Included were the Waltham 18s, 1883 model, Crescent Street Grade, and the B.W. Raymond, 18s, both in open and hunter cases with lever set or pendant set.

By the mid 1890s hunter cases were being turned down as well as pendant set. Watches meeting approval then included Waltham, 18s, 1892 model; Elgin, 7th model; and Hamilton, 17j, open face, lever set.

Hamilton Grade 992, 17 size, 21 jewels, nickel ¾ plate movement, lever set only, gold jewel settings, gold center wheel, steel escape wheel, micrometric regulator, compensating balance. Adjusted to temperature, isochronism and 5 positions.

By 1900 the double roller sapphire pallets and steel escape wheels with a minimum of five positions were required.

The early Ball Watch Co. movements, made by Howard, used initials of railroad labor organizations such as "B. of L.E. Standard" and "B. of L.F. Standard." Ball also used the trademark "999" and "Official Railroad Standard." Some watches may turn up that are marked as "loaners." These were issued by the railroad inspectors when a watch had to be kept for repairs.

By 1920 the 18 size watch had lost popularity with the railroad men and by 1950 most railroad companies were turning them down all together.

In 1936 duties on Swiss watches were lowered by 50 percent, and by 1950 the Swiss imports had reached a level of five million a year.

In 1969 the last American railroad pocket watch was sold by Hamilton Watch Co.

RAILROAD GRADE WATCH ADJUSTMENTS

The railroad watch, as well as other fine timepieces, had to compensate for several factors in order to be reliable and accurate at all times. These compensations, called adjustments, were for heat and cold, isochronism, and five to six different positions. These adjustments were perfected only after experimentation and a great deal of careful hand labor on each individual movement.

All railroad grade watches were adjusted to a closer rate to compensate for heat and cold. The compensation balance has screws in the rim of the balance wheel which can be regulated by the watchmaker. The movement was tested in an ice box and in an oven, and if it did not keep the same time in both temperature extremes, as well as under average conditions, the screw in the balance wheel was shifted or adjusted until accuracy was achieved.[1]

The isochronism adjustment maintained accuracy of the watch both when the mainspring was fully wound up and when it was nearly run down. This was achieved by selecting a hairspring of exact proportions to cause the balance wheel to give the same length of arc of rotation regardless of the amount of the mainspring that had been spent.

Railroad watches were adjusted to be accurate whether they were laying on their face or back, or being carried on their edges with pendants up or down, or with the three up or the nine up. These adjustments were accomplished by having the jewels, in which the balance pivots rest, of proper thickness in proportion to the diameter of the pivot and, at the same time, equal to the surface on the end of the

[1] Railroad grade watches had a compensation balance made of brass and steel. Brass was used on the outside rim and steel on the inside. Brass is softer than steel, and steel is more sensitive to temperature changes. The rim on the balance was cut to form two pieces and had two arms. Each piece was independent of the other so the rim was free to be influenced through expansion or contraction. (A small balance wheel with the same hairspring would run faster than a large balance wheel.) At a high temperature the entire balance wheel would expand in bulk and thus run slower. That is why a compensation balance was necessary. When the bulk of the balance wheel expands, the expansion of the brass on the outside of the rim is greater than that of the steel on the inside; thus it throws the loose ends of the rim toward the center. Consequently this makes the circumference smaller and therefore compensation for the increased volume is achieved.

pivot which rests on the cap jewel. To be fully adjusted for positions, the balance wheel and the pallet and escape wheel must be perfectly poised. Perfect poise is achieved when the pivots can be supported on two flat surfaces, perfectly smooth and polished and when the wheel is placed in any position, it will remain exactly as it is placed. If it is not perfectly poised, the heaviest part of the wheel will always turn to the point immediately under the lines of support.

The micrometric regulator or the patent regulator is a device used on all railroad grade and higher grade watches for the purpose of assisting in the finer manipulation of the regulator. It is arranged so that the regulator can be moved the shortest possible distance without fear of moving it too far. There is always a fine graduated index attached which makes it possible to determine just how much the regulator has been moved.

E. Howard Watch Co. Railroad Chronometer, Series 11, 16 size, 21 jewels, expressly designed for the railroad trade.

The hairspring used on the so-called ordinary and medium-grade watches is known as the flat hairspring. The Breguet hairspring was an improvement over the flat hairspring and was used on railroad and high-grade watches. The inside coil of any hairspring is attached to a collet on the balance staff and the end of the outside coil of the hairspring is attached to a stud which is held firmly by a screw in the balance wheel bridge. Two small curb pins are fastened to the regulator. These pins clasp the outer side of the hairspring a short distance from the hairspring stud. If the regulator index is moved toward the "S," the curb pins will move, allowing the hairspring to lengthen and the balance wheel to make a longer arc of rotation. This causes the watch to run slower because it requires a longer time for the wheel to perform the longer arc.

When the regulator is moved toward the "F" these curb pins are moved from the stud which shortens the hairspring and makes shorter arcs of the balance wheel, thus causing the movement to run faster. Sometimes, after a heavy jolt, the coil next to the outside one will catch between these curb pins and this will shorten the length of the hairspring just one round, causing a gaining rate of one hour per day. When this occurs, the hairspring can be easily released and will resume its former rate.

The Breguet hairspring, which is used on railroad grade movements, prevented the hairspring from catching on the curb or guard pins and protected against any lateral or side motion of the balance wheel ensuring equal expansion of the outside coil.

Railroad grade watches also used the patent or safety pinion which was developed to protect the train of gears from damage in the event of breakage of the mainspring.

Some railroad grade watches had non-magnetic movements. This was achieved by the use of non-magnetic metals for the balance wheel, hairspring, roller table and pallet. Two of the metals used were iridium and paladium, both very expensive.

Rockford Grades 805-Hunting & 905-Open Face, 18 size, 21 extra fine ruby jewels in gold settings, beautifully damaskeened nickel plates, gold lettering, adjusted to temperature, isochronism and 5 positions, Breguet hair spring, double roller escapement, steel escape wheel, sapphire pallets, micrometric regulator, compensating balance in recess.

RAILROAD WATCH DIALS

Railroad watch dials are distinguished by their simplicity. A true railroad watch dial contained no fancy lettering or beautiful backgrounds. The watches were designed to be functional and in order to achieve that, the dials contained bold black Arabic numbers against a white background. This facilitated ease of reading the time under even the most adverse conditions.

True railroad watches had the winding stem at the 12 o'clock position. The so-called "side winder," that winds at the 3 o'clock position, was not approved for railroad use. (The side winder is a watch movement designed for a hunter case but one that has been placed in an open-faced case.)

One railroad watch dial design was patented by a Mr. Ferguson. On this dial, the five minute numbers were much larger than the hour numbers which were on the inside. This dial never became very popular.

About 1910 the Montgomery dials began to appear. The distinguishing feature of the Montgomery dial is that each minute is numbered around the hour chapter. The five-minute divisions were in red, and the true Montgomery dial has the number "6" inside the minute register. These dials were favored by the railroad men.

The so-called Canadian dial had a 24-hour division inside the hour chapter.

The double-time hands are also found on some railroad grade watches. One hour hand was in black and the other was in red, one hour apart, to compensate for passing from one time zone to another.

Ball Watch Co. Motto: "Carry a Ball and Time Them All." This case is an example of Ball's patented Stirrup Bow. With the simple easy-to-read dial, this watch was a favorite among railroad men.

RAILROAD WATCH CASES

Open face cases were the only ones approved for railroad use. Railroad men sought a case that was tough and durable; one that would provide a dust-free environment for the movement. The swing-out case offered the best protection against dust, but the screw-on back and bezel were the most popular open-face cases.

The lever-set was a must for railroad-approved watches and some of the case manufacturers patented their own styles of cases, most with a heavy bow. One example is the Stirrup Bow by the Ball Watch Co. Hamilton used a bar above the crown to prevent the stem from being pulled out. Glass was most commonly used for the crystal because it was not as likely to scratch.

RAILROAD GRADE OR
RAILROAD APPROVED WATCHES

Note: Not all watches listed here are railroad approved, even though all are railroad grade. See Ball Watch Co. for railroad standards.

BALL
All official R.R. standard with 19, 21, & 23J, hci5p, 18 & 16S, open face.

COLUMBUS WATCH CO.
Columbus King, 21, 23, 25J; Railway King, 17-25J; Time King, 21-25J, 18S; Ruby Model, 16S.

ELGIN
1. "Pennsylvania Railroad Co." on dial, 18S, 15J & 17J, key wind and set, first model "B. W. Raymond."
2. "No. 349," 18S, seventh model, 17-21J.
3. Veritas, B. W. Raymond, or Father Time, 18S, 21-23J.
4. Grades 162, 270, 280, or 342 marked on back plate, 16S, 17-21J.
5. Veritas, Father Time, or Paillard Non-Magnetic, 16S, 19-23J.
6. 571, 21J or 572, 16S, 19J.
7. All wind indicator models.

HAMILTON
1. Grade 946, 23J, 18S.
2. Grades 940, 942, 21J, 18S.
3. Grade 944, 19J, 18S.
4. Grades 924, 926, 934, 936, 938, 948, 17J, 18S.
5. Grades 950, 950B, 950E, 23J, 16S.
6. Grades 992, 992B, 992E, 954, 960, 970, 994, 990, 21J, 16S.
7. Grade 996, 19J, 16S.
8. Grades 972, 968, 964, 17J, 16S.

HAMPDEN
1. Special Railway, 17J, 21J, 23J; New Railway, 23J & 17J; North Am. RR, 21J; Wm. McKinley, 21J; John Hancock, 21J & 23J; John C. Duber, 21J, 18S.
2. 105, 21J; 104, 23J; John C. Duber, 21J; Wm. McKinley, 17, 21, & 23J; New

Railway, 21J; Railway, 19J; Special Railway, 23J, 16S.

E. HOWARD & CO.
1. All Howard models marked "Adjusted" or deer symbol.
2. Split plate models, 18S or N size; 16S or L size.

HOWARD WATCH CO.
All 16S with 19, 21, & 23J.

ILLINOIS
1. Bunn 15J marked "Adjusted," and Stuart, 15J marked "Adjusted," 18S.
2. Benjamin Franklin, 17-26J; Bunn 17, 19, 21, 24J; Bunn Special, 21-26J; Chesapeake & Ohio Sp., 24J; Interstate Chronometer, 23J;Lafayette, 24J; A. Lincoln, 21J; Paillard W. Co., 17-24J; Trainsmen, 23J; Pennsylvania Special 17-26J; The Railroader & Railroad King, 18S.
3. Benjamin Franklin, 17-25J; Bunn, 17-19J; Bunn Special, 21-23J; Diamond Ruby Sapphire, 21 & 23J; Interstate Chronometer, 23J; Lafayette, 23J; A. Lincoln, 21J; Paillard Non-Magnetic W. Co., 17 & 21J; Pennsylvania Special, 17, 21, & 23J; Santa Fe Special, 21J; Sangamo, 21-26J; Sangamo Special, 19-23J; Grades 161, 161A, 163, 163A, 187, and 189, 17J, 16S.

PEORIA WATCH CO.
15 & 17J with a patented regulator, 18S.

ROCKFORD
1. All 21 or more jewels, 16-18S, and wind indicators.
2. Grades 900, 905, 910, 912, 918, 945, 200, 205, 18S.
3. Winnebago, 17-21J, 505, 515, 525, 535, 545, 555, 16S.

SETH THOMAS
Maiden Lane, 21-28J; Henry Molineux, 20J; 260 Model, 18S.

SOUTH BEND
1. Studebaker 329, Grade Nos. 323, and 327, 17-21J, 18S.
2. Studebaker 229, Grade Nos. 223, 227, 293, 295, 299, 17-21J, 16S.
3. Polaris.

UNITED STATES WATCH CO., MARION
United States, 19J, gold train.

U. S. WATCH CO., WALTHAM
The President, 17J, 18S.

WALTHAM

1. 1857 KW with Pennsylvania R.R. on dial, Appleton Tracy & Co. on movement.
2. Crescent Street, 17-23J; 1883 & 1892 Models; Appleton Tracy & Co., 1892 Model; Railroader, 1892 Model; Pennsylvania Railroad; Special Railroad, Special RR King, Vanguard, 17-23J, 1892 Model; Grade 845, 18S.
3. American Watch Co., 17-21J, 1872 Models; American Watch Co., 17-23J, Bridge Models; Crescent Street, 17-21J, 1899 & 1908 Models; Premier Maximus; Railroader; Riverside Maximus, 21-23J; Vanguard, 19-23J; 645, 16S.
4. All wind indicators.

American Waltham Watch Co. Vanguard, 16 size, 19-23 jewels, winding indicator which alerts user to how far up or down the mainspring is wound. This watch was made to promote new sales in the railway industry.

Hamilton Watch Co. A Favorite raiload style case by Hamilton. Note the Montgomery style dial as well as the bar above the crown.

CANADIAN PACIFIC SERVICE RAILROAD APPROVED WATCHES 1899

WALTHAM

Vanguard, 18-16S, 19-21-23 jewels
Crescent St., 18S, 19J; 18-16S, 21J
Appleton-Tracy 17J; also No. 845, 21J
Riverside 16S, 19J; Riverside Maximus, 16S, 23J; and 16S, No. 645, 21J
C. P. R. 18-16S, 17J; also C. T. S. 18-16S, 17J

ELGIN
   Veritas, 18-16S, 21-23J
   B. W. R. 18-16S, 17-19-21J
   Father Time 18-16S, 21J
   Grade 349, 18S, 21J

HAMILTON
   18S, 946, 23J; 940-942, 21J; 944, 19J; 936-938, 17J
   16S, 950, 23J; 960-990-992, 21J; 952, 19J; 972, 17J

SOUTH BEND
   18S, 327-329, 21J; 323, 17J
   16S, 227-229, 21J; 223, 17J

BALL
   All Balls 18S, 16S, 17-19-21-23J

ILLINOIS
   Bunn Special, 18-16S, 21-23J; also Bunn 18-16S, 17-19J
   A. Lincoln, 18-16S, 21J
   Sangamo Special, 16S, 19-21-23J

SETH THOMAS
   Maiden Lane, 18S, 25J; No. 260, 21J; No. 382, 17J

E. HOWARD WATCH CO.
   16S Series, 0-23J, 5-19J, 2-17J, 10-21J; also No. 1, 21J

ROCKFORD
   18S, Grade 918-905, 21J; Winnebago, 17J; also Grade 900, 24J
   16S, Grades 545, 525, 515, 505, 21J; 655 W.I., 21J; and Grade 405, 17J

LONGINES
   18S, Express Monarch, 17-19-21-23J
   16S, Express Monarch, 17-19-21-23J

BRANDT-OMEGA
   18S, D.D.R., 23J; C.C.C.R., 23J; C.D.R., 19J; C.C.R., 19J

AMERICAN RAILROAD APPROVED WATCHES—1930

The following requirements for railroad approved watches are outlined by Mr. R. D. Montgomery, General Watch Inspector of the Santa Fe Railway System:

"The regulation watch designated as of 1930 to be standard is described as follows:"

"16 size, American, lever-setting, 19 jewels or more, open face, winding at '12,' double-roller escapement, steel escape wheel, adjusted to 5 positions, temperature and isochronism, which will rate within a variation not exceeding 6 seconds in 72 hour tests, pendant up, dial up and dial down, and be regulated to run within a variation not exceeding 30 seconds per week."

"The following listed makes and grades meet the requirements and comprise a complete list of watches acceptable. Watches bearing the name of jewelers or other names not standard trade marks or trade numbers will not be accepted:"

American Waltham Watch Co.
(16 Size)
23J	Premier Maximus
23J	Riverside Maximus
23J	Vanguard
	6 position
	winding indicator
23J	Vanguard
	6 position
21J	Crescent Street
21J	No. 645
19J	Vanguard
19J	Riverside

Ball Watch Co.
(16 Size)
23J	Official R.R. Standard
21J	Official R.R. Standard
19J	Official R.R. Standard

Elgin Watch Co.
(16 Size)
23J	Veritas
21J	Veritas
21J	B. W. Raymond
21J	Father Time
21J	No. 270

Hamilton Watch Co.
(16 Size)
23J	No. 950
21J	No. 990
21J	No. 992
19J	No. 952
19J	No. 996

Hampden Watch Co.
(16 Size)
23J	Special Railway
21J	New Railway
19J	Railway

Howard Watch Co.
(16 Size)
All 23J	
All 21J	
All 19J	

Illinois Watch Co.
(16 Size)
23J	Sangamo Special
23J	Sangamo
23J	Bunn Special
21J	Bunn Special
21J	Sangamo
21J	A. Lincoln
19J	Bunn

South Bend Watch Co.
(16 Size)
21J	No. 227
21J	No. 229
21J	No. 295
19J	No. 293

APPROVED POCKET WATCHES IN
CP RAIL SERVICE
AS OF FEBRUARY 1, 1957

Waltham (16 Size)
23J	Vanguard No. 29, 634, 001 and up

Elgin (16 Size)
21J	B.W.R.
21J	No. 571

Hamilton (16 Size)
23J	No. 950B
21J	No. 992B

Ball (16 Size)
21J	(Hamilton) No. 992C
21J	No. 435C

Zenith (16 Size)
21J	Extra RR 56

APPROVED WRIST WATCHES IN
CP RAIL SERVICE

Cyma
17J	RR 2852 M
25J	RR 2872 A

Girard Perregaux
17J	CP 307H.F.

Longines
17J	RR 280

Universal
19J	RR 1205

Zenith
18J	RR 120 T

APPROVED WRIST WATCHES IN
CP RAIL SERVICE
BATTERY POWERED

Bulova Accutron	**Rodania**	**Wittnauer**
17J 214	13J RR 2780 Calendar	13J RR 12 WT Calendar
17J 218 Calendar		

APPROVED WRIST WATCHES SEMI-MECHANICAL
QUARTZ ANALOG BATTERY POWERED
IN CP RAIL SERVICE AS OF 1978

Cyma	**Rodania**	**Wyler**
7J Calendar RR 9361 Q	6J Calendar 9952.111RR	7J Calendar RR 9361 Q
6J Calendar RR 960 Q	7J Calendar RR 9361 Q	

Bulova	**Rotary**	**Wittnauer**
7J Calendar RR 9362 Q	7J Calendar RR 9366 Q	7J Calendar RR 2 Q 115 C
6J Calendar RR 960.111Q		

ADJUSTMENTS

There are nine basic adjustments for watch movements. They are:

heat ... 1   positions ... 6

cold ... 1   TOTAL ... 9

isochronism ... 1

THE SIX POSITION ADJUSTMENTS ARE:

Stem UP

Stem Down

This position adjustment not required on railroad watches.

Stem Left

Stem Right

Dial Up

Dial Down

A watch with eight adjustments (the most common) will be listed in this book as: "Adj.5P" (heat, cold, isochronism, 5 positions).

The total number of pocket watches made for the railroad industry was small in comparison to the total pocket watches produced. Generally, watches defined as "Railroad Watches" fall into five categories:

1. **Railroad Approved**—Grades and Models approved by the railway companies.[1]
2. **Railroad Grade**—Those advertised as being able to pass railroad inspection.[2]
3. **Pre-Commission Watches**—Those used by the railroads before 1893.[3]
4. **Company Watches**—Those with a railroad logo or company name on the dial.[4]
5. **Train Watches**—Those with a locomotive painted on the dial or inscribed on the case.[4]

COLONIAL WATCHMAKERS

Early American watchmakers came from Europe; little is known about them, and few of their watches exist today. Their hand-fabricated watches were made largely from imported parts. It was common practice for a watchmaker to use rough castings made by several craftsmen. These were referred to as "movements in the gray." The watchmaker finished these parts and assembled them to make a complete watch. He would then engrave his name on the finished timepiece.

Some of the early American watchmakers designed the cases or other parts, but most imported what they needed. The early colonial watchmakers

---

[1]Not all railroad employees were required to purchase or use approved watches, just the employees that were responsible for schedules. But many employees did buy the approved watches because they were the standard in reliability.

[2]These were used primarily by those railroaders who were not required to submit their watches for inspection.

[3]There were many watches made for railroad use prior to 1893. Some of the key wind ones, especially, are good quality and highly collectible.

[4]Some manufacturers inscribed terms such as railroader, special railroad, dispatcher, etc. on the back plates of the movements.

showed little originality as designers and we can only guess how many watches were really made in America.

These early hand-made watches are almost non-existent; therefore, only the name of the watchmaker will be listed. This compilation comes from old ads in newspapers and journals and other sources. It is not considered to be complete.

Because of the rarity and condition of these early watches, prices may vary widely from $400 to $2,000.

Example of watch paper placed inside a pair-cased watch by a watch maker. This was a form of advertisement placed in the watch after repair was made.

Ephraim Clark, 18 size, non-jeweled, made between 1780-1790; a good example of a colonial watch. These early watches usually included chain driven fusees, verge type escapements, hand pierced balance cock, key wind & set; note the circular shaped regulator on the far left side of the illustrated example.

Nath. Hawxhurst, N.Y., 18 size, non-jeweled, ca. 1770-1780, chain driven fusee, verge type escapement, notice hand-pierced cock.

J.F. Bartlett, Clinton, Mass. Example of watch paper placed inside a pair-cased watch by the watch maker, ca. 1850.

EARLY AMERICAN WATCHMAKERS
(With Location and Approximate Date)

Adams, Nathan (Boston, MA, 1800)
Adams, William (Boston, MA, 1810)
Aldrich, Jacob (Wilmington, DE, 1802)
Allebach, Jacob (Phila., PA, 1825-1840)
Atherton, Nathan (Phila., PA, 1825)
Atkinson, James (Boston, MA, 1745)
Backhouse, John (Lancaster, PA, 1725)
Bagnall, Benjamin (Phila., PA, 1750)
Bailey, John (Boston, MA, 1810)
Bailey, William (Phila., PA, 1820)
Baker, Benjamin (Phila., PA, 1825)
Banks, Joseph (Phila., PA, 1790)
Barnhill, Robert (Phila., PA, 1775)
Barrow, Samuel (Phila., PA, 1771)
Barry, Standish (Baltimore, MD, 1785)
Basset, John F. (Phila., PA, 1798)
Belknap, William (Boston, MA, 1815)
Bell, William (Phila., PA, 1805)
Benedict, S. W. (New York, NY, 1835)
Bigger & Clarke (Baltimore, MD, 1783)
Billion, C. (Phila., PA, 1775-1800)
Bingham & Bricerly (Phila., PA, 1778-1799)
Birnie, Laurence (Phila., PA, 1774)
Blundy, Charles (Charleston, SC, 1750)
Blunt & Nichols (New York, NY, 1850)
Bond, William (Boston, MA, 1800-1810)
Bonnaud (Phila., PA, 1799)
Bower, Michael (Phila., PA, 1790-1800)
Bowman, Joseph (Lancaster, PA, 1821-1844)
Boyd & Richards (Phila., PA, 1808)
Boyter, Daniel (Lancaster, PA, 1805)
Brands & Matthey (Phila., PA, 1799)
Brandt, Aime (Phila., PA, 1820)
Brant, Brown & Lewis (Phila., PA, 1795)
Brazier, Amable (Phila., PA, 1795)
Brearley, James (Phila., PA, 1790-1800)
Brewer, William (Phila., PA, 1785-1791)
Brewster & Ingraham (Bristol, CT, 1827-1839)
Brown, Garven (Boston, MA, 1767)
Brown, John (Lancaster, PA, 1840)
Brownell, A. P. (New Bedford, MA)
Burkelow, Samuel (Phila., PA, 1791-1799)
Bush, George (Easton, PA, 1790-1800)
Campbell, Charles (Phila., PA, 1796)
Campbell, William (Carlisle, PA, 1765)
Capper, Michael (Phila., PA, 1799)
Carey, James (Brunswick, ME, 1830)
Carrell, John (Phila., PA, 1791-1793)
Carter, Jacob (Phila., PA, 1805)
Carter, Thomas (Phila., PA, 1823)
Carver, Jacob (Phila., PA, 1790)

Carvill, James (New York, NY, 1803)
Chandlee, John (Wilmington, DE, 1795-1810)
Chaudron (Phila., PA, 1799)
Chauncey & Joseph Ives (Bristol, CT, 1825)
Cheney, Martin (Windsor, VT, 1800)
Chick, M. M. (Concord, NH, 1845)
Clark, Benjamin (Wilmington, DE, 1737-1750)
Clark, Ephraim (Phila., PA, 1780-1800)
Clark, John (New York, NY, 1770-1790)
Clark, John (Phila., PA, 1799)
Clark, Thomas (Boston, MA, 1764)
Claudon, John-
Cook, William (Boston, MA, 1810)
   George (Charleston, SC, 1773)
Crow, George (Wilmington, DE, 1740-1770)
Crow, John (Wilmington, DE, 1770-1798)
Crow, Thomas (Wilmington, DE, 1770-1798)
Currier & Trott (Boston, MA, 1800)
Curtis, Solomon (Phila., PA, 1793-1795)
Dakin, James (Boston, MA, 1795)
Davis, Samuel (Boston, MA, 1820)
Delaplaine, James K. (New York, NY, 1786-1800)
DeVacht, Joseph & Frances (Gallipolis, OH, 1792)
Dix, Joseph (Phila., PA, 1770)
Downes, Anson (Bristol, CT, 1830)
Downes, Arthur (Charleston, SC, 1765)
Downes, Ephriam (Bristol, CT, 1830)
Droz, Hannah (Phila., PA, 1840)
Droz, Humbert (Phila., PA, 1793-1799)
Duffield, Edward W. (Whiteland, PA, 1775)
Dunheim, Andrew (New York, NY, 1775)
Dupuy, John (Phila., PA, 1770)
Dupuy, Odran (Phila., PA, 1735)
Dutch, Stephen, Jr. (Boston, MA, 1800-1810)
Eberman, George (Lancaster, PA, 1800)
Eberman, John (Lancaster, PA, 1780-1820)
Ellicott, Joseph (Buckingham, PA, 1763)
Elsworth, David (Baltimore, MD, 1780-1800)
Embree, Effingham (New York, NY, 1785)
Evans, David (Baltimore, MD, 1770-1773)
Fales, James (New Bedford, MA, 1810-1820)
Ferris, Tiba (Wilmington, DE, 1812-1850)
Fessler, John (Phila., PA, 1785-1820)
Feton, J. (Phila., PA, 1825-1840)
Filder, John (Lancaster, PA, 1810-1825)
Fister, Amon (Phila., PA, 1794)
Fix, Joseph (Reading, PA, 1820-1840)
Fowell, J & N (Boston, MA, 1800-1810)
Frances, Basil & Alexander Vuille (Baltimore,

MD, 1766)
Galbraith, Patrick (Phila., PA, 1795)
Gibbons, Thomas (Phila., PA, 1750)
Goodfellow, William (Phila., PA, 1793-1795)
Goodfellow & Son, William (Phila., PA,
  1796-1799)
Gooding, Henry (Boston, MA, 1810-1820)
Green, John (Phila., PA, 1794)
Groppengeiser, J. L. (Phila., PA, 1840)
Grotz, Issac (Easton, PA, 1810-1835)
Hall, Jonas (Boston, MA, 1848-1858)
Harland, Theodore (Norwich, CT, 1750-1790)
Harland, Thomas (Norwich, CT, 1802)
Harrison, James (Shrewbury, MA, 1805)
Hawxhurst, Nath. (New York, NY, 1784)
Heilig, Jacob (Phila., PA, 1770-1824)
Heilig, John (Germantown, PA, 1824-1830)
Hepton, Frederick (Phila., PA, 1785)
Heron, Isaac (New York, NY, 1770-1780)
Hodgson, William (Phila., PA, 1785)
Hoff, John (Lancaster, PA, 1800)
Hoffner, Henry (Phila., PA, 1791)
Howard, Thomas (Phila., PA, 1789-1791)
Howe, Jubal (Shrewbury, MA, 1800)
Huguenail, Charles (Phila., PA, 1799)
Hunt, Hiram (Robbinston, ME, 1800)
Hutchins, Abel (Concord, MA, 1785-1818)
Hutchins, Levi (Concord, MA, 1785-1815)
Hyde, John E. (New York, NY, 1805)
Hyde & Goodrich (New Orleans, LA, 1850)
Ingersoll, Daniel B. (Boston, MA, 1800-1810)
Ingold, Pierre Frederick (NY, NY, 1845-1850)
Ives, Chauncy & Joseph (Bristol, CT, 1825)
Jacob, Charles & Claude (Annapolis, MD,
  1775)
Jackson, Joseph H. (Phila., PA, 1802-1810)
Jessop, Jonathan (Park Town, PA, 1790)
Jeunit, Joseph (Meadville, PA, 1763)
Johnson, David (Boston, MA, 1690)
Johnson, John (Charleston, SC, 1763)
Jones, George (Wilmington, DE, 1815-1835)
Jones, Low & Ball (Boston, MA, 1830)
Keith, William (Shrewbury, MA, 1810)
Kennedy, Patrick (Phila., PA, 1795-1799)
Kincaid, Thomas (Christiana Bridge, DE,
  1775)
Kirkwood, John (Charleston, SC, 1761)
Launy, David F. (Boston & New York, 1800)
Leavenworth, Mark (Waterbury, CT, 1820)
Leavenworth, Wm. (Waterbury, CT, 1810)
Leslie & Co., Baltimore, MD, 1795)
Leslie & Price (Phila., PA, 1793-1799)
Leslie, Robert (Baltimore, MD, 1788-1791)
Levely, George (Phila., PA, 1774)

Levi, Michael & Issac (Baltimore, MD, 1785)
Limeburner, John (Phila., PA, 1790)
Lind, John (Phila., PA, 1791-1799)
Lowens, David (Phila., PA, 1785)
Ludwig, John (Phila., PA, 1791)
Lufkins & Johnson (Boston, MA, 1800-1810)
Lukins, Isaac (Phila., PA, 1825)
MacDowell, Robert (Phila., PA, 1798)
MacFarlane, John (Boston, MA, 1800-1810)
Mahve, Matthew (Phila., PA, 1761)
Manross, Elisha (Bristol, CT, 1827)
Martin, Patrick (Phila., PA, 1830)
Maunroe & Whitney (Concord, MA,
  1805-1825)
Maus, Frederick (Phila., PA, 1785-1793)
Maynard, George (New York, NY, 1702-1730)
McCabe, John (Baltimore, MD, 1774)
McDowell, James (Phila., PA, 1795)
McGraw, Donald (Annapolis, MD, 1767)
Mends, James (Phila., PA, 1795)
Merriman, Titus (Bristol, CT, 1830)
Merry, Charles F. (Phila., PA, 1799)
Meters, John (Fredricktown, MD, 1795-1825)
Miller, Abraham (Easton, PA, 1810-1830)
Mitchell & Atkins (Bristol, CT, 1830)
Mitchell, Henry (New York, NY, 1787-1800)
Mohler, Jacob (Baltimore, MD, 1773)
Moir, J & W (Waterbury, CT, 1790)
Montandon, Julien (Shrewbury, CT, 1812)
Moollinger, Henry (Phila., PA, 1794)
Morgan, Thomas (Phila. & Balti., 1774-1793)
Moris, William (Grafton, MA, 1765-1775)
Mulford, J. H. (Albany, NY, 1845)
Mulliken, Nathaniel (Boston, MA, 1765)
Munroe & Whitney (Concord, MA, 1820)
Narney, Joseph (Charleston, SC, 1753)
Neiser, Augustine (Phila., PA, 1739-1780)
Nicholls, George (New York, NY, 1728-1750)
Nicollette, Mary (Phila., PA, 1793-1799)
O'Hara, Charles (Phila., PA, 1799)
Oliver, Griffith (Phila., PA, 1785-1793)
Ormsby, James (Baltimore, MD, 1771)
Palmer, John (Phila., PA, 1795)
Palmer, John Peter (Phila., PA, 1795)
Park, Seth (Parktown, PA, 1790)
Parke, Solomon (Phila., PA, 1791-1795)
Parke, Solomon & Co. (Phila., PA, 1799)
Parker, James (Cambridge, OH, 1790)
Parker, Thomas (Phila., PA, 1783)
Parry, John J. (Phila., PA, 1795-1800)
Patton, Abraham (Phila., PA, 1799)
Patton, David (Phila., PA, 1800)
Payne, Lawrence (New York, NY, 1732-1755)
Pearman, W. (Richmond, VA, 1834)

Perkins, Thomas (Phila., PA, 1785-1800)
Perry, Marvin (New York, NY, 1770-1780)
Perry, Thomas (New York, NY, 1750-1775)
Phillips, Joseph (New York, NY, 1713-1735)
Pierret, Mathew (Phila., PA, 1795)
Pope, Joseph (Boston, MA, 1790)
Price, Philip (Phila., PA, 1825)
Proctor, Cardan (New York, NY, 1747-1775)
Proctor, William (New York, NY, 1737-1760)
Proud, R. (Newport, RI, 1775)
Purse, Thomas (Baltimore, MD, 1805)
Quimby, Phineas & William (Belfast, ME, 1825)
Reily, John (Phila., PA, 1785-1795)
Rich, John (Bristol, CT, 1800)
Richardson, Francis (Phila., PA, 1736)
Ritchie, George (Phila., PA, 1785-1790)
Roberts, John (Phila., PA, 1799)
Roberts, S & E (Trenton, NJ, 1830)
Rode, William (Phila., PA, 1785)
Rodger, James (New York, NY, 1822-1878)
Rodgers, Samuel (Plymouth, MA, 1790-1804)
Russell, George (Phila., PA, 1840)
Saxton & Lukens (Phila., PA, 1828)
Schriner, Martin (Lancaster, PA, 1790-1830)
Schriner, M & P (Lancaster, PA, 1830-1840)
Seddinger, Margaret (Phila., PA, 1846)
Severberg, Christian (NY, NY, 1755-1775)
Sherman, Robert (Wilmington, DE, 1760-1770)
Sibley, O. E. (New York, NY, 1820)
Smith, J. L. (Middletown, CT, 1830)
Smith & Goodrich (Bristol, CT, 1827-1840)
Soloman, Henry (Boston, MA, 1820)
Souza, Sammuel (Phila., PA, 1820)

Sprogell, John (Phila., PA, 1791)
Spurck, Peter (Phila., PA, 1795-1799)
Stanton, Job (New York, NY, 1810)
Stein, Abraham (Phila., PA, 1799)
Stever & Bryant (Wigville, CT, 1830)
Stillas, John (Phila., PA, 1785-1793)
Stinnett, John (Phila., PA, 1769)
Stokel, John (New York, NY, 1820-1840)
Store, Marmaduke (Phila., PA, 1742)
Strech, Thomas (Phila., PA, 1782)
Syderman, Philip (Phila., PA, 1785)
Taf, John James (Phila., PA, 1794)
Taylor, Samuel (Phila, PA, 1799)
Tonchure, Francis (Baltimore, MD, 1805)
Townsend, Charles (Phila., PA, 1799)
Townsend, David (Boston, MA, 1800)
Trott, Andrew (Boston, MA, 1800-1810)
Turrell, Samuel (Boston, MA, 1790)
Voight, Henry (Phila., PA, 1775-1793)
Voight, Sebastian (Phila., PA, 1775-1799)
Voight, Thomas (Henry's son) (Phila., PA, 1811-1835)
Vuille, Alexander (Baltimore, MD, 1766)
Warner, George T. (New York, NY, 1795)
Weller, Francis (Phila., PA, 1780)
Wells, George & Co. (Boston, MA, 1825)
Wells, J.S. (Boston, MA, 1800)
Wetherell, Nathan (Phila., PA, 1830-1840)
Wheaton, Caleb (Providence, RI, 1800)
White, Sebastian (Phila., PA, 1795)
Whittaker, William (NY, NY, 1731-1755)
Wood, John (Phila., PA, 1770-1793)
Wright, John (New York, NY, 1712-1735)
Zahm, G.M. (Lancaster, PA, 1865)

The Gruen 50th Anniversary Watch

On February 9, 1924, via a Literary Digest advertisement, the Gruen 50th Anniversary watch was first introduced to the public. This beautiful example of the watchmakers' art was to commemorate the founding of the company by Dietrich Gruen in 1874. It was to become recognized as setting a new standard for high quality watches, and was destined to become, via presentations and purchases, the "Priceless Possession of a Few" as the original and subsequent ads proclaimed.

It is believed to be the only production watch manufactured with a gold movement. The plates and bridges are 12K solid gold, for a total weight of 19 DWT, heavily hand engraved with a floral relief pattern. The extra precision movement is 17 lignes size, open face, stem wind and set, and fitted with 23 jewels—21 beautiful ruby jewels and two faceted diamond cap jewels. It has gold plated train wheels plus chronometer style balance with solid gold screws. It has a true isochronal Breguet style hairspring. The mainspring is hand rubbed steel. The movement is styled in the Veri-Thin manner with patented inverted wheel train and timed to eight adjustments, including isochronism, heat, cold, and five positions. The dial is fine silver with applied raised gold numerals and gold hands. Cases were platinum, 18K and 14K gold and 97 percent were sold in the Gruen patented pentagon shaped case.

50th Anniversary Watch. Two production runs were produced. The first production was serial numbers 1-600, while the second production was serial numbers 1-50. The watch on the left is serial number 198 from the first production. The watch on the right is serial number 19 from the second production. Identification of each production group can be determined as follows: Group 1-600 has engraved on the balance bridge "All Adjts. 8 eight." Group 1-50 has engraved "All Adjts." with "8 eight" deleted.

The Gruen Pentagon Veri-Thin shaped pocket watch was patented in March of 1922 and in 1923 production of the 50th Anniversary movement began. The first production was 600, one for each month in business, numbered 1 to 600. Another 50, one for each year, were produced, numbered 01 to 050. These 650 movements were completed by 1924. Both groups being similar, it is difficult to distinguish one from the other. The only recognizable difference is: the Group 1-600 has engraved on the balance bridge "All Adjts. 8 Eight," while Group 1-50 has engraved on the balance bridge "All Adjts." with no reference to "8 Eight."

1874 — Gruen patented the safety pinion, a technical advancement in general use today.

1878 — Gruen made the first sixteen-size watch which was destined to become the standard size railroad watch in America. The original movement is sealed in the cornerstone of the Franklin County, Ohio, courthouse to commemorate Gruen's contribution to the art of fine watchmaking.

1896 — Gruen inaugurated a new trend in watch merchandising. It was the first watch company to sell completely cased movements in beautiful boxes with the retail price established by the manufacturer.

1902 — A major contribution to watchmaking—the Gruen Veri-Thin, the first accurate thin pocket watch.

The above illustration was taken from a Gruen advertisement depicting the change in manufacturing from the old to the new streamlined very thin movements.

1908 — Introduction of ladies' wrist watches.

1910 — Gruen, the first watch company to advertise on a nation-wide scale.

1915 — The first platinized dial with numerals applied in solid gold.

1918 — Nation-wide introduction of wrist watches for men.

1921 — The first Cartouche, representing a notable advance in movement design and manufacture in that an oval movement was fitted inside an oval case.

1922 — The Pentagon Veri-Thin, manufactured to remain upright in the pocket.

1924 — The Ultra Veri-Thin, introduced as the 50th Anniversary watch.

1925 — The patented Gruen Quadron, the first rectangular movement.

1930 — Gruen contributed the Baguette movement to the science of watchmaking.

1935 — Originated the Gruen Curvex.

1936 — Gruen patented a movement which was curved at both top and bottom.

Premier Maximus, 16 size, 23 diamond, ruby, sapphire jewels, gold jewel settings, with winding indicator. Sold in a silver presentation box. Each watch came with a Kew certificate and originally sold for $620.

The Edward Howard, 16 size, 23 matched blue ruby sapphires, chronometer type balance with frosted gold bridges. Sold in a presentation box with an extra crystal and mainspring for $350.

PRESTIGE WATCHES

In 1908 Waltham's most expensive watch was a 16s, 23j, gold case (Model #1907) that was selling for about $150. That same year Waltham introduced the "Premier Maximus" which they hailed as "the finest timepiece in America." It was a 16s, 23j, diamond-end stones, 6 positions (Model #1908). The selling price was $250.

The Premier Maximus posed a challenge to the E. Howard Watch Company and, not wanting to be outdone, Howard developed the "Edward Howard" watch at a price of $350. Introduced in 1912, it was in a 18k gold case complete with matched blue sapphire jewels, freespring balance, chronometer adjustments, gold-frost finished plates, and had an extra crystal and mainspring. The Howard ads read, "The finest watch ever produced in this or any other country." By 1914 the price of the Premier Maximus had increased to $400 with a 18k gold case and a sterling silver presentation box with a "KEW Class A Certificate."

In 1922 the Elgin Watch Company introduced their "no two alike" C. H. Hulburd presentation models at $300 to $750. At the same time the Premier Maximus was selling for $750.

In 1924 the Gruen Watch Company introduced their "50th

Anniversary Watch" at $500. It was in a five-sided "Pentagon Case," about a 10s, 23j, two of the jewels were diamonds, 12k gold plates, gold-plated train.

In 1925 the 922 Masterpiece, a 12s, 23j, gold train, 5 position watch, was introduced by the Hamilton Watch Company. Hamilton ad writers labeled it, "Beauty that will always be in good taste beyond fads and passing fancies."

The marketing strategy behind the high-quality, limited production watches was to enhance the sales of their regular production line. Each company used a model that had already proved itself. Waltham's 1907 and 1908 are basically the same watch. Hamilton only added MP to the 922 model number. Marketing was intense and in 1921 Elgin and Waltham stood eye to eye in production at 24 million, but in 1922 Elgin moved ahead.

Another watch of note was the Masonic watch introduced in 1922 by the Dudley Watch Company. It was a 14s, 19j, and carried the emblem depicting the eye, compass, square, trowel, plumb, and level. In their ads, the Dudley Watch Company touted themselves as being "the makers of America's finest timepieces."

REPEATING WATCHES

Around 1675 a repeating mechanism was attached to a clock for the first time. The first repeating watch was made in about 1677 by Thomas Tompion or Daniel Quare. Five-minute, quarter-hour and half-hour repeaters were popular by 1730. The minute repeater became common about 1830.

Repeating watch by **American Waltham Watch Co.**, 16 size, 17 jewels, hunting case, stem wind, gold train.

Fred Terstegen applied for a patent in 1882 for a repeating attachment that could be used with any American watch, key wind or stem wind. He was granted three patents: No. 311,270 on January 27, 1885, No. 3,421,844 on February 18, 1890, and No. 3,436,162 in September 1890. The Waltham Watch Co. was the only watch manufacturer to produce repeating watches in America. It is not known how many repeaters were made, but 3,500 is estimated.

OUTSTANDING, HIGH-GRADE
AND SCARCE WATCHES

Note: Early American-made watches that have been recased are worth 30 to 50 percent less. The prices listed below are for watches in their original cases.

Grade or Name — Description	Avg	Ex-Fn	Mint
Adams & Perry, 20S, 20J, 18K, KW	$2,000	$2,500	$3,000
Adams & Perry, 18S, 20J	1,000	1,500	2,000
J. H. Allison, 21J, Detent Chronometer	3,000	4,500	6,800
Appleton Tracy Chronodrometer, Sporting Model, silver	1,500	2,000	2,500
Appleton Watch Co., 18S, stem attached	500	600	750
Auburndale Watch Co. (Bentley)	500	700	1,000
Auburndale Watch Co. (Lincoln)	500	700	1,000
Auburndale Watch Co. (Rotary), 20S, Detent	1,500	1,800	2,600
Aurora, 18S, marked 15 ruby jewels on movement, but a few were actually 17J, OF	800	1,000	1,300
Ball Model with wind indicator (Waltham)	2,500	3,000	4,500
Ball-E. Howard & Co. VII, HC, 18K orig. case	4,000	5,000	6,500
P. S. Barlett (Pinned Plates) Model #57	350	450	600

E.F. Bowman, 16-18 size, 17 jewels, three quarter plate, gold jewel settings, lever set, stem wind, serial number 19, c. 1880.

Grade or Name—Description	Avg.	Ex-Fn	Mint
E. F. Bowman	$7,500	$11,000	$16,000
Robert Brown & Son, Providence	2,000	2,500	3,500

Grade or Name—Description	Avg.	Ex-Fn	Mint
California Watch Co., "Berkeley"	$1,300	$1,600	$2,000
Columbus King, 25J, HC	2,000	2,500	3,500
Columbus Railway King, 25J, OF	2,000	2,500	3,500
Columbus Railway King, 25J, HC	2,500	3,000	4,000
Columbus, 16S, 21J, Ruby Model, OF	525	600	725
Columbus, 16S, 21J, Ruby Model, HC	425	500	625
Paul Cornell, San Francisco, 19J	1,500	1,800	2,500
Cornell Watch Co. (San Francisco), 15J, SW	1,300	1,500	2,200
Samuel Curtis Watch Co., S#s less than 200, original case	2,500	3,000	4,000
Jacob D. Custer	8,500	12,000	18,000
Dennison, Howard & Davis, 15J, S#s below 2,000, all original	900	1,100	1,400
Dudley Model No. 1, box & papers	3,000	3,500	4,000
Elgin (C. H. Hulburd), 12S	800	1,000	1,200
Lord Elgin, 23J, 16S, 14K	1,000	1,200	1,500
C. Fasoldt	8,000	10,000	14,500
Fellows and Schell, 15J, (Waltham)	1,500	1,700	2,400
E. H. Flint, Cincinnati, Ohio, 18S, 18K, HC	4,000	4,500	5,500
Freeport Watch Co., 18K case	4,500	5,000	6,000
Luther Goddard, with eagle bridge, S#'s 1-35	5,000	6,000	7,500
Hamilton, 7J	800	1,000	1,300
Hamilton, 11J, OF ★ ★ ★ ★	1,500	2,000	2,800
Hamilton, 11J, HC	1,200	1,400	1,700
Hamilton, 21J, 16S, Model 994,LS	700	900	1,250
Hamilton, 23J, 18S, Model 946, OF, Extra	500	575	675
Hamilton, 23J, 18S, Model 947, HC, unmarked, 14K	3,500	4,000	5,000
Hamilton, 23J, Model 947, HC, marked, 14K	5,000	6,000	7,000
Hamilton, S#s less than 400, OF	400	500	700
Hamilton, S#s less than 1300, HC	400	500	700
Hamilton, 23J, 16S, Model 951, 14K case	3,500	4,000	5,000
Hamilton—Masterpiece 922, 18K, marked	800	900	1,200
Hampden Watch Co., 15J, 14K multi-color HC, 18S	1,500	1,800	2,200
The Howard, Davis & Dennison (S#'s 1-17)	30,000	38,000	50,000
Edward Howard in box, 18K case, S#s below 300	9,000	10,000	11,000
E. Howard & Co. (KW & KS), 15J, Series I, 18K, upright pallet	2,200	2,800	3,500
Howard & Rice, S#s 6,000-6,500	1,500	1,700	2,000
H. von der Heydt (The Self-Winding Watch Co.)	2,500	3,000	4,000
Illinois Bunn Special, 24J, 18S, Adj. 5P, OF, DR	500	600	750
Illinois Bunn Special, 25J, 18S	7,000	8,000	10,000
Illinois Bunn Special, 26J, 18S	4,500	5,000	6,000
Illinois Sangamo Special, solid bow, 60 hr., marked	650	775	900
Illinois (Ben Franklin), 25J, 16S, HC	4,500	5,000	5,500
Illinois (Ben Franklin), 26J, 18S	5,000	5,500	7,500
Illinois (Ben Franklin), 21J, 18S, Adj. 6P	900	1,000	1,250
Illinois (Ben Franklin), 24J, 18S	2,000	2,400	3,000
Illinois (Penn Special), 25J, 18S	5,000	5,800	6,800
Illinois (Penn Special), 26J, 18S	4,000	4,800	5,800

Grade or Name—Description	Avg.	Ex-Fn	Mint
Illinuis 16S, 23J, Diamond Ruby Sapphire Model	$2,000	$2,200	$2,500
Illinois Keywind 18S, Stuart adjusted, 5th pinion.........	475	550	650
Illinois Model #189, marked	400	525	675
Illinois, 18S, Southern R.R. Special, 21J, HC	1,200	1,300	1,600
Illinois Watch Co., 25J, 16S, bridge movement	4,000	4,500	5,500
Illinois Watch Co., 163A, 16S, 60 hr.	600	725	875
Ingraham, Betty Boop, 1934..........................	600	750	950
Kankakee W. Co., Kankakee, Ill., 16S.................	5,500	6,000	7,500
McIntyre W. Co., Kankakee, Ill., 25J, 16S, WI..........	5,500	6,000	7,500
Mickey Mouse #1, Ingersol, 1933......................	300	350	450
Mozart Watch Co., 3 wheel	11,000	15,000	20,000
Nashua Watch Co., marked	18,000	22,000	28,000
Newark Watch Co., 15J, KW, KS, HC	350	400	500
Newark Watch Co., Arthur Wadsworth, 18S, 18K, with			
keyless watch patent, N. Y........................	800	1,000	1,250
New England, skeletonized	200	250	350
New York Watch Co., pendant crank type	500	600	850
N. Y. Standard W. Co., with worm gear...............	250	300	400
N. Y. Watch Co., 15J, wolf's teeth wind, all original.....	1,000	1,200	1,500
Otay Watch Co., California	2,000	2,200	2,500
Palmer Watch Co., 15-17J, 18K......................	1,500	1,800	2,200
Palmer Watch Co. Chronometer	4,000	4,500	6,000
C. T. Parker (Waltham)	1,200	1,400	1,800
James & Henry Pitkin, S#s 1-50......................	15,000	20,000	30,000
H & J. F. Pitkin, S#s 50-377	10,000	15,000	20,000
A. H. Potter Chronometer, N.Y., 18K case, U.S mfg.....	10,000	12,000	16,000
George P. Reed Chronometer, 18K case.................	9,000	11,500	15,000
Rockford, 21J, 18S, wind indicator, No. 950	2,000	2,500	3,500
Rockford, 23J, 16S, Doll Watch Co. dial & case.........	1,000	1,200	1,500
Rockford, 24J, 18S, marked 'R.G.,' OF	1,000	1,200	1,500
Rockford, 25J, 18S.................................	3,500	5,000	6,500
San Jose Watch Co..................................	1,500	2,000	2,500
M. S. Smith, 18S, KW, 18K case......................	2,000	2,500	3,200
South Bend, Polaris, M#1, signed Polaris	1,500	1,800	2,200
J. P. Stevens Watch Co., S#s 1-174	3,000	4,000	5,500
Seth Thomas Maiden Lane, 21J, marked...............	1,000	1,200	1,500
Seth Thomas, 23J	800	1,000	1,300

Waltham made a watch with crystal or agate (see-through) plates, a rare beauty. It was size 4, Model 1882, and size 16, Model 1872. Both were 16 jewel in gold settings, had exposed pallets and a gold train. Not many of these watches were sold because the plates did not hold up very well—they broke like glass. But it is a true collector's item. Waltham called this the "stone movement."

Grade or Name—Description	Avg.	Ex-Fn	Mint
Seth Thomas Maiden Lane, 24J, marked	$1,500	$1,700	$2,100
Seth Thomas Maiden Lane, 25J, marked	2,200	2,500	3,000
Seth Thomas Maiden Lane, 28J, marked	15,000	18,000	25,000
U. S. Watch Co. (Waltham) The President, 21J..........	700	825	1,000
U. S. Watch Co. (Marion) (Butterfly KW & KS), 19J, SW, gilded mvt..	800	1,000	1,300
U. S. Watch Co. (Marion) 19J, SW, Pen Set, 18K, U.S.W.Co. case, HC	3,000	3,500	4,500
Waltham Crystal Watch (stone movement has transparent back plates), 4 Size	3,500	4,500	6,000
Waltham Crystal Watch (stone movement has transparent back plates), 14 Size	4,500	5,000	7,000
Waltham 5-Minute Repeater, 16S, 18K A.W. case........	3,500	4,000	5,000
Waltham 1-Minute Repeater, 18K, perpetual calendar.....	30,000	35,000	45,000
Waltham Premier Maximus with original box & papers, 18K	8,000	8,500	10,000
Watson (early Waltham), marked Boston................	700	1,100	1,500
Warren Mfg. Co. (to S#29)...........................	18,000	22,000	28,000
Washington Watch Co., 18S, 24J, LaFayette	900	1,150	1,400
Western Watch Co., Chicago, 18S.....................	2,500	3,000	4,000
Wichita Watch Co., Wichita, Kansas, 18S..............	2,500	3,000	4,000

WATCH CASES

One of the most appealing aspects of the pocket watch over the years must surely have been the elaborate cases in which they were housed. The very luster of a watch case emitted a sort of status and pride. Some folks went to great lengths to have as elaborate a case as possible.

Undoubtedly the gold cases were the standard men sought to achieve in the days when the pocket watch was most prominent. Those gold cases are eagerly sought after today by collectors.

Solid gold cases were at the top of the list in value; gold-filled was next, followed by rolled gold and gold-plated cases. Solid gold cases were of 8k, 10k, 14k, 18k, and 20k. (Pure gold is 24k.) The 20k gold was too soft and was not used often. Remember, even though a case is stamped 10k, 14k, etc., it is no guarantee that the case is solid gold.

The most common type of case was the silveroid. These cases were made of 45 percent nickel, 54 percent copper, and one percent manganese. They held up extremely well, and today a silveroid case can be polished to a high gloss, that will look like new, using a household brass polish.

From as early as 1525 watch cases have been engraved. Tools were developed that would cut a fine "V"-shaped groove in the metal, producing a very delicate design. A turning lathe was used as early as 1780 to produce geometric patterns of intersecting and interlacing curved lines on the watch cases.

SOLID GOLD CASES

"Pure gold" and "solid gold" are terms often misunderstood. The terms are not interchangeable, and the differences in meaning should be noted by the collector.

Pure gold is 24 karat gold, but gold in its purest form is useless as a workable metal. Gold must be reduced to at least 22k for coinage, and is most practical at 14k to 10k for wearing.

Pure gold refers to 24k. Solid gold is anything less than 24k—but is neither gold-filled or gold-plated. Solid gold cases are made of 18k, 14k, 10k, or 8k gold throughout.

Miscellaneous Notes on Gold Cases

In 1894 solid gold cases sold for: 18 size box case $180, $200, $250; 18 size gold case $90 to $178; 6 size cases sold for $75 to $159; 0 size cases, about $45.

An 18 size movement with a full plate weighs 50 DWT; a 16 size movement with a ¾ plate weighs 35 DWT. These weights do not include the case.

Scrap gold sells for about 80 percent of the daily gold quote for 24k gold, and scrap silver brings about 85 percent of the quote.

FINENESS OF GOLD KARATS

8k	.3333%
10k	.4167%
12k	.5000%
14k	.5833%
18k	.7500%
24k	1.0000% (100%)

MULTI-COLOR GOLD CASES

Multi-color gold cases in 18k and 14k first appeared around 1879. The 18k gold case did not lend itself to the multi-color process. The beauty of the colors was not as striking as in the 14k cases, and consequently did not sell as well. Because of the natural softness of 18k gold coupled with the unpopularity of the 18k multi-colored cases, the manufacturers decided to discontinue production of them around 1882. For these reasons, 18k multi-color cases are about 100 times more scarce than the 14k cases.

The "brilliant period" for multi-color gold cases was from 1890 to 1895 which represents the peak for sales and craftsmanship. By 1910 the multi-color gold case was no longer made in the 18 and 16 sizes. However, smaller sizes continued to be produced after this date.

Determining a realistic market value for multi-color gold cases is not an easy task. The value is influenced largely by eye appeal, such as degree of height and elaborateness of decorative design. The size and condition of the case are prime factors as well. The heavier and larger the case, the greater the value. Prices can range from $600 to $7,000 depending upon the size, condition and quality of the case that you have.

It might be worth noting that when gold prices decline, the value of multi-color cases seems to show little effect. On the other hand, when gold prices go up, the multi-color cases reflect this increase.

The case value listing at the end of the case section includes for your information, estimated values of multi-color gold cases.

COMPOSITION OF MULTI-COLOR GOLD

To Achieve Multi-Color Gold	These Elements Are Added
Yellow	Silver & Copper
Red	25% Copper
Dead Leaf	30% Silver
Green	25% Silver
Water Green	40% Silver
Blue	25% Iron
Violet or Purple	Small Amount of Iron
White	Palladium, Silver, Nickel, Zinc or Platinum

Superior White Gold is 25 percent platinum.
14k gold-filled cases have about 5 percent gold.

AMERICAN MOVEMENT SIZES
LANCASHIRE GAUGE

Size	Inches	Inches	mm	Lignes	Size	Inches	Inches	mm	Lignes
18/0	18/30	.600	15.24	6 3/4	2	1 7/30	1.233	31.32	13 7/8
17/0	19/30	.633	16.08	7 1/8	3	1 8/30	1.266	32.16	14 1/4
16/0	20/30	.666	16.92	7 1/2	4	1 9/30	1.300	33.02	14 7/8
15/0	21/30	.700	17.78	7 7/8	5	1 10/30	1.333	33.86	15 1/8
14/0	22/30	.733	18.62	8 1/4	6	1 11/30	1.366	34.70	15 3/8
13/0	23/30	.766	19.46	8 5/8	7	1 12/30	1.400	35.56	15 3/4
12/0	24/30	.800	20.32	9 1/8	8	1 13/30	1.433	36.40	16 1/8
11/0	25/30	.833	21.16	9 3/8	9	1 14/30	1.466	37.24	16 1/2
10/0	26/30	.866	22.00	9 3/4	10	1 15/30	1.500	38.10	16 7/8
9/0	27/30	.900	22.86	10 1/8	11	1 16/30	1.533	38.94	17 1/4
8/0	28/30	.933	23.70	10 1/2	12	1 17/30	1.566	39.78	17 5/8
7/0	29/30	.966	24.54	10 7/8	13	1 18/30	1.600	40.64	18 1/8
6/0	1	1.000	25.40	11 1/4	14	1 19/30	1.633	41.48	18 3/8
5/0	1 1/30	1.033	26.24	11 5/8	15	1 20/30	1.666	42.32	18 3/4
4/0	1 2/30	1.066	27.08	12 1/8	16	1 21/30	1.700	43.18	19 1/8
3/0	1 3/30	1.100	27.94	12 3/8	17	1 22/30	1.733	44.02	19 1/2
2/0	1 4/30	1.133	28.78	12 3/4	18	1 23/30	1.766	44.86	19 7/8
0	1 5/30	1.166	29.62	13 1/8	19	1 24/30	1.800	45.72	20 1/4
1	1 6/30	1.200	30.48	13 1/2	20	1 25/30	1.833	46.56	20 3/4

SWISS MOVEMENT SIZES
Lignes With Their Equivalents in Millimeters and Decimal Parts of an Inch

Lignes	Inches Decimals	Millimeters
7	.622	15.79
8	.710	18.05
9	.799	20.30
10	.888	22.56
11	.977	24.81
12	1.066	27.07
13	1.154	29.32
14	1.243	31.58
15	1.332	33.84
16	1.421	36.09
17	1.510	38.35
18	1.599	40.60
19	1.687	42.86
20	1.776	45.11
21	1.865	47.37
22	1.954	49.63

GAUGES FOR MEASURING YOUR WATCH SIZE

The size of a watch is determined by measuring the outside diameter of the dial side of the lower pillar plate. The gauges below may be placed across the face of your watch to calculate its approximate size.

AMER. MOVEMENT SIZES

26/0 21/0 20/0 16/0 12/0 10/0 8/0 5/0 6 10 12 14 18
18/0   6/0 4/0 3/0   8   18
0

SWISS MOVEMENT SIZES
LIGNES

2   4   6   8   10 12 14 16 18 20
3   5   7   9   11 13 15 17 19

SOLID GOLD MARKS

GOLD-FILLED CASES

The first patent for gold-filled cases was given to J. Boss on May 3, 1859.

Gold-filled cases are far more common than solid gold cases. Only about 5 percent of the cases were solid gold. In making the gold-filled case, the following process was used: two bars of gold, 12" long, 2" wide, and ½" thick were placed on either side of a bar of base metal. The bar of base metal was ¾" thick and the same length and width as the gold bars. These three bars were soldered together under pressure at high temperature. The bars were sent through rolling mills under tremendous pressure; this rolling was repeated until the desired thickness was reached. The new sandwich-type gold was now in a sheet. Discs were punched out of the sheet and pressed in a die to form a dish-shaped cover. Finally the lip, or ridge, was added. The bezel, snap, and dust caps were added in the finishing room. Gold-filled cases are usually 10k or 14k gold. The cases were marked ten-year, fifteen-year, twenty-year, twenty-five-year, or thirty-year. The number of years indicated the duration of guarantee that the gold on the case would not wear through to the base metal. The higher the number of years indicates that more gold was used and that a higher original price was paid.

In 1924 the government prohibited any further use of the guarantee terms of 5, 10, 15, 20, 25, or 30 years. After that, manufacturers marked their cases 10k or 14k Gold-Filled and 10k Rolled Gold Plate. Anytime you see the terms "5, 10, 15, 20, 25 and 30-year" this immediately identifies the case as being gold-filled. The word "guaranteed" on the case also denotes gold-filled.

Rolled Gold

Rolled gold involved rolling gold into a micro thinness and, under extreme pressure, bonding it to each sheet of base metal. Rolled gold carried a five-year guarantee. The thickness of the gold sheet varied and had a direct bearing on value, as did the richness of the engraving.

Gold Gilding

Brass plates, wheels and cases are often gilded with gold. To do this, the parts are hung by a copper wire in a vessel or porous cell of a galvanic battery filled with a solution of offerro-cyanid of potassium, carbonate of soda, chloride of gold, and distilled water. An electric current deposits the gold evenly over the surface in about a six-minute period. One ounce of gold is enough for heavy gilding of six hundred watches. After gilding, the plates are polished with a soft buff using powdered rouge mixed with water and alcohol. The older method is fire-gilt which uses a gold and mercury solution. The metal is subjected to a high temperature so the mercury will evaporate and leave the gold plating. This is a very dangerous method, however, due to the harmful mercury vapor.

GOLD-FILLED MARKS

The following gold-filled and rolled gold plate marks are not complete, but if you have any doubt that the case is solid gold, pay only the gold-filled price.

GOLD FILLED MARKS

C.W.C.CO
★ MARK
TRADE
PIONEER

☆ 10 K ROLLED GOLD PLATE

BEE HIVE

FAHYS 14K Extra

ELGIN GIANT

(14K. Filled.)

(Jas. Boss 10K. Filled. 20 Years.)

CROWN 14K. FILLED
(25 Years.)

(Keystone Extra, Substitute for All-Gold Case.)

CROWN 10K. FILLED
(20 Years.)

ELGIN TIGER

(Rolled Gold.)

(Jas. Boss 14K. Filled. 25 Years.)

EMPRESS
(Gold Filled, 10 Years.)

FORTUNE
(Gold Filled, 20 Years.)

ELGIN COMMANDER

(14K. Filled.)

(10 Years.)

PREMIER
(Gold Filled, 25 Years.)

XV.

THE BELL 14K.
(25 Years.)

CASHIER
(Gold Filled, 25 Years.)

WARRANTED
N.A.W.Co
20 YEARS

(10K. Gold Filled.)

V.

(5 Years.)

(15 Years.)

XX.

(20 Years.)

(25 Years.)

THE COMET
(10 Years.)

SILVER CASE MARKS

AMERICAN WATCH CO.
WALTHAM, MASS.

A.W.W.CO.
WALTHAM.
STERLING.

A.W. CO.

STERLING.

A.W.W. CO. COIN.

AMERICAN WALTHAM.MASS.
WATCH CO.
STERLING

AMERICAN WATCH CO. WALTHAM. MASS.
WARRANTED
STERLING SILVER.

AMERICAN WALTHAM WATCH CO.
STERLING

AMERICAN WALTHAM WATCH CO.
STERLING

AM. WATCH CO. WALTHAM. MASS.
WARRANTED
COIN-SILVER

DUEBER STERLING

(Discontinued.)

NEWPORT COIN
(Coin Silver with Albata Cap)
(Discontinued.)

DUEBER COIN
(Coin Silver with Silver Cap)
(Discontinued.)

925
(Discontinued.)

DUEBER COIN

CHAMPION
COIN.

STAR W.C.CO.
STERLING
925/1000
FINE

(Coin Silver, with Silver Caps, Gold Joints and Crowns.)

N.A.W.Co
STERLING
(Sterling Silver.)

DUEBER STERLING

925
Sterling Silver

58

SILVER CASE MARKS

(*Sterling Silver.*)

STERLING
SILVER
UNITED STATES
ASSAY
925./1000
FINE.

ILLINOIS
W.C.CO,
ELGIN
STERLING

HUNTING CASES

A hunting case is identified by a cover over the face of the watch. The case is opened by pressing the stem of the watch. The cover was used for dress and protection and the hunter case was carried by men of status.

How To Handle A Hunting Case Watch

Hold the watch in right hand with the bow or swing ring between the index finger and thumb. Press on the stem with the right thumb to release the cover exposing the face.

When closing, don't snap the front cover. Press the crown to move the catch in, close the cover, then release the crown. This will prevent wear to the soft gold on the rim and catch.

Above: Example of a hunting case

Right: Example of a swing-out case

SWING-OUT MOVEMENTS

On some watches the movement swings out from the front. On these watches the movement can be swung out by unscrewing the crystal and pulling the stem out to release the movement. See example above.

Demi-Hunting case

Example of a 14 carat gold boxed hinged case, selling for $94 in 1890.

Below: Example of a reversible case to either hunting or open face.

Left: Example of a screw bezel and screw back case.

Note: The screw on bezel was invented by E. C. Fitch in 1886.

CASE PRICES

Case prices are for complete cases with bezel, crystal, stem, crown and bow. Hunting case must have workable lift spring.

SILVEROID CASES

Size	Avg	Ex-Fn	Mint
18S, OF, SW	$10	$15	$25
18S, OF, KW	15	20	35
18S, HC, SW	20	25	40
18S, HC, KW	22	30	50
16S, OF	8	12	18
16S, HC	10	15	22
12S, OF	3	4	6
12S, HC	5	7	10
6S, OF	3	4	6
6S, HC	5	7	10

COIN CASES

Size	Avg	Ex-Fn	Mint
18S, OF, SW	$15	$22	$35
18S, OF, KW	25	35	50
18S, HC, SW	20	27	40
18S, HC, KW	30	43	60
16S, OF	12	18	25
16S, HC	15	20	35
12S, OF	5	6	8
12S, HC	5	6	8
6S, OF	5	6	8
6S, HC	8	10	13

GOLD-FILLED CASES

Size and Style	Avg	Ex-Fn	Mint
18S, OF, Plain	$55	$65	$95
18S, OF, Fancy	65	75	115
18S, HC, Plain	75	85	135
18S, HC, Fancy	85	95	155
16S, OF, Plain	50	60	90
16S, OF, Fancy	55	65	95
16S, HC, Plain	65	75	120
16S, HC, Fancy	70	80	135
12S, OF, Plain	15	20	30
12S, OF, Fancy	20	25	35
12S, HC, Plain	25	30	45
12S, HC, Fancy	30	40	55
6S, OF, Plain	10	20	30
6S, OF, Fancy	15	25	35
6S, HC, Plain	25	30	45
6S, HC, Fancy	30	40	55

Note: Plain enamel single sunk dial brings $15 to $30.

MOVEMENT IDENTIFICATION

1. Grade Number. **2.** Nickel Motor Barrel Bridge. **3.** Center Wheel (2nd Wheel). **4.** Winding Wheel with Jewel Setting. **5.** First Barrel Wheel. **6.** Winding Click. **7.** Case Screw. **8.** Pendant Crown. **9.** Pendant Bow or Swing Ring. **10.** Crown Wheel with Screw. **11** Damaskeening-horizontal pattern. **12.** Number of Jewels. **13.** Center Wheel Jewel with Setting. **14.** Adjusted to Heat, Cold, Isochronism & 5 Positions. **15.** Patented Regulator with Index & Spring. **16.** Balance End Stones (Diamonds, Rubys, & Sapphires were used). **17.** Balance Screws. **18.** Compensating Balance Wheel. **19.** Hairspring. **20.** Escapement Bridge. **21.** Escapement Wheel Jewel with Setting (Diamonds, Rubys, & Sapphires were used). **22.** Escapement Wheel. **23.** Fourth Wheel Jewel with Setting. **24.** Third Wheel. **25.** Fourth Wheel. **26.** Fourth Wheel Bridge. **27.** Third Wheel Jewel with Setting. **28.** Center & Third Wheel Bridge. **29.** Bridge Screw. **30.** Manufacturers Name & Location. **31.** Jewel Setting Screw.

NOMENCLATURE
OF
WATCH PARTS

Ratchet Wheel

Crown or Main Wheel

Click Spring

Setting Cam

Bevel Pinion

Crown or Main
Screw Washer

Winding Arbor

Winding and
Setting Clutch

Setting
Lever

Setting Spring

Click

Setting
Spring Cam

Winding Sleeve

Clutch Lever

NOMENCLATURE
OF
WATCH PARTS

Barrel

Center Wheel

Third Wheel

Minute Wheel

Hour Wheel

Fourth Wheel

Escape Wheel

Center Arbor Washer

Third Pinion

Fourth Pinion

Center Staff

Center Pinion

Escape Pinion

Cannon Pinion

Balance Staff

Pallet Fork and Arbor

Regulator

Combination Roller

Barrel Arbor

Overcoil Hairspring

Balance Wheel

INSPECTING OPEN-FACED WATCHES

For watches with a screw-on front and back, as in railroad models, hold the watch in the left hand and, with the right hand, turn the bezel counter clockwise. While removing the bezel, hold onto the stem and swing ring in order not to drop the watch. Lay the bezel down, check the dial for cracks and crazing nicks, chips, etc. Look for lever and check to see that it will allow hands to be set. After close examination, replace the bezel and turn the watch over. Again, while holding the stem between the left thumb and index finger, remove the back cover. If it is a screw-on back cover, turn it counter clockwise. If it is a snap-on cover, look for the lip on the back and use a pocket knife to pry the back off.

DAMASKEENING

Damaskeening (pronounced dam-a-skeening) is the process of applying ornate designs on metal by inlaying gold or by etching. Damaskeening on watch plates became popular in the late 1870s. This kind of beauty and quality in the movement was a direct result of the competition in the watch industry. Illinois, Waltham, Rockford, and Seth Thomas competed fiercely for beauty. Some damaskeening was in two colors of metal such as copper and nickel. The process derives its name from Damascus, a city in Syria, most famous for its metal work. A kind of steel was made there with designs of wavy or varigated lines etched or inlaid on their swords.

Left: Example of open face case

Below: Example of Damaskeening

DISPLAY CASE WATCHES

Display case watches were used by salesmen and in jewelry stores to show the customer the movement. Both front and back had a glass crystal. These are not rare, but they are nice to have in a collection to show off a nice watch movement.

WATCH CASE PRODUCTION

Before the Civil War, watchmaking was being done on a very small scale, and most of the companies in business were making their own movements as well as their own cases. After the War, tradesmen set up shops specializing exclusively in cases, while other artisans were making the movements. The case factories, because of mass production, could supply watch manufacturers with cases more economically than the manufacturers could produce their own.

A patent was granted to James Boss on May 3, 1859, and the first gold-filled watch cases were made from sandwich-type sheets of metal. Boss was not the first to use gold-filled, but he did invent a new process that proved to be very successful, resulting in a durable metal that Boss sold with a 20-year **money-back** guarantee.

···· Gold
···· Base Metal
···· Gold

The illustrations at left is a sandwiched type gold-filled case.

GOLD CASE
WEIGHTS BY SIZE

Size & Style of Case	Pennyweights (DWT)				
	Ex. Heavy	Heavy	Medium	Light	Ex. Light
18 size Hunting Case	60 to 65	50 to 55	45 to 50	40 to 45	35
16 size Hunting Case	55 to 60	45 to 50	40 to 45	35 to 40	32
18 size Open Face Case		40 to 45	38	35	
16 size Open Face Case		40	36	30	
12 size Open Face Case (Thin)					14
6 size Hunting Case	24	22	20	18	
0 size Hunting Case					14 to 16

An 18 size movement with a full plate weighs 50 DWT; a 16 size movement with a ¾ plate weighs 35 DWT. These weights do not include the case.

CARE OF WATCHES

To some people a watch is just a device that keeps time. They do not know the history of its development nor how it operates. They have no appreciation for improvements made over the years. That the watch is a true miracle of mechanical genius and skill, is seldom more than a fleeting thought. The average person will know it must be wound to run, that it has a mainspring and possibly a hairspring. Some even realize there are wheels and gears and, by some strange method, these work in harmony to keep time. If for some reason the watch should stop, the owner will merely take it to a watch repair shop and await the verdict on damage and cost.

To be a good collector one must have some knowledge of the components of a watch and how they work and the history of the development of the watch. To buy a watch on blind faith is indeed risky, but many collectors do it every day because they have limited knowledge.

How does a watch measure time and perform so well? Within the case one can find the fulcrum, lever, gear, bearing, axle, wheel, screw, and the spring which overcomes nature's law of gravity. All these parts harmonize to provide an accurate reading minute by minute. A good collector will be able to identify all of them.

After acquiring a watch, you will want to take good care of it. A watch should be cleaned inside and out. Dirt will wear it out much faster, and gummy oil will restrict it and keep it from running all together. After the watch has been cleaned it should be stored in a dry place. Rust is the No. 1 enemy. A watch is a delicate instrument but, if it is given proper care, it will provide many years of quality service. A pocket watch should be wound at regular intervals—about once every 24 hours, early each morning—so the mainspring has its full power to withstand the abuse of daily use. Do not carry a watch in the same pocket with articles that will scratch or tarnish the case. A fully wound watch can withstand a jar easier than a watch that has been allowed to run down. Always wind a watch and leave it running when you ship it. If you are one who enjoys carrying a watch be sure to have it cleaned at least once every two years.

EXAMINATION AND INSPECTION
OF A WATCH BEFORE PURCHASING

The examination and inspection of a watch before purchasing is of paramount importance. This is by no means a simple task for there are many steps involved in a complete inspection.

The first thing you should do is to listen to a watch and see how it sounds. Many times the trained ear can pick up problems in the escapement and balance. The discriminating buyer will know that sounds cannot be relied on entirely because each watch sounds different, but the sound test is worthwhile and is comparable to the doctor putting the stethescope to a patient's heart as his first source of data.

Check the bow to see if it is securely fastened to the case and look at the case to see if correction is necessary at the joints. The case should close firmly at both the back and front. (Should the case close too firmly, rub the rim with beeswax which will ease the condition and prolong the life of the rim.)

Take note of the dents, scratches, wear and other evidences of misuse. Does the watch have a generally good appearance? Check the bezel for proper fit and the crystal to see if it is free of chips.

Remove the bezel and check the dial for chips and hairline cracks. Look for stains and discoloration; and check to see if the dial is loose. It is important to note that a simple dial with only a single sunk dial is by nature a stronger unit due to the fact that a double sunk dial is constructed of three separate pieces.

If it is a stem-winder, try winding and setting. Problems in this area can be hard to correct. Parts are hard to locate and may possibly have to be handmade. If it is a lever set, pull the lever out to see if it sets properly into gear. Also check to see that the hands have proper clearance.

Now that the external parts have been inspected, open the case to view the movement. Check to see that the screws hold the movement in place securely. Note any repair marks and any missing screws. Make a visual check for rust and discoloration, dust, dirt and general appearance. If the movement needs cleaning and oiling, this should be deducted from the price of the watch, as well as any repair that will have to be made.

Note the quality of the movement. Does it have raised gold jewel settings or a gold train (center wheel or all gears)? Are the jewels set in or pressed in? Does it have gold screws in the balance wheel? Sapphire pallets? Diamond end stones? Jeweled motor barrel? How many adjustments does it have? Does it have overall beauty and eye appeal?

Examine the balance for truth. First look directly down upon the balance to detect error truth in the roundness. Then look at it from the side to detect error in the flat swing or rotation. It should be smooth in appearance.

Examine the hairspring in the same manner to detect errors in truth. When a spring is true in the round, there will be no appearance of jumping when it is viewed from the upper side. The coils will appear to uniformly dilate and contract in perfect rhythm when the balance is in motion. Check the exposed portion of the train wheels for burred, bent, or broken teeth. Inspect pinions and pivots for wear. If a watch has complicated features such as a repeater, push the slides, plungers, and buttons to see that they are in good working order.

After the movement and case have been examined to your satisfaction and all the errors and faults are found, talk to the owner as to the history and his personal thoughts about the watch. Is the movement in the original case? Is the dial the original one? Just what has been replaced?

Has the watch been cleaned? Does it need any repairs? If so, can the seller recommend anyone to repair the watch?

Finally, see if the seller makes any type of guarantee, and get an address and phone number. It may be valuable if problems arise, or if you want to buy another watch in the future.

WATCH MOVEMENT PARTS

Mechanical watches are small engines powered by a spring, which keeps the balance in motion. The uniformity of this motion relies on the balance; the durability rests on the quality of material and construction of the complete movement.

HOW A WATCH WORKS

There are five basic components of a watch:

1. The **mainspring**, and its winding mechanism, which provides power.
2. The **train** which consists of gears, wheels and pinions that turn the hands.
3. The **escapement** consisting of the escape wheel and balance which regulates or controls.
4. The **dial and hands** which tell the time.
5. The **housing** consisting of the case and plates which protect.

The motion of the balance serves the watch the same as a pendulum serves a clock. The balance wheel and roller oscillate in each direction moving the fork and lever by means of a ruby pin. As the lever moves back and forth it allows the escape wheel to unlock at even intervals (about 1/5 sec.) and causes the train of gears to move in one direction under the power of the mainspring. Thus, the mainspring is allowed to be let down or unwind one pulse at a time.

Early style watch with a stackfreed (tear shaped cam). Note the balance is dumbell shaped.

Power unit for modern watch showing the various parts.

THE MAINSPRING

Watches were developed from the early portable clocks. The coiled spring or mainspring provided the drive power. The first coiled springs were applied to clocks about 1435. For the watch, coiled springs were first used about 1510. The power from a mainspring is not consistent and this irregular power was disastrous to the first watches. The Germans' answer to irregular power was a device called a **stackfreed**. Another apparatus employed was the **fusee**. The fusee proved to be the best choice. At first catgut was used between the spring barrel and fusee. By around 1660 the catgut was replaced by a chain. Today, the fusee is still used in naval chronometers. One drawback to the fusee is the amount of space it takes up in the watch. Generally, the simplest devices are best.

The mainspring is made of a piece of hardened and tempered steel about 20 inches long and coiled in a closed barrel between the upper and lower plates of the movement. It is matched in degree of strength, width, and thickness most suitable for the watch's need or design. It is subject to differing conditions of temperature and tensions (the wound-up position having the greatest tension). The lack of uniformity in the mainspring affects the timekeeping qualities of a watch.

The power assembly in a watch consists of the mainspring, mainspring barrel, arbor, and cap. The mainspring furnishes the power to run the watch. It is coiled around the arbor and is contained in the mainspring barrel, which is cylindrical and has a gear on it which serves as the first wheel of the train. The arbor is a cylindrical shaft with a hook for the mainspring in the center of the body. The cap is a flat disk which snaps into a recess in the barrel. A hook on the inside of the mainspring barrel is for attaching the mainspring to the barrel.

Jeweled Motor Barrel Unit: 1. Barrel top jewel screw. 2. Barrel top jewel and setting. 3. Ratchet wheel. 4. Barrel bridge. 5. Barrel hub. 6. Barrel head. 7. Mainspring (in barrel). 8. Barrel. 9. Barrel arbor (riveted to barrel). 10. Barrel lower jewel and setting. 11. Pillar plate.

The mainspring is made of a long thin strip of steel, hardened to give the desired resiliency. Mainsprings vary in size but are similar in design; they have a hook on the outer end to attach to the mainspring barrel, and a hole in the inner end to fasten to the mainspring barrel arbor.

By turning the crown clockwise, the barrel arbor is rotated and the mainspring is wound around it. The mainspring barrel arbor is held stationary after winding by means of the ratchet wheel and click. As the mainspring uncoils, it causes the mainspring barrel to revolve. The barrel is meshed with the pinion on the center wheel, and as it revolves it sets the train wheels in motion. Pocket and wrist watches, in most cases, will run up to 36 hours on one winding.

Curb pins adjusted to vary the length of hairspring

Fig. 1

Fig. 2

Fig. 1. Bottom view of hairspring & cock

Fig. 2. A side and top view of hairspring

THE HAIRSPRING

The hairspring is the brain of the watch and is kept in motion by the mainspring. The hairspring is the most delicate tension spring made. It is a piece of flat wire about 12 inches long, 1/100th of an inch wide, 2½/1,000th of an inch thick, and weighs only about 1/9,000th of a pound. Thousands of these hairsprings can be made from one pound of steel. The hairspring controls the action of the balance wheel. The hairspring steel is drawn through the diamond surfaces to a third the size of a human hair. There are two kinds of hairsprings in the watches of later times, the flat one and the Breguet. The Breguet (named for its French inventor) is an overcoil given to the spring. There are two methods for overcoil, the oldest is the way the spring is bent by hand; and with the other method the overcoil is bent or completed in a form

REGULATORS
Identification

Overcoil concentric to travel of regulator pins
Regulator pins
Curve of Hairspring overcoil
Hairspring stud
Hairspring stud screw
Regulator
Balance Cock

E. Howard & Co.

South Bend

Waltham

Breguet

Swiss

Ball Hamilton 18s

Ball Elgin 18s

Ball Hamilton 16s

Ball Illinois 16s

Ball Waltham 16s

Hampden

Marion

E. Howard & Co.

J.P. Stevens

F R S

Agassiz

Waltham

Petek Philippe

swiss- 2 piece

Fasoldt

Hampden

U.S. Waltham

U.S. Waltham

Waltham

73

REGULATORS
Identification

Fredonia & Peoria

J. Jurgensen

Keystone

Keystone

Waltham

Otay

U.S. Waltham

Elgin

Illinois

Elgin

Improved Swiss

Rockford

Thomas Tompion
1638-1700

Columbus

Hamilton

English & American 1800-1850

Underspring

Nathaniel Barrow 1750

Grossman Glasshutte

at one end and at the same time is hardened and tempered in the form. The hairspring contracts and expands 432,000 times a day.

A modern style **Regulator**. Note triangular shaped hairspring stud which is located on the balance bridge between the screw and curb pin.

THE TRAIN

The time train consists of the mainspring barrel, center wheel and pinion, third wheel and pinion, fourth wheel and pinion, and escape wheel which is part of the escapement. The function of the time train is to reduce the power of the mainspring and extend its time to 36 hours or more. The mainspring supplies energy in small units to the escapement, and the escapement delays the power from being spent too quickly.

The long center wheel arbor projects through the pillar plate and above the dial to receive the cannon pinion and hour wheel. The cannon pinion receives the minute hand and the hour wheel the hour hand. As the mainspring drives the barrel, the center wheel is rotated once each hour.

Actual alignment of **Train Unit**

The second or center wheel of the watch turns once every hour. It is the largest wheel in the train, and the arbor or post of the center wheel carries the minute hand. The center wheel pinion is in mesh with the mainspring barrel (pinions follow and the wheel supplies the power). The center wheel is in mesh with the third wheel pinion (the third wheel makes eight turns to each turn of the center wheel). The third wheel is in mesh with the fourth wheel pinion, and the fourth wheel pinion is in mesh with the escape wheel pinion. The fourth wheel post carries the second hand and is in a 1:60 ratio to the center wheel (the center wheel turns once every hour and the fourth wheel turns 60 turns every hour). The escape wheel has 15 teeth (shaped like a flat foot) and works with two pallets on the lever. The two pallet jewels lock and unlock the escape wheel at intervals (1/5 sec.) allowing the train of gears to move in one direction under the influence of the mainspring. The lever (quick train) vibrates 18,000 times to one turn of the center wheel (every hour). The hour hand works from a motion train. The mainspring barrel makes about five turns every 36 hours.

SOLID GOLD TRAIN

Some watches have a gold train instead of brass wheels. These watches are more desirable. To identify gold wheels within the train, look at a Hamilton 992; the center wheel is made of gold and the other wheels are made of brass. Why a gold train? Gold is soft, but it has a smooth surface and it molds easily. Therefore, the wheels have less friction. These wheels do not move fast, and a smooth action is more important than a hard metal. Gold does not tarnish or rust and is nonmagnetic. The arbors and pinions in these watches will be steel. Many watches have some gold in them, and the collector should learn to distinguish it.

Above: Top view of early "s" shaped cock. Note dumbbell balance and cock is pinned to the plate.

Left: Early verge style escapement with dumbbell balance. 1. Lower pallet. 2. Upper pallet. 3. Verge. 4. Dumbbell balance.

TYPES OF ESCAPEMENTS

The verge escapement is the earliest form of escapement. It was first used in clocks as far back as the early 1300s. The verge escapement consists of a crown escape wheel, a verge which has two flags called pallets, and a balance. Early German watches had a balance shaped like a dumbbell, called a "foliot." Later most other watches used a balance shaped like a wheel. The crude weights of the foliot could be adjusted closer to or farther from the center of the balance for better timekeeping. Another design from that period was the circular balance. The circular balance was used by Christiaan Huygens in 1675 when he introduced the hairspring. This remarkable invention was used from that time onward.

The verge escapement was used by Luther Goddard in America as well as most of the Colonial watchmakers.

About 1725 the cylinder escapement was invented by George Graham, an Englishman. His cylinder escapement was a great im-

A later style **Verge Escapement** with a more common balance wheel.

provement over the verge. Even so, the cylinder escapement was not popular until Abraham Louis Breguet adopted the idea about 1765. This escapement wears out rather rapidly, unfortunately.

Note: *We have never seen a Colonial watch that used a cylinder escapement in a movement. If you have one or know where one is, please contact the author.*

Cylinder Escapement

Duplex Escapement

Illustrating and American form of the **Duplex Escapement** as first employed by the Waterbury Watch Co.

78

The duplex escapement is accredited generally to Pierre LeRoy, a Frenchman, around 1750, but was never popular in France. This type of escapement was favored in England up to the mid 1850s. Thomas Tyrer patented it in England in 1782. The New England Watch Co. of Waterbury, Conn., used the duplex from 1898 until 1910. The Waterbury Watch Company used it from 1880 to 1898.

The roller and lever action escapement was invented by Thomas Mudge in 1750.

Rack and lever escapement. 1. Balance wheel pinion. 2. Rack. 3. Lever. 4. Ratchet escape wheel.

English style right angle lever which was used in earlier American made watches.

The rack lever escapement was invented by Hautefeuille in 1722. The famous Breguet used the lever early in the 1800s. By 1830 the English watchmakers had established the superiority of the lever escapement. In France and Switzerland the teeth of the lever escapement wheel were clubbed—that is to say, the point of the teeth were cut away to give a longer impulse plane. In England, pointed or ratchet teeth were preferred, and the right-angle lever was preferred over the straight line lever, also referred to as the Swiss lever. Pitkins and Custer both used the lever escapements. The right-angle lever was used in the Warren & Samuel Curtis as well as early Elgin, Newark, Tremont, New York, early Hampden, early Illinois, and Cornell watches. The American factories settled on a Swiss style escapement (straight line lever and club tooth escape wheel) by the 1870s.

Purpose of Escape Wheel

If a movement consisted only of the mainspring and a train of wheels, and the mainspring were would up, the train would run at full speed resulting in the power being spent in a few moments. For this reason, the escapement has been arranged to check it. The duty of the escapement is to allow each tooth of the escape wheel to pass at a regulated interval. The escapement is of no service alone and, therefore, must have some other arrangement to measure and regulate these intervals. This is accomplished by the balance assembly.

The escape wheel is in most cases made of steel and is staked on a pinion and arbor. It is the last wheel of the train and connects the train with the escapement. It is constructed so that the pallet jewels move in and out between its teeth, allowing but one tooth to escape at a time. The teeth are "club-shaped" because of the addition of impulse faces to the end of the teeth.

The pallet jewels are set at an angle to make their inside corners reach over three teeth and two spaces of the escape wheel. The outside corners of the jewels will reach over two teeth and three spaces of the escape wheel with a small amount of clearance. At the opposite end of the pallet, directly under the center of the fork slot, is a steel or brass pin called the guard pin. The fork is the connecting link to the balance assembly.

BALANCE AND HAIRSPRING

The rotation of the balance wheel is controlled by the hairspring. The inner end of the hairspring is pinned to the collet, and the collet is held friction-tight on the staff above the balance wheel. The outer end of the hairspring is pinned to a stud which is held stationary on the balance cock by the stud screw. The roller jewel is cemented in the large roller assembly, which is mounted on the staff directly under the balance wheel. Under the first roller is a smaller one which acts as a safety roller. This is necessary because of the crescent cut out in the roller table which allows the guard pin of the escapement assembly to pass through.

The balance wheel rotates clockwise and counterclockwise on its axis by means of the impulse it receives from the escapement. The motion of the balance wheel is constant due to the coiling and uncoiling of the hairspring. The impulse, transmitted to the roller jewel by

Modern or Swiss Lever Escapement

A. Lever
B. Entrance pallet
C. Exit pallet
D. Fork
E. Banking pins
F. Fork slot
G. Horns
H. Impulse roller jewel
K. Safety finger
L. Notch of small plate M
M. Safety roller
N. Roller table
P. Impulse plane of the teeth of the wheel
R. Escape wheel

the swinging of the pallet fork to the left, causes the balance to rotate in a counterclockwise direction. The position of the fork allows the roller jewel to move out of the slot of the fork freely and in the same direction. The fork continues on until it reaches the banking pin. Meanwhile the balance continues in the same direction until the tension of the hairspring overcomes the momentum of the balance wheel. When this occurs the balance returns to its original position, which causes the roller jewel to again enter the slot of the fork.

Pallet and Escape Tooth Action. The momentum that has been built up during the return of the balance, causes the roller pin to impart an impulse on the inside of the fork slot. This impulse is great enough to push the fork away from its position against the banking pin. As the fork is pushed away, it causes the pallet stone to slide on the toe of the escape wheel tooth. When the pallet stone has slid down to its edge, it frees the escape wheel tooth, thereby unlocking the escape wheel. The escape wheel, being impelled by the force of the mainspring, starts to rotate. As the escape wheel turns, the tooth glides along the impulse face of the pallet jewel, forcing it to move out of the way. The moving pallet carries the fork with it and imparts the impulse to the roller jewel. The right pallet stone intercepts a tooth of the escape wheel to lock it, as the fork moves toward the banking pin. Having a short "run" left to the banking pin, the pressure of the escape wheel tooth against the locking face of the pallet jewel draws the stone deeper into the escape wheel and, therefore, causes the fork to complete its run and holds it against the banking pin. Meanwhile the balance continues in a clockwise direction until the tension of the hairspring overcomes the momentum of the balance and returns it to its original position.

Rate of Escape Tooth Release. Through the motion of the escapement, the mainspring keeps the balance vibrating, and the balance regulates the train. The escape wheel has 15 teeth and is allowed to revolve 10 turns per minute. Thus, 150 teeth glide over each pallet stone in 1 minute. The gliding of the escape wheel teeth over the impulse faces of the pallet stones will cause the balance to vibrate 300 vibrations or beats per minute. These vibrations will continue until the force of the mainspring is spent.

SCREWS

Screws used in watches are very small and precise. These screws measure 254 threads to the inch and 47,000 of them can be put into a thimble. The screws were hardened and tempered and polished to a cold hard brilliance. By looking at these screws through a magnifying glass one can see the uniformity.

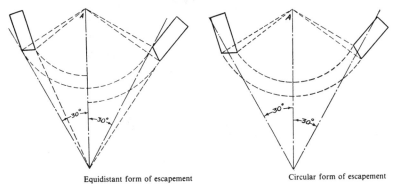

Equidistant form of escapement

Circular form of escapement

EQUIDISTANT ESCAPEMENT

The term Equidistant Escapement is a form of lever escapement. The locking of each pallet takes place at the same distance from the pallet arbor. A similar form of escapement is the circular pallet with the circular form of escapement. The impulses are given at equal distance from the center line. The Swiss preferred the equidistant while the Americans preferred the circular. There is little difference in performance between these two types of escapement.

THE PLATES

The movement of a watch has two plates and the works are sandwiched in between. The plates are called the top plate and the pillar plate. The top plate fully covers the movement. The ¾ plate watch and the balance bridge are flush and about ¼ of a full plate is cut out to allow for the balance, thus the ¾ plate. The bridge watch has two or three fingers to hold the wheels in place and together are called a bridge, just as the balance is called the balance bridge. The metal is generally brass, but on better grade watches, nickel is used. The full plate is held apart by four pillars. In older watches the pillars were very fancy, and the plates were pinned, not screwed, together. The plates can be gilded or engraved when using brass. Some of the nickel plates have damaskeening. There are a few watches with plates made of gold. The plates are also used to hold the jewels, settings, etc. Over 30 holes are drilled in each plate for pillars, pivots, and screws.

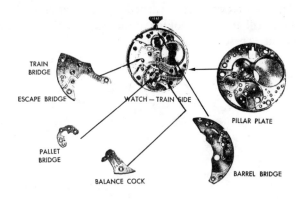

TRAIN BRIDGE

ESCAPE BRIDGE

WATCH — TRAIN SIDE

PILLAR PLATE

PALLET BRIDGE

BALANCE COCK

BARREL BRIDGE

The plates and bridges which hold all the parts in proper relation to each other.

The pinion is the smaller of the two wheels that exist on the shaft or arbor. They are small steel gears and usually have six teeth called leaves. Steel is used wherever there is great strain, but where there is much friction, steel and brass are used together; one gear of brass, and a pinion of steel. After the leaves have been cut, the pinions are hardened, tempered, and polished.

Invented in 1525

FUSEE

SPRING BARREL

THE FUSEE

A mainspring gives less and less power as it lets down. To equalize the power a fusee was first used. Fusee leverage increases as the mainspring lets down. A fusee is smaller at the top for a full mainspring. When the chain is at the bottom, the mainspring is almost spent, and the fusee has more leverage. Leonardo da Vinci is said to have invented the fusee.

When the mainspring is fully wound, it also pulls the hardest. At that time the chain is at the small end of the fusee. As the spring grows weaker, the chain descends to the larger part of the fusee. In shifting the tension, it equalizes the power.

On the American watch, the fusee was abandoned for the most part in 1850 and an adjustment is used on the hairspring and balance wheel to equalize the power through the 24 hours. When a watch is first wound the mainspring has no more power than it does when it is nearly run down. With or without the fusee, the number of parts in a watch are about the same: close to 800.

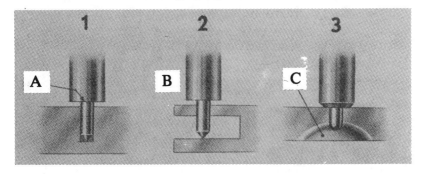

1. Illustration of pivot before 1700. **2.** Pivot used in early 1700s. **3.** Pivot used in late 1700s to present

JEWELS AND PIVOTS

Before 1700, holes were drilled only part way into the plates and the pivot rested directly on the bottom of the hole, as in Illustration No. 1. The shoulder of the pivot was above the plate, however, reducing part of the function, as in Illustration No. 1A.

In the early 1700s, a French watchmaker, Sully, improved the pivot friction as seen in Illustration No. 2B. Illustration No. 3 shows a later improvement.

N. F. de Duiller of Geneva, in conjunction with Peter and Jacob Debaufre, French immigrants living in London, developed a method of piercing jewels. This method was patented in 1704; however, it was not until around 1800 that holed jewels started to appear in watch movements and then only in high grade watches.

In the mid-1800s experiments were already being made for artificial rubies. In 1891 Fremy solved the problem and by the early 1900s the synthetic ruby was popular.

SHOCK ABSORBERS

When a watch is dropped or subjected to a hard shock, the balance and pivots usually suffer the most.

A shock-resisting device was invented by Breguet in 1789; he called it a parachute. This device was a spring steel arm supporting the end-stone. The parachute gives a cushioning effect to the balance staff.

The American pocket watch industry tried to find a device to protect pocket watch pivots, but it was the Swiss who perfected the devices for wristwatches around 1930.

Above: Incabloc
Left: Parachute
Below: Illustrates shock absorbing system. Note end stone and spring in raised position giving a cushioning effect to the balance staff.

JEWEL COUNT

Jewels are used as bearings to reduce metal-to-metal contacts which produce friction and wear. They improve the performance and accuracy of the watch, and materially prolong its usefulness. The materials used for making watch jewels are diamonds, sapphires, rubies, and garnets. The diamond is the hardest but is seldom used except for cap jewels. The sapphire is the next in hardness and is the most commonly used because of its fine texture. Garnets are softer than sapphires and rubies.

They add to the outward appearance of the watch but do not have the fine texture of the sapphire jewel.

Two views showing upper and lower jewel locations in the plates and bridges.

Types of Jewels. Watch jewels are of four distinct types, each type having a particular function.

(1) HOLE JEWELS. Hole jewels are used to form the bearing surface for wheel arbors and balance staff pivots.

(2) CAP JEWELS. Cap jewels (also called end stones) are flat jewels. They are positioned at the ends of wheel staffs, outside the hole jewels, and limit the end thrust of the staff.

(3) ROLLER JEWELS. The roller jewel (pin) is positioned on the roller table to receive the impulse for the balance from the fork.

(4) PALLET JEWELS. The pallet jewels (stones) are the angular-shaped jewels positioned in the pallet to engage the teeth of the escape wheel.

Number and Location of Jewels. Most watches have either 7, 9, 11, 15, 17, 19, 21, or 23 jewels. The location of the jewels varies somewhat in different makes and grades, but the general practice is as follows:

7-JEWEL WATCHES. Seven-jewel watches have: one hole jewel at each end of the balance staff; one cap jewel at each end of the balance staff; one roller jewel; and two pallet jewels.

9-JEWEL WATCHES. These have the seven jewels mentioned in 7-jewel watches, with the addition of a hole jewel at each end of the escape wheel.

11-JEWEL WATCHES. In these, seven are used in the escapement as in 7-jewel watches. In addition, the four top pivots (the third wheel, the fourth wheel, the escape wheel, and the pallet) are jeweled.

15-JEWEL WATCHES. These watches have the nine jewels found

in 9-jewel watches, with the addition of the following: one hole jewel at each end of the pallet staff; one hole jewel at each end of the fourth-wheel staff; and one hole jewel at each end of the third-wheel staff.

17-JEWEL WATCHES. The 15 jewels in 15-jewel watches are used with the addition of one hole jewel located at each end of the center wheel staff.

ROLLER JEWEL

Receiving pallet stone   Discharging pallet stone

19-JEWEL WATCHES. In these watches, the jewels are distributed as in the 17-jewel watch, with the addition of one for each pivot of the barrel or mainspring.

21-JEWEL WATCHES. The jewels in these are distributed as in the 17-jeweled grade, with the addition of two cap jewels each for the

Location of jewels in balance

pallet and escape wheel.

23-JEWEL WATCHES. The jewels are distributed as in the 21-jewel watch, with the addition of one for each pivot of the barrel or mainspring.

24-, 25-, and 26-JEWEL WATCHES. In all of these watches, the additional jewels were distributed as cap jewels. These were not very functional but were offered as prestige movements for the person who wanted more.

In many cases, these jewel arrangements varied according to manufacturer. All jeweled watches will not fit these descriptions.

WINDING AND SETTING

The simplest but not the most practical method for winding up

WINDING & SETTING PARTS

1. Ratchet Wheel	6. Stem and Crown	10. Clutch Lever	14. Hour Wheel
2. Crown Wheel	7. Winding Pinion	11. Clutch Lever Spring	15. Minute Wheel
3. Crown Wheel Center	8. Clutch Wheel	12. Setting Wheel	16. Dial Washer
4. Click	9. Setting Lever	13. Yoke	17. Cannon Pinion
5. Click Spring			

Winding Mechanism. a—Winding and setting clutch. p—Winding pinion. b—Barrel. r—Ratchet wheel. c—Crown or main wheel. t-Winding arbor.

the mainspring of a pocket watch was to wind the barrel staff by means of a key, but then it is necessary to open up the watch case. And the key method of winding proved unpopular, as oftentimes the key became lost.

The modern principle of the winding of the mainspring and hand-setting by pulling on the crown, dates back to 1842. We owe this combination to Adrian Philippe, associate of Patek, of Geneva.

The winding and setting mechanism consists of the stem, crown, winding pinion, clutch wheel, setting wheel, setting lever, clutch lever, clutch spring, crown wheel, and ratchet wheel. When the stem is pushed in, the clutch lever throws the clutch wheel to winding position. Then, when the stem is turned clockwise, it causes the winding pinion to turn the crown and ratchet wheels. The ratchet wheel is fitted on the square of the mainspring arbor and is held in place with a screw. When the stem and crown are turned, the ratchet wheel turns and revolves the arbor which winds the mainspring, thereby giving motive power to the train. Pulling the stem and crown outward pushes the setting lever against the clutch lever, engaging the clutch wheel with the setting wheel. The setting wheel is in constant mesh with the minute wheel; therefore, turning the stem and crown permits setting the hands to any desired time.

Setting Mechanism. Clutch **a** meshes with **m** and the minute works wheel **b**. The minute works wheel meshes with the cannon pinion **h**. The hour cannon **d** bears the hour hand **H**. **C**—Center wheel. **M**—Minute hand.

The dial train consists of the cannon pinion, minute, and hour wheels. The cannon pinion is a hollow steel pinion which is mounted on the center wheel arbor. A stud which is secured in the pillar plate holds the minute wheel in mesh with the cannon pinion. A small pinion is attached to the minute wheel which is meshed with the hour wheel.

The center arbor revolves once per hour. A hand affixed to the cannon pinion on the center arbor would travel around the dial once per hour. This hand is used to denote minutes. The hour wheel has a pipe that allows the hour wheel to set over the cannon pinion. The hour wheel meshes with the minute wheel pinion. This completes the train of the cannon pinion, minute wheel, and hour wheel. The ratio between the cannon pinion and the hour wheel is 12 to 1; therefore, the hand affixed to the hour wheel is to denote the hours. With this arrangement, time is recorded and read.

A—PINION
B—CLUTCH WHEEL
C—SETTING WHEEL
D—MINUTE WHEEL
E—CANNON PINION
F—HOUR WHEEL
G—CLUTCH LEVER
H—SETTING SPRING
J—SETTING SPRING CAM

Automatic Winding. The self-winding watch uses the movements of the body in order to wind up the mainspring slowly and nearly continuously. The first pocket self-winding watches were executed by a watchmaker from Le Locle, Abraham-Louis Perrelet, around 1770.

Early self wind pocket watch by Breguet.

Eterna-Matic Automatic Winding Mechanism. 1—Oscillating weight. 2—Oscillating gear. 3—Upper wheel of auxiliary pawl-wheel. 4—Lower wheel of auxiliary pawl-wheel. 5—Pawl-wheel with pinion. 6—Lower wheel of pawl-wheel with pinion. 7—Transmission-wheel with pinion. 8—Crown-wheel yoke. 9—Winding pinion. 10—Crown-wheel. 11—Ratchet-wheel. 12—Barrel. 13—Driving runner for ratchet-wheel. 14—Winding stem. 15—Winding button.

They were improved soon after by Abraham-Louis Breguet. In the case of the pocket watch, the movements causing the winding of the watch were essentially the result of walking. This system of winding was never widely adopted. The watch was a fancy model and not a really useful one. Herman von der Heydt was the only maker in America to work with the self-winding pocket watch. However, inventors always kept the idea of the self-winding watch in mind.

In 1923, the British firm Harwood took up once again the solution of the problem of automatic winding, for wrist watches. This was the spark which rapidly resulted in research to improve and simplify this type of mechanism. A company was formed in London to manufacture Harwood's watch, and before long over 500 jewelers in the United Kingdom were selling his automatic watch. A second company was formed in France, and a third in the United States. The business flourished about two and one-half years. Then, in 1931, these companies were liquidated.

Illustration of Self Winding mechanism used by Harwood.

This 1931 wrist watch made by Perpetual Self-Winding Watch Co. of America originally sold for $29.75.

THE BALANCE ARC OF VIBRATION

If the watch is to function with any degree of satisfaction, the proper arc of motion of a balance must be no less than 225 degrees in a single vibration direction. Wind up the watch, stop the balance; upon releasing the balance, carefully observe the extent of the swing or vibration. After 30 seconds it should have reached its maximum. If it takes longer, the full power of the mainspring is not being communicated strongly enough. With the watch fully wound, the balance should vibrate between 225 degrees and 315 degrees in a single vibration direction.

HIGH ARC   LOW ARC

COTTAGE INDUSTRY WATCHMAKING
IN COLONIAL AMERICA

The cottage industry (pre-1700s to 1800s) consisted of organized, skilled craftsmen having separate divisions for the purpose of producing watches. The movements were handmade using manpowered tools. The parts generally were not given a final finish. The cottage industries were in most countries including France, England, Switzerland, Germany, and others, but not in America. Each skilled parts maker specialized in a specific part of the watch. There were fusee makers, wheel makers, plate and cock makers, spring makers, case makers and enamelers, to name a few. In the cottage industry each maker became an expert in his field. Expenses and overhead were less because fewer tools and less labor were required. Because all components were produced separately, a larger volume of watches resulted.

The enterprising colonial watchmaker in America would order all the parts and assemble them to complete a finished movement. This finisher, or watchmaker, would detail the parts, such as filing them to fit, polishing and gilding the parts, fitting the movement to a case, installing a dial, and adjusting the movement to perform. The finisher would then engrave his name and town of manufacture to the movement or dial. The finisher determined the timekeeping quality of the completed watch, thus gaining a good reputation for some watchmakers.

Most watchmakers used this system during this period; even, to some extent, Abram Breguet. A colonial watchmaker or finisher could produce about 50 watches a year. There were few colonial watchmakers because only the wealthy could afford such a prized possession as a watch. Most colonial watchmakers struggled financially, and supplemented their businesses with repair work on European-made watches. Since most of them understood the verge escapement, and imported this type parts from England to produce watches, many colonial watches have the verge escapement. Few colonial watches survive today.

Side-view of 17th Century single-hand movement with fusee and catgut line to barrel. This three-wheel movement normally ran from 15 to 16 hours between windings. Also note the balance has no hairspring.

EBAUCHES

The stamping out of plates and bridges began with Frederic Japy of Beaucort, France, around 1770. At first, ebauches consisted of two plates with barrel and train bridges, the cock and fusee, pillars, and the clicks and assembly screws. The ebauches were stamped-out or rough movements. Japy invented machinery a common laborer could operate, including a circular saw to cut brass sheets into strips, a machine for cutting teeth in a wheel, a machine for making pillars, a press for the balance, and more. These machines were semi-automatic and hard to keep in alignment or register. But, with the aid of these new machines the principal parts of the movement could be produced in a short period of time with some precision. However, the parts of watches at this time were not interchangeable. These movements in the rough or "grey" were purchased by finishers. The finisher was responsible for fitting and polishing all parts and seeing to the freedom and depth of these working parts. He had to drill the holes to fit the dial and hands. The plates, cock and wheel, after being fitted and polished, were gilded. After the parts were gilded, the movement would be reassembled, regulated for good timekeeping, and placed in a case. The finisher had to be a master watchmaker.

In England, during the 1800s, Lancashire became the center of the movement trade. One of the better known English ebauche makers was Joseph Preston & Sons of Prescot. The movements were stamped J. P. Some Swiss ebauches would imitate or stylize the movement for the country in which they were to be sold, making it even harder to identify the origin.

As the watch industry progressed, the transformation of the ebauche to a more completed movement occurred. Automation eventually made possible the watch with interchangeable parts, standard sizing, and precision movements that did not need retouching. This automation began about 1850 with such talented mechanics as Pierre-Fredric Ingold, the Pitkins Brothers, A. L. Dennison, G. A. Leschot

Five typical Ebauches. Three with bar movements, one with a three-quarter plate, one with a half plate. Four with lever escapements, one with a cylinder escapement. The age ranges from 1860 to 1890.

with Vacheron and Constantin, Patek, Phillipe, and Frederic Japy of Beaucount (still in business today as Japy Freres). The pioneers in the 1850s who set the standards for modern watchmaking included the Pitkin Brothers, Dennison, Howard, and Jacob Custer. By 1880 most other countries had begun to follow the lead of America in the manufacture of the complete pocket watch with interchangeable parts.

 EBAUCHES S.A.

Ebauches S.A. with its main office in Neuchatel, Switzerland, consists of 17 affiliated firms:

A. Schild S.A., Grenchen

 Fabrique d'Horlogerie de
Fontainemelon, fontainemelon

 Eta S.A., Fabrique
d'Ebauches, Grenchen

 Fabrique d'Horlogerie de
Fontainemelon, Succursale
du Landeron, Le Landeron

 A. Michel S.A., Grenchen

 Felsa S.A., Grenchen

 Fabriques d'Ebauches
Bernoises S.A., Etablissement
Aurore, Villeret

 Fabrique d'Ebauches Venus
S.A., Moutier

Fabrique d'Ebauches Unitas
S.A., Tramelan

 Fabrique d'Ebauches de
Fleurier S.A., Fleurier

 Fabrique d' Ebauches de
Peseux S.A., Peseux

 Fabriques d'Ebauches Reunies
Arogno S.A., Arogno

 Fabriques d'Ebauches de
bettlach, Bettlach

 Fabrique d'Ebauches de
Chezard S.A., Chezard

 Derby S.A., La Chaux-de-
Fonds

 Nouvelle Fabrique S.A.,
Tavannes

Valjoux S.A., Les Bioux

Examples of four ebauches: **Upper left:** Example of a Chinese duplex. **Lower left:** An ebauche circa 1900-1930. **Upper right:** A three-finger bridge movement, circa 1890-1910. **Lower right:** Bridge movement, circa 1885-1900.

WORM GEAR ESCAPEMENT

This oddity was advertised as "The Watch With a Worm in It."

Robert J. Clay of Jersey City was given a patent on October 16, 1886. Mr. Clay said, "The principal object of my invention is to provide a watch movement which is very simple and has but few parts." The worm gear or continuous screw was by no means simple. Mr. Clay and William Hanson of Brooklyn revamped the original worm gear and obtained another patent on January 18, 1887.

The first watch containing a worm gear escapement reached the market in 1887. However, the New York Standard Watch Co. soon converted to a more conventional lever escapement. About 12,000 watches with the worm gear were made, but few survived.

Enlarged worm gear escapement. Note endless screw was referred to by the New York Watch Co. as "a watch with a worm in it."

Movement with top plate removed.

DIAL MAKING

Watch dials were basically hand produced. The base is copper and the coating is generally enamel. In the process the copper plate is covered

with a fine white enamel, spread with a knife to a thickness of 3/100ths
of an inch. It is then allowed to dry at which time it is placed on a
plate and inserted into a red hot furnace. The dial is turned frequently
with a pair of long tongs. The copper would melt if it were not coated
with the enamel. After the dial has been in the furnace for one minute
it is removed and the resulting enamel is soft. The dial is now baked
onto the copper plate or "set." The surface is rough after cooling, and
it is sanded smooth with sandstone and emery, then baked again. The
dial is now ready for the painter, who draws six lines across the dial
using a lead pencil. Then, with a pencil of black enamel, he traces the
numbers, finishing the ends to make them symmetrical. Then the minute
marks are made. Lastly, the name of the watch company is painted
onto the dial. The dial is glazed and fired again, then polished. The
dial artist used a magnifying glass and a fine camelhair brush to paint
the dials and produced about one dozen per hour.

Top and side view of Single and Double sunk
dial. Single sunk is one level below the hour ring.
Double sunk is two levels below the hour ring.

Single Sunk

Double
Sunk

Minute Hand

Hour Hand   Second Hand

FIRST DIALS

Henri Foucy was the first man to make enamel dials in America.
He came to New York from Geneva, Switzerland, in 1856 and was
employed by the American Watch Factory.

CRAZING

The word "craze" means a minute crack in the glaze of the enamel. This is not a crack in the dial because the dial has a backing of copper. Crazing does little damage to the structure of the enamel, even though it may go all the way through to the copper.

ENAMEL

Enamel may be transparent or colored. Enamel acts as a protective surface on the metals. It is resistant to acid, corrosion, and weather. Enamel is made of feldspar, quartz, silica, borax, lead, and mineral oxides. These materials are ground into a fine powder and then fired at a temperature of about 1500 degrees Fahrenheit. The heat melts the enamel powder and unites it with the surface of the metal.

PIN LEVER ESCAPEMENT (DOLLAR WATCHES)

The pin lever escapement is sometimes erroneously referred to as "Roskopf escapement" and watches with pin lever escapements are sometimes referred to as "Roskopf watches."

The original Roskopf watch, which was publicly exhibited at the Paris Exposition in 1867, was a rugged "poor man's watch." It had one less wheel than the conventional pocket watch. The mainspring barrel was placed in the center of the watch, and the minute wheel and pinion fastened to it friction tight. In effect, the center wheel was thereby eliminated. The watch also incorporated a pin-lever escapement, which is also used in spring-wound clocks such as alarm clocks. Watches of this type have no provision for repair or adjustments and cannot be accurately regulated. The service charge of a fine watch repairman was usually higher than the initial cost of this type watch. As a result, most of the pin lever watches were discarded after they would no longer run. Some fakes use the name "Rosskopf."

LOW COST PRODUCTION WATCHES
(DOLLAR WATCHES)

Jason R. Hopkins hoped to produce a watch that would sell for no more than 50 cents as early as the 1870s. He had a plan for which he received a patent (No. 161513) on July 20, 1875. It was a noble idea even though it was never fully realized. In 1876, Mr. Hopkins met a Mr. Fowle who bought an interest in the Hopkins watch. The movement was developed by the Auburndale Watch Co., and the Auburndale Rotary Watch was marketed in 1877. It cost $10, and 1,000 were made. The 20 size had two jewels and was open-face, pendant wind, lever set, and detent escapement. The 18 size had no jewels and was open-face.

In December, 1878, D. A. Buck introduced a new watch, at a record low price of $3.50, under the name of Benedict and Burnham Manufacturing Co. It was a rotary watch, open-face, with a skeleton dial which was covered with paper and celluloid. The movement turned around in the case, once every hour, and carried the minute hand with it. There were 58 parts and all of them were interchangeable. They had no jewels but did have a duplex style escapement. The teeth on the brass escape wheel were alternately long and short, and the short teeth were bent down to give the impulse. The main spring was about nine feet long and laid on a plate on the bed of the case. The click was also fastened to the case. The extremely long mainspring took 140 half turns of the stem to be fully wound. It came to be known as the "long wind" Waterbury and was the source of many jokes, "Here, wind my Waterbury for awhile; when you get tired, I'll finish winding it."

In 1892 R. H. Ingersoll ordered 1,000 watches produced at a cost of 85 cents each. He offered the watch for sale in his mail-order catalog

Above: Example of a Waterbury longwind showing the nine foot long spring.

Left: Face illustration of a Waterbury Longwind. The movement can be seen through open skeleton area around edge or face.

Right: Example of a two wheel train rather than the standard four wheel train.

Left: Example of the escape wheel for the duplex escapement.

for $1 each and advertised it as, "The Watch that Made the Dollar Famous." These watches were thick, sturdy and noisy and were wound from the back like a clock. The wages in 1892 were about 8 cents per hour, so it took some 13 hours of work to buy a Dollar Watch.

The E. N. Welch Manufacturing Co. was the next low cost production watch manufacturer. Then came the New York City Watch Co., who in 1895, produced a watch with a unique pendant crank to wind the movement. In 1899 came the Western Clock Mfg. Co., which later became the Westclox Corporation.

Also, among the low cost production watches were the "comic character" watches. They have become prime collectibles in recent years.

About 70 percent of the watches sold in the U. S. were Dollar-type. These watches were characterized by the pin lever, non-jeweled (for the most part), and with a face of paper or other inexpensive material. These watches were difficult to repair and the repairs cost more than the price of a new one. Thus they were thrown away, and today it is hard to find one in good condition.

DOLLAR WATCH CHARACTERISTICS:

1. Sold at a price that almost everyone could afford.
2. Used pin lever or duplex escapement.
3. Stamped or pressed out parts; also used fewer parts overall.
4. Were non-jeweled (except for a few) but rugged and practical.
5. Dial made of paper or other inexpensive material.
6. Case and movement were sold as one unit.

Personalized **watch movement by Rockford**. Engraved on movement. "W.G. Gane, Special Railway, 17j, Adj, serial No. 344551." To identify, see the Identification of Movement section of all watch companies, noting plate design & screw locations to determine that it is a **Rockford** Model No. 8.

Personalized watch movement by **Hamilton**. Engraved on movement, "Mayer, Chattanooga, Tenn., Adjusted, 21 jewels, serial No. 254507." To identify, see the Identification of Movement section of all watch companies, noting plate design & screw locations to determine that it is an 18 size, open face **Hamilton** model. Then by using the serial number, the grade can be determined.

Model 8, 18 size, Rockford, full plate, hunting, lever set. This illustration from the identification section matches the model above.

Grade 936, 18 size, Hamilton, open face. This matches the model above.

PERSONALIZED WATCHES

It was common practice for some watch manufacturers to personalize watches for jobbers, jewelry firms, and individuals. This was done either by engraving the movement or painting on the dial. Probably the Ball Watch Co. did more of this than any other jobber.

Each manufacturer used its own serial number system even though there may have been a variety of names on the movements and/or dials. Knowledge of this will aid the collector in identifying watches as well as determining age.

"Remington Watch Co."-marked on movement and case, made by N.Y. Standard Watch Co., 16 size, 11 jewels.

"E.F. Randolph"-marked on movement, made by Illinois Watch Co., 23j, hunting, model –4.

16 size, No. 390, made by New York Standard Watch Co. Watch. Same model as above.

Model 4, 16 size, made by Illinois Watch Co. Same model as above.

In order to establish the true manufacturer of the movement, one must study the construction, taking note of the shape of the balance, shape of the plates, location of jewels, etc. Compare each company in this volume until the manufacturer is located. The best place to start is at the Hamilton and Illinois sections because these two companies made most of the personalized watches.

After the correct manufacturer has been determined, the serial number can be used to determine the age. Taking the age, grade, size, and manufacturer into consideration, the approximate value can be determined by comparing similar watches from the parent company. If a jeweler's name and location are on the watch, this particular watch will command a higher price in that area.

SWISS IMPORTED FAKES

Before 1871 a flood of pocket watches were made which had names strikingly similar to many well-known American watches. These were made in foreign countries—as well as in America—and looked and sounded like high quality watches. But they were fakes, inferior in quality.

These key-wind imitations of American pocket watches are a fascinating and inexpensive watch that would make a good collection. The watches closely resembled the ones they were intended to emulate. Names such as "Hampton Watch Company" might fool the casual buyer into thinking he had purchased a watch from Hampden. "Rockville Watch Co." could easily be mistaken for the American Rockford Watch Co. Initials were also used such as H. W. Co., R. W. Co., and W. W. Co., making it even harder to determine the true identity.

In 1871 Congress passed a law requiring all watches to be marked with the country of origin. The Swiss tried to get around this by printing "Swiss" so small on the movement that it was almost impossible to see. Also the word "Swiss" was printed on the top of the scroll or on a highly engraved area of the movement, making it difficult to spot.

By 1885 these Swiss imitations were of better quality and resembled even more closely what was popular in America. But the Swiss fakes did not succeed, and by 1900 they were no longer being sold here.

Example of a Swiss imported fake. Note misspelled signature "P.S. Barrett." The authentic American Waltham watch is spelled "P.S. Bartlett."

Example of a Swiss imported fake. Note similarity to E. Howard & Co. watches.

HOW TO IDENTIFY A SWISS FAKE

1. At first they were keywind and keyset; then they became stem wind, full plate, about 18 size, large jewels on the plate side, and used Roman numerals.

2. Most had American-sounding names so close to the original that it looks merely like a misspelling.

3. The material was often crudely finished with very light gilding.

4. The dial used two feet; American watches used three.

5. The balance wheel was made to look like a compensated balance, but it was not.

6. The large flat capped jewels were blue in color.

These characteristics are not present with all imported fakes. Some or none of these factors may be present. The later the date, the more closely the fake resembled the American watch.

AMERICAN
POCKET WATCHES

AMERICAN LISTINGS
Pricing at Retail Level
(Complete Watches Only)

Watches listed in this book are priced at the retail level and as complete watches, having an original 14k gold-filled case with an original white enamel single sunk dial. The entire original movement is in good working order with no repairs needed, unless otherwise noted. Watches listed as 14k and 18k are solid gold cases. Coin or silveroid-type and stainless steel cases will be listed as such. Keywind and keyset watches are listed as having original coin silver cases. Dollar-type watches or low cost production watches are listed as having a base metal type case and a composition dial. Wrist watches are priced as having original gold-filled case with the movement being all original and in good working order, and the wrist watch band being made of leather except where bracelet is described.

Many of the watch manufacturers were commissioned to put jewelers' or jobbers' names on their movements in place of their own. Due to this practice, the true manufacturers of these movements are difficult to identify. These watch models are listed under the original manufacturer and can be identified by comparison with the model sections under each manufacturer. See "Personalized Watches" for more detailed information.

The prices shown were averaged from dealers' lists just prior to publication and are an indication of the retail level or what collectors will pay. Prices are provided in three categories: average condition, extra fine, and mint condition, and are shown in whole dollar amounts only. The values listed are a guide for the retail level and are provided for your information only. Dealers will not necessarily pay full retail price. Prices listed are for watches with **original** cases and dials.

Note: Descriptions and serial number ranges listed for early watches cannot be considered 100 percent accurate due to the manner in which records were kept by these companies.

WARNING: It has been reported to us that 24 Jeweled watches are being faked, especially in Illinois and Rockford watches. One method known is the altering of the number 21 on the movement to a 24. Before buying a 24 Jewel watch, compare the movement with a known 24 Jewel.

INFORMATION NEEDED—We are interested in any facts and information you might have that should possibly be considered for future editions. Documented facts are needed, so please send photo or sources of information. Send to: Cooksey Shugart, 780 Church Street N.E., Cleveland, Tennessee 37311. (When corresponding, please include a self-addressed, stamped envelope.)

ABBREVIATIONS USED
IN
THE OFFICIAL® PRICE GUIDE TO WATCHES

★ ★ ★ ★—Extremely rare; less than 20 known to exist.
★ ★ ★—Rare; less than 100 known to exist.
★ ★—Scarce; less than 500 known to exist.
★—Uncommon; less than 2,500 known to exist.
ADJ—Adjusted (to temperature, heat and cold, also isochronism)
BASE—Base metal used in cases; e.g., silveroid
BC—Box case
BRG—Bridge plate design movement
COIN—Coin silver
DB—Double back
DES—Diamond end stones
DMK—Damaskeened
DS—Double sunk dial
DR—Double roller
DWT—Penny weight: 1/20 Troy ounce
ETP—Estimated total production
EX—Extra nice; far above average
FULL—Full plate design movement
    ¾—¾ plate design movement
    1F brg—One finger bridge design and a ¾ plate (see Illinois 16s M#5)
    2F brg—Two finger bridge design
    3F brg—Three finger bridge design
GF—Gold filled
GJS—Gold jewel settings
G#—Grade number
GT—Gold train (gold gears)
GCW—Gold center wheel
GRO—Good running order
HC—Hunter case
HCI_P—Adjusted to heat, cold, isochronism, and positions; e.g., HCI5P
HL—Hairline crack
J—Jewel (as 21J)
K—Karat (as 14k solid gold—not gold filled)
KS—Key set
KW—Key wind
KW/SW—(Key wind/stem wind) transition

LS—Lever set
MCBC—Multi-color box case
MCC—Multi-color case
MCD—Multi-color dial
MD—Montgomery type dial
M#—Model number
Mvt. Only—Dial and movement only; no case
NI—Nickel plates or frames
OF—Open face
P—Position (5 positions adj)
PS—Pendant set
RGP—Rolled gold plate
RR—Railroad
RRA—Railroad approved
RRG—Railroad grade
S—Size
SBB—Screw back and bezel
SRC—Swing ring case
SS—Stainless steel
SW—Stem wind
S#—Serial number
TEMP—Temperature
TP—Total production
2T—Two-tone
WGF—White gold filled
WI—Wind indicator (also as up and down indicator)
WW—Wrist watch
YGF—Yellow gold filled

Abbott Stem Wind Attachment. Left: Normal view of an Illinois watch movement with 'hidden' Abbott Stem Wind Attachment (pat. Jan., 18th, 1881). Right: Same watch with dial removed exposing the Abbott Stem Wind Attachment. Serial number 52045. Add $100 to $250 to value of watch with this attachment.

ABBOTT'S STEM WIND
HENRY ABBOTT

Henry Abbott first patented his stem wind attachment on June 30, 1876. The complete Abbott's stem wind mechanism is arranged in such a way as to convert key wind to stem wind. He also made a repeater-type slide mechanism for winding. On January 18, 1881, he received a patent for an improved stem wind attachment. On the new model the watch could be wound with the crown. Abbott sold over 50,000 of these stem-wind attachments, and many of them were placed on Waltham, Elgin, and Illinois watches.

ABBOTT WATCH CO.
(MADE BY HOWARD WATCH CO.)
1908 - 1912

Abbott Sure Time Watches were made by the E. Howard Watch Co. (Keystone), and are similar to Howard Watch Co. 1905 model. These watches sold for $8.75 and had 17 jewels. The open face watches are actually hunting case models without the second bits register.

Description	Avg	Ex-Fn	Mint
Abbott Sure Time, 16S, 17J, ¾, OF, GF Case	$150	$225	$300
Abbott Sure Time, 16S, 17J, ¾, HC, GF Case	200	275	350
Abbott Sure Time, 16S, 17J, ¾, OF or HC, Coin	175	250	325
Abbott Sure Time, 16S, 17J, ¾, Silveroid..............	100	175	250

Example of **Abbott Watch Co.**, 16 size, 17 jewels, gold jeweled settings, hunting case. Note similarity to the Howard Watch Co. model 1905. Serial number 993932.

Example of **Abbott Watch Co.**, 16 size, 17 jewels, gold jeweled settings, open face. Note similarity to the Howard Watch Co. series 9.

ADAMS AND PERRY WATCH MANUFACTURING CO.
Lancaster, Pennsylvania
1874 - 1877

This company, like so many others, did not have sufficient capital to stay in business for long. The first year was spent in setting up and becoming incorporated. The building was completed in mid-1875, and watches were being produced by September. The first watches were limited to three grades, and the escapement and balance were bought from other sources. By December 1875, the company was short of money and, by the spring of 1876, they had standardized their movements to 18 size. The first movement went on sale April 7, 1876. The next year the company remained idle. In August 1877 the company was sold to the Lancaster Watch Company, after making only about 800 to 1,000 watches. In 1892 Hamilton acquired the assets.

Description		Avg	Ex-Fn	Mint
20S, 20J, GJS, PS, KW, 18K original case .... ★ ★ ★		$2,000	$2,500	$3,000
18S, 20J, GJS, PS............................ ★ ★ ★		1,000	1,500	2,000
18S, 17J, GJS, PS................................ ★ ★		700	1,200	1,700
18S, 17J, GJS, PS, Coin, Original .... ★ ★		700	1,200	1,700

Example of **Adams & Perry Watch Co.** movement. This basic model consists of 19 jewels, gold jeweled settings, key wind and pendant set, serial number 1681.

Example of **Adams & Perry Watch Co.** movement. This model consists of 20 jewels, gold jeweled settings, stem wind with micrometric regulator, 20 size.

J. H. ALLISON
Detroit, Michigan
1853 - 1890

The first watch J. H. Allison made was in 1853; it was a chronometer with full plate and a fusee with chain drive. The balance had time screws and sliding weights. In 1864, he made a ¾ plate chronometer with gold wheels. He also damaskeened the nickel movement. He produced only about 25 watches, of which 20 were chronometers. By 1883

J.H. ALLISON (continued)

he was making ¾ plate movements with a stem wind of his own design. Allison made most of his own parts and designed his own tools. He also altered some key wind watches to stem wind. Allison died in 1890.

Description		Avg	Ex-Fn	Mint
Full Plate & ¾ Plate, GT, NI, DMK . . . . ★ ★		$1,500	$2,000	$3,000
Detent Chronometer Escapement, 21J, KW/KS, GJS ★ ★ ★		3,000	4,000	5,500

AMERICAN REPEATING WATCH CO.
Elizabeth, New Jersey
1885 - 1892

Around 1675, a repeating mechanism was attached to a clock for the first time. The first repeating watch was made about 1687 by Thomas Tompion or Daniel Quare. Five-minute, quarter-hour and half-hour repeaters were popular by 1730. The minute repeater became common about 1830.

Fred Terstegen applied for a patent on August 21, 1882, for a repeating attachment that would work with any American key-wind or stem-wind watch. He was granted three patents: No. 311,270 on January 27, 1885; No. 3,421,844 on February 18, 1890; and No. 3,436,162 in September 1890. Waltham was the only watch company to fabricate repeating watches in America. It is not known how many repeaters were made, but it is estimated to be from 1,300 to 3,000.

Add $1,000 to $2,000 to value of a watch with this attachment.

American Repeating Attachment. Illustration at left shows Terstegen's patented repeating attachment only. Illustration at right shows attachment as normally found on movement. The two outside circles on left illustration are wire gongs. The hammer can be seen at upper right.

THE AMERICAN WALTHAM WATCH CO.
1851 - 1957

To trace the roots of the Waltham family one must start with the year 1850 in Roxbury, Massachusetts, No. 34 Water Street. That fall David Davis, a Mr. Dennison, and Mr. Howard together formed a watch company. Howard and Dennison had a dream of producing watches with interchangeable parts that were less expensive and did not result in less quality.

Howard served an apprenticeship to Aaron Willard Jr. in about 1829. Several years later, in 1842, Howard formed a clock and balance scale manufacturing company with Davis.

Howard and Dennison combined their ideas and, with financing provided by Samuel Curtis, the first of their watches was made in 1850. But they had problems. They were trying out ideas such as using jewels, making dials, and producing steel with mirror finishes. This required all new machinery and resulted in a great financial burden. They discovered, too, that although all watches were produced on the same machines and of the same style, each watch was individual with its own set of errors to be corrected. This they had not anticipated. It took months to adjust the watches to the point they were any better than any other timepieces on the market.

But Howard had perfected and patented many automatic watchmaking machines that produced precision watch parts. In 1851 the factory building was completed and the name American Horologe Company was chosen. It was not until late 1852 that the first watches were completed bearing the signature "The Warren Mfg. Co.," after a famed Revolutionary War hero. The first 17 watches were not placed on the market but went to officials of the company. Watches numbered 18 through 110 were marked "Warren...Boston;" the next 800 were marked "Samuel Curtis;" a few were marked "Fellows & Schell" and sold for $40.

The name was changed to the Boston Watch Company in September 1853, and a factory was built in Waltham, Massachusetts, in October 1854. The movements that were produced here carried serial numbers 1,001 to 5,000 and were marked "Dennison, Howard & Davis," "C. T. Parker," and "P. S. Bartlett."

Boston Watch Company failed in 1857 and was sold at a sheriff's auction to Royal E. Robbins. In May 1857, it was reorganized as the Appleton, Tracy & Co., and the watches produced carried serial numbers 5,001 to 14,000, model 1857. The first movements were marked Appleton, Tracy & Co. The C. T. Parker was introduced as model 1857 and sold for $12. 399 of these models were made. Also 598 chronodrometers were produced and in January 1858 the P. S. Bartlett watch was made.

Example of a **Warren** model, 18 size, 15 jewels, serial number 44. Note: This movement was made for an English case and will not fit a standard 18 size American case.

Example of a **Samuel Curtis** model, 18 size, 15 jewels, serial number 112. This movement was also made for an English case.

In January 1859 the Waltham Improvement Co. and the Appleton, Tracy & Co. merged to form the American Watch Company. In 1860, as Lincoln was elected president and the country was in Civil War, the American Watch Co. was faced with serious problems. The next year, business came to a standstill. There seemed to be little hope of finding a market for watches, and bankruptcy again seemed close at hand. At this point it was decided to cut expenditures to the lowest possible figure and keep the factory in operation.

American horology owes much to members of the Waltham Watch group such as Bacon, Church, Dennison, Fogg, Howard Marsh, Webster, and Woerd, who contributed much to its development and success.

In early 1861, the name "J. Watson" appeared on model 1857 (first run: Nos. 23,601 to 24,300—total production 1,200).

The next model 1857 was the "R. E. Robbins" of which 2,800 were made.

The William Ellery, marked "Wm. Ellery," (model 1857) was then introduced with

AMERICAN WALTHAM WATCH CO. (continued)

the first serial number of 46,201. It was key wind and key set and had 7 to 15 jewels.

A size 10 woman's watch was marketed with first serial numbers of 44,201. It was key wind and key set, ¾ plate, 13 to 15 jewels. Some were marked "P S Bartlett" and a 15 jewel was marked "Appleton, Tracy & Co."

A special model, 10 size, serial numbers of 45,801 to 46,200, is extremely rare. The first stem wind, beginning with serial number 410,698, was produced in 1868. By 1880 all watches were quick train.

The last key wind was serial No. 22,577,000, about 1919, 18 size, 1883 model, 7J, sterling, produced for export.

Factory of Boston Watch Co., 1857.

CHRONOLOGY OF THE DEVELOPMENT OF AMERICAN WATCH COMPANY

AMERICAN HOROLOGE CO.
Roxbury, Mass. 1851
"Howard, Davis & Dennison"
Serial No. 1-17

THE WARREN MANUFACTURING CO.
Roxbury, Mass. 1851-1853
"Warren"
Serial No. 18-110
"Samuel Curtis"
Serial No. 111-1,000

BOSTON WATCH CO.
Roxbury 1853-1854 & Waltham, Mass. 1854-1857
"C. T. Parker," "P. S. Bartlett,"
"Dennison, Howard & Davis"
Serial No. 1,001-5,000
"Fellows & Schell"
less than 100 made
(Serial No. 6,000-6,500 Howard & Rice)

TRACY, BAKER & CO.
Waltham, Mass. 1857

AMERICAN WALTHAM WATCH CO. (continued)

APPLETON, TRACY & COMPANY
Waltham, Mass. 1857-1859
"Appleton, Tracy & Co.," "C. T. Parker,"
"Chronodrometer," "P. S. Bartlett"
Serial No. 5,001-14,000

AMERICAN WATCH COMPANY
Waltham, Mass. 1859-1885

AMERICAN WALTHAM WATCH CO.
Waltham, Mass. 1885-1906

WALTHAM WATCH COMPANY
Waltham, Mass. 1906-1923

WALTHAM WATCH & CLOCK COMPANY
Waltham, Mass. 1923-1925

WALTHAM WATCH COMPANY
Waltham, Mass. 1925-1957

WALTHAM ESTIMATED SERIAL NUMBERS AND PRODUCTION DATES

Date	Serial No.	Date	Serial No.	Date	Serial No.
1852	50	1888	3,800,000	1924	24,550,000
1853	400	1889	4,200,000	1925	24,800,000
1854	1,000	1890	4,700,000	1926	25,200,000
1855	2,500	1891	5,200,000	1927	26,100,000
1856	4,000	1892	5,800,000	1928	26,400,000
1857	6,000	1893	6,300,000	1929	26,900,000
1858	10,000	1894	6,700,000	1930	27,100,000
1859	15,000	1895	7,100,000	1931	27,300,000
1860	20,000	1896	7,450,000	1932	27,550,000
1861	30,000	1897	8,100,000	1933	27,750,000
1862	45,000	1898	8,400,000	1934	28,100,000
1863	65,000	1899	9,000,000	1935	28,600,000
1864	110,000	1900	9,500,000	1936	29,j100,000
1865	180,000	1901	10,200,000	1937	29,400,000
1866	260,000	1902	11,100,000	1938	29,750,000
1867	330,000	1903	12,100,000	1939	30,050,000
1868	410,000	1904	13,500,000	1940	30,250,000
1869	460,000	1905	14,300,000	1941	30,750,000
1870	500,000	1906	14,700,000	1942	31,050,000
1871	540,000	1907	15,500,000	1943	31,400,000
1872	590,000	1908	16,400,000	1944	31,700,000
1873	680,000	1909	17,600,000	1945	32,100,000
1874	730,000	1910	17,900,000	1946	32,350,000
1875	810,000	1911	18,100,000	1947	32,750,000
1876	910,000	1912	18,200,000	1948	33,100,000
1877	1,000,000	1913	18,900,000	1949	33,500,000
1878	1,150,000	1914	19,500,000	1950	33,560,000
1879	1,350,000	1915	20,000,000	1951	33,600,000
1880	1,500,000	1916	20,500,000	1952	33,700,000
1881	1,670,000	1917	20,900,000	1953	33,800,000
1882	1,835,000	1918	21,800,000	1954	34,100,000
1883	2,000,000	1919	22,500,000	1955	34,450,000
1884	2,350,000	1920	23,400,000	1956	34,700,000
1885	2,650,000	1921	23,900,000	1957	35,000,000
1886	3,000,000	1922	24,100,000		
1887	3,400,000	1923	24,300,000		

The above list is provided for determining the approximate age of your watch. Match serial number with date.

AMERICAN WALTHAM WATCH CO.

(See American Waltham Watch Co. **Identification of Movements** section located at the end of the American Waltham price section to identify the movement, size, and model number of your watch.)

20 SIZE
MODEL 1862,-20-KW
T. P. 3,500

Grade or Name — Description	Avg	Ex-Fn	Mint
American Watch Co., 18K, HC, all original .... ★ ★	$2,000	$2,500	$3,000
American Watch Co., 15 & 17J, KW, KS, ¾, vibrating hairspring stud, silver case..................... ★ ★	700	1,000	1,500
American Watch Co., 15 & 17J, KW, KS, ¾, vibrating hairspring stud, 18K HC, all original .... ★ ★	2,000	2,500	3,000
American Watch Co., 15 & 17J, ¾, KW, ADJ .... ★	300	500	750
American Watch Co., 19J, ¾, KW, ADJ .... ★ ★	2,000	2,500	3,000
American Watch Co., 19J, ¾, KW, ADJ, with Maltese cross stopwork, all original .... ★ ★	2,500	3,000	3,600
American W. Co., 15J, ¾, KW............... ★	300	450	600
American W. Co., 7-11J, ¾, KW .... ★	250	400	550
Appleton, Tracy & Co., 15J, ¾, KW, with Maltese cross stopwork, all original .... ★	500	600	750
Appleton, Tracy & Co., 15 & 17J, ¾, KW, ADJ, gold balance .... ★	450	550	700
Appleton, Tracy & Co., 15 & 17J, ¾, KW..............	250	400	550
Appleton, Tracy & Co., 15 & 17J, ¾, KW, vibrating hairspring stud, silver case .... ★ ★	600	900	1,400
Appleton, Tracy & Co., 15 & 17J, ¾, KW, vibrating hairspring stud, 18K HC....................... ★ ★ ★	1,800	2,300	2,800

American Watch Co., Model 1862, 20 size, 17 jewels, gold balance and escape wheel, gold jeweled settings, key wind, key set from back, serial number 80111.

Appleton Tracy & Co., Model 20KW, 20 size, 15 jewels, serial number 125004. Note vibrating hairspring stud.

118

Appleton Tracy & Co., Model 18KW, 18 size, 15 jewels, serial number 32006. Reversible center pinion, patented Nov. 30th, 1858.

Model 1857, 18 size, 16 jewels, "Chronodrometer" on dial, "Appleton Tracy & Co." or "P.S. Bartlett on back plate, key wind & set.

18 SIZE
MODELS 1857, 18KW, 1862, 1870, 1877, 1879, 1883, 1892

Grade or Name — Description	Avg	Ex-Fn	Mint
American Watch Co., 17J, ¾, KW, M#18KW .... ★★★	$1,400	$1,700	$2,200
American Watch Co., 19J, M#18KW, ¾ .... ★★	1,600	1,900	2,400
American Watch Co., 19J, M#1883, HC, silver ...... ★★	800	1,000	1,400
American Watch Co., 17J, M#1883....................	75	100	150
American Watch Co., 21J, M#1883, ADJ, GJS	125	150	225
American Watch Co., 15J, M#18KW, ¾, Pat. Nov. 30, 1858, reverse pinion, original silver case....... ★★★	1,000	1,200	1,500
American Watch Co., 15J, M#1870, KW................	200	250	350
Am. Watch Co., 15J, M#1857, KW, KS	75	100	150
Am. Watch Co., 17J, M#1857, KW, KS .... ★	200	250	350
Am. Watch Co., 14K, HC, heavy box hinged, multi-color, (4 colors)..	2,000	2,200	2,800
Am. Watch Co., 11J, thin model, KW, ¼ plate .... ★	175	275	400
Am. Watch Co., 15 & 17J, M#1870, KW, ADJ	150	200	300
Am. Watch Co., 11J, M#1883, SW or KW..............	50	75	125
Am. Watch Co., 17J, M#1892, LS	70	90	150
Am. Watch Co., 17J, M#1892, PS	70	90	150
Am. Watch Co., 21J, M#1892, LS	90	120	185
Am. Watch Co., 21J, M#1892, PS	90	120	185
Am. Watch Co., 7J, M#1877	40	50	60
Am. Watch Co., 7J, M#1883, KW	50	75	100
Am. Watch Co., 11J, M#1877	40	50	60
Am. Watch Co., 11J, M#1883, KW	50	75	100
Am. Watch Co., 15J, M#1857, SW.................. ★	200	300	450

AMERICAN WALTHAM WATCH CO., 18 SIZE (continued)

Grade or Name—Description	Avg	Ex-Fn	Mint
Appleton, Tracy & Co., 15J, M#1857, SW	$100	$125	$175
Appleton, Tracy & Co., 7-11J, KW, M#1857	125	150	200
Appleton, Tracy & Co., 15J, M#18KW, ¼, reverse pinion, Pat. Nov. 30, 1858, orig. silver case ... ★★★	1,000	1,200	1,500
Appleton, Tracy & Co., KW, ¼ .... ★	275	350	450
Appleton, Tracy & Co., 11J, thin model, KW, ¼ ...... ★	225	350	450
Appleton, Tracy & Co., 15J, ¼, KW, with vibrating hairspring stud, orig. 18K case .... ★★★	1,200	1,500	2,000
Appleton, Tracy & Co., Sporting,(Chronodrometer) M#1857, 16J, KW, KS, orig. case, with stop feature ★★	1,500	2,000	2,500
Appleton, Tracy & Co., 15J, M#1857, KW, 18K	600	700	1,000
Appleton, Tracy & Co., 15J, M#1857, KW	100	125	175
Appleton, Tracy & Co., 11J, M#s 1877, 1879, SW	50	75	100
Appleton, Tracy & Co., 17J, M#1892, SW, Premiere	75	100	150
Appleton, Tracy & Co., 15J, M#1892, SW, OF	60	85	100
Appleton, Tracy & Co., 17J, M#1892, SW, OF	70	95	125
Appleton, Tracy & Co., 19J, M#1892, SW, OF	85	115	150
Appleton, Tracy & Co., 21J, M#1892, SW, OF	90	125	175
Appleton, Tracy & Co., 15J, M#1883, SW, OF	50	65	90
Appleton, Tracy & Co., 15J, M#1877, KW	60	75	110
Appleton, Tracy & Co., 15J, M#1879, SW, OF	50	65	90
Appleton, Tracy & Co., 17J, M#1883, OF	60	80	100
Appleton, Tracy & Co., 17J, M#1892, SW, HC..........	75	100	150
Appleton, Tracy & Co., 19J, M#1892, SW, HC..........	100	125	175
Appleton, Tracy & Co., 21J, M#1892, SW, HC..........	100	125	175
Appleton, Tracy & Co., 15J, M#1883, SW, HC..........	75	100	150
Appleton, Tracy & Co., 15J, M#1879, SW, HC..........	75	100	150
Appleton, Tracy & Co., 17J, M#1883, SW, HC..........	75	100	150

Appleton, Tracy & Co. 18 size, 15 jewels, with vibrating hairspring stud, key wind & set from back, serial number 140030.

P.S. Bartlett, Model 18KW, 18 size, 11 jewels, key wind & set from back, serial number 41597.

AMERICAN WALTHAM WATCH CO., 18 SIZE (continued)

Grade or Name—Description	Avg	Ex-Fn	Mint
A. W. W. Co., 7J, M#1883, SW, OF	$35	$45	$75
A. W. W. Co., 11J, M#1883, SW, OF	35	45	75
A. W. W. Co., 7J, M#1883, KW, OF	50	75	125
A. W. W. Co., 11J, M#1879, OF	35	45	75
A. W. W. Co., 15J, M#1879, OF	50	60	90
A. W. W. Co., 11J, M#1883, OF	35	45	75
A. W. W. Co., 15J, M#1883, OF	45	55	85
A. W. W. Co., 17J, M#1892, LS, OF	80	90	135
A. W. W. Co., 17J, M#1892, PS, OF	70	80	125
A. W. W. Co., 17J, M#1892, HC	75	100	150
A. W. W. Co., 19J, M#1892	90	115	160
A. W. W. Co., 21J, M#1892	95	125	180
A. W. W. Co., 17J, "for R.R. Service" on dial	200	250	350
A. W. W. Co., 15J, OF	50	60	90
A. W. W. Co., 15J, 14K multi-color boxcase HC	1,400	1,800	2,500
A. W. W. Co., 11J, LS, HC	75	100	150
A. W. W. Co., 15J, HC	75	100	150

P.S. Bartlett, 18 size, 15 jewels, Model 1857, Engraved on back "4 PR. Jewels." Serial number 13446.

Canadian Railway Time Service, Model 1892, 18 size, 17 jewels, serial number 22,017,534.

Grade or Name—Description	Avg	Ex-Fn	Mint
P. S. Bartlett, 7J, M#1857, KW, 1st Run	$200	$225	$325
P. S. Bartlett, 11J, M#1857, KW, 1st Run	200	225	325
P. S. Bartlett, 11J, M#1857, KW, 2nd-3rd Run	75	100	125
P. S. Bartlett, 15J, M#1857, KW, 2nd-3rd Run	100	125	150
P. S. Bartlett, 11J, LS, HC, 14K	550	650	850
P. S. Bartlett, 15J, M#1857, KW, below S#5000	200	225	325
P. S. Bartlett, 11J, M#1879, KW	50	75	125
P. S. Bartlett, 11J, M#1857, KW, Eagle inside case lid	175	200	275
P. S. Bartlett, 15J, M#1879, KW	75	100	150

AMERICAN WALTHAM WATCH CO., 18 SIZE (continued)

Grade or Name—Description	Avg	Ex-Fn	Mint
P. S. Bartlett, 15J, M#1879, SW	$55	$65	$80
P. S. Bartlett, 11-15J, M#1870, SW	75	85	100
P. S. Bartlett, 11-15J, M#1877, KW	100	125	175
P. S. Bartlett, 11J, M#1883, SW	50	70	100
P. S. Bartlett, 15J, M#1883, KW	75	100	150
P. S. Bartlett, 17J, M#1883, SW	50	70	100
P. S. Bartlett, 15J, M#1883, SW	50	70	100
P. S. Bartlett, 11J, M#18KW, ¼, thin model, KS from back	275	350	450
P. S. Bartlett, 11J, M#18KW, ¼, Pat. Nov. 30, 1858	400	500	675
P. S. Bartlett, 15J, pinned plates, KW	350	450	600
P. S. Bartlett, 15J, M#1892, SW	65	75	100
P. S. Bartlett, 17J, M#1892, SW, OF, LS	75	85	110
P. S. Bartlett, 17J, M#1892, SW, HC	125	150	175
P. S. Bartlett, 17J, M#1892, SW, OF, PS	75	80	110
P. S. Bartlett, 17J, M#1892, SW, 2-Tone	85	95	120
P. S. Bartlett, 19J, M#1892, SW	95	105	130
P. S. Bartlett, 21J, M#1892, SW	95	105	140
P. S. Bartlett, 21J, M#1892, SW, 2-Tone	100	115	150
Broadway, 7J, M#1857, KW, HC	75	100	150
Broadway, 11J, M#1857, KW, HC	75	100	150
Broadway, 11J, M#1877, KW, SW, NI, HC	75	100	150
Broadway, 7J, M#1883, KW, HC	75	100	150
Broadway, 11J, M#1883, KW, HC	75	100	150
Broadway, 11J, M#1883, SW, HC	75	100	150
Canadian Railway Time Service, 17J, M#1892, Adj.5P	300	400	500
Central Park, 15J, M#1857, KW	150	175	250
Champion, 15J, M#1877, OF	50	75	100
Crescent Park, 15J M#1857	200	250	325
Crescent Street, 15J, M#1870, KW	150	200	225
Crescent Street, 17J, M#1870, KW ★	275	375	500

Crescent Street, Model 1870, 18 size, 15 jewels, series A, Key wind & set from back, serial number 520,206.

Crescent Street, Model 1870, 18 size, 15 jewels, series B, Key wind & set from back, serial number 552,526.

AMERICAN WALTHAM WATCH CO., 18 SIZE (continued)

Grade or Name—Description	Avg	Ex-Fn	Mint
Crescent Street, 15J, M#1870, SW	$125	$145	$195
Crescent Street, 15J, M#1883, SW, non-magnetic, OF	100	140	200
Crescent Street, 15J, M#1883, SW, non-magnetic, HC	90	105	145
Crescent Street, 15J, M#1883, SW, 2-Tone	110	150	210
Crescent Street, 17J, M#1883, SW, OF	90	105	145
Crescent Street, 17J, M#1883, SW, HC	100	110	150
Crescent Street, 19J, M#1883 ★	200	260	365
Crescent Street, 17J, M#1892, SW, GJS	90	120	145
Crescent Street, 17J, M#1892, SW, OF	80	95	120
Crescent Street, 17J, M#1892, SW, HC	110	125	160
Crescent Street, 19J, M#1892, SW, Adj.5P, GJS	90	115	150
Crescent Street, 21J, M#1892, SW, Adj.5P, GJS	100	125	170
Crescent Street, 21J, M#1892, Wind Indicator	800	1,000	1,300
Crescent Street, 19J, M#1899, SW, OF	90	100	125
Crescent Street, 19J, M#1899, SW, HC	100	120	160
Crescent Street, 21J, M#1899, GJS, OF	100	125	165
Crescent Street, 21J, M#1899, GJS, HC	120	130	170
Samuel Curtis, 11-15J, M#1857, KW, S# less than 200, original 17S silver case ★★	2,500	3,000	4,000
Samuel Curtis, 11-15J, M#1857, KW, S# less than 400, original 17S silver case ★★	2,300	2,800	3,800
Samuel Curtis, 11-15J, M#1857, KW, S# less than 600, original 17S silver case ★★	2,000	2,500	3,500
Samuel Curtis, 11-15J, M#1857, KW, S# less than 1,000, original 17S silver case ★★	2,000	2,300	3,300
(Samuel Curtis not in original silver case, deduct $800 to $1,000 from value)			
Dennison, Howard, Davis, 7J, M#1857, KW ★	500	700	1,000
Dennison, Howard, Davis, 11J, M#1857, KW ★	700	900	1,200
Dennison, Howard, Davis, 15J, M#1857, KW ★	800	1,000	1,300
Dennison, Howard, Davis, 15J, M#1857, KW, S# less than 2,000, original case ★★	900	1,100	1,400
Denver & Rio Grande, 21J, M#1892, GJS, Adj.3P	900	1,200	1,600
Dominion Railway, 15J, M#1883, OF, SW, train on dial	800	1,000	1,400
Wm. Ellery, 7-11J, M#1857, Boston, Mass.	75	100	125
Wm. Ellery, 7-11J, M#1857, KW	65	90	110
Wm. Ellery, 7-11J, M#KW, ¾	200	275	375
Wm. Ellery, 7-11J, M#18KW, KW-KS from back, 18K HC	1,000	1,250	1,650
Wm. Ellery, 7J, M#1857, KW, KS from back	225	300	475
Wm. Ellery, 15J, M#1857, KW	80	90	135
Wm. Ellery, 15J, M#1857, SW ★	200	300	450
Wm. Ellery, 7-11J, M#1877, KW, M#1879, KW	60	85	100
Wm. Ellery, 11-15J, M#1877, SW	40	60	90
Wm. Ellery, 7-11J, M#1883	40	60	90
Excelsior, M#1877, KW	80	95	140
Export, 7-11J, M#1877	65	75	95
Export, 7-11J, M#1883, KW	75	100	150
Favorite, 15J, M#1877	65	75	100

Dennison, Howard, Davis, Model 1857, 18 size, 15 jewels, under sprung, key wind, serial number 1205.

Howard & Rice, Model 1857, 18 size, 15 jewels, under sprung, serial number 6003.

Grade or Name—Description	Avg	Ex-Fn	Mint
Fellows & Schell, 15J, KW, KS .... ★ ★ ★	$1,500	$1,700	$2,000
Franklin, 7J, M#1877, SW	125	150	200
Home Watch Co., 7-11J, M#1857, KW	75	100	125
Home Watch Co., 7J, M#1877, KW	75	100	125
Home Watch Co., 7-11J, M#1879, SW	100	125	150
Howard, Davis & Dennison, S#1-17 .... ★ ★ ★ ★	30,000	38,000	50,000
Howard & Rice, 15J, M#1857, KW, KS (serial numbers range from 6000 to 6500)....................... ★ ★	1,500	1,700	2,000
E. Howard & Co., Boston (on dial & mvt.), English style escape wheel, upright pallets, 15J, M#1857, KW, KS, S#s about 6,400 to 6,500 .... ★ ★ ★	2,500	2,800	3,500
Martyn Square, 7-11J, M#1857, KW, SW (exported)	125	150	200
Mermod, Jaccard & King—Paragon Timekeeper, 23J, M#1892, Vanguard, LS, GJS, HC.................	240	285	350

Pennsylvania Special, Model 1892, 18 size, 21 jewels, serial number 14,000,015.

Railroad, Model 1892, 18 size, 19 jewels, Adj5P, open face, note engine & coal car engraved on movement, serial number 10,099,625.

Grade or Name—Description	Avg	Ex-Fn	Mint
Non-Magnetic, 15J, SW, LS, NI	$100	$125	$175
Non-Magnetic, 17J, M#1892, SW, LS..................	125	150	200
Paragon, 15J, M#1883, HC	100	125	175
C. T. Parker, 7J, M#1857, KW .... ★★	1,200	1,400	1,800
Pennsylvania R.R. on dial, Appleton, Tracy & Co. on Mvt., KW, KS.................................... ★★	800	1,000	1,300
Pennsylvania Special, 21J, M#1892, HC.......... ★★★	1,400	1,600	1,900
Pennsylvania Special, 21J, M#1892, OF .... ★★★	800	1,000	1,300
Pioneer, 7J, M#1883.................................	45	60	80
Premier, 17J, M#1892, LS, OF	125	150	175
Railroad, 17J, M#1892, LS	200	250	350
Railroad, 21J, M#1892, LS	250	300	400
Railroader, 17J, M#1892, LS .... ★★	600	700	900
Railroad King, 15J, M#1883, LS	200	250	350
Railroad King, 15J, M#1883, 2-Tone	300	350	450
Railroad King, 17J, Special, M#1883, LS..............	325	375	475
Railroad Watches with R.R. names on dial and movement as follows:			
Canadian Pacific R.R., 17J, M#1883	275	325	375
Canadian Pacific R.R., 17J, M#1892	350	450	550
Canadian Pacific R.R., 21J, M#1892	450	550	650
Santa Fe Route, 17J, M#1883.....................	350	450	550
Santa Fe Route, 17J, M#1892.................... ★	600	800	1,000
Riverside, 7J, M#1857	100	125	175
Riverside, 17J, M#1892 .... ★	300	350	450
Roadmaster, 17J, M#1892, LS .... ★	300	350	450
R. E. Robbins, 11J, M#1857, KW.................... ★	400	450	550
R. E. Robbins, 15J, M#1877, KW.....................	200	250	350
R. E. Robbins, 13J, M#1883...........................	200	250	350

Sidereal, 24 hour dial used by astronomers.

Vanguard, Model 1892, 18 size, 23 jewels, diamond end stone, gold jewel settings, exposed winding gears, serial number 10,533,465.

AMERICAN WALTHAM WATCH CO., 18 SIZE (continued)

Grade or Name—Description	Avg	Ex-Fn	Mint
Sol, 7J, M#1883, OF	$50	$75	$100
Sol, 17J, OF, PS	75	100	125
Special Railroad, 17J, M#1883, LS, OF	300	350	450
Special R. R. King, 15J, M#1883	300	350	450
Sterling, 7J, M#1857, KW, Silver	100	125	150
Sterling, 7-11J, M#1877, M#1879	75	100	125
Sterling, 7-11J, M#1883, KW	75	100	125
Sterling, 11J, M#1883, SW	50	75	100
Tourist, 11J, M#1877	50	75	100
Tourist, 7J, M#1877	50	75	100
Tracy, Baker & Co., 15J, 18K original A.W.W. Co. case ★★★★	4,000	5,000	7,000
Vanguard, 17J, M#1892, GJS, HC ★★★	400	500	650
Vanguard, 17J, M#1892, LS, Adj.5P, DR, GJS, OF.. ★★	300	400	550
Vanguard, 17J, M#1892, Wind Indicator, Adj.5P, DR, GJS	900	1,000	1,200
Vanguard, 19J, M#1892, LS, Adj.5P, Diamond end stones	125	150	200
Vanguard, 19J, M#1892, LS, Adj.5P, DR, GJS, OF	125	150	200
Vanguard, 19J, M#1892, Wind Indicator, LS, Adj.5P, DR, GJS	1,000	1,100	1,400
Vanguard, 19J, M#1892, Adj.5P, GJS, HC ★	250	350	500
Vanguard, 21J, M#1892, Adj.5P, PS	100	125	175
Vanguard, 21J, M#1892, HC, GJS, Adj.5P	200	250	300
Vanguard, 21J, M#1892, LS, Adj.5P, DR, GJS, OF	100	125	175
Vanguard, 21J, M#1892, LS, Adj.5P, Diamond end stone.	125	150	200
Vanguard, 21J, M#1892, Wind Indicator, LS, Adj.5P, DR, GJS ★	1,000	1,200	1,500
Vanguard, 23J, M#1892, LS, Adj.5P, DR, GJS, OF	175	250	350
Vanguard, 23J, M#1892, LS, Adj.5P, DR, GJS, HC	250	325	425
Vanguard, 23J, M#1892, LS, Adj.5P, DR, GJS, Diamond end stone	200	275	375

American Waltham Watch Co., Model 1883, 18 size, 15 jewels, serial number 3,093,425.

845, Model 1892, 18 size, 21 jewels, railroad grade, Adj5p, serial number 15,097,475.

Grade or Name—Description	Avg	Ex-Fn	Mint
Vanguard, 23J, M#1892, PS, Adj.5P, DR, GJS, OF......	$175	$250	$350
Vanguard, 23J, M#1892, Wind Indicator, LS, Adj.5P, DR, GJS .... ★	1,100	1,300	1,600
Warren, 15J, M#1857, KW, KS, S#18-29, original 17S silver case .... ★★★	18,000	23,000	28,000
Warren, 15J, M#1857, KW, KS, S#30-60, original 17S silver case .... ★★★	10,000	15,000	18,000
Warren, 15J, M#1857, KW, KS, S#61-90, original 17S silver case .... ★★★	8,000	13,000	16,000
Warren, 15J, M#1857, KW, KS, S#91-110, original 17S silver case .... ★★★	6,000	11,000	14,000
(Warren not in original silver case, deduct $1,000 to $2,500)			
George Washington, M#1857, KW	250	350	500
J. Watson, 7J, M#1857, KW, KS, "Boston" .... ★	700	1,100	1,500
J. Watson, 7-11J, M#1857, KW, KS, "London" .... ★	700	1,100	1,500
45, 19J, GJS, 2-Tone, HC........................ ★★	800	1,000	1,400
845, 21J, M#1892, OF	100	125	175
845, 21J, M#1892, HC	200	250	300
820, 825, M#1883	50	75	100
836, 17J, DR, Adj.4P, LS, OF	75	100	125
M#1892, 19J, Sidereal, OF .... ★★★	1,200	1,500	2,000
M#1892, 17J, Astronomical Sidereal .... ★★★	1,000	1,300	1,800

Note: Some grades are not included. Their values can be determined by comparing with similar models and grades listed.

American Watch Co., Model 16KW, 16 size, 11-15 jewels, key wind and set from back, serial number 330,635.

American Watch Co., Model 1888, 16 size, 19 jewels, gold jeweled settings, gold train, hunting case. Waltham's highest grade; serial number 5,000,297.

Note: Watches listed in this book are priced at the retail level, as complete watches having an original 14k gold-filled case, an original white enamel single sunk dial, and with the entire original movement in good working order with no repairs needed.

16 SIZE
MODELS 16KW, 1868, 1872, 1888,
1899, 1908, BRIDGE MODEL

Grade or Name — Description	Avg	Ex-Fn	Mint
Am. Watch Co., 11J, M#16KW, KW & KS from back, original silver case .... ★ ★	$400	$450	$575
Am. Watch Co., 15J, M#16KW, KW & KS from back ★ ★	400	450	575
Am. Watch Co., 11J, M#1868, ¾, KW	175	200	250
Am. Watch Co., 15-17J, M#1868, ¾, KW	200	225	275
Am. Watch Co., 15J, M#1872, ¾, SW	100	125	175
Am. Watch Co., 16-17J, M#1872, ¾, SW	150	175	225
Am. Watch Co., 19J, M#1872, ¾, SW	400	500	650
Am. Watch Co., 7-11J, M#1888, ¾, SW	50	75	100
Am. Watch Co., 15J, M#1888, ¾, SW	50	75	100
Am. Watch Co., 17J, M#1899	75	100	125
Am. Watch Co., 7-11J, M#1899	50	75	100
Am. Watch Co., 13J, M#1899	50	75	100
Am. Watch Co. 15-16J, M#1899, HC..................	100	125	175
Am. Watch Co., 15J, M#1899, SW, HC	60	85	125

American Watch Co., Model 1888, 16 size, 21 jewels, gold train, note tadpole regulator.

American Watch Co., Bridge Model, 16 size, 23 jewels, gold train, Adj5p.

Grade or Name—Description	Avg	Ex-Fn	Mint
Am. Watch Co., 15J, M#1899, SW, OF	$50	$75	$100
American Watch Co., 19J, M#16KW, Maltese cross stopwork, all original 1860 Model, 18K .... ★ ★	1,500	1,800	2,200
American Watch Co., 17-19J, M#16KW, ¾, KW & KS from back, vibrating hairspring stud, 1860 Model, 18K ★ ★ ★	1,200	1,500	1,900
American Watch Co., 19J, M#16KW, ¾, KW & KS from back, 1860 Model, original case, 18K .... ★ ★ ★	2,000	2,500	3,000
American Watch Co., 15J, M#1868, ¾, KW, Silver .. ★ ★	300	350	475
American Watch Co., 17J, M#1868, ¾, KW, ADJ, Silver ★ ★	400	450	550
American Watch Co., 19J, M#1868, SW, Silver .... ★ ★ ★	450	500	600

AMERICAN WALTHAM WATCH CO., 16 SIZE (continued)

Grade or Name—Description	Avg	Ex-Fn	Mint
American Watch Co., 17J, M#1872, ¾, SW, HC, 14K . ★	$900	$1,100	$1,250
American Watch Co., 19J, M#1872, ¾, SW......★★★	600	700	900
American Watch Co., 19J, M#1872, ¾, GJS, Woerd's Pat. sawtooth balance, all original............★★★	2,000	2,500	3,200
American Watch Co., 21J, M#1872, ¾, SW.........★★	1,200	1,400	1,550
American Watch Co., 21J, M#1872, ¾, SW, 18K..★★★	1,500	1,800	2,200
American Watch Co., 19J, M#1888, 14K............★★	700	900	1,050
American Watch Co., 19J, M#1888...................★	300	400	550
American Watch Co., 21J, M#1888, NI, ¾ ....★★	400	500	650
American Watch Co., 23J, BRG, Adj.5P, GT, GJS, 14K original case ....★★★	1,500	2,000	2,500
American Watch Co., 23J, BRG, Adj.5P, GT, GJS, 18K original case ....★★★	1,800	2,300	2,800
American Watch Co., 23J, BRG, Adj.5P, GT, GJS ....★	900	1,200	1,600
American Watch Co., 21J, BRG, Adj.5P, GT, GJS ....★	500	550	650
American Watch Co., 19J, BRG, Adj.5P, GT, GJS ....★	400	450	550
American Watch Co., 17J, BRG, Adj.5P, GT, GJS ....★	300	350	450
Appleton, Tracy & Co., 15J, M#16KW, ¾, KW & KS from back, all original	400	450	575
Appleton, Tracy & Co., 15J, M#1868, ¾, KW	300	350	450
Appleton, Tracy & Co., 15J, ¾, KW, with vibrating hairspring stud, all original, silver case..........★★	600	700	900
Appleton, Tracy & Co., 15J, ¾, KW, with vibrating hairspring stud, 18K, original case...............★★	1,200	1,400	1,800
A. W. Co., 7J, M#1872, SW, HC......................	100	125	175
A. W. Co., 11J, M#1872, SW, HC......................	100	125	175
A. W. Co., 17J, M#1872, SW, DMK, GJS, DES, HC	200	300	450
A. W. Co., 7J, M#1899, SW DMK......................	40	50	75
A. W. Co., 9J, SW, NI..............................	40	50	75
A. W. Co., 11J, M#1899, SW	40	50	75
A. W. W. Co., 7J, SW, M#1888	40	50	75
A. W. W. Co., 11J, M#1888	40	50	75

P.S. Bartlett, Model 1899, 16 size, 17 jewels, serial number 10,014,478.

Crescent Street, Model 1899, 16 size, 21 jewels, Adj5p, serial number 16,179,418.

Grade or Name—Description	Avg	Ex-Fn	Mint
A. W. W. Co., 13J, M#1888, OF	$40	$50	$75
A. W. W. Co., 15J, M#1899, OF	40	50	75
A. W. W. Co., 15J, M#1888, SW, HC	50	60	95
A. W. W. Co., 16J, M#1888, SW, OF	55	65	100
A. W. W. Co., 16J, M#1899, SW, DMK, HC	65	80	125
A. W. W. Co., 17J, M#1899, SW, OF	75	85	100
P. S. Bartlett, 17J, M#1899, OF	55	65	80
P. S. Bartlett, 17J, M#1899, HC	100	125	175
P. S. Bartlett, 17J, M#1908, OF	50	75	100
Bond St., 7J, M#1888	50	70	100
Bond St., 11J, M#1888	55	75	100
Bond St. 15J, M#1888	55	75	100
Bond St., 7J, M#1899	50	75	100
Canadian Railway Time Service, M#1908 ★	400	500	650
Crescent St., 19J, M#1899, Adj.5P, LS, OF	75	100	150
Crescent St., 19J, M#1899, Adj.5P, PS, OF	75	100	150
Crescent St., 19J, M#1899, Adj.5P, LS, HC	125	150	200
Crescent St., 19J, M#1899, Adj.5P, PS, HC	125	150	200
Crescent St., 21J, M#1899, Adj.5P, PS, OF	100	125	150
Crescent St., 21J, M#1899, Adj.5P, LS, OF	100	125	150
Crescent St., 21J, M#1899, Adj.5P, PS, HC	125	150	200
Crescent St., 19J, M#1908, Adj.5P, LS, OF	100	125	150
Crescent St., 19J, M#1908, Adj.5P, PS, OF	100	125	150
Crescent St., 21J, M#1908, Adj.5P, LS, OF	100	125	150
Crescent St., 21J, M#1908, Adj.5P, PS, OF	100	125	150
Crescent St., 21J, M#1908, Adj.6P, LS, OF	100	125	150
Crescent St., 21J, M#1908, Adj.5P, PS, HC	125	150	200
Crescent St., 21J, M#1908, Adj.5P, LS, Wind Indicator	350	400	450
Crescent St., 21J, M#1912, Adj.5P, LS, Wind Indicator	350	400	450
Chronometro Superior, 21J, M#1899, LS, OF	125	150	250
Chronometro Victoria, 21J, M#1899, HC	150	175	275
Chronometro Victoria, 15J, M#1899, PS, OF	75	100	125
Diamond Express, 17J, M#1888, PS, OF, Diamond End Stones ★	400	450	525
Electric Railway, 17J, OF, LS, Adj.3P	100	125	150
Equity, 7-11J, PS, OF, 16½ Size	45	55	65
Equity, 7-11J, PS, HC, 16½ Size	40	50	75
Equity, 15-17J, PS, OF, 16½ Size	55	65	75
Equity, 15-17J, PS, HC, 16½ Size	65	75	90
Hillside, 7J, M#1868, ADJ	100	125	175
Hillside, 7J, M#1868, sweep sec. ★ ★	250	300	475
Marquis, 15J, M#1899, PS	65	75	100
Marquis, 15J, M#1908, PS	65	75	100
Non-Magnetic, 15J, NI, HC	135	155	185
Park Road, 16-17J, M#1872, PS	100	120	150

Note: Some grades are not included. Their values can be determined by comparing with similar models or grades listed.

Premier Maximus, "Premier" on movement. "Maximus" on dial, 16 size, 23 jewels (two diamond end stones), open face, pendant set, serial number 17,000,014.

American Waltham Watch Co., 5 minute repeater, 16 size, 21 jewels, ¾ plate, grade 1888, adj, 2 gongs, ca. 1900.

Grade or Name—Description	Avg	Ex-Fn	Mint
Park Road, 11-15J, M#1872, PS	$90	$110	$135
Premier, 9J, M#1908, PS, OF	35	45	75
Premier, 11J, M#1908	35	45	75
Premier, 15J, M#1908, LS, OF	70	85	100
Premier, 17J, M#1908, PS, OF	70	90	105
Premier, 17J, M#1908, PS, OF, Silveroid	45	60	70
Premier, 21J, M#1908, Silveroid	55	75	80
Premier, 21J, M#1908, LS, OF	80	95	125
Premier Maximus, 23J, M#1908, GT, gold case, LS, GJS, Adj.6P, WI, DR, 18K Maximus case, box & papers ★ ★	8,000	9,000	10,000
Premier Maximus, 23J, M#1908, GT, gold case, LS, GJS, Adj.6P, WI, DR, 18K Maximus case, no box.... ★ ★	7,500	8,000	9,000
Premier Maximus, 23J, M#1908, GT, gold case, LS, GJS, Adj.6P, WI, DR, 18K Maximus case, sterling box and papers, extra crystal & mainspring.............. ★ ★	9,000	9,500	11,000
Premier Maximus, 23J, M#1908, GT, YGF recased ... ★ ★	2,000	2,500	3,000
Railroader, 17J, M#1888, LS, NI................... ★ ★	300	350	535
Railroad King, 17J, 2-Tone........................ ★	195	240	375
Railroad Watches with R. R. names on dial and movement, such as Canadian Pacific RR, Santa Fe Route, etc., M#s 1888, 1899, 1908........................... ★	255	450	750
Repeater, 16J, M#1872, original coin case, 5 min..... ★ ★	2,000	2,200	2,700
Repeater, 16J, M#1872, 5 min., 18K................ ★ ★	4,000	5,000	6,500
Repeater, 16J, M#1872, 5 min., chronograph with register, 18K....................................	4,000	5,500	7,000
Repeater, 1 min. moon phase, M#1872, Perpetual Cal., 18K case, all original .... ★ ★ ★ ★	30,000	35,000	45,000

(Prices are with gold filled cases except where noted.)

Grade or Name—Description	Avg	Ex-Fn	Mint
Riverside, 15J, M#1872, PS, NI, OF	$75	$100	$125
Riverside, 15J, M#1872, PS, gilted, OF	75	100	125
Riverside, 16-17J, M#1888, NI, OF, 14K	400	475	600
Riverside, 16-17J, M#1888, NI, OF	75	100	125
Riverside, 17J, M#1888, gilded, OF	75	100	125
Riverside, 15J, M#1888, gilded, OF	75	100	125
Riverside, 17J, M#1888, checker goldtone DMK, raised gold jewel settings, OF	150	175	225
Riverside, 17J, M#1899, LS, DR, OF	75	100	125
Riverside, 17J, M#1899, LS, DR, HC	100	125	150
Riverside, 19J, M#1899, LS, DR, OF	100	125	150
Riverside, 19J, M#1899, PS, DR, OF	100	125	150
Riverside, 21J, M#1899, LS, DR, OF	100	125	150
Riverside, 19-21J, M#1908, Adj.5P, LS, DR	100	125	150
Riverside, 19J, M#1908, Adj.5P, PS, DR, OF	100	125	150
Riverside Maximus, 21J, M#1888, LS, ADJ, GJS, GT, DR, HC, GF ★ ★	600	700	850
Riverside Maximus, 21J, M#1888, LS, ADJ, GJS, GT, DR, HC, 14K ★ ★	1,000	1,100	1,250
Riverside Maximus, 21J, M#1899, PS, Adj.5P, GJS, GT, DR	300	400	550
Riverside Maximus, 21J, M#1899, LS, Adj.5P, GJS, GT, DR	350	450	600
Riverside Maximus, 23J, M#1899, LS, Adj.5P, GJS, GT, DR	400	500	650
Riverside Maximus, 23J, M#1908, PS, Adj.5P, GJS, GT, DR	400	500	650
Riverside Maximus, 23J, M#1908, LS, Adj.5P, GJS, GT, DR	400	500	650
Riverside Maximus, 23J, M#1908, PS, Adj.5P, GJS, GT, DR, HC, GF ★	500	600	750
Riverside Maximus, 23J, M#1908, PS, Adj.5P, GJS, GT, DR, 14K, HC ★	900	1,000	1,150
Riverside Maximus, 21J, M#1888, LS, GT, Diamond end stones, OF ★ ★	500	600	750

Royal. Model 1888, 16 size, 17 jewels, adjusted, serial number 6,125,840.

Vanguard, Model 1908, 16 size, 23 jewels, diamond end stone, gold jewel settings, exposed winding gears, serial number 11,012,533.

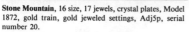

Stone Mountain, 16 size, 17 jewels, crystal plates, Model 1872, gold train, gold jeweled settings, Adj5p, serial number 20.

Vanguard, 16 size, 23 jewels, Adj6p, note pressed-in jewels rather than gold jewel settings. c. 1945.

Grade or Name—Description	Avg	Ex-Fn	Mint
Riverside Maximus, 21J, M#1899,LS,GT,Diamond end stone, OF .... ★	$375	$475	$625
Riverside Maximus, 21J, M#1899, LS, GT, Diamond end stone, HC .... ★	500	600	750
Riverside Maximus, 23J, M#1908, LS, Adj.5P, Wind Indicator .... ★ ★	2,500	2,800	3,500
Roadmaster, 17J, M#1899, LS, OF GJS .... ★	200	250	350
Royal, 15J, M#1872, PS, OF	75	100	125
Royal, 17J, M#1888, PS, OF	75	100	125
Royal, 17J, M#1888, PS, HC	100	125	150
Royal, 17J, M#1899, Adj.3P, OF	65	85	110
Royal, 17J, M#1899, LS, Adj.5P......................	75	100	125
Royal, 17J, M#1899, PS, Adj.5P......................	75	100	125
Royal Special, 17J, M#1888	100	125	175
Sol, 7J, M#1888......................................	50	75	100
Sol, 7J, M#1908......................................	50	75	100
Stone Mountain, 17J, M#1872, GT, Crystal plates . ★ ★ ★	5,500	6,000	7,000
Traveler, 7J, M#1888, 1899, 1908	40	50	65
Vanguard, 19J, M#1899, PS, LS, Adj.5P, GJS, DR, OF..	100	125	170
Vanguard, 19J, M#1899, PS, LS, Adj.5P, GJS, DR, HC .	150	175	225
Vanguard, 21J, M#1899, Adj.5P	100	125	175
Vanguard, 23J, M#1899, Adj.5P, HC...................	250	275	350
Vanguard, 23J, M#1899, Adj.6P, OF	175	200	250
Vanguard, 23J, M#1899, LS, Adj.5P, GJS, DR, OF......	150	175	200
Vanguard, 23J, M#1899, PS, Adj.5P, GJS, DR, OF......	150	175	200
Vanguard, 23J, M#1899, PS, Wind Indicator, Adj.5P, GJS, DR...	350	400	450
Vanguard, 19J, M#1908, LS & PS, Adj.5P, GJS, DR	100	125	175

Grade or Name—Description	Avg	Ex-Fn	Mint
Vanguard, 21J, M#1908, Adj.5P, GJS, DR, Diamond end stone	$125	$150	$175
Vanguard, 21J, M#1908, Adj.5P, GJS, DR, PS, LS, OF..	75	100	125
Vanguard, 21J, M#1908, Adj.5P, GJS, DR, PS, LS, HC .	125	175	200
Vanguard, 23J, M#1908, LS, Adj.5P, GJS, DR, OF......	150	175	200
Vanguard, 23J, M#1908, LS, Adj.5P, GJS, DR, HC	250	275	300
Vanguard, 23J, M#1908, PS, Adj.5P, GJS, DR..........	150	175	200
Vanguard, 23J, M#1908, Adj.5P, Wind Indicator, GJS, DR	350	400	450
Vanguard, 23J, M#1908, Adj.5P, GJS, Diamond end stone	150	175	200
Vanguard, 23J, M#1908, Adj.5P, GJS, HC	275	300	400
Vanguard, 23J, OF, LS or PS, 14K	500	550	675
Vanguard, 23J, M#1908, Adj.6P, Wind Indicator, GJS, DR	360	400	450
Vanguard, 23J, M#1908, Adj.6P, Wind Indicator, Lossier, GJS, DR	350	400	450
Vanguard, 23J, M#1912, Press Jewels...................	100	125	150
Vanguard, 23J, M#1912, PS, military (case), Wind Indicator	400	385	475
George Washington, 11J, M#1857	125	150	200
Weems, 23j, Navigation watch, Wind Indicator ...... ★ ★	400	450	530
M#665, 19J, GJS, BRG, HC .... ★ ★	700	800	1,000
M#1888, G #s 650, 640..............................	60	70	85
M#1899, G #s 610, 615, 618, 620, 625, 628, 630	60	70	85
M#1908, G #s 610, 611, 613, 614, 618, 620, 621, 623, 625, 628, 630, 635, 636, 637, 640, 641, 642	60	70	85
M#645, 21J, GCW, OF, LS	85	110	145
M#645, 19J, OF, LS.................................	80	105	130
M#16-A, 22J, Adj.3P, 24 hr. dial	100	125	150
M#16-A, 17J, Adj.5P................................	65	75	80
M#1621, 21J, Adj.5P	85	110	145
M#1623, 23J, Adj.5P	150	175	200

Weems Navigation watch, 21j, Weems pat. seconds dial, pusher for seconds scale setting, ca. 1942.

Grade 645, Model 1899, 16 size, 21 jewels, Adj5p, gold center wheel.

14 SIZE
MODELS 14KW, 1874, FULL PLATE
1884, 1895, 1897, COLONIAL-A

Grade or Name — Description	Avg	Ex-Fn	Mint
Adams Street, 7J, M#14KW, ¾, KW, Coin	$100	$125	$175
Adams Street, 11J, M#14KW, ¾, KW, Coin	100	125	175
Adams Street, 15J, M#14KW, ¾, KW	100	125	175
A. W. Co., 7J, M#14KW, ¾, KW	50	75	100
A. W. W. Co., 7J, M#1874, SW, LS, HC	75	100	125
A. W. Co., 15-16J, M#1874, ¾, SW	50	65	85
A. W. Co., 7-11J, M#s FP, 1884, & 1895	40	50	65
A. W. Co., 13J, M#1884	40	50	65
A.W.Co., 19J, GJS, GCW	65	75	95
Am. Watch Co., 7-11J, KW, ¾	35	45	60
Am. Watch Co., 13J, M#1874, ¾, SW	70	80	100
Am. Watch Co., 15J, M#1874, ¾	70	80	100
Am. Watch Co., 16J, M#1874, ¾, SW	70	80	100
Am. Watch Co., 7-11J, M#FP, KW	50	75	100
Am. Watch Co., 16J, M#1884, ¾, SW	50	75	100
Am. Watch Co., 15J, M#1897, SW....................	40	60	90
Bond St., 7J, M#1895, ¾, SW.......................	40	55	75
Bond St., 9J, M#1884, ¾, KW	75	100	125
Bond St., 7J, M#1884, ¾, SW, PS...................	50	60	90
Beacon, 15J, M#1897, ¾, SW	50	60	90
Chronograph, 13J, M#1884, 14K, OF, Am. W. Co. case..	600	800	1,000
Chronograph, 13J, M#1884, 14K, HC, Am. W. Co. case .	700	900	1,100
Chronograph, 13J, M#1884, 18K, HC, Am. W. Co. case★	1,000	1,200	1,400
Chronograph, 13J, M#1884, 14K OF with register,			
Am. W. Co. case	750	950	1,150

Chronograph, Model 1874, split-second, 14 size. Note two split second hands on dial.

Bond St., 14 size, 7 jewels, stem wind, open face, note pin set, serial number 2,437,666. c. 1884.

Grade or Name—Description	Avg	Ex-Fn	Mint
Chronograph, 13J, M#1884, 14K HC with register, Am. W. Co. case	$850	$950	$1,350
Chronograph, 13J, M#1884, 18K HC with register, Am. W. Co. case	1,100	1,200	1,650
Chronograph, 13J, M#1884	175	235	335
Chronograph, 15J, M#1884	185	250	365
Chronograph, 17J, M#1884	195	270	385
Chronograph, 17J, M#1874, split second .... ★	300	375	475
Chronograph, 15J, M#1874, split second, 14K, HC... ★★	1,200	1,350	1,600
Chronograph, 15J, M#1874, split second, min. register, 14K Am. W. Co. HC .... ★★	1,300	1,475	1,800
(Above in 18K case, add $250 to $400 to value)			
Chronograph, 16J, double dial, M#1874, 18K, Am. W. Co. case .... ★★	2,000	2,500	3,300
Chronometro Victoria, 15J, M#1897, ¾	65	75	95
Church St., 7J, M#1884, ¾	40	60	75
Crescent Garden, 7-11J, M#14KW, KW	60	75	100
Crescent Garden, 7J, M#FP, KW	60	75	90
Wm. Ellery, 7J, M#1874, SW	35	45	75
Gentleman, 7J, M#1884, SW	35	45	75
Hillside, 7-15J, M#1874, SW	35	45	75
Hillside, 7-11J, M#FP, SW	35	45	75
Hillside, 7-13J, M#1884, ¾, KW	35	45	75
Hillside, 11J, M#1884, ¾, KW	35	45	75
Hillside, 15J, M#1884, ¾, SW	65	75	100
Maximus, 21J, M#Colonial A	145	185	275
Maximus, 21J, M#Colonial A, 14K	300	400	575
Night Clock, 7J, M#1884, KW	65	75	95
Repeater (5 min.), 16J, M#1884, SW, LS, 14K	3,500	4,000	5,000
Repeater (5 min.), 16J, M#1884, SW, LS, 18K .... ★	3,800	4,800	6,300

Chronograph, Model 1874-double dial, 14 size, 15 jewels, hunting. case.

Chronograph, Model 1874-Split Second, 14 size, 15 jewels, open face, gold escape wheel, gold train, serial number 303,094.

Five Minute Repeater, Model 1884, 14 size, 13-15 jewels, hunting case, slide actuated, serial number 2,809,551.

Grade or Name—Description	Avg	Ex-Fn	Mint
Repeater (5 min.), 16J, M#1884, SW, LS, chronograph with register, 14K Am. W. Co. case	$4,000	$5,000	$6,500
Repeater (5 min.), 16J, M#1884, SW, LS, chronograph with register, 18K Am. W. Co. case	4,500	5,500	6,000
Repeater (5 min.), 16J, M#1884, SW, LS, Coin, original	2,000	2,200	2,700
Repeater (5 Min.), 18K, HC ★★	3,800	4,800	6,300
Repeater (1 Min.), perpetual calendar, moon phase, 18K ★★★	30,000	35,000	45,000
Riverside, 11-15J, M#s 1874, HC ★	150	175	250
Riverside, 15J, M#1884, OF	55	60	80
Riverside, 19-21J, M#Colonial A, OF ★★	150	175	250
Royal, 11-13J, M#s 1874, 1884	40	55	65
Seaside, 7-11J, M#1884, SW	40	55	65
Special, 7J, M#1895, HC	75	100	125
Sterling, 7J, M#1884	40	55	65
Stone Movement, 16J, M#1874, crystal top & bottom plates, 14K ★★★	4,500	5,000	7,000
Waltham, Mass., 7J, Full Plate, KW	75	100	125

12 SIZE
MODELS KW, 1894, BRIDGE, COLONIAL SERIES

Grade or Name — Description	Avg	Ex-Fn	Mint
A. W. W. Co., 7J, M#1894, 14K, OF	$200	$225	$275
A. W. W. Co., 11J, M#1894, Colonial	40	50	60
A. W. W. Co., 15J, M#1894, Colonial	40	50	60
A. W. W. Co., 15J, M#1894, Colonial, 14K, HC	250	275	350
A. W. W. Co., 17J, M#1894, Colonial	40	50	60
A. W. W. Co., 17J, M#1894, Colonial, 14K OF	200	225	275
P. S. Bartlett, 19J, M#1894, 14K, HC	275	300	375
P. S. Bartlett, 19J, M#1894	50	60	70
Bond St., 7J, M#1894	40	50	60

Actual size illustration of a cushion style shaped watch depicting thinness with emphasis on style and beauty. This watch was popular in the 1930s.

Grade or Name—Description	Avg	Ex-Fn	Mint
Bridge Model, 19J, GJS, Adj.5P, GT...................	$75	$100	$125
Bridge Model, 19J, GJS, Adj.5P, GT, 18K, HC	500	550	575
Bridge Model, 21J, GJS, Adj.5P, GT, OF	75	100	125
Bridge Model, 21J, GJS, Adj.5P, GT, HC, 14K .....★★	600	700	850
Bridge Model, 23J, GJS, Adj.5P, GT...................	125	150	175
Duke, 7-15J, M#1894	40	50	70
Digital Hour & Second Window, 17J	75	100	125
Elite, 17J, OF	40	50	70
Ensign, 7J, OF......................................	40	50	70
Martyn Square, 7-11J, M#KW	100	125	175
Maximus, 21J, GJS, GT	200	250	325
Premier, 17-19J, M#1894............................	65	80	100
Premier, 21J, M#1894	65	80	100
Riverside, 17-19J, M#1894, Colonial	60	70	80
Riverside, 19-21J, M#1894, Colonial	70	80	90

A.W.W.Co., Model 1894, 12 size, 7-11 jewels, open face, serial number 7,565,004.

Riverside, Colonial series, 12 size, 19 jewels, open face or hunting, Adj5p, double roller.

AMERICAN WALTHAM WATCH CO., 12 SIZE (continued)

Grade or Name—Description	Avg	Ex-Fn	Mint
Riverside, 19-21J, M#1894, Colonial, 14K, HC	$225	$275	$375
Riverside Maximus, 21J, M#1894, Colonial, GT, GJS, 14K	400	475	575
Riverside Maximus, 21J, M#1894, Colonial, GT, GJS	175	225	325
Riverside Maximus, 23J, M#1894, Colonial, GT, GJS .. ★	225	275	375
Riverside Maximus, 23J, M#1894, Colonial, GT, GJS, 14K	425	475	575
Royal, 17J, OF, PS	40	50	60
Royal, 19J, OF, PS	50	60	75

10 SIZE
MODEL KW, 1861, 1874

NOTE: These watches (excluding Colonial) are usually found with solid gold cases, and are therefore priced accordingly. Without cases, these watches have very little value due to the fact that the cases are difficult to find. Many of the cases came in octagon, decagon, hexagon, cushion and triad shapes.

Grade or Name — Description	Avg	Ex-Fn	Mint
Am. W. Co., 7-15J, M#1874, KW, 14K.................	$200	$250	$350
American Watch Co., 11-15J, M#1874, 14K, HC	275	325	425
Appleton, Tracy & Co., 15J, M#1861 or 1874, 14K	200	250	350
Appleton, Tracy & Co., 15J, M#1861, 18K multi-color box case	650	750	900
P. S. Bartlett, 11J, M#1861, KW, 14K	275	300	375
P. S. Bartlett, 13J, M#KW, gold balance, 1st S#45,801, last 46,200, 14K, Pat. Nov. 3, 1858 .... ★ ★	300	375	525
P. S. Bartlett, 13J, M#KW, gold balance, 1st S#45,801, last 46,200, 18K.................................	400	475	625
P. S. Bartlett, 13J, M#1861, KW, 14K.................	200	250	300
Crescent Garden, 7J, M#1861, KW, 14K	200	250	300
Wm. Ellery, 7,11,15J, M#1861, KW, 14K	200	250	300
Home W. Co., 7J, M#1874, KW, 14K	200	250	300
Martyn Square, 7-11J, M#1861, 14K....................	200	250	300
Maximus "A", 21J, 14K......................... ★ ★	400	475	600

Appleton Tracy & Co., Model 10KW, 10 size, 11-15 jewels, key wind and set from back, serial number 370,411.

Am. W. Co., Model 1873, 8 size, 15 jewels, serial number 691,001.

AMERICAN WALTHAM WATCH CO., 10 SIZE (continued)

Grade or Name — Description	Avg	Ex-Fn	Mint
Maximus "A", 23J, 14K .... ★ ★	$425	$500	$600
Riverside, 19J, HCI5P, GF	65	75	100
Riverside Maximus, 19-21J, Adj.5P, GJS, GF	125	200	275
Riverside Maximus, 19-21J, Adj.5P, GJS, 18K..........	450	525	625
Riverside Maximus, 23J, Adj.5P, GJS, GF	200	250	375
Royal, 15J, Adj.5P, GF..............................	55	65	80

8 SIZE
MODEL 1873

NOTE: Collectors usually want solid gold cases in small watches. The gold case value must be added to price listed.

Grade or Name — Description	Avg	Ex-Fn	Mint
Am. W. Co., 15J, M#1873, 14K, Multi-Color Box Hinge Case	$500	$600	$750
Am. W. Co., 15J, M#1873	65	75	85
P. S. Bartlett, 15-16J, M#1873	40	50	60
Wm. Ellery, 7-11J, M#1873	40	50	60
Wm. Ellery, 7J, 14K, HC	200	275	350
Riverside, 7-11J, M#1873, 18K, HC, 24 DWT	325	400	475
Riverside, 7-11J, M#1873............................	65	75	85
Royal, 7-13J, M#1873................................	40	50	60

Wm. Ellery, Model 1873, 8 size, 7 jewels, ¾ plate, serial number 2,679,907.

Riverside, Model 1873, 8 size, 7 jewels, serial number 931,395.

6 SIZE
MODEL 1873, 1889

Grade or Name — Description	Avg	Ex-Fn	Mint
A,B,C,D,E,F,G,H,J,K	$65	$70	$85
A,B,C,D,E,F,G,H,J,K, 14K, HC......................	200	275	325
A. W. W. Co., 19J, 18K, HC	325	400	475
A. W. W. Co., 19J, 14K, Multi-Color gold case	500	600	800
A. W. W. Co., 7J, M#1873	65	70	85

AMERICAN WALTHAM WATCH CO., 6 SIZE (continued)

Grade or Name—Description	Avg	Ex-Fn	Mint
A. W. W. Co., 15J, multi-color GF HC	$175	$200	$275
A. W. W. Co., 11J, HC, LS	75	100	150
Am. W. Co., 7J, M#1889	40	50	60
American W. Co., 7J, KW & KS from back, 10K, HC ...	175	225	275
Wm. Ellery, 7J, M#1873	55	60	75
Lady Waltham, 16J, M#1873, Demi, HC, 14K...........	275	300	350
Lady Waltham, 16J, M#1873, 18K	300	325	375
Riverside Maximus, 21J, GT, DR	225	250	300
Riverside, 15-17J, PS	50	75	100
Seaside, 7J, M#1873	40	45	55

American Watch Co., Model 1889, 6 size 7 jewels, serial number 4,700,246.

Stone Movement, Crystal Plate, size 4, 16 jewels, gold train, open face, serial number 28.

4 SIZE

Grade or Name — Description	Avg	Ex-Fn	Mint
Stone Movement, 4 size, crystal, 16 ruby jewels in gold settings, gold train, exposed pallets, compensation balance adjusted to temperature, isochronism, position, Breguet hairspring, and crystal top plate, 14K . ★★★	$3,500	$4,500	$6,000

NOTE: Watches listed in this book are priced at the retail level, as complete watches having an original 14k gold-filled case, an original white enamel single sunk dial, and with the entire original movement in good working order with no repairs needed, unless otherwise noted.

0 SIZE
MODELS 1882, 1891, 1900, 1907

Grade or Name — Description	Avg	Ex-Fn	Mint
A.W.Co., 7-15J, multi-color 14K HC..................	$350	$475	$600
A. W. Co., 7J, 14K, HC............................	175	275	350
A. W. Co., 7J, SW.................................	40	50	60
A. W. Co., 11J, ¾, SW, HC.........................	75	100	150
American Watch Co., 15J, ¾, SW, OF & HC...........	75	100	150

Lady Waltham, Model 1900, 0 size, 16 jewels, open face or hunting, adjusted, stem wind, pendant set.

A.W. Co., Model 1891, 0 size, 7 jewels, stem wind, originally sold for $13.00.

Grade or Name—Description	Avg	Ex-Fn	Mint
American Watch Co., 15J, ¾, SW, 14K, HC............	$175	$275	$350
P. S. Bartlett, 11J, M#1891, OF, 14K	125	150	175
P. S. Bartlett, 16J, 14K, HC	175	275	350
Lady Waltham, 15J, ¾, SW, 14K, HC	175	275	350
Lady Waltham, 15-16J, ¾, SW, HC	100	125	175
Maximus, 19J, ¾, SW, HC	100	125	175
Riverside, 15,16,17J, ¾, SW, HC.....................	100	125	175
Riverside, 15,16,17J, ¾, SW, HC, 14K	175	275	350
Riverside Maximus, 21J, GT, multi-color gold HC, 14K ★ ★	500	675	850
Riverside Maximus, 21J, ¾, GT	125	150	175
Riverside Maximus, 19J, ¾, SW, HC	150	175	250
Riverside Maximus, 19J, ¾, HC, 14K .... ★	275	350	475
Royal, 16J, ¾, SW, HC	75	100	125
Seaside, 15J, ¾, SW, HC, 14K	175	275	350
Seaside, 11J, ¾, SW, OF, multi-color dial, no chips	125	175	200
Seaside, 11J, ¾, SW, HC.............................	75	100	125
Seaside, 7J, ¾, HC	75	100	125
Seaside, 7J, ¾, HC, 14K.............................	175	275	350
Special, 11J, M#1891, OF, 14K	125	175	200

Riverside, Jewel Series, 6/0 size, 17 ruby jewels, raised gold settings, gold center wheel.

Ruby, Jewel Series, 6/0 size, 15 jewels, adjusted to temperature, open face or hunting.

JEWEL SERIES 6/0

Grade or Name — Description	Avg	Ex-Fn	Mint
Riverside J Size, 17J, HC, 14K	$200	$250	$300
Ruby J Size, 15J, OF, 14K	150	200	250
Sapphire, 15J, OF, 14K	150	200	250
Diamond, 15J, HC, 14K	200	250	300

AMERICAN WALTHAM WATCH CO.
IDENTIFICATION OF MOVEMENTS
BY MODEL NUMBER

How to Identify Your Watch: Compare the movement of your watch with the illustrations in this section. Upon matching the movement exactly, the model number and size can be determined. While comparing, note the location of the balance, jewels, screws, gears and type of back plate (Full, ¾, Bridge) which will be clues to identifying the movement you have. Having determined the size and model number, you can now find your watch in the main price listing by name or number (which is engraved on the movement).

20 size, 1862 or KW 20 model. Note vibrating hairspring stud. 1st serial number 50,001

18 size, key wind model
1st serial number 28,821

Model 1857, KW, KS. 1st serial number 1,001

Model 1870, KW, KS from back
1st serial number 500,001

143

Model 1877, 18 size

Model 1879, 18 size

Model 1883, hunting
1st serial number 2,354,001

Model 1883, open face

Model 1892, open face

Model 1892, hunting.
1st serial number 6,026,001

AMERICAN WALTHAM WATCH CO. (continued)

16½ size, Equity open face

Model 1868 or Model 16KW,
16 size

Model 1872, 16 size

Stone Mountain crystal plates,
16 size

Model 1888, 16 size, hunting

Bridge Model, 16 size

Model 1899 or Model 1908,
16 size, spen face

Model 1899 or Model 1908,
16 size, hunting

Model 1899 or Model 1908,
16 size, open face

Model 16-A, 16 size

Deck Watch, 16 size, sweep second

Model 1874 & 1884, 14 size

Model 1874, 14 size, hunting

Model 1884, 14 size, open face

5 Minute Repeater, 14 size

5 Minute Repeater, 14 size

Model 1874, 14 size

Model 1884, 14 size

**Model 1895, 14 size,
open face**

Model 1897, 14 size

Colonal A Model, 14 size

Colonial Series, 14 size

Model 1924, The Colonial

Model 1894, 12 size

Model 1894, 12 size

Model 10KW, 10 size

Colonial A, 10 size

Model 1873, 8 size

Model 1873, 8&6 size

Model 1889, 6 size

Model 1890, 6 size

Model 1890, 6 size

Stone Mtn, 4 size

Model 1882, 1 size

Model 1891, 0 size

Model 1900, 0 size   Model 1907, 0 size   Jewel Series

Model 1900, 0/3 size,   Model 1907, 0/3 size,   Model 1898 & 1912,
open face   hunting   0/6 size, hunting

Model 1898 & 1912,   10½ ligne   10 ligne
0/6 size, open face

ANSONIA CLOCK CO.
Brooklyn, New York
1904 - 1929

The Ansonia Watch Co. was owned by the Ansonia Clock Company in Ansonia, Connecticut. Ansonia started making clocks in about 1850 and began manufacturing watches in 1904. They produced about 10,000,000 dollar-type watches. The company was sold to a Russian investor in 1930. "Patented April 17, 1888," is on the back plate of some Ansonia watches.

Some of the watches produced by Ansonia were marketed under different labels: Ascot, Bonnie Laddie Shoes, Dispatch, Loeser, Lenox, Picadilly, Mentor, Guide, Rural, H. Rosenburg Special, Tutor, Superior, and The Sesqui-Centennial.

Ansonia Watch Company. Example of a basic movement, 16 size, stem wind.

Ansonia Watch Co., Sequi-Centennial model.

Grade or Name—Description	Avg	Ex-Fn	Mint
Ansonia White Dial	$40	$50	$70
Ansonia Radium Dial	45	55	75
Ansonia in NI case, Black Dial	40	45	60
Ascot	40	55	75
Bonnie Laddie Shoes	60	95	115
Dispatch	30	40	60
Faultless	40	45	55
Guide	40	55	70
Lenox	35	40	50
Mentor	35	45	55
Picadilly	45	60	75
Rural	35	47	70
Sesqui-Centennial	250	275	350
Superior	45	60	75
Tutor	45	60	75

APPLETON WATCH CO.
(REMINGTON WATCH CO.)
Appleton, Wisconsin
1901 - 1903

In 1901, O. E. Bell bought the machinery of the defunct Cheshire Watch Company and moved it to Appleton, Wisconsin, where he had organized the Remington Watch Company. The first watches were shipped from the factory in February 1902; production ceased in mid-1903 and the contents were sold off before the end of that year. Most movements made by this firm were modified Cheshire movements and were marked "Appleton Watch Company." Advertisements for the firm in 1903 stated that they made 16 and 18 size movements with 11, 15, or 17 jewels. Serial numbers range from 90,000 to 104,950. During the two years they were in business, the company produced about 2,000 to 3,000 watches.

Appleton Watch Co., 18 size, 7 jewels, "The Appleton Watch Co." on dial. Engraved on movement "Appleton Watch Co., Appleton, Wis." Note that the stem is attached to movement. Serial number 93,106.

Description	Avg	Ex-Fn	Mint
18S, 7J, OF, NI, ¾, DMK, SW, PS, stem attached ★★★	$500	$600	$750
18S, 7J, OF, NI, ¾, DMK, SW, PS, Coin, OF....★★★	475	525	725
18S, 15J, NI, LS, SW, ¾, M#2................★★★★	600	700	850
16S, 7-11J, ¾, stem attached ....★★★	500	600	750

Note: Prices are for watches with original cases. This case is difficult to find.

AUBURNDALE WATCH CO.
Auburndale, Massachusetts
1876 - 1883

This company was the first to attempt an inexpensive watch. Jason R. Hopkins was issued two patents in 1875 covering the "rotary design." The rotary design eliminated the need of adjusting to various positions, resulting in a less expensive watch. The company was formed about 1876, and the first watches were known as the "Auburndale Rotary." In 1876, equipment was purchased from the Marion Watch Co., and the first rotary designed watches were placed on the market for $10 in 1877. Auburndale produced about 3,230 watches before closing in 1883.

AUBURNDALE WATCH CO. (continued)

Auburndale Timer, 18 size, 7 jewels, stem wind, 10 minute, ¼ second jump timer.

Auburndale Rotary, 20 size, 2 jewels, lever set, stem wind, detent escapement.

Grade or Name — Description	Avg	Ex-Fn	Mint
Auburndale Rotary, 20S, 2J, LS, SW, NI case, detent ★ ★ ★	$1,550	$1,800	$2,600
Auburndale Rotary, 18S, 2J, SW, LS, NI case, lever . ★ ★	1,000	1,400	1,800
Bentley, 18S, 7J, LS, NI case, SW, ¾ .... ★ ★	500	700	1,000
Lincoln, 18S, 7J, LS, NI case, KW, ¾ .... ★ ★	500	700	1,000
Auburndale Timer, 18S, 7J, SW, NI case, 10 min. timer, ¼ sec. jump, Chronograph........................	200	250	375
Auburndale Timer, 18S, 7J, KW, NI case, 10 min. timer, ¼ sec. jump with split seconds, Chronograph ....★	375	425	550

Bentley, 18 size, 7 jewels, ¾ plate, stem wind, serial number 2.

Auburndale Rotary, 18 size, 2 jewels, stem wind, lever set, serial number 448.

AURORA WATCH CO.
Aurora, Illinois
1883 - 1890

Aurora Watch Co. was organized in mid-1883 with the goal of getting one jeweler

AURORA WATCH CO. (continued)

in every town to handle Aurora watches. The first movements were 18S, full plate, and were first sold in the fall of 1884. There were several watches marked No. 1. The total production was about 215,000; over 100,000 were 18S, and some were 6S ladies' watches. For the most part Aurora produced medium to low grade; and at one time made about 150 movements per day. The Hamilton Watch Co. purchased the company on June 19, 1890.

The "Guild" watch was made under special contract for the U. S. Jewelers Guild and carried the Guild trademark.

Eleven grades of hunter cases and open faces with stem wind, seven grades of key wind, and five grades with Breguet hairsprings for railroad service were made.

AURORA WATCH CO.
Estimated Serial Nos. and Production Dates

1885 - 60,000	1887 - 160,000	1889 - 215,000
1886 - 110,000	1888 - 200,000	

Aurora Watch Co., 18 size, 15 jewels, serial number 142,060. Made for railroad service.

Aurora Watch Co., 18 size, 15 jewels, Adj, engraved on movement "Made expressly R.J.A.," serial number 73,529.

Description	Avg	Ex-Fn	Mint
18S, 7J, OF, KW	$175	$225	$300
18S, 11J, OF, KW	185	235	310
18S, 11J, 5th pinion model, OF	200	250	325
18S, 15J, OF, KW	200	250	325
18S, marked 15 Ruby Jewels but has 17J, 5th pinion, HC ★	600	700	900

(The 5th pinion model is marked 15 ruby jewels, but some actually had 17 jewels. This was Aurora's highest grade.)

Description	Avg	Ex-Fn	Mint
18S, 15 Ruby Jewels but has 17J, 5th pinion, OF .... ★ ★	700	800	1,000
18S, marked 15 Ruby Jewels & has only 15J, HC	350	450	575
18S, marked 15 Ruby Jewels & has only 15J, OF	375	475	600
18S, 11J, OF, SW, Gilded, Coin	125	150	200
18S, 11J, OF, SW, Gilded	125	150	200
18s, 15J, OF, SW, Gilded	150	175	225

AURORA WATCH CO. (continued)

Aurora Watch Co., 18 size, 17 jewels (marked 15 Ruby jewels). Aurora's highest grade.

Aurora Watch Co., 18 size, 15 jewels, serial number 45,204. Made expressly for the Guild.

Description	Avg	Ex-Fn	Mint
18S, 15J, Chronometer, ADJ, SW/LS, HC, NI	$375	$450	$575
18S, 15J, NI, HC, made expressly for the guild	375	450	575
18S, 15J, gilt, HC, made expressly for the guild	325	400	525
18S, 15J, OF, DMK, NI, GJS	225	275	375
6S, 11-15J, HC	125	150	200

BALL WATCH CO.
Cleveland, Ohio
1879 - 1969

The Ball Watch Company did not manufacture watches but did help formulate the specifications of watches used for railroad service. Webb C. Ball of Cleveland, Ohio, was the general time inspector for over 125,000 miles of railroad in the U. S., Mexico, and Canada. In 1891 there was a collision between the Lake Shore and Michigan Southern Railways at Kipton, Ohio. The collision was reported to have occurred because an engineer's watch had stopped, for about four minutes, then started running again. The railroad officials commissioned Ball to establish the timepiece inspection system. Ball knew that the key to safe operations of the railroad was the manufacturing of sturdy, precision timepieces. He also knew they must be able to withstand hard use and still be accurate. Before this time, each railroad company had its own rules and standards. After Ball presented his guidelines, most American manufacturers set out to meet these standards and soon a list was made of the manufacturers that produced watches of the grade that would pass inspection. Each railroad employee had a card that he carried showing the record of how his watch performed on inspection. Ball was also instrumental in the formation of the Horological Institute of America.

A 1902 advertisement for Ball Watch Company read, "We do not sell movements or cases separately."

200,000 railroad watches, plus 150,000 non-railroad grade watches, were made and

BALL WATCH CO. (continued)

sold by the Ball Watch Co., totaling approximately 350,000.

Ball Watch Co. Dial (Brotherhood of RR Trainsmen), 18 size.

Ball Watch Co. Dial (Order of Railroad Conductors), 18 size.

BALL'S FIRST STANDARDS FOR R.R. USE

1. Must be 18 or 16 size.
2. Must have a minimum of 17 jewels.
3. Must be a single roller.
4. Must be lever set.
5. Must have a Breguet hairspring.
6. Must have a patent regulator.
7. Must be adjusted to isochronism and 5 positions.
8. Must be adjusted to a rate of within 30 seconds a week.
9. Must have a standard mark or number stamped on back plate.

BALL ADDED THESE LATER:

10. Must have "adjusted 5 positions" stamped on the plate.
11. Must be a double roller.
12. Must have a plain Arabic dial.
13. Must have the winding stem at 12 o'clock.
14. Must be temperature adjusted for accuracy from 30 to 95 degrees F.
15. Must have a minimum of 19 jewels.

NOTE: Ball Watches are difficult to identify at first, but if one studies the market he can soon identify most of them. The manufacturer's serial number list can be useful. Prices shown are for watches with original Ball cases, which bring top dollar and are preferred by most collectors.

BALL WATCH COMPANY
ESTIMATED SERIAL NUMBERS AND PRODUCTION DATES
FOR RAILROAD GRADE WATCHES

Hamilton		Waltham		Elgin
Date	**Serial No.**	**Date**	**Serial No.**	**Date**
1895	13,000	1900	060,700	1904 - 1906
1897	20,500	1905	202,000	S# range:
1900	42,000	1910	216,200	11,853,000 - 12,282,000
1902	170,000	1915	250,000	
1905	462,000	1920	260,000	**E. Howard & Co.**
1910	600,000	1925	270,000	**Date**
1915	603,000			1893 - 1895
1920	610,000	**Illinois W. Co.**		S# range:
1925	620,000	**Date**	**Serial No.**	226,000 - 308,000
1930	637,000	1929	800,000	
1935	641,000	1930	801,000	**Hampden**
1938	647,000	1931	803,000	**Date**
1939	650,000	1932	804,000	1890 - 1892
1940	651,000			S# range:
1941	652,000			626,750 - 657,960 -
1942	654,000			759,720

BALL—AURORA
18 SIZE

Description		Avg	Ex-Fn	Mint
17J, OF, marked Ball............................★ ★		$1,500	$1,750	$2,000

Ball-Elgin, Grade 333, 18 size, 17 jewels, rare hunting case model, serial number 11,958,002.

Ball-Elgin, Grade 333, 18 size, 17 jewels, open face model, serial number 11,856,801.

BALL—ELGIN
18 SIZE G. F. CASES

Description		Avg	Ex-Fn	Mint
16J, G#327, OF, LS ....★		$275	$350	$475
17J, G#328, OF, LS ....★		300	375	500

BALL-ELGIN (continued)

Description	Avg	Ex-Fn	Mint
17J, G#328, Coin, OF, LS .... ★	$250	$325	$450
17J, G#329, NI, Adj.5P, LS, HC .... ★	1,200	1,500	1,850
21J, G#330, LS, official RR std., HC .... ★ ★ ★	2,000	2,500	3,000
16J, G#331, NI, OF, Adj.5P, PS, Commercial Std. .. ★ ★	375	400	550
17J, G#331, NI, OF, Adj.5P, PS......................	165	255	325
17J, G#332, OF, PS .... ★	300	350	400
17J, G#333, NI, OF, Adj.5P, LS.....................	175	200	275
17J, G#333, NI, HC, Adj.5P, LS .... ★ ★	1,700	1,900	2,100
21J, G#333, NI, OF, Adj.5P, LS.....................	200	250	325
21J, G#334, NI, OF, Adj.5P, LS.....................	325	375	425

Note: 18 Size Ball watches in hunting cases are scarce.

BALL—HAMILTON
18 SIZE G. F. CASES

Description	Avg	Ex-Fn	Mint
17J, M#999, Commercial Standard .... ★ ★	$400	$475	$575
17J, M#999, NI, OF, Adj.5P, LS, Coin................	150	200	275
17J, M#999, NI, OF, Adj.5P, LS	150	200	275

Ball-Hamilton, Grade 999, 18 size, 17 jewels, serial number 458,623.

Ball-Hamilton, Grade 999, 18 size, 17 jewels, marked "Railroad Watch Co." serial number 20,793.

Description	Avg	Ex-Fn	Mint
17J, M#999, NI, OF, Adj.5P, marked "Loaner" on case .	$200	$275	$375
19J, M#999, NI, OF, Adj.5P, LS	175	225	300
21J, M#999, NI, OF, Adj.5P, LS	225	275	375
23J, M#999, NI, OF, Adj.5P, LS .... ★ ★ ★	6,000	7,500	10,000
23J, M#999, NI, HC, Adj.5P, LS	7,000	9,000	12,000
Ball & Co., 17J, SR, Coin	450	600	800
Brotherhood of Locomotive Engineers, 17J, OF	400	500	650
Brotherhood of Locomotive Engineers, 19J, OF	500	600	750

Ball Watch Co., Brotherhood of RR trainmen, 18 size, 17 jewels; movement made by Hamilton, serial number 13,020.

Ball Watch Co. (Hamilton). Grade 999, 18 size, 21 jewels, sun ray damaskeening, serial number 548,157, c.1906.

Description	Avg	Ex-Fn	Mint
Brotherhood of Locomotive Engineers, 21J, OF	$600	$700	$850
Brotherhood of Locomotive Firemen, 17J, OF	400	500	650
Brotherhood of Locomotive Firemen, 19J, OF	500	600	750
Brotherhood of Locomotive Firemen, 21J, OF	600	700	850
Brotherhood of Railroad Trainmen, 17J, OF	400	500	650
Brotherhood of Railroad Trainmen, 19J, OF	500	600	750
Brotherhood of Railroad Trainmen, 21J, OF	600	700	850
Order of Railroad Conductors, 17J, OF................	400	500	650
Order of Railroad Conductors, 19J, OF................	500	600	750
Order of Railroad Conductors, 21J, OF................	600	700	850
Order of Railroad Telegraphers, 17J, OF...............	400	500	650
Order of Railroad Telegraphers, 19J, OF...............	500	600	750
Order of Railroad Telegraphers, 21J, OF...............	600	700	850
Railroad Watch Co., 16J, OF, LS.................. ★★	900	1,200	1,750
Railroad Watch Co., 17J, OF, LS.................. ★★	1,000	1,300	1,850
17J, Off. Ball marked jewelers name on dial & mvt., OF★	350	450	575
17J, M#999, adjusted "A," OF .... ★	400	500	625

BALL—DeLONG ESCAPEMENT
16 SIZE

Description	Avg	Ex-Fn	Mint
21J, 14K OF Case..................................	$2,000	$2,500	$3,200

Ball-Hamilton, Model 998 Elinvar, 16 size, 23 jewels, with center bridge.

BALL—HAMILTON
16 SIZE G. F. CASES

Description	Avg	Ex-Fn	Mint
16J, M#976, 977, NI, OF, LS.........................	$125	$150	$200
17J, M#974, NI, OF, LS	125	150	200
17J, Official RR Standard, OF........................	150	175	225
19J, Official RR Standard, OF........................	300	350	425
19J, M#999, NI, OF, LS	150	175	225
21J, M#999, NI, OF, LS	175	200	250
21J, M#999B (marked), NI, OF, LS, Adj.6P	300	350	400
21J, M#999, Coin case................................	150	175	225
21J, M#999 Loaner, marked case......................	175	200	250
23J, M#999B, NI, OF, LS, Adj.6P	500	600	675
23J, M#998 Elinvar, Adj.6P	475	575	650
23J, M#999, NI, OF, LS	450	550	625
21J, M#992-B, NI, OF, LS, Webb C. Ball .... ★ ★ ★	600	750	1,000
Brotherhood of Locomotive Engineers, OF	300	350	500
Brotherhood of Locomotive Firemen, OF	300	350	500
Brotherhood of Railroad Trainmen, OF.................	300	350	500
Order of Railroad Conductors, OF	300	350	500

BALL—HAMPDEN
18 SIZE

Description	Avg	Ex-Fn	Mint
17J, LS, SW, OF, marked "Superior Grade"...... ★ ★ ★	$1,250	$1,400	$1,850
17J, LS, SW, OF, **not** marked "Superior Grade" .... ★ ★	1,000	1,200	1,600
15J, LS, SW, OF .... ★	200	250	300
15J, LS, SW, HC .... ★ ★ ★	400	500	650

BALL-HAMPDEN (continued)

Ball-Hampden, 18 size, 17 jewels, serial number 759,728.

Ball-Hampden, marked "Superior Grade," 18 size, 17 jewels, serial number 626,754.

BALL—E. HOWARD & CO.
18 SIZE

Description	Avg	Ex-Fn	Mint
17J, ¾, HC, PS, GJS, 18K, VII, orig. gold HC ... ★ ★ ★	$4,000	$5,000	$6,500
17J, ¾, OF, PS, GJS, 14K, VIII, orig. gold OF case. ★ ★	2,500	3,000	5,000
17J, ¾, OF, PS, GJS, 14K, VIII, Brotherhood of Locomotive Engineers	3,000	4,000	6,000

Ball & Co. (E. Howard & Co.), Series VIII, 18 size, 17 jewels. Order of Railway Conductors, serial number 307,488. c.1900.

Ball-E. Howard Watch Co., 16 size, 21 jewels (Keystone). This watch believed to be one-of-a-kind prototype, serial number 982,201.

BALL—E. HOWARD WATCH CO.
16 SIZE

Description	Avg	Ex-Fn	Mint
17J, OF, GJS	$2,000	$2,500	$3,500
21J, OF, GJS .... ★★★	2,500	3,000	4,000

Ball Watch Co., Illinois Model, 16 size, 23 jewels. To identify, note back plates that circle around balance wheel, serial number B801,758.

BALL—ILLINOIS
16 SIZE

Description	Avg	Ex-Fn	Mint
23J, ¾, LS, OF, GJS .... ★★	$895	$975	$1,175
23J, ¾, LS, OF, GJS, marked 60 hr .... ★★	1,200	1,400	1,800

Top Left: Ball-Hamilton, 16 size, 23 jewels. Bottom left: Ball-Illinois, 16 size, 23 jewels. Above: Ball-Waltham, 16 size, 23 jewels. These three movements are similar in appearance. To identify, note where the hair spring stud attaches to the balance bridge, which is slightly different on each movement.

162

BALL—SETH THOMAS
18 SIZE

Description	Avg	Ex-Fn	Mint
17J, M#3, LS, OF, ¾, GJS ....★★	$1,500	$2,000	$2,800

BALL—WALTHAM
18 SIZE

Description	Avg	Ex-Fn	Mint
1892, 15J, OF, LS, SW, marked Webb C. Ball, Cleveland ....★★	$1,500	$1,800	$2,200

BALL—WALTHAM
16 SIZE

Description	Avg	Ex-Fn	Mint
15J, HC, GCW ....★★	$325	$400	$550
17J, OF, LS, ¾, Adj.5P, Multi-color case, GF	250	300	400
17J, OF, LS, ¾, Adj.5P	150	200	275
17J, official RR std., HC ....★★	800	1,000	1,300
17J, commercial std., OF	75	100	150

Ball-Waltham, 16 size, 19 jewels, ORC (Order of Railroad Conductors), serial number B204,475.

Description	Avg	Ex-Fn	Mint
19J, BLF&E	$450	$500	$650
21J, Brotherhood, marked ORC, BOFLE	500	600	750
19J, Hunting case ....★★	900	1,100	1,400
19J, OF, LS, 14K	575	650	750
19J, OF, LS, stirrup style case	150	200	225

BALL-WALTHAM (continued)

Description	Avg	Ex-Fn	Mint
19J, OF, LS, Coin	$100	$125	$175
19J, OF, LS, ¾, Adj.5P	150	200	275
19J, OF, LS, ¾, Adj.5P, Wind Indicator ★★	2,500	3,000	4,500
21J, OF, LS, ¾, Adj.5P	225	250	300
21J, LS, OF, Adj.5P, marked Loaner	250	275	350
23J, LS, OF, Adj.5P, NI, GJS ★	550	650	850

Ball Watch Co. by Waltham, 12 size, 19 jewels, open face, digital seconds

12 SIZE
(Not Railroad Grade)

Description	Avg	Ex-Fn	Mint
19J, Illinois, OF, PS	$135	$175	$250
19J, Illinois, HC, PS	200	300	450
19J, Waltham, OF, PS, rotating digital sec	150	200	275

0 SIZE
(Not Railroad Grade)

Description	Avg	Ex-Fn	Mint
17-19J, Waltham, OF, PS	$225	$275	$375
19J, HC, PS, "Queen" in Ball case	350	400	550

FOR CANADA R.R. SERVICE

Description	Avg	Ex-Fn	Mint
16S,¾,LS,OF,GJS	$500	$600	$775

RAILROAD INSPECTOR'S OR JEWELRY CO. NAME
ON DIAL AND MOVEMENT

Description	Avg	Ex-Fn	Mint
18S, 17J, Adj.5P, OF	$700	$850	$1,000

BALL WATCH CO. (continued)

Ball-Audemars Piguet & Co., 14 size, 31 jewels, minute repeater, open face, serial number 4,220.

Ball-Vacheron & Constantin, 43mm, 18 jewels, hunting; note wolf-teeth winding.

BALL—SWISS
16 SIZE

Description	Avg	Ex-Fn	Mint
21J, M#435-B, OF, LS, Adj.6P, Ball case, stirrup bow ...	$185	$235	$285
21J, M#435-C, OF, LS, Adj.6P, Ball case, stirrup bow ...	185	235	285
21J, M#477-B, Adj.6P (BXC-Record Watch Co.)	150	175	225
17J, "Garland"	100	125	175
40mm Audemar Piguet, min. repeater, jeweled thru hammers, 18K, OF, triple signed Webb C. Ball	6,000	7,500	9,500
43mm Vacheron & Constantin, 18J, HC, 18K	800	900	1,100

BANNATYNE WATCH CO.
1905 - 1911

Mr. Bannatyne had previously worked for Ansonia, in charge of watch production. Bannatyne made non-jeweled watches that sold for about $1.50. Ingraham bought this company in 1912.

ESTIMATED SERIAL NUMBERS AND PRODUCTION DATES

Date	Serial No.	Date	Serial No.	Date	Serial No.
1906	40,000	1908	140,000	1910	250,000

Description		Avg	Ex-Fn	Mint
18S, OF, SW, NI case .... ★		$500	$600	$800

Bannatyne Watch Co. (left), Ingraham Watch Co. (right). Note similarity of movements. Both patented Aug. 27th, 1907 & Sept. 3rd, 1907.

BENEDICT & BURNHAM MFG. CO.
Waterbury, Connecticut
1878 - 1880

This name will be found on the dial of the first 1,000 "long wind" Waterbury watches made in 1878. These watches had skeleton type movements with open dials that made the works visible. They contained 58 parts and were very attractive. The company was reorganized in March 1880 as the Waterbury Watch Co. and in 1886 became the New England Watch Co.

Benedict & Burnham Mfg. Co. dial & movement, 18 size, long wind, skeletonized dial.

Description		Avg	Ex-Fn	Mint
18S, long wind, NI case .... ★ ★		$700	$800	$1,000

BOWMAN WATCH CO.
Lancaster, Pennsylvania
1877 - 1882

In March 1879, Ezra F. Bowman, a native of Lancaster, Pa., opened a retail jewelry and watch business. He employed William H. Todd to supervise his watch manufacturing. Todd had previously been employed by the Elgin and Lancaster Watch companies. Bowman made a 17S, ¾ plate, fully-jeweled movement. The escape wheel was a star-tooth design, fully capped, similar to those made by Charles Frodsham, an English watchmaker. They were stem wind with dials made by another company. Enough parts were made and bought for 300 watches, but only about 50 watches were completed and sold. Those performed very well. The company was sold to J. P. Stevens of Atlanta, Ga.

Description	Avg	Ex-Fn	Mint
18S, 17J, Hamilton 928, OF, marked E. F. Bowman	$300	$400	$550
17S, 19-21J, ¾, GJS, NI, LS, SW .... ★ ★ ★	7,500	11,000	16,000
16S, 21J, Hamilton 960, OF, marked E. F. Bowman	300	400	550

Bowman Watch Co., 16-18 size, 17 jewels, ¾ plate, gold jewel settings, lever set, stem wind. Note free sprung balance. Serial number 17, c.1880.

ROBERT BROWN & SON
1833 - 1856
J. R. BROWN & SHARPE
1856
Providence, Rhode Island

Description		Avg	Ex-Fn	Mint
18S, KW, KS, FULL .... ★ ★ ★		$2,000	$2,500	$3,500

California Watch Co., 18 size, 15 jewels, full plate.

California Watch Co., 18 size, 7 jewels, full plate, serial number 29,029.

CALIFORNIA WATCH CO.
Berkeley, California
1876 - 1877

The Cornell Watch Co. was reorganized in early 1876 as the California Watch Co. The new company bought machinery to make watch cases of gold and silver. In a short time the company was in bad financial trouble and even paid its employees with watches. The business closed in the summer of 1876. Albert Troller bought the unfinished watches that were left. In about four months, he found a buyer in San Francisco. The factory was then closed and sold to the Independent Watch Co. Only about 5,000 watches were made by the California Watch Company. Serial numbers range from 25,115 to 30,174. Inscribed on the movements is "Berkeley."

Description	Avg	Ex-Fn	Mint
18S, 15J, FULL, KW, KS, "Berkeley" ....★★	$1,300	$1,600	$2,000
18S, 11J, FULL, KW, KS ....★	1,000	1,200	1,600

CHESHIRE WATCH CO.
Cheshire, Connecticut
1883 - 1890

In October 1883, the Cheshire Watch Company was formed by George J. Capewell with D. A. Buck (designer of the long-wind Waterbury) as superintendent. Their first movement was 18S, ¾ gilt plate, stem wind, stem set, with the pendant attached to the movement. It fit into a nickel case which was also made at the Cheshire factory. The first watches were completed in April 1885. A new 18S nickel movement with a second hand was made to fit standard size American cases, and was introduced in 1887. By that

CHESHIRE WATCH CO. (continued)

date production was at about 200 watches per day. Serial numbers range from 201 to 89,650. All Cheshire watches were sold through L. W. Sweet, general selling agent, in New York City. The factory closed in 1890, going into receivership. The receiver had 3,000 movements finished in 1892. In 1901 O. E. Bell bought the machinery and had it shipped to Appleton, Wisconsin, where he had formed the Remington Watch Company. The watches produced by Remington are marked "Appleton Watch Co." on the movements.

Cheshire Watch Co., 18-20 size, 4 jewels, model number 1. Note stem attached and will not fit standard size case, serial number 201.

Description	Avg	Ex-Fn	Mint
20S, 4-7J, FULL, OF, SW, NI case, stem attached, 1st model, closed top plate .... ★ ★ ★	$450	$550	$700
18S, 4-7J, ¾, SW, OF, NI case, stem attached, 2nd model ★	300	375	475
18S, 7J, OF, fits standard case...................... ★	250	300	375
18S, 11J, OF, SW, standard case, 3rd model .... ★	275	325	400
18S, 15J, OF, NI, ADJ, standard case, 3rd model ..... ★	300	350	450
18S, 21J, OF, SW, Coin, standard case, 3rd model... ★ ★	400	450	550
6S, ¾, OF, SW, NI case .... ★	200	275	350

Cheshire Watch Co., 18 size, 4-7 jewels. This model number 2 was manufactured with the stem attached and requires a special case.

Cheshire Watch Co., 18 size, 4-7 jewels. This model fits standard 18 size cases. Model number 3.

CHICAGO WATCH CO.
Chicago, Illinois
1895 - 1903

The Chicago Watch Company's watches were 18S, 7J, open-faced, had silveroid type cases, and were produced at low cost. They are believed to have been made by another manufacturer and sold by Chicago Watch Co.

Description	Avg	Ex-Fn	Mint
18S, 7J, OF	$100	$150	$200
18S, 7-11J, HC or OF, Swiss fake.....................	30	40	55
18S, 11J, KW...	325	375	450
18S, 15J, OF, SW.....................................	175	200	300
Columbus, 18S, 15J, SW, NI, HC .... ★ ★	200	225	325
Illinois, 18S, 11J, SW, NI .... ★ ★	200	225	325
Waltham, 18S, 15J .... ★ ★	200	225	325
12S, 15J	125	150	200
12S, YGF, HC..	200	225	275

COLUMBIA WATCH CO.
Waltham, Massachusetts
1896 - 1899

The Columbia Watch Company was organized in 1896 by Edward A. Locke, formerly General Manager of the Waterbury Watch Company. The firm began manufacturing an 0-size, 4-jewel gilt movement with duplex escapement in 1897. These movements were marked "Columbia Watch Co./Waltham, Mass." The firm also made movements marked "Hollers Watch Co./Brooklyn, NY," as well as nickeled movements marked "Cambridge Watch Co./New York."

Locke turned the business over to his son-in-law, Renton Whidden, in 1898, and

COLUMBIA WATCH CO. (continued)

the firm changed to an 0-size, 7-jewel nickel movement with lever escapement called the Suffolk. The firm name was not changed until early 1901.

Description	Avg	Ex-Fn	Mint
0S, 4J, SW, OF, HC, Duplex, gilded	$50	$60	$75
0S, 7J, SW, OF, lever escapement.....................	60	75	85

Columbia Watch Co., 0 size, 4 jewels, stem wind, open face and hunting, duplex escapement.

COLUMBUS WATCH CO.
Columbus, Ohio
1882 - 1903

The Columbus Watch Co. grew from the Columbus Watch Mfg. Co. which was started in 1876 by D. Gruen and W. J. Savage. The company finished Swiss-imported movements in 8, 16, and 18 sizes to fit American-made cases. They continued to import movements until Nov. 18, 1882, at which time a factory was built. By Aug. 18, 1883, the first movements had been produced. There are several features that separate the Columbus from other American watches. The train is different because the barrel has 72 teeth, the center wheel 72, center pinion 11, third wheel 11 leaves. No cases were made by the company, and the mainsprings and hairsprings, as well as the jewels, were imported. The company started making its own dials in 1884. They were producing watches at the rate of 150 a day in 1888. Serial numbers range from 20,000 to 383,000 for standard grade movements. In 1894 a block of numbers from 500,000 to 505,800 was assigned to some higher grade movements. Also in that year some movements bore the name "New Columbus Watch Co." In 1903 the Columbus Watch Co. was sold to the South Bend Watch Co.

18 SIZE

Grade or Name — Description	Avg	Ex-Fn	Mint
Champion, 15J, NI, FULL, HC	$125	$150	$175
Champion, 15J, gilt, FULL, HC	125	150	175
Champion, 15J, gilt, FULL, Coin, OF..................	100	125	150
Champion, 16J, NI, ADJ, FULL, DMK, OF	85	110	140
Columbus W. Co., 15J, OF, LS	85	110	140
Columbus W. Co., 16J, OF, LS	95	120	150
Columbus W. Co., 17J, OF, LS	100	125	160
Columbus W. Co., 17J, OF, LS, 2-Tone...............	135	160	200
Columbus W. Co., 16J, KW, KS, HC ....★★★	400	550	775

Columbus Watch Co., 18 size, 15 jewels, key wind and set, "Ohio Watch Co." on dial, "Col. Watch Co." on movement.

Columbus Watch Co., Railway King, 18 size, 23 jewels, with choo choo dial.

Grade or Name—Description	Avg	Ex-Fn	Mint
Columbus W. Co., 11-15J, KW, KS, HC	$200	$300	$450
Columbus W. Co., 15J, KW, KS, 18K, HC	700	800	950
Columbus W. Co., 15J, HC, LS, KW/SW Trans.........	125	150	200
Columbus W. Co., 15J, Multi-color 14K box hinge HC...	1,600	1,800	2,500
Columbus W. Co., 15J, Coin.........................	75	100	150
Columbus W. Co., 15J, "New Columbus W. Co." on mvt.	75	100	150
Columbus W. Co., 11J, Coin.........................	75	100	150
Columbus W. Co., 11J, HC, LS	125	150	200
Columbus W. Co., 13J, HC, LS	125	150	200
Columbus W. Co., 17J, HC, LS, Trans.	125	150	200
Columbus King, 17J, HC	250	275	350
Columbus Watch Co., 17J, NI, 14K Multi-color box hinge HC	1,600	1,800	2,200
Columbus King, 21J, HC	275	300	375
Columbus King, 23J, HC	700	1,000	1,350
Columbus King, 25J, HC .... ★ ★	2,000	2,500	3,500
Jay Gould, 15J, OF	200	275	375
Jackson Park, 15J, NI, ADJ, OF	200	275	375
North Star, 11J, NI, FULL, HC	75	100	125
North Star, 11J, gilt, FULL, HC.....................	75	100	125
North Star, 15J, gilt, FULL, Coin, HC	75	100	125
North Star, 15J, NI, FULL, HC	75	100	125
Ohio Watch Co., 13J, OF, KW, KS .... ★ ★	300	375	475
Ohio Watch Co., 11-13J, OF, transition KW/KS to SW/LS .... ★	200	275	375

COLUMBUS WATCH CO., 18 SIZE (continued)

Grade or Name—Description	Avg	Ex-Fn	Mint
Railroad Monarch, 17J, ADJ, OF......................	$200	$275	$375
Railway King, 16J, ADJ, GJS, 2-Tone, Choo Choo dial, HC	250	325	425
Railway King, 17J, ADJ, GJS, Choo Choo dial, HC	250	325	425
Railway King, 17J, 2-Tone, HC........................	175	225	300
Railway King, 19J, GJS, Adj.5P, HC ....★★	500	600	700
Railway King, 19J, GJS, Adj.5P, OF..............★★	500	600	700
Railway King, 21J, GT, Adj.6P, DMK, GJS, HC........	200	275	375
Railway King, 21J, GT, Adj.6P, DMK, GJS, 2-Tone, HC	225	300	400
Railway King, 23J, Adj.6P, DMK, GJS, HC ....★	800	1,100	1,450
Railway King, 25J, GT, Adj.6P, DMK, GJS, OF ....★★	2,000	2,500	3,500
Railway King, 25J, GT, Adj.6P, DMK, GJS, HC..★★★	2,500	3,000	4,000
Railway King Special	200	275	375
R. W. K. Special, 17J, OF, LS, 2-Tone.................	225	300	400
R. W. K. Special, 19J, HC, LS, 2-Tone.................	250	325	425
Railway Regulator, 17J, OF	200	275	375
Railway Time Service, 17J, OF, NI.....................	175	225	300
Time King, 17J, 2-Tone, OF...........................	150	200	275
Time King, 21J, GT, Adj.6P, DMK, GJS, 2-Tone, HC ...	225	300	400
Time King, 23J, GT, Adj.6P, DMK, GJS, HC	800	1,100	1,450
Time King, 25J, GT, Adj.6P, DMK, GJS ....★★	2,000	2,500	3,500
G#18, 16J, HC, Adj.6P, GJS, DMK, NI................	150	175	200
G#20-21, 7-11J, HC	100	125	175
G#28, 16J, HC, FULL, ADJ, GJS, DMK	125	150	175
G#34, 15J, HC, FULL, NI	125	150	175
G#32, 15J, HC, FULL, gilded	125	150	175
G#90, 7J, gilt, OF, FULL.............................	75	100	125
G#90, 7J, gilt, OF, Coin	75	100	125
G#93, 15J, gilt, OF, FULL............................	75	100	125
G#94, 15J, NI, OF, FULL	75	100	125

Columbus King, 18 size, 25 jewels, hunting case, stem wind, serial number 503,094.

Railway King, 18 size, 23 jewels, adjusted, stem wind, open face, serial number 503,315.

COLUMBUS WATCH CO., 18 SIZE (continued)

Grade or Name—Description	Avg	Ex-Fn	Mint
G#95, 15J, NI, OF, FULL, ADJ, GJS	$75	$100	$125
G#98, 16J, NI, OF, FULL, ADJ, GJS, DMK	75	100	125
G#99, 16J, NI, OF, FULL, Adj.6P, GJS, DMK	100	125	150
G#105, 19J, GJS, 2-Tone, HC ★	1,000	1,200	1,500
Swiss-made 18S, 7J, HC, SW, LS, ¾ Plate	75	100	125
Swiss-made 18S, 11J, HC, SW, LS, ¾ Plate	75	100	125
Swiss-made 18S, 15J, HC, SW, LS, ¾ Plate	75	100	125
Swiss-made 18S, 16J, HC, SW, LS, ¾ Plate	75	100	125

Columbus Watch Co., 16 size, 17 jewels, gold train, serial number 228,188.

Columbus Watch Co., Ruby Model, 16 size, 21 jewels, three quarter plate, gold jewel settings, gold train, Adj6p.

16 SIZE

Grade or Name — Description	Avg	Ex-Fn	Mint
New Columbus Watch Co., 11J, ¾, OF	$50	$75	$100
New Columbus Watch Co., 15J, ¾, OF	50	75	100
New Columbus Watch Co., 16J, ¾, OF	50	75	100
New Columbus Watch Co., 17J, 14K, Multi-color HC	1,000	1,200	1,500
New Columbus Watch Co., 17J, 2-Tone	75	100	125
Ruby Model, 21J, ¾, NI, GJS, GT, OF, 2-tone ★ ★	525	600	725
Ruby Model, 21J, ¾, NI, GJS, Adj.6P, GT, HC ★	425	500	625
G#41, 11J, gilt, ¾, HC	75	100	125
G#43, 11J, NI, ¾, HC	75	100	125
G#44, 15J, NI, GJS, ADJ, ¾, HC	75	100	125
G#45, 19J, GJS, 2-Tone, HC ★ ★	800	1,000	1,300
G#46, 15J, NI, GJS, ADJ, ¾, HC	75	100	125
G#47, 16J, NI, ADJ, GJS, ¾, HC	75	100	125
G#81, 11J, OF, gilt, ¾	50	75	100
G#83, 11J, OF, NI, ¾	50	75	100
G#84, 15J, OF, NI, GJS, ADJ, ¾	50	75	100
G#86, 15J, OF, NI, GJS, ADJ, ¾	75	100	125
G#87, 16J, OF, Adj.3P, GJS, ¾, NI, DMK	75	100	125
G#88, 16J, OF, Adj.6p, 14K, GJS, ¾, DMK, NI	475	500	600

COLUMBUS WATCH CO., 16 SIZE (continued)

Grade or Name—Description	Avg	Ex-Fn	Mint
Swiss-made 16S, 15J, SW, LS, OF	$50	$75	$100
Swiss-made 16S, 15J, SW, LS, HC	75	100	125
Swiss-made 16S, 16J, SW, LS, OF	50	75	100
Swiss-made 16S, 16J, SW, LS, HC	75	100	125

Columbus Watch Co., 6 size, 15 jewels, ¾ plate, stem wind, serial number 377,489.

New Columbus Watch Co. Example of a basic model for 6 size. ¾ plate, 7-16 jewels, gilded and nickel.

6 SIZE

Grade or Name — Description	Avg	Ex-Fn	Mint
G#102-G#50, 7J, gilded, HC...........................	$75	$100	$125
G#101-G#51, 11J, gilded, HC..........................	75	100	125
G#53, 11J, NI, HC	75	100	125
G#55, 15J, GJS, NI, 18K, HC	375	425	575
G#55, 15J, GJS, NI, HC...............................	75	100	125
G#104-G#57, 16J, GJS, DMK, NI, HC	75	100	125
Swiss made 6S, 11-15J, SW, LS, HC	50	75	100

4 SIZE

Grade or Name—Description	Avg	Ex-Fn	Mint
Columbus Watch Co., 15J, HC, gilt mvt.	$100	$150	$200
Columbus Watch Co., 15J, HC, nickel mvt.............	110	160	220

COLUMBUS
ESTIMATED SERIAL NUMBERS AND PRODUCTION DATES

Date	Serial No.	Date	Serial No.	Special Block of Serial Nos.	
1883	23,000	1893	207,000		
1884	30,000	1894	229,000		
1885	40,000	1895	251,000	**Date**	**Serial No.**
1886	53,000	1896	273,000	1894	500,001
1887	75,000	1897	295,000	1896	501,500
1888	97,000	1898	317,000	1898	503,000
1889	119,000	1899	339,000	1900	504,500
1890	141,000	1900	361,000	1902	505,800
1891	163,000	1901	383,000		
1892	185,000				

CORNELL WATCH CO.
Chicago, Illinois
1870 - 1874
San Francisco, California
1875 - 1876

The Cornell Watch Co. bought the Newark Watch Co. and greatly improved the movements being produced. In the fall of 1874, the company moved to San Francisco, Calif., with about 60 of its employees. The movements made in California were virtually the same as those made in Chicago. The company wanted to employ Chinese who would work cheaper, but the skilled employees refused to go along and went on strike. The company stayed alive until 1875 and was sold to the California Watch Co. in January 1876. But death came a few months later.

The Chronology of the Development of Cornell Watch Co.:
Newark Watch Co. 1864-1870; S#s 6901-12,000
Cornell Watch Co., Chicago, Ill. 1870-1874; S#s 12,001 to 25,000;
Cornell Watch Co., San Francisco, Calif. 1874-Jan. 1876; S#s 25,001 to 35,000;
California Watch Co., Jan. 1876-mid 1876.

Cornell Watch Co., J.C. Adams, 18 size, 11 jewels, key wind & set, made in Chicago, Ill, serial number 13,647.

Cornell Watch Co., 18 size, 15 jewels, key wind & set, marked "John Evans," serial number 16,868.

18 SIZE

Grade or Name — Description		Avg	Ex-Fn	Mint
J. C. Adams, 11J, KW .... ★		$400	$500	$650
C. T. Bowen, FULL, KW .... ★		350	450	600
C. M. Cady, 15J, SW .... ★		300	400	550
Cornell, 7J, San Francisco on mvt., KW .... ★		900	1,100	1,400
Cornell, 11J, KW		300	400	550
Cornell, 11J, San Francisco on mvt., KW		900	1,100	1,400
Cornell, 15J, KW .... ★		350	450	600
Cornell W. Co., 15J, San Francisco on mvt., KW...... ★		1,100	1,300	1,600

176

CORNELL WATCH CO., 18 SIZE (continued)

Grade or Name—Description	Avg	Ex-Fn	Mint
Cornell W. Co., 15J, San Francisco on mvt., SW .. ★ ★ ★	$1,200	$1,400	$1,800
Paul Cornell, 19J, GJS, HCI5P, SW .... ★ ★	1,500	1,800	2,500
John Evans, 15J, KW .... ★	350	450	600
Excelsior, 15J, FULL, KW, KS	300	400	550
H. N. Hibbard, 11J, KW, ADJ .... ★	350	450	600
George F. Root, 15J, KW .... ★	350	450	600
George Waite, 7J, (Hyde Park), KW .... ★	400	550	650
E. J. Williams, 7J, KW .... ★	350	500	600
Ladies Stemwind .... ★	150	200	300

JACOB D. CUSTER
Norristown, Pennsylvania
1840 - 1845

At the age of 19, Jacob Custer repaired his father's watch. He was then asked to repair all the watches within his community. Custer was basically self-taught and had very little formal education and little training in clocks and watches. He made all the parts except the hairspring and fusee chains. The watches were about 14 size, and only 12 to 15 watches were made. The 14S fusee watches had lever escapement, ¾ plate and were sold in his own gold cases. He made a few chronometers, one with a helical spring.

J.D. Custer, 14-16 size, engraved on movement "J.D. Custer, Morristown, Pa. Patented Feb. 4, 1843.

Description	Avg	Ex-Fn	Mint
14S, OF, engraved on mvt. "J. D. Custer, Patented Feb. 4, 1843, #2,939" .... ★ ★ ★	$8,500	$12,000	$18,000

DUDLEY WATCH CO.
Lancaster, Pennsylvania
1920 - 1925

William Wallace Dudley became interested in watches and horology at the age of 13 and became an apprentice making ship chronometers in Canada. When he moved to America, he worked for the South Bend and Illinois Watch companies and the Trenton Watch Co. before going to Hamilton Watch Co. in Lancaster. He left Hamilton at age 69 to start his own watch company. In 1922 his first watches were produced; they were 14S, 19J, and were labeled Models 1894 and 1897. Watch parts, dials and hands were Swiss made. The winding mechanism was made at the Dudley factory. The cases came from Wadsworth Keystone and the Star Watch Case Co. Dudley also made a 12S, 19J watch. By 1924, the company was heavily in debt, and on February 20, 1925, a petition for bankruptcy was filed. The Masonic Watch was his most unusual.

Dudley Watches

				Total Production
Dudley Watch Co.	1920-1925	Model No. 1	S# 500-1,900	1,400
P. W. Baker Co.	1925-1935	Model No. 2	S# 2,001-4,800	1,600
XL Watch Co., N.Y.	1935-1976	Model No. 3	S# 4,801-6,500	1,000
			Total	4,000

Model No. 1, 14S, 19J, OF, can be distinguished by the "Holy Bible" engraved on the winding arbor plate.

Model No. 2, 12S, 19J, used the 910 and 912 Hamilton wheels and escapement, has a flat silver-colored Bible.

Model No. 3, 12S, can be distinguished by the silver Bible which was riveted in place and was more three-dimensional.

The earliest Model 1 serial number is 507. The earliest Model 2 serial number is 2,015. The XL Watch Co. serial numbers ran from 4,801 to 6,500. The highest serial number was on a Model 2: 6,404.

The distinguishing thing about the Masonic watch is that the movement is constructed by using the symbols of the Masons: trowel, plumb, level, square and compass. The square and compass support the mainspring barrel and the trowel supports the balance.

Dudley Watch Co., Model 1, 14 size, 19 jewels, open face, flip back, serial number 1232.

12 SIZE - 14 SIZE
"MASONS" MODEL

Grade or Name—Description		Avg	Ex-Fn	Mint
14S, Dudley, 19J, 14K, flip open back, Serial #1 (made 5 experimental models with Serial #1)..........★ ★ ★		$5,000	$7,000	$10,000
14S, M#1, 19J, OF, 14K, flip open back ....★		2,500	2,800	3,200
12S, M#1, 19J, OF, 14K, flip open back, w/box & papers★		3,000	3,500	4,000
12S, M#2, 19J, OF, flip open back, GF...............★		1,600	1,800	2,200
12S, M#2, 19J, OF, 14K, flip open back case..........★		1,850	2,000	2,400
12S, M#2, 19J, OF, 14K display case ....★		1,850	2,200	2,400
12S, M#3, 19J, OF, display case, GF ....★		1,600	1,800	2,200
12S, M#3, 19J, OF, 14K flip open case ....★		1,850	2,000	2,400

Dudley Watch Co., Model 2, 12 size, 19 jewels, open face, serial number 2,420.   Dudley Watch Co., Model 3, 12 size, 19 jewels, open face.

ELGIN WATCH CO.
(NATIONAL WATCH CO.)
Elgin, Illinois
1864 - 1964

This was the largest watch company in terms of production; in fact, Elgin produced half of the total number of pocket watches (dollar-type not included). Some of the organizers came from Waltham Watch Co., including P. S. Bartlett, D. G. Currier, Otis Hoyt, Charles H. Mason and others. The idea of beginning a large watch company for the mid-West was discussed by J. C. Adams, Bartlett and Blake. After a trip to Waltham, Adams went back to Chicago and approached Benjamin W. Raymond, a former mayor of Chicago, to put up the necessary capital to get the company started. Adams and Raymond succeeded in getting others to pledge their financial support also. The National Watch Co. (Elgin) was formed in August 1864. The factory site was in Elgin, Illinois, where the city had donated 35 acres of land. The factory was completed in 1866,

ELGIN WATCH CO. (continued)

and the first movement was a B. W. Raymond, 18S, full plate design. The first watches were put on the market in 1867, selling for about $115, and all were quick train. The first stem wind model was an H. L. Culver with serial No. 155,001, lever set and quick train. In 1874 the name was changed to the Elgin National Watch Co. and they produced watches into the 1950s.

The first wrist watch made by Elgin was sold in 1910. This watch, Serial No. 101, sold for $12,000 in 1988.

Elgin Movements

	1st App.	1st S#		1st. App.	1st. S#
18S B. W. Raymond	April 1867	101	10S Lady Elgin	Jan. 1869	40,001
18S H. L. Culver	July 1867	1,001	10S Frances Rubie	Aug. 1870	50,001
18S J. T. Ryerson	Oct. 1867	5,001	10S Gail Borden	Sept. 1871	185,001
18S H. H. Taylor	Nov. 1867	25,001	10S Dexter Street	Dec. 1871	201,001
18S G. M. Wheeler	Nov. 1867	6,001	First Stem Wind	June 1873	
18S Matt Laflin	Jan. 1868	9,001	1st Nickel Movement	Aug.15, 1879	
18S Father Time	No date	2,300,001	Convertible	Fall 1878	
18S Veritas	No date	8,400,001			

Some Serial Nos. have the first two numbers replaced by a letter; i.e., 39,482,000 would be X482,000.

X—39	V—46
C,E,T&Y—42	H—47
L—43	N—48
U—44	F—49
J—45	S—50

ELGIN ESTIMATED SERIAL NUMBERS AND PRODUCTION DATES

Date	Serial #	Date	Serial #	Date	Serial #
1867	10,000	1897	7,100,000	1926	29,100,000
1868	35,000	1898	7,550,000	1927	30,050,000
1869	65,000	1899	8,200,000	1928	31,500,000
1870	95,000	1900	9,000,000	1929	32,000,000
1871	120,000	1901	9,250,000	1930	32,500,000
1872	155,000	1902	9,700,000	1931	33,000,000
1873	170,000	1903	10,100,000	1932	33,800,000
1874	210,000	1904	10,900,000	1933	35,100,000
1875	320,000	1905	11,900,000	1934	35,000,000
1876	390,000	1906	12,600,000	1935	35,750,000
1877	475,000	1907	12,900,000	1936	36,200,000
1878	500,000	1908	13,550,000	1937	37,100,000
1879	580,000	1909	14,000,000	1938	37,900,000
1880	750,000	1910	14,900,000	1939	38,200,000
1881	900,000	1911	15,900,000	1940	39,100,000
1882	1,000,000	1912	16,500,000	1941	40,200,000
1883	1,300,000	1913	17,200,000	1942	41,100,000
1884	1,500,000	1914	17,900,000	1943	42,200,000
1885	1,700,000	1915	18,400,000	1944	42,600,000
1886	2,000,000	1916	19,500,000	1945	43,200,000
1887	2,400,000	1917	20,100,000	1946	43,800,000
1888	2,900,000	1918	21,000,000	1947	44,200,000
1889	3,400,000	1919	22,000,000	1948	45,100,000
1890	3,900,000	1920	23,000,000	1949	46,000,000
1891	4,500,000	1921	24,050,000	1950	47,000,000
1892	4,800,000	1922	25,100,000	1951	48,000,000
1893	4,900,000	1923	26,050,000	1952	49,000,000
1894	5,550,000	1924	27,000,000	1953	50,000,000
1895	5,900,000	1925	28,050,000	1956	55,000,000
1896	6,550,000				

ELGIN WATCH CO. (continued)

Some collectors seek out low serial numbers and will usually pay a premium for them. The lower the number, the more desirable the watch. The table shown below lists the first serial number of each size watch made by Elgin.

Size	1st Serial Nos.	Size	1st Serial Nos.
18	101	10	40,001
17	356,001	6	570,001
16	600,001	0	2,889,001
14	351,001		

Elgin Watch Co., Lord Elgin, Grade 351, 16 size, 23 jewels, gold train, raised gold jewel settings, serial number 12,718,340 (1st run).

18 SIZE

Grade or Name — Description	Avg	Ex-Fn	Mint
Advance, 11J, gilded, KW, HC, FULL	$75	$100	$150
Age, 7J, gilded, KW, FULL, HC	75	100	150
Atlas Watch Co., 7J, HC, LS, FULL	75	100	125
California Watch, 15J, gilded, HC, KW, KS, FULL	125	150	200
Chief, 7J, gilded, KW, FULL, HC	75	100	125
Convertible, 7J, G–98	75	100	125
H. L. Culver, 15J, gilded, KW, KS, FULL, HC, ADJ, low S–	200	250	325
H. L. Culver, 15J, gilded, KW, KS, FULL, HC, ADJ	125	150	200
H. L. Culver, 15J, KW, KS, 14K, HC	525	550	600
H. L. Culver, 15J, gilded, KW, KS, FULL, HC	100	125	175
H. L. Culver, 15J, gilded, SW, FULL, HC	75	100	150
H. L. Culver, 15J, gilded, KW, FULL, LS, HC	75	100	150
Elgin W. Co., 7J, OF, SW	50	75	100
Elgin W. Co., 7J, KW, gilded, HC	75	100	150
Elgin W. Co., 11J, KW, LS	50	75	100
Elgin W. Co., 11J, LS, SW, HC, 9K-10K	325	375	475
Elgin W. Co., 11J, LS, SW, HC, Silveroid	40	50	65
Elgin W. Co., 11J, LS, , SW, OF	50	70	100
Elgin W. Co., 13J, SW, PS/LS, Silveroid	40	50	65
Elgin W. Co., 13J, SW, PS/LS	50	75	100

ELGIN WATCH CO., 18 SIZE (continued)

California Watch, 18 size, 15 jewels, gilded, key wind & set, serial number 200,700.

Convertible, 18 size, 21 jewels, converts to either hunting or open face.

Grade or Name—Description	Avg	Ex-Fn	Mint
Elgin W. Co., 15J, KW, LS, HC	$75	$100	$150
Elgin W. Co., 15J, SW, LS, OF	50	75	100
Elgin W. Co., 15J, SW, LS, YGF, Multi-color box	300	325	500
Elgin W. Co., 15J, SW, LS, OF, Silveroid	50	60	75
Elgin W. Co., 15J, SW, LS, HC	75	100	150
Elgin W. Co., 15J, KW, hidden key	125	150	175
Elgin W. Co., 17J, SW, LS, Silveroid	50	60	75
Elgin W. Co., 17J, SW, LS or PS, OF	50	75	100
Elgin W. Co., 17J, SW, Multi-color, 14K, HC	1,500	1,800	2,200
Elgin W. Co., 21J, SW, LS or PS, OF	100	125	175
Elgin W. Co., 21J, SW, LS, box case, GF	175	200	275
Elgin W. Co., 21J, LS, HC, 14K	575	600	675
Elgin W. Co., 21J, SW, LS, Silveroid	60	70	90
Elgin W. Co., 21J, SW, LS, HC	125	150	175

Elgin W. Co., Grade 297, 18 size, 15 jewels.

Charles Fargo, 18 size, 7 jewels, gilded, key wind & set, hunting case.

Pennsylvania Railroad Co. on dial. **B.W. Raymond** on movement. One of the first railroad watches commissioned by Penn. RR Co., 18 size, 15 jewels, key wind and set, serial number 123,245, c. 1874.

Grade or Name—Description	Avg	Ex-Fn	Mint
Elgin W. Co., 21J, Wind Indicator	$600	$800	$1,000
Elgin W. Co., 21J, Wind Indicator, free sprung	600	800	1,000
Charles Fargo, 7J, gilded, KW, HC	150	175	200
J. V. Farwell, 11J, gilded, KW, HC .... ★	250	300	375
Father Time, 17J, NI, KW, FULL, HC, DMK........ ★	250	350	450
Father Time, 17J, NI, FULL, OF, DMK...............	100	125	175
Father Time, 17J, SW, OF, Silveroid	50	60	80
Father Time, 17J, SW, HC..........................	125	150	200
Father Time, 20J, NI, SW, FULL, HC, DMK .... ★	250	300	375
Father Time, 21J, NI, SW, FULL, OF, GJS, DMK	150	175	200
Father Time, 21J, NI, SW, ¾, GJS, DMK, HC	125	150	200
Father Time, 21J, NI, SW, ¾, OF, GJS, DMK..........	125	150	200
Father Time, 21J, GJT, HCI5P, Diamond end stone	125	150	200
Father Time, 21J, NI, SW, ¾, OF, GJS, Wind Indicator .	800	1,000	1,300
Father Time, 21J, SW, ¾, GJS, wind indicator, HC	1,000	1,200	1,500
Father Time, G#367, 21J, NI, SW, ¾, OF, GJS, military wind indicator, free sprung, 602 sterling case	1,200	1,400	1,700
W. H. Ferry, 15J, gilded, KW, HC	125	150	175
W. H. Ferry, 11J, gilded, KW, HC	125	150	175
Mat Laflin, 7J, gilded, KW, HC	125	150	175
National W. Co., 7J, KW, KS	75	100	125
National W. Co., 11J, KW, KS	75	100	125
National W. Co., 15J, KW, KS	75	100	125
M. D. Ogden, 15J, KW, HC	125	150	175
M. D. Ogden, 11J, gilded, KW, HC...................	225	150	175
Overland, 17J, NI, KW, HC, DMK	150	175	200
Overland, 17J, NI, SW, HC, DMK....................	100	125	175
Pennsylvania Railroad Co. on dial, B. W. Raymond on mvt., 15J, KW, KS (1st RR watches)................ ★ ★ ★	600	700	900
Railway Timer, 15J, FULL, HC .... ★	300	350	400

B.W. Raymond, 18 size, 23 jewels, wind indicator. Note small winding indicator gear next to crown wheel.

H.H. Taylor, 18 size, 15 jewels, key wind & set, serial number 288,797.

Grade or Name—Description	Avg	Ex-Fn	Mint
B. W. Raymond, 15-17J, KW, low S# under 1000	$300	$400	$550
B. W. Raymond, 15J, gilded, KW, FULL, HC	125	150	175
B. W. Raymond, 17J, gilded, KW, FULL, HC	125	150	175
B. W. Raymond, 15J, SW, HC	75	100	125
B. W. Raymond, 17J, NI, FULL, OF	50	75	100
B. W. Raymond, 17J, Silveroid	40	60	80
B. W. Raymond, 17J, NI, FULL, HC	100	125	175
B. W. Raymond, 15J, box case, 14K	700	800	1,200
B. W. Raymond, 17J, gilded, NI, SW, FULL, ADJ	75	100	125
B. W. Raymond, 19J, NI, ¾, SW, OF, GJS, DMK, GT . .	75	100	150
B. W. Raymond, 19J, NI, ¾, SW, OF, GJS, Wind Indicator, DMK	500	600	850
B. W. Raymond, 19J, ¾, GJS, GT, Diamond end stone . .	75	100	125
B. W. Raymond, 21J, ¾, GJS, GT, Diamond end stone, OF	125	150	175
B. W. Raymond, 21J, SW, Silveroid	75	100	125
B. W. Raymond, 21J, SW, GJS, GT, DES, HC	175	200	250
B. W. Raymond, 21J, NI, ¾, SW, GJS, DMK, GT	100	125	175
B. W. Raymond, 21J, NI, ¾, SW, GJS, Wind Indicator, DMK	650	750	950
J. T. Ryerson, 7J, gilded, FULL, KW, HC	75	100	125
Solar W. Co., 15J, Multi-color dial	75	100	150
Standard, 17J, OF, LS	100	125	150
Sundial, 7J, SW, PS	50	60	75
H. H. Taylor, 15J, gilded, FULL, KW, HC	100	125	175
H. H. Taylor, 15J, NI, FULL, KW, HC, DMK	100	125	175
H. H. Taylor, 15J, NI, FULL, SW, HC, DMK, quick train	100	125	175
H. H. Taylor, 15J, SW, Silveroid	40	50	65
H. H. Taylor, 15J, SW, slow train	60	70	85
Veritas, 21J, SW, PS, HC	175	225	300
Veritas, 21J, SW, LS, GJS, GT, HC	175	225	300

Veritas, 18 size, 23 jewels, solid gold train, gold jewel settings, diamond end stone, serial number 9,542,678.

G.M. Wheeler, Grade 369, 18 size, 17 jewels, open face, gold jewel settings, serial number 14,788,315

Grade or Name—Description	Avg	Ex-Fn	Mint
Veritas, 21J, ¾, NI, GJS, OF, DMK, GT..............	$100	$125	$175
Veritas, 21J, ¾, GJS, GT, Diamond end stones	100	125	175
Veritas, 21J, ¾, GJS, GT, Diamond end stones, HC.....	175	225	300
Veritas, 21J, ¾, NI, GJS, OF, Wind Indicator, DMK	1,000	1,100	1,300
Veritas, 21J, ¾, NI, GJS, HC, Wind Indicator, DMK....	1,000	1,200	1,400
Veritas, 23J, ¾, NI, GJS, OF, DMK, GT..............	175	225	300
Veritas, 23J, ¾, GJS, HC, GT	250	275	350
Veritas, 23J, ¾, NI, GJS, OF, DMK, GT, Diamond end stone	200	225	300
Veritas, 23J, ¾, Wind Indicator, GJS, OF, DMK, GT, 14K	1,400	1,600	2,000
Veritas, 23J, G#214, ¾, NI, GJS, OF, Wind Indicator, DMK	1,100	1,300	1,500
Veritas, 23J, G#214, SW, OF	125	150	200
Veritas, 23J, SW, NI, GJS, GT, LS, HC................	250	275	350
Veritas, 23J, SW, OF, 14K	550	575	650
G. M. Wheeler, 11J, gilded, KW, HC	75	100	150
G. M. Wheeler, 13-15J, gilded, FULL, KW	75	100	150
G. M. Wheeler, 15J, NI, FULL, KW, DMK, HC	75	100	150
G. M. Wheeler, 15J, SW, NI, FULL, DMK, OF.........	50	75	100
G. M. Wheeler, 17J, KW, NI, FULL, DMK, OF	100	125	175
G. M. Wheeler, 17J, SW, NI, FULL, DMK, OF.........	50	75	100

MOVEMENTS WITH NO NAME

	Avg	Ex-Fn	Mint
No. 5 & No. 17, 7J, gilded, FULL, HC.................	$50	$75	$125
No. 23 & No. 18, 11J, gilded, FULL, HC...............	50	75	125
No. 69, 15J, M#1, KW, quick train, HC................	50	75	125
No. 316, 15J, NI, FULL, HC, DMK	75	100	150
No. 317, 15J, NI, FULL, ADJ, OF, DMK	75	100	150

ELGIN WATCH CO., 18 SIZE (continued)

Grade or Name—Description	Avg	Ex-Fn	Mint
No. 316 & No. 317, 15J, Silveroid	$40	$50	$65
No. 326, 15J, OF	60	70	80
No. 327, 15J, HC	75	100	150
No. 335, 17J, HC	75	100	150
No. 336, 17J, NI, FULL, OF, DMK	50	75	150
No. 345, 19J, GJS, 2-Tone, HC .... ★	800	1,000	1,200
No. 348, 21J, NI, FULL, HC, GJS, DMK	100	125	175
No. 349, 21J, OF	50	75	150
No. 378, 19J, NI, FULL, HC, DMK	75	100	150
No. 379, 19J, OF	50	75	125

Elgin Watch Co., 17 size, 11 jewels, key wind & set, made for English market, serial number 418,220.

Elgin Watch Co., 17 size, 7 jewels, key wind & set, serial number 199,076. Made for Kennedy & Co.

17 SIZE

Grade or Name — Description	Avg	Ex-Fn	Mint
Avery, 7J, gilded, KW, FULL, HC....................	$75	$100	$150
Leader, 7J, gilded, KW, FULL, HC....................	75	100	150
Leader, 7J, gilded, KW, FULL, HC, early movement	75	100	150
Sunshine, 15J, KW, KS from back	100	125	175
M#11, 14, 15, 51, 59: 7J, gilded, KW, FULL, HC	100	125	175
17 Size, KW, Silveroid	50	60	75

16 SIZE

Grade or Name — Description	Avg	Ex-Fn	Mint
Blind Man's Watch, 17J, HC	$75	$100	$150
Convertible Model, 13J, BRG, OF	50	75	125
Convertible Model, 15J, BRG, ADJ, 14K, HC..........	450	475	525
Convertible Model, 15J, ADJ, DMK, 3F BRG, HC	75	100	150
Convertible Model, 15J, ¾, ADJ, DMK, GJS	75	100	150

Elgin Watch Co., 16 size, 21 jewels, converts to open face or hunting case, serial number 607,061.

Elgin W. Co., 16 size, 21 jewels, three-fingered bridge model, adjusted, gold jewel settings, gold train, serial number 6,469,814.

Grade or Name—Description	Avg	Ex-Fn	Mint
Convertible Model, 15J, Silveroid	$50	$60	$90
Convertible Model, 15J, 3F BRG, OF	50	75	125
Convertible Model, 21J, 3F BRG	900	1,100	1,450
Convertible Model, 21J, G#72, ¾, ADJ, DMK, GJS	1,000	1,200	1,500
Convertible Model, 21J, G#91, 3F BRG, 14K	1,600	1,800	2,200
Doctors Watch, 15J, 4th Model, NI, GT, sweep second hand, GF case	150	175	225
Doctors Watch, 15J, 4th Model, gilded, sweep second hand, coin silver case	125	150	200
Doctors Watch, 15J, 4th Model, sweep second hand, 14K	525	550	600
Elgin W. Co., 7J, OF	50	75	125
Elgin W. Co., 7J, HC	75	100	150

Doctors Watch, 16 size, 15 jewels, fourth model, gold jewel settings, gold train, sweep second hand, serial number 926,458.

Grade or Name—Description	Avg	Ex-Fn	Mint
Elgin W. Co., 9J, OF...............................	$50	$75	$125
Elgin W. Co., 11J, OF..............................	50	75	125
Elgin W. Co., 11J, HC	75	100	150
Elgin W. Co., 13J, OF..............................	50	125	125
Elgin W. Co., 13J, OF, Silveroid	40	50	70
Elgin W. Co., 13J, HC	75	100	150
Elgin W. Co., 15J, HC	75	100	150
Elgin W. Co., 15J, OF, Silveroid	40	50	70
Elgin W. Co., 15J, OF..............................	50	75	125
Elgin W. Co., 15J, HC, 14K	400	450	550
Elgin W. Co., 17J, OF..............................	50	75	125
Elgin W. Co., 17J, 14K, HC	400	450	550
Elgin W. Co., 17J, G#280, 9th model, ADJ5P...........	100	125	175
Elgin W. Co., 17J, HC	100	125	175
Elgin W. Co., 19J, OF, LS...........................	75	100	150
Elgin W. Co., 21J, HC	150	175	225
Elgin W. Co., 21J, OF, Silveroid	50	60	75
Elgin W. Co., 21J, OF..............................	100	125	175
Elgin W. Co., 17J, LS, multi-color HC, GF.............	250	300	400
Elgin W. Co., 17J, multi-color HC, 14K	1,000	1,200	1,600
3F Bridge Model, 15J, NI, DMK.......................	50	75	100
3F Bridge Model, 17J, Adj.3P, NI, DMK, GJS..........	50	75	100
3F Bridge Model, 17J, Adj.5P, NI, DMK, GJS, GT......	75	100	150
3F Bridge Model, 21J, Adj.5P, NI, DMK, GJS, GT......	200	250	325
Father Time, 17J, ¾, NI, OF, GJS, DR, DMK..........	100	125	175
Father Time, 21J, ¾, NI, HC, GJS, DR, DMK	175	200	275
Father Time, 21J, ¾, NI, OF, GJS, DR, Wind Indicator .	400	450	500
Father Time, 21J, Silveroid...........................	60	70	80
Father Time, 21J, NI, GJS, DR, OF	100	125	175
Lord Elgin, 21J, GJS, DR, Adj.5P, 3F BRG, 14K ...★★	1,000	1,200	1,500

Father Time, 16 size, 21 jewels, gold train; Note up and down wind indicator.

Father Time, 16 size, 21 jewels, gold train; Note up and down wind indicator, serial number 18,106,465.

Lord Elgin, 16 size, 23 jewels, gold train, raised gold jewel settings, serial number 12,718,340.

B.W. Raymond, 16 size, 19 jewels, gold jewel settings, serial number 17,822,991.

Grade or Name—Description	Avg	Ex-Fn	Mint
Lord Elgin, 23J, GJS, DR, Adj.5P, ¾, 14K, OF .... ★ ★	$1,100	$1,300	$1,600
B. W. Raymond, 17J, ¾, GJS, 14K, OF...............	475	525	650
B. W. Raymond, 17J, ¾, GJS, SW, HC...............	200	275	350
B. W. Raymond, 17J, 3F BRG .... ★ ★	400	500	650
B. W. Raymond, 17J, M#8, LS, NI, Wind Indicator	300	350	400
B. W. Raymond, 17J, GJS, SW, OF	150	200	250
B. W. Raymond, 17J, ¾, GJS, DR, Adj.5P, DMK	175	225	275
B. W. Raymond, 19J, ¾, GJS, DR, Adj.5P, DMK, OF ..	75	100	150
B. W. Raymond, 19J, OF, 14K, 30 DWT	400	450	500
B. W. Raymond, 19J, ¾, GJS, DR, HCI5P, DMK, Wind Indicator	350	400	450
B. W. Raymond, 19J, M#8, G#240, OF, Adj.5P	75	100	150
B. W. Raymond, 19J, GJS, Adj.5P, HC...............	150	175	225
B. W. Raymond, 21J, 14K, OF	425	475	525
B. W. Raymond, 21J, G#389, OF	100	125	175
B. W. Raymond, 21J, G#571, ¾, Adj.5P, OF...........	100	125	175
B. W. Raymond, 21J, ¾, GJS, DR, Adj.5P, HC	175	225	275
B. W. Raymond, 21J, ¾, GJS, DR, Adj.5P, DMK, OF ..	100	125	175
B. W. Raymond, 21J, ¾, GJS, DR, Adj.5P, DMK, Wind Indicator	350	400	450
B. W. Raymond, 22J, WWII Model, sweep second hand..	125	150	175
B. W. Raymond, 23J, ¾, GJS, DR, Adj.5P, DMK	250	300	375
B. W. Raymond, 23J, ¾, GJS, DR, Adj.5P, DMK, Wind Indicator	475	525	600
B. W. Raymond, 23J, ¾, GJS, DR, Adj.5P, DMK, Wind Indicator, military style.....................	425	475	550
Repeater, Terstegen, 5 min., 21J, 2 gongs .... ★ ★	2,000	3,000	4,500
Veritas, 21J, 3F brg, GJS .... ★	225	275	350
Veritas, 21J, GJS, DR, Adj.5P, DMK, ¾, HC	250	300	375

Veritas, 16 size, 23 jewels, solid gold train, gold jeweled settings, Adj5p, serial number 16,678,681.

Grade 340, 16 size, 17 jewels, three-fingered bridge model, open face.

Grade or Name—Description	Avg	Ex-Fn	Mint
Veritas, 21J, GJS, DR, Adj.5P, DMK, ¾, Wind Indicator	$550	$600	$700
Veritas, 21J, GJS, SW, Grade 360 ....★	375	400	475
Veritas, 21J, GJS, SW, Adj.5P, OF, Grade 270..........	125	150	200
Veritas, 23J, GJS, Adj.5P, 14K, OF...................	575	675	800
Veritas, 23J, GJS, Adj.5P, HC	300	400	500
Veritas, 23J, GJS, DR, Adj.5P, DMK, ¾, OF, Grade 376★	350	400	500
Veritas, 23J, GJS, DR, Adj.5P, DMK, ¾, Diamond end stone, Grade 350 ....★	375	425	525
Veritas, 23J, GJS, DR, Adj.5P, DMK, ¾, Wind Indicator	600	650	750
G. M. Wheeler, 17J, DR, Adj.3P, DMK, ¾	50	75	125
G. M. Wheeler, 17J, 3F BRG.........................	50	75	125
G. M. Wheeler, 17J, HC, 14K	450	475	525
WWII Model, 17J, OF...............................	100	125	175
WWII Model, 21J, OF...............................	125	150	200
M#13, 9J, HC	75	100	150
M#48, 13J, HC	75	100	150

(Add $50 to hunting case models listed as open face)

MODELS WITH NO NAMES

	Avg	Ex-Fn	Mint
Grade #72-91, 21J, 3F BRG ....★ ★	$450	$550	$700
Grade #145, 19J, GJS, BRG, HC ....★ ★	650	750	900
Grade #156, 21J, ¾, NI, DR, DMK, GT, GJS, OF	150	175	225
Grade #156, 21J, ¾, NI, DR, DMK, GT, GJS, HC, 14K .	475	500	625
Grade #162, 21J, SW, PS, NI, GJS, GT	225	275	350
Grade #270, 21J, 3F BRG, GJS, marked mvt.	150	175	225
Grade #280, 17J, marked on mvt.......................	125	150	200
Grade #290 & #291, 7J, OF, ¾, NI, DMK	50	75	125

ELGIN WATCH CO., 16 SIZE (continued)

Grade or Name—Description	Avg	Ex-Fn	Mint
Grade #291, 7J, ¾, HC, 14K	$400	$450	$550
Grade #312 & #313, 15J, ¾, NI, DR, DMK, OF.........	50	75	100
Grade #372, 19J, M#15, LS, OF, Adj.5P	250	300	375
Grade #374, 21J, M#15, LS, OF, Adj.5P	275	325	400
Grade #381 & #382, 17J, ¾, NI, DR, DMK, OF.........	50	75	100
Grade #391, 21J, M#15, LS, OF, Adj.5P	300	350	450
Grade #145, 19J, GJS, BRG, HC .... ★★	900	1,000	1,200
Grade #156, 21J, ¾, NI, DR, DMK, GT, GJS, HC......	175	200	250
Grade #156, 21J, ¾, NI, DR, DMK, GT, GJS, HC, 14K .	475	500	550
Grade #162, 21J, SW, PS, NI, GJS, GT, OF	200	250	325
Grade #72, 21J, ADJ, ¾, HC .... ★	400	450	525
Grade #91, 21J, 3F BRG, HC .... ★★	700	800	1,000
Grade #571, 21J, Adj.5P, OF.........................	100	125	175

14 SIZE

Grade or Name — Description	Avg	Ex-Fn	Mint
Lord Elgin, 17J, SS, ¾, OF...........................	$200	$225	$275
7J, ¾, M#1, gilded, KW, 14K, HC	300	350	400
7J, ¾, M#1, gilded, KW, YGF, HC...................	75	100	150
11J, ¾, M#1, gilded, KW, YGF, HC..................	75	100	150
11J, ¾, M#1, gilded, KW, YGF, OF	50	75	100
13J, ¾, M#1, gilded, KW, OF.......................	50	75	100
15J, ¾, M#1, gilded, KW, OF.......................	50	75	100
7J, ¾, M#2, SW, OF................................	50	75	100
15J, ¾, M#2, SW, OF...............................	50	75	100
15J, ¾, M#2, SW, 14K, HC	275	325	375

12 SIZE

Grade or Name — Description	Avg	Ex-Fn	Mint
Eight Day, 21J, 8-Day Wind Indicator, BRG ....★★★★	$2,000	$2,500	$3,000

Elgin Eight Day, 12 size, 21 jewels, wind indicator, bridge movement, open face, serial number 12,345,678.

ELGIN WATCH CO., 12 SIZE (continued)

Example of a 12 size 17 jewel Elgin with a personalized logo on dial.

Lord Elgin, 12 size, 21 jewels, gold train, gold jewel settings, serial number 24,999,947.

Grade or Name—Description	Avg	Ex-Fn	Mint
Elgin W. Co. #30, 7J, ¾, gilded, KW, OF	$45	$55	$85
Elgin W. Co. #189, 19J, HC, ¾, NI	75	100	150
Elgin W. Co. #190-194, 23J, OF, GJS, ¾, Adj.5P, NI, DMK, GT	125	150	200
Elgin W. Co. #190-194, 23J, HC, GJS, ¾, Adj.5P, NI, DMK, GT	150	175	225
Elgin W. Co. #236 & #237, 21J, OF, GJS, ¾, Adj.5P, NI, DMK, GT	75	100	150
Elgin W. Co. #236 & #237, 21J, HC, GJS, ¾, Adj.5P, NI, DMK, GT	100	125	175
Elgin W. Co. #301 & #302, 7J, ¾, HC, NI	50	75	125
Elgin W. Co. #314 & #315, 15J, ¾, HC, NI	50	75	125
Elgin W. Co. #383 & #384, 17J, ¾, HC, NI	50	75	125
Elgin W. Co., 15J, 14K, Multi-color	500	600	750
Elgin W. Co., 15J, OF, GF	50	60	75
Elgin W. Co., 15J, HC, 14K	300	350	425
Elgin W. Co., 17J, OF, 14K	275	300	350
Elgin W. Co., 19J, HC, 14K	325	375	450
Elgin W. Co., 19J, 14K, OF	275	300	350
C. H. Hulburd, 19J, thin BRG model, 14K case ★	800	1,000	1,200
C. H. Hulburd, 19J, thin BRG model, 18K ★	1,000	1,200	1,400
Lord Elgin, 23J, HC, GJS, DR, Adj.5P, DMK, NI	175	200	275
Lord Elgin, 17J, HC	75	100	150
Lord Elgin, 19J, HC	75	100	150
Lord Elgin, 21J, 14K, OF	275	300	375
Lord Elgin, 21J, HC	75	100	150

Lord Elgin, 12 size, 23 jewels, gold jewel settings, Adj5p, originally sold for $110.00.

G.M. Wheeler, 12 size, 17 jewels, Adj3p, originally sold for $27.00.

Grade or Name—Description	Avg	Ex-Fn	Mint
B. W. Raymond, 19J, HC, ¾, GJS, Adj.5P, DR, DMK, NI	$75	$100	$125
G. M. Wheeler, 17J, ¾, DR, Adj.5P, DMK, NI, OF	40	60	75
G. M. Wheeler, 17J, ¾, DR, Adj.5P, DMK, NI, HC	65	90	110

Frances Rubie, Grade 23, 10 size, 15 jewels, key wind & set.

Gail Borden, Grade 22, 10 size, 11 jewels, key wind & set, serial number 947,696.

10 SIZE
(HC)

Grade or Name — Description	Avg	Ex-Fn	Mint
Dexter St., 7J, KW, HC, 14K	$200	$275	$325
Dexter St., 7J, KW, HC, 18K	250	325	375
Dexter St., 7J, ¾, gilded, KW, HC, gold filled	50	75	125
Frances Rubie, 15J, ¾, gilded, KW, HC, 14K .... ★	550	600	700
Frances Rubie, 15J, KW, HC, 18K .... ★ ★	600	650	750

ELGIN WATCH CO., 10 SIZE (continued)

Grade or Name—Description	Avg	Ex-Fn	Mint
Gail Borden, 11J, ¾, gilded, KW, HC, 14K	$200	$275	$325
Gail Borden, 11J, ¾, KW, HC, gold filled	50	75	125
Gail Borden, 11J, KW, HC, 18K	250	325	375
Lady Elgin, 15J, ¾, gilded, KW, HC, 14K	200	275	325
Lady Elgin, 15J, KW, HC, 18K	250	325	375
21 or 28, 7J, ¾, gilded, KW, HC, gold filled	50	75	125
Elgin, multi-color case, gold filled, HC	200	225	275
Elgin, 15J, Silveroid, HC	30	40	50
Elgin, 15J, YGF, HC	50	75	125

Elgin W. Co., Grade 121, 6 size, 15 jewels, hunting, serial number 4,500,445.

Elgin W. Co., Grade 67, 6 size, 11 jewels, serial number 1,149,615.

6 SIZE
(HC Only)

Grade or Name — Description	Avg	Ex-Fn	Mint
Atlas, 7J, HC	$50	$75	$125
Elgin W. Co. #286, 7J, HC, ¾, DMK, NI	50	75	125
Elgin W. Co. #295, 15J, HC, ¾, DMK, NI	50	75	125
Elgin W. Co., 7J, HC, 10K	150	175	225
Elgin W. Co., 7J, HC, ¾, 14K	175	225	300
Elgin W. Co., 15J, SW, HC, Enamel case, 18K	800	1,000	1,300
Elgin W. Co., 15J, YGF, HC	50	75	125
Elgin W. Co., 15J, HC, ¾, 14K	175	225	300
Elgin W. Co., 15J, HC, ¾, 10K	150	175	225
Elgin W. Co., 15J, HC, ¾, 18K	250	325	375
Elgin W. Co., 15J, HC, GF multi-color case	200	225	275
Elgin W. Co., 11J, HC, 14K	175	225	300
Elgin W. Co., 15J, demi-HC	75	100	150
Elgin W. Co., 15J, 14K, Multi-color HC	450	500	650

ELGIN WATCH CO. (continued)

Elgin W. Co., 6 size, 15 jewels

Elgin W. Co., Grade 201-HC, 205-OF, 0 size, 19 jewels, gold train.

Elgin W. Co., Grade 200-HC, 204-OF, 0 size, 17 jewels, gold jewel settings.

0 SIZE

Grade or Name — Description	Avg	Ex-Fn	Mint
Atlas W. Co., 7J, HC	$75	$100	$150
Elgin W. Co., 7J, NI, ¾, DR, DMK, OF	35	40	50
Elgin W. Co., 15J, NI, ¾, DR, DMK, OF	40	45	55
Elgin W. Co., 15J, NI, ¾, DR, DMK, HC	75	100	150
Elgin W. Co., 17J, NI, ¾, DR, DMK, ADJ, OF	50	60	80
Elgin W. Co., 19J, NI, ¾, DR, DMK, GJS, ADJ, OF	55	65	85
Elgin W. Co., 15J, HC, 14K	175	225	300
Elgin W. Co., 15J, HC, multi-color GF	175	200	250
Elgin W. Co., 15J, OF, multi-color dial	100	125	175
Elgin W. Co., 11J, HC, 14K	175	225	300
Elgin W. Co., 7J, HC, 10K	150	175	225
Elgin W. Co., 15J, 14K, Multi-color	400	450	525
Elgin W. Co., 15J, 14K, Multi-color + diamond	500	550	625
Frances Rubie, 19J, HC ★	200	225	300

Lady Elgin, 5/0 size, 17 jewels, gold jewel settings, originally sold for $42.50.

Lady Raymond, 5/0 size, 15 jewels, originally sold for $24.20.

3/0 and 5/0 SIZE
(HC ONLY)

Grade or Name—Description	Avg	Ex-Fn	Mint
Lady Elgin, 15J, PS, HC	$75	$100	$150
Lady Elgin, 15J, 14K, HC	200	225	275
Lady Raymond, 15J, PS, HC	75	100	150
Elgin W. Co., 7J, HC	75	100	150

How to Identify Your Watch: Compare the movement of your watch with the illustrations in this section. Upon matching the movement exactly, the model number and size can be determined. While comparing, note the location of the balance, jewels, screws, gears and type of back plate (Full, ¾, Bridge) which will be clues in identifying the movement you have. Having determined the size and model number, you can now find your watch in the main price listing by name or number (which is engraved on the movement).

Model 1, 18 size, full plate, hunting, key wind & set, first serial number 101, Apr., 1867.

Model 2-4, 18 size, full plate, hunting, lever set, first serial number 155,001, June, 1873.

Model 5, 18 size, full plate, open face, pendant set, first serial number, 2,110,001, Grade 43, Dec., 1885.

Model 6, 18 size, three-quarter plate, hunting, open face, pendant set.

Model 7, 18 size, full plate, open face, lever set, first serial number 6,563,821, Grade 265, Apr., 1897.

Model 8, 18 size, three-quarter plate, open face, lever set, first serial number 8,400,001, Grade 214, Dec., 1900.

Model 8, 18 size, three-quarter plate, open face, lever set with winding indicator.

Model 9, 18 size, three-quarter plate, hunting, lever set, first serial number 9,625,001, Grade 274, May, 1904.

Model 9, 18 size, three-quarter plate, hunting, lever set with winding indicator.

Model 1, 17 size, full plate, hunting, key wind and set.

Model 2, 17 size, full plate, hunting, lever set.

Model 1, 16 size, three-quarter plate, hunting & open face, lever set.

Model 2, 16 size, three-quarter plate, bridge, hunting & open face, lever set.

Model 3, 16 size, three-quarter plate, hunting, lever set, first serial number 625,001, Grade 1, Feb., 1879.

Model 4, 16 size, three-quarter plate, sweep second, hunting & open face, lever set.

Model 5, 16 size, three-quarter plate, open face, pendant set.

Model 5, 16 size, three-quarter plate, open face, pendant set, first serial number 2,811,001, Grade 105, Oct., 1887.

Model 6, 16 size, three-quarter plate, hunting, pendant set, first serial number 6,458,001, Grade 151, Aug., 1895.

Model 6, 16 size, three-quarter plate, bridge, hunting, pendant set, first serial number 6,463,001, Grade 156, May, 1896.

Model 7, 16 size, three-quarter plate, open face, pendant set, first serial number 6,464,001. Grade 157, Sept., 1895.

Model 7, 16 size, three-quarter plate, bridge, open face, pendant set, first serial number 6,469,001, Grade 162, Apr., 1896.

Model 8, 16 size, three-quarter plate, bridge, hunting, lever set, serial number 12,283,001, Grade 341, Jan., 1907.

Model 9, 16 size, three-quarter plate, bridge, open face, lever set, first serial number 9,250,001, Grade 270, July, 1902.

Model 13, 16 size, three-quarter plate, open face, lever set, first serial number 12,717,001, Grade 350, June, 1908.

Model 14, 16 size, three-quarter plate, hunting, lever set.

Model 15, 16 size, three-quarter plate, open face, lever set.

Model 17, 16 size, three-quarter plate, hunting, lever set.

Model 19, 16 size, three-quarter plate, open face, lever set with winding indicator.

Model 20, 16 size, three-quarter plate, open face, Grades 571, 572, 573, 574, 575, 616.

Model 1, 14 size, three-quarter plate, hunting, key wind and set.

Model 2, 14 size, three-quarter plate, open face, pendant set.

Model 1, 12 size, three-quarter plate, hunting, key wind and set.

Model 2, 12 size, three-quarter plate, hunting, pendant set, first serial #7,410,001, Grade 188, Dec., 1897.

Model 2, 12 size, three-quarter plate, spread to 16 size, hunting, pendant set.

Model 3, 12 size, three-quarter plate, open face, pendant set, serial number 7,423,001, Grade 192, May 1898.

Model 3, 12 size, three-quarter plate, spread to 16 size, open face, pendant set.

Model 4, 12 size, three-quarter plate, open face, pendant set, serial number 16,311,001, Grade 392, July, 1912.

Model 1, 10 size, three-quarter plate, style 1, hunting, key wind and set.

Model 2, 10 size, three-quarter plate, hunting, key wind and set.

ELGIN WATCH CO. (continued)

Model 3, 10 size, three-quarter plate, hunting, key wind and set.

Model 4, 10 size, three-quarter plate, hunting, key wind and set.

Model 5 & 6, 10 size, three-quarter plate, Grades 546, 542, 543.

Model 1, 6 size, three-quarter plate, hunting, lever set.

Model 1, 6 size, three-quarter plate, hunting, lever set.

Model 2, 6 size, three-quarter plate, hunting, pendant set, first serial number 4,449,001, Grade 117, March, 1891.

Model 1, 0 size, three-quarter plate, hunting, pendant set, first serial number 2,889,001, Grade 198, Dec., 1898.

Model 2, 0 size, three-quarter plate, hunting, pendant set, first serial number 7,868,001, Grade 198, Dec., 1898.

Model 2, 0 size, three-quarter plate, spread to 12 size, hunting, pendant set.

Model 3, 0 size, three-quarter plate, open face, pendant set.

Model 3, 0 size, three-quarter plate, spread to 12 size, open face, pendant set.

Model 2, 3-0 size, three-quarter plate, hunting, pendant set, first serial number 18,149,001, Grade 413, Feb., 1915.

Charles Fasoldt, 18-20 size, 16 jewels, gold jewel settings, key wind & set, bar movement, serial number 90.

Charles Fasoldt, 18-20 size, 16 jewels, key wind & set, bar movement; note patented regulator, series II.

CHARLES FASOLDT WATCH CO.
Rome, New York
1849 - 1861
Albany, New York
1861 - 1878

Charles Fasoldt came to the United States in 1848. One of his first watches, Serial No. 27, was for General Armstrong and was an eight-day movement. At about that same time, he made several large regulators and a few pocket chronometers. He displayed some of his work at fairs in Utica and Syracuse and received four First-Class Premiums and two diplomas. In 1850, he patented a micrometric regulator (generally called the Howard Regulator because Howard bought the patent). He also patented a chronometer escapement in 1855-1865, a watch regulator in 1864, and a hairspring stud in 1877. He was also known for his tower clocks, for which he received many awards and medals. He made about 500 watches in Albany and about 50 watches in Rome.

Charles Fasoldt, 18-20 size, 16 jewels, stem wind, key set, bar movement, series III.

Charles Fasoldt, 18-20 size, 16 jewels, stem wind, key set, bar movement, series III.

Year	Model	Style	Serial # Range
1855 - 1864	Series I	KW, ½ plate	5- 40
1865 - 1868	Series II	KW, Bar	41-330
1868 - 1878	Series III	SW, Bar	331-540

Grade or Name — Description	Avg	Ex-Fn	Mint
18—20 SIZE, 16J, GJS, KW, KS ....★ ★ ★	$8,000	$10,000	$14,500
10—12 SIZE, 16J, GJS, KW & SW, KS, 14K...........	3,500	4,000	5,000
Otto H. Fasoldt, 18S, 15J, SW, Swiss made or American .	175	200	250

FITCHBURG WATCH CO.
Fitchburg, Massachusetts
1875 - 1878

In 1875 S. Sawyer decided to manufacture watches. He hired personnel from the U. S. Watch Company to build the machinery, but by 1878 the company had failed. It is not known how many, if any, watches were made. The equipment was sold to Cornell and other watch companies.

E.H. Flint dial and movement, 18 size, 4-7 jewels, open face, key wind & set, "Lancaster Pa." on dial, "Patented Sept. 18th, 1877" on movement.

E. H. FLINT
Cincinnati, Ohio
1877 - 1879

The Flint watch was patented September 18, 1877, and about 50 watches were made. The serial number is found under the dial.

Grade orName — Description	Avg	Ex-Fn	Mint
18 Size, 4-7J, KW, Full Plate, OF, Coin ....★ ★ ★	$2,000	$2,500	$3,500
18 Size, 4-7J, KW, Full Plate, 18K, HC...........★ ★ ★	4,000	4,500	5,500

Fredonia Watch Co., 18 size, 15 jewels, signature on movement "Cyrus N. Gibbs, Mas," key wind & set, serial number 4403.

Fredonia Watch Co., 18 size, 15 jewels, adjusted, serial number 8,368.

FREDONIA WATCH CO.
Fredonia, New York
1883 - 1885

This company sold the finished movements acquired from the Independent Watch Co. These movements had been made by other companies. The Fredonia Watch Company was sold to the Peoria Watch Co. in 1885, after having produced approximately 20,000 watches.

Chronology of the Development of Fredonia:

Independent Watch Co.	1880-1883
Fredonia Watch Co.	1883-1885
Peoria Watch Co.	1885-1895

Fredonia Watch Co., with a reversible case; changes to either hunting or open face.

206

FREDONIA WATCH CO. (continued)

Grade or Name — Description	Avg	Ex-Fn	Mint
18S, 7J, SW, OF	$100	$125	$175
18S, 7J, SW, HC	125	150	200
18S, 9J, SW, OF	100	125	175
18S, 9J, SW, HC	125	150	200
18S, 11J, SW, OF	100	125	175
18S, 11J, KW, KS, HC, Coin	125	150	200
18S, 15J, SW, Multi-color, 14K, HC	1,600	1,800	2,200
18S, KW, Reversible case	300	350	450
18S, 15J, SW, LS, Gilt, OF	100	125	175
18S, 15J, straight line escapement, NI	300	350	450
18S, 15J, HC, low serial number	300	350	450
18S, 15J, personalized mvt	200	250	350
18S, 15J, KW, HC, marked Lakeshore W. Co.	250	300	400

FREEPORT WATCH CO.
Freeport, Illinois
1874 - 1875

Probably less than 20 watches made by Freeport have survived. Their machinery was purchased from Mozart Co., and a Mr. Hoyt was engaged as superintendent. The building erected was destroyed by fire on Oct. 21, 1875. A safe taken from the ruins contained 300 completed movements which were said to be ruined.

Grade or Name — Description	Avg	Ex-Fn	Mint
18S, 15J, KW, KS, gold train, 18K case ★★★	$4,500	$5,000	$6,000

Freeport Watch Co.. Example of a basic movement, 18 size, 15 jewels, key wind & set, pressed jewels, gold train, high grade movement, serial number 11.

SMITH D. FRENCH
Wabash, Indiana
1866 - 1878

On August 21, 1866, Mr. French was issued a patent for an improved escapement for watches. The escape wheel has triangular shaped pins and the lever has two hook-

SMITH D. FRENCH (continued)

shaped pallets. The pin wheel escapement was probably first used by Robert Robin, about 1795, for pocket watches. Antoine Tavan also used this style escape wheel around 1800. Mr. French's improved pin wheel and hook shaped lever (about 70 total production) can be seen through a cutout in the plates of his watches.

Illustration from the patent office, patent number 57,310, patented Aug. 21, 1866. Note pin wheel escapement with adjustable hook shaped lever.

Grade or Name — Description		Avg	Ex-Fn	Mint
18S, 15J, ¾, KW, KS, gilt, pin wheel escapement, Silver	★ ★ ★	$2,000	$2,500	$3,500
18S, 15J, ¾, KW, KS, gilt, pin wheel escapement, 18K	★ ★ ★	3,000	3,500	4,500

S.D. French, about 18 size, 15 jewels, gilt ¾ movement, key wind & set, with pin wheel escapement, engraved on movement "S.D. French, Walbash Ind., Aug. 21. 1866, No. 24."

LUTHER GODDARD
Shrewsbury, Massachusetts
1809 - 1825

The first significant attempt to produce watches in America was made by Luther Goddard. William H. Keith, who became president of Waltham Watch Co. (1861-1866) and was once apprenticed to Goddard, said that the hands, dials, round and dove-tail brass,

LUTHER GODDARD (continued)

steel wire, mainsprings and hairsprings, balance verge, chains, and pinions were all imported. The plates, wheels, and brass parts, however, were cast at the Goddard shop. He also made the cases for his movements which were of the usual style—open faced, double case—and somewhat in advance of the prevalent style of thick bull's eye watches of the day. About 600 watches were made that were of high quality and more expensive than the imported type. The first watch was produced about 1812 and was sold to the father of ex-governor Lincoln of Worcester, Massachusetts. In 1820 his watches sold for about $60.

D. Goddard, 18-20 size, 15 jewels, "Worcester, Mass." on movement, key wind & set, solid balance, under sprung, serial number 8.

L. Goddard & Co., 16-18 size, pair case, open face-thick bulls-eye type, and of high quality for the time.

About 1870 Goddard built a shop one story high with a hip roof about 18' square, and a lean-to at the back for casting. The building was intended for making clocks, but a need for watches developed and Goddard made watches there. He earned the distinction of establishing the first watch factory in America.

His movements were marked as follows: L. Goddard, L. Goddard & Co., Luther Goddard & Son, P. Goddard, L & P Goddard, D. P. Goddard & Co., P. & D. Goddard.

Frank A. Knowlton purchased the company and operated it until 1933.

Chronology of the Development of Luther Goddard:

Luther Goddard,		D. Goddard & Son	1842-1850
"L Goddard,"		Luther D. Goddard	1850-1857
Luther Goddard & Son	1809-1825	Goddard & Co.	1857-1860
L Goddard & Co.	1817-1825	D. Goddard & Co.	
P & D Goddard	1825-1842	(also Benjamen Goddard)	1860-1872

NOTE: Watches listed below are with original silver cases.

Grade or Name — Description	Avg	Ex-Fn	Mint
Benjamin Goddard .... ★ ★	$2,000	$2,500	$3,000
Luther Goddard, S#1-35 with eagle on balance bridge ★ ★ ★	5,000	6,000	7,500
Luther Goddard, without eagle on cock .... ★	3,000	3,500	4,500
Luther Goddard, L. Goddard, Luther Goddard & Son, ★ ★	3,000	3,500	4,500

L. Goddard & Son. Example of basic movement, about 18 size, open face, pair case; most of the parts are made in America but resemble the English style.

L. Goddard & Son, about 18 size, pair case, verge escapement, engraved on movement "L. Goddard & Son, Shrewsbury," serial number 460.

Grade or Name—Description	Avg	Ex-Fn	Mint
L. Goddard & Co., P & D Goddard, D. Goddard & Son ★	$2,000	$2,500	$3,000
Luther D. Goddard, Goddard & Co., D. Goddard & Co. .... ★	2,000	2,500	3,000
P. Goddard, with eagle on cock .... ★	1,500	2,000	2,500

JONAS G. HALL
Montpelier, Vermont
1850 - 1870
Millwood Park, Roxbury, Vermont
1870 - 1890

Jonas G. Hall was born in 1822 in Calais, Vermont. He opened a shop in Montpelier where he sold watches, jewelry, silverware, and fancy goods. While at this location, he produced more than 60 full plate, lever style watches. Hall later established a business in Roxbury where he manufactured watch staking tools and other watchmaking tools. At Roxbury, he made at least one watch which watch which was a three-quarter plate model. He also produced a few chronometers, about 20-size with a fusee and detent escapement and a wind indicator on the dial.

Hall was employed by the American Waltham Watch Co. for a short time and helped design the first lady's model. He also worked for Tremont Watch Co., E. Howard & Co., and the United States Watch Co. of Marion, New Jersey.

Style or Name—Description	Avg	Ex-Fn	Mint
18S, 15J, full plate, KW, KS	$1,000	$1,500	$2,200
18S, 15J, ¾, gilt, KW, KS	2,000	2,500	3,000

J.G. Hall, 18 size, 15 jewels, full plate, key wind & set, engraved on movement "J.G. Hall, Montpelier, VT.," serial number 25, ca. 1857.

J.G. Hall, 18 size, 15 jewels, ¾ plate, key wind and set, engraved on movement "J.G. Hall, Millwood Park, Roxbury, VT," no serial number, ca. 1880.

HAMILTON WATCH CO.
Lancaster, Pennsylvania
December 14, 1892 - Present

Hamilton's roots go back to the Adams & Perry Watch Manufacturing Co. On Sept. 26, 1874, E. F. Bowman made a model watch, and the first movement was produced on April 7, 1876. It was larger than an 18S, or about a 19S. The movement had a snap-on dial and the patented stem-setting arrangement. They decided to start making the watches a standard size of 18, and no more than 1,000 of the large-size watches were made. Work had commenced on Sept. 1, 1877, at the Lancaster Watch Co. The watches were designed to sell at a cheaper price than normal. It had a one-piece top ¾ plate and a pillar plate that was fully ruby-jeweled (4½ pairs). It had a gilt or nickel movement and a new stem-wind device designed by Mosely & Todd. By mid-1878, the Lancaster Watch Co. had made 150 movements. Four grades of watches were produced: Keystone, Fulton, Franklin, and Melrose. In September 1879 the company had manufactured 334 movements. In 1880 some 1,250 movements had been made. In mid-1882, about 17,000 movements had been assembled. All totaled, about 20,000 movements were made.

Grade 936, 18 size, 17 jewels, serial number 1. c. 1893.   Grade 936, 18 size, 17 jewels, serial number 2, c. 1893.

The first Hamilton movement to be sold was No. 15 to W. C. Davis on January 31, 1893. The No. 1 movement was finished on April 25, 1896, and was never sold. The No. 2 was finished on April 25, 1893, and was shipped to Smythe & Ashe of Rochester, N. Y. Nos. 1 & 2 are at the N.A.W.C.C. museum.

Chronology of the Development of Hamilton:

Adams & Perry Watch Co.	Sept. 1874-May 1876
Lancaster, Pa., Watch Co.	Aug. 1877-Oct. 1887
Lancaster, Pa., Watch Co.	Nov. 1877-May 1879
Lancaster Watch Co.	May 1883-1886
Keystone Standard Watch Co.	1886-1890
Hamilton Watch Co.	Dec. 14, 1892-1969

In 1893 the first watch was produced with the Hamilton label. The watches became very popular with railroad men and by 1923 some 53 percent of Hamilton's production was railroad watches. The 940 model watch was discontinued in 1910. Most Hamilton

Grade 937, 18 size, 17 jewels, hunting case. Note serial number 1047. Hunting case models began with 1001.   Hamilton Watch Co., 18 size, 7 jewels, serial number 2934.

HAMILTON WATCH CO. (continued)

movements were fitted with a 42-hour mainspring. The Elinvar hairspring was patented in 1931 and used in all movements thereafter. On October 15, 1940, Hamilton introduced the 992B which were fitted with the Elinvar hairspring. Elinvar and Invar are tradenames and are the same 36 percent nickel steel. Although the Hamilton Watch Co. is still in business today making modern type watches, they last produced American-made watches in 1969.

HAMILTON ESTIMATED SERIAL NUMBERS
AND PRODUCTION DATES

Date	Serial No.	Date	Serial No.	Date	Serial No.	Date	Serial No.
1893	1-2,000	1906	590,000	1919	1,700,000	1932	2,500,000
1894	5,000	1907	756,000	1920	1,790,000	1933	2,600,000
1895	10,000	1908	921,000	1921	1,860,000	1934	2,700,000
1896	14,000	1909	1,087,000	1922	1,900,000	1935	2,800,000
1897	20,000	1910	1,050,500	1923	1,950,000	1936	2,900,000
1898	30,000	1911	1,290,500	1924	2,000,000	1937	3,000,000
1899	40,000	1912	1,331,000	1925	2,100,000	1938	3,200,000
1900	50,000	1913	1,370,000	1926	2,200,000	1939	3,400,000
1901	90,000	1914	1,410,500	1927	2,250,000	1940	3,600,000
1902	150,000	1915	1,450,500	1928	2,300,000	1941	3,800,000
1903	260,000	1916	1,517,000	1929	2,350,000	1942	4,025,000
1904	340,000	1917	1,580,000	1930	2,400,000		
1905	425,000	1918	1,650,000	1931	2,450,000		

NOTE: The serial numbers and dates listed above are only close approximations. The actual date of your watch could vary 2 to 3 years from the listed date.

The Hamilton Masterpiece

The adjoining illustration shows the Masterpiece in a platinum case. The dial is sterling silver with raised gold numbers and solid gold hands. This watch sold for $685.00 in 1930. All 922 MP Models included the following: 23 jewels, were adjusted to heat, cold, isochronism, and five positions, with a motor barrel, solid gold train, steel escape wheel, double roller, sapphire pallets and a micrometric regulator.

HAMILTON SERIAL NUMBERS AND GRADES

To help determine the size and grade of your watch, the following serial number list is provided. Serial numbers 30,001 through 32,000, which are omitted from the list, were not listed by Hamilton. To identify your watch, simply look up its serial number which will identify the grade. After determining the grade, your watch can be easily located in the pricing section.

No.	Grade	No.	Grade	No.	Grade
1-20	936	22801-23000	935	52501-700	974
21-30	932	23001-200	928	52701-800	966
31-60	936	23201-500	7J	52801-53000	976
61-400	932	24001-500	926	53001-53070	16s
401-1000	936	24501-25000	934	53071-53500	977
1001-20	937	25001-100	11J	53501-900	975
1021-30	933	25101-400	927	53901-54000	967
1031-60	937	25401-800	931	54001-200	972
1061-1100	933	25801-26000	935	54201-300	974
1101-300	937	26001-500	930	54301-500	976
1301-600	933	26501-27000	928	54501-700	974
1601-2000	937	27001-28000	929	54701-800	968
2001-3000	7J	28001-29000	999	54801-55000	976
3001-100	931	29001-800	927	55001-300	973
3101-500	935	29801-30000	935	55301-600	977
3501-600	931	32001-300	926	55601-700	969
3601-900	935	32301-700	930	55701-800	977
3901-4000	931	32701-33000	934	55801-56000	975
4001-300	930	33001-500	931	56001-300	974
4301-5100	934	33501-800	927	56301-500	976
5101-400	926	33801-34000	935	56501-600	966
5401-600	934	34001-500	928	56601-800	972
5601-6000	930	34501-700	930	56801-900	974
6001-600	936	34701-800	926	56901-57000	976
6601-700	938	34801-35000	934	57001-300	977
6701-800	936	35001-800	931	57301-500	975
6801-7000	932	35801-36000	935	57501-600	973
7001-10	17J	36001-37000	928	57601-800	975
7011-600	937	37001-38000	929	57801-58000	977
7601-700	939	38001-500	926	58001-100	972
7701-800	937	38501-600	930	58101-200	974
7801-8000	933	38601-900	934	58201-300	972
8001-700	936	38901-39000	926	58301-400	966
8701-800	938	39001-200	931	58401-500	976
8801-9000	936	39201-500	935	58601-600	972
9001-300	937	39501-700	927	58601-800	974
9301-600	939	39701-900	935	58801-59000	976
9601-800	937	39901-40000	931	59001-300	973
9801-900	933	40001-200	930	59301-500	967
9901-10000	939	40201-500	934	59501-700	975
10001-200	938	40501-41000	926	59701-60000	977
10201-400	936	41001-500	929	60001-500	976
10401-50	932	41501-42000	927	60501-700	974
10451-500	936	42001-43000	999	60701-61000	976
10501-700	938	43001-300	941	61001-200	975
10701-900	936	43301-500	943	61201-500	977
10901-11000	938	43501-700	937	61501-600	973
11001-12000	936	43701-900	941	61601-800	975
12001-200	939	43901-44000	943	61801-62000	977
12201-13000	937	44001-02	21J	62001-100	972
13001-400	999	44003-400	938	62101-300	974
13401-14000	938	44401-500	942	62301-500	976
14001-15000	999	44501-45000	936	62501-700	974
15001-300	939	45001-46000	929	62701-900	972
15301-15401	21J	46001-500	926	62901-63000	974
15302-700	937	46501-800	934	63001-500	977
15701-16000	939	46801-47000	930	63501-600	975
16001-100	931	47001-500	927	63601-800	977
16101-200	930	47501-700	935	63801-900	975
16201-300	927	47701-48000	931	63901-64000	973
16301-400	931	48001-05	942	64001-100	976
16401-600	927	48006-300	940	64101-200	972
16601-17000	931	48301-500	942	64201-300	974
17001-500	929	48501-900	940	64301-600	972
17501-18000	931	48901-49000	942	64601-700	976
18001-200	928	49001-400	927	64701-900	974
18201-300	926	49401-900	925	64901-65000	976
18301-500	928	49901-50	11J	65001-200	973
18501-19500	930	50071-500	962	65201-300	977
19501-700	926	50501-750	960	65301-400	975
19701-20000	930	50751-50850	964	65401-500	973
20001-300	934	50851-51000	960	65501-700	977
20301-500	926	51001-51300	16s	65701-900	975
20501-21000	999	51301-400	963	65901-66000	977
21001-300	935	51401-650	961	66001-200	976
21301-500	927	51651-750	965	66201-300	974
21501-800	935	51751-52000	961	66301-500	972
21801-22500	927	52001-300	16s	66501-600	976
22501-800	931	52301-500	976	66601-700	974

No.	Grade	No.	Grade	No.	Grade
66701-800	972	89001-500	941	149001-150000	925
66801-67000	974	89501-90000	937	150001-151000	924
67001-100	977	90001-100	926	151001-400	927
67101-300	975	90101-950	999	151401-500	935
67301-600	973	91001-92000	925	151501-152000	927
67601-800	975	92001-200	940	152001-153000	936
67801-68000	977	92201-93000	936	153001-154000	941
68001-800	960	93001-94000	927	154001-155000	936
68801-69000	964	94001-003	934	155001-156000	927
69001-100	977	94004-95000	928	156001-157000	940
69101-200	975	95001-96000	923	157001-158000	925
69201-400	973	96001-100	942	158001-159000	940
69401-600	975	96101-700	940	159001-160000	941
69601-70000	977	96701-97000	936	160001-161000	940
70001-200	976	97001-900	929	161001-162000	941
70201-400	970	97901-98000	927	162001-163000	926
70401-600	968	98001-99000	924	163001-164000	943
70601-900	972	99001-100000	925	164001-165000	940
70901-71000	974	100001-101000	924	165001-166000	925
71001-200	975	101001-102000	925	166001-167000	924
71201-500	971	102001-103000	922	167001-168000	927
71501-700	975	103001-104000	927	168001-169000	940
71701-90	973	104001-105000	940	169001-400	935
71791-800	969	105001-500	925	169401-170000	927
71801-900	977	105501-106000	927	170001-171000	999
71901-72000	975	106001-107000	940	171001-172000	925
72001-100	974	107001-400	941	172001-100	934
72101-300	976	107401-500	943	172101-173000	926
72301-600	974	107501-800	941	173001-174000	925
72601-700	968	107801-108000	943	174001-175000	924
72701-900	976	108001-200	928	175002-176000	HWW*
72901-73000	972	108201-109000	926	175001-699	HWW*
73001-200	975	109001-500	927	176001-177000	940
73201-300	973	109501-110000	925	177001-178000	927
73301-74000	977	110001-900	940	178001-179000	942
74001-400	974	110901-111000	942	179001-500	935
74401-600	972	111001-500	937	179501-180000	927
74601-75000	976	111501-112000	941	180001-181000	940
75001-76799	HWW*	112001-200	928	181001-182000	941
76002-76800	HWW*	112201-113000	926	182001-300	926
77001-100	969	113001-114000	925	182301-400	934
77101-300	973	114001-003	940	182401-183000	926
77301-500	975	114004-115000	936	183001-184000	941
77501-600	971	115001-116000	927	184001-185000	940
77601-700	973	116001-117000	940	185001-186000	925
77701-900	975	117001-118000	925	186001-187000	942
77901-78000	977	118001-119000	999	187001-188000	927
78001-500	970	119001-120000	925	188001-189000	924
78501-700	972	120001-121000	924	189001-190000	925
78701-900	974	121001-500	941	190001-191000	926
78901-79000	976	121501-122000	943	191001-192000	927
79001-100	973	122001-300	940	192001-193000	924
79101-300	975	122301-400	942	193001-194000	925
79301-700	977	122401-123000	940	194001-195000	928
79701-900	975	123001-124000	941	195001-500	935
79901-80000	973	124001-100	942	195501-196000	927
80001-200	972	124101-800	940	196001-197000	926
80201-400	974	124801-125000	942	197001-198000	937
80401-600	970	125001-126000	927	198001-199000	936
80601-700	972	126001-127000	924	199001-200000	925
80701-900	974	127001-128000	941	200001-201000	926
80901-81000	976	128001-129000	936	201001-202000	925
81001-300	961	129001-130000	925	202001-500	926
81301-500	965	130001-500	924	202501-203000	934
81501-82000	961	130501-131000	926	203001-204000	927
82001-300	972	131001-132000	925	204001-100	934
82301-500	974	132001-100	926	204101-500	926
82501-600	970	132101-200	934	204501-205000	934
82601-700	972	132201-500	926	205001-206000	941
82701-800	974	132501-133000	924	206001-207000	940
82801-900	968	133001-134000	937	207001-208000	927
82901-83000	976	134001-135000	924	208001-900	999
83001-400	977	135001-136000	925	208901-209000	940
83401-500	971	136001-137000	926	209001-210000	925
83501-700	975	137001-100	11J	210001-211000	940
83701-800	973	137101-138000	927	211001-212000	927
83801-900	975	138001-139000	940	212001-213000	940
83901-84000	969	139001-140000	937	213001-500	941
84001-400	974	140001-300	938	213501-600	937
84401-500	970	140301-141000	942	213601-214000	925
84501-700	972	141001-142000	941	214001-215000	924
84701-800	968	142001-143000	940	215001-216000	927
84801-85000	976	143001-100	927	216001-217000	940
85001-200	937	143101-144000	925	217001-218000	927
85201-900	941	144001-145000	924	218001-219000	940
85901-86000	943	145001-146000	925	219001-220000	925
86001-87000	928	146001-400	934	220001-221000	924
87001-88000	929	146401-147000	924	221001-222000	927
88001-500	926	147001-148000	927	222001-223000	926
88501-89000	930	148001-149000	940	223001-02	927

No.	Grade	No.	Grade	No.	Grade
223003-04	941	300501-900	974	331201-400	975
223005	937	300901-301000	968	331401-500	969
223006-224000	927	301001-400	975	331501-700	971
224001-225000	924	301401-500	971	331701-800	973
225001-226000	927	301501-302000	973	331801-332000	975
226001-227000	940	302001-100	990	332001-200	992
227001-228000	925	302101-200	992	332201-800	972
228001-229000	924	302201-300	990	332801-333000	974
229001-230000	925	302301-900	992	333001-500	975
230001-500	926	302901-303000	990	333501-700	971
230501-231000	924	303001-100	973	333701-900	973
231001-565	937	303101-300	971	333901-334000	975
231566-232000	927	303301-800	975	334001-200	972
232001-233000	940	303801-304000	973	334201-800	992
233001-234000	941	304001-100	970	334801-335000	990
234001-235000	940	304101-400	972	335001-600	975
235001-236000	941	304401-305000	974	335601-800	971
236001-237000	936	305001-100	973	335801-900	973
237001-238000	941	305101-200	971	335901-336000	975
238001-239000	926	305201-300	969	336001-200	972
239001-500	943	305301-900	975	336201-337000	974
239501-240000	941	305901-306000	973	337001-338000	975
240001-241000	940	306001-400	972	338001-200	974
241001-242000	941	306401-307000	974	338201-900	992
242001-243000	940	307001-100	975	338901-339000	990
243001-244000	927	307101-300	971	339001-300	971
244001-245000	936	307301-400	975	339301-500	973
245001-246000	925	307401-500	973	339501-340000	975
246001-247000	940	307501-600	975	340001-200	974
247001-248000	927	307601-700	971	340201-300	972
248001-249000	940	307701-900	975	340301-600	970
249001-250000	927	307901-308000	969	340601-341000	974
250001-251000	926	308001-700	990	341001-200	973
251001-252000	927	308701-309000	992	341201-342000	975
252001-253000	924	309001-100	971	342001-300	990
253001-254000	925	309101-400	973	342301-343000	992
254001-255000	940	309401-310000	975	343001-344000	975
255001-256000	925	310001-400	970	344001-200	970
256001-257000	926	310401-311000	974	344201-400	972
257001-258000	941	311001-700	975	344401-345000	974
258001-259000	924	311701-312000	973	345001-346000	975
259001-260000	941	312001-200	970	346001-300	992
260001-261000	940	312201-500	972	346301-347000	974
261001-262000	927	312501-600	968	347001-180	993
262001-263000	926	312601-313000	974	347181-200	991
263001-264000	925	313001-100	973	347201-300	975
264001-265000	940	313101-400	971	347301-400	973
265001-266000	927	313401-600	969	347401-700	993
266001-267000	940	313601-314000	975	347701-900	991
267001-268000	925	314001-600	974	347901-348000	973
268001-269000	940	314601-900	972	348001-200	970
269001-270000	927	314901-315000	970	348201-800	974
270001-271000	940	315001-100	971	348801-349000	972
271001-272000	925	315101-400	973	349001-350000	975
272001-273000	926	315401-316000	975	350001-300	990
273001-274000	941	316001-200	992	350301-400	974
274001-275000	924	316201-300	972	350401-600	990
275002-100	H W W*	316301-500	992	350601-351000	992
275102-200	H W W*	316501-317000	972	351001-352000	975
275202-460	H W W*	317001-600	975	352001-100	968
275462-500	H W W*	317601-700	969	352101-353000	974
276001-277000	940	317701-318000	973	353001-354000	975
277001-278000	941	318001-100	972	354001-400	992
278001-279000	940	318101-900	974	354401-355000	974
279001-280000	925	318901-319000	970	355001-800	975
280001-281000	936	319001-100	971	355801-900	973
281001-282000	927	319101-320000	975	355901-356000	993
282001-283000	926	320001-300	972	356001-500	990
283001-284000	925	320301-400	968	356501-357000	974
284001-500	934	320401-321000	974	357001-358000	975
284501-900	924	321001-200	973	358001-359000	974
284901-285000	999	321201-322000	975	359001-360000	975
285001-286000	925	322001-323000	974	360001-550	960
286001-287000	940	323001-700	975	360801-361000	960
287001-288000	927	323701-324000	973	361001-100	993
288001-289000	940	324001-325000	960	361101-300	991
289001-290000	927	325001-100	965	361301-400	993
290001-800	936	325101-326000	961	361401-700	975
290801-291000	938	326001-327000	974	361701-20	973
291001-292000	925	327001-300	971	361721-362000	975
292001-500	940	327301-500	973	362001-900	974
292501-293000	942	327501-328000	975	362901-363000	990
293001-294000	925	328001-300	992	363001-364000	975
294001-295000	926	328301-500	990	364001-365000	974
295001-296000	927	328501-329000	992	365001-100	975
296001-297000	940	329001-330000	975	365101-300	973
297001-298000	927	330001-100	992	365301-366000	975
298001-299000	940	330101-500	990	366001-367000	974
299001-300000	925	330501-331000	992	367001-500	975
300001-300	972	331001-200	973	367501-368000	993
300301-500	970			368001-369000	974

HAMILTON WATCH CO. (continued)

No.	Grade	No.	Grade	No.	Grade
369001-370000	992	434501-600	942	536001-537000	936
370001-100	990	434601-435000	946	537001-538000	924
370101-400	992	435001-436000	924	538001-543000	940
370401-500	974	436001-438500	940	543001-544000	927
370501-800	990	438501-800	946	544001-200	934
370801-371400	992	438801-900	942	544201-545000	926
371401-500	972	438901-440000	946	545001-546000	925
371501-373500	974	440001-441000	924	546001-547000	924
373501-700	990	441001-442000	940	547001-548000	926
373701-374000	992	442001-400	946	548001-549000	999
374001-200	974	442401-500	942	549001-551000	946
374201-700	990	442501-443000	946	551001-553000	944
374701-375000	974	443001-444000	926	553001-555000	940
375001-100	993	444001-445000	924	555001-556000	936
375101-500	991	445001-446000	927	556001-558000	924
375501-376000	975	446001-447000	924	558001-560000	925
376001-200	972	447001-448000	925	560001-561000	999
376201-500	974	448001-449000	926	561001-562000	926
376501-377000	992	449001-450000	924	562001-564000	924
377001-200	973	450001-451000	926	564001-565000	926
377201-378000	975	451001-452000	925	565001-568000	940
378001-379000	974	452001-453000	940	568001-569000	936
379001-380800	992	453001-454000	924	569001-571000	924
380801-381000	990	454001-456000	940	571001-576000	940
381001-382000	992	456001-457000	999	576001-200	942
382001-100	990	457001-458000	940	576201-578000	940
382101-383000	974	458001-459000	999	578001-580000	924
383001-300	992	459001-110	946	580001-582000	926
383301-700	990	459119-200	942	582001-584000	925
383701-384000	972	459111-118	946	584001-585000	927
384001-700	974	459201-700	942	585001-587000	999
384701-900	972	459701-460000	946	587001-592000	940
384901-385000	974	460001-461900	940	592001-593000	926
385001-600	972	461901-462000	940	593001-594000	924
385601-800	974	462001-463000	999	594001-601000	940
385801-386000	990	463001-500	940	B600001-601000	999 Ball
386001-800	974	463501-464000	940	601001-601800	926
386801-900	992	464001-466000	926	B601001-601800	999 Ball
386901-387000	972	466001-467000	924	601801-602000	934
387001-100	990	467001-468000	926	B601801-602000	999 Ball
387101-900	992	468001-469000	940	602001-603000	926
387901-388000	972	469001-470000	924	B602001-603000	999 Ball
388001-400	990	470001-471000	926	603001-604000	926
388401-389000	992	471001-472000	946	B603001-604000	999 Ball
389001-391000	974	472001-473000	924	604001-605000	926
391001-300	972	473001-474000	940	B604001-605000	999 Ball
391301-392000	974	474001-475000	924	605001-606000	925
392001-800	992	475001-476000	940	B605001-606000	999 Ball
392801-393000	990	476001-477000	924	606001-607000	925
393001-400	975	477001-478000	940	B606001-607000	999 Ball
393401-600	973	478001-479000	926	607001-608000	925
393601-394000	993	479001-480000	944	B607001-608000	999 Ball
394001-200	972	480001-481000	926	608001-613000	924
394201-395000	974	481001-482000	927	B608001-613000	999 Ball
395001-100	993	482001-483000	924	613001-614000	925
395101-900	991	483001-484000	926	B613001-614000	999 Ball
395901-396000	993	484001-485000	940	614001-616500	924
396001-397000	992	485001-486000	925	B614001-616500	999 Ball
397001-200	990	486001-487000	999	616501-617000	934
397201-398000	992	487001-488000	924	B616501-617000	999 Ball
398001-200	972	488001-489000	999	617001-619000	926
398201-399000	992	489001-492000	924	B617001-619000	999 Ball
399001-600	993	492001-493000	940	619001-620000	927
399601-400000	975	493001-494000	946	B619001-620000	999 Ball
400001-401000	924	494001-495000	944	620001-622700	940
401001-402000	940	495001-496000	940	B620001-622700	999 Ball
402001-404000	924	496001-497000	925	622701-623000	942
404001-405000	926	497001-498000	999	B622701-623000	999 Ball
405001-406000	924	498001-499000	936	623001-624000	941
406001-407000	940	499001-501000	940	B623001-624000	999 Ball
407001-408000	926	501001-900	926	624001-625000	936
408001-416000	940	501901-502000	934	B624001-625000	999 Ball
416001-417000	926	502001-503000	926	625001-626000	925
417001-418000	940	503001-504000	999	B625001-626000	999 Ball
418001-419000	926	504001-507000	940	626001-627000	926
419001-420000	941	507001-508000	999	B626001-627000	999 Ball
420001-421000	940	508001-509000	940	627001-628000	924
421001-422000	926	509901-510000	942	B627001-628000	999 Ball
422001-423000	924	510001-511500	940	628001-630800	925
423001-425000	926	511501-700	942	B628001-630800	999 Ball
425001-426000	924	511701-517000	940	631001-636000	940
426001-500	936	517001-519000	924	B631001-636000	999 Ball
426501-427000	944	519001-521000	925	636001-637000	941
427001-428000	924	521001-523000	944	B636001-637000	999 Ball
428001-429000	926	523001-524000	946	637001-638000	936
429001-430000	925	524001-531000	940	B637001-638000	999 Ball
430001-431000	924	531001-532000	926	638001-639000	926
431001-432000	925	532001-10	934	B638001-639000	999 Ball
432001-433000	940	532011-533000	926	639001-640000	925
433001-434000	924	533001-535500	999	B639001-640000	999 Ball
434001-500	940	535501-536000	940		

No.	Grade	No.	Grade	No.	Grade
640001-642000	924	736001-738000	975	783001-600	992
B640001-644400	999 Ball	738001-739000	974	783601-784000	974
644401-645000	940	739001-740000	975	784001-785000	992
645001-645500	927	740001-100	974	785001-500	952
B645001-645500	999 Ball	740101-200	972	785501-786000	950
645501-646000	925	740201-900	974	786001-787000	992
B645501-646000	999 Ball	740901-741000	975	787001-400	974
646001-647000	926	741001-742000	992	787401-788000	972
B646001-647000	999 Ball	742001-743000	974	788001-791300	992
647001-648000	940	743001-300	975	791301-792600	974
B647001-648000	999 Ball	743301-400	993	792601-900	972
648001-649000	940	743401-744000	975	792901-793700	992
B648001-649000	998 Ball	744001-500	974	793701-900	990
B649001-650000	998 Ball	744501-745000	992	793901-794000	992
B650001-651000	999 Ball	745001-747000	975	794001-200	972
651001-652000	940	747001-700	974	794201-795000	974
B651001-652000	998 Ball	747701-748000	972	795001-796400	992
652001-652700	924	748001-749500	992	796401-800	972
B652001-652700	998 Ball	749501-750000	974	796801-797200	974
652701-652800	924	750001-100	961	797201-500	954
652801-652900	927	750101-200	961	797501-798000	974
652901-653000	937	750201-700	950	798001-500	990
653001-655000	940	750701-751000	952	798501-800	972
B653001-655000	999 Ball	751001-752000	960	798801-799000	974
655001-655200	924	752001-500	952	799001-200	954
B655001-655200	999 Ball	752501-753000	950	799201-600	992
655201-656000	924	753001-500	952	799601-800000	954
656001-657000	926	753501-754000	950	800001-802000	974
657001-659000	927	754001-100	960	802001-200	954
659001-660000	925	754101-500	952	802201-2	972
660001-661000	927	754501-755000	960	802203-300	954
661001-662000	924	755001-400	992	802301-500	972
662001-664000	940	755401-500	974	802501-803700	974
664001-666000	924	755501-700	972	803701-804200	954
666001-667000	940	755701-900	974	804201-806000	974
667001-668000	941	755901-756000	972	806001-807000	975
668001-669000	926	756001-757000	974	807001-500	993
669001-670000	999	757001-300	975	807501-808800	975
670001-100	937	757301-500	993	808801-809000	993
670501-673000	925	757501-758000	975	809001-500	974
673001-675000	926	758001-100	972	809501-600	972
675001-677000	940	758101-759000	992	809601-810000	974
677001-678000	924	759001-760000	975	810001-300	990
678001-679200	927	760001-400	992	810301-812000	974
679201-680000	926	760401-600	972	812001-700	992
680001-685000	924	760601-800	974	812701-813000	974
685001-687000	940	760801-761000	992	813001-814000	974P
687001-688000	925	761001-400	975	814001-800	974L
688001-689000	946	761401-600	993	814801-815900	992
689001-694000	940	761601-762000	975	815901-816000	974L
694001-696000	924	762001-200	992	816001-817000	974P
696001-697000	941	762201-300	972	817001-819000	974L
697001-700000	924	762301-763000	974	819001-820000	974P
700001-702000	974	763001-300	993	820001-821500	974L
702001-703800	992	763301-60.	973	821501-822000	990L
703801-704000	990	763601-7640	975	822001-700	992L
704001-400	992	764001-300	992	822701-823000	974L
704401-705000	990	764301-400	972	823001-824000	974P
705001-700	972	764401-765000	974	824001-826000	975P
705701-706000	974	765001-300	992	826001-500	975L
706001-707000	990	765301-767000	974	826501-827000	993
707001-800	972	767001-600	992	827001-828000	975P
707801-708000	990	767601-800	972	828001-829000	974L
708001-709500	975	767801-768000	974	829001-830000	974P
709501-710000	973	768001-769000	975	830001-500	990L
710001-800	993	769001-700	992	830501-831000	992L
710801-711000	991	769701-770000	972	831001-100	954P
711001-300	973	770001-100	974	831101-200	972P
711301-712000	975	770101-771200	992	831201-500	954P
712001-600	993	771201-400	972	831501-832000	974P
712601-713000	991	771401-772000	974	832001-400	974L
713001-714900	975	772001-773000	975	832401-833000	992L
714901-715000	991	773001-800	992	833001-834000	990L
715001-716000	993	773801-774000	972	834001-600	974P
716001-100	972	774001-775000	975	834601-800	974L
716101-717000	974	775001-500	952	834801-835000	974P
717001-200	991	775501-776000	950	835001-600	992L
717201-718000	975L	776001-300	973	835601-800	990L
718001-721500	974	776301-700	993	835801-836000	974L
721501-722000	992	776701-777000	975	836001-500	974P
722001-724000	974	777001-300	972	836501-900	954P
724001-725000	972	777301-778300	974	836901-837000	974P
725001-726000	974	778301-800	992	837001-838000	975P
726001-727000	992	778801-900	972	838001-839000	975L
727001-728000	974	778901-779300	974	839001-400	974L
728001-729000	992	779301-780100	992	839401-700	992L
729001-730000	975	780101-300	972	839701-840000	990L
730001-731000	992	780301-781300	992	840001-400	952L
731001-732000	975	781301-400	972	840401-900	950L
732001-734000	992	781401-500	974	840901-841000	952L
734001-735000	975	781501-782000	992	841001-842000	975P
735001-736000	974	782001-783000	975		

No.	Grade	No.	Grade	No.	Grade
842001-843000	974L	937001-939000	940	1057001-1061300	992
843001-844000	974P	939001-941000	924	1061301-1062300	972
844001-200	993	941001-944000	940	1062301-1066000	992
844201-845000	975	944001-949000	926	1066001-1068000	974
845001-200	992	949001-952000	925	1068001-1069000	975
845201-400	972	952001-958000	924	1069001-1070000	974
845401-700	954	958001-960000	926	1070001-1071000	992L
845701-846000	972	960001-968000	940	1071001-1073000	975P
846001-500	952	968001-970000	926	1073001-1075000	992
846501-847000	950	970001-971700	924	1075001-1076200	974L
847001-200	972	971701-972000	948	1076201-700	972L
847201-849000	974	972001-973000	924	1076701-1077000	978L
849001-850000	975	973001-974000	936	1077001-1079000	974P
850001-300	992	974001-975400	924	1079001-1080000	992L
850301-800	990	975401-25 Spec.	926	1080001-100	952L
850801-851000	972	975426-976000	924	1080101-200	960L
851001-400	993	976001-979000	940	1080201-400	994L
851401-852000	975	979001-100	942	1080401-1081000	950L
852001-853000	992	979101-981000	940	1081001-1082000	978L
853001-854000	974	981001-982000	948	1082001-400	993L
854001-600	950	982001-984000	924	1082401-1083000	973L
854601-900	952	984001-986000	940	1083001-1084000	990L
854901-855100	960L	986001-987000	946	1084001-1085000	992L
855101-856000	950L	987001-988000	936	1085001-1086000	992L
856001-857840	975	988001-992000	940	1086001-1088000	974P
857841-858000	975L	992001-996000	924	1088001-1091000	992L
858001-500	974	996001-999998	940	1091001-200	978L
858501-859000	972	999999-1000000	947	1091201-1092000	974L
859001-860000	974	1000001-1000300	992	1092001-1093000	992L
860001-862300	992	1000301-1003000	992	1093001-1095000	974P
862301-400	954	1003001-1004000	974	1095001-1096000	992P
862401-500	972	1004001-900	992	1096001-400	974L
862501-600	954	1004901-1007100	974	1096401-1097000	974P
862601-800	972	1007101-1008300	992	1097001-1098000	992L
862801-863000	974	1008301-1009500	974	1098001-400	975P
863001-864000	992	1009501-1010700	992	1098401-1099000	975L
864001-865000	975	1010701-1011200	972	1099001-600	993L
865001-866000	992	1011201-1012700	974	1099601-1100000	975P
866001-600	974	1012701-1013000	992	1100001-1104000	992L
866601-700	954	1013001-1015000	978	1104001-1105000	974P
866701-867000	972	1015001-300	974	1105001-1106000	992L
867001-868000	975	1015301-1016000	992	1106001-500	978L
868001-869000	992	1016001-300	975	1106501-1107000	992L
869001-870000	975	1016301-600	973	1107001-1109000	992L
870001-872000	992	1016601-1018000	993	1109001-1111000	972L
872001-200	993	1018001-1020000	992	1111001-112000	974L
872201-874000	975	1020001-1022600	950	1112001-1113000	974P
874001-800	974	1022601-1023000	952	1113001-1116000	992L
874801-875000	975	1023001-700	992	1116001-900	974P
875001-300	952	1023701-1024500	974	1116901-1117000	974L
875301-876000	975	1024501-600	974	1117001-1119000	992L
876001-600	993	1024601-1025000	972	1119001-1120000	978L
876601-877000	975	1025001-1027000	975	1120001-1122000	992L
877001-400	992	1027001-400	993	1122001-1123000	974P
877401-700	975	1027401-1029600	975	1123001-500	972P
877701-878000	993	1029601-1030000	973	1123501-1125000	974P
878001-879400	975	1030001-1032000	992	1125001-1127000	992L
880001-600	992	1032001-1033000	974	1127001-128000	972L
880601-882400	974	1033001-200	972	1128001-1129000	974L
882401-883400	992	1033201-800	954	1129001-1130500	974P
883401-884100	974	1033801-1035300	974	1130501-1131000	956P
884101-885300	992	1035301-600	972	1131001-1132000	992L
885301-886000	974	1035601-1036000	974	1132001-1133000	990L
886001-887000	992	1036001-300	972	1133001-1134000	978L
887001-300	974	1036301-800	954	1134001-1135000	972L
887301-890300	992	1036801-1037000	992L	1135001-1137000	992L
890301-891000	974	1037001-1038000	974	1137001-1138000	956P
891001-600	992	1038001-1039000	992	1138001-1139000	956P
891601-892200	978	1039001-200	972	1139001-1140000	978L
892201-896200	992	1039201-500	978	1140001-1141000	972L
896201-897800	974	1039501-1040300	974	1141001-1142000	956P
897801-898000	972	1040301-1041000	992	1142001-500	974P
898001-899100	992	1041001-1042000	974	1142501-1145000	974L
899101-500	978	1042001-700	992	1145001-1146000	975P
899501-900000	974	1042701-1043000	972	1146001-500	956P
900001-902000	940	1043001-700	978	1146501-1149000	974P
902001-904000	926	1043701-1044000	992	1149001-1150000	974L
904001-906000	924	1044001-1045000	974	1150001-600	950L
906001-914000	940	1045001-1046000	992	1150601-1151800	952L
914001-916000	926	1046001-1047000	975	1151801-1152000	952P
916001-917000	927	1047001-1048000	974L	1152001-900	950P
917001-919000	925	1048001-1049000	992	1152901-1153200	952P
919001-921000	940	1049001-500	990	1153201-300	
921001-923000	924	1049501-1051000	992	1153301-500	994P
923001-500	999	1051001-200	975	1153501-800	994L
923501-924000	925	1051201-1052000	993	1153801-1154000	960L
924001-926000	940	1052001-500	972P	1154001-500	950L
926001-100	927	1052501-900	954	1154501-1155000	950P
927001-929000	926	1052901-1053000	974	1155001-200	994P
929001-933000	924	1053001-1054000	992	1155201-500	994L
933001-935000	925	1054001-1056000	974	1156001-1158000	996L
935001-937000	926	1056001-1057000	975	1158001-1160000	974P

No.	Grade	No.	Grade	No.	Grade
1160001-1162000	992L	1271701-1272000	974P	1354701-1355000	974P
1162001-500	993L	1272001-1274000	996L	1355001-1356000	992L
1162501-1164000	992L	1274001-500	993L	1356001-1357000	974P
1164001-1166000	974P	1274501-700	992L	1357001-1359800	992L
1166001-1167000	974L	1274701-1275000	992L	1359801-1361000	996L
1167001-1168000	956P	1275001-1276000	972L	1361001-1362000	992L
1168001-1169000	975P	1276001-1277000	974L	1362001-600	974P
1169001-1170000	974P	1277001-1278000	992L	1362601-1363000	956P
1170001-1174000	956P	1278001-1279000	975P	1363001-1364000	992L
1174001-1176000	974P	1279001-1280000	974P	1364001-1365000	975P
1176001-1177000	992L	1280001-1281000	992L	1365001-800	956P
1177001-1178000	956P	1281001-800	974P	1365801-1367000	974P
1178001-1179000	974P	1281801-1282000	956P	1367001-1369400	992L
1179001-1181000	996L	1282001-1284000	996L	1369401-1370000	996L
1181001-1182000	992L	1284001-1285000	992L	1370001-1371000	974L
1182001-1183000	996L	1285001-1286000	956P	1371001-600	996L
1183001-1184400	974P	1286001-1288000	978L	1371601-1373000	992L
1184401-1185400	956P	1288001-500	993L	1373001-1374000	975P
1185401-1186000	974P	1288501-1289100	992L	1374001-1375000	992L
1186001-1187000	992L	1289101-700	990L	1375001-1376000	950L
1187001-1188000	996L	1289701-1290000	992L	1376001-1377000	992L
1188001-1189000	992L	1290001-1291500	974P	1377001-1378300	974P
1189001-1190000	974P	1291501-1292000	992P	1378301-1379000	956P
1190001-1192000	996L	1292001-1297000	992L	1379001-1380200	972L
1192001-1193000	975P	1297001-1298000	974P	1380201-1381000	978L
1193001-1194000	974P	1298001-1299000	992L	1381001-500	956P
1194001-1195000	956P	1299001-1300000	975P	1381501-1383000	974P
1195001-1196000	974P	1300001-1301000	974P	1383001-1384000	992L
1196001-1199000	992L	1301001-1302000	974L	1384001-1386100	974P
1199001-1201000	974P	1302001-500	992L	1386101-1387000	956P
1201001-1202000	975P	1302501-1303000	990L	1387001-1388000	992L
1202001-1203000	992L	1303001-500	972L	1388001-400	978L
1203001-1204000	974P	1303501-1304000	972P	1388401-1389000	978L
1204001-500	956P	1304001-1305000	978L	1389001-300	956P
1204501-1206000	974P	1305001-1306000	956P	1389301-1390000	956P
1206001-1207000	992L	1306001-307000	974P	1390001-1391000	992L
1207001-1210000	974P	1307001-1308500	992L	1391001-500	956P
1210001-1212000	992L	1308501-1309000	993L	1391501-1392000	974P
1212001-1213000	974P	1309001-1310000	974L	1392001-1393000	992L
1213001-500	996L	1310001-1311000	972L	1393001-1394000	974P
1213501-1214000	992L	1311001-1312000	992L	1394001-1396000	992L
1214001-1214600	993L	1312001-800	974P	1396001-500	972L
1214601-1215000	975P	1312801-1313000	956P	1396501-1398000	974P
1215001-1216000	974L	1313001-1317000	992L	1398001-400	974P
1216001-1219000	992L	1317001-1318000	956P	1398401-1399000	956P
1219001-1220000	974P	1318001-1321000	992L	1399001-1400000	992L
1220001-1221000	992L	1321001-300	990L	1400001-1401000	936
1221001-1223500	974P	1321301-1322000	992L	1401001-1403000	924
1223501-1224000	956P	1322001-700	974L	1403001-1409000	940
1224001-1227000	992L	1322701-1323000	972L	1409001-500	946
1227001-1228000	972L	1323001-1324000	992L	1409501-1410000	940
1228001-700	992L	1324001-1325000	996L	1410001-1414000	924
1228701-1229000	990L	1325001-1326500	975P	1414001-300	941
1229001-500	956P	1326501-1327000	993L	1414501-1415000	925
1229501-1230000	974P	1327001-300	956P	1415001-1417000	924
1230001-1231000	974L	1327301-1329000	974P	1417001-1419000	940
1231001-1232000	992L	1329001-1330000	992L	1419001-1420000	924
1232001-1233000	974P	1330001-1331300	974L	1420001-1421000	940
1233001-1236000	992L	1331301-800	972L	1421001-1422000	924
1236001-500	974P	1331801-1332000	978L	1422001-1424000	940
1236501-1237000	956P	1332001-1334000	992L	1424001-1428000	924
1237001-500	996L	1334001-400	974P	1428001-1430000	940
1237501-1238000	992L	1334401-1335000	956P	1430001-200	924
1238001-1239000	956P	1335001-300	978L	1430201-400	948
1239001-1241000	992L	1335301-1336000	972L	1430401-1431000	924
1241001-1242000	975P	1336001-1337000	992L	1431001-1433000	940
1242001-400	974L	1337001-1338200	996L	1433001-1438000	924
1242401-1243000	972L	1338201-1339000	996L	1438001-500	926
1243001-500	996L	1339001-1340000	956P	1438501-1439500	924
1243501-1244000	992L	1340001-1341000	992L	1439501-1440000	926
1244001-1245000	974P	1341001-300	972L	1440001-1441000	940
1245001-1246000	992L	1341301-500	974L	1441001-1442000	924
1246001-300	974P	1341501-1342000	978L	1442001-500	926
1246301-800	956P	1342001-1343000	992L	1442501-1444000	924
1246801-1247000	974L	1343001-400	956P	1444001-1445000	940
1247001-1248000	992L	1343401-1344000	974P	1445001-1447000	924
1248001-1249700	974P	1344001-1345000	992L	1447001-1448200	940
1249701-1250000	956P	1345001-600	974L	1449001-1450500	924
1250001-1252000	983	1345601-1346000	972L	1500001-600	974P
1252001-1253000	985	1346001-1348000	975P	1500601-1501200	956P
1253001-1257000	983	1348001-1349000	974P	1501201-1502000	974P
1257001-900	985	1349001-1350000	992L	1502001-1503000	993L
1260001-970	Chro.*	1350001-600	972L	1503001-1504000	996L
1260971-1265000		1350601-1351000	974L	1504001-500	974L
1265001-1266000	956P	1351001-1352000	993L	1504501-1505200	972L
1266001-1267000	974P	1352001-1352300	974L	1505201-700	978L
1267001-1268200	978L	1352301-800	978L	1505701-1506000	974L
1268201-1269000	978L	1352801-1353000	974L	1506001-1507000	975P
1269001-600	992L	1353001-500	972P	1507001-1508000	992L
1269601-1270000	992L	1353501-1354200	956P	1508001-400	974P
1270001-1271700	956P	1354201-700	992P	1508401-1509000	956P

No.	Grade	No.	Grade	No.	Grade
1509001-1510000	992L	1615001-1625000	992L	1839001-500	914
1510001-1511000	974L	1625001-200	950L	1839501-1844700	910
1511001-1512000	975P	1625201-1626000	952L	1844701-1845700	914
1512001-1513200	992L	1626001-1627000	974P	1845701-1848300	910
1513201-600	992P	1627001-1633000	992L	1848301-1849500	914
1513601-1514000	992L	1633001-1635000	950L	1849501-1851900	910
1514001-200	956P	1635001-1636000	992L	1851901-1853100	914
1514201-1515000	974P	1636001-1637000	956P	1853101-1856800	910
1515001-1516000	992L	1637001-1638000	974P	1856801-1857900	914
1516001-1517000	974P	1638001-1642800	992L	1857901-1860300	910
1517001-1520000	992L	1642801-1643000	992P	1860301-1861000	914
1520001-1521200	974L	1643001-1644000	992L	1861001-1863000	900
1521201-1522000	978L	1644001-1646000	974L	1863001-700	920
1522001-600	974P	1646001-1648000	972L	1863701-1864300	900
1522601-1525000	956P	1648001-1649000	992L	1864301-1865000	920
1525001-1527000	996L	1649001-1652000	974P	1865001-500	914
1527001-1528000	992L	1652001-1653000	950L	1865501-1870300	910
1528001-1531000	974P	1653001-1654000	956P	1870301-1871500	914
1531001-1533000	992L	1654001-1657000	974P	1871501-1875100	910
1533001-600	974P	1657001-1660000	992L	1875101-600	914
1533601-1534000	956P	1660001-1661000	978L	1875601-1876500	910
1534001-100	975P	1661001-1663000	974P	1876501-1877500	914
1535101-200	975P	1663001-1664000	974L	1877501-1878700	910
1535201-600	975P	1664001-1665000	950L	1878701-1880000	914
1535601-1536000	993L	1665001-1666000	974P	1880001-300	920
1536001-1537000	972L	1666001-1667000	956P	1880301-1881500	900
1537001-1538000	992L	1667001-1669000	974P	1881501-700	920
1538001-800	956P	1669001-1670000	978L	1881701-900	900
1538801-1539000	974P	1670001-1671000	974P	1881901-1882900	920
1539001-1540000	992L	1671001-300	992L	1882901-1885000	900
1540001-500	992P	1671301-900	992P	1885001-1887400	910
1540501-1541000	992L	1671901-1672000	992L	1887401-1888600	914
1541001-1542200	974P	1672001-1676000	974P	1888601-1891000	910
1542201-800	956P	1676001-1678000	992L	1891001-1892200	914
1542801-1543000	974P	1678001-1679000	974P	1892201-1894600	910
1543001-1544000	996L	1679001-1681000	974L	1894601-1895800	914
1544001-1545000	992L	1681001-1682000	974P	1895801-1899000	910
1545001-400	978L	1682001-1683000	956P	1899001-300	900
1545401-1546000	974L	1683001-1685000	974P	1899301-1900000	920
1546001-1548000	992L	1685001-1686000	992L	1900001-400	910
1548001-600	974L	1686001-1688000	974P	1900401-1902100	914
1548601-1549000	972L	1688001-500	978L	1902101-1907000	910
1549001-1550000	974P	1689001-600	975P	1907001-1909000	914
1550001-500	972P	1690001-1691000	956	1909001-1910000	910
1550501-1552000	974P	1691001-1693000	992L	1910001-500	920
1552001-1555000	992L	1693001-1696000	956P	1910501-1911000	900
1555001-1557000	993P	1696001-1699000	992L	1911001-1913000	920
1557001-800	972L	1699001-1703000	974P	1913001-1914000	900
1557801-1558000	974L	1703001-1704000	992L	1914001-1920000	910
1558001-500	956	1704001-1705000	956P	1920001-1922000	920
1558501-1559700	956P	1705001-1706000	974P	1922001-1924000	910
1559701-1560000	974P	1706001-1707100	992L	1924001-1925000	900
1560001-1561000	975P	1708001-1714000	992L	1925001-1936000	910
1561001-1563000	992L	1714001-1715000	974P	1936001-1937000	920
1563001-1565000	978L	1715001-1717000	992L	1937001-900	900
1565001-1567000	992L	1717001-800	956	1940001-1941000	914
1567001-1568000	974L	1718001-1750000	992L	1941001-1944000	910
1568001-1569000	992L	1756001-1761000	900	1944001-1950000	914
1569001-1571000	972L	1761001-1765000	914	1950001-1962000	910
1571001-1572000	974P	1765001-1767000	920	1962001-1963000	914
1572001-1573000	975P	1767001-1768000	914	1963001-1975000	910
1573001-1575000	974P	1768001-1769000	900	1975001-1976000	914
1575001-400	950L	1769001-1770000	920	1976001-1980000	910
1575401-1576000	950P	1770001-1778200	914	1980001-1981000	914
1576001-1577000	950L	1778201-1779000	910	1981001-1988500	910
1577001-1578000	975P	1779001-1780000	920	1989001-400	914
1578001-1580000	992L	1780001-1782000	910	2000001-2001700	988
1580001-1581200	974L	1782001-500	920	2001701-2002400	986
1581201-1582000	956P	1782501-1783000	900	2002401-800	988
1582001-1583000	974P	1783001-1808000	910	2002801-2003100	986
1583001-1584000	992L	1808001-1810000	914	2004001-2035000	986
1584001-1585000	978L	1810001-1811000	910	2035001-2037200	981
1585001-1586000	972L	1811001-1813000	900	2040001-2064900	986
1586001-1587000	992L	1813001-1818000	910	2100001-2191300	986A
1587001-500	992P	1818001-1819000	914	2200001-2248000	987
1587501-1589000	992L	1819001-1821000	910	2248001-2300000	987F
1589001-500	956P	1821001-1822000	914	2300001-2311000	992L
1589501-1590000	974P	1822001-1827000	910	2311001-2312000	974L
1590001-1591000	974L	1827001-600	914	2312001-2321700	992L
1591001-1592000	992L	1827601-1829100	910	2321701-2323000	974L
1592001-1593000	974P	1829101-500	914	2323001-2326000	992L
1593001-1595000	992L	1829501-1830000	910	2326001-2327000	974P
1595001-200	974P	1830001-1831000	900	2327001-2333000	992L
1595201-900	956P	1831001-1832000	920	2333001-2336000	974P
1595901-1596000	974P	1832001-700	910	2336001-2338000	992L
1596001-1611000	992L	1832701-1833300	914	2338001-2339000	974P
1611001-1612100	974P	1833301-1834500	910	2339001-2340000	974L
1612101-1613000	956P	1834501-1835400	914	2340001-2341000	974P
1613001-600	996L	1835401-1836900	910	2341001-2346000	992L
1614001-900	956P	1836901-1837400	914	2346001-2347000	974P
1614901-1615000	974P	1837401-1839000	910	2347001-2356000	992L

No.	Grade
2356001-2358000	974P
2358001-2364000	992L
2364001-2365000	974P
2365001-2374000	992L
2374001-2375000	974P
2375001-2378000	992L
2378001-2380000	974L
2380001-2383000	992L
2383001-2384000	950L
2384001-2385000	992L
2385001-2396000	974P
2386001-2390000	992L
2390001-2391000	974P
2391001-2393000	992L
2393001-2395000	974P
2395001-2397000	992L
2397001-2398000	974L
2398001-2401000	992L
2401001-2402000	974P
2402001-2407000	992L
2407001-2409000	974P
2409001-2413000	992L
2413001-2414000	974P
2414001-2415000	974L
2415001-2418000	992L
2418001-2420000	974P
2420001-2422000	992L
2422001-2423000	974P
2423001-2432000	992L
2432001-2433000	974P
2433001-2434000	992L
2434001-2435000	974P
2435001-2437000	992L
2437001-2438000	974P
2438001-2442000	992L
2442001-2445000	974P
2445001-2451000	992L
2451001-2453000	974P
2453001-2455000	992L
2455001-2456000	974P
2456001-2457000	992L
2457001-2458000	950L
2458001-2459000	974L
2459001-2461000	992L
2461001-2462000	974L
2462001-2464000	992L
2464001-2466000	974P
2466001-2468000	992L
2468001-2469000	974P
2469001-2472000	992L
2472001-2473000	974P
2473001-2474000	992L
2474001-2475000	974P
2475001-2476000	992L
2476001-2477000	974P
2477001-2490000	992L
2490001-2492000	974L
2492001-2504000	992L
2504001-2505000	950L
2505001-300	950L
2506001-2526000	992L

No.	Grade
2526001-2528000	974P
2528001-2533000	992L
2533001-2534000	974P
2534001-2535000	992L
2535001-2536000	974P
2536001-2537000	974L
2537001-2538000	974P
2538001-2539000	974L
2539001-2542000	974P
2542001-2543000	992L
2543001-2545000	974P
2545001-2547000	992L
2547001-2548400	974P
2548401-2548600	974L
2548601-2548700	974P
2548701-2550000	974L
2550001-2551000	992L
2551001-2552000	974L
2552001-2555000	992L
2555001-2555600	974L
2555701-2558000	974L
2558001-2560000	992L
2560001-2561000	974L
2561001-2563000	992L
2563001-2564000	974L
2564001-2566000	992L
2566001-2566800	974L
2567001-2581000	992L
2581001-2583900	992E
2583901-2584300	992L
2584301-2596000	992E
2596001-2597000	974L
2597001-2608000	992E
2608001-2608800	974L
2609001-2611000	992E
2611001-2611400	950L
2611401-2613000	950E
2613001-2618000	992E
2618001-2619000	950E
2619001-2631000	992E
2631001-2631600	950E
2631801-2632000	950E
2632001-2639000	992E
2639001-2641000	950E
2641001-2649000	992E
2649001-2650600	950E
2651001-2655300	992E
2906001-2911500	979
2911601-2931900	979F
3000001-3002300	922
3002301-3002500	922M.P.
3002501-3003800	922
3003801-3004000	922M.P.
3004001-3006100	922
3006101-3006300	922M.P.
3006301-3008000	922
3008001-3008600	922M.P.
3008601-3010000	922
3010001-3010500	922
3010501-3010700	922M.P.
3010701-3011900	922

No.	Grade
3011901-3012500	922M.P.
3012501-3013100	922
3013101-3013700	922M.P.
3013701-3015700	922
3050001-3054800	902
3054801-3056000	922
3056001-3060800	902
3061001-3065100	904
3100001-3133800	916
3135001-3152700	918
3200001-3460900	912
4000001-4447201	987F
4447301-4523000	987E
A-001 to A-8450	980B
1B-001 to 1B-4000	999B
2B-001 to 2B-700	999B
2B-701 to 2B-800	950B
C-001 to C-169000	992B
E-001 to E-114000	989
E-114001 to E-140400	989E
F-101 to F-57600	995
F-57601 to F-59850	995A
F-59851 to F-62000	995
F-62001 to F-63000	995A
F-63001 to F-63800	995
F-63801 to F-286200	995A
G-001 to G-13600	980
G-13601 to G-14600	980 & 980A
G-14601 to G-44500	980
G-44501 to G-45000	980A
G-45001 to G-47400	980
G-47401 to G-48400	980A
G-48401 to G-55200	980
G-58201 to G-58700	980A
G-58701 to G-61600	980
G-61601 to G-62500	980A
G-62501 to G-67500	980
G-67501 to G-68600	980A
G-68601- to G-486000	980
H-001 to H-1000	921
H-1001 to H-1800	400 & 921
H-1801 to H-2000	921
H-2001 to H-2800	400 & 921
H-2801 to H-3500	400
H-3501 to H-30000	921
H-50001 to H-57500	401
J-001 to J-320000	982
M-001 to M-58000	982M
N-001 to N-223000	721
O-1 to 0408000	987A
R-001 to R-1400	923
S-001 to S-3400	950B
SS-001 to SS-71500	987S
T-001 to T-312000	911
V-001 to V-38000	911M
X-001 to X-125000	917

*Hamilton 36 size chronometer watch

*Haydn W. Wheeler model

NOTE: The above serial number and grade listing is an actual Hamilton factory list and is accurate in most cases. However, it has been brought to our attention that in rare cases the serial number and grade number do not match the list. One example is the Hayden W. Wheeler model.

(See Hamilton Watch Co. **Serial Numbers and Grades** section located at the end of the Hamilton Watch price section to identify the movement, size and grade of your watch.)

NOTE: Watches listed in this book are priced at the retail level, as complete watches having an original 14k gold-filled case, an original white enamel single sunk dial, and with the entire original movement in good working order with no repairs needed.

HAMILTON WATCH CO. (continued)

Grade 925, 18 size, 17 jewels, hunting case, serial number 101,495.

Grade 932, 18 size, 16 jewels, open face, serial number 6,888.

HAMILTON
18 SIZE

Grade or Name — Description	Avg	Ex-Fn	Mint
7J, OF, LS, FULL .... ★ ★	$800	$1,000	$1,300
11J, HC, LS, FULL .... ★ ★ ★	1,200	1,400	1,700
11J, OF, LS, FULL .... ★ ★ ★ ★	1,500	2,000	2,800
922, 15J, OF .... ★	375	450	575
923, 15J, HC .... ★	475	550	675
924, 17J, NI, OF, DMK	50	75	100
925, 17J, NI, HC, DMK	100	125	175
926, 17J, NI, OF, DMK, ADJ	50	75	100
927, 17J, NI, HC, DMK, ADJ........................	100	125	175
928, 15J, NI, OF..................................	125	150	200
929, 15J, NI, HC, 14K.............................	500	600	750
929, 15J, NI, HC	175	225	300
930, 16J, NI, OF..................................	150	200	275
931, 16J, NI, HC	200	250	325
932, 16J, NI, OF................................ ★ ★	400	450	525
932 *(S#s less than 400 up to $1,200)*			
933, 16J, NI, HC .... ★ ★	500	550	625
933 *(S#s less than 1,300 up to $1,400)*			
934, 17J, NI, OF, DMK, DR, Adj.5P	100	125	175
934, 17J, NI, OF, Adj.5P, Coin	75	100	150
935, 17J, NI, HC, DMK, DR, Adj.5P .... ★	250	300	375
936, 17J, NI, OF, DMK, DR	75	100	150
936 *(Early S#s less than 400 up to $1,200)*			
937, 17J, NI, HC, DMK, DR.........................	150	200	275
937 *(S#s less than 1,300 up to $1,200)*			

HAMILTON WATCH CO., 18 SIZE (continued)

Grade or Name—Description	Avg	Ex-Fn	Mint
938, 17J, NI, OF, DMK, DR . . . . ★ ★	$500	$600	$775
939, 17J, NI, HC, DMK, DR . . . . ★ ★	600	700	875
940, 21J, NI, OF, Mermod Jaccards St. Louis Paragon Time Keeper & an hour glass on mvt.	275	325	400
940, 21J, NI, OF, DMK, DR, Adj.5P, GJS	125	175	250
940, 21J, NI, OF, 2-Tone	150	200	275
940, 21J, NI, OF, Extra.	175	225	300
940, 21J, NI, OF, Coin	75	100	150
940, 21J, NI, OF, Special	175	225	300
941, 21J, NI, HC, GJS, Marked	125	175	250
941, 21J, NI, HC, GJS, Special	275	350	450
941, 21J, NI, HC, DMK, DR, Adj.5P, GJS	200	275	375
942, 21J, NI, OF, DMK, DR, Adj.5P, GJS	175	250	300
943, 21J, NI, HC, DMK, DR, Adj.5P, GJS . . . . ★	225	300	350
943, Burlington Special, 21J	550	650	800
944, 19J, NI, OF, DMK, DR, Adj.5P, GJS	150	200	275
945, 19J, GJS, 2-Tone, HC. . . . . ★ ★	1,000	1,200	1,500
946, Anderson (jobber name on movement), 14K	800	1,000	1,300
946, 23J, Extra, OF, GJS	500	550	625
946, 23J, "Loaner" on case	425	475	575
946, 23J, NI, OF, DMK, DR, Adj.5P, GJS	400	450	525
946, 23J, NI, OF, DMK, Adj.5P, GJS, unmarked	300	350	425
947, 23J, NI, HC, DMK, DR, Adj.5P, GJS, not marked "947" . . . . ★	3,500	4,000	5,000

Note: Some movements are marked with grade numbers, some are not. Add $25 to $75 for a marked movement. The first **hunting case** was a Model number 937 which begins with serial number 1001.

Grade 947 (marked), 18 size, 23 jewels, gold jewel settings, hunting case, Adj6p, serial number 163,219.

Burlington Special, 18 size, 21 jewels, Grade 943, open face, serial number 121,614.

NOTE: Watches listed in this book are priced at the retail level, as complete watches having an original 14k gold-filled case, an original white enamel single sunk dial, and with the entire original movement in good working order with no repairs needed, unless otherwise noted.

Grade or Name—Description	Avg	Ex-Fn	Mint
947, 23J, NI, HC, Adj.5P, GJS, marked "947" ..... ★ ★	$4,500	$5,500	$6,500
947, 23J, Extra, NI, GJS, marked 947, 14K, HC... ★ ★ ★	5,000	6,000	7,500
948, 17J, NI, OF, DMK, DR, Adj.5P, GJS .... ★	300	350	425
948, 17J, NI, DMK, DR, Adj.5P, GJS, OF, Coin...... ★	300	350	425
The Banner, 928, 15J, NI, OF	125	150	200
The Banner, 940, 21J, NI, OF	150	175	225
The Banner, 941, 21J, NI, HC......................	200	225	275
The Banner, 17J, M#927, HC, ADJ	125	150	200
Burlington Special, 17J, Adj.5P, OF..................	200	250	325
Burlington Special, 17J, Adj.5P, HC	250	300	375
Burlington Special, 21J, Adj.5P, OF..................	300	350	425
Burlington Special, 21J, Adj.5P, HC	350	400	475
Inspectors Standard, 21J, OF	300	350	475
The Union, 17J	125	150	200
The Union Special, 17J	125	150	200
The Union, 17J, G#925, HC........................	200	225	275

Grade 950, 16 size, 23 jewels, pendant set, gold train, gold jewel settings, serial number 1,020,650.

Grade 961, 16 size, 21 jewels, gold train, gold jewel settings, serial number 81,848.

16 SIZE

Grade or Name — Description	Avg	Ex-Fn	Mint
950, 23J, LS, DR, GT, 14K	$700	$775	$900
950, 23J, LS, DR, OF, BRG, GJS, Adj.5P, NI, GT......	325	375	450
950, 23J, PS, DR, OF, GJS, BRG, Adj.5P, NI, GT......	350	400	475
950B, 23J, LS, OF, Adj.5P, NI, DR, BRG..............	350	400	450
950E, 23J, LS, OF, Adj.5P, NI, DR, BRG..............	325	375	425
951, 23J, LS, Adj.5P, NI, GT, GJS, DR, HC ..... ★ ★ ★	2,800	3,400	4,000
951, 23J, PS, HC, Adj.5P, NI, GT, GJS, DR ..... ★ ★ ★	3,000	3,500	4,500
951, 23J, PS, HC, Adj.5P, NI, GT, GJS, DR, 14K ★ ★ ★	3,500	4,000	5,000
952, 19J, LS or PS, OF, BRG, Adj.5P, NI, GJS, DR	175	200	275
952, 19J, LS or PS, Adj.5P, OF, 14K	475	525	600
953, 19J, LS or PS, HC, GJS, GT .... ★ ★	2,000	2,500	3,000

Grade or Name — Description	Avg	Ex-Fn	Mint
954, 17J, LS or PS, OF, ¾, DR, Adj.5P	$75	$100	$150
956, 17J, PS, OF, ¾, DR, Adj.5P	75	100	150
960, 21J, PS, OF, BRG, GJS, GT, DR, Adj.5P .... ★	300	325	400
960, 21J, LS, OF, BRG, GJS, GT, DR, Adj.5P .... ★	325	350	425
961, 21J, PS & LS, HC, BRG, GJS, GT, DR, Adj.5P .. ★	400	450	500
962, 17J, PS, OF, BRG .... ★★	500	650	600
963, 17J, PS, HC, BRG .... ★★	550	600	700
964, 17J, PS, OF, BRG .... ★★	650	700	800
965, 17J, PS, HC, BRG .... ★★	500	550	650
966, 17J, PS, OF, ¾ .... ★★	600	650	750
967, 17J, PS, HC, ¾ .... ★★	625	675	775
968, 17J, PS, OF, ¾ .... ★	325	375	475
969, 17J, PS, HC, ¾ .... ★	425	450	500
970, 21J, PS, OF, ¾	150	175	225
971, 21J, PS, HC, ¾	175	200	250
972, 17J, PS & LS, OF, ¾, NI, GJS, DR, Adj.5P, DMK .	100	125	175
973, 17J, PS & LS, HC, ¾, NI, DR, Adj.5P	150	175	225
974, 17J, LS, OF, ¾, NI, Adj.3P	50	75	100
974, 17J, OF, PS, Adj.3P	50	75	100
974, 17J, OF, 2-tone	125	150	200
2974B, 17J, OF, Adj.3P	100	125	175
975, 17J, PS & LS, HC, ¾, NI, Adj.3P	75	100	150
976, 16J, PS, OF, ¾	150	175	225
977, 16J, PS, HC, ¾	150	175	225
978, 17J, LS, OF, ¾, NI, DMK	50	75	100
990, 21J, LS, OF, GJS, DR, Adj.5P, DMK, NI, ¾, GT ..	150	175	225
991, 21J, LS, HC, ¾, GJS, Adj.5P, DMK, NI, GT	175	200	250
992, 21J, OF, ¾, LS, GJS, Adj.5P, DR, NI, DMK	100	125	175
992, 21J, OF, ¾, PS & LS, GJS, Adj.5P, DR, NI, DMK, 2-Tone	150	175	225
992, 21J, Extra, OF, ¾, PS & LS, GJS, Adj.5P, DR, NI, DMK	150	175	225

Grade 992B, 16 size, 21 jewels, Adj5p.

Grade 4992B, 16 size, 22 jewels, Adj6p.

Grade 996, 16 size, 19 jewels, open face, gold jewel settings, serial number 152,060.

Hayden W. Wheeler, 16 size, 17 jewels, adjusted to heat & cold, serial number 76,029.

Grade or Name—Description	Avg	Ex-Fn	Mint
992, 21J, ¾, PS, GJS, Adj.5P, OF	$100	$150	$200
992, 21J, Elinvar, ¾, GJS, Adj.5P....................	150	175	200
992, 21J, Special, OF, ¾, PS & LS, GJS, Adj.5P, DR, NI, DMK, 'Adj. for RR Service' on dial................	350	400	500
992B, 21J, 2-Tone...................................	200	250	300
992B, 21J, LS, OF, ¾	150	175	225
992B, 21J, OF, ¾, silver case	75	100	175
3992B, 22J, Adj.6P, 12 hr. dial ....★	150	200	275
4992B, 22J, LS, OF, ¾, Adj.6P, 24-hour dial, Greenwich Civil Time..	125	150	200
993, 21J, PS, HC, GJS, Adj.5P, DR, NI, DMK	200	225	275
993, 21J, LS, HC, GJS, Adj.5P, DMK, DR, NI	175	200	250
993, 21J, LS, HC, GJS, Adj.5P, DMK, DR, NI, 14K	550	600	700

Grade 994, 16 size, 21 jewels, pendent set, gold train, gold jewel settings, serial number 1,153,431.

Chronograph, Grade 23, 16 size, 19 jewels, start-stop-reset to 0.

HAMILTON WATCH CO., 16 SIZE (continued)

Grade or Name—Description	Avg	Ex-Fn	Mint
993, 21J, LS, HC, GJS, Adj.5P, DMK, DR, NI, GF multi-color case	$275	$325	$400
994, 21J, BRG, OF, GJS, GT, DR, Adj.5P, DMK, PS . ★	600	750	900
994, 21J, BRG, OF, GJS, GT, DR, Adj.5P, DMK, LS . ★	700	850	950
995, 19J, GJS, BRG, HC ....★ ★	900	1,000	1,200
996, 19J, LS, OF, ¾, GJS, DR, Adj.5P, DMK..........	125	150	200
DeLong Escapement, 21J, 992-B ....★ ★ ★	1,000	1,100	1,300
Electric Interurban, 17J, G#974, OF	50	75	100
Official Standard, 17J, OF	175	200	275
Union Special, 17J	100	125	200
Hayden W. Wheeler, 17J, OF ....★	400	500	650
Hayden W. Wheeler, 17J, HC ....★	450	550	700
Hayden W. Wheeler, 21J...........................★	600	700	850
Hayden W. Wheeler, 21J, 14K H.W.W. case	1,000	1,100	1,300
Swiss Mfg., 17J, Adj.2P, GF case.....................	85	100	145

CHRONOGRAPH
Grade 23

Grade or Name — Description	Avg	Ex-Fn	Mint
16S, 19J, start-stop-reset to 0	$175	$200	$300

12 SIZE

(Some cases were octagon, decagon, cushion, etc.)

Grade or Name — Description	Avg	Ex-Fn	Mint
900, 19J, BRG, DR, Adj.5P, GJS, OF, 14K.............	$275	$300	$375
900, 19J, BRG, DR, Adj.5P, GJS, OF	75	100	175
902, 19J, BRG, DR, Adj.5P, GJS.....................	100	125	200

Grade 918, 12 size, 19 jewels, Adj3p, serial number 3,136,257.

Grade 920, 12 size, 23 jewels, gold train, gold jewel settings, serial number 1,863,381.

Grade or Name—Description	Avg	Ex-Fn	Mint
902, 19J, BRG, DR, Adj.5P, GJS, 14K	$300	$325	$375
904, 21J, BRG, DR, Adj.5P, GJS, GT	100	125	175
910, 17J, ¾, DR, ADJ	40	50	70
912, 17J, Digital model, rotating seconds, OF	50	60	80
912, 17J, ¾, DR, ADJ	40	50	70
914, 17J, ¾, DR, Adj.3P, GJS	40	50	70
914, 17J, ¾, DR, Adj.3P, GJS, 14K	225	250	300
916, 17J, ¾, DR, Adj.3P	40	50	70
916, 17J, Adj.3P, silver case.........................	30	40	60
918, 19J, Adj.3P, WGF.............................	75	100	150
918, 19J, ¾, DR, Adj.3P, GJS, OF	75	100	150
920, 23J, BRG, DR, Adj.5P, GJS, GT, OF	200	250	325
920, 23J, BRG, DR, Adj.5P, GJS, GT, 14K.............	400	450	525
922, 23J, BRG, DR, Adj.5P, GJS, GT, 14K.............	400	450	525
922, 23J, BRG, DR, Adj.5P, GJS, GT, OF	200	250	325
922 MP, 18K case	800	900	1,100
922 MP, GF, Hamilton case..........................	300	400	550
400, 21J, ¾, ADJ.................................★	300	400	550

Grade 922MP, 12 size, 23 jewels, serial number 3,013,390, c. 1930.

Grade 912, 12 size, 17 jewels, with Secometer dial, originally sold for $88.70.

10 SIZE

Grade or Name — Description	Avg	Ex-Fn	Mint
917, 17J, ¾, DR, Adj.3P	$40	$50	$70
917, 17J, ¾, DR, Adj.3P, 14K	200	225	300
921, 21J, BRG, DR, Adj.5P..........................	60	70	90
923, 23J, BRG, DR, Adj.5P..........................	150	175	250
923, 23J, M.P.G.F..................................	275	300	375
923, 23J, M.P., 18K, and box	600	700	900
945, 23J, Adj.5P	125	150	225

HAMILTON WATCH CO. (continued)

Example of Hamilton's thin model, 12-10 size, in a decagon case, 14k gold filled, originally sold for $52.00.

Grade 983HC, 982OF, 0 size, 17 jewels, gold jewel settings.

0 SIZE

Grade or Name — Description	Avg	Ex-Fn	Mint
981, 17J, ¾, Adj.3P, DR, 18K, HC	$275	$300	$350
983, 17J, Adj.3P, DR, GJS, 18K, HC	275	300	350
985, 19J, BRG, Adj.3P, DR, GJS, GT, 18K, HC	300	325	375
Lady Hamilton, 14K case, OF	200	225	300

Top: **Pocket Chronometer**, 36 size, 21 jewels, gold jewel settings, Adj5p, serial number 1,260,382.

Right: **Chronometer** in gimbles and box, 35 size, wind indicator.

CHRONOMETER

Grade or Name — Description	Avg	Ex-Fn	Mint
35S, M#22, 21J, Wind Indicator, Adj.6P, in gimbles and box, lever	$350	$400	$500
35S, M#22, 21J, Wind Indicator, Adj.6P, in a large base metal OF case	275	300	400
36S, M#36, 21J, Wind Indicator, in gimbles and box	1,000	1,200	1,400
36S, M#36, 21J, Wind Indicator, in Hamilton sterling pocket watch case with bow	1,200	1,400	1,700
85S, M#21, 14J, KW, KS, Fusee, Detent Escapement with boxes	1,300	1,500	1,800

How to Identify Your Watch: Compare the movement with the illustrations in this section. While comparing, note the location of the balance, jewels, screws, gears, and back plate (Full, ¼, Bridge) which will be clues in identifying the movement you have. Having determined the size, the Grade can also be found by looking up the serial number of your watch in the Hamilton Serial Number and Grades list.

Grade 936, 18 size

Open face, 17 jewels, single roller before No. 426,001, double roller after No. 426,000.

Grade 925, 18 size

Hunting, 17 jewels, single roller

Grade 971, 16 size

Hunting, 21 jewels, ¼ plate movt.

Grade 992, 16 size

Open face, ¼ plate movt., 21 jewels, single roller before No. 377,001, double roller after No. 379,000.

Grade 992B, 16 size
Open face, ¾ plate movt., 21 jewels, double roller

Grade 950, 16 size
Open face, bridge movt., 23 jewels, double roller

Grade 950B, 16 size
Open face, bridge movt., 23 jewels, double roller

Grade 902, 12 size
Open face, bridge movt., 19 jewels, double roller

Grade 912, 12 size
Open face, ¾ plate movt., 17 jewels, double roller

Grade 918, 12 size
Open face, ¾ plate movt., 19 jewels, double roller

HAMILTON WATCH CO. (continued)

Grade 922, 12 size
Open face, bridge movt., 23 jewels, double roller

Grade 917, 10 size
Open face, ¾ plate movt., 17 jewels, double roller

Grade 921, 10 size
Open face, bridge movt., 21 jewels, double roller

Grade 923, 10 size
Open face, bridge movt., 23 jewels, double roller

Grade 983, 0 size
Hunting, bridge movt., 17 jewels, double roller

Grade 979,6/0 size
Hunting, ¾ plate movt., 19 jewels, double roller

Grade 986, 6/0 size
Open face, ¾ plate movt., 17 jewels, double roller

HAMPDEN WATCH CO.
(DUEBER WATCH CO.)
Springfield, Massachusetts
Canton, Ohio
1876 - 1930

The New York Watch Co. preceded Hampden, and before that Don J. Mozart (1864) produced his three-wheel watch. Mozart was assisted by George Samuel Rice of New York and, as a result of their joint efforts, the New York Watch Co. was formed in 1866 in Providence, Rhode Island. It was moved in 1867 to Springfield, Massachusetts. Two grades of watches were decided on, and the company started with a 18S, ¾ plate engraved "Springfield." They were sold for $60 to $75. The 18S, ¾ plate were standard production, and the highest grade was a "George Walker" that sold for about $200 and a 16S, ¾ plate "State Street" which had steel parts and exposed balance and escape wheels that were gold plated.

John C. Dueber started manufacturing watch cases in 1864 and bought a controlling interest in a company in 1886. At about this time a disagreement arose between Elgin, Waltham, and the Illinois Watch companies. Also, at this time, an anti-trust law was passed, and the watch case manufacturers formed a boycott against Dueber. Dueber was faced with a major decision, whether to stay in business, surrender to the watch case companies or buy a watch company. He decided to buy the Hampden Watch Co. of Springfield, Mass. By 1889 the operation had moved to Canton, Ohio. By the end of the year the company was turning out 600 watches a day. The first 16 size watch was produced in 1890. In 1894 Hampden introduced the first 23J movement made in America.

HAMPDEN ESTIMATED SERIAL NUMBER
AND PRODUCTION DATES

Date	Serial No.	Date	Serial No.	Date	Serial No.
1877	60,000	1893	775,000	1909	2,536,000
1878	91,000	1894	833,000	1910	2,664,000
1879	122,000	1895	888,500	1911	2,792,000
1880	153,000	1896	944,000	1912	2,920,000
1881	184,000	1897	1,000,000	1913	3,048,000
1882	215,000	1898	1,128,000	1914	3,176,000
1883	250,000	1899	1,256,000	1915	3,304,000
1884	300,000	1900	1,384,000	1916	3,432,000
1885	350,000	1901	1,512,000	1917	3,560,000
1886	400,000	1902	1,642,000	1918	3,680,000
1887	450,000	1903	1,768,000	1919	3,816,000
1888	500,000	1904	1,896,000	1920	3,944,000
1889	555,500	1905	2,024,000	1921	4,072,000
1890	611,000	1906	2,152,000	1922	4,200,000
1891	666,500	1907	2,280,000	1923	4,400,000
1892	722,000	1908	2,408,000	1924	4,600,000

Chronology of the Development of Hampden Watch Co.:
The Mozart Watch Co., Providence, R. I. — 1864-1866
New York Watch Co., Providence, R. I. — 1866-1867
New York Watch Co., Springfield, Mass. — 1867-1875
New York Watch Mfg. Co., Springfield, Mass. — 1875-1876
Hampden Watch Co., Springfield, Mass. — 1877-1886
Hampden-Dueber Watch Co., Springfield, Mass. — 1886-1888

 Issued 1890

 Issued 1892

HAMPDEN WATCH CO. (continued)

Hampden Watch Co., Canton, Ohio — 1888-1923
Dueber Watch Co., Canton, Ohio — 1888-1923
Dueber-Hampden Watch Co., Canton, Ohio — 1923-1931
Amtorg, U.S.S.R. — 1930-Present

Issued 1895

Dueber Watch Co., 18 size, 15 jewels, nickel movement. Model 3, hunting case.

Dueber Grand, 18 size, 17 jewels, open face, originally sold for $20.00.

HAMPDEN
18 SIZE

Grade or Name — Description	Avg	Ex-Fn	Mint
Anchor, 17J, ADJ, GJS, DMK, OF	$75	$100	$150
"3" Ball, 17J, ADJ, NI, DMK, OF	100	125	175
Champion, 7J, ADJ, FULL, gilded, NI, OF............	50	75	125
Correct Time, 15J, HC	125	150	200
Dueber, 16J, gilded, DMK, OF	75	100	150
Dueber, 17J, gilded, DMK, OF	75	100	150
John C. Dueber, 15J, gilded, DMK, OF	75	100	150
John C. Dueber, 17J, gilded, ADJ, DMK, OF...........	75	100	150
John C. Dueber, Sp., 17J, gilded, ADJ, DMK, OF	75	100	150
John C. Dueber, 17J, HC	100	125	175
Dueber Grand, 17J, OF	75	100	150
Dueber Grand, 17J, ADJ, HC	100	125	175
Dueber Grand, 21J, ADJ, DMK, NI, HC	150	175	225
Dueber W. Co., 11J, OF	75	100	150
Dueber W. Co., 15J, DMK, OF	75	100	150
Dueber W. Co., 16J	750	100	150
Dueber W. Co., 17J, DMK, ADJ, OF	75	100	150
Dueber W. Co., 17J, Gilded	75	100	150
Dueber W. Co., 17J, DMK, ADJ, HC.................	100	125	175
Dueber W. Co., 19J, ADJ, GJS, HC ....★	400	475	550
Dueber W. Co., 21J, Adj.5P, GJS, OF	100	125	175

John C. Dueber Special, 18 size, 17 jewels, serial number 949,097.

Oriental, 18 size, 15 jewels, open face, serial number 117,825.

Grade or Name—Description	Avg	Ex-Fn	Mint
Dueber W. Co., 21J, GJS, Adj.5P, HC	$150	$175	$225
Homer Foot, gilded, KW, OF (Early)	150	175	225
Gladiator, KW, OF	75	100	150
Gladiator, 11J, NI, DMK, OF	75	100	150
Gulf Stream Sp., 21J, OF, LS	200	250	325
Hampden W. Co., 7J, KW, KS, OF	75	100	150
Hampden W. Co., 7J, SW, OF	50	75	100
Hampden W. Co., 11J, OF, KW	75	100	150
Hampden W. Co., 11J, HC, KW	100	125	175
Hampden W. Co., 11J, OF, SW	75	100	150
Hampden W. Co., 15J, OF, KW	100	125	175
Hampden W. Co., 15J, OF, KW	75	100	150
Hampden W. Co. 15J, HC, KW	100	125	175
Hampden W. Co., 15J, HC, SW	100	125	175
Hampden W. Co., 15J, SW, Gilded, OF	75	100	150
Hampden W. Co., 15J, SW, NI, OF	75	100	150
Hampden W. Co., 15J, Multi-color, 14K, HC	1,600	1,800	2,200
Hampden W. Co., 16J, OF	75	100	150
Hampden W. Co., 17J, SW, Gilded	75	100	150
Hampden W. Co., 17J, SW, NI, OF	75	100	150
Hampden W. Co., 17J, HC, SW	100	125	175
Hampden W. Co., 17J, LS, HC, 14K	500	550	625
Hampden W. Co., 17J, LS, HC, 10K	350	400	475
Hampden W. Co., 21J, OF, HC, SW	150	125	225
John Hancock, 17J, GJS, Adj.3P, OF	75	100	150
John Hancock, 21J, GJS, Adj.3P, OF	125	150	200
John Hancock, 23J, GJS, Adj.5P, OF	200	250	325
Hayward, 15J, KW	100	125	200
Hayward, 11J, SW	75	100	150

Menlo Park, 18 size, 17 jewels, serial number 1,184,116.

New Railway, 18 size, 23 jewels, open face only, gold jewel settings, originally sold for $50.00, Model 2.

Grade or Name—Description	Avg	Ex-Fn	Mint
Lafayette, 11J, NI	$100	$125	$175
Lafayette, 15J, NI, KW	125	150	200
Lafayette, 15J, NI	100	125	175
Lakeside, 15J, NI, SW	100	125	175
M. J. & Co. Railroad Watch Co., 15J, HC	300	400	525
Menlo Park, 17J, NI, ADJ, OF	100	125	175
Mermod, Jaccard & Co., 15J, KW, HC	125	150	200
Metropolis, 15J, NI, SW, OF	75	100	150
Wm. McKinley, 17J, Adj.3P, OF	75	100	150
Wm. McKinley, 21J, GJS, Adj.5P	125	150	200
New Railway, 17J, GJS, Adj.5P, OF	75	100	150
New Railway, 19J, GJS, Adj.5P, OF	150	175	225
New Railway, 19J, GJS, Adj.5P, HC	150	175	225

Railway, 18 size, 17 jewels, key wind & set; early railroad watch.

Special Railway, 18 size, 23 jewels, Adj5p, serial number 3,357,284.

Grade or Name—Description	Avg	Ex-Fn	Mint
New Railway, 21J, GJS, Adj.5P, HC	$125	$150	$200
New Railway, 21J, GJS, Adj.5P, OF	100	125	175
New Railway, 23J, GJS, Adj.5P	175	225	300
New Railway, 23J, GJS, Adj.5P, 14K, OF	550	575	625
North Am. RR, 21J, GJS, Adj.5P, OF, LS	125	150	200
North Am. RR, 21J, GJS, Adj.3P, HC, PS	150	175	225
Pennsylvania Special, 17J, GJS, Adj.5P, DR, NI .... ★ ★	700	900	1,200
J. C. Perry, 15J, KW, gilded, HC	125	150	200
J. C. Perry, 15J, NI, SW, OF	70	80	95
J. C. Perry, 15J, gilded, SW, OF	75	100	150
Railway, 15J, gilded, OF	75	100	150
Railway, 17J, NI, OF	75	100	150
Railway, 15J, KW, marked on mvt., HC............ ★ ★	600	700	850
Railroad with R.R. names on dial and movement:			
Canadian Pacific RR, 17J, OF.................. ★	275	300	400
Canadian Pacific RR, 21J, OF.................. ★	375	400	500
Special Railway, 17J, GJS, Adj.5P, NI, DR, OF.........	75	100	150
Special Railway, 21J, GJS, Adj.5P, NI, DR, 2-Tone, OF .	125	150	200
Special Railway, 23J, GJS, Adj.5P, NI, DR, 2-Tone, OF .	200	275	375
Special Railway, 23J, Adj.5P, HC	225	300	400
Special Railway, 23J, 14K, HC	625	675	750
Springfield, 7-11J, KW, gilded, HC	100	125	175
Springfield, 7-11J, SW, NI, HC	100	125	175
Standard, 15J, gilded, HC	100	125	175
State Street, 15J, NI, LS, (Early KW)	150	175	225
Theo. Studley, 15J, KW, KS, HC	125	150	200
Tramway Special, 17J, NI	125	150	200
Woolworth, 11J, KW	100	125	175
Grade 45 HC & 65 OF, 11J	75	100	150
Grade 60, 15J, LS, OF	75	100	150
Grade 80 & 81, 17J, ADJ, OF	75	100	150
Grade 85, 19J, GJS, 2-Tone, HC .... ★ ★	500	600	750
Grade 95, 21J, GJS, OF	100	125	175
Grade 125, 21J, Adj.3P, OF	125	150	200

16 SIZE

Grade or Name — Description	Avg	Ex-Fn	Mint
Champion, 7J, NI, ¾, gilded, coin, OF	$50	$75	$125
Champion, 7J, NI, ¾, gilded, OF	50	75	100
Champion, 7J, NI, ¾, gilded, HC	100	125	175
Chronometer, 21J, NI, Adj.3P, GJS	150	175	225
John C. Dueber, 17J, GJS, NI, Adj.5P, ¾	75	100	150
John C. Dueber, 21J, GJS, NI, Adj.5P, ¾	100	125	175
John C. Dueber, 21J, GJS, NI, Adj.5P, DR, BRG	125	150	200
Dueber Watch Co., 17J, ADJ, ¾	75	100	150

HAMPDEN WATCH CO., 16 SIZE (continued)

Hampden W. Co., Bridge Model, 16 size, 23 jewels, 2-tone movement, serial number 1,899,430.

Hampden W. Co., 16 size, 17 jewels, gold jewel settings, serial number 3,075,235.

Grade or Name—Description	Avg	Ex-Fn	Mint
Hampden W. Co., 7J, SW, OF	$50	$75	$125
Hampden W. Co., 7J, SW, HC	75	100	150
Hampden W. Co., 11J, SW, OF	50	75	125
Hampden W. Co., 11J, SW, HC	75	100	150
Hampden W. Co., 15J, SW, OF	50	75	125
Hampden W. Co., 15J, SW, HC	75	100	150
Hampden W. Co., 17J, SW, OF	50	75	125
Hampden W. Co., 17J, 14K, Multi-color, HC	1,200	1,300	1,600
Hampden W. Co., 17J, SW, HC	75	100	150
Hampden W. Co., 21J, SW, HC	125	150	200
Hampden W. Co., 21J, SW, OF	100	125	175
Hampden W. Co., 23J, Adj.5P, GJS, ¾	200	225	300
Hampden W. Co., 23J, Series 2, HC "Freesprung", GJS, GT ★★	375	450	550
Masonic Dial, 23J, GJS, 2-Tone porcelain dial	350	400	500

Hampden W. Co., Series I, 16 size, 15 jewels, stem wind, open face.

Railway, 16 size, 17 jewels, Adj5p, serial number 2,271,866.

Grade 104, 16 size, 23 jewels, gold jewel settings, gold train, Adj5p, serial number 2,801,184.

Grade 108, 16 size, 17 jewels, open face and hunting, serial number 1,042,051.

Grade or Name—Description	Avg	Ex-Fn	Mint
Wm. McKinley, 17J, GJS, Adj.5P, NI, DR, ¾	$75	$100	$150
Wm. McKinley, 21J, GJS, Adj.5P, NI, DR, ¾	100	125	175
Wm. McKinley, 21J, GJS, Adj.5P, NI, DR, ¾, Coin	75	100	150
Wm. McKinley, 21J, GJS, Adj.5P, NI, DR, BRG........	100	125	175
New Railway, 21J, GJS, Adj.5P	100	125	175
New Railway, 23J, GJS, Adj.5P, LS, HC	250	300	375
Ohioan, 21J, Adj.3P, GJS, ¾	150	175	225
Railway, 19J, GJS, Adj.5P, BRG, DR.................	125	150	175
Special Railway, 23J, Adj.5P, NI, BRG, DR	225	275	350
Gen'l Stark, 15J, DMK, BRG	75	100	150
Gen'l Stark, 17J, DMK, BRG	75	100	150
95, 21J, marked "95", GJS	125	150	175
97 HC, 98 HC, & 108 OF, 17J, Adj.3P, NI, ¾, DMK ...	75	100	150
99, 15J, ¾, HC.....................................	100	125	175
103, 21J, GJS, Adj.5P, NI, BRG, DR	100	125	175
104, 23J, GJS, Adj.5P, NI, BRG, DR, DMK...........	225	275	350
105, 21J, GJS, Adj.5P, NI, ¾, DR, DMK	100	125	175
106, 107 OF, & 108, 17J, SW, NI	75	100	150
109, 15J, ¾, OF	75	100	150
110, 11J, ¾	75	100	150
115-120, 21J, SW, NI, OF...........................	100	125	175
340, 17J, SW, NI	75	100	150
440, 15J, 2-tone...................................	100	125	175
555, 21J, GT, GJS, Chronometer on dial & mvt.	200	250	325
600, 17J, SW, NI	75	100	150

12 SIZE

Grade or Name — Description	Avg	Ex-Fn	Mint
Champion, 7J, SW	$40	$50	$75

HAMPDEN WATCH CO., 12 SIZE (continued)

Dueber Grand, 12 size, 17 jewels, gold jewel settings, hunting case, serial number 1,737,354.

Dueber Grand, 12 size, 17 jewels, gold jewel settings, open face, pin set, serial number 1,732,255.

Grade or Name—Description	Avg	Ex-Fn	Mint
Dueber Grand, 17J, BRG	$40	$50	$75
Hampden W. Co., 7J, SW, OF	40	50	75
Hampden W. Co., 17J, 14K, Multi-color, HC	700	800	1,000
John Hancock, 21J, BRG	55	65	85
Gen'l Stark, 15J, BRG	40	50	75
Gen'l Stark, 15J, pin set	40	50	75
207-300 HC & 302 OF, 7J, ¾ (add $25 for HC)	40	50	75
304 HC & 306 OF, 15J, ¾ (add $25 for HC)	40	50	75
305-308 HC & 310 OF, 17J, ¾	40	50	75
307, 17J	40	50	75
312 HC & 314 OF, 21J, ¾, Adj.5P (add $25 for HC)	50	75	125
31 OF, 17J, SW, 14K	275	325	400

Paul Revere. Example of Hampden Watch Co.'s thin series showing face and movement, 12 size, 17-19 jewels, Adj5p.

12 SIZE (THIN MODEL)

Grade or Name — Description	Avg	Ex-Fn	Mint
Aviator, 17J, Adj.4P	$40	$50	$75
Aviator, 19J, Adj.4P	40	50	75
Beacon, 17J	40	50	75
Nathan Hale, 15J	40	50	75
Minuteman, 17J	50	60	85
Paul Revere, 17J, 14K, OF	275	325	400
Paul Revere, 17J	50	60	85
Paul Revere, 19J	60	70	95

Note: Some 12 Sizes came in cases of octagon, decagon, hexagon, triad, and cushion shapes, and these usually bring slightly higher prices.

6 SIZE

Grade or Name — Description	Avg	Ex-Fn	Mint
200, 7J (add $25 for HC)	$40	$50	$75
206, 11J (add $25 for HC)	40	50	75
213, 15J (add $25 for HC)	40	50	75
220, 17J (add $25 for HC)	40	50	75
Hampden W. Co., 15J, multi-color GF, HC	150	200	275
Hampden W. Co., 15J, Multi-color, 14K, HC	375	425	500

Top left: **Molly Stark**, 000 size, 7 jewels, hunting or open face, originally sold for $12.00.

Bottom left: **Four Hundred Series**, 000 sizes, 11, 15 & 16 jewels, gold jewel settings, originally sold for from $20.25.

000 SIZE

Grade or Name — Description	Avg	Ex-Fn	Mint
Diadem, 15J, 14K, OF Case	$100	$150	$200

HAMPDEN WATCH CO., 000 SIZE (continued)

Grade or Name—Description	Avg	Ex-Fn	Mint
Diadem, 15J, HC, 14K	$200	$250	$325
Diadem, 15J, HC	100	125	175
Molly Stark, 7J, HC................................	100	125	175
Molly Stark, 7J, 14K, HC..........................	200	250	325
Molly Stark, 7J, Pin Set, OF	50	75	125
Four Hundred, 11, 15, 16, & 17J, HC	100	125	175
14K Multi-color, HC	375	425	500

HAMPDEN WATCH CO.
IDENTIFICATION OF MOVEMENTS

How to Identify Your Watch: Compare the movement of your watch with the illustrations in this section. While comparing, note the location of the balance, jewels, screws, gears, and type of back plate (Full, ¾, Bridge) which will be clues in identifying the movement you have.

Series I, 18 size
Hunting or open face, key wind & set

Series II, 18 size
Hunting, stem wind, pendant or lever set

Series III, 18 size
Hunting, stem wind, pendant or lever set

Series IV, 18 size
Open face, stem wind, lever set

245

Series 1, 16 size
Open face, stem wind, pendant or lever set

Series II, 16 size
Hunting, stem wind, pendant or lever set

Series III, 16 size
Open face, stem wind, pendant set

Series IV, 16 size
Hunting, stem wind, pendant or lever set

Series V, 16 size
Open face, stem wind, pendant or lever set

Series VI, 16 size
Hunting, stem wind, pendant set

Series VII, 16 size
Open face, stem wind, pendant set

Series III, 12 size
Open face, stem wind, pendant set

Series I, 12 size
Hunting, stem wind, lever set

Series II, 12 size
Open face, stem wind, lever set

Series IV, 12 size
Open face, stem wind, pendant

Series V, 12 size
Open face, stem wind, pendant
set

Series I, 6 size
Open face, stem wind

Series I, 3/0 size
Hunting, stem wind

Series II, 3/0 size
Open face, stem wind, pendant
set

Series III, 3/0 size
Hunting, lever or pendant set

Series IV, 3/0 size
Hunting, stem wind, pendant
or lever set

HERMAN VON DER HEYDT
Chicago, Illinois
1883

Herman von der Heydt patented a self-winding watch on Feb. 19, 1884. A total of 35 watches were hand-made by von der Heydt. The watches were 18S, full plate, lever escapement and fully-jeweled. The wind mechanism was a gravity type made of heavy steel and shaped like a crescent. The body motion let the heavy crescent move which was connected to a ratchet on the winding arbor, resulting in self-winding. Five movements were nickel and sold for about $90; the gilded model sold for about $75.

Grade or Name — Description		Avg	Ex-Fn	Mint
18S, 19J, FULL, NI . . . . ★ ★ ★		$4,500	$5,000	$6,500
18S, 19J, FULL, gilded . . . . ★ ★ ★		3,000	3,500	4,000

Example of **Herman Von Der Heydt** patented self winding watch, 18 size, 19 jewels, crescent shaped winding weight.

E. HOWARD & CO.
Boston (Roxbury), Massachusetts
December 11, 1858 - 1903

After the failure of the Boston Watch Company (1853-57), Edward Howard decided to personally attempt the successful production of watches using the interchangeable machine-made parts system. He and Charles Rice, his financial backer, were unable to buy out the defunct watch company in Waltham, however, they did remove (per a prior claim) the watches in progress, the tools and the machinery to Howard and Davis' Roxbury factory (first watch factory in America), in late 1857. During their first year, the machinery was retooled for the production of a revolutionary new watch of Howard's design. Also, the remaining Boston Watch Co. movements were completed (E. Howard & Co. dials, Howard & Rice on the movement). By the summer of 1858, Edward Howard had produced his first watch. On December 11, 1858 the firm of E. Howard & Co. was formed for the manufacture of high-grade watches. Howard's first model was entirely different from any watch previously made. It introduced the more accurate "quick beat" train to American watchmaking. The top plate was in two sections and had six pillars instead of the usual four pillars in a full plate. The balance was gold or steel at first, then later it was a compensation balance loaded with gold screws. Reed's patented barrel was used for the first time. The size, based on the Dennison system, was a little larger than the regular 18 size. In 1861, a ¾ plate model was put on the market. Most movements were being stamped with "N" to designate Howard's 18 size. On February 4, 1868 Howard patented a new steel motor barrel which was to supersede the Reed's, but not before some 28,000 had been produced. Also, in 1868 Howard introduced the stemwinding movement and was probably the first company to market such a watch in the U. S. By 1869, Howard was producing their "L" or 16 size as well as their first nickel movements. In 1870, G. P. Reed's micrometer regulator was patented for use by E. Howard & Co. The Reed style "whiplash" regulator has been used in more pocket watches, worldwide, than any other type. In 1878, the manufacturing of keywind movements was discontinued. Mr. Howard retired in 1882, but the company continued to produce watch movements of the grade and style set by him until 1903. This company was the first to adjust to all six positions. Their dials were always a hard enamel and always bore the name "E. Howard & Co., Boston." In 1903, the company transferred all rights to use the name "Edward Howard," in conjunction with the production of watches, to the Keystone Watch Case Co. Most of their models were stamped "Howard" on the dial and "E. Howard Watch Co., Boston. U.S.A." on the movement. Edward Howard's company never produced its own watch cases, the great majority of which were solid gold or silver. Keystone, however, produced complete watches, many of which were gold filled.

CHRONOLOGICAL DEVELOPMENT OF E. HOWARD & CO.:
Howard, Davis & Dennison, Roxbury, Mass., 1850
American Horologue Company, Roxbury, Mass., 1851
Warren Manufacturing Company, Roxbury, Mass., 1851-53
Boston Watch Co., Roxbury, Mass. — 1853-1854/Waltham, Mass., 1854-57
Howard & Rice, Roxbury, Mass., 1857-58 (E. Howard & Co. on dials)
E. Howard & Co., Roxbury, Mass. — 1858-1903
Keystone Watch Case Co. (Howard line), Jersey City, N. J., 1903-30

E. HOWARD & CO.
15 JEWELS
APPROXIMATE DATES, SERIAL NOS., AND TOTAL PRODUCTION

Serial Number	Date	Series	Total Prod.
131-1,800	-1860	I (18S)	1,800
1,801-3,000	1860-1861	II (18S)	1,200
3,001-3,200	1861	K(14S)	100
3,201-3,400	1861	i(10S)	100
3,501-28,000	1861-1871	III (18S)	24,500
30,001-50,000	1868-1882	IV (18S)	20,000
50,001-71,000	1869-1899	V (16S)	21,000
100,001-105,500	1869-1899	VI (6S)	5,500
200,001-227,000	1880-1899	VII (18S)	27,000
*228,001-231,000	1895	VII (18S)	3,000
300,001-309,000	1884-1899	VIII (18S)	9,000
*309,001-310,000	1895	VIII (18S)	1,000
400,001-405,000	1890-1895	IX (18S)	5,000
500,001-501,500	1890-1899	X (12S)	1,500
*600,001-601,500	1896	XI (16S)	1,500
*700,001-701,500	1896	XII (16S)	1,500
Approx.			
Total Production			**123,700**

* ¼ Split Plates with 17 Jewels

E. HOWARD & CO. WATCH SIZES

Letter	Inches	Approx. Size
N	1 13/16	18
L	1 11/16	16
K	1 10/16	14
J	1 9/16	12
I	1 8/16	10
H	1 7/16	8
G	1 6/16	6
F	1 5/16	4
E	1 4/16	2
D	1 3/16	0

Standard Escapement

Deer	Horse	Hound
Adjusted to	Adjusted to	Unadjusted
HcI6P	HCI-No	
	positions	

Coles Escapement

The above symbols appear on some E. Howard & Co. models and refer to the grade and adjustments. On some of the earlier movements, "adjusted," and "heat and cold" appear on the balance bridge rather than the above symbols. "Adjusted" refers to isochronism, heat and cold, and positions. "Heat and cold" refers to adjustment to temperature and isochronism. The plain movement with no symbols or wording on the bridge are adjusted only to isochronism.

Prices are for complete watches with specially made Howard cases and dials.

NOTE: Watches listed in this book are priced at the retail level, as complete watches having an original 14k gold-filled case, an original white enamel single sunk dial, and with the entire original movement in good working order with no repairs needed, unless otherwise noted.

NOTE: E. Howard & Co. movements will not fit standard cases properly.

E. HOWARD & CO.
N SIZE (18)
(In Original Cases)

Series or Name — Description	Avg	Ex-Fn	Mint
E. Howard & Co. on dial and movement, 1857 Model, upright pallets, English style escape wheel, KW & KS, silver case .... ★ ★	$2,200	$2,800	$3,500
I, Isochronism, 15J, gilded, KW, helical hairspring . ★ ★ ★	4,000	5,000	7,000

E. HOWARD & CO., N (18) SIZE (continued)

Series I, 18 size, 15 jewels, note the compensating balance on this early movement, serial number 133.

Series II, 18 size, 15 jewels, key wind & set, serial number 2,477.

Grade or Name—Description	Avg	Ex-Fn	Mint
I, 15J, gilded, KW, 18K, HC or OF, upright pallets .. ★ ★	$2,200	$2,800	$3,500
I, 15J, gilded, KW, 18K, HC or OF, horizontal pallets . ★	1,800	2,000	2,500
I, 15J, gilded, KW, silver HC........................ ★	1,000	1,200	1,400
I, 15J (movement only) .... ★	350	400	500
II, 15J, gilded, KW, 18K, HC or OF .... ★	1,400	1,600	1,900
II, 15J, gilded, KW, silver HC...................... ★	800	1,000	1,200
II, 15J (movement only) .... ★	200	250	325
III, 15J, gilded, KW, 18K, HC	1,300	1,500	1,800
III, 15J, gilded, KW, silver case.....................	600	800	1,000
III, 15J, nickel, KW, silver case.....................	700	900	1,100
III, 15J, gilded, KW, 18K, Mershon's Patent	1,500	1,800	2,200
III, 15J, gilded, KW, 18K, Coles Escapement...........	1,600	1,900	2,300
III, 15J (movement only)............................	175	225	350
IV, 15J, gilded or nickel, KW, 18K, HC	1,200	1,400	1,700
IV, 15J, gilded or nickel, SW, 18K, HC	1,000	1,200	1,400

Series III, 18 size, 15 jewels, note center wheel rack regulator, serial number 22,693.

Series III, 18 size, 15 jewels, note high balance wheel over center wheel, serial number 7,000.

Series IV, 18 size, 15 jewels, key wind and set, serial number 37,893.

Series VII, 18 size, 15 jewels, nickel movement, note running deer on movement, "adjusted" on bridge, serial number 219,304.

Series or Name—Description	Avg	Ex-Fn	Mint
IV, personalized with jobber's name, silver . . . . ★ ★	$500	$600	$800
IV, 15J (movement only)	150	200	300
VII, 15J, gilded or nickel, SW, 14K, HC	1,000	1,200	1,500
VII, 17J, nickel, split plate, SW, 14K, HC . . . . ★	1,200	1,400	1,700
VII, 17J, nickel, split plate, SW, silver, HC . . . . ★	600	700	900
VII, 19J, nickel, split plate, SW, 14K HC . . . . ★ ★ ★	2,500	3,000	4,000
VII, 15J (movement only)	110	150	225
VII, Ball, 17J, nickel, SW, 14K, HC . . . . ★ ★ ★	3,500	4,000	6,000
VII, Ball, 17J, nickel, SW, GF, HC . . . . ★ ★ ★	2,200	2,800	3,500
VIII, 15J, gilded or nickel, SW, 14K, OF	900	1,000	1,400
VIII, 17J, nickel, split plate, SW, 14K, OF . . . . ★	1,200	1,400	1,700
VIII, 17J, nickel, split plate, SW, silver, OF . . . . ★	425	525	650
VIII, 15J (movement only)	100	125	175
VIII, Ball, 17J, nickel, SW, 14K, OF . . . . ★ ★	3,000	3,500	4,000
VIII, Ball, 17J, nickel, SW, GF, OF . . . . ★ ★	1,000	1,500	2,000

Series VII, 18 size, 17 jewels, ¾ split plate, serial number 228,055.

Series VIII, 18 size, 15 jewels, serial number 308,455.

Series VIII, 18 size, 17 jewels, split plate model, gold jewel settings, serial number 309,904.

Series IX, 18 size, 15 jewels, hunting. This series is guilded only and hound grade exclusively, serial number 402,873.

Series or Name—Description	Avg	Ex-Fn	Mint
IX, 15J, gilded, SW, 14K, HC	$900	$1,100	$1,400
IX, 15J, gilded, SW, silver, HC	425	525	650
IX, 15J (movement only)	100	125	175

L SIZE (16)
(In Original Cases)

Series or Name — Description	Avg	Ex-Fn	Mint
V, 15J, gilded, KW, 18K, HC	$1,000	$1,200	$1,500
V, 15J, gilded, KW, 18K, Coles Escapement ★	1,300	1,500	1,800
V, 15J, gilded or nickel, SW, 14K, HC	800	1,000	1,300
V, 15J, gilded, SW, 14K, Coles Escapement ★	1,100	1,300	1,600

Series V, 16 or L size, Prescott Model, 15 jewels, hunting, serial number 50,434.

Series XI, 16 size, 17 jewels, split plate model, nickel movement, gold jewel settings, serial number 600,021.

Series XII, L-16 size, 21 jewels, split plate model, nickel movement, gold lettering, gold jewel settings, serial number 700,899.

Series K, 14 or K size, 15 jewels, key wind & set, serial number 3,005.

Series or Name—Description	Avg	Ex-Fn	Mint
V, 15J (movement only)	$100	$150	$175
XI, 17J, nickel, split plate, SW, 14K, HC ★	1,100	1,300	1,600
XI, 17J, nickel, split plate, SW, silver, HC ★	400	500	650
XI, 17J (movement only)	200	300	450
XII, 17J, nickel, split plate, SW, 14K, OF ★	1,000	1,200	1,500
XII, 17J, nickel, split plate, SW, silver, OF ★	375	475	625
XII, 17J (movement only)	100	150	175
XII, 21J, nickel, split plate, SW, 14K OF ★★★	2,500	3,000	4,000

K SIZE (14)
(In Original Cases)

Series or Name — Description	Avg	Ex-Fn	Mint
K, 15J, gilded, KW, 18K, HC ★★★	$2,500	$3,000	$4,000

J SIZE (12)
(In Original Cases)

Series or Name — Description	Avg	Ex-Fn	Mint
X, 15J, nickel, hound, SW, 14K, OF ★	$700	$900	$1,200
X, 15J, nickel, horse, SW, 14K, OF ★	800	1,000	1,300
X, 15J, nickel, deer, SW, 14K, OF ★	900	1,100	1,400
X, 15J, hound (movement only) ★	200	250	300

E. HOWARD & CO. (continued)

Series X, 12 or J size, 15 jewels, note deer on movement, serial number 501,361.

I size (10 size), 15 jewels, guilded, key wind, serial number 3,404.

I SIZE (10)
(In Original Cases)

Series or Name — Description		Avg	Ex-Fn	Mint
I, 15J, gilded, KW, 18K HC...................★★★		$2,500	$3,000	$4,000

G SIZE (6)
(In Original Cases)

Series or Name — Description		Avg	Ex-Fn	Mint
VI, 15J, gilded, KW, 18K, HC...................★★		$1,400	$1,800	$2,400
VI, 15J, gilded or nickel, SW, 18K, HC		1,000	1,200	1,500
VI, 15J, gilded or nickel, SW, 14K, HC		800	1,000	1,300
VI, 15J (movement only)		175	200	300

Series VI, 6 or G size, 15 jewels, stem wind.

Series VI, 6 or G size, 15 jewels, stem wind, serial number 104,520.

E. HOWARD WATCH CO.
Waltham, Massachusetts
1902 - 1930

The Howard name was purchased by the Keystone Watch Case Co. in 1902. The watches are marked "E. Howard Watch Co. Boston, U. S. A." There were no patent rights transferred, just the Howard name. The "Edward Howard" chronometer was the highest grade, 16 size, and was introduced in 1912 for $350.

Keystone Howard gained control of U. S. Watch Co. of Waltham and N. Y. Standard Watch Co.

ESTIMATED SERIAL NUMBERS AND PRODUCTION DATES

Date	Serial No.
1902	850,000
1903	900,000
1909	980,000
1912	1,100,000
1915	1,285,000
1917	1,340,000
1921	1,400,000
1930	1,500,000

The opposite arrows denote number of jewels and adjustments in each grade.

Cross—23 jewel, 5 positions

Star—21 jewel, 5 positions

Triangle—19 jewel, 5 positions

Circle—17 jewel, 3 positions

Series 1905, 16 size, 17 jewels. This model can be identified by the slant parallel damaskeening. This represents the middle grade.

Series 9, 16 size, 17 jewels. This model can be identified by the checkerboard damaskeening. This represents the top grade.

Series 3, 16 size, 17 jewels. This model can be identified by the circular damaskeening. This represents the lowest grade of the three.

E. Howard Watch Co., Series 0, 16 size, 23 jewels, in original E. Howard Watch Co. swing-out movement Keystone Extra gold filled OF case.

E. Howard Watch Co., Series 0 (not marked), 16 size, 23 jewels, HC.

E. HOWARD WATCH CO.
(KEYSTONE)
16 SIZE

Series or Name — Description	Avg	Ex-Fn	Mint
No. 0, 23J, BRG, Adj.5P, DR, OF	$425	$500	$600
Series 0, 23J, BRG, Adj.5P, DR, Ruby banking pins	425	500	600
Series 0, 23J, BRG, Adj.5P, DR, jeweled barrel	450	525	625
Series 0, 23J, BRG, Adj.5P, DR, OF, 14K	700	900	1,200
Series 0, 23J, BRG, Adj.5P, DR, HC, 14K..............	750	950	1,250
No. 1, 21J, BRG, Adj.5P, DR...................... ★	275	300	375
Series 1, 21J, BRG, Adj.5P, DR	275	300	375
Series 2, 17J, BRG, Adj.5P, DR, HC	175	200	275

Note: Add $75-$100 for original box and papers. Add $50 for hunting case models listed as open face.

Series II, Railroad Chronometer, 16 size, 21 jewels, Adj5p, serial number 1,217,534.

Edward Howard Model, 16 size, 23 blue sapphire jewels, frosted gold bridge, wolfteeth wind, serial number 77. c.1914.

E. Howard Watch Co., 16 size, 23 jewels, by Waltham, raised gold jewel settings, Adj5p, hunting case, bridge style movement.

E. Howard Watch Co., 16 size 19 jewels, by Waltham, gold jewel settings, Adj3p, hunting case, ¼ plate movement.

Series or Name—Description	Avg	Ex-Fn	Mint
Series 2, 17J, BRG, Adj.5P, DR, OF	$125	$150	$175
Series 3, 17J, ¾, Adj.3P, circular DMK	100	125	150
Series 3, 17J, OF, Adj.3P, 14K, circular DMK..........	500	525	550
No. 5, 19J, GJS, BRG, HC .... ★	400	425	450
Series 5, 19J, BRG, Adj.5P, DR, 14K	550	575	600
Series 5, 19J, BRG, Adj.5P, DR, 1907 Model	200	225	275
1905, 17J, ¾, Adj.5P, DR, RGJS, slant parallel DMK, OF	125	150	175
1905, 17J, ¾, Adj.5P, DR, RGJS, slant parallel DMK, HC	175	200	150
Series 9, 17J, ¾, Adj.5P, DR, LS, checkerboard DMK ...	175	200	250
Series 9, 17J, ¾, Adj.5P, DR, 14K, checkerboard DMK			
(railroad grade)	475	500	550
Series 10, 21J, BRG, Adj.5P, DR	250	300	375
No. 10, 21J, BRG, Adj.5P, DR.......................	250	300	375
Series 11, 21J, R.R. Chrono., Adj.5P, DR	300	350	425
"Edward Howard," 23 blue sapphire J, Adj.6P, GJS, GT,			
DR — Serial numbers below 300, without box ... ★ ★	8,000	9,000	10,000
"Edward Howard," 23 blue sapphire J, Adj.6P, GJS, GT,			
DR — Serial numbers below 300, with original box			
and papers, 18K the Edward Howard case .... ★ ★ ★	9,000	10,000	11,000
23J, E. Howard W. Co. on movement (mfg. by			
Waltham), 14K, Brg model .... ★ ★	1,200	1,400	1,700
23J, E. Howard W. Co. on movement (mfg. by			
Waltham), OF, gold filled	500	600	700
23J, E. Howard W. Co. on movement (mfg. by			
Waltham), HC, gold filled	600	700	800
21J, Waltham Model, ¾, OF..........................	275	300	350
19J, Waltham Model, ¾, OF..........................	275	300	350

E. HOWARD WATCH CO., 16 SIZE (continued)

Series or Name—Description	Avg	Ex-Fn	Mint
17J, Waltham Model, ¾, OF	$225	$250	$300
Unmarked, 23J, BRG, Adj.5P, DR, OF	425	450	500

Note: Add $100 for original wood box and papers on 16 size watches.

12 SIZE

Series or Name — Description	Avg	Ex-Fn	Mint
Series 6, 19J, BRG, DR, Adj.5P, 1908 Model, 14K, HC	$300	$350	$425
Series 6, 19J, BRG, DR, Adj.5P, 14K, OF	200	250	325
Series 6, 19J, BRG, DR, Adj.5P, OF	75	100	150
Series 7, 17J, BRG, DR, Adj.3P, 14K, OF	200	250	325
Series 7, 17J, BRG, DR, Adj.3P, OF	75	100	150
Series 8, 21J, BRG, DR, Adj.5P, OF	100	125	175
Series 8, 23J, BRG, DR, Adj.5P, 14K, OF	350	400	475
Series 8, 23J, BRG, DR, Adj.5P, OF	150	200	275
Series 8, 23J, BRG, DR, Adj.5P, 14K, HC	450	500	575

NOTE: Add $25 for gold filled hunting case.

Series 8, 12 size, 21 jewels, open face, stop works, extra thin.

E. Howard Watch Co., 10 size, 17 jewels, Adj3p, serial number 61,230. (Serial numbers started at about 1,001 on this model.)

10 SIZE

Series or Name — Description	Avg	Ex-Fn	Mint
Thin Model, 21J, ADJ, 14K case, OF	$250	$275	$325
Thin Model, 19J, ADJ, 14K case, OF	225	250	300
Thin Model, 17J, ADJ, 14K case, OF	200	225	275

NOTE: Serial numbers start at about 1,001 on this model.

ILLINOIS WATCH CO.
Springfield, Illinois
1869 - 1927

The Illinois Watch Company was organized mainly through the efforts of J. C. Adams. The first directors were J. T. Stuart, W. B. Miller, John Williams, John W. Bunn, George Black and George Passfield. In 1879 the company changed all its watches to a quick train movement by changing the number of teeth in the fourth wheel. The first mainspring made by the company was used in 1882. The next year soft enamel dials were used.

The Illinois Watch Co. used more names on its movements than any other watch manufacturer. To identify all of them requires extensive knowledge by the collector plus a good working knowledge of watch mechanics. Engraved on some early movements, for example, are "S. W. Co." or "I. W. Co., Springfield, Ill." To the novice these abbreviations might be hard to understand, thus making Illinois watches difficult to identify. But one saving clue is that the location "Springfield, Illinois" appears on most of these watches. It is important to learn how to identify these type watches because some of them are extremely collectible. Examples of some of the more valuable of these are: the Benjamin Franklin (size 18 or 16, 25 or 26 jewels), Paillard's Non-Magnetic, Pennsylvania Special, C & O, and B & O railroad models.

The earliest movements made by the Illinois Watch Co. are listed below. They made the first watch in early 1872, but the company really didn't get off the ground until 1875. Going by the serial number, the first watch made was the Stuart. Next was the Mason, followed by the Bunn, the Miller, and finally the Currier. The first stem-wind was made in 1875.

The Illinois Watch Company was sold to Hamilton Watch Co. in 1927. The Illinois factory continued to produce Illinois watches under the new management until 1932. After 1933 Hamilton produced watches bearing the Illinois name in their own factory until 1939.

Illinois made watches for other companies which are listed below. These watches, for the most part, did not contain the Illinois name. But most all contain the Illinois

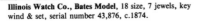

Illinois Watch Co., Bates Model, 18 size, 7 jewels, key wind & set, serial number 43,876, c.1874.

Bunn, 18 size, 16 jewels, hunting case, serial number 1,185,809.

ILLINOIS WATCH CO. (continued)

serial numbers (exceptions: Ball, Paillard, & J. P. Stevens). Their age can be determined by simply looking up the serial numbers on the Illinois Serial Numbers List, and the model can be compared to the Illinois model diagrams for identification purposes.

CHRONOLOGY OF THE DEVELOPMENT OF ILLINOIS WATCH CO.:
Illinois Springfield Watch Co. 1869-1879
Springfield Illinois Watch Co. 1879-1885
Illinois Watch Co. 1885-1927
Illinois Watch Co. was sold to Hamilton Watch Co. in 1927.

ILLINOIS ESTIMATED SERIAL NUMBERS
AND PRODUCTION DATES

Date	Serial No.	Date	Serial No.	Date	Serial No.
1872	5,000	1893	1,120,000	1914	2,600,000
1873	20,000	1894	1,160,000	1915	2,700,000
1874	50,000	1895	1,220,000	1916	2,800,000
1875	75,000	1896	1,250,000	1917	3,000,000
1876	100,000	1897	1,290,000	1918	3,200,000
1877	145,000	1898	1,330,000	1919	3,400,000
1878	210,000	1899	1,370,000	1920	3,600,000
1879	250,000	1900	1,410,000	1921	3,750,000
1880	300,000	1901	1,450,000	1922	3,900,000
1881	350,000	1902	1,500,000	1923	4,000,000
1882	400,000	1903	1,650,000	1924	4,500,000
1883	450,000	1904	1,700,000	1925	4,700,000
1884	500,000	1905	1,800,000	1926	4,800,000
1885	550,000	1906	1,840,000	1927	5,000,000
1886	600,000	1907	1,900,000	(Sold to Hamilton)	
1887	700,000	1908	2,100,000	1928	5,200,000
1888	800,000	1909	2,150,000	1929	5,350,000
1889	900,000	1910	2,200,000	1930	5,400,000
1890	1,000,000	1911	2,300,000	1931	5,500,000
1891	1,040,000	1912	2,400,000	1932	5,600,000
1892	1,080,000	1913	2,500,000		

ILLINOIS
18 SIZE

Grade or Name — Description	Avg	Ex-Fn	Mint
Alleghany, 11J, KW, gilded, OF	$50	$75	$125
Alleghany, 11J, M#1, NI, KWM#	100	125	175
Alleghany, 11J, M#2, NI, Transition	100	125	175
America, 7J, M#3, Silveroid	50	75	100
America, 7J, M#1-2, KW, FULL	100	125	175
America Special, 7J, M#1-2, KW, FULL	150	175	225
Army & Navy, 19J, GJS, Adj.5P, FULL	225	250	300
Army & Navy, 21J, GJS, Adj.5P, FULL	275	300	350
Baltimore & Ohio R.R. Special, 17J, GJS, ADJ	500	600	750
Baltimore & Ohio R.R. Special, 21J, GJS, NI, ADJ	800	900	1,050
Baltimore & Ohio R.R. Standard, 24J, GJS, ADJ	1,300	1,400	1,550
Bates, 7J, M#1-2, KW, FULL	125	150	200
Benjamin Franklin U.S.A., 17J, ADJ, NI	500	600	750

Illinois Watch Co., 18 size, railroad watch with a Ferguson dial.

Army and Navy, 18 size, 19 jewels, engraved on movement "Washington Watch Co.," serial number 1,606,612.

Grade or Name—Description	Avg	Ex-Fn	Mint
Benjamin Franklin U.S.A., 21J, GJS, Adj.6P, NI......★	$900	$1,000	$1,150
Benjamin Franklin U.S.A., 21J, GJS, Adj.5P, NI......★	800	900	1,050
Benjamin Franklin U.S.A., 24J, GJS, Adj.6P, FULL, NI, DMK ....★	2,000	2,400	3,000
Benjamin Franklin U.S.A., 25J, GJS, Adj.6P, FULL, NI, DMK ....★★★★	6,000	6,500	8,500
Benjamin Franklin U.S.A., 26J, GJS, Adj.6P, FULL, DR, NI, DMK ....★★★	5,000	5,500	7,500
Bunn, 15J, M#1, KW, KS, FULL, OF..................	500	600	775
Bunn, 15J, M#1, KW, KS, ADJ, FULL	550	650	825
Bunn, 15J, KW/SW transition	375	400	500
Bunn, 15J, M#1, KW, Coin	500	600	775
Bunn, 15J, KW, M#1, HC	550	650	825
Bunn, 16J, KW, OF	500	600	775
Bunn, 16J, KW, HC.................................	550	650	825
Bunn, 17J, SW, M#1, HC..........................★	650	750	925
Bunn, 17J, M#2, SW, NI, FULL, HC	150	200	275
Bunn, 17J, SW, NI, Coin	125	150	200
Bunn, 17J, SW, M#3, 5th pinion, gilded, OF	350	400	475
Bunn, 17J, M#4, SW, NI, FULL, OF	125	150	200
Bunn, 17J, M#5, SW, NI, FULL, HC	150	200	275
Bunn, 17J, M#6, SW, NI, FULL, OF	125	150	200
Bunn, 19J, SW, NI, FULL, OF, DR, LS, GJS, Adj.5P, J. barrel	250	300	325
Bunn, 19J, SW, OF, Adj.6P, DR, J. barrel	300	350	425
Bunn, 19J, SW, GJS, FULL, HC, DR, Adj.5P, J. barrel ....★	350	400	475
Bunn Special, 21J, SW, Coin	150	175	225
Bunn Special, 21J, GJS, ADJ, HC	300	350	400

Bunn Special, 18 size, 24 jewels, adjusted, serial number 1,413,435

Bunn Special, 18 size, 26 Ruby jewels, "J. Home & Co." on dial, adjusted to six positions, gold jewel settings, serial number 2,019,415.

Grade or Name—Description	Avg	Ex-Fn	Mint
Bunn Special, 21J, GJS, ADJ, DR, OF	$150	$175	$225
Bunn Special, 21J, GJS, DR, Adj.5P, OF	155	180	230
Bunn Special, 21J, GJS, DR, Adj.6P, OF	160	185	235
Bunn Special, 21J, GJS, Adj.5P, HC, 14K	700	750	825
Bunn Special, 21J, GJS, ADJ, 2-Tone	175	200	250
Bunn Special, 21J, GJS, Adj.5P, DR	175	200	250
Bunn Special, 21J, Extra, GJS	275	300	350
Bunn Special, 23J, GJS, ADJ, DR, OF	350	375	425
Bunn Special, 23J, GJS, Adj.6P, DR, OF	375	400	450
Bunn Special, 23J, GJS, Adj.6P, DR, 2-Tone, OF	375	400	450
Bunn Special, 23J, GJS, ADJ, DR, HC ★	1,800	2,200	2,500
Bunn Special, 24J, GJS, Adj.5P, DR, HC	600	700	850
Bunn Special, 24J, GJS, Adj.5P, DR, 14K, HC	1,300	1,400	1,600
Bunn Special, 24J, GJS, Adj.5P, DR, OF	475	525	600
Bunn Special, 24J, GJS, Adj.6P, DR, OF	500	600	700
Bunn Special, 24J, GJS, Adj.5P, single roller	425	475	550
Bunn Special, 25J, GJS, Adj.6P, DR ★★★	5,000	6,000	7,500
Bunn Special, 26J, GJS, Adj.6P, DR ★★	4,500	5,000	6,000
Central Truck Railroad, 15J, KW, KS	350	400	475
Chesapeake & Ohio, 17J, ADJ, OF	300	350	425
Chesapeake & Ohio Special, 21J, GJS, 2-Tone ★	900	1,100	1,400
Chesapeake & Ohio Special, 24J, NI, ADJ, GJS ★	1,600	1,800	2,100
Chronometer, 15J, M#2, HC	150	175	225
Columbia, 11J, M#3, 5th Pinion	100	125	175
Columbia, 11J, M#1 & 2, FULL, KW	100	125	175
Columbia, 11J, M#1 & 2, Silveroid	75	100	150
Columbia Special, 11J, M#1-2-3, FULL, KW	100	125	175
Columbia Special, 11J, M#1-2-3, FULL, KW, transition	75	100	125
Comet, 11J, M#3, OF, LS, SW	75	100	125

Diurnal, 18 size, 7 jewels, key wind & set, only one run, total production 2,000, serial number 86,757.

Emperor, 18 size, 21 jewels, Adj3p, serial number 2,396,628.

Grade or Name—Description	Avg	Ex-Fn	Mint
Commodore, 17J, HC	$150	$175	$225
Currier, 11J, KW, FULL, OF	100	125	175
Currier, 11J, KW, FULL, Coin	100	125	175
Currier, 11J, KW, HC	125	175	225
Currier, 11J, KW/SW, HC	100	150	200
Currier, 11J, transition, OF	75	100	125
Currier, 11J, M#3, OF	75	100	125
Currier, 13J, M#3, OF	75	100	125
Dauntless, 11J	75	100	125
Dean, 15J, M#1, KW, FULL, HC	150	175	225
Diurnal, 7J, KW, KS, HC, Coin ★	200	250	325
Dominion Railway, with train on dial	800	900	1,150
Eastlake, 11J, SW, KW, Transition	100	125	175
Emperor, 21J, M#6, LS, SW, ADJ	150	175	225
Enterprise, M#2, ADJ	100	125	175
Eureka, 11J	100	125	175
Forest City, 11J, SW, LS, HC	125	150	200
General Grant or General Lee, 11J, M#1, KW	225	250	300
Hoyt, 9-11J, M#1-2, KW, FULL	75	100	150
Illinois Watch Co., 11J, M#1-2, KW, FULL	75	100	125
Illinois Watch Co., 11J, M#3	50	75	100
Illinois Watch Co., 13J, M#1-2, KW, FULL	100	125	175
Illinois Watch Co., 15J, M#1-2, KW, FULL	100	125	175
Illinois Watch Co., 15J, G#106, KW, ADJ, FULL, NI	125	150	200
Illinois Watch Co., 17J, M#3, 5th Pinion	200	225	275
Illinois Watch Co., 15J, SW, ADJ, DMK, NI	75	100	125
Illinois Watch Co., 15J, transition	50	75	100
Illinois Watch Co., 15J, SW, Silveroid	50	60	75
Illinois Watch Co., 15J, SW, 9K, HC	300	400	550
Illinois Watch Co., 17J, SW, Silveroid	50	60	75

Ill. W. Co., 18 size, 17 jewels, adjusted, 2-tone movement, serial number 1,404,442.

Miller, 18 size, 17 jewels, 5th pinion model which changes hunting case to open face.

Grade or Name—Description	Avg	Ex-Fn	Mint
Illinois Watch Co., 17J, SW, ADJ	$75	$100	$125
Illinois Watch Co., 17J, transition	75	100	125
Illinois Watch Co., 19J, OF	150	175	225
Illinois Watch Co., 21J, OF	150	175	225
Illinois Watch Co., 21J, HC	175	200	250
Interior, 7J, KW, FULL	100	125	175
Interior, 7J, M#3	75	100	150
Interstate Chronometer, 17J, HC	400	500	650
Interstate Chronometer, 17J, OF	300	400	550
Interstate Chronometer, 23J, Adj.5P, GJS, NI, OF	850	950	1,150
Interstate Chronometer, 23J, Adj.5P, GJS, NI, HC	950	1,050	1,250
Iowa W. Co., 7J, M#1-2, KW, FULL	175	200	250
Iowa W. Co., 11J, M#1-2, KW	175	200	250
King of the Road, 16&17J, NI, OF & HC, LS, FULL, ADJ ★	400	500	625
Lafayette, 24J, GJS, Adj.6P, NI, SW, OF	950	1,050	1,250
Lakeshore, 17J, OF, LS, NI, FULL, SW	100	125	175
Landis W. Co., 7-11J	75	100	150
Liberty Bell, 17J, NI, SW, FULL	100	125	175
Liberty Bell, 17J, Silveroid	75	100	150
A. Lincoln, 21J, Silveroid	75	100	150
A. Lincoln, 21J, Adj.5P, NI, DR, GJS, HC	250	300	375
A. Lincoln, 21J, Adj.5P, NI, FULL, DR, OF, GJS	150	175	225
Maiden Lane, 17J, 5th Pinion	400	475	600
Manhatten, 11J, HC, NI, FULL, KW, LS	125	150	200
Mason, 7J, KW, KS, HC, FULL	125	150	200
Miller, 15J, Silveroid	75	100	125
Miller, 15J, M#1, HC, KW, FULL	150	175	225
Miller, 15J, M#1, HC, KW, FULL, ADJ	175	200	250
Miller, 15J, KW, FULL, OF	125	150	200

Paillard Non-Magnetic W. Co., 18 size, 24 jewels, gold jewel settings, serial number 1,397,812.

Pennsylvania Special, 18 size, 26 jewels, Adj6p, 2-tone movement, serial number 1,742,913.

Grade or Name—Description	Avg	Ex-Fn	Mint
Miller, 17J, 5th Pinion, ADJ	$275	$300	$375
Monarch W. Co., 17J, NI, ADJ, SW, FULL	125	150	200
Montgomery Ward, 17J, OF, GJS......................	125	150	200
Montgomery Ward, 21J..............................	150	175	225
Montgomery Ward Timer, 21J, Silveroid...............	125	150	200
Montgomery Ward, 24J, OF..........................	950	1,050	1,250
Montgomery Ward, 24J, HC .... ★	1,200	1,400	1,700
Muscatine W. Co., 15J, LS, NI, HC	150	175	225
The National, 11J, SW, LS, OF	75	100	150
Non-Magnetic W. Co., 21J, OF.......................	225	275	350
Paillard Non-Magnetic W. Co., 15J, NI, OF	75	100	150
Paillard Non-Magnetic W. Co., 17J, GJS, NI, Adj.5P, OF	100	125	175
Paillard Non-Magnetic W. Co., 21J, GJS, NI, Adj.5P, OF	200	250	325
Paillard Non-Magnetic W. Co., 23J, GJS, NI, Adj.5P, OF	850	900	1,150
Paillard Non-Magnetic W. Co., 24J, GJS, NI, Adj.5P, OF	950	1,050	1,250
Pennsylvania Special, 17J, GJS, Adj.3P.............. ★	600	750	900
Pennsylvania Special, 21J, DR, Adj.5P .... ★	1,200	1,400	1,800
Pennsylvania Special, 24J, DR, GJS, ADJ .... ★	1,800	2,000	2,400
Pennsylvania Special, 25J, DR, GJS, ADJ, NI... ★ ★ ★ ★	5,000	5,800	6,800
Pennsylvania Special, 26J, DR, GJS, ADJ, NI....... ★ ★	4,000	4,800	5,800
Pierce Arrow, 17J, "automaker logo"	350	425	575
Plymouth W. Co., 17J, SW, FULL	75	100	150
Potomac, 17J, OF, FULL, ADJ, NI....................	125	150	200
The President, 15J, FULL, NI, OF.....................	125	150	200
The President, 17J, DMK, FULL, 14K gold case.........	600	700	850
Railroad Construction, 17J, OF	200	250	325
Railroad Dispatcher Extra, 17J, OF	200	250	325
Railroad King, 15-17J, FULL, NI, ADJ	300	350	425
The Railroader, 15J, OF, FULL, ADJ, NI	250	300	375
Railway Engineer, 15J	250	300	375

The President, 18 size, 17 jewels, chalmer patented regulator, serial number 1,240,909.

Railroad King, 18 size, 17 jewels, Fifth Pinion Model, adjusted. Note chalmer patented regulator, serial number 1,160,836.

Grade or Name—Description	Avg	Ex-Fn	Mint
Railway Regulator, 15J, KW, KS, gilt	$400	$500	$675
S. W. Co., 15J, M#1, KW, HC	125	150	200
Sears & Roebuck Special, 17J, GJS, NI, DMK, ADJ	125	150	200
Senate, 17J, NI, DMK, FULL	125	150	200
Southern R.R. Special, 21J, LS, ADJ, OF .... ★	800	1,000	1,250
Southern R.R. Special, 21J, M#5, LS, ADJ, HC .... ★	1,200	1,400	1,650
Star Light, 17J, 5th pinion, Chalmers Reg. OF	175	225	300
J. P. Stevens, 17J, SW. FULL, NI	600	700	850
Stuart, 15J, M#1, KW, KS	500	600	750
Stuart, 15J, M#1, KW, KS, transition .... ★	300	350	450
Stuart, 15J, M#1, KW, KS, marked ADJ .... ★ ★	500	650	825
Stuart, ADJ, KW, Abbotts Conversion, 18K, HC .... ★ ★	1,500	1,700	2,000
Stuart, 15J, M#1, KW, KS, Coin.................. ★ ★	500	600	775

Sears & Roebuck Special, 18 size, 17 jewels, serial number 1,481,879.

Washington Watch Co., Lafayette model, 18 size, 24 Ruby jewels, gold jewel settings, adjusted, serial number 3,392,897.

Vault Time Lock for Mosler Lock Co., Covington, Ky. Movement is 18 size, 15 jewels, open face, Model number 6, serial number 4,576,540. Note 72 hour dial. Strong arm rooms first used vault time locks in the 1870s.

Grade or Name—Description	Avg	Ex-Fn	Mint
Stuart, 17J, M#3, 5th Pinion ★★	$300	$400	$475
Stuart, 17J, M#3, 5th Pinion, ADJ ★★	375	425	500
Transition Models, 17J, OF	100	125	175
Time King, 17J, OF, LS, FULL, NI	150	175	250
Time King, 21J, OF, LS, FULL	175	200	275
Vault Time Lock for Mosler, 15J, 72 hr.	100	125	175
Washington W. Co. (See Army & Navy, Liberty Bell, Lafayette, Senate)			
65, 15J, HC, LS, M#2	75	100	150
101, 11J, FULL, SW, KW, OF	75	100	150
101, 11J, SW, KW, Silveroid	40	60	85
101, 11J, SW, KW, HC	75	100	150
102, 13J, SW, KW, Silveroid	40	60	85
102, 13J, SW, KW, OF	75	100	150
102, 13J, FULL, SW, KW, HC	100	125	175
104, 15J, M#2, HC ★★	250	300	375
104, 17J, M#3, OF ★★★	300	350	425
105, 17J, M#3, OF ★★★	300	350	425
105, 15J, M#2, GJS, ADJ, FULL, KW, KS, HC ★★	275	325	400
106, 15J, ADJ, FULL, KW, KS	100	125	175
444, 17J, OF, NI, ADJ, FULL	50	75	125
445, 19J, GJS, 2-Tone, HC ★★	1,000	1,200	1,500
1905 Special, 21J, OF, NI, Adj.5P	300	400	550

NOTE: Watches listed in this book are priced at the retail level, as complete watches having an original 14k gold-filled case, an original white enamel single sunk dial, and with the entire original movement in good working order with no repairs needed, unless otherwise noted.

ILLINOIS WATCH CO. (continued)

ILLINOIS
16 SIZE

Note: Bunn Special original cases were marked Bunn Special except for Elinvars (Hamilton cased).

Grade or Name — Description	Avg	Ex-Fn	Mint
Adams Street, 17J, ¾, SW, NI, DMK, HC	$175	$225	$300
Adams Street, 21J, 3F brg, NI, DMK	250	300	375
Ak-Sar-Ben (Nebraska backward), 17J, OF, GCW	150	175	225
Ariston, 11J, OF	50	75	125
Ariston, 15J, OF	50	75	125
Ariston, 17J, 3F brg, HC	175	225	300
Ariston, 17J, Adj.3P, OF	150	175	225
Ariston, 19J, Adj.3P, OF	150	175	225
Ariston, 21J, GJS, Adj.6P, OF	300	375	450
Ariston, 23J, GJS, Adj.6P, OF	500	600	750
Ariston, 23J, GJS, Adj.6P, HC	700	800	950
Arlington Special, 17J, OF	75	100	150
Arlington Special, 17J, OF, Silveroid	50	75	125
Army & Navy, 19J, GJS, Adj.5P, NI, 1F brg	200	250	325
Army & Navy, 21J, GJS, Adj.5P, 1F brg	250	300	375
B & M Special, 17J, BRG, Adj.4P	200	250	325
B & O Standard, 21J	350	400	525
Benjamin Franklin, 17J, ADJ, DMK, ¾	300	325	400
Benjamin Franklin, 21J, GJS, Adj.5P, DR, GT, ¾	500	550	625
Benjamin Franklin, 25J, GJS, Adj.6P, DR, GT, ¾, OF ★ ★	3,000	3,500	4,000
Benjamin Franklin, 25J, GJS, Adj.6P, DR, GT, ¾, HC ★ ★ ★	3,500	4,000	4,500
Bunn, 17J, LS, OF, NI, ¾, GJS, Adj.5P	100	125	175
Bunn, 17J, LS, NI, ¾, Adj.5P, HC	450	500	575
Bunn, 19J, LS, OF, NI, ¾, GJS, Adj.5P	100	125	175

Ben Franklin, 16 size, 25 jewels, gold jewel settings, gold train, serial number 2,242,138.

Bunn Special, Model 163, 16 size, 23 jewels, gold jewel settings, gold train, 60 hour movement, serial number 5,421,504.

Left: Standard style escapement. **Right:** DeLong style escapement.

Illinois Watch Co., 16 size, 25 jewels, three-fingered bridge, gold train, hunting, note serial number S731,870.

Grade or Name—Description	Avg	Ex-Fn	Mint
Bunn, 19J, LS, NI, ¼, Adj.5P, HC....................	$450	$500	$575
Bunn, 19J, LS, OF, NI, ¼, GJS, Adj.5P, 60 hour.......	300	350	425
Bunn, 19J, marked Jeweled Barrel	175	200	250
Bunn Special, 19J, LS, OF, NI, ¼, Adj.6P, GT.........	125	150	200
Bunn Special, 19J, LS, OF, NI, ¼, Adj.6P, GT, 60 hour.	300	350	425
Bunn Special, 21J, NI, GJS, HC.....................★	400	450	525
Bunn Special, 21J, LS, OF, NI, ¼, GJS, Adj.6P, GT....	125	150	175
Bunn Special, 21J, LS, OF, NI, ¼, GJS, Adj.6P, GT, 60 hour	200	225	275
Bunn Special, 21J, LS, OF, NI, ¼, GJS, Adj.6P, GT, 60 hr. Elinvar...................................	275	300	375
Bunn Special, 21J, 60 hr., 14K, OF, Bunn Special case .★	675	725	800
Bunn Special, 23J, LS, OF, NI, ¼, GJS, Adj.6P, GT....	300	375	425
Bunn Special, 23J, LS, OF, NI, ¼, GJS, Adj.6P, GT, 60 hour	350	425	475
Bunn Special, 23J, LS, OF, NI, ¼, GJS, Adj.6P, GT, with 23J 60-hour on dial	450	475	525
Bunn Special, 23J, LS, NI, GJS, HC ....★	1,200	1,300	1,500
161 Bunn Special, 21J, ¼, Adj.6P, 60 hour	250	300	375
161A Bunn Special, 21J, ¼, Adj.6P, 60 hour (Elinvar signed under balance or on top plate)...............	325	375	450
161 Elinvar Bunn Special, 21J, ¼, Adj.6P, 60 hour (Elinvar signed at bottom of bridge)...............	375	425	500
161B, Bunn Special, 21J, 60 hour, pressed jewels ..★★★	1,000	1,200	1,500
163 Bunn Special, 23J, GJS, Adj.6P, ¼, 60 hour	400	475	575
163 Elinvar Bunn Special, 23J, GJS, Adj.6P, 60 hour (Elinvar signed at bottom of bridge) ....★	900	950	1,050

Grade or Name—Description	Avg	Ex-Fn	Mint
163A Elinvar Bunn Special, 23J, GJS, Adj.6P, ¼, 60 hour (Elinvar signed under balance)	$800	$850	$950
163A Elinvar Bunn Special, 23J, Adj.6P, ¼, 60 hour (Elinvar signed on top plate)......................	800	850	950
Burlington, 15J, OF	50	75	125
Burlington, 15J, HC................................	125	150	200
Burlington, 17J, OF	50	75	125
Burlington, 17J, HC................................	125	150	200
Burlington W. Co., 19J, ¼, NI, Adj.3P	75	100	150
Burlington W. Co., 19J, BRG, NI, Adj.3P..............	75	100	150
Burlington W. Co., 19J, ¼, HC	125	150	200
Burlington W. Co., 19J, 3F brg, NI, Adj.3P	75	100	125
Burlington W. Co., 21J, ¼, NI, Adj.3P	100	125	175
Burlington W. Co., 21J, Adj.6P, GJS .... ★ ★	200	225	275
Burlington, Bull Dog, 21J, SW, LS, GJS, GT	200	275	350
C & O Special, 21J, ¼, NI, ADJ	600	700	900
Capitol, 19J, OF, ¼, NI, Adj.5P	100	125	175
Central, 17J, SW, PS, OF............................	50	75	125
Craftsman, 17J, OF	50	75	125
DeLong Escapement, 21J, GJS, Adj.6P, 14K OF .. ★ ★ ★	1,500	1,600	1,800
Diamond, Ruby, Sapphire, 21J, GJS, GT, Adj.6P, NI, BRG, DR .... ★	800	900	1,100
Diamond, Ruby, Sapphire, 23J, GJS, GT, Adj.6P, NI, BRG, DR .... ★ ★	1,500	1,700	2,000
Dispatcher, 19J, Adj.3P.............................	50	75	125
Forest City, 17J, KW/SW, gilted, FULL................	150	175	225
Franklin Street, 15J, ¼, NI, ADJ	75	100	150
Getty Model, 21J....................................	150	175	225
Getty Model, 17J....................................	75	100	150

Interstate Chronometer, 16 size, 23 jewels, one-fingered bridge, serial number 2,327,614.

A. Lincoln, 16 size, 21 jewels, gold jewel settings, gold train, Adj5p, serial number 2,237,406.

Grade or Name—Description	Avg	Ex-Fn	Mint
Great Northern Special, 17J, BRG, ADJ	$250	$275	$325
Great Northern Special, 19J, BRG, ADJ	275	300	350
Great Northern Special, 21J, BRG, ADJ, Adj.3P	300	325	375
Illinois Central, 17J, 2-Tone, GT......................	100	125	175
Illinois Watch Co., 7J, M#1-2-3.......................	50	75	125
Illinois Watch Co., 11J, M#1-2-3......................	80	75	125
Illinois Watch Co., 11J, ¼, OF........................	50	75	125
Illinois Watch Co., 11J, M#7, ¼, OF	50	75	125
Illinois Watch Co., 11J, M#6, ¼, HC	100	125	175
Illinois Watch Co., 15J, M#2, OF......................	50	75	125
Illinois Watch Co., 15J, M#1, HC	100	125	175
Illinois Watch Co., 15J, M#3, OF......................	50	75	125
Illinois Watch Co., 15J, ¼, ADJ	50	75	125
Illinois Watch Co., 15J, 3F brg, GJS	50	75	125
Illinois Watch Co., 17J, 14K, HC	400	450	525
Illinois Watch Co., 17J, M#2-3, SW, OF...............	50	75	125
Illinois Watch Co., 17J, M#6, SW, HC	100	125	175
Illinois Watch Co., 17J, M#7, OF	75	100	150
Illinois Watch Co., 17J, M#5, ¼, ADJ, HC............	100	125	175
Illinois Watch Co., 17J, M#4, 3F brg, GJS, Adj.5P, HC .	100	125	175
Illinois Watch Co., 19J, M#1, ¼, GJS, Adj.5P	75	100	150
Illinois Watch Co., 19J, ¼, BRG, Adj.3P	75	100	150
Illinois Watch Co., 21J, ADJ, OF.....................	175	200	250
Illinois Watch Co., 21J, GJS, HC.....................	150	175	225
Illinois Watch Co., 21J, ¼, GJS, Adj.5P	100	125	175
Illinois Watch Co., 21J, 3F brg, GJS, Adj.5P	125	150	200
Illinois Watch Co., 23J, GJS	250	300	375
Illinois Watch Co., 25J, 3F brg, GJS, Adj.5P .... ★ ★	3,000	3,500	4,000
Imperial Sp, 17J, SW, LS, Adj.4P, OF	75	100	150
Interstate Chronometer, 17J, GCW, Adj.5P, HC	275	300	325
Interstate Chronometer, 17J, GCW, Adj.5P, OF	250	275	300
Interstate Chronometer, 23J, 1F brg, ADJ, OF	600	700	850
Interstate Chronometer, 23J, 1F brg, ADJ, HC	900	1,000	1,150
Lafayette, 23J, 1F brg, GJS, Adj.5P, GT	750	850	1,000
Lakeshore, 17J, OF	75	100	150
Lakeshore, 17J, HC	150	175	225
Landis W. Co., 15J	75	100	150
Liberty Bell, 17J	100	125	175
A. Lincoln, 21J, ¼, GJS, Adj.5P	125	150	200
Marine Special, 21J, ¼, Adj.3P	250	275	325
Monroe, 17J, NI, ¼, OF (Washington W. Co.)..........	100	125	175
Monroe, 15J, ¼, OF (Washington W. Co.)	75	100	150
Our No. 1, 15J, HC, M#1.............................	150	200	275
Paillard Non-Magnetic Watch Co., 11J, ¼	75	100	150
Paillard Non-Magnetic Watch Co., 15J, ¼	75	100	150
Paillard Non-Magnetic Watch Co., 17J, ¼, Adj.5P, DMK	100	125	175

Sangamo, 16 size, 23 jewels, Adj6p, gold jewel settings, gold train, serial number 2,222,797.

Sangamo Special, 16 size, 19 jewels, 60 hour movement, Adj6p, gold jewel settings, gold train, serial number 4,720,522.

Grade or Name—Description	Avg	Ex-Fn	Mint
Paillard Non-Magnetic Watch Co., 21J, ¾, GJS, Adj.5P, DMK	$300	$325	$375
Pennsylvania Special, 23J, ¾, GJS, Adj.5P	1,200	1,300	1,450
Plymouth W. Co., 17J, OF (Add $25 for HC)	75	100	125
Precise, 21J, OF, LS, Adj.3P	125	150	200
Quincy Street, 17J, ¾, NI, DMK, ADJ	75	100	125
Railroad Dispatcher, 11J, HC	150	175	225
Railroad King, 17J, HC	200	225	275
Railroad Official, 23J, 3F brg ★★	800	900	1,050
Railway King, 17J, OF	150	175	225
Sangamo, 21J, GJS, HC	275	300	350
Sangamo, 21J, GJS, Adj.5P, OF	150	175	225
Sangamo, 21J, ¾, GJS, DR, Adj.6P, OF	150	175	225
Sangamo, 23J, ¾, GJS, DR, Adj.6P, OF	250	275	325
Sangamo, 23J, ¾, GJS, DR, Adj.6P, HC	425	475	550
Sangamo, 25J, M#5, ¾, GJS, DR, Adj.6P ★★★	4,000	5,000	6,500
Sangamo, 26J, M#5, ¾, GJS, DR, Adj.6P ★★★	5,000	6,000	7,500
Sangamo Extra, 21J, ¾, GJS, DR, Adj.6P	400	500	650
Sangamo Special, 19J, BRG, GJS, GT, Adj.6P	350	375	425
Sangamo Special, 19J, BRG, GJS, GT, Adj.6P, 60 hour	450	475	525
Sangamo Special, 19J, BRG, GJS, GT, Adj.6P, HC	800	850	950
Sangamo Special, 21J, M#7, OF	325	375	450
Sangamo Special, 21J, M#8, BRG, HC ★★★	700	800	950
Sangamo Special, 21J, M#9, BRG, GJS, GT, Adj.6P, OF	325	375	450
Sangamo Special, 21J, BRG, GJS, GT, Diamond end cap	350	400	475
Sangamo Special, 23J, M#9-10, BRG, GJS, GT, Adj.6P, Sangamo Special case	400	450	525

Grade or Name—Description	Avg	Ex-Fn	Mint
Sangamo Special, 23J, BRG, GJS, GT, Adj.6P, Diamond end stone, screw back, Sangamo Special case	$400	$450	$525
Sangamo Special, 23J, BRG, GJS, GT, Adj.6P, marked 60 hour, rigid bow, Sangamo Special case	700	750	825
Sangamo Special, 23J, BRG, GJS, GT, Adj.6P, *not* marked 60 hour, rigid bow, Sangamo Special case	450	550	575
Sangamo Special, 23J, M#8, BRG, GJS, GT, Adj.6P, HC .... ★ ★ ★	1,000	1,200	1,500
Santa Fe Special, 17J, BRG, Adj.3P...................	150	175	225
Santa Fe Special, 21J, ¾, Adj.5P, OF.................	275	300	350
Santa Fe Special, 21J, ¾, Adj.5P, HC	450	500	575
Sears, Roebuck & Co. Special, 17J, ADJ	75	100	150
Senate, 17J, OF, NI, ¾	75	100	150
Standard, 15J.......................................	50	75	125
Sterling, 19J, SW, PS, Adj.3P, OF....................	50	75	125
Stewart, 17J	50	75	125
Stewart Special, 17J	50	75	125
Time King, 17J, OF	75	100	150
Victor, 21J, ¾, Adj.5P	75	100	150

Grade 163, 16 size, 23 jewels, adjusted to 6 positions, motor barrel, 60 hour model, serial number 5,421,504.

Grade 187, 16 size, 17 Ruby jewels, three-fingered bridge model, gold jewel settings, gold train, Adj5p, serial number 2,487,510.

Grade or Name—Description	Avg	Ex-Fn	Mint
161 through 163A—See Bunn Special			
167L, 17J, marked	$125	$150	$175
167, 17J..	50	75	125
169, 19J, Adj.3P, OF...............................	100	125	175
174, 23J, LS, GJS, Adj.5P, OF, marked............ ★ ★	675	725	800
175, 19J, GJS, BRG, HC .... ★	900	975	1,100
177, 19J, SW, LS, 60 hour, Adj.5P, OF	400	500	650

ILLINOIS WATCH CO., 16 SIZE (continued)

Grade or Name—Description	Avg	Ex-Fn	Mint
179, 21J, HC, 3F brg, marked Ruby Jewels .... ★	$300	$400	$550
187, 17J, 3F brg, Adj.5P, GJS, GT, HC................	225	275	350
189, 21J, 3F brg, Adj.6P, GJS, GT, DR, marked Ruby Jewels, HC................................	400	450	525
333, 15J, HC	100	125	175
555, 17J, ¾, ADJ...................................	75	100	150
777, 17J, ¾, ADJ...................................	75	100	150
900, 19J, LS, Adj.3P	100	125	175

Illinois Watch Co., 14 size, 16 jewels, Adj5p.

Illinois Watch Co., 14 size, 21 jewels, adjusted, nickel movement, gold jewel settings, serial number 1,029,204.

ILLINOIS
14 SIZE

Grade or Name — Description	Avg	Ex-Fn	Mint
Illinois Watch Co., 7J, M#1-2-3, SW, OF	$40	$50	$65
Illinois Watch Co., 11J, M#1-2-3, SW, OF	50	60	75
Illinois Watch Co., 15J, M#1-2-3, SW, OF	60	70	90
Illinois Watch Co., 16J, M#1-2-3, SW, OF	75	80	115
Illinois Watch Co., 21J, M#1-2-3, SW, OF	90	110	135
Illinois Watch Co., 21J, Silveroid	60	70	90

NOTE: Add $25 for above watches in hunting case.

ILLINOIS
12 SIZE and 13 SIZE

Grade or Name — Description	Avg	Ex-Fn	Mint
Aristocrat, 19J, OF...................................	$40	$50	$70
Ariston, 11-17J, OF	60	70	85
Ariston, 19J, OF.....................................	75	100	150
Ariston, 21J, OF.....................................	85	110	160
Ariston, 23J, OF.....................................	175	200	250

Ben Franklin, 12 size, 17 jewels, open face, gold train, serial number 2,366,286.

Illini, 12 size, 21 jewels, bridge model, serial number 3,650,129. Note five tooth click.

Grade or Name—Description	Avg	Ex-Fn	Mint
Autocrat, 17J, Adj.3P, ¾	$60	$70	$85
Autocrat, 19J, Adj.3P, ¾	65	75	95
Benjamin Franklin, 17J, OF	200	250	325
Burlington W. Co., 21J, OF	60	70	85
Central, 17J, OF, 2-Tone	40	50	70
Diamond Ruby Sapphire, 21J, Adj.5P, GJS	300	350	425
Elite, 19J, OF	60	70	85
Illini, 13 Size, 21J, Adj.5P, 14K, HC	275	325	400

Example of Illinois Thin Model, 12 size, 17 jewels, adjusted to 3 positions.

Maiden America, 12 size, 17 jewels, serial number 2,820,499.

Santa Fe Special, 12 size, 21 jewels, three-quarter plate, serial number 3,414,422.

Grade or Name—Description	Avg	Ex-Fn	Mint
Illini, 13 Size, 21J, Adj.5P, BRG, GJS	$75	$100	$150
Illini Extra, 13 Size, 21J, Adj.5P, OF	75	100	150
Illini, 13 Size, 23J, Adj.5P, BRG, GJS	125	150	200
Illinois Watch Co., 15J, OF	40	50	70
Illinois Watch Co., 17J, OF, 14K	250	275	325
Illinois Watch Co., 17J, HC, GF	75	100	150
Illinois Watch Co., 19J, OF	60	70	85
Illinois Watch Co., 21J, OF	70	80	95
Illinois Watch Co., 21J, HC	100	125	175
Interstate Chronometer, 21J, GJS, OF	150	175	225
Interstate Chronometer, 21J, GJS, HC	200	225	275
A. Lincoln, 19J, Adj.5P, GJS, DR, ¾, marked on mvt...	60	70	85
A. Lincoln, 21J, Adj.5P, DR, GJS	70	80	95
Maiden America, 17J, ADJ	60	70	85
Marquis Autocrat, 17J, OF	60	70	85
Master, 21J, GT, GJS, OF	70	80	95
Masterpiece, 19J, Adj.3P, OF	65	75	100
Railroad Dispatch Special, 17J, SW, GT	70	80	95
Santa Fe Special, 21J	75	100	150
Sterling, 17J, OF	40	50	65
Stewart Special, 17J, SW, Adj.3P	50	60	75
Stewart Special, 19J, SW, OF, GT	55	65	80
Time King, 19J, SW, Adj.3P	60	70	85
Time King, 21J, SW, Adj.3P	70	80	95
Transit, 19J, OF, PS	60	70	85
Vim, 17J, ADJ, BRG, GJS, DR, OF	50	60	75
Washington W. Co., 11J, HC	100	125	175
Washington W. Co., Army & Navy, 19J	100	125	175
Washington W. Co., Senate, 17J, M#2, PS, HC	60	70	85

ILLINOIS WATCH CO., 12 & 13 SIZE (continued)

Grade or Name—Description	Avg	Ex-Fn	Mint
121, 21J, Adj.3P	$70	$85	$95
127, 17J, ADJ	60	70	85
129, 19J, Adj.3P	60	70	85
219, 11J, M#1	50	60	75
403, 15J, BRG	60	70	85
405, 17J, BRG, ADJ, OF	60	70	85
409, 21J, BRG, Diamond, Ruby, Sapphire, Adj.5P, GJS .	275	325	400
410, 23J, BRG, GJS, Adj.6P, DR......................	150	200	275
410, 23J, BRG, GJS, Adj.6P, DR, 14K, OF.............	250	300	375

ILLINOIS
8 SIZE

Grade or Name — Description	Avg	Ex-Fn	Mint
Arlington, 7J, ¾ ....★	$125	$150	$200
Rose LeLand, 13J, ¾ ....★ ★	225	250	300
Stanley, 7J, ¾ ....★ ★ ★	250	300	350
Mary Stuart, 15J, ¾ ....★ ★	200	250	300
Sunnyside, 11J, ¾ ....★	150	200	250
151, 7J, ¾	40	50	65
152, 11J, ¾	50	60	75
155, 11J, ¾	60	70	85
155, 11J, ¾, Coin...................................	30	40	55

Note: Add $10 more for above watches in hunting case.

Illinois Watch Co., 8 size, 7 jewels

Grade 144, 6 size, 15 jewels, serial number 5,902,290.

ILLINOIS
6 SIZE

Grade or Name — Description	Avg	Ex-Fn	Mint
Illinois W. Co., 7J, LS, HC, 14K	$200	$225	$300
Illinois W. Co., 7J, HC..............................	50	75	125

ILLINOIS WATCH CO., 6 SIZE (continued)

Grade or Name—Description	Avg	Ex-Fn	Mint
Illinois W. Co., 7J, OF, Coin	$35	$45	$60
Illinois W. Co., 11J, OF, HC	50	75	125
Illinois W. Co., 15J, OF, HC, 14K	200	250	325
Illinois W. Co., 17J, OF, HC	50	75	125
Illinois W. Co., 19J, OF, HC	75	100	150
Washington W. Co., 15J, HC, Liberty Bell	125	150	200

ILLINOIS
4 SIZE

Grade or Name — Description	Avg	Ex-Fn	Mint
Illinois W. Co., 7J, LS, HC	$50	$55	$95
Illinois W. Co., 11J, LS, HC	50	75	125
Illinois W. Co., 15J, LS, HC	50	75	125

ILLINOIS
0 SIZE

Grade or Name — Description	Avg	Ex-Fn	Mint
Illinois W. Co., 7J, LS, HC, 14K	$175	$225	$300
201, 11J, BRG, NI	75	100	150
203, 15J, BRG, NI	75	100	150
204, 17J, BRG, NI	75	100	150
Interstate Chronometer, 15J, HC, SW	175	200	275
Interstate Chronometer, 17J, HC, SW	185	210	285
Washington W. Co., Liberty Bell, 15J, ADJ	150	175	250
Washington W. Co., Mt. Vernon, 17J, ADJ	160	185	275

Grade 201, 0 size, 11 jewels, originally sold for $8.10.

Grade 203, 0 size, 15 jewels, originally sold for $10.40

Grade 204, 0 size, 17 jewels, originally sold for $12.83.

ILLINOIS SPRINGFIELD WATCH CO.
IDENTIFICATION OF MOVEMENTS
BY MODEL NUMBER

How to Identify Your Watch: Compare the movement of your watch with the illustrations in this section. Upon matching the movement exactly, the model number and size can be determined. While comparing, note the location of the balance, jewels, screws, gears, and type of back plate (Full, ¾, Bridge) which will be clues in identifying the movement you have. Having determined the size and model number, you can now find your watch in the main price listing by name or number (which is engraved on the movement).

THE ILLINOIS WATCH CO. GRADE AND MODEL CHART

Size	Model	Plate Design	Setting	Hunting or Open Face	Type Barrel	Started w/ Serial No.	Remarks
18	1	Full	Key	Htg	Reg	1	Course train
	2	Full	Lever	Htg	Reg	38,901	Course train
	3	Full	Lever	OF	Reg	46,201	Course train, 5th pinion
	4	Full	Pendant	OF	Reg	1,050,001	Fast train
	5	Full	Lever	Htg	Reg	1,256,101	Fast train, RR Grade
	6	Full	Lever	OF	Reg	1,144,401	Fast train, RR Grade
16	1	Full	Lever	Htg	Reg	1,030,001	Thick model
	2	Full	Pendant	OF	Reg	1,037,001	Thick model
	3	Full	Lever	OF	Reg	1,038,001	Thick model
	4	¼ & brg	Lever	Htg	Reg	1,300,001	Getty model
	5	¼ & brg	Lever	OF	Reg	1,300,601	Getty model
	6	¼ & brg	Pendant	Htg	Reg	2,160,111	DR & Improved RR model
	7	¼ & brg	Pendant	OF	Reg	2,160,011	DR & Improved RR model
	8	¼ & brg	Lever	Htg	Reg	2,523,101	DR & Improved RR model
	9	¼ & brg	Lever	OF	Reg	2,522,001	DR & Improved model
	10	Cent brg	Lever	OF	Motor	3,178,901	Also 17S Ex Thin RR gr 48 hr
	11	¼	Lever & Pen	OF	Motor	4,001,001	RR grade 48 hr
	12	¼	Lever & Pen	Htg	Motor	4,002,001	RR grade 48 hr
	13	Cent brg	Lever	OF	Motor	4,166,801	Also 17S RR grade 60 hr
	14	¼	Lever	OF	Motor	4,492,501	RR grade 60 hr
	15	¼	Lever	OF	Motor	5,488,301	RR grade 60 hr Elinvar
14	1	Full	Lever	Htg	Reg	1,009,501	Thick model
	2	Full	Pendant	OF	Reg	1,000,001	Thick model
	3	Full	Lever	OF	Reg	1,001,001	Thick model
13	1	brg	Pendant	OF	Motor		Ex Thin gr 538 & 539
12	1	¼	Pendant	OF	Reg	1,685,001	
Thin	2	¼	Pendant	Htg	Reg	1,748,751	
	3	Cent brg	Pendant	OF	Reg	2,337,011	Center bridge
	4	Cent brg	Pendant	Htg	Reg	2,337,001	Center bridge
	5	Cent brg	Pendant	OF	Motor	3,742,201	Center bridge
	6	Cent brg	Pendant	Htg	Motor	4,395,301	Center bridge
12T	1	True Ctr brg	Pendant	OF	Motor	3,700,001	1 tooth click, Also 13S
	2	True Ctr brg	Pendant	OF	Motor	3,869,301	5 tooth click
	3	¼	Pendant	OF	Motor	3,869,201	2 tooth click
8	1	Full	Key or lever	Htg	Reg	100,001	Plate not recessed
	2	Full	Lever	Htg	Reg	100,101	Plate is recessed
6	1	¼	Lever	Htg	Reg	552,001	
4	1	¼	Lever	Htg	Reg	551,501	
0	1	¼	Pendant	OF	Reg	1,815,901	
	2	¼	Pendant	Htg	Reg	1,749,801	
	3	Cent brg	Pendant	OF	Reg	2,644,001	
	4	Cent brg	Pendant	Htg	Reg	2,637,001	

Model 1, 18 size, hunting, key wind & set.

Model 2, 18 size, hunting, lever set, coarse train.

Model 3, 18 size, open face, lever set, coarse train, with fifth pinion.

Model 4 18 size, open face, pendant set, fine train.

Model 5, 18 size, hunting, lever set, fine train.

Model 6, 18 size, open face, lever set, fine train.

Model 1, 16 size, hunting, lever set.

Model 2, 16 size, open face, pendant set.

Model 3, 16 size, open face, lever set

Model 4, 16 size, three-quarter plate, hunting, lever set.

Model 4, 16 size, three-quarter plate, bridge, hunting, lever set.

Model 5, 16 size, three-quarter plate, open face, lever set.

ILLINOIS SPRINGFIELD WATCH CO. (continued)

Model 5, 16 size, three-quarter plate, bridge, open face, lever set.

Model 6, 16 size - Pendant set
Model 8, 16 size - Lever set
hunting, three-quarter plate

Model 6, 16 size - Pendant set
Model 8, 16 size - Lever set
hunting, bridge model

Model 7, 16 size - Pendant set
Model 9, 16 size - Lever set
open face, three-quarter plate

Model 7, 16 size - Pendant set
Model 9, 16 size - Lever set
open face, bridge model

Model 10, 16 size, bridge, extra thin, open face, lever set, motor barrel.

Model 11, 16 size, three-quarter plate, open face, pendant set, motor barrel.

Model 12, 16 size, three-quarter plate, hunting, pendant set, motor barrel.

Model 13, 16 size, bridge, open face, lever set, motor barrel.

Model 14, 16 size, three-quarter plate, open face, lever set, 60-hour motor barrel.

Model A, 16 size, open face.

Model B, 16 size, hunting case.

Model C, 16 size, open face

Model D, 16 size, open face

Model 1, 14 size, hunting, lever set.

Model 2, 14 size, open face, pendant set.

Model 3, 14 size, open face, lever set.

Model 1, 13 size, bridge, extra thin, open face, pendant set, motor barrel.

Model 1, 12 size, three-quarter plate, open face, pendant set.

Model 1, 12 size, three-quarter plate, bridge, open face, pendant set.

Model 2, 12 size, three-quarter plate, hunting, pendant set.

Model 2, 12 size, three-quarter plate, bridge, hunting, pendant set.

Model 3, 12 size, **Model 4**, 12 & 14 size, bridge, open face, pendant set.

Model 4, 12 size, bridge, hunting, pendant set.

Model 5, 12 size, bridge, open face, pendant set, motor barrel.

Model 1, 12 size, extra thin, bridge, open face, pendant set, motor barrel.

Model 2, 12 size, extra thin, bridge, open face, pendant set, motor barrel.

Model 3, 12 size, extra thin, three-quarter plate, open face, pendant set, motor barrel.

Model A, 12 size, bridge, open face.

Model 1, 8 size, hunting, key or lever set.

Model 2, 8 size, hunting, lever set.

Model 1, 6 size, hunting, lever set.

Model 1, 4 size, hunting, lever set.

Model 1, 0 size, three-quarter plate, open face, pendant set

Model 2, 0 size, three-quarter plate, hunting, pendant set.

Model 3, 0 size, bridge, open face, pendant set.

Model 4, 0 size, bridge, hunting, pendant set.

Model 3, 3/0 size, bridge, open face, pendant set.

Model 4, 3/0 size, bridge, hunting, pendant set.

Model 1, 6/0 size, three-quarter plate, open face, pendant set.

Model 2, 6/0 size, bridge, open face, pendant set.

288

INDEPENDENT WATCH CO.
Fredonia, New York
1880 - 1885

The California Watch Company was idle for two years before it was purchased by brothers E. W. Howard and C. M. Howard. They had been selling watches by mail for sometime and started engraving the Howard Bros. name on them and using American-made watches. Their chief supply came from Hampden Watch Co., Illinois, U. S. Watch Co. of Marion, and Cornell Watch Co. The brothers formed the Independent Watch Co. in 1880, but it was not a watch factory in the true sense. They had other manufacturers engrave the Independent Watch Co. name on the top plates and on the dials of their watches. These watches were sold by mail order and sent to the buyer C. O. D. The names used on the movements were "Mark Twain," "Howard Bros.," "Independent Watch Co.," "Fredonia Watch Co.," and "Lakeshore Watch Co., Fredonia, N. Y."

The company later decided to manufacture watches and used the name Fredonia Watch Co. But they found that selling watches two different ways was no good. The business survived until 1885 at which time the owners decided to move the plant to a new location at Peoria, Illinois. Approximately 350,000 watches were made that sold for $16.

CHRONOLOGY OF THE DEVELOPMENT OF INDEPENDENT WATCH CO.:

Independent Watch Co.	1880-1883
Fredonia Watch Co.	1883-1885
Peoria Watch Co.	1885-1895

Grade or Name — Description	Avg	Ex-Fn	Mint
18S, 7J, KW, KS, OF, by U.S. W. Co. Marion, with butterfly cutout .... ★	$450	$550	$675
18S, 11J, KW, KS, by Hampden	200	250	325
18S, 11J, KW, KS, Coin	150	175	225
18S, 11J, KW, KS...................................	150	175	225
18S, 15J, KW, KS...................................	160	185	235

Independent Watch Co., 18 size, 11 jewels, key wind & set, made by Hampden Watch Co. (Model Number 1), serial number 170,844.

Independent Watch Co., 18 size, 15 jewels, key wind, made by U.S. Marion Watch Co., note butterfly cuttout, serial number 192,661.

Grade or Name—Description	Avg	Ex-Fn	Mint
18S, Howard Bros., 11J, KW, KS	$250	$300	$375
18S, Independent W. Co., 11J	150	175	225
18S, Lakeshore W. Co., 15J, KW, HC, by N.Y. W. Co.	200	275	350
18S, Mark Twain, 11J, KW, KS	350	400	475

ROBERT H. INGERSOLL & BROS.
New York, New York
1892 - 1922

In 1892 this company published a catalog for the mail order trade. It listed men's watch chains and a "silverine" watch for $3.95. It was not a true Ingersoll but a "Universal," introduced that same year to the dealers. The first $1 watches were jeweled; "Reliance" had seven jewels. In 1916, Ingersoll's production was 16,000 a day. The slogan was "The Watch that Made the Dollar Famous." The first 1,000 watches were made by Waterbury Clock Co. By 1922 the Ingersoll line was completely taken over by Waterbury. U. S. Time Corp. acquired Waterbury in 1944 and continued to use the Ingersoll name on certain watches.

ESTIMATED SERIAL NUMBERS
AND PRODUCTION DATES

Date	Serial No.	Date	Serial No.	Date	Serial No.
		1905	10,000,000	1918	47,500,000
1892	150,000	1906	12,500,000	1919	50,000,000
1893	310,000	1907	15,000,000	1920	55,000,000
1894	650,000	1908	17,500,000	1921	58,000,000
1895	1,000,000	1909	20,000,000	1922	60,500,000
1896	2,000,000	1910	25,000,000	1923	62,000,000
1897	2,900,000	1911	30,000,000	1924	65,000,000
1898	3,500,000	1912	38,500,000	1925	67,500,000
1899	3,750,000	1913	40,000,000	1926	69,000,000
1900	6,000,000	1914	41,500,000	1927	70,500,000
1901	6,700,000	1915	42,500,000	1928	71,500,000
1902	7,200,000	1916	45,500,000	1929	73,500,000
1903	7,900,000	1917	47,000,000	1930	75,000,000
1904	8,100,000			1944	95,000,000

Ingersoll Back Wind & Set, patent date Dec. 23, 1890 and Jan. 13, 1891, c. late 1890s.

Ingersoll Blind Man's Watch.

INGERSOLL
DOLLAR TYPE

NOTE: Prices are for complete watch in good running order. In some specialty markets, the comic character watches may bring higher prices in top condition.

Grade or Name — Description	Avg	Ex-Fn	Mint
Ingersoll Back Wind.............................★	$100	$125	$175
Admiral Dewey, "Flagship Olympia" on back of case	125	150	200
American Pride.....................................	75	100	125
Are U My Neighbor	35	45	65
B. B. H. Special, Backwind	65	75	95
Blind Man Pocket Watch	40	50	60
Buck...	25	30	40
Champion (many models)	50	75	125
Chancery..	50	75	125
Chicago Expo. 1933	175	200	275
Climax...	40	45	65
Clock Watch, pat. 1878-90-91.......................	65	75	95
Cloverine..	60	70	85
Colby...	20	25	35
Columbus	45	60	85
Columbus (3 ships on back of case), 1893	200	275	350
Connecticut W. Co.	30	40	50
Cord..	20	30	45
Crown	20	25	35
Dan Dee	25	35	50
Defiance	30	40	55
Delaware W. Co.....................................	25	30	40
Devon Mfg. Co.	20	25	35

Scout watch (Be prepared)

Yankee watch with bicycle on dial.

INGERSOLL DOLLAR TYPE (continued)

Ingersoll Premium, early back wind & set.

Ingersoll Triumph, note pin for setting.

Grade or Name—Description	Avg	Ex-Fn	Mint
Eclipse (many models)	$25	$30	$40
Eclipse Radiolite	30	35	40
Ensign	30	35	40
Escort	25	30	40
Fancy Dials unfaded to be mint	100	145	200
Freedom	30	35	40
Gotham	15	20	35
Graceline	45	50	65
Gregg	15	25	35
Junior (several models)...............................	15	25	35
Junior Radiolite	35	40	55
Kelton	10	15	25
Lapel Watches	25	45	65
Leeds	15	20	25
Liberty U.S.A., backwind	75	100	150
Liberty Watch Co.	35	45	75
Limited, lever set....................................	40	50	60
Major..	10	15	20
Maple Leaf	25	30	40
Master Craft...	10	15	20
Midget (several models)	25	40	55
Monarch	20	25	30
New West	30	45	65
New York World's Fair, 1939.........................	275	325	425
Overland	35	40	50
Pan American Expo., Buffalo	200	275	350
Paris World Expo., 1900	250	325	400
Patrol...	35	45	65
Perfection	35	45	55
Pilgram	40	50	55
Premier, back wind, eagle on back, c. 1894	70	100	120

INGERSOLL DOLLAR TYPE (continued)

Left: **Ingersoll Back Wind**, c. 1895. Right: **Yankee Back Wind**, c. 1893.

Grade or Name—Description	Avg	Ex-Fn	Mint
Premium Back Wind and Set	$50	$75	$100
Progress, 1933 World's Fair Chicago	200	275	350
Puritan	35	50	75
Quaker	40	45	60
Radiolite	30	35	45
Reliance, 7J	35	45	85
Remington W. Co. USA	60	75	95
Rotary International, c. 1920	40	45	65
Royal	10	15	25
St. Louis World's Fair (two models)	225	250	300
St. Louis World's Fair, 1904	100	150	200
The Saturday Post	150	175	225
Scout "Be Prepared"	250	300	375
Senator	35	40	50
Senior	25	30	40
Sir Leeds	25	30	40
Solar	25	30	40
Souvenir Special	35	45	60
Sterling	35	40	50
Ten Hune	60	70	85
Traveler with Bed Side Stand	35	45	65
Triumph	75	85	100
Triumph Penset	150	175	225
True Test	25	30	40
Trump	35	45	55
USA (two models)	50	75	100
Universal, 1st model	200	250	300
Uncle Sam	40	50	60
George Washington	150	175	225
Waterbury (several models)	40	60	90

INGERSOLL DOLLAR TYPE (continued)

Grade or Name—Description	Avg	Ex-Fn	Mint
Waterbury Back Wind, 35 Size........................	$100	$150	$200
Winner...	20	25	35
Winner with S.B.B....................................	40	45	55
Yankee Backwind	85	95	150
Yankee Bicycle Watch (sold for $1.00 in 1896)...........	150	175	225
Yankee Radiolite	40	55	75
Yankee Radiolite with S.B.B.	45	50	60
Yankee Special (many models)	75	100	150
Yankee, Perpetual calendar on back of case	75	100	150

Exmple of an Ingersoll moveable calendar for years
1929-1951 located on back of case.

Example of an Ingersoll watch made in Great Britain.

INGERSOLL LTD.
(GREAT BRITAIN)

Grade or Name — Description	Avg	Ex-Fn	Mint
Ingersoll Ltd. (many models)	$50	$75	$100
Coronation, Elizabeth II on watch	175	200	250
Coronation, June 2, 1953 on dial	175	200	250
16S, 7J, 3F Brg	55	60	85
16S, 15J, 3F Brg	75	85	110
16S, 17J, 3F Brg, ADJ...............................	115	145	175
16S, 19J, 3F Brg, Adj5P	200	250	350
12S, 4J	25	30	45

Example of an **Ingraham movement**.　　**New York to Paris**, airplane model commemorating Lindbergh's famous flight.

E. INGRAHAM CO.
Bristol, Connecticut
1912 - 1968

The E. Ingraham Co. purchased the Bannatyne Co. in 1912. They produced their first American pocket watch in 1913. A total of about 65 million American-made pocket watches and over 12 million wrist watches were produced before they started to import watches in 1968.

Grade or Name — Description	Avg	Ex-Fn	Mint
Ingraham W. Co. (many models)	$25	$35	$50
Aristocrat Railroad Sp.	25	30	40
Autocrat	15	20	25
Beacon	15	20	25
Biltmore	10	15	20
Biltmore Radium	10	15	20
Bristol	15	20	25
Clipper	20	25	35
Comet	15	20	25
Companion, sweep second hand	15	20	30
Cub	15	20	25
Demi-hunter cover	10	15	20
Dixie	10	15	20
Dot	10	20	25
Endura	10	15	20
Everbrite (all models)	15	25	30
Ingraham USA	10	15	20

E. INGRAHAM CO. (continued)

Grade or Name—Description	Avg	Ex-Fn	Mint
Jockey	$15	$20	$25
Laddie	25	30	40
Laddie Athlete	40	45	55
Lady's Purse Watch, with fancy bezel	45	50	60
Lendix Extra	25	30	40
Master	10	15	20
Miss Ingraham	25	30	40
New York to Paris	200	250	300
Overland	30	35	45
The Pal	20	30	45
Pastor, stop watch	45	55	70
Pathfinder, compass on pendant	65	75	95
Patriot	125	150	250
Peerless	30	35	55

Example of **Path Finder** showing compass in crown.   Printed on dial, "Unbreakable crystal," ca. 1924.

Grade or Name—Description	Avg	Ex-Fn	Mint
Pilot	$30	$40	$55
Pocket Pal	15	20	25
Pony	25	30	40
Pride	20	25	35
Princess	20	30	45
Pup	25	30	40
Reliance	45	50	60
Rex	15	20	25
Rite Time	25	30	40
St. Regis	15	20	25
Secometer	20	25	35
Sentinel	15	20	25

Grade or Name—Description	Avg	Ex-Fn	Mint
Sentinel Click	$20	$25	$35
Sentinel Fold Up Travel	45	50	60
Sentry	25	30	35
Silver Star	15	25	30
Sterling	20	25	35
Sterling W. Co. Stop Watch, fly back to zero	45	50	75
Sturdy	10	15	20
Target	10	15	20
Time Ball	25	30	40
Time & Time	30	40	55
Top Flight	20	25	35
Top Notch	35	45	50
Tower	15	20	25
Trail Blazer	150	200	275
Unbreakable Crystal	45	60	75
Uncle Sam (all models)	50	75	95
Uncle Sam Backwind & Set	85	110	145
Viceroy	20	25	35
Victory	25	30	55
Zep	150	200	275

Left: Example of a basic **International Watch Co.** movement with patent dates of Aug. 19, 1902, Jan. 27, 1903 & Aug. 11, 1903. Right: Example of a **Highland.**

INTERNATIONAL WATCH CO.
Newark City, New Jersey
1902 - 1907

This company produced only non-jeweled or low-cost production type watches that were inexpensive and nickel plated. Names on their watches include: Berkshire, Madison, and Mascot.

Grade or Name — Description		Avg	Ex-Fn	Mint
Berkshire, OF....................................... ★		$75	$100	$150
Highland .... ★		65	90	140
Madison, 18S, OF .... ★		75	100	150
Mascot, OF .... ★		50	75	125

KANKAKEE WATCH CO.
Kankakee, Illinois
1900

This company reportedly became the McIntyre Watch Co. Little other information is available.

Grade or Name — Description	Avg	Ex-Fn	Mint
16S, BRG, NI .... ★ ★ ★	$5,500	$6,000	$7,000

Kelly Watch Co., 16 size, aluminum movement, straight line lever, quick train, porcelain dial, stem set, reversible ratchet stem wind, originally sold for $2.20, c. 1900.

KELLY WATCH CO.
Chicago, Illinois
c. 1900

Grade or Name — Description	Avg	Ex-Fn	Mint
16S, aluminum movement and OF case	$50	$75	$125

KEYSTONE STANDARD WATCH CO.
Lancaster, Pennsylvania
1886 - 1890

Abram Bitner agreed to buy a large number of stockholders' shares of the Lancaster Watch Co. at 10 cents on the dollar; he ended up with 5,625 shares out of the

KEYSTONE STANDARD WATCH CO. (continued)

8,000 that were available. Some 8,900 movements had been completed but not sold at the time of the shares purchase. The company Bitner formed assumed the name of Keystone Standard Watch Co. as the trademark but in reality existed as the Lancaster Watch Co. The business was sold to Hamilton Watch Co. in 1891. Total production was 48,000.

Example of a basic **Keystone** movement, about 16-18 size, 7-11 jewels, stem wind, serial number 420,843, c. 1888.

Keystone Watch Co., dust proof model, 18 size, 15 jewels, serial number 352,766.

Grade or Name — Description		Avg	Ex-Fn	Mint
18S, 20J, ¾, LS, HC	★ ★	$500	$550	$650
18S, 7-15J, OF, KW		50	75	125
18S, 15J, dust proof, ADJ		125	150	200
18S, 15J, dust proof, OF		100	125	175
18S, 15J, dust proof, HC		150	175	225
18S, West End, 15J, HC		75	125	175
18S, 11J, dust proof		100	125	175
18S, 7-15J, OF, SW, ¾, LS		50	75	125
6S, 7-10J, HC		100	125	175

Example of a basic **Knickerbocker** movement, 16-18 size, 7 jewels, duplex escapement.

Example of a basic **Knickerbocker** movement with a duplex escapement, 16-18 size.

KNICKERBOCKER WATCH CO.
New York, New York
1890 - 1930

This company imported and sold Swiss and low-cost production American watches.

Grade or Name — Description	Avg	Ex-Fn	Mint
6S, Duplex	$40	$50	$65
10S, Barkley "8 Day"	75	100	125
12S, 7J, OF	45	55	85
18S, 7J, OF, PS, NI, duplex escapement	50	60	80
16S, 7J	45	55	75

LANCASTER WATCH CO.
Lancaster, Pennsylvania
1877 - 1886

Work commenced on Sept. 1, 1877, at the Lancaster Watch Co. The watches produced there were designed to sell at a cheaper price than normal. They had a solid top, ¾ plate, and a pillar plate that was fully ruby-jeweled (4½ pairs). They had a gilt and nickel movement and a new stem-wind device, modeled by Mosly & Todd. By mid-1878 the Lancaster Watch Co. had produced 150 movements. Four grades of watches were made: Keystone, Fulton, Franklin, and Melrose. In September 1879 the company had made 334 movements. In 1880 the total was up to 1,250 movements, and by mid-1882 about 17,000 movements had been produced. All totaled, about 20,000 watch movements were made.

About 75 8-size ladies' watches were also made.

CHRONOLOGY OF THE DEVELOPMENT OF THE LANCASTER WATCH CO.:
> Adams and Perry Watch Mfg. Co. — 1874-1876
> Lancaster Watch Co. — 1877-1878
> Lancaster Pa. Watch Co. — 1878-1879
> Lancaster Watch Co. — 1879-1886
> Keystone Standard Co. — 1886-1890
> Hamilton Watch Co. — 1892-1958

LANCASTER
18 SIZE
(All ¾ Plate)

Grade or Name — Description	Avg	Ex-Fn	Mint
Chester, 7J, KW, gilded	$125	$150	$200
Comet, 7J, NI	125	150	200
Delaware, 20J, ADJ, SW, gilded	300	375	450
Denver, 7J, gilded	75	100	125
Denver, 7J, gilded, Silveroid	40	50	65
Elberon, 7J, dust proof	125	150	200
Ben Franklin, 7J, KW, gilded	250	300	375
Ben Franklin, 11J, KW, gilded	300	350	425
Fulton, 7J, ADJ, KW, gilded	125	150	200
Fulton, 11J, ADJ, KW, gilded	125	150	200
Girard, 15J, ADJ, gilded	100	150	200
Hoosac, 11J, OF	125	175	225
Keystone, 15J, ADJ, gilded, GJS, dust proof	100	125	175
Keystone, 15J, ADJ, gilded, GJS, Silveroid	60	70	85
Lancaster, 7J, SW	40	50	65
Lancaster, 15J, SW, Silveroid	60	70	85
Lancaster, 15J, OF	75	100	150
Lancaster Pa., 20J, ADJ, NI ★ ★	400	500	650

Lancaster Watch Co., 18 size, 20 jewels, gold jeweled settings, stem wind & pendant set, serial number 1747.

Stevens Model, 18 size, 15 jewels, adjusted, dust proof model, swing-out movement, c.1886.

Grade or Name—Description	Avg	Ex-Fn	Mint
Lancaster Watch, 20J, DR, ADJ, NI, GJS, 14K HC . ★ ★	$700	$800	$950
Malvern, 7J, gilded	60	70	85
Melrose, 15J, NI, ADJ, GJS	100	125	175
Nation Standard American Watch Co., 7J, HC	200	225	275
New Era, 7J, gilded, KW, HC	75	100	150
New Era, 7J, gilded, KW, Silveroid	40	60	90
Paoli, 7J, NI	50	75	125
Wm. Penn, 20J, ADJ, NI, dust proof	400	500	650
Radnor, 7J, gilded	100	125	175
Record, 7J, Silveroid	40	50	65
Record, 15J, NI	75	100	150

West End, 18 size, 15 jewels, key wind & set, serial number 158,080, c. 1878.

Example of a basic Lancaster movement, 8-10 size, 15 jewels, serial number 317,812.

LANCASTER WATCH CO. (continued)

Grade or Name—Description	Avg	Ex-Fn	Mint
Ruby, 16J, NI	$275	$325	$400
Sidney, 15J, NI	100	125	175
Stevens, 15J, ADJ, NI, dust proof	150	175	225
West End, 19J, HC, KW, gilded .... ★★	450	500	575
West End, 15J, HC, KW, KS.........................	175	200	250
West End, 15J, SW	175	200	250
West End, 15J, SW, Silveroid	40	60	85

8 SIZE

Grade or Name — Description	Avg	Ex-Fn	Mint
Flora, gilded..	$75	$100	$150
Lady Penn, 20J, GJS, ADJ, NI.......................	300	350	425
Lancaster W. Co., 7J	75	100	125

Manhattan Watch Co., Chronograph, 18-16 size, note two buttons on top; one sets hands, the other starts and stops watch, serial number 117,480.

Manhattan Watch Co., 18 size, Chronograph. Note two buttons on top; one sets hands, the other starts and stops watch.

MANHATTAN WATCH CO.
New York, New York
1883 - 1891

The Manhattan Watch Co. made mainly low cost production watches. A complete and full line of watches was made, and most were cased and styled to be sold as a complete watch. The watches were generally 16S with full plate movements. The patented winding mechanism was different. These watches were in both the hunter and open-face cases and later had a sweep second hand. Total production was 160,000 or more watches.

16 SIZE

Grade or Name — Description	Avg	Ex-Fn	Mint
OF, with back wind .... ★	$250	$300	$400
OF, stop watch .... ★	200	250	350
7J, 2 button, sweep sec., OF .... ★	125	175	225
7J, 2 button, sweep sec., HC .... ★	200	250	300
Stallcup, 7J, OF .... ★	150	200	250

12 SIZE

Grade or Name — Description	Avg	Ex-Fn	Mint
12S .... ★	$125	$200	$275

MANISTEE WATCH CO.
Manistee, Michigan
1908 - 1912

The Manistee watches, first marketed in 1909, were designed to compete with the low-cost production watches. Dials, jewels, and hairsprings were not produced at the factory. The first movement was 18S, 7J, and sold for about $5. Manistee also made 5J, 15J, 17J, and 21J watches in cheap cases in sizes 16 and 12. Estimated total production was 60,000. Most were sold by Star Watch Case Co.

18 TO 12 SIZE

Grade or Name — Description	Avg	Ex-Fn	Mint
18S, 7J, ¾, LS, HC................................ ★	$325	$375	$425
18S, 7J, ¾, LS, OF .... ★	275	325	375
16S, 15J, HC .... ★	225	250	325
16S, 7J, OF .... ★	200	250	325

Example of a basic **Manistee** movement, 16-18 size, 17 jewels, open face, three-quarter plate.

Grade or Name—Description		Avg	Ex-Fn	Mint
16S, 15-17J, OF	★	$225	$250	$325
16S, 19J, HC	★	300	350	425
16S, 21J, OF	★	325	375	450
12S, 15J	★	150	175	225

McIntyre Watch Co., 16 size, 25 jewels, adjusted to 5 positions with wind indicator, with equidistant escapement, manufactured about 1909. Above illustration taken from a blue print.

McINTYRE WATCH CO.
Kankakee, Illinois
1905 - 1911

This company probably bought the factory from Kankakee Watch Co. In 1908 Charles DeLong was made master watchmaker, and he designed and improved the railroad watches. Only a few watches were made, estimated total production being about ten watches.

Grade or Name — Description		Avg	Ex-Fn	Mint
16S, 21J, BRG, NI, WI	★ ★ ★	$4,500	$5,000	$6,500
16S, 25J, BRG, NI, WI, Adj.5P, equidistant escapement	★ ★ ★	5,500	6,000	7,500
12S, 19J, BRG	★ ★ ★	2,000	2,500	3,500

MELROSE WATCH CO.
Melrose, Massachusetts
1866 - 1868

Melrose Watch Co. began as Tremont Watch Co. and imported the expansion balances and escapements. Dials were first made by Mr. Gold and Mr. Spear, then later by Mr. Hull and Mr. Carpenter. Tremont had hoped to produce 600 sets of trains per month. They were 18S, key wind, fully jeweled movements and were engraved "Tremont Watch Co." In 1866 the company moved, changed its name to Melrose Watch Co., and started making complete watch movements, including a new style 18S movement engraved "Melrose Watch Co." About 3,000 were produced. Some watches are found with "Melrose" on the dial and "Tremont" on the movement. Serial numbers start at about 30,000.

Example of a basic **Melrose Watch Co.** movement, 18 size, 15 jewels, key wind & set.

Grade or Name — Description		Avg	Ex-Fn	Mint
18S, 7J, KW, KS	★ ★	$300	$350	$425
18S, 11J, KW, KS, OF	★ ★	325	375	450
18S, 15J, KW, KS	★ ★	350	400	475
18S, 15J, KW, KS, Silveroid	★ ★	250	300	375

Note: Add $25.00 to values of above watches in hunting case.

MOZART WATCH CO.
Providence, Rhode Island
Ann Arbor, Michigan
1864 - 1870

In 1864 Don J. Mozart started out to produce a less expensive three-wheel watch in Providence, R. I. Despite his best efforts, the venture was declared a failure by 1866. Mozart left Providence and moved to Ann Arbor, Mich. There, again, he started on a three-wheel watch and succeeded in producing thirty. The three-wheel watch was not a new idea except to American manufacturers. Three-wheel watches were made many decades before Mozart's first effort, but credit for the first American-made three-wheel watch must go to him. The size was about 18 and could be called a ¾ or full plate move-

MOZART WATCH CO. (continued)

ment. The balance bridge was screwed on the top plate, as was customary. The round bridge partially covered the opening in the top plate and was just large enough for the balance to oscillate. The balance was compensated and somewhat smaller in diameter than usual. Mozart called it a chronolever, and it was to function so perfectly it would be free from friction. That sounded good but was in no way true. The watch was of the usual thickness of the American watches of 18S. The train had a main wheel with the usual number of teeth and a ten-leaf center pinion, but it had a large center wheel of 108 teeth and a third wheel of 90 teeth, with a six-leaf third (escape) pinion. The escape wheel had 30 teeth and received its impulse directly from the roller on the staff, while the escape tooth locked on the intermediate lever pallet. The escape pinion had a long pivot that carried the second hand, which made a circuit of the dial, once in 12 seconds. The total number of Mozart watches produced was 165, and about 30 of these were the three-wheel type.

Grade or Name — Description		Avg	Ex-Fn	Mint
18S, ¾, KW, KS, 3-wheel.......................★ ★ ★				
		$11,000	$15,000	$20,000
18S, ¾, KW, KS................................★ ★		6,000	7,000	8,000

Example of a basic **Mozart Watch Co.** movement, 18 size, three-quarter plate, key wind & set, three-wheel train, "Patent Dec. 24th, 1868" engraved on back plate.

Nashua Watch Co. (marked), 20 size, 19 jewels, key wind & set from back, serial number 1,057.

NASHUA WATCH CO.
Nashua, New Hampshire
1859 - 1862

One of the most important contributions to the American Watch industry was made by the Nashua Watch Co. of Nashua, New Hampshire. Founded in 1859 by B. D. Bingham, the company hired some of the most innovative and creative watchmakers in America and produced an extremely high grade American pocket watch.

His company included N. P. Stratton, C. V. Woerd, Charles Moseley, James H. Gerry, and James Gooding, among others. Most of the people connected with the Nashua Watch Company became famous for various advances in watch manufacture, at one time or another. Many had extremely important American patents on various inventions that came to be regarded as a benchmark of the best watches America was capable of making at the time.

The Nashua Watch Co. is important for many reasons. It was the first American company to produce a truly superior high grade movement; the ¾ plate design used by Nashua became the standard for over 40 years in the American marketplace. Perhaps most importantly, the watches designed by the Nashua Watch Co., and later by the Nashua division of the American Watch Co., became the leaders in the production of the highest quality watches made in America and forced the entire Swiss watch industry to change their technology to compete with the Nashua designs.

Nashua continually won awards for their various models of watches both here and in Europe. By virtue of their sheer technical superiority and classical elegance, Nashua became known universally as the most innovative producer of watches America ever knew.

The original Nashua company produced material for about 1,000 movements but, except for a handful, almost the entire production was finished by the American Watch Company at Waltham, Mass., after R. E. Robbins took over Nashua in 1862 when the company was in grave financial difficulty. Robbins was very happy about the arrangement since he got back almost all the watchmaking geniuses who had left him in 1859 to join Nashua. Robbins incorporated the Nashua Division into the American Watch Company as its high grade experimental division.

Over the years, many of the major advances were made by the Nashua division of Waltham, including the 1860 model 16-size keywind keyset, the 1862 model 20-size keywind keyset, the 1870 model 18-size keywind keyset, pin set, and lever set (which became the first American advertised Railroad watch), the 1868 model 16-size stemwind, and the 1872 model 17-size stemwind. The Nashua division also greatly influenced the 1888 model and the 1892 model by Waltham.

Since almost all the production material made by Nashua from 1859 until its incorporation into the American Watch Co. in 1862 was unfinished by Nashua, only about four examples of the 20-size keywind keyset from the back signed Nashua Watch Co. are known to exist.

Grade or Name — Description		Avg	Ex-Fn	Mint
Nashua (marked), 19J, KW, KS, ¾, 18K . . . . ★ ★ ★	$18,000	$22,000	$28,000
Nashua (unmarked), 15J, KW, KS, ¾, silver case . . . . ★ ★	3,000	4,000	5,000

NEWARK WATCH CO.
Newark, New Jersey
1864 - 1870

Arthur Wadsworth, one of the designers for Newark Watch Co., patented an 18 Size full plate movement. The first movements reached the market in 1867. This company produced only about 4,000 watches before it was sold to the Cornell Watch Co.

CHRONOLOGY OF THE DEVELOPMENT OF NEWARK WATCH CO.:
Newark Watch Co. 1864-1870; S#s 6,901 to 12,000;

NEWARK WATCH CO. (continued)

Cornell Watch Co., Chicago, Ill. 1870-1874; S#s 12,001 to 25,000;
Cornell Watch Co., San Francisco, Calif. 1874-Jan. 1876; S#s 25,001 to 35,000;
California Watch Co., Jan. 1876-mid 1876.

Example of a basic **Newark Watch Co.** movement, 18 size, 7-15 jewels, key wind & set.

Grade or Name — Description		Avg	Ex-Fn	Mint
18S, 15J, KW, KS, HC	★ ★	$350	$400	$500
18S, 15J, KW, KS, OF	★ ★	300	350	425
18S, 7J, KW, KS	★ ★	300	350	425
J. C. Adams, 11J, KW, KS	★ ★	350	400	475
J. C. Adams, 11J, KW, KS, Coin	★ ★	350	400	475
Edward Biven, 15J, KW, KS	★ ★	350	400	475
Robert Fellow, KW, KS	★ ★	400	450	525
Keyless Watch Co., 15J, LS, SW		300	350	425
Newark Watch Co., 7-15J, KW, KS	★ ★	350	400	475
Arthur Wadsworth, SW	★ ★	300	350	425
Arthur Wadsworth, 18S, 15J, 18K, HC ("Arthur Wadsworth, New York" on dial; "Keyless Watch, Patent #3655, June 19, 1866" engraved on movement)	★ ★	800	1,000	1,250

NEW ENGLAND WATCH CO.
Waterbury, Connecticut
1898 - 1914

The New England Watch Co., formerly the Waterbury Watch Co., made a watch with a duplex escapement, gilt, 16S, open faced. Watches with the skeletonized movement are very desirable. The company later became Timex Watch Co.

Grade or Name — Description		Avg	Ex-Fn	Mint
16S, OF, duplex, skeleton, good running order	★	$200	$250	$325
12S, 16S, 18S, OF, pictures on dial: ladies, dogs, horses, trains, flags, ships, cards, etc.		100	125	150
12S, 16S, 18S, OF, duplex escapement, good running order		30	40	60
12S, 16S, 18S, OF, pin lever escapement, good running order		15	25	45

NEW ENGLAND WATCH CO. (continued)

Front and back view of a skeletonized New England Watch Co. movement. This watch is fitted with a glass back and front, making the entire movement and wheels visible, 4 jewels, silver hands, black numbers, originally sold for $10-13.

Grade or Name—Description	Avg	Ex-Fn	Mint
6S, duplex	$35	$40	$55
Addison	35	40	55
Alden	35	40	55
Ambassador, 12S, duplex	25	30	40
Americus, duplex	20	25	30
Avour, duplex escapement	35	40	55
Berkshire, duplex, 14K, GF	60	70	85

New England Watch co., 16 size, 7 jewels, open face, double roller, Dan Patch stop watch.

New England Watch Co., Scout, about 16 size, 4 jewels, duplex escapement, New England base metal case.

New England Watch Co., multi-colored paper dials, showing an assorted selection. Watches complete with these type dials bring $125 - $175.00.

Grade or Name—Description	Avg	Ex-Fn	Mint
Cadish, duplex escapement	$35	$40	$55
Cavour	45	50	60
Columbian	15	20	30
Cruiser, duplex	45	50	69
Dan Patch, 7J ★	275	350	425
Excelsor, 7J	65	70	95
Fancy dial, "unfaded"	100	145	200
Gabour	65	70	85
General	20	30	45
Hale, 7J	25	30	45
Jockey, duplex	55	60	75
Oxford	15	20	30
Padishah, duplex	45	50	65
Putnam	65	70	85
Rugby, stop watch	65	70	85
Scout, 12 Size, duplex escapement, HC	40	45	60
Senator, duplex escapement	40	45	55
Trump, duplex	15	20	30
Tuxedo	15	20	35

NEW HAVEN CLOCK AND WATCH CO.
New Haven, Connecticut
1853 - 1956

The company started making watches in early 1880 in New Haven and produced the regular 16S, lever watch. These sold for $3.75. The company soon reached a production of about 200 watches per day, making a total of some 40 million watches.

New Haven Clock & Watch Co., **Angelus**, with rotating dials, patented Jan 23, 1900.

Example of a **New Haven** movement.

Grade or Name — Description	Avg	Ex-Fn	Mint
Always Right	$45	$55	$75
Angelus, 2 rotating dials	45	55	75
Babe Ruth	125	175	245
Beardsley—Radiant	45	50	65
Buddy	35	40	45
Bull Dog	40	45	60
Captain Scout	85	100	150
Chronometer	45	85	100
Elite	30	40	55
Fancy dials, no fading	100	145	200
Football Timer	45	55	75
Ford Special	75	85	100
Hamilton	35	45	60
Handy Andy	40	45	50
Jerome USA	35	40	50
Kaiser Wilhelm ★ ★	175	250	325

NEW HAVEN CLOCK & WATCH CO. (continued)

Example of **Kaiser Wilhelm.**

Example of **Traveler.**

Grade or Name—Description	Avg	Ex-Fn	Mint
Kermit	$40	$45	$55
Laddie	25	30	40
Leonard Watch Co.	25	40	50
Leonard	25	35	45
Mastercraft Rayolite	35	45	60
Miracle	25	30	40
Nehi	45	60	75
New Haven, pin lever, SW	50	75	100
New Haven, back wind	85	115	165
Panama Official Souvenir, 1915	200	250	350
Pastor Stop Watch	65	85	100
Playing cards on dial	100	175	300
Sports Timer	65	75	95
Surity	15	20	30
Tip Top	15	20	30
Tip Top Jr.	15	20	30
Tommy Ticker	30	35	40
Traveler, with travel case	40	45	60
True Time Teller Tip Top	40	45	60
USA	30	35	40

NEW HAVEN WATCH CO.
New Haven, Connecticut
1883 - 1887

This company was organized October 16, 1883 with the intention of producing W. E. Doolittle's patented watch; however, this plan was soon abandoned. They did produce a "Model A" watch, the first was marketed in the spring of 1884. Batch or lot numbers were used instead of serial numbers, and watches can be found bearing the same batch number. Estimated total production was 2,000 to 3,000. The original capital became absorbed by Trenton Watch Co.

Example of a basic **New Haven Watch Co.** movement with batch or lot number 65. Note this is not a serial number.

Grade or Name — Description	Avg	Ex-Fn	Mint
"A" Model, about 18S, pat. Dec. 27, '81 . . . . ★ ★ ★	$200	$275	$475
Alpha Model, pat. Dec. 27, '81 . . . . ★ ★ ★	200	275	475

New York City Watch Co., 20 size, "Lever Winder" on dial. This watch is wound by cranking the pendant, pin lever escapement, patent number 526,871.

NEW YORK WATCH CO.
and
NEW YORK CITY WATCH CO.
New York, New York
1890 - 1897

This company manufactured the Dollar-type watches, which had a pendant-type crank. The patent number 526,871, dated October 1894, was held by S. Schisgall.

Grade or Name — Description	Avg	Ex-Fn	Mint
20S, no jewels, good running order............★ ★ ★ ★	$450	$600	$850

N.Y. Chronograph Watch Co., dial and movement, 16 size, 7 jewels, open face, sweep second hand, serial number 174,484.

NEW YORK CHRONOGRAPH WATCH CO.
New York, New York
1883 - ?

This company sold about 18,000 watches marked "New York Chronograph Watch Co," manufactured by Manhattan Watch Co. They used a sweep second hand.

Grade or Name — Description	Avg	Ex-Fn	Mint
18S, 7J, HC	$100	$175	$250
18S, 7J, OF ....★	100	175	250
16S, 7J, SW, OF...................................★	100	175	250
16S, 9J, SW, OF...................................★	100	175	250
16S, 9J, SW, OF, time only sweep sec.	100	175	250

New York Chronograph Watch Co. dial and movement, 7 jewels, open face, buttons at the top of case set hands and stop watch.

NEW YORK STANDARD WATCH CO.
Jersey City, New Jersey
1885 - 1929

The first watch reached the market in early 1888 and was a 18S. The most interesting feature was a straight line lever with a "worm gear escapement." This was patented by R. J. Clay. All watches were quick train and open-faced. The company also made its own cases and sold a complete watch. A prefix number was added to the serial number after the first 10,000 watches were made. Estimated total production was 7,000,000.

Chronograph, 16-18 size, 7 jewels, stem wind, second hand start-stop and fly back, three-quarter plate, serial number 5,334,322.

Example of a basic **New York Standard** movement, 18 size, 7 jewels, stem wind, serial number 296,893.

N. Y. STANDARD
16 AND 18 SIZE

Grade or Name — Description	Avg	Ex-Fn	Mint
18S, 7J, N. Y. Standard, KW, KS	$250	$300	$375
18S, 7J, N. Y. Standard, SW	40	60	85
18S, 15J, N. Y. Standard, SW, LS, HC	100	125	175
Chronograph, 7J, ¾, NI, DMK, SW, second hand stop, and fly back	125	175	250
Chronograph, 13J, sweep sec., stop & fly back	135	185	260
Chronograph, 15J, ¾, NI, DMK, SW, second hand stop, and fly back	150	200	275
Columbus, 7J	40	60	85
Crown W. Co., 7J, OF or HC	40	60	85
Crown W. Co., 15J, HC	50	75	125
Dan Patch, 7J, stop watch ★	275	350	425
Dan Patch, 17J, stop watch ★ ★	375	450	525
Edgemere, 7J, OF & HC	40	60	85
Excelsior, 7J, OF or HC	40	60	85

New York Standard, with worm gear (located under cut-out star), 18 size, 7 jewels, serial number 31,138.

Remington W. Co. (marked on movement & case), 16 size, 11 jewels, 2-tone damaskeening, serial number CC021,331.

Grade or Name—Description	Avg	Ex-Fn	Mint
Hi Grade	$40	$60	$85
Ideal	40	60	85
New Era, 7J, OF or HC, skeletonized (Poor Man's Dudley)	250	275	325
New York Standard W. Co., 11J, ¾	50	75	125
New York Standard, 7J, ¾	50	75	125
New York Standard, 15J, BRG	75	100	150
New York Standard, with worm gear ★	300	350	425

NEW YORK STANDARD WATCH CO., 16 & 18 SIZE (continued)

Grade or Name—Description	Avg	Ex-Fn	Mint
Pan American, 7J, OF	$50	$75	$125
Perfection, 7J, OF or HC	40	60	85
Perfection, 15J, OF or HC, NI	50	75	125
Remington W. Co., 11J, marked mvt. & case	75	100	150
Solar W. Co., 7J	40	60	85
18S Tribune USA, 23J, HC or OF, Pat. Reg. Adj.	150	175	225
Wilmington	40	60	85

Note: For watches with O'Hara Multi-Color Dials, add $75 to value in mint condition; add $5 for Hunting Cases.

12 SIZE

Grade or Name — Description	Avg	Ex-Fn	Mint
N. Y. Standard, 7J, OF	$25	$30	$45
N. Y. Standard, 7J, HC, Multi-Color dial	100	125	175

New York Standard Watch Co., 12 size, 7 jewels, open face, serial number 1021224.

6 SIZE AND 0 SIZE

Grade or Name — Description	Avg	Ex-Fn	Mint
Empire State W. Co., 7J	$40	$50	$65
Standard USA, 7J	40	50	65
6S, Columbia, 7J, HC	60	70	85
6S, N. Y. Standard, 7J, HC	60	70	85
6S, Orient, SW	30	40	55
6S, Progress, 7J, YGF	40	50	65
0S, Ideal, 7J, HC	60	70	85
0S, N. Y. Standard, 7J, HC	60	70	85

NOTE: Watches listed in this book are priced at the retail level, as complete watches having an original 14k gold-filled case, an original white enamel single sunk dial, and with the entire original movement in good working order with no repairs needed, unless otherwise noted.

How to Identify Your Watch: Compare the movement of your watch with the illustrations in this section. Upon matching the movement exactly, the model number and size can be determined. While comparing, note the location of the balance, jewels, screws, gears, and type of back plate (Full, ¾, Bridge) which will be clues in identifying the movement you have. Having determined the size and model number, you can now find your watch in the main price listing by name or number (which is engraved on the movement).

18 size, 5th model, hunting

18 size, 6th model, open face

18 size, No. 80

18 size, No. 64

18 size, No. 360

18 size, No. 60

18 size, No. 165

18 size, 4th Model

16 size, No. 94

16 size, No. 91

16 size, 1st Model,
converts to open
or hunting

16 size, No. 1516

16 size, No. 390

12 size, No. 170

12 size, No. 1570

12 size, hunting

12 size, No. 1512

12 size, No. 370

6 size, No. 146

6 size, No. 44

0 size, No. 300

3/0 size, No. 730

10/0 size, No. 1015

NEW YORK SPRINGFIELD WATCH CO.
Springfield, Massachusetts
1866 - 1876

The New York Watch Co. had a rather difficult time getting started. The name of the company was changed from the Mozart Watch Co. to the New York Watch Co., and it was located in Rhode Island. Before any watches had been produced, they moved to Springfield, Mass., in 1867. A factory was built there, but only about 100 watches were produced before a fire occurred on April 23, 1870. Shortly after the fire, in 1870, a newly-designed watch was introduced. The first movements reached the market in 1871, and the first grade was a fully-jeweled adjusted movement called "Frederick Billings." The standard 18S and the Swiss Ligne systems were both used in gauging the size of these watches. The New York Watch Co. used full signatures on its movements. The doors closed in the summer of 1876.

In January 1877, the Hampden Watch Co. was organized and commenced active operation in June 1877.

CHRONOLOGY OF THE DEVELOPMENT OF NEW YORK WATCH CO.

The Mozart Watch Co., Providence, R. I. — 1864-1866
New York Watch Co., Providence, R. I. — 1866-1867
New York Watch Co., Springfield, Mass. — 1867-1875
New York Watch Mfg. Co., Springfield, Mass. — 1875-1876
Hampden Watch Co., Springfield, Mass. — 1877-1886
Hampden-Dueber Watch Co., Springfield, Mass. — 1886-1888
Hampden Watch Co., Canton, Ohio — 1888-1923
Dueber Watch Co., Canton, Ohio — 1888-1923
Dueber-Hampden Watch Co., Canton, Ohio — 1923-1931
Amtorg, U.S.S.R. — 1930-

NEW YORK WATCH CO.—SPRINGFIELD
ESTIMATED SERIAL NUMBERS
AND PRODUCTION DATES

Date	Serial No.	Date	Serial No.
1866	1,000	1871	20,000
1867	3,000	1872	30,000
1868	5,000	1873	40,000
1869	7,000	1874	50,000
1870	10,000	1875	60,000

N. Y. W. SPRINGFIELD
18 TO 20 SIZE

Grade or Name — Description	Avg	Ex-Fn	Mint
Aaron Bagg, 7J, KW, KS ....★	$200	$250	$325
Frederick Billings, 15J, KW, KS ....★	200	250	325
E. W. Bond, 15J, ¾ ....★★	300	350	425
J. A. Briggs, 11J, KW, KS, from back ....★★	300	350	425

322

E.W. Bond movement, 18 size, 7 jewels, three-quarter plate.

Chas. F. Hayward, 18 size, 15 jewels, key wind & set, serial number 18,733.

Grade or Name—Description	Avg	Ex-Fn	Mint
Albert Clark, 15J, KW, KS, from back, ¾ . . . . ★ ★	$300	$350	$425
Homer Foot, 15J, KW, KS, from back, ¾ . . . . ★ ★	300	350	425
Herman Gerz, 11J, KW, KS . . . . ★	200	250	325
John Hancock, 7J, KW, KS	100	200	275
John Hancock, 7J, KW, KS, Silveroid	100	150	225
John Hancock, 7J, KW, KS, Coin	150	200	275
Chas. E. Hayward, 15J, KW, KS, long balance cock	150	200	275
Chas. E. Hayward, 15J, KW, KS, Coin	150	200	275
John L. King, 15J, KW, KS, from back, ¾ . . . . ★ ★	300	350	425
New York Watch Co., 7J, KW, KS . . . . ★	150	200	275
New York Watch Co., 15J, KW, KS, (Serial #s below 75) .	1,300	1,500	1,800
New York Watch Co., 15J, KW, KS, Wolf's Teeth winding, all original . . . . ★ ★ ★	1,000	1,200	1,500
New York Watch Co., 11J, KW, KS . . . . ★ ★	300	350	375
H. G. Norton, 15J, KW, KS, from back, ¾ . . . . ★ ★	300	350	425

H.G. Norton, 18 size, 15 jewels, three-quarter plate, gold escape wheel, serial number 6592.

New York Watch Co., 18 size, 15-19 jewels, stem wind, hunting, note wolf teeth winding, serial number 978.

State Street movement, 18 size, 11 jewels, three-quarter plate.

Theo E. Studley movement, 18 size, 15 jewels, key wind & set, full plate.

Grade or Name—Description	Avg	Ex-Fn	Mint
J. C. Perry, 15J.................................... ★	$150	$200	$275
J. C. Perry, 15J, Silveroid........................... ★	100	125	175
Railway, 15J, KW, FULL, Coin .... ★	600	650	725
Railway, 15J, KW, KS, FULL .... ★	600	650	725
Geo. Sam Rice, 7J, KW, KS......................... ★	300	350	425
Springfield, 19J, KW, KS, from back, ADJ, Wolfsteeth wind, serial Nos. below 1,000................ ★ ★ ★	1,300	1,500	1,800
State Street, 11J, ¾, SW........................... ★	250	275	325
State Street, 11J, ¾, SW, Silveroid.................. ★	200	225	275
Theo E. Studley, 15J, KW, Coin.....................	100	125	175
Theo E. Studley, 15J, KW, KS	100	125	175
George Walker, 17J, KW, ¾, ADJ....................	250	275	325
Chester Woolworth, 15J, KW, KS....................	100	125	175
Chester Woolworth, 11J, KW, KS....................	100	125	175
Chester Woolworth, 11J, KW, KS, Silveroid...........	75	100	150
Chester Woolworth, 11J, KW, KS, ADJ	150	175	225
#4, 15J, ADJ, KW, KS	125	150	200
#5, 15J, KW, KS...................................	100	125	175
#6, 11J, KW, KS...................................	100	125	175
#6, 11J, KW, KS, Silveroid..........................	75	100	150

NOTE: Some KW, KS watches made by the New York Watch Co. have a hidden key. If you unscrew the crown, and the crown comes out as a key, add $100 to the listed value.

NOTE: Watches listed in this book are priced at the retail level, as complete watches having an original 14k gold-filled case, an original white enamel single sunk dial, and with the entire original movement in good working order with no repairs needed, unless otherwise noted.

NON-MAGNETIC WATCH CO.
Geneva and America
1887 - 1905

The Non-Magnetic Watch Co. sold and imported watches from the Swiss as well as contracted watches made in America. Geneva Non-Magnetic marked watches appear to be the oldest type of movement. This company sold a full line of watches, high grade to low grade, as well as repeaters and ladies watches. An advertisement appeared in the monthly journal of "Locomotive Engineers" in 1887. The ad states that the "Paillard's patent non-magnetic watches are uninfluenced by magnetism of electricity." Each watch contains the Paillard's patent non-magnetic, inoxydable compensation balance and hairspring. An ad in 1888 shows prices for 16 size Swiss style watches as low as $15 for 7 jewels and as high as $135 for 20 jewels.

18 SIZE
(must be marked Paillard's Patent)

Grade or Name — Description	Avg	Ex-Fn	Mint
Elgin, 17J, FULL, SW, LS, OF	$100	$125	$175
Elgin, 17J, FULL, SW, LS, HC	125	150	225
Elgin, 15J, FULL, SW, LS, OF	75	100	150
Elgin, 15-17J, FULL, SW, LS, HC	100	125	175
Illinois, 24J, GJS, NI, Adj.5P, OF	800	850	925
Illinois, 24J, GJS, NI, Adj.5P, HC	900	950	1,025
Illinois, 23J, GJS, NI, Adj.5P, OF	700	750	925
Illinois, 23J, GJS, NI, Adj.5P, HC ★★★	1,600	1,800	2,100
Illinois, 21J, GJS, NI, Adj.5P, OF	200	250	325
Illinois, 21J, GJS, NI, Adj.5P, HC	250	300	325
Illinois, 17J, NI, ADJ, OF	100	125	175
Illinois, 17J, NI, ADJ, HC	125	150	225
Illinois, 15J, NI, OF	75	100	150
Illinois, 15J, NI, HC	100	125	175
Illinois, 11J, OF	75	100	150

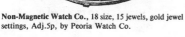

Non-Magnetic Watch Co., 18 size, 15 jewels, gold jewel settings, Adj.5p, by Peoria Watch Co.

Non-Magnetic Watch Co., 18 size, 21 Ruby jewels, Adj.5p, note "Paillard" engraved on movement.

Non-Magnetic Watch co., 18 size, 16 jewels, ½ plate, hunting, note "Geneva" engraved on movement, serial number 6113.

Non-Magnetic Watch Co., 18 size, 16 jewels, bridge model, example of a Swiss Ebauche.

Grade or Name—Description	Avg	Ex-Fn	Mint
Illinois, 11J, HC	$100	$125	$175
Peoria, 17J, FULL, SW, LS, OF	325	350	400
Peoria, 15J, FULL, SW, LS, OF	300	325	375
Peoria, 15J, FULL, SW, LS, HC	400	425	475
Peoria, 11J, FULL, SW, LS, OF	100	125	175
Peoria, 11J, FULL, SW, LS, HC	175	200	250
Swiss, 16J, ½ plate, SW, LS, OF	60	70	85
Swiss, 16J, ½ plate, SW, LS, HC	75	100	150
Swiss, 15J, bar bridge, SW, LS, OF	55	65	80
Swiss, 15J, bar bridge, SW, LS, HC	75	100	150
Swiss, 11J, ½ plate, SW, LS, OF, HC	75	100	150
Swiss, 11J, bar bridge, SW, LS, OF, HC	75	100	150

Non-Magnetic Watch Co., 16 size, 21 Ruby jewels, adjusted, made by Illinois Watch Co.

Non-Magnetic Watch Co., 16 size, 20 jewels in gold jewel settings, stem wind, open or hunting. Swiss made.

16 SIZE
(must be marked Paillard's Patent)

Grade or Name — Description	Avg	Ex-Fn	Mint
Illinois, 21J, GJS, ¾, DR, Adj.6P, OF	$200	$250	$325

Non-Magnetic Watch Co., 16 size, three-quarter plate, 15 jewels, adjusted.

Non-Magnetic Watch Co., 16 size, three-quarter plate, 15 jewels, note "Paillard's Patent, Balance And Spring" engraved on movement.

Grade or Name—Description	Avg	Ex-Fn	Mint
Illinois, 21J, GJS, ¾, DR, Adj.6P, HC	$300	$350	$425
Illinois, 17J, ¾, DR, ADJ, OF	75	100	150
Illinois, 17J, ¾, DR, ADJ, HC.......................	100	125	175
Illinois, 15J, HC	75	100	125
Illinois, 15J, OF	50	75	125
Illinois, 11J, OF	50	75	125
Illinois, 11J, HC	75	100	150
Swiss, 20J, GJS, DR, Adj.6P, NI, OF	75	100	150
Swiss, 20J, GJS, DR, Adj.6P, NI, HC	100	125	175
Swiss, 18J, GJS, DR, Adj.6P, NI, OF	75	100	150
Swiss, 18J, GJS, DR, Adj.6P, NI, HC	100	125	175
Swiss, 16J, GJS, DR, Adj.6P, NI, OF	75	100	150
Swiss, 16J, GJS, DR, Adj.6P, NI, HC	75	100	150
Swiss, 15J, DR, NI, OF..............................	75	100	150
Swiss, 15J, DR, NI, HC	100	125	175
Swiss, 11J, NI, OF	75	100	150
Swiss, 11J, NI, HC..................................	100	125	175
Swiss, 7J, OF & HC	75	100	150

OTAY WATCH CO.
Otay, California
1889 - 1894

This company produced about 1,000 watches with a serial number range of 1,000 to 1,500 and 30,000 to 31,000. The company was purchased by a Japanese manufacturer in 1894. Names on Otay movements include: Golden Gate, F. A. Kimball, Native Sun, Overland Mail, R. D. Perry, and P. H. Wheeler.

OTAY WATCH CO. (continued)

Otay Watch Co. Dial; note hunting case style and lever for setting hands.

Otay Watch Co., F.A. Kimball, 18 size, 15 jewels, lever set, hunting, serial number 1,264.

18 SIZE

Grade or Name — Description		Avg	Ex-Fn	Mint
California, 15J, LS, HC, NI	★★★	$2,000	$2,200	$2,500
Golden Gate, 15J, LS, HC, OF, NI	★★★	1,600	1,800	2,100
F. A. Kimball, 15J, LS, HC, Gilt	★★	1,200	1,400	1,700
Native Son, 15J, LS, HC, NI	★★	1,600	1,800	2,100
Overland Rail, 15J, LS, HC, NI	★★	1,800	2,000	2,300
R. D. Perry, 15J, LS, HC, Gilt	★★	1,200	1,400	1,700
P. H. Wheeler, 15J, LS, HC, Gilt	★★	1,200	1,400	1,700

D. D. PALMER WATCH CO.
Waltham, Massachusetts
1864 - 1875

In 1858, at age 20, Mr. Palmer opened a small jewelry store in Waltham, Mass. Here he became interested in pocket chronometers. At first he bought the balance and jewels from Swiss manufacturers. In 1864 he took a position with the American Watch Co. and made the chronometers in his spare time (only about 25 produced). They were 18S, ¾ plate, gilded, key wind, and some were nickel. At first they were fusee driven, but he mainly used going barrels. About 1870, Palmer started making lever watches and by 1875 he left the American Watch Co. and started making a 10S keywind, gilded-movement, and a 16S, ¾ plate, gilt and nickel, and a stem wind of his own invention (a vibrating crown wheel). In all he made about 1,500 watches. The signature appearing on the watches was "Palmer W. Co. Wal., Mass."

He basically had three grades of watches: Fine—Solid Nickel; Medium—Nickel Plated; and Medium—Gold Gilt. They were made in open-face and hunter cases.

D.D. PALMER WATCH CO. (continued)

D.D. Palmer Watch Co., 18 size, 15 jewels, "Palmer's Pat. Stem Winder" on movement, serial number 1,007.

Grade or Name — Description		Avg	Ex-Fn	Mint
18S, 15-17J, ¾ Plate, KW, Chronometer .... ★ ★ ★		$4,000	$4,500	$6,000
16S, 17J, NI, OF, 18K........................... ★ ★		1,500	1,800	2,200

PEORIA WATCH CO.
Peoria, Illinois
1885 - 1895

The roots of this company began with the Independent Watch Co. (1880-1883). These watches marked "Marion" and "Mark Twain" were made by the Fredonia Watch Co. (1883-1885). Peoria Watch Co. opened Dec. 19, 1885, and made one model of railroad

Peoria Watch Co., 18 size, 15 jewels, nickel damaskeening plates, hunting, note patented regulator, serial number 11,532.

PEORIA WATCH CO. (continued)

watch in 1887. They were 18S, quick train, 15 jewel, and all stem wind. These watches are hard to find, as only about 3,000 were made. Peoria also made railroad watches for A. C. Smith's Non-Magnetic Watch Co. of America, from 1884-1888. The 18S watches were full plate, adjusted, and had whiplash regulator.

The Peoria Watch Co. closed in 1889, having produced about 47,000 watches.

Grade or Name — Description	Avg	Ex-Fn	Mint
18S, 11J, SW, OF	$125	$150	$225
18S, 15J, SW, personalized name	150	175	250
18S, Peoria W. Co., 15J, SW, OF	175	200	275
18S, Peoria W. Co., 15J, SW, HC	225	250	325
18S, Peoria W. Co., 15J, SW, low S#	325	350	400
18S, Anti-Magnetic, 15J, SW	325	350	400
18S, Non-Magnetic Watch Co. of America, 15J, NI, SW, GJS, Adj.5P, OF	350	375	425
18S, 15J, Non-Magnetic Watch Co. of America, NI, SW, GJS, Adj.5P, HC	400	425	475
18S, Made for Railway Service, 15J, NI, GJS, Adj.5P, OF	300	350	425
18S, Made for Railway Service, NI, GJS, Adj.5P, HC	350	400	475

PHILADELPHIA WATCH CO.
Philadelphia, Pennsylvania
1874 - 1886

Eugene Paulus organized the Philadelphia Watch Co. about 1874. Most all the parts were made in Switzerland, and finished and cased in this country. The International Watch Co. is believed to have manufactured the movements for Philadelphia Watch Co. Estimated total production of the company is 12,000 watches.

Philadelphia Watch Co., 16 size, 15 jewels, gold jewel settings, hunting case model. "Paulus Patents 1868. Aug. 25th, Nov. 3rd" on movement, serial number 5,751.

Grade or Name — Description		Avg	Ex-Fn	Mint
18S, 15J, SW, HC	★	$350	$450	$575
18S, 15J, KW, KS	★	275	375	500
18S, 15J, SW, OF	★	325	425	525
18S, HC, KW, KS, 18K original case marked				
Philadelphia Watch Co.	★	1,200	1,400	1,800
18S, 11J, KW, KS	★	150	175	225
16S, 15J, KW, KS	★	150	175	225
16S, 19J, KW, KS, GJS	★	375	475	600
8S-6S, 11J, HC	★	150	175	225
8S-6S, 15J, HC	★	150	175	225
8S-6S, Paulus, 19J, KW, KS	★	225	300	400
000S, 7J, HC, PS	★	125	200	300

JAMES & HENRY PITKIN
Hartford, Connecticut
New York, New York
1838 - 1852

Henry Pitkin was the first to attempt to manufacture watches by machinery. The machines were of Pitkin's own design and very crude, but he had some brilliant ideas. His first four workers were paid $30 a year plus their board. After much hardship, the first watches were produced in the fall of 1838. The watches had going barrels, not the fusee and chain, and the American flag was engraved on the plates to denote they were American made and to exemplify the true spirit of American independence in watchmaking.

The first 50 watches were stamped with the name "Henry Pitkin." Others bore the firm name "H & J F Pitkin." The movements were about 16S and ¾ plate. The plates were rolled brass and stamped out with dies. The pinions were lantern style with tight leaves. The movement had a slow train of 14,400 beats per hour. Pitkin's first plan was to make the ends of the pinions conical and let them run in the ends of hardened steel screws, similar to the Marine clock balances. A large brass setting was put in the plates and extended above the surface. Three screws, with small jewels set in their ends, were

Example of a basic **Henry Pitkin** movement, 16 size, key wind & set.

JAMES & HENRY PITKIN (continued)

inserted so that they closed about the pivot with very small end shake. This proved to be too expensive and was used in only a few movements. Next, he tried to make standard type movements extend above the plates with the end shake controlled by means of a screw running down into the end of the pivots, reducing friction. This "capped jewel train" was used for a while before he adopted the standard ways of jeweling. The escape wheels were the star type, English style. The balance was made of gold and steel. These movements were fire gilded and not interchangeable. The dials, hands, mainsprings and hairsprings were imported. The rounded pallets were manufactured by Pitkin,and the cases for his watches were made on the premises. As many as 900 watches could have been made by Pitkin.

Grade or Name — Description		Avg	Ex-Fn	Mint
Henry Pitkin S#1-50 . . . . ★ ★ ★ ★		$15,000	$20,000	$30,000
H. & J. F. Pitkin & Co., S#50-377 . . . . ★ ★ ★		10,000	15,000	20,000
Pitkin & Co., New York, S#378-900 . . . . ★ ★ ★		4,500	6,000	7,500
W. Pitkin, Hartford, Conn., S# approx. 40,000, fusee lever,				
KW, Coin . . . . ★ ★		450	500	600

Albert H. Potter, 18 size, 22 jewels, pat. Oct. 11, 1875 & June 4, 1876, helical hairspring, detent escapement, made in Geneva, serial number 14.

A.H. Potter Watch Co., Boston, 18 size, about 6 jewels, detent escapement, note similarity to E.H. Howard & Co. early watches, serial number 5.

ALBERT H. POTTER WATCH CO.
New York, New York
1855 - 1875

Albert Potter started his apprenticeship in 1852. When this was completed he moved to New York to take up watchmaking on his own. He made about 35 watches in all that sold for $225 to $350. Some were chronometers, some were lever escapements, key wind, gilded movements, some were fusee driven, both bridge and ¼ plate. Potter was a contemporary of Charles Fasoldt and John Mulford, both horological inventors from Albany, N. Y. Potter moved to Cuba in 1861 but returned to New York in 1868. In 1872 he worked in Chicago and formed the Potter Brothers Company with his brother William. He moved to Geneva about 1876. His company produced a total of about 600 watches, but only about 40 of those were made in the U. S.

ALBERT H. POTTER WATCH CO. (continued)

Grade or Name — Description	Avg	Ex-Fn	Mint
18S, 29J, 18K HC, 1 min. repeater, Geneva	$5,500	$6,500	$8,000
18S, BRG lever, Chronometer, signed A. H. Potter, New York, 18K Potter case, U.S. mfg. .... ★ ★ ★ ★	10,000	12,000	16,000
18S, BRG lever with wind indicator, 18K Potter case ★ ★ ★	5,000	6,500	7,500
18S-20S, Tourbillion, signed A. H. Potter, Boston, gilded, 18K Potter case, U.S. mfg. .... ★ ★ ★ ★	15,000	17,000	20,000
16S-18S, 22J, helical spring, detent chronometer escapement, Geneva, 18K	40,000	50,000	65,000
4S, 21J, ¼ hour repeater, Geneva, 18K Potter HC	3,000	3,500	4,500

George P. Reed, 18 size, 15 jewels, key & stem wind, key & lever set, lever escapement, 48 hour up and down wind indicator, serial number 262.

George P. Reed, 18 size, 15 jewels, key & stem wind, key & lever set, lever escapement, 48 hour up and down wind indicator, serial number 5.

GEORGE P. REED
Boston, Massachusetts
1865 - 1885

In 1854, George P. Reed entered the employment of Dennison, Howard and Davis, in Roxbury, Mass., and moved with the company to Waltham, Mass. Here he was placed in charge of the pinion finishing room. While there he invented and received a patent for the mainspring barrel and main timing power combination. This patent was dated February 18, 1857. Reed returned to Roxbury with Howard who purchased his patented barrel. He stayed with the Howard factory as foreman and adjuster until 1865, when he left for Boston to start his own account.

He obtained a patent on April 7, 1868, for an improved chronometer escapement which featured simplified construction. He made about 100 chronometers with his improved escapement, to which he added a stem-wind device. His company turned out about 100 watches the first three years. Most, if not all, of his watches run for two days and have up and down indicators on the dial. They are both 18S and 16S, ¾ plate, nickel, and are artistically designed. Reed experimented with various combinations of lever and chronometer escapements. One was a rotary watch he made in 1862 and called the "Monitor." It was the first rotary watch made in America. In all, Reed made a total of about 550 watches, and these are valuable to collectors.

Grade or Name — Description	Avg	Ex-Fn	Mint
18S, 15J, LS, OF or HC, Wind Indicator, chronometer escapement, 18K case .... ★ ★ ★	$9,000	$11,500	$15,000
16S, 15J, LS, OF or HC, **not** chronometer, 18K case ★ ★ ★	6,500	7,000	9,000
16S, 15J, LS, OF, 31 day calendar, 18K case ...... ★ ★ ★	6,500	7,000	9,000

ROCKFORD WATCH CO.
Rockford, Illinois
1873 - 1915

The Rockford Watch Company's equipment was bought from the Cornell Watch Co., and two of Cornell's employees, C. W. Parker and P. H. Wheeler, went to work for Rockford. The factory was located 93 miles from Chicago on the Rock River. The first watch was placed on the market on May 1, 1876. They were key wind, 18S, full plate expansion balance. By 1877 the company was making ¾ plate nickel movements that fit standard size cases. Three railroads came through Rockford, and the company always advertised to the railroad men—and was very popular with them. The company had some problems in 1896, and the name changed to Rockford Watch Co. Ltd. It closed in 1915.

ROCKFORD ESTIMATED SERIAL NUMBERS AND PRODUCTION DATES

Date	Serial No.	Date	Serial No.	Date	Serial No.	Date	Serial No.
1876	5,000	1886	110,000	1896	290,000	1906	620,000
1877	15,000	1887	125,000	1897	320,000	1907	650,000
1878	25,000	1888	140,000	1898	350,000	1908	690,000
1879	35,000	1889	150,000	1899	385,000	1909	730,000
1880	50,000	1890	165,000	1900	415,000	1910	765,000
1881	60,000	1891	175,000	1901	450,000	1911	820,000
1882	70,000	1892	195,000	1902	480,000	1912	850,000
1883	80,000	1893	200,000	1903	515,000	1913	880,000
1884	90,000	1894	230,000	1904	550,000	1914	930,000
1885	100,000	1895	260,000	1905	580,000	1915	1,000,000

(See Rockford Watch Co. **Identification of Movements** section located at the end of the Rockford price section to identify the movement, size, and model number of your watch.)

(Prices are with gold filled cases except where noted.)

NOTE: Some grades are not included. Their values can be determined by comparing with similar models or grades listed.

ROCKFORD
18 SIZE

Grade or Name — Description	Avg	Ex-Fn	Mint
Belmont USA, 21J, LS, OF, NI, M#7	$200	$250	$325
Chronometer, 17J, ADJ, OF, G925	275	350	500
Dome Model, 9J, brass plates....................... ★	150	175	225

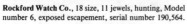

Rockford Watch Co., 18 size, 11 jewels, hunting, Model number 6, exposed escapement, serial number 190,564.

Special Railway, 18 size, 17 jewels, hunting, Model number 8, serial number 344,551.

Grade or Name—Description	Avg	Ex-Fn	Mint
King Edward, Plymouth W. Co., 21J, 14K HC	$700	$800	$975
King Edward (Sears), 21J, GJS, ADJ, NI, OF	275	350	475
King Edward (Sears), 21J, GJS, ADJ, NI, HC...........	300	325	500
Pennsylvania Special, 25J, LS, Adj.6P, OF........ ★★★	3,000	4,000	6,000
Railway King, 21J, OF................................	475	600	750
The Ramsey Watch, 11J, NI, KW or SW	100	125	150
The Ramsey Watch, 15J, NI, KW or SW	100	125	150
The Ramsey Watch, M#7, 21J, OF, NI, ADJ............	350	375	450
Rockford Early KW-KS, M#1-2, with low Serial #s less than 500....................................★	400	500	675
Rockford Early KW-KS, M#1-2, with low Serial #s less than 500, Coin ....★	400	500	675
Rockford Early KW-KS, M#1-2, with reversible case	275	325	400
Rockford Early KW-KS, M#1-2, S#s less than 100....★★	1,000	1,400	2,000
Rockford, 7J, SW, FULL, OF.........................	75	100	150
Rockford, 7J, KW, FULL, OF	75	100	150
Rockford, 7J, KW, FULL, Silveroid...................	40	60	85
Rockford, 9J, SW, FULL, HC	100	125	175
Rockford, M#1, 9J, KW, FULL, HC...................	150	175	225
Rockford, 11J, SW, FULL, OF........................	75	100	150
Rockford, M#1-2, 11J, KW, FULL.....................	150	175	225
Rockford, M#1-2, 11J, transition case, FULL	100	125	175
Rockford, 11J, KW, Coin HC	150	175	225
Rockford, 11-15J, KW, HC, M#5, ¾ Plate, Coin......★	275	350	550
Rockford, 13J, HC.................................	100	125	175
Rockford, 15J, SW, FULL	75	100	150
Rockford, 15J, KW, FULL, multi-color dial.............	275	350	425
Rockford, 15J, SW, 2-Tone movement.................	100	125	175

Rockford movement, 18 size, 7 jewels, model 5, hunting, lever set, three-quarter plate.

Grade 900, 18 size, 24 jewels, Adj5p. Warning: 24 jewel fakes have been made from 21 jewel movements. The fakes are missing the eliptical jewel setting on the barrel bridge.

Grade or Name—Description	Avg	Ex-Fn	Mint
Rockford, 15J, KW, FULL, ADJ	$175	$225	$350
Rockford, 15J, KW/SW	100	150	200
Rockford, 15J, KW/SW, Silveroid	60	70	85
Rockford, 15J, M#6, exposed escapement wheel, FULL, HC, LS, nickel mvt...............................	275	300	350
Rockford, 15J, M#6, exposed escapement wheel, FULL, HC, LS, gilded mvt...............................	175	200	250
Rockford, 15J, M#6, exposed wheel, nickel mvt., Coin ...	175	200	250
Rockford, M#1, 15J, KW, FULL	100	125	175
Rockford, 16J, GJS, NI, DMK, SW....................	75	100	150
Rockford, 16J, GJS, NI, DMK, SW, Silveroid...........	50	75	125
Rockford, 16J, GJS, NI, DMK, SW, Coin	75	100	150
Rockford, 17J, NI, DMK, SW, OF....................	75	100	150
Rockford, 17J, GJS, NI, DMK, SW, Adj.5P	100	125	175
Rockford, 17J, GJS, NI, SW, 2-Tone, OF	125	150	200
Rockford, M#1-2, 19J, KW, FULL, GJS, ADJ	1,200	1,400	1,700
Rockford, 19J, transition, HC, GJS	400	500	650
Rockford, 21J, SW, Silveroid.........................	75	100	150
Rockford, 21J, GJS, OF, Adj.5P, wind indicator .... ★ ★	2,500	3,000	3,500
Rockford, 21J, SW, DMK, ADJ, HC	275	325	400
Rockford, 21J, NI, DMK, ADJ, OF...................	175	225	300
Rockford, 21J, GJS, NI, DMK, Adj.5P, marked "RG" ..	200	250	325
Rockford, 24J, GJS, SW, LS, Adj.5P, marked "RG," OF	900	1,000	1,200
Rockford, 24J, GJS, SW, LS, Adj.5P, marked "RG," HC..★	1,200	1,400	1,700
Rockford, 25J, GJS, SW, LS, Adj.5P, NI, DMK .... ★ ★	3,500	5,000	6,500
Rockford, 26J, GJS, SW, LS, Adj.5P, NI, DMK .. ★ ★ ★	8,000	10,000	16,000

Rockford Watch Co., 18 size, 15 jewels, ¾ plate, key & stem wind.

Rockford Watch Co., 18 size, 15 jewels, model 4, open face, lever set, serial number 227,430.

Grade or Name--Description	Avg	Ex-Fn	Mint
Special Railway, 17J, ADJ, 2-tone, SW, HC	$300	$400	$550
The Syndicate Watch Co., M#7, 15J, LS, NI, HC	150	200	275
Winnebago, 17J, LS, GJS, Adj.5P, DR, NI, DMK.......	150	175	225
Winnebago, 17J, LS, GJS, Adj.5P, DR, NI, DMK, Silveroid	100	125	175
24 Hour Dial, 15J, SW or KW	150	175	225
40, 15J, M#3, HC .... ★ ★	250	300	375
43, 15J, M#3, HC, 2-Tone	100	125	175
66, 11J, M#7, OF	75	100	150
66, 11J, M#7, OF, Silveroid	35	45	60
66, 11J, M#7, HC	75	100	150
81, 9J, M#3, HC, Gilt	100	125	175
82, Special, 21J, SW.......................... ★ ★	400	500	650
83, 15J, M#8, HC, 2-Tone	125	150	200
86, 15J, M#7, OF, NI	50	75	125
93, 9J, M#8, HC, Gilt	100	125	175
94, 9J, M#7, OF	50	75	125
200-205, 17J, M#9, OF, NI, LS	75	100	150
245, 19J, HC, GJS, 2-Tone.......................... ★	1,000	1,200	1,600
800, 24J, GJS, DR, Adj.5P, DMK, HC............... ★	1,200	1,400	1,700
805, 21J, GJS, Adj.5P, NI, DMK, HC, marked "RG" ...	200	250	325
810, 21J, NI, DMK, ADJ, HC........................	250	300	375
820, 17J, HC, SW............................... ★ ★	300	350	425
825, 17J, HC, FULL	125	150	200
830, 17J, HC, FULL	100	125	175
835, 17J, HC, FULL	100	125	175
835, 17J, HC, FULL, Silveroid	50	75	125
845, 21J, HC, GJS, FULL .... ★	400	475	550
870, 7J, HC, FULL	75	100	150

ROCKFORD WATCH CO., 18 SIZE (continued)

Grade or Name—Description		Avg.	Ex-Fn	Mint
900, 24J, GJS, DR, Adj.5P, OF, NI, DMK ....★★		$1,000	$1,200	$1,500
900, 24J, GJS, DR, Adj.5P, 14K, OF case ....★★		1,400	1,600	1,900
905, 21J, GJS, DR, Adj.5P, OF, NI, DMK		250	275	350
910, 21J, NI, DMK, 1 ADJ, OF		150	175	250
912, 21J, OF ....★★		425	475	600
915, 17J, M#9, OF, SW........................★★★		450	500	625
918, 21J, OF, NI, GJS, Adj.5P, DR		150	175	225
918, 21J, OF, NI, GJS, Adj.5P, DR, Silveroid		100	125	175
918, 21J, OF, NI, GJS, Adj.5P, DR, Coin		125	175	225
930, 17J, OF		175	225	275
935, 17J, OF		75	100	125
945, 21J, M#9, OF, SW............................		150	175	225
950, 21J, OF, NI, GJS, Adj.5P, DR, Wind Indicator.★★		2,500	3,000	4,200
970, 7J, OF		60	70	90
970, 7J, OF, Silveroid		40	50	70

16 SIZE

Grade or Name — Description	Avg	Ex-Fn	Mint
Commodore Perry, 21J, OF, GJS, GT, marked "RG" ...	$350	$450	$600
Cosmos, 17J, OF, GJS, LS, DMK, marked dial & mvt. ..	225	350	500
Doll Watch Co., 23J, marked dial & mvt..........★★★	1,000	1,200	1,500
Dome Model, 15J	60	75	100
Dome Model, 17J	65	80	120
Dome Model, 17J, 2-tone, HC........................	200	250	325
Iroquois, 17J, DR, 14K, HC........................	525	575	675
Iroquois, 17J, DR	150	175	225
Peerless, 17J, OF, NI, LS, DMK......................	75	100	125
Pocahontas, 17-21J, GJS, Adj.5P, DR.................	225	250	375
Prince of Wales (Sears), 21J	225	250	375
Prince of Wales (Sears), 21J, 14K	525	550	675

Example of a **Cosmos** face and movement, 16 size, 17 jewels, open face, gold jewel settings.

ROCKFORD WATCH CO., 16 SIZE (continued)

Example of a Rockford movement, 16 size, 21 jewels, three-quarter plate, serial number 842,520.

Grade 500-HC, 505-OF, 16 size, 21 jewels, gold jewel settings, gold train, Adj6p, marked "RG," originally sold for $100.00

Grade or Name—Description	Avg	Ex-Fn	Mint
Rockford 7J, ¾, HC	$100	$125	$175
Rockford, 9J, ¾, SW, OF	40	60	85
Rockford, 9J, SW, Silveroid	30	40	60
Rockford, 9J, SW, HC	100	125	175
Rockford, 11J, SW, Silveroid	40	60	85
Rockford, 11J, ¾, HC	100	125	175
Rockford, 15J, ¾, ADJ, OF	75	100	150
Rockford, 15J, ¾, ADJ, Silveroid	40	60	85
Rockford, 15J, ¾, ADJ, HC	100	125	175
Rockford, 16J, ¾, SW, Silveroid	40	60	85
Rockford, 16J, ¾, ADJ, NI, DMK	75	100	150
Rockford, 17J, ¾	75	100	150
Rockford, 17J, ¾, 2-Tone, marked "RG"	125	150	200
Rockford, 17J, BRG, Adj.3P, DR	100	125	175
Rockford, 17J, GJS, Adj.5P, DR, Wind Indicator	400	450	525
Rockford, 17J, BRG, Silveroid	40	60	85
Rockford, 17J, ¾, Silveroid	40	60	85
Rockford, 21J, ¾, SW, Silveroid	75	100	150
Rockford, 21J, BRG, SW, Silveroid	75	100	150
Rockford, 21J, ¾, GJS, Adj.5P	125	150	200
Rockford, 21J, BRG, GJS, Adj.5P, GT, DR	150	175	225
Rockford, 21J, GJS, Adj.5P, DR, Wind Indicator	500	600	750
Winnebago, 17J, BRG, GJS, Adj.5P, NI	150	175	225
Winnebago, 21J, BRG, GJS, Adj.5P, NI	175	200	275
100, 16J, M#1, HC, ¾, 2-Tone	175	200	250
100S, 21J, Special, HC, ¾, LS	200	250	325
102, 15J, HC, M#1 ★	250	300	375
103, 15J, HC, M#1	125	150	200
115-125, 17J, Special, HC ★ ★ ★	500	600	750
120-130, 17J, HC ★ ★ ★	400	500	650

Pocahontas, 16 size, 21 jewels, hunting case, bridge model, Adj.5pserial number 670,203.

Rockford movement, 16 size, 17 jewels, ¾ plate, hunting, lever set, serial number 556,064.

Grade or Name—Description	Avg	Ex-Fn	Mint
400 & 405, 17J, NI, Adj.5P, GJS, DR, BRG	$100	$125	$175
445, 19J, HC, GJS, BRG .... ★ ★	850	1,000	1,200
500, 21J, BRG, NI, GJS, Adj.5P, GT, HC......... ★ ★	500	550	625
501, 21J, GJS, HC .... ★ ★ ★	900	1,100	1,250
505, 21J, BRG, NI, GJS, Adj.5P, GT, OF .... ★ ★	400	500	650
510, 21J, BRG, NI, GJS, Adj.5P, GT, HC........... ★	300	400	550
515 & 525, 21J, OF, ¾	150	175	225
520, 21J, HC, ¾	200	250	325
520, 21J, BRG, NI, GJS, Adj.5P, HC .... ★	400	450	525
530, 21J, HC, GJS, Adj.5P, marked "RG" .... ★	300	350	425
535, 21J, OF, ¾ .... ★	225	275	350
537, 21J, OF, GJS, Adj.5P .... ★ ★	500	600	775
545, 21J, OF	150	175	225
561, 17J, BRG............................	125	150	200
566, 17J, BRG	125	150	200
572, 17J, BRG, NI, GJS, Adj.5P	75	100	150
573, 17J, BRG, NI	75	100	150
578-579, 17J, PS, GJS .... ★ ★	300	350	475
584 & 585, 15J, ¾, NI......................	40	60	85
620-625, 21J, HC, ¾ .... ★	300	400	525
655, 21J, OF, Wind Indicator, marked 655 .... ★	500	600	750

12 SIZE
All ¾ Bridge

Grade or Name — Description	Avg	Ex-Fn	Mint
Iroquois, 17J, BRG, DR, ADJ...................	$60	$70	$100
Pocahontas, 21J, GJS, Adj.5P, BRG, DR..............	100	125	125

Rockford Watch co., 12 size, 15 jewels, model 1, hunting, pendant set.

Rockford Watch Co., 12 size, 15 jewels, model 2, open face, pendant set.

Grade or Name—Description	Avg	Ex-Fn	Mint
Rockford, 15J, BRG	$35	$40	$55
Rockford, 17J, BRG, NI, DR, ADJ	50	60	75
Rockford, 21J, BRG, NI, DR, ADJ	70	80	110
Rockford, 21J, BRG, NI, DR, ADJ, Silveroid	40	60	85
Winona, 15J, BRG	45	55	80
300, 23J, ¾, HC, GJS, Adj.5P ★★★	300	350	425
305, 23J, BRG, NI, GJS, Adj.5P, GT, OF ★★★	300	350	425
310(HC)-315(OF), 21J, BRG, NI, GJS, Adj.5P	75	100	150
320(HC)-325(OF), 17J, BRG, NI, ADJ, DR	40	60	85
330, 17J, BRG, NI, DR, OF	40	60	85
335, 17J, BRG, NI, DR, HC	40	60	85
340(HC)-345(OF), 21J, M#1 ★	200	225	300
350, 17J, OF	40	60	85
355, 17J, HC	40	60	85

Note: Add $10 to above watches with hunting case.

8 SIZE

Grade or Name — Description	Avg	Ex-Fn	Mint
15J, ¾, HC, LS, 14K, 40 DWT	$375	$400	$475
15J, ¾, HC, LS	100	125	175

6 SIZE

Grade or Name — Description	Avg	Ex-Fn	Mint
9J, HC, NI	$75	$100	$150

Rockford movement, 6 size, 17 jewels, quick train, straight line escapement, compensating balance, adjusted to temperature, micrometric regulator, three-quarter damaskeened plates.

Grade or Name—Description	Avg	Ex-Fn	Mint
15J, ¾, NI	$40	$60	$85
16J, ¾, NI	70	90	115
17J, ¾, ADJ, NI	80	100	125

0 SIZE

Grade or Name — Description	Avg	Ex-Fn	Mint
Plymouth Watch Co., 15J, HC	$200	$225	$275
7J, BRG, HC	150	175	225
11J, BRG, NI, DR, HC	160	185	235
15J, BRG, NI, DR, HC	170	195	245
17J, BRG, NI, DR, HC	180	205	255
17J, BRG, NI, DR, in marked Rockford HC in dust cover ring	325	350	375

ROCKFORD WATCH CO.
IDLENTIFICATION OF MOVEMENTS
BY MODEL NUMBER

How to Identify Your Watch: Compare the movement of your watch with the illustrations in this section. Upon matching the movement exactly, the model number and size can be determined. While comparing, note the location of the balance, jewels, screws, gears, and type of back plate (Full, ¾, Bridge) which will be clues in identifying the movement you have. Having determined the size and model number, you can now find your watch in the main price listing by name or number (which is engraved on the movement).

ROCKFORD WATCH CO. (continued)

Model 1, 18 size, full plate, hunting, key wind & set.

Model 2, 18 size, full plate, hunting, lever set.

Model 3, 18 size, full plate, hunting, lever set.

Model 4, 18 size, full plate, open face, lever set.

Model 5, 18 size, three-quarter plate, hunting, lever set.

Model 6, 18 size, full plate, hunting, lever set, exposed escapement.

Model 7, 18 size, full plate, open face, lever set.

Model 8, 18 size, full plate, hunting, lever set.

Model 9, 18 size, full plate, open face, lever set.

Model 10, 18 size, full plate, hunting, lever set.

Model 1, 16 size, three-quarter plate, hunting, lever set.

Model 2, 16 size, three-quarter plate, open face, pendant & lever set.

Model 3, 16 size, three-quarter plate, hunting, pendant & lever set.

Model 4, 16 size, three-quarter plate, bridge, hunting, pendant & lever set.

Model 5, 16 size, three-quarter plate, bridge, open face, pendant & lever set.

Model 1, 12 size, three-quarter plate bridge, hunting, pendant set.

Model 2, 12 size, three-quarter plate bridge, open face, pendant set.

Model 1, 6 & 8 size, three-quarter plate, hunting, lever set.

Model 2, 6 size, three-quarter plate, hunting, lever set.

Model 1, 0 size, three-quarter plate, bridge, hunting, pendant set.

Model 2, 0 size, three-quarter plate, bridge, open face, pendant set.

SAN JOSE WATCH CO.
San Jose, California
1891

Very few watches were made by the San Jose Watch Co., and very little is known about them.

Grade or Name — Description		Avg	Ex-Fn	Mint
16S, SW .... ★ ★ ★		$1,500	$2,000	$2,500

Example of a basic **M.S. Smith & Co.** movement, 18 size, 15 jewels, three-quarter plate, key wind & set.

M. S. SMITH & CO.
Detroit, Michigan
1870 - 1874

Eber B. Ward purchased the M. S. Smith & Co. which was a large jewelry firm. These watches carried the Smith name on them. A Mr. Hoyt was engaged to produce these watches and about 100 were produced before the Freeport Watch Co. purchased the small firm.

Left: FREEPORT WATCH CO., 18 size, 15 pressed jewels, gold train, lever set, three-quarter plate; no more than 20 watches with the FREEPORT name was made. Similar to a Swiss "ebauche," ca. 1874, serial number 11. *Right:* NEWARK WATCH CO., 18 size, 15 jewels, lever set, "ROBERT FELLOWS" engraved on movement, gilt full plate, ca. 1866, serial number 11707.

Left: AUBURNDALE WATCH CO., about 18 size, 2 jewels, lever set, stem wind, lever escapement, "ROTARY" marked on movement. The rotary design was created to eliminate watch position errors in the same way as a tourbillon, ca. 1876, serial number 448. *Right:* AUBURNDALE WATCH CO., 18 size, 7 jewels, "BENTLEY" engraved on movement, gilt three-quarter plate movement, ca.1888, serial number 2.

Top Left: Face. *Top Right:* Back of case. *Left:* Movement. Engraved on movement, "TEMPOR WATCH CO., 15 jewels, 3 adjs.," case signed "G. SCHWAB LOEILLE GENEVA," Masonic triangular pocket watch with Masonic symbols on face and case; engraved on dial, "love your fellow man, lend him a helping hand," ca. 1900.

BRONNIKOFF, signed wooden works watch with the case made of wood; note spoke on balance is missing, some bone was used, and the hairspring is made of metal, ca. 1860.

Left: J. G. HALL, 18 size, 15 jewels, gilt full plates, key wind and set, slow train, club tooth lever escapement, compensation balance, ca. 1860, serial number 25. *Right:* "J. G. HALL, MILLWOOD PARK, ROXBURY, VT" engraved on movement, 18 size, gilt three-quarter plate movement, 15 jewels, quick train, with compensating balance, ca. 1875, no serial number.

Right: E. GUBELIN, "world time," 24-hour dial, 56 cities listed on bezel that may be rotated to show a different time zone for each location, 18k gold case. *Bottom Left:* HAMILTON WATCH CO., "VENTURA ELECTRIC," grade 500, hacking sweep second hand, ca. 1958. *Bottom Right:* HAMILTON WATCH CO., tonneau-style case with chased engraving bezel, grade 987, 17 jewels, with a solid gold movement, ca. 1928.

Left: WALTHAM WATCH CO., rectangular-style 14k case, riverside rectangular grade movement, 21 jewels, ca. 1930s. *Right:* ELGIN WATCH CO., rectangular-style 14k case, Lord Elgin grade, two-toned silver hourglass-style dial, 21 jewels.

Left: TIFFANY & CO., large minute repeating and automaton wristwatch, two cherubs striking a bell. *Bottom Left:* Movement jeweled to the hammers; note two hammers and gongs. *Bottom Right:* TIFFANY & CO., 18k rose gold, round-style case, thin model.

Top Left: LONGINES, 14k white gold case, 36-diamond dial, auxiliary seconds dial. *Top Right:* LONGINES, 14k white gold rectangular case, 11-diamond dial, heavy lugs. *Right:* LONGINES, small WEEMS patented navigator's wristwatch, bezel may be rotated, auxiliary seconds dial may be rotated with stem at 2 o'clock, 14k gold case.

Bottom Left: OMEGA, 14k gold rectangular, heavy lugs, ca. 1930s. *Bottom Right:* WITTNAUER, 14k rectangular case, with hidden lugs, faceted crystal, ca. 1930s.

Left: GRUEN, 14k roped, carved bezel, auxiliary second dial, ca. 1950s. *Right:* INTERNATIONAL WATCH CO., SCHAFFAUSEN, 18k, date, automatic, watertight screw on back, sweep second.

JEAN LOUIS, duo-dial, Swiss-made watch, hour dial at top, minute dial at bottom, sweep 1/5 seconds outer dial.

Bottom Left: CARTIER, 18k rectangular case, black line from 12 to 6 and 9 to 3, hinged back. *Bottom Right:* ESKA, chronometer, day-date-month, moon phases, chronograph, two registers.

Left: LE COULTRE, 10k gold-filled rectangular case, moon phase, day-date-month, bezel marked to show hours. *Right:* BULOVA, 14k rectangular case; dial has black lines in shape of hourglass.

JULES JURGENSEN, 14k rectangular case, heavy, deep carved lugs.

Bottom Left: PIAGET, 18k oval-style case, automatic, with black dial and gold hands, ca. 1970s. *Bottom Right:* BUCHERER, 18k rectangular engraved case, eight-day movement, ca. 1930s.

Top Left: ROLEX, 18k case and bracelet, day-date, 10-diamond dial, oyster, perpetual, ca. 1960s. *Top Right:* ROLEX, 18k case and president bracelet, day-date, 10-diamond dial, 44-diamond bezel, oyster, perpetual. *Below Left:* ROLEX, 18k case, two round-button chronograph, day-date-month, three registers. *Below Right:* ROLEX, 18k rectangular style, "PRINCE," duo-dial, doctor's style watch, ca. 1930s.

EBERHARD & CO., early one-button chronograph; dial has snail-shaped tachometer, ca. 1930s.

M.S. SMITH & CO. (continued)

Grade or Name — Description	Avg	Ex-Fn	Mint
18S, 15J, ¾, KW, KS, 18K case	$2,000	$2,500	$3,200
18S, 15J, ¾, KW, KS .... ★ ★ ★	1,200	1,700	2,400
6S, 15J, SW, 18K case	700	800	1,000
6S, 15J, SW .... ★ ★	400	500	700

SOUTH BEND WATCH CO.
South Bend, Indiana
March 1903 - December 1929

Three brothers, George, Clement and J. M. Studebaker, purchased the successful Columbus Watch Co. The first South Bend watches were full plate and similar to the Columbus watches. The serial numbers started at 380,501 whereas the Columbus serial numbers stopped at about 500,000. The highest grade watch was a "Polaris," a 16S, ¾ plate, 21 jewels, and with an open face. This watch sold for about $100. The 227 and 229 were also high grade. The company identified its movements by model numbers 1, 2, and 3, and had grades from 100 to 431. The even numbers were hunting cases, and the odd numbers were open-faced cases. The lowest grade was a 203, 7J, that sold for about $6.75. The company closed on Dec. 31, 1929.

SOUTH BEND ESTIMATED SERIAL NUMBERS
AND PRODUCTION DATES

Date	Serial No.	Date	Serial No.	Date	Serial No.	Date	Serial No.
1903	380,501	1910	620,000	1917	865,000	1924	1,110,000
1904	410,000	1911	655,000	1918	900,000	1925	1,145,000
1905	445,000	1912	690,000	1919	935,000	1926	1,180,000
1906	480,000	1913	725,000	1920	970,000	1927	1,215,000
1907	515,000	1914	760,000	1921	1,005,000	1928	1,250,000
1908	550,000	1915	795,000	1922	1,040,000	1929	1,275,000
1909	585,000	1916	825,000	1923	1,075,000		

SOUTH BEND
18 SIZE

Grade or Name — Description	Avg	Ex-Fn	Mint
South Bend, 15J, OF	$75	$100	$150
South Bend, 15J, HC	100	125	175
South Bend, 17J, OF	75	100	150
South Bend, 17J, HC...............................	100	125	175
South Bend, 21J, OF	150	175	225
South Bend, 21J, HC, 14K	550	600	675
South Bend, 21J, OF, HC, Silveroid...................	75	100	125
South Bend, 21J, SW, HC	200	225	275
The Studebaker, G#323, 17J, OF, GJS, NI, Adj.5P	200	250	325
The Studebaker, G#328, 21J, HC, GJS, NI, FULL, Adj.5P	275	325	400
The Studebaker, G#329, 21J, OF, GJS, NI, FULL, Adj.5P	225	275	350
304, 15J, HC	100	125	175

South Bend movement, 18 size, 17 jewels, stem wind, hunting, serial number 426,726.

Studebaker, 18 size, 17 jewels, gold jewel settings, stem wind.

Grade or Name—Description	Avg	Ex-Fn	Mint
305, 15J, OF	$75	$100	$150
305, 15J, OF, Silveroid	40	50	65
309, 17J, OF	75	100	150
312, 17J, HC, NI, ADJ	100	125	175
313, 17J, OF, NI, ADJ, marked 313 .... ★	200	250	325
327, 21J, OF, Adj.5P................................	125	150	200
327, 21J, OF, Adj.5P, Silveroid......................	75	100	150
330, 15J, M#1, LS, HC .... ★★	300	350	425
331, 15J, M#1, LS, OF .... ★★	275	325	400
332, 15J, HC .... ★★	275	325	400
333, 15J, OF	75	100	150
337, 17J, OF	75	100	150
340, 17J, M#1, Adj.3P, NI, HC	125	150	200
341, 17J, M#1, ADJ, NI, Adj.3P, OF	100	125	175
342, 17J, M#1, LS	75	100	150
343, 17J, M#1, LS, OF	75	100	150
344, 17J, HC, NI, Adj.3P.......................... ★★	300	350	425
345, 17J, OF, NI, Adj.3P .... ★★	275	325	400
346, 17J, HC, NI .... ★★	300	350	425
347, 17J, OF, NI...................................	75	100	125
355, 19J, GJS, 2-Tone, HC........................ ★★	1,000	1,200	1,500

(Prices are with gold filled cases except where noted.)

NOTE: Some grades are not included. Their values can be determined by comparing with similar models or grades listed.

SOUTH BEND WATCH CO. (continued)

Grade 211, 16 size, 17 jewels, three-quarter plate, serial number 703,389.

Grade 295, 16 size, 21 jewels, first model, gold jewel settings, gold train, open face, serial number 518,022.

16 SIZE

Grade or Name — Description	Avg	Ex-Fn	Mint
Polaris, 21J, M#1, Adj.5P, ¾, NI, DR, GJS, GT.... ★ ★	$1,500	$1,800	$2,200
South Bend, 7J, OF	50	75	125
South Bend, 7J, HC	75	100	150
South Bend, 9J, OF	50	75	125
South Bend, 9J, HC	75	100	150
South Bend, 15J, OF	50	75	125
South Bend, 15J, HC	75	100	150
South Bend, 15J, OF, Silveroid	40	60	85
South Bend, 17J, OF	50	75	125
South Bend, 17J, HC, ADJ	100	125	175
South Bend, 17J, 14K HC	475	500	575
South Bend, 21J, OF	100	125	175
South Bend, 21J, HC, ADJ	200	250	325
The Studebaker 223, M#2, 17J, Adj.5P, BRG, GJS, DR, GT	275	300	375
The Studebaker 229, 21J, M#2, Adj.5P, BRG, GJS, DR, GT	300	325	400
203, 7J, ¾, NI, OF	50	75	125
204, 15J, ¾, NI, HC	75	100	150
207, 15J, OF, PS	50	75	125
209, 9J, M#2, OF, PS	50	75	125
211, 17J, M#2, ¾, NI, OF	50	75	125
212, 17J, M#2, HC, LS, heat & cold	100	125	175
215, 17J, M#2, OF, LS, heat & cold	50	75	125

South Bend Watch Co., **Polaris**, 16 size, 21 jewels, model number 1, Adj5p, gold jewel settings, gold train, open face, serial number 518,236.

Grade 227, 16 size, 21 jewels, gold jewel settings, Adj5p, serial number 1,222,843.

Grade or Name—Description	Avg	Ex-Fn	Mint
215, 17J, M#2, OF, Silveroid	$40	$50	$65
217, 17J, M#2, OF, BRG, NI, DR, Adj.3P..............	75	100	150
219, 19J, M#2, OF, NI, DR, Adj.4P	100	125	175
223, 17J, M#2, OF, LS, Adj.5P.......................	50	75	125
227, 21J, M#2, BRG, NI, LS, OF, DR, Adj.5P..........	125	150	200
229, 21J, M#2, BRG, GJS, ADJ, HC .... ★ ★	300	350	425
245, 19J, GJS, BRG, HC .... ★ ★	600	700	850
260, 7J, M#1, Adj.3P, OF	50	75	125
261, 7J, M#1, Adj.3P, HC	75	100	125
280, 15J, M#1, BRG, Adj.3P	75	100	150
281, 15J, M#1, OF	50	75	125
290, 17J, M#1, LS, Adj.3P, HC .... ★ ★	200	250	325
291, 17J, M#1, OF, Adj.3P .... ★ ★	175	200	275
292, 19J, M#1, HC, ¾, GJS, NI, DR, Adj.5P .... ★	250	300	375
293, 19J, M#1, OF, ¾, GJS, NI, DR, Adj.5P .... ★	175	225	275
294, 21J, M#1, Adj.5P, GJS, GT, HC, marked 294 .. ★ ★	300	350	475
295, 21J, M#1, OF, LS, Adj.5P, GJS, GT, marked 295 ★	250	300	425
298, 17J, M#1, HC, Adj.3P .... ★ ★	200	250	325
299, 17J, M#1, OF, Adj.3P .... ★ ★	175	225	275

12 SIZE
(OF Only)

Grade or Name — Description	Avg	Ex-Fn	Mint
Chesterfield, 15J, BRG, NI, DR	$50	$60	$75
Chesterfield, 17J, BRG, NI, GJS, DR, Adj.3P	60	70	85
Chesterfield, 21J, BRG, NI, GJS, DR, Adj.5P	75	100	125
Digital, 21J, GJS, DR, BRG, Adj.5P .... ★ ★	200	250	325

Grade 411., 12 size, 17 jewels, open face, double roller.

Chesterfield, 12 size, 21 jewels, open face only, bridge, gold jewel settings, pendant set, double roller, Adj5p.

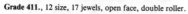

Grade or Name—Description	Avg	Ex-Fn	Mint
South Bend, 15J	$35	$45	$60
South Bend, 17J	40	50	65
South Bend, 17J, Silveroid	30	40	55
South Bend, 19J	60	70	85
South Bend, 21J	70	80	95
Studebaker, 21J, ¾, NI, Adj.5P, GJS	125	150	200
407, 15J, Silveroid	30	35	45
407, 15J	35	45	60
411, 17J, DR, GJS	40	50	65
415, 17J, ADJ to temp. ★★	125	150	200
419, 17J, Adj.3P ★★	125	150	200
429, 19J, Adj.4P, GT, GJS ★	100	125	175
431, 21J, Adj.5P, DR, GJS ★★	125	150	200
431, 21J, Adj.5P, Silveroid	40	50	65

6 SIZE

Grade or Name — Description	Avg	Ex-Fn	Mint
South Bend, 11J, G#180, HC	$100	$125	$175
South Bend, 15J, G#170, HC	100	125	175
South Bend, 17J, G#160, HC	100	125	175
South Bend, 17J, G#160, 14K	200	250	325

South Bend, 6 size, 15 jewels.

Grade 120-HC, 121-OF, 0 size, 17 jewels, bridge, nickel, double roller, pendant set.

0 SIZE

Grade or Name — Description	Avg	Ex-Fn	Mint
South Bend, 15J, OF, PS	$50	$60	$75
Grade 100 HC & 101 OF, 7J, PS	75	100	150
Grade 110 HC & 111 OF, 15J, 3F Brg, DR .... ★	125	150	200
Grade 120 HC & 121 OF, 17J, BRG, NI, DR, PS.... ★★	125	150	200
Grade 150 HC & 151 OF, 17J, BRG, NI, PS .... ★★	125	150	200

Note: Add $20 to above watches with hunting case; add $40 for hunting cases marked South Bend.

SOUTH BEND WATCH CO.
IDENTIFICATION OF MOVEMENTS
BY MODEL NUMBER

How to Identify Your Watch: Compare the movement of your watch with the illustrations in this section. Upon matching the movement exactly, the model number and size can be determined. While comparing, note the location of the balance, jewels, screws, gears, and type of back plate (Full, ¾, Bridge) which will be clues in identifying the movement you have. Having determined the size and model number, you can now find your watch in the main price listing by name or number (which is engraved on the movement).

18 SIZE—MODEL 1
Open Face and Hunting. Lever Set
Grade Numbers and Description of Movements

No. 341—Open Face, 17 Jewels, Lever Set, Adjusted to Temperature & 3 Positions.

SOUTH BEND WATCH CO. (continued)

No. 340—Hunting, 17 Jewels, Lever Set, Adjusted to Temperature & 3 Positions.
No. 343—Open Face, 17 Jewels, Lever Set.
No. 331—Open Face, 15 Jewels, Lever Set.

Model 1, Full Plate, Open face.

Model 1 , Full Plate, Hunting

18 SIZE—MODEL 2

Open Face and Hunting. Lever Set

Grade Numbers and Description of Movements

No. 329—21J, Open Face, "Studebaker," Adjusted to Temperature and 5 Positions.
No. 328—21J, Hunting, Adjusted to Temperature and 5 Positions.
No. 327—21J, Open Face, Adjusted to Temperature and 5 Positions.
No. 323—17J, Open Face, "Studebaker," Adjusted to Temperature and 5 Positions.
No. 345—17J, Open Face, Adjusted to Temperature and 3 Positions.
No. 344—17J, Hunting, Adjusted to Temperature and 3 Positions.
No. 313—17J, Open Face, Adjusted to Temperature.
No. 312—17J, Hunting, Adjusted to Temperature.

Model 2, Full Plate, Open face.

Model 2, Full Plate, Hunting.

Nos. 309, 337, 347—17J, Open Face.
No. 346—17J, Hunting.
Nos. 333, 305—15J, Open Face.
Nos. 332, 304—15J, Hunting.

16 SIZE—MODEL 1
Open Face and Hunting. Pendant and Lever Set
Grade Numbers and Description of Movements

No. 295—Open Face, 21 Jewels, Adjusted to Temperature and 5 Positions.
No. 294—Hunting, 21 Jewels, Adjusted to Temperature and 5 Positions.
No. 293—Open Face, 19 Jewels, Adjusted to Temperature and 5 Positions.
No. 292—Hunting, 19 Jewels, Adjusted to Temperature and 5 Positions.
No. 299—Open Face, 17 Jewels, Adjusted to Temperature and 3 Positions.
No. 298—Hunting, 17 Jewels, Adjusted to Temperature and 3 Positions.
No. 291—Open Face, 17 Jewels, Adjusted to Temperature and 3 Positions.
No. 290—Hunting, 17 Jewels, Adjusted to Temperature and 3 Positions.
No. 281—Open Face, 15 Jewels.
No. 280—Hunting, 15 Jewels.
No. 261—Open Face, 7 Jewels.
No. 260—Hunting, 7 Jewels.

Model 1, ¾ Plate, Open Face.   **Model 1,** ¾ Plate, Hunting.

16 SIZE—MODEL 2
Open Face and Hunting. Pendant and Lever Set.
Grade Numbers and Description of Movements

No. 229—21J, Open Face, Lever Set, "Studebaker," Adjust. to Temp. and 5 Positions.
No. 227—21J, Open Face, Lever Set, Adjusted to Temperature and 5 Positions.
No. 219—19J, Open Face, Pendant Set, Adjusted to Temperature and 4 Positions.
No. 223—17J, Open Face, Lever Set, "Studebaker," Adjust. to Temp. and 5 Positions.

No. 217—17J, Open Face, Lever Set, Adjusted to Temperature and 3 Positions.
No. 215—17J, Open Face, Pendant Set, Adjusted to Temperature.
No. 212—17J, Hunting, Lever Set, Adjusted to Temperature.
No. 211—17J, Open Face, Pendant Set.
No. 207—15J, Open Face, Pendant Set.
No. 204—15J, Hunting, Lever Set.
No. 209— 9J, Open Face, Pendant Set.
No. 203— 7J, Open Face, Pendant Set.

Model 2, ¾ Plate, Hunting.   **Model 2**. ¾ Plate, Open Face.

Model 2, Bridges, Open Face.

12 SIZE — MODEL 1
Chesterfield Series
and Grade 429 Special

Made in Pendant Set, Open Face Only
Grade Numbers and Description of Movements

No. 431—21J, Adjusted to Temperature and 5 Positions.
No. 429—19J, Adjusted to Temperature and 4 Positions.

SOUTH BEND WATCH CO. (continued)

No. 419—17J, Adjusted to Temperature and 3 Positions.
No. 415—17J, Adjusted to Temperature.
No. 411—17J.
No. 407—15J.

Model 1, Bridges, Open Face

Model 1, Lower Plate, Dial Side

6 SIZE—MODEL 1

Hunting

Grade No. 180, 17 Jewels
Grade No. 170, 15 Jewels
Grade No. 160, 11 Jewels

Serial Number Range
380,501 to 389,900

Model 1, ¼ Plate, 6
size

0 SIZE — MODEL 1

Open Face, No second hand, Hunting has second hand

Model 1, Open Face, ¼ Plate, 7 jewels.   **Model 1**, Hunting, Bridges, 15-17 jewels.

SOUTH BEND WATCH CO. (continued)

Model numbers 1 & 2 serial numbers under 659,700. All open face and hunting parts for this model except dial and fourth pinion are interchangeable.

0 SIZE—MODEL 2
Open Face, No second hand, Hunting has second hand

No. 100, 7 Jewels, Hunting, ¾ Bridge.
No. 101, 7 Jewels, Open Face, ¾ Plate.
No. 110, 15 Jewels, Hunting, ¾ Bridge.
No. 111, 15 Jewels, Open Face, ¾ Plate.
No. 120, 17 Jewels, Hunting, ¾ Bridge.
No. 121, 17 Jewels, Open Face, ¾ Plate.

Model 2, Open Face, ¾ Plate.   **Model 2**, Hunting, ¾ Bridge.

0 SIZE — MODEL 3
Both Open Face and Hunting have second hand
Grade Numbers and Description of Movements

No. 151—21J, Open Face, Bridge Model.
No. 150—21J, Hunting, Bridge Model.
No. 121—17J, Open Face, Bridge Model.
No. 120—17J, Hunting, Bridge Model.

Model 3, Open Face, Bridges.   **Model 3**, Hunting, Bridges.

Example of a basic original **J. P. Stevens** movement, 18 size, 15 jewels, note patented eccentric style regulator, serial number 65.

J.P. Stevens Watch Co. movement by Waltham, 18 size, 11 jewels, serial number 1,240,058.

J. P. STEVENS & CO.
Atlanta, Georgia
1882 - 1887

In mid-1881 J. P. Stevens bought part of the Springfield Watch Co. of Massachusetts; and some unfinished watch components from E. F. Bowman. He set up his watchmaking firm above his jewelry store in Atlanta, Ga., and started to produce the Bowman unfinished watches which were 16 size and 18 size, to which was added the "Stevens Patent Regulator." This regulator is best described as a simple disc attached to the plate which has an eccentric groove cut for the arm of the regulator to move in. This regulator is a prominent feature of the J. P. Stevens, and only the top is jeweled. These watches were 16S, ¾ plate, stem wind and had a nickel plate with damaskeening. The pallets were equidistant locking and needed greater accuracy in manufacturing. About 50 of these watches were made. A line of gilt movements was added. The pallet and fork are made of one piece aluminum. The aluminum was combined with 1/10 copper and formed an exceedingly tough metal which will not rust or become magnetized. The lever of this watch is only one-third the weight of a steel lever. The aluminum lever affords the least possible resistance for overcoming inertia in transmitting power from the escape wheel to the balance. In 1884, the company was turning out about ten watches a day at a price of $20 to $100 each. In the spring of 1887 the company failed. Only 174 true Stevens watches were made, but other watches carried the J. P. Stevens name.

16 TO 18 SIZE

Grade or Name — Description		Avg	Ex-Fn	Mint
Original Model, Serial Nos. 1 to 174 ....★ ★ ★		$3,000	$4,000	$5,500

J.P. STEVENS WATCH CO., 16-18 SIZE (continued)

Grade or Name—Description	Avg	Ex-Fn	Mint
Original Model, Serial Nos. 1 to 174 with original J. P. Stevens 18K case	$4,000	$5,000	$6,500
Aurora, 17J ★	350	400	525
Columbus W. Co., 17J ★	400	450	575
Elgin, 17J ★	300	350	425
Hamilton, 17J ★	400	450	525
Hampden, 17J ★	300	350	425
Illinois, 17J ★	600	650	725
N. Y. W. Co., 17J, Full Plate, S#s range in 500s	700	750	825
N. Y. W. Co. "Bond" Model, S#s range in 500s ★ ★	850	950	1,100
Rockford, 15J, Full Plate, HC ★	400	450	625
16S Swiss, 17J, Longines ★	175	200	250
Waltham, 17J ★	400	450	625

J.P. Stevens movement made by **Hampden**, 18 size, 17 jewels, note eccentric style regulator, serial number 1695.

J.P. Stevens Watch Co., 6 size, 11 jewels, exposed winding gears.

6 SIZE

Grade or Name — Description	Avg	Ex-Fn	Mint
Ladies Model, 15J, LS, HC, 14K	$500	$575	$650
Ladies Model, 15J, LS, GF case, HC	225	275	350
Ladies Model, 15J, LS, GF cases, OF	200	250	325
Ladies Model, 15J, LS, GF cases, Swiss made	175	225	325

SUFFOLK WATCH CO.
Waltham, Massachusetts
c. 1899 - 1901

The Suffolk Watch Company officially succeeded the Columbia Watch Company in March 1901. However, the Suffolk 0-size, 7-jewel nickel movement with lever escapement was being manufactured in the Columbia factory before the end of 1899. More than 25,000 movements were made. The factory was closed after it was purchased by the Keystone Watch Case Company on May 17, 1901. The machinery was moved to the nearby factory of the United States Watch Company (purchased by Keystone in April 1901), where it was used to make the United States Watch Company's 0-size movement, introduced in April 1902.

Both the Columbia Watch Company and the Suffolk Watch Company made 0-size movements only.

Suffolk Watch Co., 0 Size, 7 jewels, serial number 216,841.

Grade or Name — Description		Avg	Ex-Fn	Mint
0S, 7J, NI, HC .... ★ ★		$500	$600	$775

SETH THOMAS WATCH CO.
Thomaston, Connecticut
1883 - 1915

Seth Thomas is a very prominent clock manufacturer, but in early 1883, the company made a decision to manufacture watches. The watches were first placed on the market in 1885. They were 18S, open face, stem wind, ¾ plate, and the escapement was between the plates. The compensating balance was set well below the normal. They were 11J, 16,000 bpm train, but soon went to 18,000 or quick train. In 1886, the company started to make higher grade watches and produced four grades: 7J, 11J, 15J, and 17J. That year the output was 100 watches a day.

SETH THOMAS ESTIMATED SERIAL NUMBERS
AND PRODUCTION DATES

Date	Serial No.	Date	Serial No.	Date	Serial No.	Date	Serial No.
1885	5,000	1893	510,000	1901	1,230,000	1909	2,500,000
1886	20,000	1894	600,000	1902	1,320,000	1910	2,725,000
1887	40,000	1895	690,000	1903	1,410,000	1911	2,950,000
1888	80,000	1896	780,000	1904	1,500,000	1912	3,175,000
1889	150,000	1897	870,000	1905	1,700,000	1913	3,490,000
1890	235,000	1898	960,000	1906	1,900,000	1914	3,600,000
1891	330,000	1899	1,050,000	1907	2,100,000		
1892	420,000	1900	1,140,000	1908	2,300,000		

S. Thomas movement, 18 size, 7 jewels, model 9, serial number 574,714.

Edgemere, 18 size, 17 jewels, serial number 786,773.

18 SIZE

Grade or Name — Description	Avg	Ex-Fn	Mint
Century, 7J, OF	$50	$75	$125
Century, 7J, HC	75	100	150
Century, 15J, OF	50	75	125
Century, 15J, HC	75	100	150
Chautauqua, 15J, GJS, M#5	125	150	225
Eagle Series, No. 36, 7J, OF	50	75	125
Eagle Series, No. 37, 7J, HC	75	100	150
Eagle Series, No. 106, 11J, OF	50	75	125
Eagle Series, No. 107, 11J, HC	75	100	150
Eagle Series, No. 206, 15J, OF	50	75	125

Liberty, 18 size, 7 jewels, hunting or open face, eagle on movement.

Maiden Lane, 18 size, 28 jewels, gold jewel settings, Adj5p, dated 8,1.99. No serial number.

Henry Molineux, 18 size, 17 jewels, "Corona W. Co. USA" on dial, open face, serial number 54,951.

Seth Thomas, 18 size, 23 jewels, gold jewel settings, adjusted, serial number 298,333.

Grade or Name—Description	Avg	Ex-Fn	Mint
Eagle Series, No. 207, 15J, HC	$100	$125	$175
Eagle Series, No. 210, 17J, OF	75	100	150
Eagle Series, No. 211, 17J, HC	150	175	225
Eagle Series, 17J, NI, ¾, OF.........................	75	100	150
Edgemere, 11J	50	75	125
Edgemere, 17J	75	100	150
Keywind M#4, 7J, 11J, & 15J, ¾	250	300	375
Lakeshore, 17J, GJS, ADJ, NI	200	250	300
Liberty, 7J, ¾, eagle on back plate	75	100	125
Maiden Lane, 17J, GJS, DR, Adj.6P, NI, marked ... ★ ★	900	1,100	1,500
Maiden Lane, 19J, GJS, DR, Adj.6P, NI, marked . ★ ★ ★	1,000	1,200	1,600
Maiden Lane, 21J, GJS, DR, Adj.6P, NI, marked ..... ★	1,000	1,200	1,500
Maiden Lane, 24J, GJS, DR, Adj.6P, marked ..... ★ ★ ★	1,500	1,700	2,000
Maiden Lane, 25J, GJS, DR, Adj.6P, NI, marked ... ★ ★	2,400	2,500	3,000
Maiden Lane, 28J, GJS, DR, Adj.5P, NI, marked ★ ★ ★	15,000	18,000	25,000
Henry Molineux, M#3, 17J, ¾, GJS, ADJ .... ★ ★	500	550	650
Henry Molineux, M#2, 17J, GJS, ADJ .... ★ ★	500	550	650
Henry Molineux, M#2, 20J, GJS, ADJ .... ★ ★ ★	1,000	1,200	1,500
Monarch Watch Co., 7-15J, 2-tone	75	100	150
Republic USA, 7J, OF................................	50	75	125
S. Thomas, 7J, ¾, multi-color dial.....................	150	200	275
S. Thomas, 7J, ¾	50	75	125
S. Thomas, 11J, ¾, HC	75	100	150
S. Thomas, 11J, ¾, OF..............................	50	75	125
S. Thomas, 15J, ¾, HC	100	125	175
S. Thomas, 15J, ¾, gilded, OF	50	75	125
S. Thomas, 15J, ¾, OF..............................	50	75	125
S. Thomas, 16J, ¾	75	100	150
S. Thomas, 17J, ¾, OF, nickel	100	125	175

Grade or Name—Description	Avg	Ex-Fn	Mint
S. Thomas, 17J, ¾, 2-Tone	$125	$150	$200
S. Thomas, 17J, ¾, OF, gilded	75	100	150
S. Thomas, 17J, ¾, HC	125	150	175
S. Thomas, 21J, GJS, DR, Adj.5P	275	325	400
S. Thomas, 23J, GJS, DR, Adj.5P .... ★ ★	800	1,000	1,300
20th Century (Wards), 11J	75	100	150
20th Century (Wards), 11J, 2-Tone	100	125	175
Wyoming Watch Co., 7J, OF..........................	125	150	200
33, 7J, ¾, gilded, OF	50	75	125
37, 7J, ¾, NI, HC..................................	75	100	150
44, 11J, ¾, gilded, OF	50	75	125
47, 7J, gilded, FULL, OF	50	75	125
58, 11J, FULL, gilt, OF	50	75	125
70, 15J, ¾, gilded, OF	50	75	125
80, 17J, ¾, gilded, ADJ, HC........................	75	100	150
101, 15J, ¾, gilded, ADJ, OF	50	75	125
149, 15J, gilded, FULL, OF	50	75	125
159, 15J, NI, FULL, OF	50	75	125
169, 17J, NI, FULL, OF	75	125	150
170, 15J, ¾, NI, OF	50	100	125
179, 17J, ¾, NI, ADJ, OF	75	125	150
180, 17J, ¾, NI, HC	75	125	150
182, 17J, DR, NI, FULL, OF	100	125	175
201, 15J, ¾, NI, ADJ, OF...........................	75	100	150
245, 19J, GJS, 2-Tone, HC..........................	1,000	1,200	1,500
260, 21J, DR, Adj.6P, NI, FULL, OF.................	225	275	350
281-282, 17J, OF, LS, FULL, DR, Adj.3P, OF, 2-tone ...	150	175	225
382, 17J, OF, LS, FULL, DR, Adj.5P, OF, 2-tone.......	150	175	225

Centennial, 16 size, 7 jewels, three-quarter nickel plate.

Grade 36, 16 size, 7 jewels, open face, three-quarter nickel plate.

16 SIZE
(OF Only)

Grade or Name — Description	Avg	Ex-Fn	Mint
Centennial, 7J, ¾, NI, OF	$50	$75	$125
Locust, 7J, NI, ¾, OF	50	75	125
Locust, 17J, NI, ADJ, ¾, OF	75	100	175
Republic USA, 7J, OF	50	75	125
25, 7J, BRG, OF...................................	50	75	125
26, 15J, BRG, GJS, OF.............................	50	75	125
27, 17J, BRG, GJS, OF.............................	50	75	125
28, 17J, BRG, Adj.3P, GJS, OF	75	100	150
326, 7J, ¾, NI, OF	50	75	125
328, 15J, ¾, NI, OF	50	75	125
332, 7J, ¾, NI, OF	50	75	125
334, 15J, NI, ADJ, ¾, DMK, OF	75	100	150
336, 17J, ADJ, ¾, DMK, OF	100	125	150

Seth Thomas, 12 size, 7 jewels, open face, pendant set.

Seth Thomas, 12 size, 17 jewels, gold jewel settings, gold center wheel, open face, Adj3p.

12 SIZE
(OF Only)

Grade or Name — Description	Avg	Ex-Fn	Mint
Republic USA, 7J, OF	$40	$50	$65
25, 7J, BRG, OF...................................	40	50	65
26, 15J, BRG, GJS, OF.............................	45	55	70
27, 17J, BRG, GJS, OF.............................	50	60	75

SETH THOMAS WATCH CO., 12 SIZE (continued)

Grade or Name—Description	Avg	Ex-Fn	Mint
28, 17J, OF, BRG, Adj.3P, GJS	$55	$65	$80
326, 7J, OF, ¾, NI	40	50	65
328, 15J, OF, ¾, NI	45	55	70

Example of a basic **Seth Thomas** movement, 6 size, 7 jewels, serial number 441,839. Sometimes appears in a 12 size case.

Grade 45, 6 size, 7 jewels, open face, three-quarter nickel plate.

6 SIZE
(Some 6 Size were used to fit 12 Size cases)

Grade or Name — Description	Avg	Ex-Fn	Mint
Century, 7J, NI, ¾	$45	$50	$65
Eagle Series, 7J, No. 45, ¾, NI, DMK, OF	55	60	75
Eagle Series, 7J, No. 205, ¾, HC	75	100	150
Eagle Series, 15J, No. 35, ¾, NI, DMK, OF	65	70	85
Eagle Series, 15J, No. 245, ¾, HC	75	100	150
Republic USA, 7J	45	50	65
Seth Thomas, 7J, ¾, HC, 14K, 26 DWT	250	275	325
Seth Thomas, 11J, ¾, HC	75	100	150
Seth Thomas, 11J, ¾, OF	45	55	65
35, 7J, HC, NI, DMK, ¾	75	100	150
119, 16J, HC, GJS, NI, DMK, ¾	100	125	175
205, 15J, HC	75	100	150
320, 7J, OF, NI, DMK, ¾	50	65	85
322, 15J, OF	55	60	70

NOTE: Add $25 for HC.

0 SIZE

Grade or Name — Description	Avg	Ex-Fn	Mint
Seth Thomas, 7J, OF, No. 1	$60	$70	$85
Seth Thomas, 7J, HC, No. 1	75	100	150
Seth Thomas, 15J, OF, GJS, No. 3	60	70	85
Seth Thomas, 15J, HC, No. 3	75	100	150
Seth Thomas, 17J, OF, GJS, PS, No. 9	60	70	85
Seth Thomas, 17J, HC, GJS, PS, No. 9	75	100	150

NOTE: Add $25 for HC.

SETH THOMAS WATCH CO.
IDENTIFICATION OF MOVEMENTS
BY MODEL NUMBER

How to Identify Your Watch: Compare the movement of your watch with the illustrations in this section. Upon matching the movement exactly, the model number and size can be determined. While comparing, note the location of the balance, jewels, screws, gears, and type of back plate (Full, ¾, Bridge) which will be clues in identifying the movement you have. Having determined the size and model number, you can now find your watch in the main price listing by name or number (which is engraved on the movement).

Model 1, 18 size, Open Face

Model 2, 18 size, Hunting

Model 3, 18 size, Open Face

Model 4, 18 size, Key Wind

Model 5, 18 size, Maiden Lane Series, Open Face.

Model 6, 18 Size, Open Face

Model 7 & 9, 18 size

Model 8, 18 size

Model 10, 18 size, Open Face

Model 11, 18 size, Hunting

Model 13, 18 size, Hunting

16 Size

16 Size, Open Face

12 Size, Open Face

6 Size, Open face

Model 14, 6 size

Model 16 & 17, 6 size

TREMONT WATCH CO.
Boston, Massachusetts
1864 - 1866

In 1864 A. L. Dennison thought that if he could produce a good movement at a reasonable price, there would be a ready market for it. Dennison went to Switzerland to find a supplier of cheap parts, as arbors were too high in America. He found a source for parts, mainly the train and escapement and the balance. About 600 sets were to be furnished. In 1865, the first movements were ready for the market. They were 18S, key wind, fully jeweled, and were engraved "Tremont Watch Co." In 1886, the company moved from Boston to Melrose. Another 18S was made, and the company made its own train and escapement. The watches were engraved "Melrose Watch Co., Melrose, Mass." The Tremont Watch Co. produced about 5,000 watches before being sold to the English Watch Co.

Tremont Watch Co., with "Washington Street Boston" engraved on movement, 18 size, 15 jewels, key wind and set, serial number 5,264.

Example of a basic **Tremont** movement, 18 size, 15 jewels, key wind & set, serial number 8,875.

Grade or Name — Description		Avg	Ex-Fn	Mint
18S, 7J, KW, KS	★ ★	$250	$275	$350
18S, 11J, KW, KS	★ ★	250	275	350
18S, 15J, KW, KS, Silveroid, recased	★	150	175	225
18S, 15J, KW, KS, gilded	★	250	275	350
18S, 15J, KW, KS, HC, 14K	★	650	675	750
18S, 15J, KW, KS, gilded, Washington Street	★ ★	350	375	450
18S, 17J, KW, KS, gilded	★	300	325	400
18S, 15J, KW, KS from back, ¼ plate	★ ★ ★	1,500	1,700	2,000

NOTE: Watches listed in this book are priced at the retail level, as complete watches having an original 14k gold-filled case, an original white enamel single sunk dial, and with the entire original movement in good working order with no repairs needed, unless otherwise noted.

TRENTON WATCH CO.
Trenton, New Jersey
1885 - 1908

Trenton watches were marketed under the following labels: Trenton, Ingersoll, Fortuna, Illinois Watch Case Company, Calumet U.S.A., Locomotives Special, Marvel Watch Co., and Reliance Watch Co.

Serial numbers started at 2,001 and ended at 4,100,000. Total production was about 1,934,000.

CHRONOLOGY OF THE DEVELOPMENT OF TRENTON WATCH CO.:

New Haven Watch Co., New Haven, Conn. — 1883-1887
Trenton Watch Co., Trenton, N. J. — 1887-1908
Sold to Ingersoll — 1908-1922

TRENTON MODELS AND GRADES
With Years of Manufacture and Serial Numbers

Date	Numbers	Size	Model	Date	Numbers	Size	Model
1887-1889	2,001- 61,000	18	1	1900-1903	2,000,001-2,075,000	6	2
1889-1891	64,001- 135,000	18	2	1902-1905	2,075,001-2,160,000	6	3 LS
1891-1898	135,001- 201,000 *[1]	18	3			12	2 LS
1899-1904	201,001- 300,000	18	6	1905-1907	2,160,001-2,250,000	6	3 PS
1891-1900	300,001- 500,000	18	4			12	2 PS
1892-1897	500,001- 600,000	6	1	1899-1902	2,500,001-2,600,000	3/0	1
1894-1899	650,001- 700,000	16	1	ca. 1906	2,800,001-2,850,000	6	3 PS
1898-1900	700,001- 750,000	6	2			12	2 PS
1900-1904	750,001- 800,000 *[2]	18	4	1900-1904	3,000,001-3,139,000	16	2
1896-1900	850,001- 900,000	12	1	1903-1907	3,139,001-3,238,000	16	3 OF
1898-1903	900,001-1,100,000	18	5	1903-1907	3,500,001-3,600,000	16	3 HC
1902-1907	1,300,001-1,400,000	18	6	1905-1907	4,000,001-4,100,000	0	1

[1] 7 jewel grades made only during 1891; 9 jewel chronograph made 1891-1898.
[2] A few examples are KWKS for export to England.

Trenton movement, 18 size, 4 jewels, serial number 4,744.

Trenton movement, 18 size, 7 jewels, 4th model, serial number 788,313.

18 SIZE

Grade or Name — Description	Avg	Ex-Fn	Mint
M#1-2, gilded, OF................................★	$150	$175	$250
M#3, 7J, ¾	50	75	125
M#3, 9J, ¾	50	75	125
M#4, 7J, FULL....................................	50	75	125
M#4, 11J, FULL...................................	50	75	125
M#4, 15J, FULL...................................	50 .	75	125
M#4-5, FULL, OF, NI..............................	50	75	125
New Haven Watch Co. style, M#1, 4J ....★★★	225	300	425
Trenton, 7J, KW, KS..............................★	225	300	425

Note: Add $25 to value of above watches in hunting case.

Trenton movement, 18 size, 7 jewels, serial number 148,945.

Chronograph, 16 size, 9 jewels, third model; start, stop & fly back, sweep second hand.

16 SIZE

Grade or Name — Description	Avg	Ex-Fn	Mint
M#1-2, 7J, ¾, NI, OF..............................	$50	$75	$125
M#3, 7J, 3F BRG	50	75	125
M#3, 11J, 3F BRG	50	75	125
M#3, 15J, 3F BRG	50	75	125
7,11,15J, 3F BRG, NI	50	75	125
Chronograph, 9J, start, stop, & fly back	150	175	225
Convertible Model, 7J, OF	100	125	175
Grade #30 & 31, 7J................................	50	75	125
Grade #35, 36 & 38, 11J	50	75	125
Grade #45, 16J....................................	75	100	150
Grade #125, 12J...................................	50	75	125
Ingersoll Trenton, 7J, 3F BRG.....................	50	75	125

Ingersoll Trenton movement, 16 size, 19 jewels, three-fingered bridge, adjusted, serial number 3,419,771.

Ingersoll Trenton movement, 16 size, 12 jewels; "Edgemere" engraved on movement.

Grade or Name—Description	Avg	Ex-Fn	Mint
Ingersoll Trenton, 15J, 3F BRG, NI, ADJ	$75	$100	$150
Ingersoll Trenton, 17J, 3F BRG, NI, ADJ	75	100	150
Ingersoll Trenton, 19J, 3F BRG, NI, Adj.5P	150	175	225
Peerless, 7J, SW, LS	50	75	125
Reliance, 7J	50	75	125

Note: Add $25 to value of above watches in hunting case.

Reliance, 16 size, 7 jewels, serial number 241,265.

Trenton movement, convertible model, 16 size, 7 jewels.

12 SIZE

Grade or Name — Description	Avg	Ex-Fn	Mint
"Fortuna," 7J, BRG	$40	$50	$65

TRENTON WATCH CO., 12 SIZE (continued)

Grade or Name—Description	Avg	Ex-Fn	Mint
M#1, 7J, ¾	$40	$50	$65
Monogram, 7J, SW	40	50	65

Note: Add $25 to value of above watches in hunting case.

Example of a basic **Trenton Watch Co.** movement, 6 size, 7 jewels, open face & hunting, nickel damaskeened.

6 SIZE

Grade or Name — Description	Avg	Ex-Fn	Mint
7J, ¾, NI	$30	$40	$55
7J, 3F BRG	40	50	65
15J, 3F BRG	40	50	65

Note: Add $25 to value of above watches in hunting case.

0 SIZE

Grade or Name — Description	Avg	Ex-Fn	Mint
7J, 3F BRG	$40	$50	$65
15J, 3F BRG	50	60	75

Note: Add $25 to value of above watches in hunting case.

UNITED STATES WATCH CO.
Marion, New Jersey
1865 - 1877

The United States Watch Company was chartered in 1865, and the factory building was started in August 1865 and was completed in 1866. The first watch, called the "Frederic Atherton," was not put on the market until July 1867. It was America's **first** mass-produced stem winding watch. This first grade was 18S, 19J, full plate and a gilt finish movement. A distinctive feature of the company's full plate movements was the butterfly shaped patented opening in the plate which allowed escapement inspection. That same year a second grade called the "Fayette Stratton" was introduced. It was also

UNITED STATES WATCH CO. (continued)

a gilt finish, full plate movement. Most of these were 15J, but some of the very early examples have been noted in 17J. In 1868 the "George Channing," "Edwin Rollo," and "Marion Watch Co." grades were introduced. All were 18S, 15J, full plate movements in a gilt finish. In February 1869 the gilt version of the "United States Watch Co." grade was introduced. It was 18S, 19J, full plate and was the company's first entry into the prestige market. Later that year the company introduced their first nickel grade, a 19J, 18S, full plate movement called the "A. H. Wallis." About this same time, in December 1869, they introduced America's most expensive watch, the first nickel, 19J, 18S, full plate "United States Watch Co." grade. Depending on case weight, these prestige watches retailed between $500 and $600, more than the average man earned in a year at that time. The company also introduced damaskeening to the American market; first on gilt movements and later on the nickel grades. The United States and Wallis 19J prestige grades were beautifully finished with richly enameled engraving including a variety of unique designs on the balance cock. It is significant to note that "no" solid gold trains have been seen with these prestige items in the extant examples presently known.

Example of a **Frederick Atherton & Co.** movement, 18 size, 19 jewels, gold jewel settings, key wind & pin set. Note butterfly cut-out.

In 1870 the company introduced their first watch for ladies, a 10S, 15J, ¼ plate, cock & bridge movement which was made to their specifications in Switzerland. This model was first introduced in two grades, the "R. F. Pratt" and "Chas. G. Knapp," both in a 15J, gilt finish movement. Later it was offered in a high grade, 19J "I. H. Wright" nickel finish movement. During 1870 and 1871 several other full plate grades in both gilt and nickel finish were introduced. In 1871 development on a new line of full plate, ¾ plate, and ¼ plate & bridge was started but not introduced to the market until late in 1872 and early in 1873. The 10S and 16S new grades in ¼ plate and bridge were probably delayed well into 1873 and were not available long before the "Panic of 1873" started in September; this explains their relative scarcity.

By July 1874 the "Panic" had taken its toll and it was necessary for the company to reorganize as the Marion Watch Company, a name formerly used for one of their grades. At this time jewel count, finish standards, and prices were lowered on the full plate older grades, but this proved to be a mistake. That same year they introduced a

UNITED STATES WATCH CO. (continued)

cased watch called the "North Star," their cheapest watch at $15 retail. The year of 1875 hit the watch industry the hardest; price cutting was predatory and the higher priced watches of the United States Watch Co. were particulary vulnerable. Further lowering of finish standards and prices did not help and in 1876 the company was once again reorganized into the Empire City Watch Co. and displayed their products at the Centennial that year. The Centennial Exhibition was not enough to save the faltering company and they finally closed their doors in 1877. The Howard brothers of Fredonia, New York (Independent and Fredonia Watch Co.) purchased most of the remaining movement stock and machinery. In the ten year period of movement production, current statistical studies indicate an estimated production of only some 60,000 watches, much smaller than the number deduced from the serial numbers assigned up to as high as 289,000.

NOTE: *The above historical data and estimated production figures are based on data included in the new NAWCC book* **MARION, A History of the United States Watch Company** *by William Muir and Bernard Kraus. This definitive work is available from NAWCC, Inc., 514 Poplar St., Columbia, PA. (Courtesy, Gene Fuller, MARION book editor.) This book is recommended by Mr. Shugart and Mr. Engle for your library.*

KEY FEATURES USED TO DISTINGUISH USWC MODELS

'66 Model

★ Lower barrel bridge is straight or "bar" shaped.
★ Mechanism gears mounted on top of yoke plate.
★ Yoke plate is not secured on pillar plate and has two sets of intermediate gears mounted on it.
★ Barrel arbor flush with barrel plate and flush cannon pinion, so STEM WIND AND SET only with no provision for key wind and set (early '66 models).
★ Slipping yoke plate and poor gear ratios caused binding, wear and breakdown of gears.

'68 Model

★ Lower barrel bridge is bent or "horseshoe" shaped.
★ Mechanism gears mounted under the yoke plate for improved gear action.
★ Longer arms on yoke plate, now clearly a "3 arm" yoke plate; reduced number of intermediate gears mounted on yoke plate.
★ Stationary intermediate gear mounted on pillar plate to engage cannon pinion.
★ Stem wind/set watches were given key wind/set capability.

'71 Model

★ Streamlined and simplified mechanisms, reduced number of components under dial.
★ Minute wheel relocated to also act as the stationary intermediate gear in setting system.
★ Redesigned 1-piece click spring served as a click and as a device to maintain power on the yoke plate.

UNITED STATES WATCH CO. (continued)

★ Streamlined yoke plate either with extended arm for "side set" or crescent shaped for conventional "lever set."

★ Redesigned pillar plate permitting removal of lower barrel and jewel bridges.

North Star

★ Streamlined and simplified '71 Model, **stem wind and key set**, or key wind and set.

★ Crown wheel directly engages main wheel for stem winding (one way).

★ Back to 2-piece click spring.

★ $10/week average wages, still a week and a half of work to purchase the $15 watch.

Trading down on finish and jewel standards

★ Took place 1874-1876 **only** on **full plate** models.

★ Coupled with lower prices, led to failure of the company in 1877.

Table I
USWC MODELS

Model	Sizes	Movement Style	Reference*
1865**	18s	¾ Plate	MKB 39-40
1866	18s	Full Plate	MKB 49-53
1868	18s	Full Plate	MKB 53-56
1870	10s	¼ Plate, Cock & Bridge	MKB 66-67
1871	18s	Full Plate	MKB 85-94
1871	14s & 18s	¾ Plate	MKB 85-94
1871	10s & 16s	¼ Plate & Bridge	MKB 85-94

NOTES:

* Page numbers in Muir Kraus book "MARION." Also see Table IV, MKB 134-136 for breakdown into grades and model variations.

** Deduction based on available evidence; no actual examples known.

Table II
USWC MODELS and KEY PATENTS

Model	Patent	Date	Inventor and Feature
1865	47,412	Apr. 25, 1865	Frederick A. Giles, Stemwind/set
1865	D2,055	May 9, 1865	Frederick A. Giles, Top plate
1866	49,397	Aug. 15, 1865	Frederick A. Giles, Stemwind/set
1866	D2,281	Mar. 13, 1866	Frederick A. Giles, "Butterfly"
1868	Improved	Dec. 22, 1868	No patent filed on this improvement to stemwinding mechanism.
1870	D3,885-6	Mar. 8, 1870	Fayette S. Giles, Top plate
1871	74,041	Feb. 4, 1868	Belding D. Bingham, Dust band
1871	100,511	Mar. 8, 1870	Julius Elson, Double Index Reg.
1871	145,939	Pat. Appl. For Dec. 30, 1873	Frederick A. Giles, Reversible Barrel

UNITED STATES WATCH CO. (continued)

NOTE: Also see MKB 127-128

Table III
USWC DEVELOPMENTS and REORGANIZATIONS
1872 - 1877

Year	Major Events
1872	**Sept.**—Along with introduction of the new '71 models, FA & Co and AHW jeweled down from 19 to 17J while ER grade is jeweled down from 15 to 11J.
1873	**May**—USWC jeweled down from 19 to 15J.
	Sept.—PANIC of 1873 begins.
1874	"North Star" introduced as cased watch for $15. **July**—Marion Watch Co. formed. "Trading Down" in jewel count **and** finish standards begins.
1875	Further step downs in finish standards. Sale of 16s, ¼ plate and bridge machinery.
1876	Empire City Watch Co. formed—Royal Gold American Watch connection with Elias Bros. CENTENNIAL. Sale of 18s, ¾ plate machinery.
1877	Factory closes.

Table IV
EMPIRE CITY W. CO. & EQUIVALENT U.S.W.CO. GRADES
See Table VIII, MKB 179

Empire City W. Co.	United States W. Co.
W. S. Wyse	A. H. Wallis
L. W. Frost	Henry Randel
Cyrus H. Loutrel	Wm. Alexander
J. L. Ogden	S. M. Beard
E. F. C. Young	John W. Lewis
D. C. Wilcox	George Channing
Henry Harper	Asa Fuller
Jesse A. Dodd	Edwin Rollo
E. C. Hine	J. W. Deacon
New York Belle	A. J. Wood
The Champion	G. A. Read
Black Diamond	Young America

NOTE: *Tables I, II, III, and IV courtesy Gene Fuller, NAWCC "MARION" book editor.*

United States Watch Co. movement, 18 size, 19 jewels, gold jewel settings, key wind. Their highest grade watch.

United States Watch Co. double sunk dial, hunting, note pin setting at 4 o'clock.

MARION
18 SIZE
(All with Butterfly Cutout
Except for ¾ Plate)

Grade or Name — Description	Avg	Ex-Fn	Mint
Wm. Alexander, 15J, NI, KW, HC	$275	$350	$425
Wm. Alexander, 15J, NI, KW, OF	200	250	325
Wm. Alexander, 15J, NI, SW, OF	225	275	350
Frederic Atherton & Co., 15J, SW, gilded	250	325	400
Frederic Atherton & Co., 17J, KW, gilded, HC	300	350	425
Frederic Atherton & Co., 17J, KW, gilded, OF	250	300	375
Frederic Atherton & Co., 17J, SW, gilded, HC	300	350	425
Frederic Atherton & Co., 17J, SW, gilded, OF	250	325	400

U.S. Watch Co., dial and movement, 18 size, 20 jewels, hunting case, ¾ plate, engraved on movement "N.D. Godfrey," serial number 72,042. Painted on the dial "New York 1873." The dial consists of day-date-month and moon phases.

Grade or Name—Description	Avg	Ex-Fn	Mint
Frederic Atherton & Co., 19J, SW, gilded, ... ★ ★ ★ ★	$800	$1,000	$1,300
Frederic Atherton & Co., 19J, KW, gilded .... ★ ★	600	700	850
BC&M R.R., 11J, KW......................, ... ★ ★ ★ ★	1,600	1,800	2,100
BC&M R.R., 15J, gilded, KW .... ★ ★ ★ ★	1,600	1,800	2,100
S. M. Beard, 15J, KW, NI, OF	250	300	375
S. M. Beard, 15J, SW, NI, OF	250	300	375
S. M. Beard, 15J, SW or KW, HC	300	350	425
Centennial Phil., 11-15J, SW or KW, NI........ ★ ★ ★ ★	1,800	2,000	2,300
George Channing, 15J, KW, NI........................	250	300	375
George Channing, 15J, KW, gilded....................	225	275	325
George Channing, 15J, KW, NI, ¾ Plate .... ★ ★	350	400	475
George Channing, 17J, KW, NI.......................	275	325	400
J. W. Deacon, 11-13J, KW, gilded	175	225	300
J. W. Deacon, 15J, KW, gilded.......................	175	225	300
J. W. Deacon, 11-15J, KW, ¾ Plate .... ★	275	325	400
Empire City Watch Co., 11J, SW, no cutout	175	225	300
Empire City Watch Co., 15J, SW, NI, no cutout	200	250	325
Empire Combination Timer, 11J, FULL, time & distance on dial..	400	500	650
Empire Combination Timer, 15J, ¾, time & distance on dial..	600	750	1,000
Fellows, 15J, NI, KW	400	450	525
Benjamin Franklin, 15J, KW	400	450	525
Asa Fuller, 7-11J, gilded, KW	200	225	275
Asa Fuller, 15J, gilded, KW	200	225	275
Asa Fuller, 15J, gilded, KW, ¾ Plate .... ★ ★	300	325	350
N. D. Godfrey, 20J, NI, ¾ plate, day date month, moon phases, c. 1873, HC, 18K .... ★ ★ ★ ★	3,500	4,000	4,800
John W. Lewis, 15J, NI, KW.........................	225	275	350
John W. Lewis, 15J, NI, SW	250	300	375

Edwin Rollo, 18 size, 15 jewels, gilded, key wind & set, note butterfly cut-out, serial number 110,214.

Marion Watch Co. personalized Watch, 18 size, about 15 jewels, pin set, note butterfly cut-out, serial number 106,761.

UNITED STATES WATCH CO., 18 SIZE (continued)

Empire City Watch Co. on movement, U.S. Marion Watch Co. on dial, 18 size, 15 jewels, note no butterfly cut-out on this model.

United States Watch Co., 18 size, 19 jewels, gold jewel settings, key wind & pin set, serial number 24,054.

Grade or Name—Description		Avg	Ex-Fn	Mint
John W. Lewis, 15J, NI, ¾ Plate	★★	$350	$400	$475
Marion Watch Co., 11J, KW, gilded		200	250	325
Marion Watch Co., 15J, KW, gilded		200	250	325
Marion Watch Co., 15J, SW, gilded, ¾ Plate	★★	300	350	425
Marion Watch Co., 17-19J, KW, gilded	★	300	350	425
N.J. R.R.&T. Co., 15J, gilded, KW		1,200	1,400	1,700
Newspaper Special Order, 11-15J, gilded, SW or KW		325	375	450
North Star, 7J, KW, NI case		300	350	425
North Star, 7J, SW, KS		300	350	425
North Star, 7J, ¾ Plate		325	375	450
Pennsylvania R.R., 15J, NI, KW	★★★★	2,500	2,800	2,900
Personalized Watches, 7-11J, KW, ¾ Plate	★	250	300	375
Personalized Watches, 11J, KW, gilded	★	250	300	375
Personalized Watches, 15J, KW, gilded	★	250	300	375
Personalized Watches, 15J, KW, NI	★	275	325	400
Personalized Watches, 15J, KW, ¾ Plate	★	300	350	425
Personalized Watches, 19J, KW, Full Plate	★	400	450	525
Henry Randel, 15J, KW, NI		250	300	375
Henry Randel, 15J, SW, NI		250	300	375
Henry Randel, 15J, ¾ Plate	★★	350	400	475
Henry Randel, 17J, KW, NI	★	275	325	400
G. A. Read, 7J, gilded, KW		200	250	325
G. A. Read, 7J, ¾ Plate		300	350	425
Edwin Rollo, 11J, KW, gilded		200	250	325
Edwin Rollo, 15J, KW, gilded		200	250	325
Edwin Rollo, 15J, SW, gilded		200	250	325
Edwin Rollo, 15J, ¾ Plate	★	300	350	425
Royal Gold, 11J, KW		300	350	425
Royal Gold, 15J, KW		300	350	425
Royal Gold, 15J, ¾ Plate	★★	400	450	525

A.H. Wallis on movement, **Empire City Watch Co.** on dial, 18 size, 19 jewels, three-quarter plate, hunting. This combination timer has listed on the dial, 16 cities showing the time of day and distance in comparison with New York City, serial number 54,409.

Grade or Name—Description	Avg	Ex-Fn	Mint
Rural New York, 15J, gilded	$250	$300	$375
Fayette Stratton, 11J, gilded	250	300	375
Fayette Stratton, 15J, KW, gilded	250	300	375
Fayette Stratton, 15J, SW, gilded	250	300	325
Fayette Stratton, 17J, KW, gilded	275	325	400
Fayette Stratton, 17J, SW, gilded	300	350	425
Union Pacific R.R., 15J, KW, gilded .... ★ ★ ★ ★	1,800	2,000	2,300
United States Watch Co., 15J, NI, KW	500	550	625
United States Watch Co., 15J, NI, SW	600	650	725
United States Watch Co., 15J, ¾ Plate, NI	600	650	725
United States Watch Co., 15J, ¾ Plate, gilded	600	650	725
United States Watch Co., 19J, GJS, Adj.5P, 18K HC, dial			
mvt. & case all marked, Pin Set, SW .... ★ ★ ★	4,000	4,300	4,800
United States Watch Co., 19J, NI, KW .... ★ ★	750	950	1,200
United States Watch Co., 19J, NI, SW .... ★ ★	900	1,100	1,350
A. H. Wallis, 15J, KW, NI............................	250	300	375
A. H. Wallis, 15J, SW, NI	250	300	375
A. H. Wallis, 17J, KW, NI............................	275	325	400
A. H. Wallis, 17J, SW, NI	300	350	425
A. H. Wallis, 19J, KW, NI..................... ★ ★ ★	600	650	725
A. H. Wallis, 19J, SW, NI .... ★ ★ ★	650	700	775
D. C. Wilcox, 15J, SW, no butterfly cutout	250	300	375
I. H. Wright, 11J, KW, gilded	225	275	350
I. H. Wright, 15J, KW, gilded	225	275	350

Note: 18S, ¾ plate are scarce. Add $25 to $50 for listed open face watches with hunting cases.

NOTE: Watches listed in this book are priced at the retail level, as complete watches having an original 14k gold-filled case, an original white enamel single sunk dial, and with the entire original movement in good working order with no repairs needed, unless otherwise noted.

16 SIZE
¼ Plate

Grade or Name — Description	Avg	Ex-Fn	Mint
S. M. Beard, 15J, NI, KW, ¼ Plate............ ★ ★ ★ ★	$400	$450	$525
John W. Lewis, 15J, ¼ Plate, NI, KW .... ★ ★ ★ ★	400	450	525
Personalized Watches, 15J, ¼ Plate, NI, SW.... ★ ★ ★ ★	400	450	525
Edwin Rollo, 15J, ¼ Plate, KW .... ★ ★ ★ ★	400	450	525
United States Watch Co., 15J, ¼ Plate, NI, SW. ★ ★ ★ ★	600	700	850
A. H. Wallis, 19J, NI, SW, ¼ Plate .... ★ ★ ★ ★	600	700	850

Note: 16S, ¼ plate are the scarcest of the U.S.W.Co.-Marion watches.

Asa Fuller, 16 size, 15 jewels, stem wind, one-quarter plate, serial number 280,018.

United States Watch Co., 14 size, 15 jewels, three-quarter plate, engraved on movement "Royal Gold American Watch, New York, Extra Jeweled."

14 SIZE
¾ Plate

Grade or Name — Description	Avg	Ex-Fn	Mint
Centennial Phil., 11J, KW, ¾ Plate, gilded	$400	$500	$750
J. W. Deacon, 11J, ¾ Plate.........................	250	300	375
Asa Fuller, 15J, ¾ Plate .... ★ ★	350	400	475
John W. Lewis, 15J, ¾ Plate, NI .... ★ ★	300	350	400
North Star, 15J, ¾ Plate...........................	250	300	375
Personalized Watches, 7-11J, ¾ Plate .... ★ ★	350	400	475
Edwin Rollo, 15J, ¾ Plate .... ★	300	350	425
Royal Gold, 15J, ¾ Plate......................... ★	350	400	475
Young America, 7J, ¾ Plate, gilded.................	300	350	425

10 SIZE
¼ **Plate**

Grade or Name — Description	Avg	Ex-Fn	Mint
Wm. Alexander, 15J, KW, NI	$200	$250	$325
Empire City Watch Co., 15J, KW.....................	200	250	325
Chas. G. Knapp, 15J, Swiss, ¼ Plate, KW.............	100	150	225
Personalized Watches, 11-15J, ¼ Plate	200	250	325
R. F. Pratt, 15J, Swiss, ¼ Plate, KW	100	150	225
Edwin Rollo, 11-15J, ¼ Plate .... ★	250	300	375
A. H. Wallis, 17-19J, KW, ¼ Plate	225	275	350
A. J. Wood, 15J, ¼ Plate, KW .... ★ ★ ★	300	350	425
I. H. Wright, 19J, Swiss, NI, ¼ Plate, KW .... ★ ★ ★	500	550	625

United States Watch Co., 10 size, 15-19 jewels, key wind
& set from back, one-quarter plate. Swiss model.

U. S. WATCH CO.
OF WALTHAM
Waltham, Massachusetts
1884 - 1905

The business was started as the Waltham Watch Tool Co. in 1879. It was organized as the United States Watch Co. in 1884. The first watches were 16S, ¾ plate pillar movement in three grades. They had a very wide mainspring barrel (the top was thinner than most) which was wedged up in the center to make room for the balance wheel. These watches are called dome watches and are hard to find. The fork was made of an aluminum alloy with a circular slot and a square ruby pin. The balance was gold at first, as was the movement which was a slow train, but the expansion balance was changed when they went to a quick train. The movement required a special case which proved unpopular. By 1887, some 3,000 watches had been made. A new model was then produced, a 16S movement that would fit a standard case. These movements were quick train expansion balance with standard type lever and ¾ plate pillar movement. The company had a top production of ten watches a day. It was sold to the E. Howard Watch Co. in 1903. The United States Watch Co. produced some 802,000 watches total. Its top grade watch was the "President."

U. S. WATCH CO. OF WALTHAM
ESTIMATED SERIAL NUMBERS
AND PRODUCTION DATES

Date	Serial No.	Date	Serial No.
1887	3,000	1896	300,000
1888	6,500	1897	350,000
1889	10,000	1898	400,000
1890	30,000	1899	500,000
1891	60,000	1900	600,000
1892	90,000	1901	700,000
1893	150,000	1902	750,000
1894	200,000	1903	800,000
1895	250,000		

U.S. Watch Co. of Waltham, The President, 18 size, 17 jewels, hunting, serial number 150,000.

U.S. Watch Co. of Waltham, The President, 18 size, 17 jewels, open face, 2-tone, adj., note regulator, serial number 150,350.

18 SIZE

Grade or Name — Description	Avg	Ex-Fn	Mint
Express Train, 15J, OF, ADJ	$275	$325	$400
Express Train, 15J, HC, ADJ	375	425	500
The President, 17J, HC ★ ★	500	550	625
The President, 21J, GJS, Adj.6P, DR, 14K ★ ★	900	950	1,025
The President, 17J, GJS, Adj.6P, DR, NI, DMK, OF ★	500	550	625
U. S. Watch Co., 15J, OF, 2-tone, stem attached ★	250	300	375
Washington Square, 15J, HC	150	200	275
39 (HC) & 79 (OF), 17J, GJS, ADJ, NI, DMK, Adj.5P, BRG	100	125	175
40 (HC) & 80 (OF), 17J, GJS	100	125	175
48 (HC) & 88 (OF), 7J, gilded, FULL	100	125	175
48 (HC) & 88 (OF), 7J, gilded, FULL, Silveroid	50	75	125
52 (HC)	125	150	200
92 (OF), 17J, Silveroid	50	75	125

U.S. WATCH CO. OF WALTHAM, 18 SIZE (continued)

Grade or Name—Description	Avg	Ex-Fn	Mint
52 (HC) & 92 (OF), 17J	$100	$125	$175
53 (HC) & 93 (OF), 15J, NI, FULL, DMK	100	125	175
54 (HC) & 94 (OF), 15J	100	125	175
56 (HC) & 96 (OF), 11J	100	125	175
57 (HC) & 97 (OF), 15J	100	125	175
58 (HC) & 98 (OF), 11J, NI, FULL, DMK	100	125	175

(Prices are with gold filled cases except where noted; add $25 to value of above watches with hunting case.)

NOTE: Some grades are not included. Their values can be determined by comparing with similar models or grades listed.

U.S. Watch Co. of Waltham, 16 size, 7 jewels, guilded, note raised dome on center of movement, engraved on movement "Chas. V. Woerd's Patents," serial number 3,564.

U.S. Watch Co. of Waltham, 16 size, 7 jewels, "A New Watch Company At Waltham, Est'd 1885" on movement, serial number 770,771.

16 SIZE

Grade or Name — Description	Avg	Ex-Fn	Mint
Dome Plate Model, 7J, gilded	$125	$150	$200
Early KW-KS, 7J, S– below 100	500	700	1,000
103, 17J, NI, ¾, ADJ	50	75	125
104, 17J, NI, ¾	50	75	125
104, 17J, NI, ¾, Silveroid	40	65	115
105, 15J, NI, ¾, HC	125	150	200
105, 15J, NI, ¾, OF	50	75	125
105, 15J, NI, ¾, Silveroid	40	65	115
106, 15J, gilded, ¾, Silveroid	40	65	115
106, 15J, gilded, ¾	50	75	125
108, 11J, gilded, ¾	50	75	125
109, 7J, NI, ¾	50	75	125
110, 7J, ¾, HC	50	75	125
110, 7J, ¾, OF	50	75	125

Note: Add $20 to value of above watches in hunting case.

U.S. Watch Co., 16 size, 15 jewels, three-quarter plate.

6 SIZE

Grade or Name — Description	Avg	Ex-Fn	Mint
60, 17J, GJS, NI, ¾, Adj.3P	$40	$60	$85
60, 17J, GJS, NI, ¾, Adj.3P, HC, 14K	225	275	350
62, 15J, NI, ¾	40	60	85
63, 15J, gilded	40	60	85
64, 11J, NI	40	60	85
65, 11J, gilded	40	60	85
66, 7J, gilded	40	60	85
66, 7-11J, NI, ¾	40	60	85
68, 16J, GJS, NI, ¾	50	75	125
69, 7J, NI, HC	75	100	150
69, 7J, NI, OF	40	60	85

Note: Add $10 to value of above watches in hunting case.

Grade 64, 6 size, 11 jewels

U.S. Watch Co. of Waltham, 0 size, 7 jewels, serial number 808,231.

0 SIZE

Grade or Name — Description	Avg	Ex-Fn	Mint
Betsy Ross, HC	$125	$150	$200
U. S. Watch Co., 15J, HC	100	125	175
U. S. Watch Co., 7-11J, HC	100	125	175

THE WASHINGTON WATCH CO.
Washington, D. C.
1872 - 1874

J. P. Hopkins, though better known as the inventor of the Auburndale Rotary Watch, was also connected with the Washington Watch Co. which made about fifty watches. They were 18S, key wind, ¾ plate and had duplex escapements. Before Hopkins came to Washington Watch Co. he had handmade about six fine watches. Most of the materials used to produce the watch movements were purchased from the Illinois Watch Co. The company had a total production of 45 movements with duplex escapements.

Grade or Name — Description		Avg	Ex-Fn	Mint
18S, 15J, ¾, KW, KS	★ ★ ★	$2,500	$3,000	$3,700

Example of a **Waterbury Long Wind** movement and dial. Note six spokes on dial.

WATERBURY WATCH CO.
Waterbury, Connecticut
1880 - 1898

The Waterbury Watch Co. was formed in 1880, and D. A. Buck made its first watch. The watches were simple and had only fifty parts. The mainspring was about nine feet long and coiled around the movement. It had a two-wheel train rather than the standard four-wheel train. The Waterbury long wind movement revolved once every hour and had a duplex escapement. The dial was made of paper, and the watch was priced at $3.50 to $4. Some of these watches were used as giveaways.

CHRONOLOGY OF THE DEVELOPMENT OF THE WATERBURY WATCH CO.:
Waterbury Watch Co., Waterbury, Conn. — 1880-1898
New England Watch Co. — 1898-1912
Purchased Ingersoll — 1914
Became U. S. Time Corp. (maker of Timex) — 1944

Example of a basic **Waterbury Watch Co.** movement, Series C.

Series L, Waterbury W. Co. Duplex Escapement, about 18 size.

18 TO 0 SIZES

Grade or Name — Description	Avg	Ex-Fn	Mint
35S, 1890-1891, back wind	$100	$150	$200
Long wind, skeletonized, 3 spokes.................... ★	350	400	550
Long wind, skeletonized, 4 spokes................. ★ ★	600	750	1,000
Long wind, skeletonized, 6 spokes.................... ★	350	400	550
Series A, long wind, skeletonized.................... ★	350	400	550
Series B, long wind.................................	200	225	300
Series C, long wind.................................	200	225	300
Series D, long wind.................................	225	250	350
Series E, long wind (discontinued 1890)	250	275	350

Series I, The Trump, about 18 size, no jewels, pin lever escapement.

Series T, Oxford Duplex Escapement, about 18 size, no jewels.

Grade or Name—Description	Avg	Ex-Fn	Mint
Series G, ¾ lever escapement . . . . ★	$200	$225	$300
Series H, Columbian Duplex. . . . . ★ ★	250	275	350
Series I, Trump, ¾	85	95	110
Series J, Americus Duplex	85	95	110
Series K, Charles Benedict Duplex	100	125	150
Series L, Waterbury W. Co. Duplex	85	100	125
Series N, Addison Duplex	60	80	95
Series P, Rugby Duplex	80	90	120
Series R, Tuxedo Duplex	70	80	100
Series S, Elfin	65	75	85
Series T, Oxford Duplex	65	75	85
Series W, Addison.	65	75	85
Series Z	65	85	95
Oxford.	55	80	95
The Trump	50	75	90
Waterbury W. Co., 7J, ¾, low Serial No.	300	375	500

NOTE: Dollar watches must be in running condition to bring these prices.

E. N. WELCH MFG. CO.
Bristol, Connecticut
1834 - 1897

Elisha Welch founded this company about 1834. His company failed in 1897, and the Sessions Clock Co. took over the business in 1903. E. N. Welch Mfg. Co. produced the large watch which was displayed at the Chicago Exposition in 1893. This watch depicted the landing of Columbus on the back of the case.

E.N. WELCH MFG. CO. (continued)

E.N. Welch Mfg. Co., 36 size, back wind & set, made for the Chicago Exposition in 1893. Die debossed back depicting the landing of Columbus in America, Oct, 12th, 1492.

Grade or Name — Description	Avg	Ex-Fn	Mint
36S, Columbus exhibition watch	$200	$225	$300

WESTCLOX

United Clock Co.
Westclox & Western Clock Co.
General Time Corp.
Athens, Georgia
1899 - Present

The first Westclox pocket watch was made about 1899; however, the Westclox name did not appear on their watches until 1906. In 1903 they were making 100 watches a day, and in 1920 production was at 15,000 per day. This company is still in business today in Athens, Georgia.

Grade or Name — Description	Avg	Ex-Fn	Mint
M#1, SW, push to set, GRO...........................	$75	$100	$125
M#2, SW, back set, GRO	50	60	75
18S, Westclox M#4, OF, GRO	50	60	75
1910 Models to 1920, GRO...........................	35	45	60
Anniversary	35	45	60
Antique...	20	30	45
Boy Proof...	35	45	60
Bingo...	30	40	55
Bulls Eye (several models)	10	25	40
Country Gentleman...................................	40	50	60
Dax (many models)...................................	10	20	30

WESTCLOX (continued)

Boy Proof Model, about 16 size, designed to be tamper proof.

Example of a basic **Westclox** movement, stem wind, back set.

Grade or Name—Description	Avg	Ex-Fn	Mint
Elite	$25	$35	$40
Everbrite (several models)	15	20	30
Explorer	200	250	300
Farm Bureau	65	85	100
Glo Ben	65	85	100
Ideal	30	35	40
Lighted Dial	25	30	40
Mark IV	35	45	55
Maxim	30	40	50
Mickey Mouse (1960 to Present)	35	45	65
Military Style, 24 hour	65	75	95

Example of a basic **Westclox** movement, about 16 size, stem wind, lever escapement.

Explorer, back of case and dial, "Wings Over The Pole, The Explorer" on back of case.

WESTCLOX (continued)

Example of a basic Westclox movement, stem wind & set.

Zep, about 16 size with radiant numbers and hands, c. 1929.

Grade or Name—Description	Avg	Ex-Fn	Mint
Mustang	$40	$45	$60
NAWCC, ETP 1,000	40	45	50
Pocket Ben (many models)	20	35	60
Ruby	25	30	45
Scotty (several models)	10	15	20
Smile	25	30	40
Sun Mark	30	35	40
Team Mate (various major league teams)	25	35	40
Tele Time	25	35	45
Texan	35	45	65
Tiny Tim	150	200	275
Victor	80	100	130
Vote	25	35	45
Westclox	15	20	25
Zep	200	250	325

WESTERN WATCH CO.
Chicago, Illinois
1880

Albert Trotter purchased the unfinished watches from the California Watch Co. Mr. Trotter finished and sold those watches. Later he moved to Chicago and, with Paul Cornell and others, formed the Western Watch Company. Very few watches were completed by the Western Watch Co.

Grade or Name — Description		Avg	Ex-Fn	Mint
Western Watch Co., 18S, FULL .... ★ ★ ★		$2,500	$3,000	$4,000

Example of a **Western Watch Co.** movement, 18 size, 15 jewels, key wind & set.

WICHITA WATCH CO.
Wichita, Kansas
July, 1887 - 1888

This company completed construction of their factory in Wichita, Kansas in June 1888, and only a half dozen watches were produced during the brief period the company was in operation. The president was J. R. Snively. These watches are 18S, half plate, adjusted, 15 jewels.

Grade or Name — Description		Avg	Ex-Fn	Mint
18S, 15J, ½ plate, ADJ........................ ★ ★ ★		$2,500	$3,000	$4,000

NOTE: Watches listed in this book are priced at the retail level, as complete watches having an original 14k gold-filled case, an original white enamel single sunk dial, and with the entire original movement in good working order with no repairs needed, unless otherwise noted.

COMIC AND CHARACTER WATCHES

Note: To be mint condition, character watches must have unfaded dials, and boxes must have all inserts. *(PW = Pocket Watch; WW = Wrist Watch)*

Big Bad Wolf & 3 Pigs, ca. 1936.

Buck Rogers with lightning bolt hands, ca. 1935.

Style or Grade—Description	Avg	Ex-Fn	Mint	Mint + Box
Alice in Wonderland, WW, c. 1951, by U.S. Time .	$15	$25	$45	$350
Alice, Red Riding Hood, & Marjory Daw, WW, c. 1953, by Bradley	20	30	55	150
Alice in Wonderland, WW, c. 1958, by Timex	10	20	35	250
Babe Ruth, WW, c. 1948, by Exacta Time, box baseball pledge card	45	95	250	550
Bambi, WW, c. 1949, by U.S. Time	20	60	250	450
Batman, WW, c. 1970 by Gilbert (band in shape of bat)	45	65	85	150
Batman, WW, c. 1978, by Timex	10	20	35	55
Betty Boop, PW, c. 1934, by Ingraham (with die-debossed back)	350	500	750	1,000
Big Bad Wolf & 3 Pigs, PW, c. 1936, by Ingersoll .	300	350	500	800
Big Bad Wolf & 3 Pigs, WW, c. 1936, by Ingersoll.	350	400	550	850
Buck Rogers, PW, c. 1935, by Ingraham (lightning bolt hands)	250	300	500	750
Bugs Bunny, WW, c. 1951, by Ingersoll (carrot-shaped hands)	100	125	150	350
Bugs Bunny, WW, c. 1951, by Ingersoll (without carrot hands)	45	65	100	200
Buster Brown, PW, c. 1928, by Ingersoll (2 models)	125	175	250	300
Buzz Corey, WW, c. 1952, by U.S. Time	20	45	95	325
Captain Liberty, WW, c. 1950, by U.S. Time	15	40	80	200
Captain Marvel, PW, c. 1945, by New Haven	100	125	200	400

Buster Brown & his dog Tige, ca. 1925.

Coca Cola, by Ingersoll, ca. 1948.

Style or Grade—Description	Avg	Ex-Fn	Mint	Mint +Box
Captain Marvel, WW, c. 1948, by New Haven (small watch, plastic box)	$75	$150	$175	$350
Captain Marvel, WW, c. 1948, by New Haven (larger size watch)	100	125	200	450
Captain Midnight, PW, c. 1948, by Ingraham	250	300	350	400
Cinderella, WW, c. 1950, by U.S. Time (slipper box)	15	25	60	350
Cinderella, WW, c. 1955, by Timex (box with imitation cel)	15	25	60	200
Cinderella, WW, c. 1958, by Timex (box with plastic statue)	15	25	60	250
Cinderella, WW, c. 1958, by Timex (box with porcelain statue)	15	25	60	300

Dick Tracy, New Haven, ca. 1950.

Dizzy Dean, Ingersoll, ca. 1935.

Style or Grade—Description	Avg	Ex-Fn	Mint	Mint + Box
Coca Cola, PW, c. 1948, by Ingersoll	$125	$150	$200	$300
Daisy Duck, WW, c. 1947, by Ingersoll (tonneau style)	100	135	200	300
Daisy Duck, WW, c. 1955, by U.S. Time (fluted bezel, bithday series)	75	100	150	200
Dale Evans, WW, c. 1949, by Bradley (western style leather band)	50	60	75	250
Dale Evans, WW, c. 1949, by Bradley (metal band)	15	25	55	200
Dan Dare, PW, c. 1950, by Ingersoll Ltd. (made in England) (action arm)......................	150	200	285	400
Davy Crockett, WW, c. 1955, by U.S. Time (came with powder horn).........................	15	25	55	350
Davy Crockett, WW, c. 1956, by Bradley (watch barrel shaped dial).........................	75	100	150	400
Dennis the Menace, WW, c. 1970, by Bradley	20	35	55	75
Dick Tracy, PW, c. 1948, by Ingersoll	200	250	350	500
Dick Tracy, WW, c. 1950, by New Haven.........	75	100	175	400
Dick Tracy, WW, c. 1952, by New Haven (six shooter action arm)	150	200	275	450
Dizzy Dean, PW, c. 1935, by Ingersoll............	150	225	325	500
Dizzy Dean, WW, c. 1938, by Ingersoll	200	250	300	550
Donald Duck, PW, c. 1939, by Ingersoll (Mickey on back)	200	300	400	575
Donald Duck, WW, c. 1939, by Ingersoll (Mickey on second hand)	200	235	300	650
Donald Duck, WW, c. 1948, by U.S. Time (tonneau style, silver tone)	100	150	250	350
Donald Duck, WW, c. 1948, by U.S. Time (tonneau style, gold tone)...........................	150	200	300	450

Donald Duck, with Mickey on the back of the watch, made by Ingersoll, ca. 1940.

Style or Grade—Description	Avg	Ex-Fn	Mint	Mint + Box
Donald Duck, WW, c. 1948, by Ingersoll (fluted bezel, birthday series)	$150	$175	$250	$450
Donald Duck, WW, c. 1955, by U.S. Time, (plain bezel, pop-up in box)	25	40	75	250
Dopey, WW, c. 1948, by Ingersoll (fluted bezel, birthday series)	100	125	175	400
Flash Gordon, c. 1939, by Ingersoll	200	275	375	450
Gene Autry, WW, c. 1936, by Ingersoll (Gene and Champion on dial)	75	100	150	250
Gene Autry, WW, c. 1939, by Ingersoll	75	100	150	300
Gene Autry, WW, c. 1950, by New Haven, (six shooter watch)	150	175	225	450
Goofy, WW, c. 1972, by Helbros, 17J (watch runs backward)	350	400	450	500
Hopalong Cassidy, WW, by U.S. Time (metal watch, box with saddle)	15	35	65	450
Hopalong Cassidy, WW, by U.S. Time (plastic watch, box with saddle)	5	20	35	450
Hopalong Cassidy, WW, by U.S. Time (small watch, leather Western band, flat rectangular box)	25	45	75	300
Hopalong Cassidy, WW, by U.S. Time (regular size watch, black leather cowboy strap)	15	35	65	300
Hopalong Cassidy, PW, c. 1950, by U.S. Time (rawhide strap and fob)	150	200	275	400
Howdy Doody, WW, c. 1954, by Ingraham (with moving eyes)	100	125	175	400
Howdy Doody, WW, c. 1954, by Ingraham (with friends)	75	100	150	550

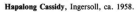

Hapalong Cassidy, Ingersoll, ca. 1958.   **Lone Ranger**, New Haven, ca. 1939.

COMIC AND CHARACTER WATCHES (continued)

Lone Ranger, New Haven, ca. 1939.   Mickey Mouse, fluted bezel, birthday series, ca. 1948.

Style or Grade—Description	Avg	Ex-Fn	Mint	Mint + Box
James Bond 007, WW, c. 1972, by Gilbert	$15	$20	$40	$75
Jeff Arnold, WW, c. 1952, by Ingersoll (English watch with moving gun)	150	200	275	335
Joe Carioca, WW, c. 1952, by U.S. Time (fluted bezel, birthday series)	100	125	200	400
Joe Palooka, WW, c. 1948, by New Haven	100	125	200	400
Li'l Abner, WW, c. 1948, by New Haven (waving flag)	150	175	200	400
Li'l Abner, WW, c. 1948, by New Haven (moving mule)	150	175	200	400
Little King, WW, c. 1968, by Timex	35	45	60	75
Lone Ranger, PW, c. 1939, by New Haven (with fob)	150	175	200	325
Lone Ranger, WW, c. 1938, by New Haven	125	150	175	400

Mickey Mouse, Ingersoll. **Left: Mickey** no. 1, ca. 1933. **Right: Mickey** no. 2, ca. 1933. Note tall stem on **Mickey** no. 1.

Mickey Mouse, Ingersoll. Model no. 3 is illustrated on the left. Model no. 4 is shown with lapel button.

Style or Grade—Description	Avg	Ex-Fn	Mint	Mint + Box
Mary Marvel, WW, c. 1948, by U.S. Time	$75	$85	$125	$300
Mary Marvel, WW, c. 1948, by U.S. Time (plastic box)	75	85	125	300
Mickey Mouse, PW, c. 1933, by Ingersoll, #1&2 (tall stem)	250	300	400	600
Mickey Mouse, PW, c. 1936, by Ingersoll, #3&4 (short stems).............................	200	225	300	400
Mickey Mouse, PW, c. 1936, by Ingersoll (Mickey decal on back)	250	300	400	700

Mickey Mouse, bicentennial model, Bradley. Note the seconds dial on illustration to the right.

Style or Grade—Description	Avg	Ex-Fn	Mint	Mint + Box
Mickey Mouse, PW, c. 1933, by Ingersoll Ltd. (English)	$200	$300	$450	$700
Mickey Mouse, PW, c. 1976, by Bradley (bicentennial model)	15	20	30	45
Mickey Mouse, PW, c. 1974, by Bradley (no second hand)	15	20	30	45
Mickey Mouse, PW, c. 1974, by Bradley ("Bradley" printed at 6)	15	20	30	45
Mickey Mouse, WW, c. 1933, by Ingersoll (metal band with Mickey)	50	100	200	350
Mickey Mouse, WW, c. 1936, by Ingersoll (one Mickey for second hand)	175	200	250	650
Mickey Mouse, WW, c. 1936, by Ingersoll (girl's watch, 1 Mickey for second hand)	175	200	250	650
Mickey Mouse, WW, c. 1948, by Ingersoll (fluted bezel, birthday series)	150	175	200	450
Mickey Mouse, WW, c. 1946, by U.S. Time (10k gold plated)	100	125	200	250
Mickey Mouse, WW, c. 1947, by U.S. Time (tonneau, plain, several styles)	50	75	150	350
Mickey Mouse, WW, c. 1947, by U.S. Time (same as above, gold tone)	50	75	150	250
Mickey Mouse, WW, c. 1950s, by U.S. Time (round style)	25	35	55	300
Mickey Mouse, WW, c. 1958, by U.S. Time (statue of Mickey in box)	15	25	45	250

Mickey Mouse, Bradley, ca. 1955.   **Mickey Mouse,** with wide bezel, Ingersoll, ca. 1948.

Style or Grade—Description	Avg	Ex-Fn	Mint	Mint + Box
Mickey Mouse, WW, c. 1965, by Timex (Mickey Mouse electric)	$100	$125	$155	$250
Mickey Mouse, WW, c. 1965, Timex (manual wind)	35	55	75	200
Mickey Mouse, WW, c. 1970s, by Bradley	10	15	35	80
Mickey Mouse, WW, c. 1980, by Bradley (colored min. chapter)	50	65	85	200
Mickey Mouse, WW, c. 1983, by Bradley (limited commemorative model)	100	125	150	200
Mickey Mouse, WW, c. 1985, by ETA (clear plastic bezel and band)	15	20	35	75
Minnie Mouse, WW, c. 1958, by U.S. Time (statue of Minnie in box)	25	35	50	250
Moon Mullins, PW, c. 1938, by Ingersoll	250	300	400	450
Orphan Annie, WW, c. 1940, by New Haven (large style)	100	125	155	400
Orphan Annie, WW, c. 1948, by New Haven smaller model)	100	125	155	350
Orphan Annie, WW, c. 1968, by Timex	35	45	65	95
Peter Pan, PW, c. 1948, by Ingraham	100	150	200	300
Pinocchio, WW, c. 1948, by Ingersoll (fluted bezel, birthday series)	125	160	200	325
Pinocchio, WW, c. 1948, by U.S. Time (Happy Birthday cake box)	125	150	200	450
Pluto, WW, c. 1948, by U.S. Time	75	125	200	300
Popeye, PW, c. 1935, by New Haven (with friends on dial)	200	250	350	475
Popeye, PW, c. 1940, by New Haven (plain dial)	200	235	300	400

Left: **Orphan Annie**, New Haven, ca. 1940. **Middle: Popeye** with friends, New Haven, ca. 1935. **Right: Popeye** with friends, New Haven, ca. 1936.

Roy Rogers, Ingraham, ca. 1960.   Skeezix, Ingraham, ca. 1936.

Style or Grade—Description	Avg	Ex-Fn	Mint	Mint + Box
Popeye, WW, c. 1936, by New Haven (tonneau style, with friends on dial)	$150	$175	$250	$450
Popeye, WW, c. 1952, by U.S. Time (round style)	100	125	165	300
Porky Pig, WW, c. 1948, by Ingraham (tonneau)	100	125	150	350
Porky Pig, WW, c. 1949, by U.S. Time (round)	100	125	150	350
Puss-N-Boots, WW, c. 1959, by Bradley	50	75	100	200
Robin, WW, c. 1978, by Timex	25	35	50	75
Robin Hood, WW, c. 1955, by Bradley (tonneau style)	75	100	150	300
Robin Hood, WW, c. 1958, by U.S. Time (round)	75	100	150	300
Rocky Jones Space Ranger, WW, c. 1955, by Ingraham	100	125	150	300
Roy Rogers, WW, c. 1954, by Ingraham (Roy and rearing Trigger)	50	75	100	250
Roy Rogers, WW, c. 1954, by Ingraham (Roy and Trigger)	50	75	100	250
Roy Rogers, WW, c. 1954, by Ingraham (expansion band)	50	75	100	250
Roy Rogers, WW, c. 1956, by Ingraham (round dial)	50	75	100	200
Skeezix, PW, c. 1936, by Ingraham	125	150	200	300
Smitty, WW, c. 1936, by New Haven	100	125	200	450
Smokey Stover, WW, c. 1968, by Timex	35	45	60	75
Snow White, WW, c. 1938, by Ingersoll (tonneau)	100	125	200	400
Snow White, WW, c. 1952, by U.S. Time (round)	25	35	50	350
Snow White, WW, c. 1956, by U.S. Time (statue in box)	25	35	50	250
Snow White, WW, c. 1962, by U.S. Time (plastic watch)	25	35	50	250
Superman, PW, c. 1956, by Bradley	150	200	250	450

Style or Grade—Description	Avg	Ex-Fn	Mint	Mint + Box
Superman, WW, c. 1938, by New Haven..........	$150	$200	$250	$450
Superman, WW, c. 1946, by Ingraham (lightning bolt hands)	150	175	200	400
Superman, WW, c. 1978, by Timex (large size)	35	50	75	100
Superman, WW, c. 1978, by Timex (small size)	35	50	75	100
Three Little Pigs, PW, c. 1936, by Ingersoll	350	400	500	850
Tom Corbett, WW, c. 1954, by Ingraham	75	100	150	450
Tom Mix, WW, c. 1936, by Ingersoll	75	125	175	250
Tom Mix, PW, c. 1936, by Ingersoll (with fob)	200	275	400	775
Woody Woodpecker, WW, c. 1952, by Ingraham ..	75	100	150	300
Yogi Bear, WW, c. 1964, by Bradley	15	20	35	65
Zorro, WW, c. 1956, by U.S. Time	25	35	50	250

Robin Hood, Swiss made, center seconds, ca. 1950.

Smitty, New Haven, ca. 1936.

EUROPEAN
POCKET WATCHES

EARLY ANTIQUE WATCHES

The early antique watches looked quite similar to small table clocks. These drum-shaped watches were about two inches in diameter and usually over one-half inch thick. The drum-shaped watch lost popularity in the late 1500s. The earliest portable timepieces did not carry the maker's name, but initials were common. The cases generally had a hinged lid which covered the dial. This lid was pierced with small holes to enable ready identification of the position of the hour hand. They also usually contained a bell. The dial often had the numbers "I" to "XII" engraved in Roman numerals and the numbers "13" to "24" in Arabic numbers with the "2" engraved in the form of a "Z." Even the earliest of timepieces incorporated striking. The oldest known watch with a date engraved on the case was made in 1548. A drum-shaped watch with the initials "C. W.," it was most likely produced by Casper Werner, a protege of Henlein.

Early pocket watches were designed to run from 12 to 16 hours. The pinions usually bore five leaves, the great wheel 55 teeth, the second wheel 45 teeth, the third wheel 40 teeth, and the escape wheel 15 teeth. With one less pinion and wheel the escape wheel ran reverse to a standard four-wheel watch. During the 1500s, 1600s, and much of the 1700s, it was stylish to decorate not only the case and balance cock but all parts including the clicks, barrel, studs, springs, pillars, hands, and stackfreed. The plates themselves were decorated with pierced and engraved metal scrolls, and in some instances the maker's name was engraved in a style to correspond with the general decoration of the movement. During these periods the most celebrated artists, designers, and engravers were employed. The early watches were decorated by famous artists such as Jean Vauquier 1670, Daniel Marot

1700, Gillis l'Egare 1650, Michel Labon 1630, Pierre Bourdon 1750, and D. Cochin 1750. Most of the artists were employed to design and execute pierced and repouse cases.

THE MID-1700s

In the mid-1700s relatively minor changes are noticed. Decoration became less distinctive and less artistic. The newer escapements resulted in better timekeeping, and a smaller balance cock was used. The table and foot became smaller. The foot grew more narrow, and as the century and the development of the watch advanced, the decoration on the balance cock became smaller and less elaborate. About 1720 the foot was becoming solid and flat. No longer was it hand pierced; however, some of the pierced ones were produced until about 1770. Thousands of these beautiful hand pierced watch cocks have been made into necklaces and brooches or framed. Sadly, many of the old movements were destroyed in a mad haste to cater to the buyers' fancy.

THE 1800s

As the 1800s approached the balance cocks became less artistic as the decoration on movements gradually diminished. Breguet and Berthoud spent very little time on the beauty or artistic design on their balance cocks or pillars. But the cases were often magnificient in design and beauty, made with enamels in many colors and laden with precious stones. During this period the movements were plain and possessed very little artistic character.

Exposed illustration of an early watch movement, c. 1800-1850. Note that movement is key wind and set from the dial side. The illustrated example is a chain driven fusee with a verge escapement: **a**-Main spring barrel and chain. **b**-Fusee. **c**-Verge escapement. **d**-Balance wheel. **e**-Dial. **f**-Hour hand. **g**-Minute hand. **h**-Winding arbor. **i**-Setting arbor.

As early as 1820 three-quarter and one-half plate designs were being used with the balance cock lowered to the same level as the other wheels. The result was a slimmer watch.

CLUES TO DATING YOUR WATCH

To establish the age of a watch there are many points to be considered. The dial, hands, pillars, balance cock and pendant, for example, contain important clues in determining the age of your watch. However, no one part alone should be considered sufficient evidence to draw a definite conclusion as to age. The watch as a whole must be considered. For example, an English-made silver-cased watch will have a hallmark inside the case. It is quite simple to refer to the London Hallmark Table for hallmarks after 1697. But this hallmark will reveal the age of the case only. This does not fix the age of the movement. Many movements are housed in cases made years before or after the movement was produced. An informed collector will note that a watch with an enamel dial, for instance, could not have been made before 1635. A pair of cases indicates it could not have been made prior to 1640. The minute hand was introduced in 1687. The presence of jewels would indicate it was made after 1700. A dust cap first appeared in 1774. Keyless winding came into being after 1820 but did not gain widespread popularity until after 1860. All of these clues and more must be considered before accurately assessing the age of a watch.

Example of an early pocket watch with a stackfreed design to equalize power much as a fusee does. Note dumbbell shaped foliot which served as a balance for verge escapement, and the tear shaped cam which is part of the stackfreed.

PILLARS

Pillars are of interest and should be considered as one of the elements in determining age. Through the years small watches used round pillars, and the larger watches generally used a square type engraved pillar.

(Illus. 1) This pillar is one of the earliest types and used in the 1800s as well. This particular pillar came from a watch which dates about 1550. It is known that this type pillar was used in 1675 by Gaspard Girod of France and also in 1835 by James Taylor of England.

(Illus. 2) This style pillar is called the tulip pattern. Some watchmakers preferred to omit the vertical divisions. This style was popular between 1660 and 1750 but may be found on later watches. It was common practice to use ornamentation on the tulip pillar.

(Illus. 3) The ornament shown was used by Daniel Quare of London from 1665 to 1725 and by the celebrated Tompion, as well as many others.

(Illus. 4) This type pillar is referred to as the Egyptian and dates from 1630 to the 1800s. The squared Egyptian pattern was introduced about 1630 and some may be found with a wider division with a head or bust inserted. This style was used by D. Bouquet of London about 1640 and by many other watchmakers.

Illus. 1   Illus. 2   Illus. 3   Illus. 4

(Illus. 5) This pillar was used by Thomas Earnshaw of London about 1780. The plain style was prominent for close to two hundred years—1650 to 1825.

Illus. 5   Illus. 6   Illus. 7   Illus. 8

(Illus. 6) This style was popular and was used by many craftsmen. Nathaniel Barrow of London put this in his watches about 1680.

(Illus. 7) This pillar may be seen in watches made by Pierre Combet of Lyons, France, about 1720. It was also used by many others.

(Illus. 8) This style pillar and the ornament were used by John Ellicott of England and other watchmakers from 1730 to 1770.

These illustrations represent just a few of the basic pillars that were used. Each watchmaker would design and change details to create his own individual identity. This sometimes makes it more difficult to readily determine the age of watches.

BALANCE COCKS OR BRIDGES

The first balance cocks or bridges used to support the balance staff were a plain "S" shape. The cocks used on the old three-wheel watches were very elaborate; hand-pierced and engraved. At first no screws were used to hold the cock in place. It is noteworthy that on the three-wheel watch the regulator was a ratchet and click and was used on these earlier movements to adjust the mainspring. About 1635 the balance cock was screwed to the plate and pinned on its underside, which helped steady the balance. The first cock illustrated is a beautifully decorated example made by Josias Jeubi of Paris about 1580. Note that it is pinned to a stud which passes through a square cut in the foot of the cock. Next is a balance cock made by Bouquet of London about 1640. The third balance cock is one made by Jean Rousseau and dates around 1650. The fourth one dates around 1655.

The next two bridges are supported on both sides of the balance cock by means of screws or pins. They are strikingly different and usually cover much of the plate of the movement. This style of balance cock was used around 1675 and was still seen as late as 1765.

The beautiful balance cock below at left, with the ornate foot, dates about 1660. The next illustrated balance cock with the heavy ornamentation was used from about 1700 to 1720 or longer. By 1720 a face was added to the design. The face shows up where the table terminates on most balance cocks.

Cylinder escapement

Invented in 1695

Virgule Escapement

Rack and lever escapement

Invented in 1722

Duplex escapement

Invented in 1750

EARLY EUROPEAN WATCHMAKERS

Note abbreviations used:
enamel = enamel case painter or artist
pat. = patent or inventor
ca. = circa or about
since = founded to present

Achard, J. Francois (Geneva, ca. 1750)
Addison, J. (London, 1760-1780)
Adamson, Gustave (Paris, 1775-1790)
Alfred, W. Humphreys (London, ca. 1905)
Alibut (Paris, ca. 1750s)
Allier, Bachelard & Teron Co. (French, ca. 1830)
Amabric, Abraham (Geneva, ca. 1750-1800)
Amabric, Freres (Geneva, ca. 1760-1795)
Amon (Paris, 1913)
Andre, Jean (enamel) (Geneva, 1660-1705)
Anthony, Willams (London, 1785-1840)
Antram, J. (London, ca. 1700-1730)
Appleby, Edward (London, ca. 1675)
Appleby, Joshua (London, ca. 1720-1745)
Ardin, Coppet (ca. 1710)
Arland, Benjamin (London, c. 1680)

Arlaud, Louis (Geneva, ca. 1750)
Arnold & Frodsham, Charles (London, 1845)
Arnold, Henery (London, ca. 1770-1780)
Arnold, John (London, ca. 1760-1790)
Arnold, John Roger (London, ca. 1800-1830)
Arnold, Nicolas (ca. 1850)
Arnold & Lewis, Lote Simmons (Manchester, ca. 1860)
Arnold & Son (London, ca. 1787-1799)
Assman, Julius (Glasshutte, 1850-1885)
Auber, Daniel (London, ca. 1750)
Aubert, D. F. (Geneva, ca. 1825)
Aubert, Ferdinand (1810-1835)
Aubert & Co. (Geneva, ca. 1850)
Aubry, Irenee (Geneva, 1885-1910)
Audebert (Paris, 1810-1820)

Audemars, Freres (Swiss, 1810 until company splits in 1885)
Audemars, Louis-Benjamin (Swiss, 1811-1867)
Aureole (Swiss, 1921)
Auricoste, Jules (Paris, ca. 1910)
Bachhofen, Felix (Swiss, 1675-1690)
Badollet, Jean-Jacques (Geneva, 1779-1891)
Baillon, Jean-Hilaire (Paris, ca. 1727)
Baird, Wm. (London, 1815-1825)
Balsiger & Fils (ca. 1825)
Barberet, J. (Paris, ca. 1600)
Barbezat, Bole (Swiss, 1870)
Baronneau, Jean-Louis (France, 1675-1700)
Barraud & Lunds (1812-1840)
Barraud, Paul-Philip (London, 1752-1820)
Barrow, Edward (London, ca. 1650-1710)
Barrow, Nathaniel (London, 1653-1689)
Barry, M. (French, ca. 1620)
Bartholony, Abraham (Paris, 1750-1752)
Barton, James (London, 1760-1780)
Barwise (London, 1800)
Bassereau, Jean-Hilaire (Paris, ca. 1800-1810)
Bautte, Jean-Francois (Geneva, 1800-1835)
Bautte & Moynier (Geneva, ca. 1825)
Beaumarchais, Caron (Paris, 1750-1795)
Beauvais, Simon (London, ca. 1690)
Beckman, Daniel (London, 1670-1685)
Beckner, Abraham (London, ca. 1640)
Beliard, Dominique (Paris, ca. 1750)
Bell, Benj. (London, 1650-1668)
Bennett, John (London, 1850-1895)
Benson, J. W. (London, 1825-1890)
Benson, J. W. (London, 1850-1900)
Bergstein, L. (London, ca. 1840)
Bernard, Nicholas (Paris, 1650-1690)
Bernoulli, Daniel (Paris, 1720-1780)
Berrollas, J. A. (Denmark, 1800-1830)
Berthound, Augusta-Louis (Paris, ca. 1875)
Berthound, Ferdinand (Paris, 1750-1805)
Beihler & Hartmann (Geneva, ca. 1875)
Blanc, Henri (Geneva, ends 1964)
Blanc, Jules (Geneva, 1929-1940)
Blanc & Fils (Geneva, 1770-1790)
Bock, Johann (German, 1700-1750)
Bockel (London, ca. 1650)
Bolslandon, Metz (ca. 1780)
Bolviller, Moise (Paris, 1840-1870)
Bommelt, Leonhart (Nuremburg, Ger., ca. 1690)
Bonney (London, ca. 1790)
Bonniksen, Bahne (England, 1890-1930)
Booth, Edward (name change to Barlow)
Bordier, Denis (France, ca. 1575)
Bordier, Freres (Geneva, 1787-1810)
Bordier, Jacques (enamel) (ca. 1670)
Bornand, A. (Geneva, 1895-1915)
Boubon (Paris, 1810-1820)
Bouquet, David (London, ca. 1630-1650)
Bovet, Edouard (Swiss, 1820-1918)
Bovier, G. (enamel painter) (Paris, c. 1750)
Brandt, Iacob (Swiss, ca. 1700)
Brandt, Robert & Co. (Geneva, ca. 1820)
Breitling, "Leon" (Swiss, since 1884)
Brockbank (London, 1776-present)
Brocke (London, ca. 1640)
Brodon, Nicolas (Paris, 1674-1682)

Bronikoff, a Wjatka (Russia, 1850 "watches of wood")
Bruguier, Charles A. (Geneva, 1800-1860)
Bull, Rainulph (one of the first British) (1590-1617)
Burgis, Eduardus (London, 1680-1710)
Burgis, G. (London, 1720-1740)
Burnet, Thomas (London, ca. 1800)
Busch, Abraham (Hamburg, Ger., ca. 1680)
Buz, Johannes (Augsburg, Bavaria, ca. 1625)
Cabrier, Charles (London, ca. 1690-1720)
Capt, Henry Daniel (Geneva, 1802-1880)
Caron, Augustus (Paris, ca. 1750-1760)
Caron, Francois-Modeste (Paris, 1770-1788)
Caron, Pierre (Paris, ca. 1700)
Caron, Pierre Augustin (Paris, 1750-1795) (pat. virgule escapement)
Carpenter, William (London, 1750-1800)
Carte, John (England, 1680-1700)
Champod, P. Amedee (enamel) (Geneva, 1850-1910)
Chapponier, Jean (Geneva, 1780-1800)
Charman (London, 1780-1800)
Charrot (Paris, 1775-1810)
Chartiere (enamel) (France, ca. 1635)
Chaunes (Paris, ca. 1580-1600)
Chavanne & Pompejo (Vienna, 1785-1800)
Cheneviere, Louis (Geneva, 1710-1740)
Cheneviere, Urbain (Geneva, 1730-1760)
Cheriot or Cherioz, Daniel (ca. 1750-1790)
Cheuillard (Blois, France, ca. 1600)
Chevalier & Co. (Geneva, 1795-1810)
Cisin, Charles (Swiss, 1580-1610)
Clark, Geo. (London, 1750-1785)
Clerc (Swiss, ca. 1875)
Clouzier, Jacques (Paris, 1690-1750)
Cochin, D. (Paris, ca. 1800)
Cocque, Geo. (ca. 1610)
Cogniat (Paris, ca. 1675)
Coladon, Louis (Geneva, 1780-1850)
Cole, James Ferguson (London, 1820-1875)
Cole, Thomas (London, 1820-1864)
Collins, Clement (London, ca. 1705)
Collins, John (London, ca. 1720)
Collins, R. (London, ca. 1815)
Colondre & Schnee (ca. 1875)
Combet, Pierre (Lyons, France, ca. 1610-1625)
Cotton, John (London, ca. 1695-1715)
Coulin, Jaques & Bry, Amy (Paris & Geneva, 1780-1790)
Court, Jean-Pierre (ca. 1790-1810)
Courvosier, Freres (Swiss, 1810-1852)
Courvoisier & Houriet (Geneva, ca. 1790)
Cox, James (London, 1760-1785)
Csacher, C. (Prague, Aus., ca. 1725)
Cumming, Alexander (London, 1750-1800)
Cummins, T. (London, 1820)
Cuper, Barthelemy (French, 1615-1635)
Curtis, John (London, ca. 1720)
Cusin, Charles (Geneva, ca. 1587)
Darling, William (British, ca. 1825)
De Baghyn, Adriaan (Amsterdam, ca. 1750)
Debaufre, Peter (French, 1690-1720) (Debaufre escapement)
Debaufre, Pierre (Paris, London, Geneva, 1675-1722)
De Bry, Theodore (German, 1585-1620)

De Charmes, Simon (London, France, 1690-1730)
De Choudens (Swiss & French, 1760-1790)
Decombaz, Gedeon (Geneva, 1780-1820)
Degeilh & Co. (ca. 1880-1900)
De Heca, Michel (Paris, ca. 1685)
De L Garde, Abraham (Paris, "Blois," ca. 1590)
Delynne, F. L. (Paris, ca. 1775)
Dent, Edward John (London, 1815-1850)
Derham, William (English, ca. 1677-1730)
Deroch, F. (Swiss, 1730-1770)
Des Arts & Co. (Geneva, 1790-1810)
Desquivillons & DeChoudens (Paris, ca. 1785)
Destouches, Jean-Francois-Albert (Holland, ca. 1760)
Devis, John (London, 1770-1785)
Dimier & Co. (Geneva, 1820-1925)
Dinglinger (enamel) (Dresden, Ger., ca. 1675)
Ditisheim & Co. "Maurice" (Swiss, 1894)
Ditisheim, Paul (Swiss, 1892)
Dobson, A. (London, 1660-1680)
Droz, Daniel (Chaux-de-Fonds, Sw., ca. 1760)
Droz, Henri (Chaux-de-Fonds, Sw., ca. 1775)
Droz, Pierre Jacquet (Chaux-de-Fonds, Sw., 1750-1775)
Droz, Pierre (Swiss, 1740-1770)
Droz & Co. (Swiss, ca. 1825)
Dubie (enamel) (Paris, ca. 1635)
Dubois & Fils (Paris, ca. 1810)
Duchene & Co. "Louis" (Geneva, 1790-1820)
Ducommun, Charles (Geneva, ca. 1750)
Duduict, Jacques (Blois, France, ca. 1600)
Dufalga, Philippe (Geneva, 1730-1790)
Dufalga, P. F. (Geneva, ca. 1750)
Dufour, Foll & Co. (Geneva, 1800-1830)
Dufour, J. E. & Co. (ca. 1890)
Dufour & Ceret (Ferney, Fr., ca. 1770-1785)
Dufour & Zentler (ca. 1870)
Duhamel, Pierre (Paris, ca. 1680)
Dupin, Paul (London, 1730-1765)
Dupont (Geneva, ca. 1810-1830)
Dupont, Jean (enamel) (Geneva, 1800-1860)
Duru (Paris, ca. 1650)
Dutertre, Baptiste (ca. 1730) (pat. duplex escapement)
Dutton, William (London, 1760-1840)
Earnshaw, Thomas (London, 1760-1842)
East, Edward (London, 1630-1670)
Edmonds, James (London to U.S.A., 1720-1766)
Edward, George & Son (London, ca. 1875)
Ekegren, Henri-Robert (Geneva, 1860)
Ellicott, John (London, 1728-1810)
Emery, Josiah (Geneva, 1750-1800)
Esquivillon & De Choudens (Paris, 1710-1780)
Ester, Jean Henry (Geneva, 1610-1665)
Etherlington, George (London, 1680-1730)
Etienne Guyot & Co. (Geneva, ca. 1880)
Facio De Duillier, Nicholas (British, 1665-1710)
Fallery, Jacques (Geneva, ca. 1760)
Farmer, G. W. (wooden watches) (Germany, ca. 1650-1675)
Fatio, Alfred (Geneva, 1920-1940)
Fatton, Frederick Louis (London, ca. 1822)
Favre Marius & Fils (Geneva, 1893)
Fenie, M. (ca. 1635)
Ferrero, J. (ca. 1854-1900)
Fiacre, Clement (Paris, ca. 1700)

Fitter, Joseph (London, ca. 1660)
Fontac (London, ca. 1775)
Forfaict, Nicolas (Paris, 1573-1619)
Fowles, Allen (Kilmarnock, Scot., ca. 1770)
French (London, 1810-1840)
Fureur (Swiss, 1910)
Gallopin "Henri Capt" (Geneva, 1875)
Gamod, G. (Paris, ca. 1640)
Garnier, Paul (Paris, 1825) (pat. Garnier escapement)
Garrault, Jacobus (Geneva, ca. 1650)
Garty & Constable (London, ca. 1750)
Gaudron, Antoine (Paris, 1675-1707)
Gaudron, Pierre (Paris, 1695-1740)
Geissheim, Smod (Augsburg, Ger., ca. 1625)
Gent, James & Son (London, 1875-1910)
Gerbeau, V. (Paris, 1900-1930)
Gerrard (British, 1790-1820)
Gibs, William (Rotterdam, ca. 1720)
Gibson & Co., Ltd. (Ireland, ca. 1875-1920)
Gidon (Paris, ca. 1700)
Gillespy, Charles (Ireland, 1774-1171)
Girard, Perregaux (Swiss, 1856)
Girard, Theodore (Paris, 1623-1670)
Girardier, Charles (Geneva, 1780-1815)
Girod, B. (Paris, ca. 1810)
Girod, Gaspard (Paris, ca. 1670-1690)
Godod, E. (Paris, ca. 1790)
Godon, F. L. (Paris, ca. 1787)
Golay, A. Leresche & Fils (Geneva, 1844-1857)
Golay, H. (Swiss, 1969-1911)
Golay, Stahl & Fils (1878-1914)
Gollons (Paris, ca. 1663)
Gounouilhou, P. S. (Geneva, 1815-1840)
Gout, Ralph (London, 1790-1830)
Graham, George (London, 1715-1750)
Grandjean, Henri (Swiss, 1825-1880)
Grandjean, L. C. (Swiss, 1890-1920)
Grant, John & Son (English, 1780-1867)
Grantham, William (London, ca. 1860)
Grasset, Isaac (Geneva, ca. 1896)
Gray & Constable (London, ca. 1750)
Grazioza (Swiss, ca. 1901)
Grebauval, Hierosme (ca. 1575)
Gregory, Jermie (London, ca. 1652-1680)
Gregson, Jean P. (Paris, 1770-1790)
Griblin, Nicolas (French, 1650-1716)
Griessenback, Johann G. (Bavaria, ca. 1660)
Grignion "family" (London, 1690-1825)
Grignion, Daniel & Thomas (London, 1780-1790)
Grosclaude, Ch. & Co. (Swiss, ca. 1865)
Grosjean, Henry (French, ca. 1865)
Gruber, Hans (Nurnberg, Ger., ca. 1520-1560)
Gruber, Michel (Nurnberg, Ger., ca. 1605)
Gruet (Geneva, Sw., ca. 1664)
Gubelin, E. (Lucern, Switzerland, ca. 1832)
Guillaume, Ch. (pat. Invar, Elinvar)
Haas Nevevx & Co. (founder B. J. Haas) (Geneva, 1828-1925)
Hagen, Johan (German, ca. 1750)
Haley, Charles (London, 1781-1825)
Hallewey (London, 1695-1720)
Hamilton & Co. (London, 1865-1920)
Harper, Henry (London, ca. 1665-1700)
Harrison, John (England, 1710-1775) (pat. comp. balance)
Hasluck Brothers (London, ca. 1695)

Hautefeuille, Jean (Paris, 1670-1722)
Hautefeuille, John (Paris, 1660-1700)
Hawley, John (London, ca. 1850)
Hebert, Juliette (enamel) (Geneva, ca. 1890)
Helbros (Geneva, since 1918)
Hele or Henlein, Peter (Nurnberg, 1510-1540)
Heliger, J. (Zug, Sw., ca. 1575)
Henner, Johann (Wurtzburg, Ger., ca. 1730)
Henry, F. S. (Swiss, ca. 1850)
Hentschel, J. J. (French, ca. 1750)
Hess, L. (Zurich, Sw., ca. 1780)
Hessichti, Dionistus (ca. 1630)
Higgs & Evans (London, 1775-1825)
Hill, Ben. (London, 1640-1670)
Hoguet, Francois (Paris, ca. 1750)
Hooke, Robert (England, 1650-1700)
Hoseman, Stephen (London, ca. 1710-1740)
Houghton, James (England, ca. 1800-1820)
Houghton, Thomas (Chorley, England,
   ca. 1820-1840)
Houriet, Jacques Frederic (Paris 1810-1825)
Huaud, Freres (enamel) (Geneva, ca. 1685)
Huber, Peter (German, ca. 1875)
Hubert, David (London, 1714-1747)
Hubert, Oliver (London, ca. 1740)
Hubert, Etienne (French, 1650-1690)
Hues, Peter (Augsburg, Ger., ca. 1600)
Huguenin, David L. (Swiss, 1780-1835)
Humbert-Droz, David (Swiss, ca. 1790)
Huygens, Christian (Paris, 1657-1680)
Iaquier or Jacquier, Francois (Geneva,
   1690-1720)
Ilbery, William (London, 1800-1835)
Ingold, Pierre-Frederic (Swiss, Paris, London,
   1810-1870)
Invicta ("R. Picard") (Swiss, 1896)
Jaccard, E. H. & Co. (Swiss, ca. 1850)
Jacot, Charles-Edouard (Swiss, 1830-1860)
   (pat. Chinese duplex)
Jaeger, Edmond (Paris, 1875-1920)
Jaeger Le Coultre & Co. (Swiss, since 1833)
Jamison, Geo. (London, 1786-1810)
Janvier, Antide (Paris, 1771-1834)
Japy, Frederic & Sons "family" (French, Swiss,
   ca. 1776)
Jaquet, Pierre (Swiss, 1750-1790)
Jean Richard, Daniel (Swiss, 1685-1740)
Jean Richard, Edouard (Swiss, 1900-1930)
Jeannot, Paul (ca. 1890)
Jefferys & Gildert (London, 1790)
Jesop, Josias (London, 1780-1794)
Jeubi, Josias (Paris, ca. 1575)
Joly, Jacques (Paris, ca. 1625)
Jovat (London, ca. 1690)
Jones, Henry (London, ca. 1665-1690)
Jump, Joseph (English, ca. 1827-1850)
Junod, Freres (Geneva, ca. 1850)
Jurgensen, Urban & Jules (Copenhagen, Swiss,
   1745-1912)
Just & Son (London, 1790-1825)
Juvet, Edouard (Swiss, 1844-1880)
Juvet, Leo (Swiss, 1860-1890)
Keates, William (London, ca. 1780)
Keely, W. (London, ca. 1790)
Kendall, Larcum (London, ca. 1786)
Kendall, James (London, 1740-1780)
Kessels, H. J. (Holland, 1800-1845)
Kirkton, R. (London, ca. 1790)
Klein, Johann Heinr (Copenhagen, Den., ca.
   1710)
Klentschi, C. F. (Swiss, 1790-1840)
Koehn, Edward (Geneva, 1860-1908)
Kreizer, Conard (German, 1595-1658)
Kuhn, Jan Hendrik (Amsterdam, 1775-1800)
Kullberg, Victor (Copenhagen to London,
   1850-1890)
Lamy, Michel (Paris, 1767-1800)
Lang & Padoux (ca. 1860)
Larcay (Paris, ca. 1725)
Lardy, Francois (Geneva, ca. 1825)
Larpent, Isacc & Jurgensen (Copenhagen,
   1748-1811)
Laurier, Francois (Paris, 1654-1675)
Le Baufre (Paris, ca. 1650)
Lebet (Geneva, ca. 1850)
Lebet & Fils (Swiss, 1830-1892)
Le Coultre, Ami (Geneva, ca. 1887)
Le Coultre, Eugene (Geneva, ca. 1850)
Leekey, C. (London, ca. 1750)
Leeky, Gabriel (London, ca. 1775-1820)
Lepaute, Jean-Andre (Paris, 1750-1774)
Lepine, Jean-Antoine (Paris, 1744-1814)
Le Puisne, Huand (enamel) (Blois, Fr., ca. 1635)
Leroux, John (England, 1758-1805)
Le Roy & Co. (Paris, ca. 1853)
Le Roy, Charles (Paris, 1733-1770)
Le Roy, Julien (Paris, 1705-1750)
Le Roy, Pierre (French, 1710-1780)
   (improved duplex escapement)
Levy, Hermanos (Hong Kong, "Swiss,"
   1880-1890)
L'Hardy, Francois (Geneva, 1790-1825)
Lichtenauer (Wurzberg, Ger., ca. 1725)
Lindesay, G. (London, ca. 1740-1770)
Lindgren, Erik (England, 1735-1775) (pat. rack
   lever)
Litherland, Peter (English, 1780-1876)
Loehr, (Von) (Swiss, ca. 1880)
Long & Drew (enamel) (London, ca. 1790-1810)
Losada, Jose R. (London, 1835-1890)
Lowndes, Jonathan (London, ca. 1680-1700)
MacCabe, James (London, 1778-1830)
Maillardet & Co. (Swiss, ca. 1800)
Mairet, Sylvain (Swiss, 1825-1885) (London,
   1830-1840)
Malignon, A. (Geneva, ca. 1835)
Marchand, Abraham (Geneva, 1690-1725)
Margetts, George (London, 1780-1800)
Markwick Markham, "Perigal" "Recordon"
   (London, 1780-1825)
Marshall, John (London, ca. 1690)
Martin (Paris, ca. 1780)
Martin, Thomas (London, ca. 1870)
Martineau, Joseph (London, 1765-1790)
Martinot, "family" (Paris, 1570-1770)
Martinot, James (London, ca. 1780)
Mascarone, Gio Batt (London, ca. 1635)
Massey, Edward (England, 1800-1850)
Massey, Henry (London, 1692-1745)
E. Mathey-Tissot & Co. (Swiss, 1886-1896)
Matile, Henry (Swiss, ca. 1825)
Maurer, Johann (Fiessna, Ger., ca. 1640-1650)
May, George (English, 1750-1770)
Mayr, Johann Peter (Augsburg, Ger., ca. 1770)
McCabe, James (London, 1780-1710)
McDowall, Charles (London, ca. 1820-1860)
Meak, John (London, ca. 1825)

Mecke, Daniel (ca. 1760)
Melly, Freres (Geneva, Paris, 1791-1844)
Mercier, A. D. (Swiss, 1790-1820)
Mercier, Francois David (Paris, ca. 1700)
Meuron & Co. (Swiss, ca. 1784)
Meylan, C. H. "Meylan W. Co." (Swiss, ca. 1880)
Michel, Jean-Robert (Paris, ca. 1750)
Miller, Joseph (London, ca. 1728)
Milleret & Tissot (ca. 1835)
Miroir (London, ca. 1700-1725)
Mistral (Swiss, ca. 1902)
Mobilis (Swiss, ca. 1910)
Modernista (Swiss, ca. 1903)
Moillet, Jean-Jacques (Paris, 1776-1789)
Molina, Antonio (Madrid, Spain, ca. 1800)
Molinie (Swiss, ca. 1840)
Molyneux, Robert (London, ca. 1825-1850)
Montandon, Chs. Ad. (Swiss, 1800-1830)
Morand, Pierre (Paris, ca. 1790)
Moricand & Co. (Swiss, ca. 1780)
Moricand & Desgranges (Geneva, 1828-1835)
Moricand, Christ (Geneva, 1745-1790)
Morin, Pierre (English, French & Dutch style, ca. 1700)
Morliere (enamel) (Blois, Fr., ca. 1636-1650)
Moser, George Michael (London, ca. 1716-1730)
Motel, Jean Francois (French, 1800-1850)
Moulineux, Robert (London, 1800-1840)
Moulinier, Aine & Co. (Swiss, 1828-1851)
Moulinier, Freres & Co. (Swiss, ca. 1822)
Mudge, Thomas (London, 1740-1790)
Mulsund (enamel) (Paris, ca. 1700)
Munoz, Blas (Madrid, Spain, ca. 1806-1823)
Mussard, Jean (Geneva, 1699-1727)
Musy Padre & Figlo (Paris, 1710-1760)
Myrmecide (Paris, ca. 1525)
Nardin, Ulysse (Swiss, ca. 1846)
Nelson, W. (London, 1777-1818)
Nocturne (ca. 1920)
Noir, Jean-Baptiste (Paris, 1680-1710)
Norris, J. (Dutch, 1680-1700)
Nouwen, Michael (1st English, 1580-1600)
Noyean (ca. 1850)
Oldnburg, Johan (German, ca. 1648)
Oudin, Charles (Paris, 1807-1900)
Owen, John (English, ca. 1790)
Palmer, Samuel (London, ca. 1790-1810)
Panier, Iosue "Josue" (Paris, ca. 1790)
Papillon (ca. 1690)
Papillon, Francesco (Florence, ca. 1705)
Parr, Thomas (London, ca. 1735-1775)
Payne, H. & John (London, ca. 1735-1775)
Pellaton, Albert (Swiss, ca. 1873)
Pellaton, James (Swiss, 1903) (Tourbillon)
Pendleton, Richard (London, 1780-1805)
Pennington, Robert (English, 1780-1816)
Perigal, Francis (English, 1770-1790)
Pernetti, F. (Swiss, ca. 1850)
Perrelet, Abram (Swiss, 1780) (self wind)
Perret, Edouard (Swiss, 1850)
Perrin, Freres (Swiss, 1810)
Phillips, Edouard (Paris, ca. 1860)
Phleisot (Dijon, Fr., ca. 1540)
Piaget, George (Swiss, ca. 1881)
Picard, James (Geneva, ca. 1850)
Piguet & Capt (Geneva, 1802-1811)

Piguet & Meylan (Geneva, 1811-1828)
Piguet, Victorin-Emile (Geneva, 1870-1935)
Plairas, Solomon (Blois, Fr., ca. 1640)
Plumbe, David (ca. 1730)
Poitevin, B. (Paris, 1850-1935)
Poncet, J. F. (Dresden, 1750)
Poncet, Jean-Francois (Swiss, 1740-1800)
Potter, Harry (London, 1760-1800)
Pouzait, Jean-Moise (Geneva, 1780-1800)
Poy, Gottfrey (London, ca. 1725-1730)
Prest, Thomas (English, 1820-1855)
Prevost, Freres (ca. 1820)
Prior, Edward (London, 1825-1865)
Prior, George (London, 1800-1830)
Pyke, John (English, 1750-1780)
Quare, Daniel (London, 1700-1724)
Quarella, Antonio (ca. 1790)
Racine, Cesar (Swiss, ca. 1902)
Racine, Charles Frederic (Chaux-de-Fonds, Sw., ca. 1810-1832)
Raillard, Claude (Paris, 1662-1675)
Raiss (1890-1910) (enamel)
Rait, D. C. (German, ca. 1866)
Ramsay, David (Scotland, France, London, 1590-1654)
Ramuz, Humbert U. & Co. (Swiss, ca. 1882)
Ratel, Henri (Paris, 1850-1900)
Recordon, Louis (London, 1778-1824)
Redier, Antoine (Paris, 1835-1883)
Renierhes (London, ca. 1850)
Rey, Jn. Ante, & Fils (Paris, 1790-1810)
Reynaud, P. & Co. (1860)
Rich, John (Geneva, London, 1795-1825)
Richard, Daniel Jean (1685-1740)
Richter, Jean Louis (enamel) (Geneva, 1786-1840)
Rigaud, Pierre (Geneva, 1750-1800)
Rigot, Francois (Geneva, ca. 1825)
Robert & Courvoisier & Co. (Paris, 1781-1832)
Robin, Robert (Paris, 1765-1805)
Robinet, Charles (Paris, ca. 1640)
Robinson, Olivier & Fredmahn (Naples, 1727-1790)
Rogers, Isaac (London, 1770-1810)
Romilly, Sieur (Geneva, ca. 1750-1775)
Rooker, Richard (London, 1790-1810)
Rose, Joseph (London, 1752-1795)
Rosier, John (Geneva, ca. 1750)
Roskell, Robert (London, 1798-1830) (rack-lever)
Roskopf, G. (German to Swiss, 1835-1885)
Rosselet, Louis (Geneva, 1855-1900) (enamel)
Rousseau, Jean (Paris, 1580-1642)
Roux, Bordier & Co. (Geneva, ca. 1795)
Ruegger, Jacques (ca. 1800-1840)
Ruel, Samuel (Rotterdam, ca. 1750)
Rugendas, Nicholas (Augsburg, Ger., ca. 1700-1750)
Rundell & Bridge (London, ca. 1772-1825)
Sailler, Johann (Vienna, Aus., ca. 1575)
Sanchez, Cayetano (Madrid, Spain, c. 1790-1800)
Sandoz, Henri F. (Tavannes W. Co.) (ca. 1840)
Savage, George (London, 1808-1855) (Inv. pin lever)
Savage, William (London 1800-1850)
Savile, John (London, ca. 1656-1679)
Schatck, Johann Engel (Prague, ca. 1650)

Schultz, Michael (ca. 1600-1650)
Schuster, Caspar (Nunburg, ca. 1570)
Sermand, J. (Geneva, ca. 1640)
Sherman De Neilly (Belfort, ca. 1910)
Sherwood, J. (London, ca. 1750-1775)
Solson (London, 1750)
Soret (Geneva, ca. 1810)
Soret, Frederic II (1735-1806)
Soret, Isaac & Co. (1690-1760)
Spencer & Perkins (London, 1790-1808)
Stadlin, Francois (Swiss, 1680-1735)
Staples, James (1755-1795)
Stuffer, M. T. (Swiss, 1830-1855)
Stauffer "Stauffer Son & Co." (London, 1880)
Strasser & Rohde (Glashutte, 1875)
Sudek, J. (ca. 1850)
Sully, Henry (French, London, 1700-1725)
Swift, Thomas (London, ca. 1825-1865)
Tavan, Antoine (Geneva, 1775-1830)
Tavernier, Jean (Paris, 1744-1795)
Tempor Watch Co. (1930) (Masonic watch)
Terond, Allier & Bachelard (ca. 1805-1830)
Terrot & Fazy (ca. 1767-1775)
Terrot, Philippe (Geneva, ca. 1732)
Terroux (ca. 1776)
Theed & Pikett (ca. 1750)
Thierry, J. (London, ca. 1760)
Thierry, Niel (ca. 1810)
Thiout, Antoine (Paris, 1724-1760)
Thorne, Robert (London, 1850)
Thoroton, James (London, 1860)
Thuret, Jacques (Paris, ca. 1695)
Thompion, Thomas (English, 1671-1713)
Timing & Repeating W. Co. (Geneva, 1900)
Tonkin, Tho. (London, ca. 1760)
Toutaia, Henri (French, 1650) (enamel)
Toutin, Jean (enamel) (Blois, Fr., ca. 1630)
Treffler, Sebastain (ca. 1750)
Tregent, J. (English, 1765-1800)
Truitte, Louis & Mourier (Geneva, ca. 1780)
Tyrer, Thomas (London, ca. 1782)

Uhren Fabrik Union (Glashutte, 1893-1970)
Ullman, J. & Co. (Swiss, 1893)
Ulrich, Johann (London, 1820-1870)
Upjohn, W. J. (London, 1815-1824)
Vacheron, Abraham Girod (German, 1760-1843)
Valere (Paris, 1860)
Vallier, Jean (Lyons, Fr., ca. 1630)
Valove, James (London, ca. 1740)
Vanbroff, James (Germany, ca. 1600)
Van Ceule, J. (ca. 1799-1725)
Vandersteen (ca. 1725)
Vaucher, C. H. (Geneva, ca. 1835)
Vaucher, Daniel (Paris, 1767-1790)
Vaucher, Freres (Swiss, 1850)
Vauquer, Robert (French, ca. 1650) (enamel)
Veigneur, F. I. (ca. 1780)
Vernod, Henriette (Paris, ca. 1790)
Vigne, James (London, ca. 1770)
Vrard, L., & Co. (Pekin, 1860-1872)
Vulliamy, Justin (London, ca. 1830-1854)
Vully, Jaques (ca. 1890-1900)
Vuolf (Swiss, ca. 1600)
Waldron, John (London, 1760)
Wales, Giles & Co. (Swiss, ca. 1870)
Waltrin (Paris, ca. 1820)
Weston, D. & Willis (enamel) (London, ca. 1800-1810)
Whitthorne, James (Dublin, since 1725)
Willats, John (London, ca. 1860)
Williamson, Timothy (London, 1770-1790)
Wilter, John (London, ca. 1760)
Winckles, John (London, 1770-1790)
Winnerl, Joseph Thaddeus (Paris, 1829-1886)
Wiss, Freres & Menu (Swiss, ca. 1787-1810)
Wiss, G. (Geneva, ca. 1750)
Wright, Charles (London, 1760-1790)
Wright, Thomas (English, ca. 1770-1790)
Young, Richard (London, 1765-1785)
Zech, Jacob (Prague, Aus. 1525-1540)
Zolling, Ferdinand (Frankfurt, Ger. ca. 1750)

PROTECTING ANTIQUE WATCH MOVEMENTS

Many collectors of antique watches have purchased movements without cases. One cause is rooted in the Great Depression of the 1930s when watchmakers stripped the movements from pocket watches that had been traded for the increasingly popular wrist watch. The pocket watch cases were sold for their gold content. The movements, respected as fine pieces of workmanship, were stored for use as parts. This devastating occurrence was repeated, during the last five years, as the price of gold reached unprecedented levels, and many cases were once again scrapped for the gold content.

A display watch case is one excellent way to handle antique pocket watch movements. These cases hold the movements securely and protect the hands, dial, and movement from accidental damage from moisture or dropping. This case, which has see-through panels on both the front and back, permits the collector to show a prospective buyer the face and back of the movement without exposing it to dirt or taking a chance of damage.

An antique watch movement can also be protected during travel with an inexpensive clear plastic shipping case which is available in both 18 size and 16 size (the 16 size will also adapt to the 12 size movement).

HALLMARKS OF LONDON

Hallmarks were used on gold and silver cases imported from England. These marks, when interpreted, will give you the age of the case and location of the assay office.

The date-marks used 20 letters of the alphabet, A-U, never using the letters W, X, Y, or Z. The letters J & I or U & V, because of their similarity in shape, were never used together within the same 20-year period. A total of four marks can be found on English cases, which are:

The Maker's Mark The Standard Mark

The Assay Office Mark The Date Letter Mark

1822-up   1478 to 1821

The **Maker's Mark** was used to denote the manufacturer of the case.

The **Standard Mark** was used to denote a guarantee of the quality of the metal.

The **Assay Office Mark** (also known as the town mark) was used to denote the location of the assay office.

The **Date Letter Mark** was a letter of the alphabet used to denote the year in which the article was stamped. The stamp was used on gold and silver cases by the assay office.

SWISS HALLMARKS

18k .750   14k .585   Platinum

Sterling Silver   Silver .800

Year	Year	Year	Year	Year	Year	Year	Year	Year
1551	1589	1627	1666	1709	1752	1797	1841	1884
1552	1590	1628	1667	1710	1753	1798	1842	1885
1553	1591	1629	1668	1711	1754	1799	1843	1886
1554	1592	1630	1669	1712	1755	1800	1844	1887
1555	1593	1631	1670	1713	1756	1801	1845	1888
1556	1594	1632	1671	1714	1757	1802	1846	1889
1557	1595	1633	1672	1715	1758	1803	1847	1890
1558	1596	1634	1673	1716	1759	1804	1848	1891
1559	1597	1635	1674	1717	1760	1805	1849	1892
1560	1598	1636	1675	1718	1761	1806	1850	1893
1561	1599	1637	1676	1719	1762	1807	1851	1894
1562	1600	1638	1677	1720	1763	1808	1852	1895
1563	1601	1639	1678	1721	1764	1809	1853	1896
1564	1602	1640	1679	1722	1765	1810	1854	1897
1565	1603	1641	1680	1723	1766	1811	1855	1898
1566	1604	1642	1681	1724	1767	1812	1856	1899
1567	1605	1643	1682	1725	1768	1813	1857	1900
1568	1606	1644	1683	1726	1769	1814	1858	1901
1569	1607	1645	1684	1727	1770	1815	1859	1902
1570	1608	1646	1685	1728	1771	1816	1860	1903
1571	1609	1647	1686	1729	1772	1817	1861	1904
1572	1610	1648	1687	1730	1773	1818	1862	1905
1573	1611	1649	1688	1731	1774	1819	1863	1906
1574	1612	1650	1689	1732	1775	1820	1864	1907
1575	1613	1651	1690	1733	1776	1821	1865	1908
1576	1614	1652	1691	1734	1777	1822	1866	1909
1577	1615	1653	1692	1735	1778	1823	1867	1910
1578	1616	1654	1693	1736	1779	1824	1868	1911
1579	1617	1655	1694	1737	1780	1825	1869	1912
1580	1618	1656	1695	1738	1781	1826	1870	1913
1581	1619	1657	1696	1739	1782	1827	1871	1914
1582	1620	1658	1697	1739	1783	1828	1872	1915
1583	1621	1659	1698	1740	1784	1829	1873	1916
1584	1622	1660	1699	1741	1785	1830	1874	1917
1585	1623	1661	1700	1742	1786	1831	1875	1918
1586	1624	1662	1701	1743	1787	1832	1876	1919
1587	1625	1663	1702	1744	1788	1833	1877	1920
1588	1626	1664	1703	1745	1789	1834	1878	1921
		1665	1704	1746	1790	1835	1879	1922
			1705	1747	1791	1836	1880	1923
			1706	1748	1792	1837	1881	1924
			1707	1749	1793	1838	1882	1925
			1708	1750	1794	1839	1883	1926
				1751	1795	1840		
					1796			

EUROPEAN WATCHES
COLLECTED IN AMERICA

Auguste Agassiz of Saint Imier and Geneva started manufacturing quality watches in 1832. They later became interested in making a flat style watch which proved to be very popular. Some of these movements can be fitted inside a $20 gold piece.

The company was inherited by Ernest Francillion who built a factory called Longines. The Longines factory continued the Agassiz line until the Great Depression.

Agassiz, 43mm, 17 jewels, stem wind, 14 carat case, open face, serial number 39,863.

Julius Assmann began producing watches with the help of Adolf Lange in 1852. His watches are stylistically identical to those produced by Lange. Later on he adopted his own lever style. Assmann made highly decorative watches for the South American market which are highly regarded by German collectors.

Audemars, Piguet & Cie. was founded in 1875 by Jules Audemars and Edward Piguet, both successors to fine horological families. This company produced many fine high grade and complicated watches, predominantly in nickel and, with a few exceptions, fully jeweled. Their complicated watches are more sought after than the plain timepieces. They also produced some very handsome wrist watches.

The Swiss company of **Blancpain** was founded in 1735 by **Jean-Jacques Blancpain**. The company still produces mechanical watches of the greatest craftsmanship, and does not make a quartz-type watch.

Abraham-Louis Breguet, one of the worlds most celebrated watchmakers.

Abraham-Louis Breguet was born at Neuchatel in 1747 and died in 1823. He was perhaps the greatest horologist of all time in terms of design, elegance, and innovation. He is responsible for the development of the tourbillion, the perpetual calendar, the shock-proof parachute suspension, the isochronal overcoil, and many other improvements. It is difficult to include him in this section because of the complexity surrounding identification of his work which was frequently forged, and the fact that so many pieces produced by his shop were unique. Suffice it to say that the vast majority of watches one encounters bearing his name were either marketed only by his firm or are outright fakes made by others for the export market. Much study is required for proper identification.

As early as 1884 **Leon Breitling** made chronographs using his own name. The Swiss company made chronographs during World War I for different governments, gaining important acceptance in this field. One such model is the "Chronomat."

Henry Daniel Capt of Geneva was an associate of Isac Daniel Piguet for about 10 years from 1802 to 1812. Their firm produced quality watches and specialized in musicals, repeaters, and chronometers. By 1844 his son was director of the firm, and around 1880 the firm was sold to Gallopin.

Cartier was a famous artisan from Paris who first made powder flasks. By the mid-1840s the family became known as the finest goldsmiths of Paris. Around the turn of the century the Cartier firm was designing watches and in 1904 the first wrist watches were being made. In 1917 Cartier created a watch design that was to become known as the tank-style case. The tank-style case was made to look like tank caterpillars of the U. S. This style is still popular today.

The **Chopard** family made and crafted many fine watches as early as 1860 and by the 1920s were making watches for the Swiss Railway. The company was sold to a German company in 1960 and still produces very fine watches.

Edward John Dent worked with Vulliamy and Barraud separately before joining J. R. Arnold in 1830. After 10 successful years in that association, he established his own firm, **E. Dent & Co.**, which continued after his death in 1853. His name is associated with Big Ben, although his successor is responsible for the execution of that contract. Dent's chronometers and complicated watches are particularly desirable, whereas the later products of the company are less so.

Paul Ditisheim founded his company in 1892 at La Chaux de Fonds in Switzerland. He made extremely small watches, some as small as 6.75 millimeters. The company later became Vulcain et Volta, Ditisheim & Co.

Henry Robert Ekegren, a Swiss maker of quality watches, started in business around 1870. The firm specialized in flat watches, chronometers, and repeaters. Ekegren became associated with F. Koehn in 1891.

John Ellicott, an Englishman, made watches from 1706 to 1772. One of his most notable developments was the cylinder escapement. After Ellicott's death the company was named John Ellicott & Son.

J. Girard and A. Schild started a small company in the mid-1800s making movements only, and by 1906 the name was changed to **Eterna**. The company was well known for its precision pocket watches. By 1930 the company decided to make a small wrist watch, which they call the "baguette," and an eight-day alarm. Both proved to be very popular. A movement named the "Eterna-Matic" was being produced by 1948, and their first electronic watch was made in 1974, followed by the quartz "Kontiki" produced in 1976. This Swiss company still produces quality watches, both jeweled and electronic.

Charles Frodsham followed in the footsteps of his father William, whose father was close with Earnshaw. Charles became the most eminent of the family, producing very fine chronometers and some rare tourbillions and complicated watches. He died in 1871. The following code was used to denote the year in which the watch was made:

F R O D S H A M Z   Thus, FMHZ = 1860
1 2 3 4 5 6 7 8 0

Charles Frodsham, 55mm, jeweled through center wheel, engraved on movement "By appointment to the king, A.D. FMSZ" [5] 1850. Note Karrusel at top of movement. Included within the Karrusel are the balance and escape wheel. The whole mechanism revolves about once every 60 minutes.

In 1856 the Constant Girard and Henry Perragaux families founded the Swiss firm of **Girard-Perregaux**. About 1880 the firm made a tourbillion with three golden bridges. A replica of this watch was made in 1982. Both were a supreme expression of horological craftsmanship. In 1906 the company purchased the Hecht factory in Geneva. Girard-Perregaux has been recognized many times and still makes prestigious quartz and mechanical watches.

Jacques Edouard Gubelin joined the firm of Mourice Brithschmid in Lucerne around 1854. By 1919 Edouard Gubelin headed the firm. In 1921 they opened an office in New York and produced fine jewelry and watches for five generations.

The founder of the prestigious Swiss **International Watch Co.** was an American engineer F. A. Jones from Boston. The company began in 1868 and in 1879 was sold to Mr. J. Rauschenbach. The company today is still making precision, handcrafted watches. IWC is well known for its super-light watch constructed of titanium.

E. Gubelin, 54mm, 33 jewels, minute repeater, split second chronograph.

Right: Jules Jurgensen example of his famous bow setting feature.

The firm of **Jules Jurgensen** was an extension of the earlier firm of Urban Jurgensen & Sons, which was located, at various times, in Copenhagen and Le Locle. Jules ultimately established his firm in Le Locle after his father's death in the early 1830s. From that time forward the company produced, generally speaking, very fine watches that were high grade and complicated. It appears that by 1850 the company had already established a strong market in America, offering beautiful heavy 18k gold watches of exemplary quality. Until around 1885 most stem-winding watches exhibited the bow-setting feature. Almost any collectable Jurgensen watch will be fully signed on the dial and movement, with an impressively embossed "JJ" stamping on all covers of the case. Watches not so marked should be examined carefully; and untypical or inelegant stampings should be viewed suspiciously, as there has been some forgeries of these fine watches. Frequently one finds the original box and papers accompanying the watch, which exhances the value. After 1885, as the firm started to buy movements from other companies, we begin to see variations in Jurgensen watches. By 1930, Jurgensen watches barely resembled the quality and aesthetics of the early period, and they are not particularly desirable to the collector.

Jules Jurgensen, 17 jewels, rectangular 14k case.

Adolf Lange, 49mm, jeweled through the center wheel, gold escape and pallet, gold jeweled settings, gold train, diamond end stones, 14k hunting case, serial number 9,524.

A. Lange & Sohne was established with the aid of the German government at Glashutte, Germany in 1845. Lange typically produced ¾ plate lever watches in gilt finish for the domestic market, and in nickel for the export market. High grade and very practical, these watches had a banking system for the pallet that was later used briefly by E. Howard in America. Lange complicated watches are scarce and very desirable.

Le Coultre and Co. was founded by Antoine Le Coultre in 1833. A fine clockmaker, he created a machine to cut pinions from solid steel as well as other machines for manufacturing clocks and watches. By 1900 they were making flat or thin watches. They made parts for Patek Philippe & Co., Tissoy, Vacheron & Constantin, Omega, Paul Ditisheim, Agassiz, Longines and others.

Le Coultre round 18k gold case with sweep center second and date.

426

Le Roy et Cie. was the final product of a dynasty of great watchmakers, starting with Julien Le Roy and his son Pierre, whose credits are numerous in the development of horology in the 18th century. There is, however, much confusion and hooplah over "Le Roy" watches. Frequently you will see watches signed "Le Roy" that have nothing to do with the original family. These watches are unimportant. You have to distinguish between the works of Julien, of Pierre, of Charles; and of their contemporary namesakes. The modern firm, Le Roy et Cie., established in the late 19th century, contracted and finished some very fine and, in some cases, extremely important complicated watches, using imported Swiss ebauches.

The beautiful **Fabrique des Longines** is situated in St. Imier, Switzerland. The company was founded by Ernest Francillon in 1866. They manufacture all grades of watches.

Meylan Watch Co., founded by C. H. Meylan in 1880, manufactured fine watches, with complications, in Le Brassus, Switzerland.

Movado pocket watch, 42mm, 15 jewels, 8 day with alarm.

L. A. Ditisheim & Freres founded their company in 1881 and the name **Movado** ("always in motion") was adopted in 1905. The Swiss company invented a system of watch making which they called "Polyplan." This was an arrangement of three different angles to the watch movement which produced a curve effect to the case so as to fit the curvature of the arm. Another unusual watch produced by this company in 1926 was the "Ermeto." This watch was designed to be protected while inside a purse or pocket, and each time the cover was opened to view the time, the watch was partially wound.

Ulysse Nardin, 12 & 16 size, 19 jewels, adjusted to heat, cold & six positions. Illustrated example was used as a pocket and deck watch.

Ulysse Nardin was born in 1823. The company he started in 1846 produced many fine timepieces and chronometers, as well as repeaters and more complicated watches. This firm, as did Assmann, found a strong market in South America as well as other countries. Ulysse's son Paul David Nardin succeeded him, as did Paul David's sons after him. The firm also made wrist watches.

Omega Watch Co. was founded by Louis Brandt in 1848. They produced watches of different grades. By 1920 Omega had manufactured about 5,000,000 watches; by 1923, 6,000,000; and by 1931, 10,000,000.

Patek, Philippe & Cie. has produced some of the world's most desirable factory-made watches. Antoine Norbert de Patek began contracting and selling watches in the 1830s, later became partners with Francois Czapek, and generally produced lovely decorative watches for a high class of clientel. In 1845 Adrien Philippe, inventor of the modern stem-winding system, joined the firm of Patek & Cie., and in 1851 the firm established its present name. Between Philippe's talent as a watch-maker and Patek's talent as a businessman with a taste for the impeccable, the firm rapidly established an international reputation which lasts to this day.

Patek, Philippe & Co., 39 jewels, self wind movement, 18k case.

Early Patek, Philippe & Cie. watches are generally signed only on the dust cover, but some are signed on the dial and cuvette. It was not until the 1880s that the practice began of fully signing the dial, movement and case—perhaps in response to some contemporary forgery, but more likely a necessity to conform to customs' regulations for their growing international market. Many early and totally original Patek watches have suffered from the misconception that all products of this company are fully signed. Nevertheless, collectors find such pieces more desirable. It requires more experience, however, to determine the originality of the earlier pieces. As with Vacheron & Constantin, some watches were originally cased in America, but this lowers their value in general.

The Swiss company **Piaget** was founded by Georges Piaget who has a history of employing master goldsmiths. They have always produced watches in limited amounts, and watch collectors seek out these watches of *D'art*.

Rolex was founded by Hans Wilsdorf in 1919. In 1926 they made the first real waterproof wrist watch and called it the "oyster." In 1931, Rolex introduced a self-wind movement which they called "perpetual." In 1945 they introduced the "datejust" which showed the day of the month. The "submariner" was introduced in 1953 and in 1954 the "GMT Master" model. In 1956 a "day-date" model was released which indicates the day of the month (in numbers) and the day of the week (in letters).

In 1837 **Charles Lewis Tiffany** opened a store with John P. Young. They enlarged this operation in 1841, with the help of J. L. Eliss, and imported fine jewelry, watches and clocks from Europe. They incorporated as **Tiffany & Co.** in 1853. Tiffany made clocks, on special order, in New York around the mid-1880s. About 1874 Tiffany & Co. started a watch factory in Geneva but with little success. Four years later Patek, Philippe & Co. assumed the management of their Geneva watch business. The watch machinery was returned to America. Tiffany, Young & Ellis had been a client of Patek, Philippe & Co. since 1849. Tiffany & Co. introduced Patek, Philippe to the American market in 1851. Audemars, Piguet and International Watch Co. also made watches for this esteemed company. Tiffany & Co. sell watches of simple elegance as well as watches with complications such as chronographs, moonphases, repeaters, etc.

Vacheron & Constantin, about 38-39mm, 21 jewels, nickel bridge movement, wolf tooth wind, 18k case, serial number 386,637.

The firm of **Vacheron & Constantin** was officially founded by Abraham Vacheron in 1785, but the association bearing the name today did not come into being until 1819. In these early periods, different grades of watches produced by Vacheron & Constantin bore different names. The firm produced several hundred thousand watches. The association with Leschot, around 1840, catapulted the firm into its position as a top quality manufacturer. Before that time, their watches were typical of Genevese production. Vacheron & Constantin exported many movements to the United States to firms such as Bigelow, Kennard & Co., which were cased domestically, typically in the period 1900-1935. In its early period the firm produced some lovely ladies' enameled watches, later it produced high grade timepieces and complicated watches, and to this day produces fine wrist watches.

Zenith Watch and clock factory was founded in 1865 by George Farvre Jacot. They mass produced watches of different grades in large quantities. By 1920 they had manufactured 2,000,000 watches.

Example of **Split Second & Fly-Back Movement** with a minute repeater, c. 1890.

Example of **English Clock Watch**, 20 size, jeweled through hammers, minute repeater. Note two train movement.

REPEATING WATCHES

Repeating watches or repeaters are those watches which will sound the time at the wish of the user. The repeating mechanism is operated by either a slide, plunger, or button in the case of the watch. There are basically five types of repeating mechanisms, some more common than others:

(1). QUARTER REPEATERS—The quarter repeater strikes the previous hour and quarter hour. In the older watches—usually verge— the striking is on a single bell attached to the inside of the case and the hour and quarter striking uses the same tone. There is first a series of hammer blows on the bell to indicate the hours, followed, after a short pause, by up to three twin strikes to denote the number of quarters elapsed. In later watches the striking is on wire gongs attached to the movement itself. The hours are struck on a single deep gong and the quarters on a higher-pitched gong followed by the deeper gong, producing a "ting-tang" sound.

(2). HALF-QUARTER REPEATERS—These strike the hours, the last quarter (ting-tang) and the previous half-quarter; i.e., seven and a half minutes. Half-quarter repeaters are mostly all verge escapement watches and are quite rarely seen by the average collector.

(3). FIVE-MINUTE REPEATERS—These fall into two types. One system is similar to the half-quarter repeater but follows the quarter "ting-tang" by a single higher-pitched strike for each five minute interval elapsed since the last quarter. The other system strikes the hours on a deep gong and follows this with a single higher note for each five minute period after the hour, omitting a quarter striking.

(4). MINUTE REPEATERS—This is the most complicated of the repeating mechanisms and is similar to the quarter repeater with the addition of the minutes being struck on the higher-pitched gong after the quarters.

(5). CLOCK WATCHES—The clock watch is essentially a repeater with the features of a striking clock. Whereas the above-mentioned repeaters are all operated by a plunger or slide which winds the repeating function and which runs down after the last strike, the clock watch is wound in the same way as the going train—usually with a key—and is operated by the touch of a button in the case. The repeat function can be operated many times before the watch needs to be rewound. The "clock" part of the name comes from the watch also striking the hours and sometimes the quarters or half hour in passing. The clock watch is easily recognizable by the two winding holes in either the case or the dial.

In addition to the five types described above, the features of striking are sometimes found with not only two but three and even four gongs, this producing a peal of notes. These repeaters are known as "carillons."

At the other end of the scale from the carillon is the "dumb" repeater. This strikes on a block of metal in the case or on the movement and is felt rather than heard. It is said that the idea was to produce a watch that would not embarrass its owner when he wished to know when to slip away from boring company. Although the dumb repeater is less desirable for the average collector, it should certainly not be avoided—Breguet himself made dumb repeaters.

A BIT OF HISTORY

Now that we have seen what repeaters are supposed to do, it might be in order to look briefly at their origins.

Before the days of electric light, it was a major project to tell the time at night, since striking a tinderbox was said to have taken up to fifteen minutes to accomplish. Clocks, of course, had striking mechanisms, but they tended to keep the occupants of the house awake listening for the next strike. The repeating addition to the clock meant that the master of the house could silence the passing strike at night and, at his whim, simply pull a cord over his bed to activate the striking in another part of the house and thus waking everyone. To silence those members of the household who did not appreciate a clock booming out in the early hours of the morning, the horologists of the day turned their thoughts to the idea of a repeating watch.

The first mention of repeating watches is in the contest between Daniel Quare (1649-1724) and the Rev. Edward Barlow (1639-1719) to miniaturize the repeating action of a clock. Barlow, who for some reason had changed his name from Booth, was a theoretical horologist of outstanding ability. Barlow's design—made for him by Thomas Tompion—and Quare's watch were both submitted to King James II and the Privy Council for a decision as to whom should be granted a patent. The King chose Quare's design because the repeating mechanism was operated by a single push-button, whereas Barlow's required two. Quare was granted a patent in 1687. Barlow had had his share of fame earlier, however, with the invention of rack-striking for clocks in 1676.

Quare went into production with his new repeater watches, but changed the design to replace the push-button in the case with a pendant that could be pushed in. The first of these watches showed a fault that is still found on the cheaper repeaters of this century—that is, if the pendant was not pushed fully in, then the incorrect hours were struck. To overcome this problem, he invented the so-called "all-or-nothing" piece. This is a mechanism whereby if the pendant was not pushed fully home, then the watch would not strike at all.

The half-quarter appeared shortly after the all-or-nothing piece, and then by about 1710 the five-minute repeater was on the market. Some five years after this, a "deaf-piece" was often fitted to the watch. This was a slide or pin fitted to the case which, when activated, caused the hammers to be lifted away from the bell and had the same effect as a dumb repeater.

Sometime around 1730, Joseph Graham decided to dispense with the idea of a bell and arranged for the hammers to strike a dust-cover, thus making the watch slimmer and preventing dust from entering the pierced case.

About the middle of the century, the French master Le Roy carried the idea a stage further and dispensed with both bells and dust-covers, and used a metal block which revolutionized the thickness of the repeating watch and introduced the dumb repeater. Breguet used wire gongs around 1789 and the pattern for the modern repeater was set. The minute repeater came into more common use after 1800, and earlier examples are definitely very rare, although it is known that Thomas Mudge made a complicated watch incorporating minute repeating for Ferdinand VI of Spain about 1750.

By the last quarter of the 1700s, Switzerland had gone for the repeater in a big way and the centre of fine craftsmanship for complicated watches was in the Valley of Joux. Here the principle of division of labour was highly refined and whole families were hard at work producing parts for repeating and musical watches. Since one person concentrated only on one part of the watch, it is hardly surprising that parts of excellent quality were turned out. The basic movements were then sold to watchmakers/finishers all over the Continent and even to England, where the principle of one man, one watch, among the stubborn majority eventually led to the downfall of what had once been the greatest watchmaking nation in history.

The greatest popularity of the repeater came, however, in the last quarter of the 1800s, when Switzerland turned them out in the tens of thousands. Although there were many different names on the dials of the watches, most seem to have been produced by the company "Le Phare" and only finished by the name on the dial. The production of repeaters in quantity seems to have ground to a finish in about 1921 due to (a) the invention of luminous dials and universal electric or gas lighting, and (b) a lack of watchmakers willing to learn the highly demanding skills. The interest in horology over the past decade has, however, revived the idea of the repeater and several companies in Switzerland are now producing limited editions of expensive models.

BUYING A REPEATER

Since so many repeaters seem to have been repaired by incompetent watchmakers at some time in the past, it is often too expensive a purchase if the buyer does not know what he is doing.

Rule One should be: if it does not work perfectly, avoid it like the plague unless a competent repairer first gives you an estimate which suits your pocket. All too ofen, a past repairer was under the impression that metal grows with age and he has filed the teeth of a rack in order to get the full striking to work again. When it then dawns on him that the problem was a worn bearing, the tooth is stretched with a punch, refiled, and is weakened. It is then goodbye to a fine piece of craftsmanship.

A better quality repeater is usually one which is "jewelled to the hammers." This simply means that the hammers have jewelled bearing—which can be seen by searching the movement for the hammers, locating the pivots around which they swing, and looking for the jewelled bearing in which they sit.

All repeaters have some system for regulating the speed of the repeating train. On the older fusee types, there was usually a rather primitive arrangement of a pinion in an eccentric bushing which could be turned to increase or decrease the depth of engagement of the pinion with the next wheel. Another system, a little better, uses an anchor and a toothed wheel as in an alarm clock. This system is usually located under the dial but can be detected by the buzzing sound it makes when the train is operated. The far superior system is the centrifugal governor which can be seen whizzing around in the top plate of the watch when the repeating action is operated. On the whole, the watch with the centrifugal governor is more desirable, although it must be mentioned that the Swiss turned out some quite inferior watches with this system.

If possible—and it should be possible if you are investing a lot of money—have a watchmaker look under the dial to see if the watch is jewelled throughout. Many are only jewelled in the places the owner can see and leave much to be desired in the "blind" places.

Test the watch by operating the repeating train over a full hour, seeing that the quarters and minutes function correctly, then test each individual hour. Finally, set the hands to just before 1 o'clock and test the striking. Any defect due to dirt or worn bearings will show up by the final blow(s), being either sluggish or not striking at all. If there is incorrect striking, have an expert look at it before you buy.

Try a partial operation of the slide or push-piece. If the watch has an all-or-nothing piece (as a reasonable grade movement should have), then the watch will not strike. Partial striking indicates either a low-grade watch or a non-functioning all-or-nothing piece.

Additional features such as chronograph functions, calendar, moon phase, etc., will obviously affect the price of the watch and one must be guided by current price listings from reputable dealers.

Remember Rule One, though—if any function does not work, BEWARE!

Example of a 33 minute karrusel by **Russell & Son**, makers to the Queen (London), 55mm, 16 jewels, open face.

Tourbillon

A. Fixed fourth wheel
B. Third wheel
C. Carriage (one revolution per minute)
D. Carriage pinion
E. Escape Wheel & pinion
F. Arbor for seconds hand
G. Escape cock
H. Lever & pallets

Note: Approximately 50-60 per cent of pocket watch repeaters were manufactured by LePhare and about 20 per cent by LeCoultre.

Calibre OV., open face

Calibre LV., open face

Calibre EV., open face

Calibre JV., open face

Calibre DV., open face

Open face

Calibre E., open face

Calibre L., open face

Calibre D., open face

Calibre J., open face

Calibre YM.

Calibre YMC.

Calibre 110M.   Calibre 105.

Calibre 115V.   Calibre LVC.

Calibre EVC.   Calibre LVCC.

Calibre EVCC.

Calibre EC.

Calibre OVC.

Calibre JC.

Calibre DC.

Calibre OC.

Dial side, triple date
moon phase

Calibre LC.

Calibre JVCC.

Calibre DVCC.

Calibre JVC.

Calibre DVC.

Calibre ZM.

Calibre ZMC.

LECOULTRE

Calibre 43

Calibre 44

Calibre 45

Calibre 46

Calibre 49

Calibre 48

Calibre 30

Calibre 31

Calibre 32

Calibre 33

Calibre 43

Calibre 46

Calibre 47

AUDEMARS, PIGUET

Calibre SMCCRV

Calibre SCCV & SCCRV

Calibre SCCV & SCCRV

Calibre SMCCRS

Calibre SMV

Calibre SMS

Patek, Philippe

Patek, Philippe

Patek, Philippe

C.H. Meylan

Picard & Co.

Picard & Co.

Invicta

Invicta

Invicta

Nathan Weil

Longines, open face

Longines, hunting

Longines

W. Golay

447

Walter Meylan

Walter Meylan

Martel W. Co.

Martel W. Co.

Martel W. Co.

Martel W. Co.

TOURBILLON

Breguet invented the tourbillon in 1795. A tourbillon is a device designed to reduce the position errors of a watch. This device has the escape wheel, lever and balance wheel all mounted in a carriage of light frameworks. This carriage makes one complete turn every minute. The fourth wheel is fixed and is concentric with the carriage pinion and arbor. The escape wheel pinion meshes with the fourth wheel and will roll around the fixed fourth wheel. The escape wheel and lever are mounted on the carriage, and the third wheel drives the carriage pinion, turning the carriage once every minute. This rotation of the escapement will help reduce the position errors of a watch. One of the major objections is that the carriage and escapement weight mass must be stopped and started at each release of the escapement. The tourbillon design requires extreme skill to produce and is usually found on watches of high quality. Somewhat similar to the tourbillon is the karrusel, except it rotates about once per hour and the fourth wheel is not fixed. It also takes less skill to produce.

MUSICAL WATCHES
(Three basic types)

Stacked Tooth

Disc Type with individual teeth

Pinned Cylinder & Comb

PRODUCTION TOTALS

PATEK PHILIPPE

1840	100
1845	1,200
1850	3,000
1855	8,000
1860	15,000
1865	22,000
1870	35,000
1875	45,000
1880	55,000
1885	70,000
1890	85,000
1895	100,000
1900	110,000
1905	125,000
1910	150,000
1915	175,000
1920	190,000
1925	200,000
1950	700,000
1955	725,000
1960	750,000
1965	775,000
1970	795,000

1920	800,000
1925	805,000
1930	820,000
1935	824,000
1940	835,000
1945	850,000
1950	860,000
1955	870,000
1960	880,000
1965	890,000
1970	895,000
1940	900,000
1945	915,000
1950	930,000
1955	940,000
1960	960,000
1965	975,000
1970	995,000
1960	1,100,000
1965	1,130,000
1970	1,250,000
1975	1,330,000
1980	1,400,000

A. LANGE

1870	5,000
1875	10,000
1880	20,000
1885	25,000
1890	30,000
1895	35,000
1900	40,000
1905	50,000
1910	60,000
1915	70,000
1920	75,000
1925	80,000
1930	85,000
1935	90,000
1940	100,000

LONGINES

1870	20,000
1880	200,000
1890	600,000
1900	1,200,000
1910	2,000,000
1920	3,000,000
1930	5,000,000
1940	6,000,000

The above list is provided for determining the approximate age of your watch. Match serial number with date.

EUROPEAN POCKET WATCH LISTINGS
Pricing at Retail Level
(Complete Watches Only)

Unless otherwise noted, watches listed in this section are priced at the retail level and as complete watches having an original 14k gold-filled case with an original white enamel single sunk dial, and the entire original movement in good working order with no repairs needed. Watches listed as 14k and 18k are solid gold cases. Coin or silveroid-type and stainless steel cases will be listed as such. Keywind and keyset pocket watches are listed as having original coin silver cases. Dollar-type watches, or low cost production watches, are listed as having a base metal type case and a composition dial.

Many of the watch manufacturers were commissioned to put jewelers' or jobbers' names on their movements in place of their own. Because of this practice, the true manufacturers of these movements are difficult to identify. These watch models are listed under the original manufacturer and can be identified by comparison with the model sections under each manufacturer. See "Personalized Watches" for more detailed information.

The prices shown were averaged from dealers' lists just prior to publication and are an indication of the retail level or what collectors will pay. Prices are provided in three categories: average condition, extra fine, and mint condition, and are shown in whole dollar amounts only. The values listed are a guide for the retail level and are provided for your information only. Dealers will not necessarily pay full retail price. Prices listed are for watches with **original** cases and dials.

Note: Descriptions and serial number ranges listed for early watches cannot be considered 100 percent accurate due to the manner in which records were kept by these companies.

INFORMATION NEEDED—This price guide is interested in any facts and information you might have that should possibly be considered for future editions. Documented facts are needed. Please send photo or sources of information to Cooksey Shugart, 780 Church Street N.E., Cleveland, Tennessee 37311.

AGASSIZ

Swiss

Agassiz, 43mm, 18 jewels, serial number 44,844.

Agassiz, 43mm, 21 jewels, ¾ plate, serial number 39,863.

Size and Description	Avg	Ex-Fn	Mint
52mm, split sec. chronograph, 14K, OF, register	$600	$750	$1,000
50mm, art deco, "Cartier," 1925, 19J, Adj.5P, 18K......	1,000	1,400	1,800
43mm, 17J, nickel mvt., 14K, OF	325	400	550
43mm, 21J, nickel mvt., 18K, OF, WI, 8 day............	700	850	1,050
40mm, 19J, World Time, 32 Cities, 14K, OF	3,000	3,600	4,250
40mm, 19J, World Time, 32 Cities, 18K, OF	3,600	4,200	5,000
37mm, 21J, 8 day, wind indicator, OF, 18K	650	775	950
Lady's, 40mm, HC, 18K, white enamel dial	300	350	475

Agassiz, 43mm, 17 jewels, World Time, 42 towns, ca. 1940.

Assmann, 44mm, 21 jewels, serial number 19,539, ca. 1914.

ASSMANN
GLASSHUTTE

Size and Description	Avg	Ex-Fn	Mint
44mm, elaborate chasing, fancy dial, for South American market, 18K, HC	$3,200	$3,900	$4,750
42mm, SW, Timepiece, OF, 18K	1,800	2,200	2,800

Assmann, 50mm, 19 jewels, diamond cap jewels, gold jewel settings, gold lever escapement, serial number 3,086, ca. 1855.

Assmann, 50mm, 19 jewels, diamond cap jewels, gold jewel settings, gold lever escapement, serial number 3,739, ca. 1857.

AUDEMARS, PIGUET
SWISS

Size and Description	Avg	Ex-Fn	Mint
46mm, OF, min. repeater, chronograph, register, 18K	$3,000	$3,700	$4,600

Audemars, Piguet, 46mm, 20 jewels, minute repeater. Note governor at right-hand side of balance bridge.

Audemars, Piguet, 48mm, 30 jewels, minute repeater, serial number 4,155, ca. 1890.

AUDEMARS, PIGUET (continued)

Size and Description	Avg	Ex-Fn	Mint
46mm, OF, min. repeater, split chronograph, register, 18K	$4,000	$4,600	$5,500
46mm, min. repeater, 18K, HC	3,200	3,800	4,600
46mm, 20J, ¼ repeater, OF, 18K	1,800	2,200	2,600
44-45mm, OF, timepiece, 18K	550	650	850
44mm, OF, min. repeater	2,600	3,000	3,600
44mm, OF, 5-min. repeater	2,200	2,800	3,200
40mm, 31J, min. repeater, 18K, OF, c. 1875	3,000	3,600	4,500

Audemars, Piguet, 46mm, 36 jewels, minute repeater, split-second chronograph, serial number 3853, ca. 1888.

Audemars, Piguet, about 16 size, 18 jewels, adj.6P, jumping hour, day-date-month windows, ca. 1925.

J. W. BENSON
LONDON

Size and Description	Avg	Ex-Fn	Mint
58mm, Grande & Petite Sonnerie, min. repeater, perpetual calendar, moonphases	$52,000	$58,000	$67,000
40mm, KW, KS, fusee, lever, wind indicator, free sprung, 18K, HC	1,200	1,400	1,800

BULOVA
SWISS AND U.S.A.

Size and Description	Avg	Ex-Fn	Mint
40mm, 18J, "Phantom," c. 1920, OF platinum case ★ ★ ★	$550	$750	$950

HENRY CAPT
GENEVE

Size and Description	Avg	Ex-Fn	Mint
52mm, min. repeater, perpetual calendar, moon phases, 18K hunting case	$19,000	$22,000	$25,000
Lady's, OF, 1 min. repeater, 18K	2,800	3,200	3,700

Henry Capt, 52mm, 32 jewels, minute repeater, serial number 34,711, ca. 1900.

Cartier, 59mm, 19 jewels, art deco black onyx, gold, enamel and diamonds on case (European W. Co.).

CARTIER
PARIS

Size and Description	Avg	Ex-Fn	Mint
49mm, 19J, art deco, black onyx, gold, enamel & diamonds on case	$3,000	$4,000	$5,000

H. R. EKEGREN
GENEVE

Size and Description	Avg	Ex-Fn	Mint
55mm, min. repeater, jeweled to hammers, 18K case, OF	$3,000	$3,400	$4,200

H.R. EKEGREN (continued)

H.R. Ekegren, 39mm, minute repeater, slide activated, jeweled through hammers, open face, serial number 78,268.

H.R. Ekegren, 43mm, minute repeater, jeweled through hammers, hunting case.

Size and Description	Avg	Ex-Fn	Mint
43mm, min. repeater, 18K, HC, jeweled to hammers	$3,400	$3,800	$4,500
42mm, 18K, OF, fully jeweled, SW, LS	600	750	950
39mm, min. repeater, jeweled to hammers, OF, 18K	2,600	3,000	3,400

Frodsham, 44mm, jeweled through center wheel. Movement shows coded date under serial number. He used his name 'Frodsham' for numbers 1-8, and Z for 0. For example "AD. FMSZ" means the year 1850, serial number 04172.

Frodsham, 55mm, 60 minute karrusel, 15 jewels, stem wind, open face, 18k gold case, c. 1850.

FRODSHAM
LONDON

Size and Description	Avg	Ex-Fn	Mint
55mm, min. repeater, jeweled thru hammers, DES, 18K, HC	$4,200	$4,800	$5,800
55mm, 16J, 59 min., Karrusel, 18K case	4,400	5,000	5,600
54mm, one min., tourbillon, ¾ plate, signed, 18K, OF ...	22,000	26,000	32,000
44mm, detent escapement, 18K, HC	1,800	2,000	2,600
42mm, 17J, ¾ plate, GJS, DES, 18K, HC	900	1,100	1,400
42mm, KW, KS, wind indicator, free sprung, 18K, OF ...	1,200	1,400	1,650
35mm, ¼ & 5 min. repeater, by Thomas Frodsham, 18K, HC	4,500	5,000	5,800

D. Gruen & Son, 44mm, jeweled through center wheel, made for railroad service, serial number 62,428.

Gruen 50th Anniversary Watch, 10 size, 21 jewels, (two diamonds) placed in a five-sided pentagon case, solid gold bridges.

GRUEN
SWISS AND U.S.A.

Size and Description	Avg	Ex-Fn	Mint
45mm, 14K, HC, by D. Gruen & Son, 21J, GJS, gold escape wheel, "Dresden," by Assman	$900	$1,100	$1,400
44mm, made for R.R. Service, GF	135	195	275
40mm, 19J, "Precision," SW, LS, YGF	100	120	145
40mm, 50th Anniversary, 21J, including 2 diamonds, 18K, OF	2,500	2,900	3,400
40mm, "Detrich Gruen," marked Extra Precision, 31J, min. repeater, 18K, OF	2,400	2,700	3,200
38mm, 17J, pentagon case, veri thin style, YGF..........	75	85	95
38mm, 17J, pentagon case, veri thin style, 14K	250	325	400
38mm, 17J, pentagon case, veri thin style, 18K	325	400	475
38mm, 21J, RGJ, GT, Adj.5P, YGF	75	110	145
38mm, 19J, GT, Adj.5P	65	95	110
38mm, 15J, ADJ.....................................	50	60	75

E. GUBELIN
SWISS

Size and Description	Avg	Ex-Fn	Mint
54mm, min. repeater, 33J, split sec. chronograph, GT	$3,000	$3,500	$4,200
54mm, 28J, min. repeater, OF, 18K	2,400	2,700	3,200
38mm, 21J, deco style, Adj.5P, perpetual calendar, 18K, OF	4,400	5,200	6,000

E. Gubelin, 54mm, 33 jewels, minute
repeater, jeweled through the hammers,
split second chronograph.

E. Gubelin, 54mm, 33 jewels, minute repeater, jeweled through the hammers, split second chronograph.

C.L. Guinand, 50mm, split-second chronograph, serial number 44,109.

C. L. GUINAND
SWISS

Size and Description	Avg	Ex-Fn	Mint
50mm, 34J, min. repeater, split sec. chronograph, 18K, OF	$3,000	$3,500	$4,200

HAAS, NEVEUX & CO.
SWISS

Size and Description	Avg	Ex-Fn	Mint
42mm, 18K, HC, cover wind	$2,200	$2,600	$3,200
40mm, 31J, min. repeater, 18K hunting case............	2,800	3,400	4,000
40mm, 31J, min. repeater, 18K, OF	2,400	2,900	3,500
34mm, $20 gold piece form watch....................	1,200	1,500	1,900

Haas, Neveux & Co., 40mm, 31 jewels, minute repeater, 18k open face case, serial number 11,339.

Hebdomas novelty watch, 8-day movement, balance can be seen from dial side.

HEBDOMAS
SWISS

Style or Grade—Description	Avg	Ex-Fn	Mint
50mm, 7J, 8 day, balance seen from dial................	$100	$125	$165

INTERNATIONAL WATCH CO.
SWISS

Size and Description	Avg	Ex-Fn	Mint
54mm, 17J, lever escapement, GJS, 14K, HC............	$475	$550	$650
42mm, early mvt., 18K, HC..........................	550	750	950

International Watch Co., 42mm, 18 size, 15 jewels, serial number 7,609.

International Watch Co., 54mm, 17 jewels, adj.6P, serial number 741,073.

JULES JURGENSEN
SWISS

Size and Description	Avg	Ex-Fn	Mint
55mm, OF, detent chronometer, KW, 18K	$2,800	$3,200	$3,800
55mm, OF, detent chronometer, SW, 18K..............	4,500	4,800	5,400
55mm, HC, detent chronometer, SW, 18K	5,000	5,800	6,800
50mm, OF, timepiece, enamel dial, 18K................	1,800	2,200	2,800
49mm, ¼ repeater, c. 1880, nickel lever mvt., gold train, 18K HC..	2,400	2,800	3,400
46mm, OF, min. repeater, chronograph, register, 18K	4,600	5,200	6,000
46mm, OF, min. repeater, split chrono., register, 18K	5,400	6,200	7,200
46mm, HC, min. repeater, 18K	4,800	5,500	6,500
46mm, HC, min. repeater, chronograph, 18K............	5,000	5,500	6,800
46mm, HC, min. repeater, split chronograph, register, 18K	7,000	8,000	11,000
46mm, OF, chronograph, timepiece, register, 18K	2,200	2,600	3,400

Jules Jurgensen, 1 minute repeater, popular bow set, triple signed case, movement & dial, 18k hunting case, serial number 13,824.

Jules Jurgensen, 46mm, 21 jewels, hand-setting by inclination of pendant ring, serial number 14,492, ca. 1890.

Size and Description	Avg	Ex-Fn	Mint
46mm, OF, split chronograph, timepiece, register	$2,800	$3,400	$4,200
46mm, HC, chronograph, timepiece, register	2,600	3,000	3,800
46mm, HC, split chronograph, timepiece, register	3,400	4,000	4,800
45mm, OF, timepiece, enamel dial.....................	1,600	2,000	2,400
45mm, HC, timepiece, enamel dial	1,800	2,200	2,800
45mm, OF, KW, timepiece, enamel dial.................	750	850	950
45mm, OF, min. repeater, enamel dial	3,600	4,200	5,000
44mm, OF, 5-min. repeater...........................	3,000	3,600	4,200
40mm, OF, timepiece, enamel dial.....................	1,100	1,400	1,750
40mm, HC, timepiece, enamel dial	1,400	1,700	2,200

A. LANGE
GERMANY

Size and Description	Avg	Ex-Fn	Mint
55mm, min. repeater, 18K, HC, jeweled thru hammers, GJS, NI, GT, gold escape & pallet, DES, 1st quality mvt. .	$18,000	$20,000	$24,000
55mm, ¼ repeater, NI, DES, 1st quality mvt., HC.......	8,500	9,500	11,000
54mm, ¼ repeater, DES, jeweled thru hammers, OF	6,800	7,800	9,000
53mm, 18K case, c. 1885, GJS, GT, DES, gold pallet and escape wheel	2,200	2,700	3,200
52mm, World War II model, WI, OF, silver case	1,200	1,400	1,800

A. Lange & Sohne, 52mm, wind indicator, World War II model, open face.

A. Lange & Sohne, 48mm, three-quarter plate, engraved on movement "Deutsche Uhren Fabrikation Glashutte," serial number 58,398.

Size and Description	Avg	Ex-Fn	Mint
49mm, 18K case, 17J, GJS, GT, gold escape wheel & pallet, c. 1914, OF....................................	$1,650	$2,000	$2,400
49mm, 18K case, HC, gild mvt., 17J, GJS, DES, gold lever and escape wheel	1,850	2,200	2,600
49mm, min. repeater, 3rd grade mvt., gilt, 14K, triple sized HC	8,500	9,500	11,500
48mm, ¾ plate, Deutsche Uhren Fabrikation, silver	450	550	700

LE COULTRE & CO.
SWISS

Size and Description	Avg	Ex-Fn	Mint
57mm, 32J, min. repeater, slide repeat, 14K, HC	$2,500	$2,800	$3,200
57mm, 32J, min. repeater, slide repeat, 18K, HC	2,600	3,000	3,500
55mm, 31J, min. repeater, day-date-month, moon phase, 18K, HC	3,800	4,500	5,500
54mm, min. repeater, gilt, lever escapement, 14K, HC	1,800	2,200	2,700

LE COULTRE & CO. (continued)

Le Coultre & Co., 57mm, 32 jewels, minute repeater, exposed winding gears, 14k hunting case.

Le Coultre & Co., 55mm, 31 jewels, day, date, month and moon phases, 18k hunting case, minute repeater.

Style or Grade—Description	Avg	Ex-Fn	Mint
52mm, ¼ repeater, double dial, calendar, moon phase, 18K, HC	$3,200	$3,700	$4,300
49mm, nickel mvt., 18K, OF	500	650	800

LE ROY
SWISS

Size and Description	Avg	Ex-Fn	Mint
55mm, musical, plays on demand, repeater, 18K	$2,400	$2,800	$3,500
20mm, ¼ repeater, exposed repeat work on back plate, pear bezel, 18K	3,200	3,800	4,500

Leroy, 50mm, minute repeater, two train, tandem winding wheels, jump center seconds.

LONGINES
SWISS

Size and Description	Avg	Ex-Fn	Mint
59mm, 30J, min. repeater, chronograph, calendar & moon moon phases, 18K HC	$3,200	$4,000	$5,000
55mm, OF, 18K, split chronograph, 2 registers	1,200	1,400	1,800
50mm, chronograph with register, nickel mvt., silver	150	175	195
50mm, 8 day, wind indicator, 15J, Adj.3P, silver	325	425	550
46mm, 21J, "Express Monarch," R.R. approved, Adj.5P .	175	195	235
46mm, rectangular case, 30 small diamonds on case, 15J . .	700	900	1,200
44mm, 15J, 3 ADJ, 8 day, WI, 14K	500	600	750
44mm, "U. S. Army," sweep sec. hand, WI, Adj.5P	300	350	425
26mm, lady's pendant, 18K, OF, enamel & diamonds	600	700	850

Longines, 44mm, 21 jewels, U.S. Army AC, adjusted to temp. & 5 positions, World War II model, serial number 5,939,626.

Longines, 59mm, 26 jewels, minute repeater, chronograph, two registers, ca. 1910.

MATHEY-TISSOT
SWISS

Size and Description	Avg	Ex-Fn	Mint
52mm, ¼ jump sec. chronograph, tandem wind, 2 train, 18K	$2,400	$2,800	$3,400
48mm, min. repeater, 14K, OF	1,800	2,200	2,600

C. H. MEYLAN
SWISS

Style or Grade — Description	Avg	Ex-Fn	Mint
50mm, min. repeater, OF, 18K, jeweled to hammers	$2,400	$2,850	$3,400
50mm, min. repeater, HC, 18K, chronograph, fully jeweled	2,800	3,250	3,850

C.H. MEYLAN (continued)

Mathey-Tissot, 52mm, 27 jewels, quarter jump sweep-second chronograph, two train, 18k hunting case.

C.H. Meylan, 44mm, 21 jewels, straight line lever escapement.

Style or Grade—Description	Avg	Ex-Fn	Mint
48mm, split sec. chronograph, register, OF, 18K	$900	$1,150	$1,400
48mm, chronograph, register, OF, 14K	600	750	950
46mm, platinum & sapphire dress watch, c. 1925.........	1,200	1,600	2,050
44mm, min. repeater, 14K, OF.......................	1,800	2,250	2,750
44mm, timepiece, 18K, thin model	350	450	550

Ulysse Nardin, 50mm, 15 jewels, made for Corps. of Engineers, USA, World War I, serial number 691,527-H6.

Ulysse Nardin Chronometer, 55mm, 21 jewels, ultra-high grade movement, c. 1878, serial number 7,685.

ULYSSE NARDIN
SWISS

Size and Description	Avg	Ex-Fn	Mint
Deck chronometer w/mahogany box, detent mvt., silver dial	$1,000	$1,200	$1,500
50mm, 15J, made for Corps of Engineers, U.S.A., WWI .	175	225	275
50mm, min. repeater, jeweled thru hammers, HC, 18K ...	3,250	3,800	4,400
45mm, split chronograph, 2 registers, 14K, OF	750	950	1,100
45mm, detent chronometer, KW, KS, 18K..............	450	575	725
45mm, SW, timepiece only, 18K, OF	550	675	800
45mm, SW, timepiece only, 14K	350	400	475
42mm, perpetual calendar, moon phases, OF, 18K	5,500	6,500	7,500
42mm, moon phases, perpetual calendar, 18K, HC	7,500	9,500	11,500
40mm, 29J, min. repeater, Adj.5P, 18K, OF	2,500	2,800	3,500

OMEGA
SWISS

Size and Description	Avg	Ex-Fn	Mint
45mm, 15J, lever escapement, silver	$55	$75	$95
45mm, 17J, OF, 14K	275	325	375
45mm, 17J, HC, 14K	325	375	450
38mm, 15J, OF	55	75	95

Omega pocket watch, 38mm, 15 jewels, serial number 9,888,934.

Patek Philippe & Co., 38-39mm, 18 jewels, deco bridge movement, 8 adj., 18k open face case, serial number 196,051.

PATEK, PHILIPPE & CO.
SWISS

Size and Description	Avg	Ex-Fn	Mint
56mm, 22J, "Chronometro Gondolo," 24 hr. dial, 18K, OF, c. 1890s...................................	$1,650	$2,000	$2,450

PATEK, PHILIPPE & CO. (continued)

Patek, **Philippe** dial and movement, minute repeater, 29 jewels, perpetual calendar, day, date, month, moon phase, adjusted to 5 positions, 18k solid gold case.

Size and Description	Avg	Ex-Fn	Mint
55mm, astronomic, perpetual calendar, min. repeater, 1897, white enamel dial, 3 registers, split sec. chronograph, moon phases, 38J, slide repeat, original box and papers	$80,000	$88,000	$98,000
54mm, split sec. chronograph, 14K, OF	1,800	2,100	2,700
52mm, split sec. chronograph, 18K, OF, Tiffany & Co., register	2,400	2,800	3,250
51mm, 22J, independent dead seconds, 2 train, heavy 18K HC, c. 1890 ★★★★	20,000	25,000	33,000
51mm, 18K, HC, gilt, lever mvt.	1,400	1,600	1,800
48mm, 18K, HC, nickel mvt.	1,500	1,700	2,000
48mm, early chronograph, fly back sec. hand, 18K, OF, wolf's teeth winding	1,800	2,000	2,400
47mm, 1 min. tourbillon, by James Pellaton, c. 1920, 18K case ★★★	75,000	85,000	99,000
46mm, OF, timepiece, enamel dial	950	1,100	1,300
46mm, two train, min. repeater, Tiffany & Co.	7,000	8,500	11,000
46mm, "Gondolo," OF, timepiece, enamel dial, 18 size	1,100	1,300	1,500
46mm, 18K, OF, 18J, Adj.5P, cam regulator	950	1,100	1,300
46mm, OF, min. repeater, split chronograph, registers	9,000	10,000	12,000
46mm, HC, min. repeater, split chronograph, registers	10,500	12,000	14,000
46mm, HC, min. repeater, split chronograph, perpetual calendar, moon phase	72,000	80,000	90,000
45mm, 18J, 18K, OF, Tiffany & Co.	1,000	1,100	1,400
45mm, 18K, HC, 1860, SW & set, wolf tooth wind	1,200	1,400	1,800
45mm, OF, split chronograph, timepiece, register	2,400	2,800	3,400
45mm, OF, perpetual calendar, timepiece, metal dial	8,500	10,000	12,000
45mm, OF, perpetual calendar, timepiece, enamel dial	9,500	10,500	13,000
45mm, OF, timepiece, gilt dial, 14K	500	600	750

PATEK, PHILIPPE & CO. (continued)

Patek Philippe & Co., 38-39mm, 18 jewels, nickel bridge movement, wolf tooth wind, cam regulator, serial number 124,348.

Patek, Philippe & Co., 42mm, Chronograph, 17 jewels, triple signed case (18k), dial & movement, serial number 94,290.

Style or Grade—Description	Avg	Ex-Fn	Mint
45mm, HC, min. repeater, chronograph	$5,500	$6,500	$7,500
45mm, HC, chronograph, timepiece, register	2,400	2,800	3,300
45mm, HC, split chronograph, timepiece, register	2,800	3,200	3,800
45mm, HC, min. repeater, split chronograph, perpetual calendar, register + moon phases	74,000	82,000	92,000
44mm, OF, timepiece, gilt, enamel dial, 18K	900	1,000	1,200
44mm, OF, timepiece, nickel, enamel dial, 18K	1,000	1,100	1,300
44mm, HC, min. repeater	4,500	5,000	6,500
44mm, OF, 5 min. repeater	3,800	4,200	5,200
44mm, OF, 5 min. repeater, chronograph	4,000	4,700	5,500
44mm, OF, min. repeater	4,500	5,000	5,800
44mm, OF, min. repeater, chronograph	5,000	5,500	6,500
44mm, OF, min. repeater, split chrono., register	8,500	10,000	12,000
42mm, 14K, OF, chronometer on dial, USA cased	600	700	850
39mm, 18J, wolf tooth wind, 14K, OF, BRG, nickel mvt. USA cased	650	750	900
39mm, 18J, Adj.5P, enamel on bezel & back	1,000	1,250	1,500
38mm, "Gondolo," OF, timepiece, enamel dial, 16 Size	1,050	1,250	1,500
35mm, 29J, min. repeater, very thin, 18K, OF	4,400	5,000	5,800
32mm, 18K, HC, early bridge mvt., Tiffany & Co.	600	675	800
30mm, lady's, 18K, gold & enamel + diamonds, lapel watch	2,500	3,500	4,500
30mm, lady's, 18K, multi color gold, enamel & diamonds, matching chain & pin, OF, art nouveau	4,500	5,500	6,750
29mm, lady's, 18K, OF	500	600	700
26mm, lady's, 18K, OF, gold, seed pearls & enamel, lapel watch, matching pin	3,200	3,800	4,500

NOTE: Watches listed in this book are priced at the retail level, as complete watches having an original 14k gold-filled case, an original white enamel single sunk dial, and with the entire original movement in good working order with no repairs needed, unless otherwise noted.

ALBERT H. POTTER & CO.
GENEVA

Style or Grade—Description	Avg	Ex-Fn	Mint
45mm, 29J, min. repeater, 18K, HC	$5,500	$6,500	$8,000
43mm, 22J, helical hairspring, detent chronometer escapement, 18K, HC	40,000	50,000	65,000
33mm, 21J, ¼ repeater, 18K, HC	3,000	3,500	4,500

Albert Potter, 22 jewels, hunting case, helical hair spring, detent escapement.

Rolex, 42-43mm, 17 jewels, three adjustments, cam regulator, exposed winding gears.

ROLEX
SWISS

Size and Description	Avg	Ex-Fn	Mint
43mm, 3 ADJ, cam regulator, 14K, OF	$850	$1,050	$1,250

THOMAS RUSSEL & SONS
ENGLAND

Size and Description	Avg	Ex-Fn	Mint
52mm, ½ ¼ repeater, rachet tooth escapement, 18K, OF	$2,600	$3,000	$3,500
46mm, min. repeater, ¾ plate, 18K, HC	3,800	4,350	5,000
46mm, karrusel, 59 min., chronometer, free sprung, 18K, OF	4,500	5,000	6,500

TIFFANY & CO.
U.S.A.

Size and Description	Avg	Ex-Fn	Mint
49mm, 5 min. repeater, c. 1900, 18K, HC	$3,000	$3,500	$4,200
49mm, 1 min. repeater, 18K, OF	3,000	3,500	4,200
49mm, 1 min. repeater, 18K, HC	3,500	4,000	4,600
48mm, nickel mvt., wolf's tooth wind, 18K, OF	750	875	1,050
48mm, nickel mvt., chronograph, 18K, OF	900	1,100	1,350
48mm, nickel mvt., split sec. chronograph, 18K, OF	950	1,100	1,500
48mm, min. repeater, split sec. chronograph, day-date-month, moonphase, perpetual, 18K, OF, mvt. by Vacheron & Constantin	22,000	27,000	32,000
48mm, min. repeater, split sec. chronograph, day-date-month, moonphase, 18K, OF, mvt. by Patek Philippe	75,000	85,000	95,000
48mm, timepiece, 18K, HC, enamel dial	850	1,000	1,250
48mm, timepiece, 18K, OF, by Patek, Philippe & Co.	950	1,100	1,300
47mm, 5 min. repeater, 18K, OF	2,400	2,900	3,600
45mm, 18K, OF, by Longines	400	525	675
44mm, 18K, HC, timepiece	550	650	800
42mm, OF, 18K, timepiece	375	450	550

NOTE: Watches listed in this book are priced at the retail level, as complete watches having an original 14k gold-filled case, an original white enamel single sunk dial, and with the entire original movement in good working order with no repairs needed, unless otherwise noted.

Tiffany & Co., 50mm, 25 jewels, split-second chronograph, made by Ekegren.

Tiffany & Co., flat minute repeater, 45mm, 29 jewels, made by Patek, Philippe & Co., ca. 1911.

Touchon & Co., 47mm, 29 jewels, minute repeater, open face, jeweled through hammers.

Touchon & Co., 47mm, 29 jewels, split-second chronograph and minute repeater, ca. 1910.

TOUCHON & CO.
SWISS

Size and Description	Avg	Ex-Fn	Mint
47mm, 29J, min. repeater, thin model, 1925, 18K, OF	$1,950	$2,350	$2,850
46mm, min. repeater, jeweled thru hammers, wolf tooth wind, 18K, HC	2,250	2,700	3,250
45mm, 23J, min. repeater, 14K, OF	1,600	1,800	2,050
44mm, OF, 18K, timepiece	375	450	550
40mm, 28J, min. repeater, 14K, OF	1,700	1,900	2,200

50 pesos 24k gold coin with **Vacheron & Constantin** watch inside. The left view shows the movement inside the coin which was hollowed out to receive the Vacheron & Constantin watch.

VACHERON & CONSTANTIN
SWISS

Size and Description	Avg	Ex-Fn	Mint
59mm, chronometer escapement, with silver deck case, c. 1920	$1,200	$1,400	$1,700
55mm, min. repeater, 18K, OF, ultra high grade, nickel mvt.	3,500	3,900	4,500
51mm, 14K, HC, nickel mvt., c. 1890	700	850	1,100
50mm, min. repeater, chronograph mvt., 18K, OF, gilt	3,200	3,800	4,500
47mm, 14K, OF, c. 1900, nickel mvt.	450	550	700
43mm, 18K, OF, c. 1920, nickel lever mvt., Adj.5P	450	550	700
42mm, 14K, OF, 17J, Adj.5P, c. 1915	400	475	600

Vacheron & Constantin , 40mm, wolf tooth winding, 18k open face.

Vacheron & Constantin, 40mm, 29 jewels, minute repeater, slide repeat, wolf tooth wind, 18k open face, serial number 340,949.

Style or Grade—Description	Avg	Ex-Fn	Mint
41mm case size, 24mm mvt. size, skeletonized, c. 1930, 18J	$2,200	$2,600	$3,200
40mm, 21J, NI, BRG, wolf tooth wind, 18K, OF	550	650	800
40mm, 19J, high quality mvt., 14K, OF	400	500	650
40mm, 17J, wolf tooth wind, GF, HC	125	175	285
40mm, min. repeater, slide repeat, jeweled thru hammers, OF	2,600	3,000	3,500
40mm, 31J, min. repeater, 18K, OF, slide activated	2,500	2,800	3,200
40mm, 21J, observatory time trial, 3rd place winner, 18K	1,200	1,600	2,200
30mm, jeweled to center wheel, 18K, OF	450	500	700

MISC. ENGLISH

Size and Description	Avg	Ex-Fn	Mint
70mm, silver & horn triple cased, for Turkish market, by G. Charles, c. 1810, verge, & pierced cock, enamel dial	$600	$800	$1,000

MISC. ENGLISH (continued)

Size and Description	Avg	Ex-Fn	Mint
60mm, pair cased, silver c. 1800, hand painted battle scene on dial	$450	$550	$675
60mm, ¼ repeater, pair cased, push repeat, pierced cock, 18K, repousse case	1,850	2,250	2,850
56mm, by Robert Roskell, pair cased, 18K, full plate, dust cover, rack & lever escapement	800	1,100	1,400
55mm, min. repeater, by John Barwise, jeweled thru hammers, duplex escapement, heavy 18K case	4,000	4,500	5,200
55mm, reversible case, KW, KS, cylinder escapement, 18K	1,000	1,200	1,600
55mm, fusee, lever escapement, KW, KS, by W. Chance & Sons, 18K pair cased, repousse case	950	1,150	1,600
54mm, min. repeater, by H. C. Boddington, 18K, ¾ plate	2,500	2,900	3,400
54mm, min. repeater, 18K, HC, by H. C. Boddington, c. 1877	2,500	2,900	3,400

John Creed, 50mm, Edinburgh, c. 1820.

English watch, 55mm, with repousse case.

Size and Description	Avg	Ex-Fn	Mint
52mm, full plate, 14K, HC, by Johnson	$400	$475	$650
52mm, by Arnold & Dent, chronometer, fusee, KW, KS, OF, silver	1,250	1,500	1,850
52mm, demi-hunter, by Robert Roskell, resilient lever, silver case	750	800	1,000
52mm, gold & enamel + pearls, by John Page, c. 1800, cylinder	2,500	2,900	3,400
51mm, by Dent, OF, lever movement, 18K	500	600	750
50mm, c. 1872, WI, with resilient banking, KW, KS, 18K, HC	1,250	1,400	1,650
50mm, min. repeater, chronograph, by Dent, c. 1885, mvt. by Nicole Nielsen	3,800	4,300	5,000

MISC. ENGLISH (continued)

Cooper, 48mm, bar detached lever movement, key wind & set, parachute system at end stone, 18k open face, serial number 6631.

Wm. Hopetown, 48mm, chain driven fusee, verge escapement, dust cover, c. 1842, made in London, pair case, serial number 3865.

MISC. ENGLISH (continued)

Size and Description	Avg	Ex-Fn	Mint
50mm, by William Jones, pierced cock, chain driven fusee, c. 1842, pair cased	$100	$125	$200
50mm, ¼ repeater, silver & enamel, by Weill & Harburg, c. 1886	650	750	900
50mm, gold & enamel + pearls, by John Page, c. 1800, cylinder	2,000	2,400	2,800
50mm, gold & gems, set in OF watch, by James McCabe, c. 1820, cylinder, pierced cock, DES, gold dial, 18K, diamond on back	2,800	3,200	3,700
50mm, by Robert Gellatly, of Edinburgh, 18K, OF, free sprung, c. 1870	800	1,000	1,200
50mm, ¼ repeater, 18K, OF, by John Barwise, c. 1830, ¾ plate	1,200	1,400	1,800
50mm, 11J, lever escapement, fusee, gold balance, by Yates, 16K case	500	600	750
50mm, pair cased, by Creed, Edinburgh, AD1820, silver case	125	145	200
48mm, bar movement, by Cooper, KW, KS, 18K, OF, with parachute, gold dial	250	325	450
48mm, pair case, verge, fusee, pierced cock, silver	100	150	200
48mm, by M. I. Tobias & Co., Liverpool, lever, fusee, KW, KS, 18K, OF, multi-color gold dial	550	675	850
48mm, by William Hopetown, London, silver pair case, chain driven, fusee, verge escapement	125	150	200
48mm, 18K, OF, c. 1896, ¾ plate, GJS	400	475	575
46mm, KW, KS, c. 1865, by McPherson, lever gilt mvt., silver case	55	75	95
46mm, KW, KS, fusee, dust cover, pinned plates	55	75	95

Size and Description	Avg	Ex-Fn	Mint
46mm, KW, KS, fusee, dust cover, Scotland.............	$65	$85	$110
45mm, KW, KS, c. 1865, dust cover, lever, gilt	45	55	65
45mm, KW, KS, c. 1880, fusee, dust cover, HC	65	75	85
44mm, KW, KS, silver case, lever movement	45	55	65
44mm, fusee, lever, KW, KS, 18K, OF	400	475	575
44mm, repousse, 18K, by Williamson, pierced cock, enamel dial..	1,250	1,600	2,200
23mm, small triple case, 18K & enamel, for Turkish market, by Edward Prior, c. 1815, pierced cock, translucent pink enamel	6,000	7,500	8,500

MISC. FRENCH

Size and Description	Avg	Ex-Fn	Mint
55mm, 2 figure automaton, min. repeater, 18K, HC......	$3,800	$4,200	$5,250
55mm, 3 figure automaton, ¼ repeater, 18K, c. 1830.....	3,800	4,200	5,500
54mm, 2 figure automaton, ¼ repeater, 18K	2,200	2,600	3,250
50mm, 1 figure automaton, ¼ repeater, silver	1,500	1,700	2,000

Father & Baby Time, automated minute repeater, 54mm, note animated bell striking by father and baby time, 18k hunting case.

French made movement, 50mm, chain driven fusee, verge escapement, note hand pierced two-footed cock attached on both sides.

Size and Description	Avg	Ex-Fn	Mint
50mm, ¼ repeater, repeat on bell, c. 1780, 18K	$1,250	$1,500	$1,800
50mm, ¼ repeater, by L'Epine, parachute, cylinder escape, gold & enamel, champleve.......................	1,650	1,950	2,400
47mm, by La Cloche, ultra thin, 18K, OF, gilt movement .	350	450	575
45mm, gold champleve enamel, by LeRoy, c. 1840, cylinder escapement	1,400	1,600	1,800
44mm, signed Breguet (by Audemars), 18K, OF, digital, 19J, c. 1925	2,800	3,200	3,800

MISC. FRENCH (continued)

Size and Description	Avg	Ex-Fn	Mint
44mm, by Robin, gold enamel portrait, parachute suspension, KW, KS	$3,000	$3,500	$4,000
42mm, musical and ¼ repeater, KW, OF	1,800	2,200	2,800
41mm, ¼ repeater, c.1820, cylinder escapement, KW,KS			

LeRoy & Co., 50mm, 49 jewels, minute repeater, jump center sweep, two train, exposed winding wheels, 18k hunting case.

French watch, 42mm, musical, plays music on the hour or on demand.

Size and Description	Avg	Ex-Fn	Mint
silver	$400	$550	$750
38mm, gold & champleve enamel, by A. Verdiere, c. 1830, cylinder	1,000	1,200	1,500
36mm, ¼ repeater, ladies, by LeRoy et Fils, HC	1,600	1,800	2,400
32mm, gold enamel, "acorn form," by Ch. Oudin, Palais Royal, c. 1880, cylinder	2,200	2,800	3,500
32mm, ¼ repeater, 18K, lever mvt., slide to repeat, KW	1,000	1,200	1,400
29mm, gold & enamel with pearls, by Bovet Flevrier, c. 1810, duplex movement	1,800	2,000	2,450

James Picard, 55mm, split second chronograph, 18k hunting case, jeweled through hammers, serial number 2,697.

Swiss minute repeater, 54mm, jeweled through hammers, 18k case.

475

MISC. SWISS

Size and Description	Avg	Ex-Fn	Mint
62mm, min. repeater, calendar & moon phases, split sec., chronograph, 30 min. register, GJS, 18K, HC	$4,700	$5,500	$6,500
60mm, heavy 14K HC, spring detent, by Ulysse Breting, c. 1880, nickel mvt., gold train & escape wheel	1,400	1,700	2,200
56mm, ¼ repeater, chronograph, by R. Picard, 18K, HC .	1,400	1,650	2,000
55mm, min. repeater, by Paul Henri Mathey, 18K, heavy HC, gold train	2,450	2,850	3,450
55mm, detent, chronometer, by Emile Perret, KW, KS, 18K, HC, nickel mvt..................................	900	1,200	1,500
55mm, split sec. chronograph, by James Picard, fully jeweled, 18K, HC, min. repeater	2,600	2,850	3,450
54mm, min. repeater, moon phases, day-date-month, 18K, HC	3,000	3,500	4,200
54mm, min. repeater, jeweled thru hammers, 18K, HC ...	2,200	2,500	3,000
54mm, by Piguet & Meylan, ¼ musical repeater, c. 1815, 18K..	3,500	4,000	4,750

Record Watch Co. Sector style watch, dial and movement, hour and minute hand moves to the right, then returns to home.

Size and Description	Avg	Ex-Fn	Mint
54mm, min. repeater, 18K, HC, chronograph with calendar and moon phases................................	$3,000	$3,600	$4,250
54mm, automated min. repeater, Father & Cherub, 18K, HC	3,800	4,400	5,000
53mm, 35J, min. repeater, 1900, 18K, HC, "Zenith"	2,400	2,800	3,400
52mm, moon phase, triple date, massive 18K OF case, by Henri Grandjean	2,250	2.750	3,400
52mm, captain's watch, KW, KS, OF, 18K, 2 train, independent sec., gold dial	850	1,100	1,500
52mm, Time Zone or Captain's watch, KW, KS, 18K, HC	650	750	950

MISC. SWISS (continued)

Size and Description	Avg	Ex-Fn	Mint
52mm, by L'Epine, c. 1869, cylinder escapement, KW, KS, 18K, OF	$450	$550	$750
52mm, min. repeater, by J. Barth, 14K, HC	1,600	2,000	2,400
52mm, min. repeater, by Ernest Duval, 18K, OF	1,800	2,100	2,500
52mm, musical ¼ repeater, KW, KS	2,300	2,500	2,700
50mm, ¼ repeater, by Leresche & Fils, c. 1900, 18K, OF, slide repeat	1,000	1,200	1,500
50mm, 18K, OF, by Duchene Peyrot & Co., c. 1840, gilt, lever, parachute	450	550	750
50mm, min. repeater, Carillon chime, 18K, HC, top grade	2,800	3,100	3,800
49mm, world time watch, by Gubelin, GF, OF, 48 cities	850	1,000	1,250
49mm, by C. L. Guinand, split sec. chronograph, 18K, OF, 30 min. register	600	700	900
49mm, 18K, pocket chonometer, by Breting, Frers, c. 1840, spring detent, 15J	1,200	1,400	1,600
49mm, OF, c. 1820-30, by common maker, pierced cock, etc., silver case	85	125	175
45mm, 15J, OF, HCI4P	55	60	75
45mm, 21J, LS, SW, Railway Special, OF	85	95	110
44mm, Waltham Swiss mvt., 17J, "Incabloc"	55	65	75
44mm, 7J, SW, gold filled	50	55	60
44mm, multi-color, verge, pierced cock	1,000	1,200	1,400

Swiss, self wind, 36mm, cylinder escapement with wind indicator, gun metal case.

Swiss, early self wind, 40mm, sweep second hand.

Size and Description	Avg	Ex-Fn	Mint
44mm, ¼ repeater, 28J, by Bernard Reber, multi-color dial, gold train, 14K, HC	$1,350	$1,550	$2,000
43mm, Automaton, blacksmith with hammered gun metal, pen set	400	500	695
42mm, gold & enamel, 18K, HC	650	700	950
42mm, self wind by Von Loehr, wind indicator, silver	700	800	1,050

477

MISC. SWISS (continued)

Size and Description	Avg	Ex-Fn	Mint
42mm, 21J, "Dueber" chronometer, helical hairspring, OF	$800	$1,000	$1,400
41mm, gold champleve enamel, floral design, 18K, c. 1830	800	1,000	1,400
40mm, self wind, by Von Loehr, gun metal	500	650	900
40mm, 15J, moon phase, day, date, month, calendar, gunmetal	165	225	350
40mm, 31J, min. repeater, split sec. chronograph, register.	1,800	2,000	2,500
40mm, gilt metal & enamel, verge	300	400	550
40mm, 18K, gold & enamel + diamonds, HC, KW, KS ..	1,000	1,400	1,800
40mm, 18K, HC, enamel landscape scene on each side, c. 1860..	1,100	1,400	1,800
40mm, ¼ repeater, gold enamel + diamonds, verge, fusee movement	2,600	3,000	3,500
38mm, 15J, ¾ plate, c. 1930, YGF....................	50	70	95
36mm, self wind, cylinder escapement, gun metal case	250	350	450
30mm, 18K, enamel, OF, blue & white champleve enamel, cylinder movement	400	550	650
25mm, gold & enamel watch, matching enamel chain	1,200	1,450	1,750
25mm, gold & enamel watch, with matching chain of enamel	1,200	1,400	1,600
25mm, 18K gold & enamel, ladies, 17J, lever mvt.	700	900	1,200
25mm, 18K, OF, gold & 7 pearls, lapel watch	400	500	650
21mm, min. repeater, by Henri Grand Jean	2,250	2,850	3,450
21mm, 5 min. repeater, by James Freres, c. 1890, 18K, HC slide repeat	1,600	2,000	2,400

Centennial Watch, 55mm, Chronograph, 17 jewels, engraved on movement "Henry O. Stauffer, Ponts-Martel, pat. May 9th, 1882."

OTHER MISC. WATCHES

Size and Description	Avg	Ex-Fn	Mint
56mm, 14K, HC, min. repeater, chronograph, calendar & moon phases....................................	$3,200	$3,600	$4,200

OTHER MISC. WATCHES (continued)

Size and Description	Avg	Ex-Fn	Mint
56mm, 18K, HC, by Union Watch Co., GJS, DES, gold pallet & escape wheel	$750	$850	$950
53mm, 14K, ¼ repeater, chronograph, "Invicta," c. 1900, push button repeat, HC	1,200	1,400	1,750
50mm, ¼ hour repeater, by J. R. Losada, c. 1870, 18K, slide repeat, HC	1,500	1,700	2,000
50mm, scarab form watch, by Goering Watch Co., enamel & diamond	3,200	3,800	4,600

German Dollar Watch, 50mm, no jewels, 3 adjustments, "Gebruder, thiel, Ruhla Germany" engraved on back plate.

Chronometer, 38mm, 44 diamonds on bezel, platinum case.

Size and Description	Avg	Ex-Fn	Mint
50mm, German dollar watch	$30	$40	$55
46mm, musical ¼ hour repeater, KW, KS, 18K	2,400	2,600	2,900
46mm, min. repeater, by J. Ullman & Co., 14K, slide repeat, c. 1900, OF	1,200	1,400	1,800
45mm, min. repeater, 18K HC, case very fancy	1,800	2,500	3,000
45mm, chronometer, 15J, 14K, OF	325	375	450
45mm, lever, bar, Geneve, by Gilbert, 18K	225	275	450
44mm, ¼ repeater, 21J, recased	250	350	450
43mm, 15J, 9K, demi-hunter case	175	200	300
42mm, ¼ repeater, by Denand, 14K, OF	550	650	850
38mm, square-cut corners case, 44 diamonds on bezel, chronometer, platinum	1,200	1,600	2,200

OTHER MISC. WATCHES (continued)

Time Zone or Captain's Watch, 58mm, key wind & set, note separate registers for two time zones, 18k hunting case.

Swiss Quarter Repeater, 50mm, cylinder escapement, note parachute shock for end stone on balance bridge.

SPECIALIZED & TECHNICAL WATCHES

Size and Description	Avg	Ex-Fn	Mint
65mm, world time, double dial in multi-color, 14K, OF...	$2,200	$2,800	$3,500
58mm, 2 train, captain's watch, Courvoisier & Co., c. 1860	1,600	1,800	2,400
58mm, min. repeater, perpetual calendar, moon phases, date, date, month, chronograph, 18K, HC	12,500	14,500	17,000
55mm, 52 min. karussel, c. 1920, ¾ plat., signed T. A. Pimblett, 18K, OF................................	3,400	3,800	4,600
55mm, 40J, grand sonnerie clockwatch, carillion strike, 2 train, min. repeater, 18K, HC	6,800	7,500	9,000

12,000

Perpetual Calendar Watch, Swiss, day-date-month-moon phases, gold hands, gun metal case.

Eight Day Watch, Swiss, with exposed escapement, gun metal case.

SPECIALIZED & TECHNICAL WATCHES (continued)

Size and Description	Avg	Ex-Fn	Mint
55mm, grand & petite sonnerie clockwatch, min. repeater, 2 train, jeweled thru hammers, exposed tandem winding wheels, signed Marcks & Co., 18K, HC	$8,500	$9,500	$12,000
54mm, one min. tourbillion, ¾ plate, signed Frodsham, 18K, OF	$22,000	$26,000	$32,000
54mm, musical ¼ repeater, Piguet & Meylan, c. 1815, 18K	3,600	4,000	4,600
54mm, musical watch, with pinned cylinder, c. 1800, 18K	4,000	4,650	5,200
53mm, virgule escapement, by Lepine (inventor), c.1780, 18K	1,000	1,200	1,600
53mm, 2 train, clockwatch, hour repeater, signed Bourguin Le Jeune, c. 1800, 18K, OF	1,200	1,600	2,200
52mm, duplex with trapelozoidal weights, c. 1830, KW, KS, deck box, silver case	1,100	1,400	1,750
52mm, deck watch, resilient lever, free sprung, c. 1880	800	1,000	1,250
51mm, 15J, helical mainspring, by Isaac Gasset & Co., Geneva, 1910	1,000	1,500	2,200
50mm, detent escapement, helical hairspring, 17J, gilt mvt., 14K, HC	800	1,000	1,250
50mm, ruby duplex, min. repeater, signed J. R. Lund, 18K OF, 4 color of gold	4,000	4,500	5,500
50mm, ¼ repeater, cylinder escapement, parachute shock, c. 1800, 18K, OF	750	850	1,100
50mm, 49J, min. repeater, 2 train, tandem wind, jump center seconds, by Le Roy, 18K, HC	4,800	5,500	6,500
50mm, carillon chimes, triple repeat gongs, ¼ repeater, chronograph, 14K, HC	1,500	1,800	2,400
48mm, gold digital repeater, parachute shock, c. 1820	1,600	1,800	2,250
45mm, detent escapement, gold escape wheel, GF case, OF	225	275	350
45mm, chronometer escapement, wind indicator, by A. P. Walsh, 18K, OF	3,200	3,800	4,500

Visible Tourbillon, 53mm, 13 jewels, tourbillon system is visible from dial side, ca. 1920.

Helical Mainspring, 51mm, 15 jewels, unusual winding system, cylindrical spring replaces standard mainspring.

SPECIALIZED & TECHNICAL WATCHES (continued)

Size and Description	Avg	Ex-Fn	Mint
44mm, reverse fusee, helical hairspring, detent escapement, by J. Penlinston..................................	$1,800	$2,100	$2,400
44mm, circuit breaker, made by Nardin.................	350	400	495
41mm, 2 train, min. repeater, 18K (Wittnauer)...........	2,800	3,200	3,850

Early **French** watch movement with hour and minute hand, striking bell each hour, fluted case & gilt brass movement, catgut fusee, c. 1600s.

EARLY WATCHES

Size and Description	Avg	Ex-Fn	Mint
172mm, 4 train, coach watch, grand sonnerie, alarm, repeat, repousse case, c. 1700	$12,000	$14,000	$18,000
103mm, 3 train, coach watch, with alarm, by Higgs Evans, c. 1790..	3,500	4,000	4,800
60mm, pair case, by Richard Vick, champleve dial, c. 1700	1,200	1,300	1,500
50mm, pair case, verge fusee, by Clayton, silver, c. 1730..	250	300	425
50mm, rack & lever, fusee, by Ganthony of London, KW, KS	200	250	350
50mm pair case, verge fusee, pierced cock, by J. A. Freeman, c. 1790, silver....................................	125	165	200
50mm, ¼ repeater, pair case, silver repousse scene	800	1,000	1,200
50mm, detached lever, fusee, DES, compensating balance by Marshall, 18K	750	850	1,000
48mm, pair case, repousse, by Robert Allan, c. 1760, 20K	1,500	1,800	2,500
47mm, pair case, verge, pierced cock, Benjamin Lamb, silver	$400	$485	$600
46mm, pair case, verge fusee, by Hallifax, c. 1785, 18K, repousse..	1,200	1,600	2,200
45mm, repousse, fancy matchine chatelaine, pierced cock, by Grantham, c. 1750, 18K..........................	2,500	3,500	4,600
45mm, multi-color enamel case watch, by Berthoud, c. 1780, 18K...	1,800	2,400	2,950
45mm, multi-color gold, verge, KW, KS, by Louis Roch ..	1,800	2,200	2,600
43mm, pair cased, chatelaine, tortoise shell pique, by Cornelius Horbert, London, c. 1695, silver	1,600	2,400	3,400

Chinese Duplex, 59mm, made for Chinese market with Chinese symbols, key wind & set.

Mysterieuse on watch, 51mm, note hands are set with finger, silver case.

Size and Description	Avg	Ex-Fn	Mint
41mm, multi-color gold case, verge, pierced cock, by Romilly, KW, KS	$700	$1,000	$1,400
40mm, 3 colors gold, portrait of lady, diamonds, c. 1760 .	1,800	2,000	2,400
40mm, 3 colors gold & diamonds, ¼ repeater, by Mallet .	2,500	2,800	3,500
40mm, pearls & enamel on gold, verge, pierced cock	2,800	3,000	3,200
39mm, pair cased, Freres Esquivillons, porcelain back	1,400	1,500	1,600
39mm, pair cased, adjustable hour dial, for Japanese market, silver	2,600	3,200	4,200

Miniature skull form watch, 30-32mm, cylinder escapement, chain driven fusee, skeletonized movement, silver skull case, popular in the mid-nineteenth century.

NOVELTY WATCHES

Size and Description	Avg	Ex-Fn	Mint
67mm, barometer watch, silver case	$400	$500	$650
60mm, bar movement, day, date, month, moon phase, gun metal, pin set	95	150	225

Rare wooden works by Bronnikoff of Russia, 60-50mm, wooden wheels, balance bridge and movement, no jewels, cylinder type escapement, c. 1890.

Masonic, triangle shaped watch, by Pempor W. Co., 15 jewels, adj.3P.

Size and Description	Avg	Ex-Fn	Mint
50-60mm, wooden works, no jewels	$600	$800	$1,000
59mm, Chinese duplex, for Chinese market, silver case ...	175	225	295
55mm, 17J, "Commemorative 1776," chronograph dial, American, 14K HC	1,600	1,800	2,250
52mm, 8 day watch, balance seen from dial, GF OF	95	125	185
51mm, "Mysterieuse," mystery watch, crescent mvt.	900	1,100	1,450
51mm, "Mysterieuse," mystery watch, min. repeater, crescent mvt., silver	3,500	4,000	4,500
51mm, repeater, slide repeat, gun metal	250	300	400
50mm, digital jump hour & min., silver	150	225	300
50mm, 15J, visible tourbillon style escapement, c. 1915, gun metal	1,050	1,200	1,600
49x34mm, sector watch (fan shaped), fly back hour & min., by Record W. Co., GF	1,000	1,100	1,350
46mm, gambling devices (roulette, horse racing, & dice)...	85	120	175
46mm, blinking eye, silver case	250	300	375
46mm, blinking eye, gun metal case	175	225	275
45mm, double time watch, single train, OF, silver	250	300	425
44mm, skeletonized, open numbers, open back plates, 18K	550	650	850
42mm, plates in form of bird, 22J, KW, KS, silver	95	110	150
40mm, "Shell" watch, 7-17J, skeletonized, (Girard-Perregaux)..	100	125	175
40mm, grasshopper alarm, (cricket sound), silver case	700	900	1,100
40mm, digital watch, engraved dial, silver, c. 1900	225	300	395
40mm, compass watch, KW, KS, silver case	125	175	225

NOVELTY WATCHES (continued)

Blinking Eyes, 46mm, pin set, animated eyes.

Lock Form Watch, cylinder escapement, 18k case.

Size and Description	Avg	Ex-Fn	Mint
30mm, ball form watch, silver & enamel, c. 1870	$200	$300	$450
25mm, ball form watch, rim wind & set, small diamonds, 18K...	750	850	1,200
25mm, skull form watch, miniature, cylinder escapement, silver	800	875	950
20mm, ball form watch, Juvenia W. Co., silver & enamel, c. 1900..	175	195	275
Lock form watch, cylinder escapement, 18K & enamel	1,500	1,800	2,250
Masonic, triangular shape, by Tempor W. Co., 15J, Adj.3P, Swiss...................................	200	300	400

Ball Lapel Watch, rim wind & set, 18k with diamonds & sapphires.

Shell, 40mm, made for Shell Oil Co. as advertising premium.

NOTE: Watches listed in this book are priced at the retail level, as complete watches having an original 14k gold-filled case, an original white enamel single sunk dial, and with the entire original movement in good working order with no repairs needed, unless otherwise noted.

AMERICAN & EUROPEAN
WRIST WATCHES

ROMANCING THE WRIST WATCH

The wrist watch is considered by many watch collectors to be "today's collectable." This phenomenon is due, in part, to the development of the quartz movement which began about 20 years ago and virtually revolutionized the watch market. Although these quartz watches are quiet, accurate timekeepers, and are inexpensive to manufacture, the watches of the past hold a special fascination in the heart of the collector. They enjoy collecting the timepieces with jeweled and moving parts that produce a rhythmic heartbeat inside their gold cases.

The watch collector has seen the prices of wrist watches soar in the past 10 years, as wrist watches have become more and more in demand as an object of fashion, function and jewelry. Prices have climbed highest in just the last two or three years. This year a Patek, Philippe man's platinum minute repeater wrist watch sold for the record price of 345,000 Swiss francs, about $250,000 U.S. dollars. Not far behind this record-setting sale was a Patek, Philippe "Calatrava" that brought $198,000. A Patek, Philippe enameled white gold "World Time" man's wrist watch sold for about $130,000. Some collectors have seen the values of their wrist watches double and, in many cases, triple in recent years. For example, in the early 1980s, a Patek, Phillipe perpetual calendar chronograph watch would have sold for $10,000. In 1987, the same watch would have sold for $50,000, and in 1988 for $80,000. In 1989, the price could conceivably be $100,000. Such dramatic increases in values have brought about a feverish demand for wrist watches. The Swiss wrist watch has the attention of the wealthiest collectors, with Patek, Philippe & Co. at the top of their list and Audemars Piguet, Cartier, Rolex, and Vacheron & Constantin close behind. Other wrist watches showing appreciable value are Ebel, A. Lange, Gubelin, International Watch Co., Le Coultre, Ulysse Nardin, and Piaget. Next are Jules Jurgensen, Baume & Mercier, Gerard Perregaux, Movado, and Omega; then Benrus, Bulova, Agassiz, Elgin, Gruen, Hamilton, Illinois, Longines, and Waltham, the character watches, chronographs, and complicated watches.

Many wrist watch collectors have focused on fashion and take pride in wearing their unique watches. Women have been buying high fashion men's watches to wear, making women candidates for collecting. Young men appear to enjoy collecting wrist watches rather than pocket watches. The intense competition within their increasing numbers has influenced the rising prices. European and Japanese collectors are making the biggest impact on the wrist watch market with their volume of buying, as well as the higher prices being paid. The American collector has been inspired by the heated market which has been, in part, fueled by the weakened U.S. dollar. The general appearance of a wrist watch seems to be the main factor in the price of the watch, but high mechanical standards, along with the various functions of the watch, also determine the price. Some of these features include repeaters, chronographs, duo-dials, bubble backs, curvex, flip-up tops, reverso, day-date-month moon phase, jump hour, diamond dial, world time, sector, skeletonized, character, first versions as early autowinds, very early electronics, unusual shapes, and enamel bezels.

Ebel Watch Co., chronograph with day-date-month & moon phases, outside chapter shows tachymetre, 18k gold.

Today's watches are a "mixed bag," ranging from gold luxury watches priced at $10,000, and mid-priced watches at $1,000, to the low-end plastic quartz watches at $30, and all keep time equally well. The gold watch is still a status symbol today; a mark of affluence and of appreciation for the finer things in life. The Swiss control about 85 percent of the luxury watch market, while the Japanese have about the same percentage of the market for more moderately-priced watches. The predominant companies producing the "top of the line" watches are Patek, Phillipe & Co., Cartier, Gubelin, Audemars Piguet, Piaget, Vacheron Constantin. Just below in price, but higher in volume, are names like Rolex, International Watch Co., Girard Perregaux, and Le Coultre. Collectors are also wearing high grade new watches by Ebel, Blancpain, Gerald Genta, Hublot, Raymond Weil, and watches produced for and bearing the names of Chanel, Christian Dior, and Dunhill. Prices of Ebel watches start at about $1,000 and go upward to $24,000. This company also manufactures watches for Cartier. Patek, Philippe watches range in price from $3,000 to $100,000. Audemars

Piguet produces a tourbillon wrist watch that retails for about $28,000. Blancpain, owned by Omega, produces only about 100 ultra-thin hand-made watches per year. Rolex is the most recognizable name in today's luxury wrist watch market. The Rolex 18k gold President with fluted bezel, champagne cabochon dial, and 18k gold bracelet, sells for $9,400, while the same watch with diamond bezel and dial sells for $14,400. Rolex makes the Oyster Quartz day-date, 18k gold, pave diamond dial with sapphire, bezel case, and bracelet set with 107 diamonds totaling 8.06 carats, which bears a price tag of $100,000.

The Warhol collection, which included about 200 watches, was sold on April 27, 1988 at Sotheby's for a reported price of $461,000. The artist collected watches of various styles and types. A set of three vinyl quartz character watches brought the price of $2,400. A stainless steel Gene Autry watch listed and pre-determined to bring about $100 sold for $1,700. The so-called "heavy weight" wrist watches such as Patek Philippe, Cartier, Rolex, and Vacheron Constantin sold for two to three times the estimated prices.

The trend or vogue for older watches has motivated some watch companies to reproduce favorite watches from their past models. Companies have searched their archives to find older models that sold well, and are now marketing replicas of those watches. Hamilton Classics—Authentic Reproductions From America's Past—include the Ventura (1957), Wilshire City (1939), Cabot (1935), and Ardmore (1934). Jaeger-LeCoultre's Reverso has been reintroduced, as well as Longines' hour angle watch developed and worn by Charles Lindbergh. Also, the Lorus Company has marketed a close look-a-like to the Mickey Mouse wrist watch first sold by Ingersoll in the early 1930s.

The romancing of the wrist watch is moving at a steady upward pace. Price adjustments may be needed, but should hold for a few more years. The quality American movements may still be undervalued, and the novelty or comic character wrist watches may still be a good value for the investor.

Ebel Watch Co., time only, waterproof, self winding, date, white enamel dial, bracelet and case made of stainless steel and 18k gold.

A SHORT HISTORY OF WRIST WATCHES

In the late 1700s, Queen Elizabeth adorned her wrist with a watch heavily decorated with jewels and gold. While no one is sure who invented the wrist watch Queen Elizabeth was wearing, or even the first wrist watch ever, as few appeared around 1790. Small miniature watches had been made earlier than this, however. David Rosseau made a watch which was about 18mm in diameter (the size of a dime) in the late 1600s.

Miniaturized wrist watch by Waltham. Model number 400. Note size comparison to dime.

Miniaturization was a great challenge to many of the famous watchmakers including Louis Jaquet, Paul Ditisheim, John Arnold and Henri Capt. The smallest watch in semi-mass production was 12mm by 5mm. In early 1930, the American Waltham Watch Co. made a 9mm by 20mm Model 400 watch.

Wrist watches were at first thought to be too small and delicate to be practical for men to wear. However, during World War I a German officer was said to have strapped a small pocket watch to his wrist with a leather webbed cup. This arrangement freed both hands and proved to be most useful. After the war, the wrist watch gained in popularity. Mass production of wrist watches was started around 1880 by the Swiss industry. The Swiss introduced them to the United States around 1895, but they did not prove to be very popular at first. Around 1907 the Elgin and Illinois watch companies were manufacturing wrist watches and by 1912 Hampden and Waltham had started. By 1920 the

Breguet self-winding pocket watch, c.1785.

Rotor for self winding wrist watch.

Harwood self-winding wrist watch, c. 1928.

round styles were being replaced with square, rectangular and tonneau shapes and decorated with gems. By 1928 wrist watches were outselling pocket watches, and, by 1935, over 85 percent of the watches being produced were wrist watches.

Self-wind pocket watches were first developed by Abraham Louis Perrelet in 1770 and by Abraham Louis Breguet about 1777. Louis Recordon made improvements in 1780, but is was not until 1923 that the principle of self-winding was adapted to the wrist watch by John Harwood, an Englishman who set up factories to make his patented self-wind wrist watches in Switzerland, London, France, and the United States. His watches first reached the market about 1929. The firm A. Schild manufactured about 15,000 watches in Switzerland. Mr. Harwood's watch company removed the traditional stem or crown to wind the mainspring, but in order to set the hands it was necessary to turn the bezel. The Harwood Watch Co. failed around 1931 and the patent expired.

Early in 1930 the Rolex Watch Co. introduced the Rolex Oyster Perpetual, the first waterproof and self-winding wrist watch. By 1940 wrist watches came in all shapes and types including complicated chronographs, calendars, and repeaters; also novelties, digital jump hour and multi-dial were very popular.

A dramatic change occurred in 1957 when the Hamilton Watch Co. eliminated the mainspring and replaced it with a small battery that lasted well over one year. In 1960 the balance wheel was removed in the Accutron by Bulova and replaced by a tuning fork with miniature pawls.

1. Case number. 2. Movement serial number. 3. Caliber number. 4. Caliber number.

Some wrist watches have a grade or caliber number engraved on the movement. For example, Patek, Phillipe & Co. has a caliber number 27-460Q. The '27' stands for 27mm; the '460Q' is the grade; the 'Q' designates Quantieme (Perpetual calendar and moon phases).

AUTOMATIC WINDING

The self-winding watch uses the movements of the body in order to wind up the mainspring slowly and nearly continuously. The first pocket self-winding watches were executed by a watchmaker from Le Locle, Abraham-Louis Perrelet, around 1770. They

Early self wind pocket watch by Breguet.

Eterna-Matic Automatic Winding Mechanism. 1—Oscillating weight. 2—Oscillating gear. 3—Upper wheel of auxiliary pawl-wheel. 4—Lower wheel of auxiliary pawl-wheel. 5—Pawl-wheel with pinion. 6—Lower wheel of pawl-wheel with pinion. 7—Transmission-wheel with pinion. 8—Crown-wheel yoke. 9—Winding pinion. 10—Crown-wheel. 11—Ratchet-wheel. 12—Barrel. 13¢Driving runner for ratchet-wheel. 14—Winding stem. 15-Winding button.

were improved soon after by Abraham-Louis Breguet. In the case of the pocket watch, the movements causing the winding of the watch were essentially the result of walking. This system of winding was never widely adopted. The watch was a fancy model and not a really useful one. Herman von der Heydt was the only maker in America to work with the self-winding pocket watch. However, inventors always kept the idea of the self-winding watch in mind.

In 1923, the British firm Harwood took up once again the solution of the problem of automatic winding, for wrist watches. This was the spark which rapidly resulted in research to improve and simplify this type of mechanism. A company was formed in London to manufacture Harwood's watch, and before long over 500 jewelers in the United Kingdom were selling his automatic watch. A second company was formed in France, and a third in the United States. The business flourished about two and one-half years. Then, in 1931, these companies were liquidated.

Illustration of Self Winding mechanism used by Harwood.

This 1931 wrist watch made by Perpetual Self-Winding Watch Co. of America originally sold for $29.75.

HOW TO READ THE TACHY-TELEMETER DIAL

Tachometer

The spiral scale around center of dial indicates miles per hour, based on a trial over one mile. It indicates speeds from 400 to 20 miles per hour on three turns. Each turn of spiral corresponds to one minute (scale for first 8 seconds being omitted), the outer turn from 400 to 60 (0 to 1 minute) and the center turn from 30 to 20 miles per hour (2 to 3 minutes).

When passing the first marker of mile zone, start chronograph hand by pressing push piece. When passing following mile marker, press push piece again. The chronograph hand now indicates the speed in miles per hour on the spiral. If a mile has been made in less than one minute the speed will be indicated on outside turn of spiral; from 1 to 2 minutes on middle turn and 2 to 3 minutes on center turn.

EXAMPLE: If a mile has been made in 1 minute and 15 seconds the chronograph hand indicates 48 miles per hour on middle turn of spiral.

Telemeter

The Telemeter scale around margin of dial is based on the speed of sound compared with the speed of light. Each small division is 100 meters. The scale is read in kilometers and hundreds of meters. Approximately 16 divisions equal 1 mile.

TO DETERMINE THE DISTANCE OF A STORM: When you see the flash of lightning press push piece of chronograph. When hearing thunder press again, the chronograph hand will indicate on the Telemeter scale the distance in kilometers and hundreds of meters. One kilometer equals 5/8 of a mile.

Dial No. 1 is a simple stop watch dial. Graduated into fifths of seconds.

Dial No. 2 is used to time a car over a quarter-mile track and read the numbers of miles per hour directly from dial.

Dial No. 3 is used to measure speed in kilometers per hour over a course of one fifth of a kilometer.

Dial No. 4 used by physicians to count the pulse beats of a patient.

Dial No. 5 is used by artillery officers for determining distance by means of sound in kilometers.

Dial No. 6 shows a tachometer: many watches are made with several scales on the same dial in order to cover a greater range of functions. The figures are sometimes grouped in a spiral form or in several circles, thus the hand may make more than one complete revolution.

CHRONOGRAPH

The term chronograph is derived from the Greek words *chronos* which means "time" and *grapho* which means "to write." The first recording of intervals of time was around 1822 by the inventor Rieussec. His chronograph made dots of ink on a dial as a measure of time. Around 1862 Adolph Nicole introduced the first chronograph with a hand that returned to zero. The split second chronograph made its appearance around 1879. Today a chronograph can be described as a timepiece that starts at will, stops at will, and can return to zero at will. A mechanical chronograph had a sweep or center second hand that will start, stop, and fly back to zero. The term chronometer should not be confused with chronograph. A chronometer is a timepiece that has superior timekeeping qualities at the time it is made.

A. Day window. **B.** Split second hand. **C.** Calendar pusher. **D.** Register for seconds. **E.** Calendar pusher. **F.** Date hand. **G.** Register for total hours. **H.** Sweep center second hand. **I.** Month window. **J.** Start/stop pusher. **K.** Register for total minutes. **L.** Return pusher. **M.** Day of month.

Caliber number

Coded number

Coded symbol

Company name

MERCEDES

TRYLON

BATON (RECTILINE)

BATON

MOON

REGATE

POINTEX

LEAF

HOUR and MINUTE HANDS

ALPHA

DAUPHINE

DAUPHINE PITCHED

DIAMOND

FILS

RADIUM

INDEX

MODERN

FUSEAUX

LANCE

RADIUM DAUPHINE

SECOND HANDS

ALPHA

DAUPHINE

INDEX

MODERN

FILS

(REGULAR)

WRIST WATCH CASE AND DIAL STYLES

Barrel

Maxine

Square

Round

Square Cut Corner

Cushion

Rectangle

Flared

Tank

Curved or Curvex

Round
(Ladies style; converts to lapel or wrist)

Rectangle
Cut Corner

Tonneau

Baguette

Oval

SWISS CODE INITIALS

Some Swiss watches have three initials on the balance bridge. These initials are **not** model identification but are for house identification. Following is a list of import initials with the name of the Swiss company maker.

AOC—Roamer
AOL—Adolph Schwarcz &
    Son
AOX—Alstate W. Co.
AXA—Wittnauer
AXZ—Benrus
BOL—Bernard S. Lipman
BXC—Avia
BXJ—Midland
BXN—Benrus
BXP—Imperial, Bayer,
    Pretzfelder & Mills
BXW—Bulova
COC—Crawford
COW—Croton
CXC—Concord
CXD—Cypres
CXH—Clinton
CXV—Cort
CXW—Central; Benrus
DOB—Dreffa W. Co.
DOW—Deauville
EOE—Elrex
EON—Avalon
EOP—Harvel
EOT—Lavina
EXC—Everbrite
FXE—Provis
FXU—Louis Aisenstein &
    Bros.
FXW—Louis
GXC—Gruen
GXI—Gotham (Ollendorff)
GXM—Girard-Perregaux
GXR—Grant
GXW—Gothic
HOM—Homis
HON—Tissot; A. Hirsch

HOR—Lanco; Langendorf
HOU—Oris
HOX—Patek, Philippe
HXF—Harman
HXM—R. H. Macy & Co.
HXN—Harvel
HXO—Harold K. Oleet
HXW—Helbros
JXE—Normandie
JXJ—Jules Jurgensen
KOT—Landau
KXJ—Wm. J. Kappel
KXV—Louis
KXZ—Kelton; Benrus, Central
LOA—Emil Langer
LOD—Latham
LOE—Packard
LXA—Laco, Winton, Elbon
LXE—Evkob
LXJ—LeCoultre
LXW—Longines
MOG—Mead & Co.;
    Boulevard
MOU—Tower; Delbana
MXE—Monarch
MXH—Seeland
MXI—Movado
MXT—Mathey-Tissot
NOS—Heritage
NOU—Louvic
NXJ—National Jewelers Co.
NXO—Oris
OXG—Omega
OXL—Wyler
OYT—Shriro (Sandoz)
POY—Camy; Copley
PXA—Pierce
PXP—Patek, Philippe

PXT—Paul Breguette
PXW—Parker
PYS—Langel
QXO—Kelbert
ROC—Raleigh
ROL—Ribaux
ROP—Rodania
ROW—Rolex
RXG—R. Gsell & Co.
RXM—Galmor
RXW—Rima
RXY—Liengme
RYW—Ritex
SOA—Felca
SOE—Semca
SOW—Seeland
SOX—Cortebert, Orvin
SXE—Savoy; Banner
SXK—S. Kocher & Co.
SXS—Franco
UOA—Actua
UOB—Aero
UOW—Universal
UXM—Medana
UXN—Marsh
UYW—Stanley W. Co.
VOS—Sheffield
VXN—LeCoultre
VXT—Kingston
WOA—Tower
WOB—Wyler
WOR—Creston
WXC—Buren
WXE—Welsbro
WXW—Westfield
ZOV—Titus
ZYV—Hampden (new
    company)

Coded number

Coded
symbol

WRIST WATCH LISTINGS
Pricing at Retail Level
(Complete Watches Only)

Unless otherwise noted, wrist watches listed in this section are priced at the retail level and as complete watches having an original 14k gold-filled case with an original dial, and the entire original movement in good working order with no repairs needed. They are also priced as having a watch band made of leather except where bracelet is described. Watches listed as 14k and 18k are solid gold cases. Coin or silveroid-type and stainless steel cases will be listed as such. Dollar-type watches, or low cost production watches, are listed as having a base metal type case and a composition dial.

Many of the watch manufacturers were commissioned to put jewelers' or jobbers' names on their movements in place of their own. Because of this practice, the true manufacturers of these movements are difficult to identify. These watch models are listed under the original manufacturer and can be identified by comparison with the model sections under each manufacturer. See "Personalized Watches" and "Swiss Code Initials" for more detailed information.

The prices shown were averaged from dealers' lists just prior to publication and are an indication of the retail level or what collectors will pay. Prices are provided in three categories: average condition, extra fine, and mint condition, and are shown in whole dollar amounts only. The values listed are a guide for the retail level and are provided for your information only. Dealers will not necessarily pay full retail price. Prices listed are for watches with **original** cases and dials.

Note: Descriptions and serial number ranges listed for early watches cannot be considered 100 percent accurate due to the manner in which records were kept by these companies.

WARNING: There are currently fake wrist watches being sold on the worldwide market. These watches have the appearance of authenticity but are merely cheap imitations of prestigious companies such as Rolex (all types), Gucci, Cartier, and Piaget.

INFORMATION NEEDED—This price guide is interested in any facts and information you might have that should possibly be considered for future editions. Documented facts are needed, so please send photo or sources of information. (When corresponding, please send a self-addressed, stamped envelope.) Send to Cooksey Shugart, 780 Church Street N.E., Cleveland, Tennessee 37311.

ADMIRAL
SWISS

Style or Grade — Description	Avg	Ex-Fn	Mint
Rectangular, 17J, 14K	$65	$75	$100
Round, 17J, automatic, stainless case	5	10	18
Round, 17J, day, date, month, moonphases, GF	35	45	75

Agassiz, round, 17 jewels, World Time   Agassiz, rectangular, 17 jewels, fancy bezel

AGASSIZ
SWISS

Style or Grade — Description	Avg	Ex-Fn	Mint
Oval, 18J, Curvex, 18K	$800	$900	$1,100
Rectangular, 17J, 18K	400	500	600
Rectangular, 17J, 18K, fancy large bezel, 1940s	900	1,000	1,100
Rectangular, 17J, 18K, diamond dial	1,100	1,200	1,800
Round, 17J, World Time, 24 hr. dial, 35 cities, 18K	10,000	12,000	14,000
Ladies, rectangular, platinum case & diamonds	600	700	1,000

AGIR
SWISS

Style or Grade — Description	Avg	Ex-Fn	Mint
Round, 17J, Astronomic, moon phases, triple date, 1950, 18K	$1,000	$1,200	$1,500

AGIR WATCH Co. (continued)

Style or Grade—Description	Avg	Ex-Fn	Mint
Round, 17J, Astronomic, moon phases, triple date, 1950, 14K	$800	$1,000	$1,200
Round, 17J, Astronomic, moon phases, triple date, 1950, stainless steel	200	300	400

Alpina, round, automatic, waterproof

Alpina, square, 15 jewels, sweep second hand

ALPINA
SWISS

Style or Grade — Description	Avg	Ex-Fn	Mint
Rectangular, 15J, duo-dial, by Gruen, stainless	$350	$400	$460
Round, 17J, date, sweep sec., inner sec. track, GF	80	95	110
Round, 16J, date, c. 1955	20	25	35
Round, 16J, auto, stainless, c. 1955	20	25	35
Round, 16J, caliber 582, auto wind	20	25	35
Square, 15J, sweep sec., GF	20	25	35
Tonneau, 15J, 14K, c. 1925	150	200	275

Square, gold-filled, 6/0 size

Tonneau, gold-filled, 6/0 size

Waltham, barrel, 17 jewels, ca. 1920.   Waltham, rectangular, 17 jewels, curved back

AMERICAN WALTHAM W. CO.
U.S.A.
MAN'S WRIST WATCH

Style or Grade — Description	Avg	Ex-Fn	Mint
Barrel, Cromwell, 17J, GF	$50	$60	$75
Barrel, Oberlin, 17J, GF	50	60	75
Curvex, GF, 2+ inches long	300	400	500
Curvex, 14K case	175	200	250
Curvex, gold filled case	75	100	150
Cushion, 14K case	125	150	175
Cushion, gold filled	50	60	75
Cushion, Hilton, 17J, GF	35	40	55
Rectangular, 17J, G#750, stainless	30	40	60
Rectangular, 9J, Premier, stainless	25	35	50
Rectangular, 21J, G#750-B, sub. sec., gold border, 14K	125	175	200
Rectangular, 21J, curved back, 14K	250	300	375
Rectangular, 14K case	100	150	175

Round, military style, with 24 hour dial. Movement on right, 17 jewels, hack setting.

504

Albright, 21 jewels, 14k gold, originally sold for $150.

Allen, 17 jewels, 14k gold filled, originally sold for $80.

Jeffrey, 17 jewels, 14k gold filled, originally sold for $80.

Penton, 17 jewels, 10k gold filled, originally sold for $65.

Grade or Name—Description	Avg	Ex-Fn	Mint
Rectangular, gold filled	$50	$60	$80
Rectangular, Duke, "link style" bracelet, GF	50	60	70
Rectangular, Duxbury, 17J, GF	50	60	75
Rectangular, Fairmont, 17J, GF	75	100	125
Rectangular, Jeffery, 17J, GF	50	60	75
Rectangular, Skipper, "link style" bracelet, GF	35	40	55
Rectangular, Stanhope, 17J, GF	60	75	90
Rectangular, Viking, "link style" bracelet, GF	50	60	70
Rectangular, Winfield, 17J, GF	50	60	75
Rectangular, Wollaston, 17J, GF	75	100	125
Rectangular, York, "link style" bracelet, GF	35	40	55
Round, gold filled case	20	30	40
Round, calendar, 14K case	90	100	150
Round, doctor's, pulsation on outer rim	70	125	150
Round, military style, stainless case	50	60	75
Round, 7J, sweep sec. hand, GF	20	25	35
Round, Albright, 21J, 14K	85	95	125

Sheraton, 21 jewels, 14k gold, originally sold for $152.

Stanhope, 17 jewels, 10k gold filled, originally sold for $60.

Tulane, 21 jewels, 14k gold, originally sold for $125.

Winfield, 17 jewels, 10k gold filled, originally sold for $70.

Model 1900, 0 size

Model 1907, 0 size

Jewel Series

Model 1900, 0/3 size,
open face

Model 1907, 0/3 size,
hunting

Model 1898 & 1912,
0/6 size, hunting

Model 1898 & 1912,
0/6 size, open face

10½ ligne

10 ligne

7½ ligne

5¼ ligne

Model 400

Model 450

Model 650

Model 675

Model 750

Americus, 8 day wrist watch, 17 jewels, c. 1933.

AMERICUS
SWISS

Style or Grade — Description	Avg	Ex-Fn	Mint
Tonneau, 17J, 8 day, c. 1933, 18K case	$400	$600	$800
Tonneau, 17J, 8 day, c. 1933, stainless case	200	300	400

Angelus, round, chronograph, two registers.

ANGELUS
SWISS

Style or Grade — Description	Avg	Ex-Fn	Mint
Round, chronograph, day-date-month, 2 reg., 18K	$450	$500	$600

Angelus, 32mm, 15 jewels, chronograph.

Size and Description	Avg	Ex-Fn	Mint
Round, chronograph, day-date-month, 2 reg., 14K	$350	$400	$475
Round, chronograph, day-date-month, 2 reg., GF	75	100	150
Round, chronograph, day-date-month, 2 reg., stainless ...	60	90	130
Round, chronograph, 2 reg., 18K case	400	500	600

ANGELUS (continued)

Size and Description	Avg	Ex-Fn	Mint
Round, chronograph, 2 reg., 14K case	$300	$350	$400
Round, chronograph, 2 reg., GF	50	60	95
Round, chronograph, 2 reg., stainless..................	40	60	90
Round, 17J, pulsation respiration, chronograph	200	225	250
Round, chronograph, split sec., 2 reg., month window at 12 o'clock, day window at 6 o'clock, c. 1945, 18K ...	2,000	2,500	3,000
Round, 17J, split sec., chronograph, 1950, 18K	6,000	7,000	8,000

Arbu, round, 17 jewels, triple date, moon phase.   Arbu, round, 17 jewels, split-second chronograph.

ARBU
SWISS

Style or Grade — Description	Avg	Ex-Fn	Mint
Round, 17J, chronograph, split sec., c. 1950, 18K	$1,800	$2,000	$2,500
Round, 17J, chronograph, day date month, moon phase, 18K...	650	750	1,000
Round, 17J, chronograph, day date month, moon phase, stainless steel	200	300	400
Round, 17J, day date month, moon phase, 18K..........	400	500	650
Round, 17J, day date month, moon phase, stainless steel .	75	135	200

ARISTON
SWISS

Style or Grade — Description	Avg	Ex-Fn	Mint
Rectangular, 17J, 14K, c. 1930........................	$90	$110	$140
Tonneau, 17J, 14K, c. 1930	90	110	140

Arsa, round, day-date, moon phase

ARSA
SWISS
(Mfg. by James Choffat)

Style or Grade—Description	Avg	Ex-Fn	Mint
Round, 17J, chronograph, 2 reg., 18K	$200	$250	$340
Round, 17J, chronograph, 2 reg., SS	50	65	90
Round, 17J, chronograph, 3 reg., day date month, 18K...	300	350	425
Round, 17J, chronograph, 2 reg., day date month, SS....	85	125	200
Round, 17J, time only $ date, 18K	85	120	160
Round, 17J, time only $ date, SS	35	55	75

Audemars, Piguet, cushion, minute repeater, 29 jewels, repeats on gongs, serial number 10474, ca. 1907.

AUDEMARS, PIGUET
SWISS

MAN'S WRIST WATCH

Style or Grade — Description	Avg	Ex-Fn	Mint
Cushion, 29J, min. repeater, Adj.8P, 1925, platinum	$80,000	$90,000	$100,000
Cushion, 29J, min. repeater, for Gubelin, 18K...........	75,000	80,000	90,000
Dodecagonal, 18J, gold indexes	1,300	1,500	1,800
Dodecagonal, 17J, thin & flat, 18K, 1970s	2,500	3,000	3,500

AUDEMARS, PIGUET (continued)

Audemars, Piguet, round, chronograph, 22 jewels

Audemars, Piguet, round, chronograph, ca. 1945.

Audemars, Piguet, round, day-date, moon phase

Audemars, Piguet, round, 18 jewels, 18k, ca. 1970.

Audemars, Piguet, Dodecagonal, 17 jewels, ca. 1970.

Audemars, Piguet, Dodecagonal, black dial

Size and Description	Avg	Ex-Fn	Mint
Octagonal, 36J, astronomic moonphases, triple date, 1980, 18K band & case..........................	$15,000	$18,000	$22,000
Octagonal, 17J, bezel with small diamonds, 1980s, 18K ...	2,000	2,250	2,550
Rectangular, 18J, 18K case	800	900	1,100
Rectangular, 18J, day-date-month, moonphases, 4 registers, Adj.4P, 18K case and bracelet, c. 1940	40,000	50,000	60,000
Rectangular, 18J, digital jump, hour & min. hand, 14K ...	5,000	6,000	7,000
Rectangular, 18J, diamonds on dial & bezel, white 14K ...	1,800	2,200	2,800

AUDEMARS, PIGUET (continued)

Style or Grade—Description	Avg	Ex-Fn	Mint
Rectangular, 18J, c. 1950s, platinum....................	$3,000	$3,500	$4,000
Rectangular, 18J, Adj.7P, jumping hour, for Gubelin	16,000	18,000	22,000
Rectangular, 17J, 18K, 2-tone case	1,500	2,000	2,500
Rectangular, 17J, platinum	2,000	2,500	3,000
Round, 36J, 18K case, 22K rotor, skeletonized...........	7,000	8,000	9,000
Round, 36J, free sprung, date, 18K band & case	1,000	1,400	1,900
Round, 22J, chronograph & tachymeter, 1940, 18K	10,000	12,000	15,000
Round, 21J, Adj.4P, c. sec., c. 1950s, 18K..............	1,500	1,600	1,800
Round, auto wind, watertight, 18K heavy case...........	1,000	1,200	1,500
Round, 21J, chronograph, 3 reg., 1945, 18K	5,000	5,500	6,000

Audemars, Piguet, round, skeletonized, 18k.

Audemars, Piguet, round, skeletonized, 18k.

Audemars, Piguet, rectangular, 18k, ca. 1940.

Audermars, Piguet, rectangular, platinum, ca. 1950.

Audemars, Piguet, square, 18 jewels, 18k.

Audemars, Piguet, square, curvex, ca. 1940.

AUDEMARS, PIGUET (continued)

Audemars, Piguet, octogonal, triple date, moon ph.

Audemars, Piguet, 18 jewels, 8 positions, ca. 1940.

Audemars, Piguet, round, 21 jewels, 4 pos.

Audemars, Piguet, round, center seconds, ca. 1950.

Audemars, Piguet, round, straight line lever escap.

Audemars, Piguet, square, 18k, 18 jewels, ca. 1950.

Size and Description	Avg	Ex-Fn	Mint
Round, 20J, "Le Brassus" Fausses-Cotes decoration 1970, 18K	$3,000	$3,500	$4,000
Round, 18J, "Le Brassus" chronograph, skeletonized, 1970, 18K	12,000	15,000	18,000
Round, 18J, "Le Brassus," skeleton, 1960	5,000	6,000	7,000
Round, 18J, Adj.4P, 1950, 18K	1,500	2,000	2,500
Round, 18J, day-date-month, moonphases, 4 registers, 18K case	12,500	14,000	15,000
Round, 18J, self-wind, 18K case	800	1,000	1,400

Audemars, Piguet, round, fancy bezel, ca. 1950.

Audemars, Piguet, round, mid-size, 17 jewels, 18k.

Audemars, Piguet, round, 20 jewels, ca. 1970.

Audemars, Piguet, round, 18k case & band.

Audemars, Piguet, cushion, minute repeater.

Audemars, Piguet movement, 19 jewels, ca. 1927.

Size and Description	Avg	Ex-Fn	Mint
Round, 18J, Giromax balance	$1,200	$1,400	$1,700
Round, 18J, day date month, moonphases, 1950s, 18K ...	10,000	12,000	15,000
Round, 18J, aux. sec. dial, 1950, 18K	1,200	1,400	1,600
Round, 18J, 18K case.................................	600	700	900
Round, 18J, moonphase, day-date-month on outer ring ...	5,000	6,500	8,000
Round, 18J, 18K bracelet & case	1,200	1,400	2,000
Round, 18J, large style, sweep sec. hand, 18K case	700	800	1,100
Round, 17J, "Le Brassus," applied gold indexes, 1970, 18K...	3,000	3,500	4,000
Round, 17J, mid-sized, 1930, 18K	2,000	2,200	2,500
Round, 17J, Adj.5P, 18K band & case, 1970	1,200	1,400	1,700
Round, chronograph, 3 registers, 14K case	2,500	3,000	3,500

AUDEMARS, PIGUET (continued)

Size and Description	Avg	Ex-Fn	Mint
Round, chronograph, 3 reg., split sec., c. 1945, 18K......	$20,000	$25,000	$30,000
Round, min. repeater, 18K bracelet & case	40,000	50,000	60,000
Round, ultra thin, 18K...............................	600	700	975
Round, curvex back, 18K	1,000	1,400	1,800
Square, 18J, aux. sec., Adj.4P, 1940, 18K	2,000	2,200	2,500
Square, 18J, Adj.4P, 1950, white gold	800	1,000	1,200
Square, 18J, Adj.7P, jump hour, c. 1925, 18K...........	5,000	6,000	8,000
Square, 18J, Adj.4P, c. 1950s, 18K....................	2,000	2,200	2,600
Square, 18J, thin model, 18K case.....................	800	900	1,000
Tonneau, 18J, jump hour & min., 2 windows, 18K, 1930 .	20,000	22,000	25,000
Tonneau, enamel bezel, platinum......................	2,000	2,400	3,000

LADY'S WRIST WATCH

Style or Grade — Description	Avg	Ex-Fn	Mint
Rectangular, 17J, 18K	$600	$800	$900
Rectangular, 17J, 12 small diamonds on bezel, 14K case ..	800	1,000	1,200
Rectangular, 17J, small diamonds on case & bracelet, 14K	1,000	1,200	1,500
Rectangular, 17J, 30-50 diamond bezel, platinum	1,600	2,000	2,500

Autowrist movement, lug wind, ca. 1925

Autowrist, rectangular, 15 jewels, enamel dial.

AUTOWRIST WATCH CO.
Swiss
Wrist Watch

Style or Grade—Description	Avg	Ex-Fn	Mint
Man's rectangular, 15J, c. 1930, lug action winds watch, by Breguet	$600	$700	$800
Lady's rectangular, 15J, "Universe," early auto lug action winds watch	95	175	250

BALL WATCH CO.
U.S.A.

Style or Model — Description	Avg	Ex-Fn	Mint
Official R.R. Standard, 21J, Adj.5P, 14K case	$300	$350	$450
Official R.R. Standard, 21J, Adj.5P, 10K case	250	275	300
Official R.R. Standard, 21J, Adj.5P, gold filled	150	175	225
Official R.R. Standard, 21J, Adj.5P, stainless	100	125	150
Official R.R. Standard, 25J, Adj.5P, 10K case, E.T.A....	275	300	325
Official R.R. Standard, 25J, Adj.5P, gold filled, E.T.A...	175	200	250
Official R.R. Standard, 25J, Adj.5P, stainless, E.T.A. ...	150	175	200
17J, Self-wind, Wind Indicator, GF	100	150	225
M#433, 17J, gold filled	50	60	75
M#435B, 21J, gold filled	80	95	125
Vacheron & Constantin, 19J, GJS, 14K	600	700	850

NOTE: Prices for wrist watches are for stem wind and set, leather band, complete and in good working order.

Ball Wrist Watches by ETA, 25 jewels, auto wind.

BAUME & MERCIER
GENEVE
Man's Wrist Watch

Style or Grade — Description	Avg	Ex-Fn	Mint
Oval, 18K	$200	$250	$300
Rectangular, 18K case & bracelet......................	800	900	1,200
Rectangular, 17J, diamond bezel, 18K case	300	340	500
Round, 18K case	200	250	300
Round, 17J, chronograph, 2 reg., c. 1940s, SS..........	250	300	350
Round, 17J, chronograph, black dial, 1940, SS	500	600	700
Round, 25J, "Baumatic" autowind, date, 18K case	200	235	300
Round, 30J, "Baumatic," 18K mesh band	500	550	600
Round, skeleton, autowind, 18K	1,000	1,100	1,200
Round, moonphase, day-date-month, 1945, 18K case	1,200	1,400	1,600
Round, chronograph, 3 registers, day-date-month, 18K ...	1,000	1,200	1,400

Baume & Mercier, round, chronograph, 3 registers.

Baume & Mercier, round, triple date, ca.1945.

Baume & Mercier, round, triple date, moon phase.

Baume & Mercier, round, tachymeter, ca. 1940.

Style or Grade—Description	Avg	Ex-Fn	Mint
Square, 17J, chronograph, tachometer, 18K	$2,500	$3,000	$3,500
Tank, 18K case	300	400	500
Ladies, round, small diamonds on bezel, 18K case	200	300	400

Benrus, round, Mystery-diamond dial.

Benrus, tank, 26 diamond bezel.

BENRUS
U.S.A. & Swiss

Style or Grade — Description	Avg	Ex-Fn	Mint
Round, 16J, wind indicator, sweep sec., c. 1940	$50	$60	$75
Round, 17J, alarm	40	50	70

BENRUS (continued)

Style or Grade—Description	Avg	Ex-Fn	Mint
Round, diamond dial	$25	$35	$55
Round, 25J, autowind	10	15	22
Round, chronograph, 2 registers, 14K	400	500	600
Round, chronograph, 2 registers, stainless	75	100	125
Round, digital, "Dial-O-Rama," watertight, GF	100	125	150
Round, mystery dial, diamond dial, 18K	600	700	800
Tank, 26 diamond bezel, 14K white gold	500	600	700
Lady's, round, 15-17J	8	15	20

J. W. BENSON
LONDON

Style or Grade — Description	Avg	Ex-Fn	Mint
Cushion, 15J, Swiss movement, 9K	$350	$425	$600
Round, 18J, chronograph by Longines, c. 1925, 2 reg, 9K	1,200	1,400	1,600

BEYER
SWISS
MAN'S WRIST WATCH

Style or Grade — Description	Avg	Ex-Fn	Mint
Cushion, 15J, ¾ plate, enamel dial, c. 1930, 18K	$300	$350	$450
Rectangular, 15J, c. 1935, 14K	200	275	375
Round, 17J, chronograph, 2 reg., c. 1950, 18K	500	600	750
Round, 15J, sweep sec., enamel dial, c. 1928, 18K	300	400	500
Round, 15J, sweep sec., c. 1950, GF	30	40	55
Round, 15J, "Imperial Chrono Oyster" by Rolex, silver	400	500	600

LADY'S WRIST WATCH

Style or Grade — Description	Avg	Ex-Fn	Mint
Round, 15J, c. 1932, silver	$35	$45	$65
Round, 18J, watertight Oyster, center sec., 14K	200	300	400

BLANCPAIN
SWISS

Style or Grade — Description	Avg	Ex-Fn	Mint
Round, "53J," caliber R300, date, auto, stainless case	$150	$200	$275
Round, 23J, M#6511, by Piguet, perpetual calendar, day-date-month, moonphase, ex-thin auto, 18K	5,000	6,500	9,000
Round, 53J, "Cyclotron," autowind, c. 1965, stainless	175	200	300
Lady's, square, diamond dial & bezel, 18K case	150	185	250

BOREL
SWISS

Style or Grade — Description	Avg	Ex-Fn	Mint
Rectangular, 16J, flips up to a table side clock, 14K......	$900	$1,100	$1,500
Round, 15J, rotating sec. disc, c. 1924..................	100	120	150
Lady's, round, 16J, "fancy rotating dial," GF case	30	40	60

Breitling Watch Co., Chronograph, model 769/B, 2 registers, moveable bezel.

Breitling Watch Co., Chronograph, Cosmonaute-Navytimer, 17 jewels, 3 registers, ca. 1965.

BREITLING
SWISS

Style or Grade — Description	Avg	Ex-Fn	Mint
Rectangular, 15J, 18K case	$150	$200	$250
Round, 17J, chronograph, 2 registers, GF	150	200	250
Round, 17J, chronomat, 2 registers, slide rule bezel, 18K .	800	1,000	1,250
Round, 17J, chronomat, 2 registers, slide rule bezel, GF ..	250	300	350
Round, 17J, chronomat, 2 registers, slide rule bezel, stainless	200	250	300
Round, 17J, chronomat, 3 registers, slide rule bezel, moonphase, date, GF	800	1,000	1,200

Breitling, split sec. chronograph.

Breitling, chronograph, day-date-month, 3 registers.

Breitling, round, telemeter number 104.

Breitling, tachymeter, number 54.

Breitling, round, pulsations, number 53

Breitling, round, telemeter, number 53A

Breitling, round, chronograph, 2 registers.

Breitling, tachymeter, number 55.

Style or Grade—Description	Avg	Ex-Fn	Mint
Round, 17J, "Cadette," chronograph, tachometer, stainless	$200	$250	$350
Round, 17J, "Superocean," 60 min. counter, 200mm	195	225	275
Round, 17J, "Navitimer," chronograph, 24 hr. dial, 18K...	2,000	2,200	2,400

BREITLING (continued)

Style or Grade—Description	Avg	Ex-Fn	Mint
Round, 17J, "Navitimer," chronograph, 24 hr. dial, date, stainless	$300	$400	$550
Round, 17J, chronograph, slide rule bezel, moon phase, 18K case	2,500	3,000	3,500
Round, 17J, chronograph, slide rule bezel, moon phase, SS	800	1,000	1,200
Round, 17J, day date month, 18K	250	300	375
Round, 17J, day date month, SS	100	125	165
Round, 17J, c. sec., SS	65	75	95
Round, split sec. chronograph, 3 registers, "Duograph," 18K	2,500	2,800	3,000
Round, Unitime, chronograph, dual time, large, stainless	225	250	300
Round, chronograph, 2 reg., date, 2 pushers, stainless	200	250	345
19J, duograph, split sec., SS case	800	900	1,000
Chronograph, day date month, moon phase, 2 reg., 18K	1,000	1,200	1,700
Chronograph, day date month, moon phase, 2 reg., SS	500	600	700

Bucherer, day-date-moon phases, auto wind, 12 diamonds on dial, 18k case.

Bucherer, rectangular, 8-day, 15 jewels.

BUCHERER

Style or Grade — Description	Avg	Ex-Fn	Mint
Rectangular, 15J, 8 day, GF case	$250	$300	$450
Rectangular, 15J, 8 day, Adj.3P, 1930s, 18K	400	500	700
Round, 15J, 14K	150	175	225
Round, 15J, stainless	20	30	50
Square, 21J, day-date-month & moonphase, 12 diamond dial, 18K case	1,500	1,800	2,000
Tank, 15J, 14K	175	200	250
Tank, 15J, silver	100	125	150
Tank, 15J, stainless	75	100	125

BUCHERER (continued)

Style or Grade—Description	Avg	Ex-Fn	Mint
Ladies round, 15J, 14K	$70	$85	$125
Ladies round, 15J, silver	50	60	80

Bulova Accutron, with sweep second hands.

Bulova Accutron, Masonic dial.

Bulova, tonneau, The Governor, 14k.

Bulova, tank, The Athlete, 15 jewels.

Bulova, tonneau, The Ambassador, gold filled.

Bulova, tank, The Curtis, 17 jewels.

BULOVA
SWISS AND U.S.A.

MAN'S WRIST WATCH

Style or Grade — Description	Avg	Ex-Fn	Mint
Accutron, M#214, railroad approved, GF	$90	$100	$125
Accutron, M#218, with date, GF	60	65	80
Accutron, skeletonized, 18K case	600	700	800

BULOVA (continued)

Bulova, digital, water p., s. steel.

Bulova, Accutron, 18k, ca. 1960s

Bulova, Accutron, Alpha, water p.

Bulova, Accutron, skeletonized mvt.

Bulova, rectangular, 14k, bell-shaped lugs.

Bulova, rectangular, rose 14k, fancy lugs.

Style or Grade—Description	Avg	Ex-Fn	Mint
Accutron, skeletonized model, 14K case, "Spaceview"	$300	$350	$400
Accutron, skeletonized model, GF, "Spaceview"	100	125	175
Accutron, skeletonized model, stainless, "Spaceview"	80	100	125
Accutron, "Astronaut," M–214, 24 hr. dial, 14K	300	350	400
Rectangular, 21J, "Curvex," c. 1945, 14K	200	250	335
Rectangular, 17J, 14K case	125	150	175
Rectangular, 17J, GF	40	50	60
Rectangular, 17J, bell shaped lugs, 14K	275	350	375
Rectangular, 17J, curved, fancy lugs, 14K white gold	300	350	425
Round, 14K case	75	85	90

BULOVA (continued)

Style or Grade—Description	Avg	Ex-Fn	Mint
Round, GF	$25	$30	$40
Round, gold plate	10	15	25
Round, chronograph, c. 1945	150	175	225
Round, 30J, "Ambassador," autowind, 18K case	100	125	155
Round, 30J, sweep sec., self-wind, 14K case	100	125	135
Round, 23J, waterproof, 14K	100	125	175
Round, 23J, day, date, self-wind, GF case	50	60	75
Round, 17J, alarm, stainless	50	60	75
Square, 14K case	100	125	150
Tank, 15J, "Athlete," GF	50	60	70
Tank, 15J, "Curtis," GF	50	60	70
Tonneau, quartz, waterproof, 1960, SS	150	175	200
Tonneau, 17J, "Lone Eagle," (Lindbergh model), c. 1930, GF	125	150	175
Tonneau, 15J, "Governor," GF	50	60	70
Tonneau, 15J, Ambassador," GF	50	60	70
Tonneau, "Light Emitting Diode," 14K & stainless	75	100	135

Bulova, 22mm, 17 jewels, self wind

Bulova, 8/0 size, 17 jewels

Bulova, Rectangular, 17 jewels

LADY'S WRIST WATCH

Style or Grade — Description	Avg	Ex-Fn	Mint
Round, 14K case	$35	$45	$65
Round, GF	10	15	25
Rectangular, 14K case	35	45	75
Rectangular, small diamonds on 14K case	195	225	350

Buren, 27mm, Tonneau, 15 jewels.

Buren, 27mm, model 14LN.

Buren, 27mm, sweep second.

BUREN
SWISS

Style or Grade — Description	Avg	Ex-Fn	Mint
Rectangular, 17J, 14K case	$100	$125	$150
Rectangular, 17J, GF	25	30	40
Round, 17J, moonphase, day-date-month, c. 1940, GF ...	150	185	245

HENRY CAPT
GENEVE

Style or Grade — Description	Avg	Ex-Fn	Mint
Round, ¼ repeater, 14K case	$8,000	$10,000	$12,000
Round, 5 min. repeater, 14K Case.....................	15,000	18,000	20,000
Round, 1 min. repeater, 18K case	30,000	40,000	50,000

Cartier, Tank, 20 jewels, 18k gold case, c. 1950s.

Cartier, Tank, 18 jewels, 18k gold case, jeweled winding crown.

CARTIER
PARIS
MAN'S WRIST WATCH

Style or Grade — Description	Avg	Ex-Fn	Mint
Asymetric, 18J, signed E.W. Co., 1920s, 18K case	$6,000	$7,000	$8,000
Asymetric, 18J, E.C.& W. Co., 1928, 18K	6,500	7,000	7,500
Cushion, 17J, diamond bezel, 1970, 18K	3,000	3,200	3,500
Hexagon, 15J, Adj.3P, 1925, 18K	2,000	2,500	3,000
Min. repeater, 28J, 18K case.........................	80,000	100,000	120,000

Cartier, hexagonal, 18k, 15 jewels, ca. 1925

Cartier, asymetric, European W. Co., ca. 1928.

Cartier, square, 18k, 17 jewels, ca. 1960.

Cartier, square, 18k, 17 jewels, ca. 1960.

Cartier, tank, man's watch, ca. 1930s

Cartier, square, ladies, European W. Co.

Cartier, reversible, 17 jewels, 18k.

Cartier, Santos Lady's, self wind, ca. 1980s

Style or Grade—Description	Avg	Ex-Fn	Mint
Octagon, 15J, "Santos," self wind, 1980, 18K	$4,500	$5,000	$5,500
Rectangular, 17J, diamond bezel, 1970, 18K	2,000	2,200	2,500
Rectangular, 18K, Curvex, by the European W. Co.	15,000	18,000	22,000
Rectangular, 18K case by Le Coultre	3,000	4,000	5,000
Rectangular, "Panthere," large size, 18K band & case	6,000	7,000	8,000
Rectangular, "Santo," c. 1925, 18K	4,000	4,500	5,000
Rectangular or Square, 18K case, mvt. by E.W.C. Co. . . .	4,000	5,000	6,000
Round, quartz, 18K case & bracelet, total wt. 70 DWT . . .	3,000	3,500	4,500
Round, 29J, min. rep. by LeCoultre, 1930s, platinum	80,000	100,000	120,000
Round, 26J, split chronograph, by P.P. & Co., 2 registers	60,000	70,000	80,000
Round, 18K case	1,000	1,200	1,400
Round, "Mysterious," wind & set on back, 18K	5,000	6,000	7,500
Square, reverso type case, 2 movements, 2 dials, each dial a different color, used for 2 diff. time zones, 18K	$12,000	$15,000	$18,000
Square, with flip up top cover, free sprung, 18K case	8,000	10,000	12,000
Square, by Bueche-Girod, c. 1950s, 18K case	2,000	2,500	3,000

CARTIER (continued)

Cartier, tank, platinum band & case, ca. 1930s.

Cartier, tonneau, jump-hour & minute, ca. 1930s.

Cartier, minute repeater, platinum case, ca. 1930s.

Cartier, minute repeater, 29 jewels, 2 gongs.

Cartier, tonneau, minute repeater, ca. 1925.

Cartier, minute repeater by European W. Co.

Style or Grade—Description	Avg	Ex-Fn	Mint
Square, by Uneversal, 17J, 1960s, 18K case	$800	$900	$1,000
Tank, 18K case	1,200	1,400	1,600
Tank, 14K..	800	1,000	1,200
Tonneau, 28J, min. rep., signed E.W. Co., mid-1920s, 18K case	100,000	125,000	150,000
Tonneau, 28J, min. repeater by E.W.C., c. 1925, 18K	90,000	100,000	140,000
Tonneau, 15J, mvt. by E.W.C., day-date-month & moon-phase, c. 1945, 18K.............................	30,000	40,000	50,000
Tonneau, chronograph, 2 reg., fancy case, c. 1927, 18K ..	20,000	25,000	30,000
Tonneau, 18K case, mvt. by E.W.C. Co.	8,000	9,000	10,000

CARTIER (continued)

Style or Grade—Description	Avg	Ex-Fn	Mint
Tonneau, square dial, "Santos," c. 1925, platinum.......	$9,000	$11,000	$12,000

LADY'S WRIST WATCH

Style or Grade — Description	Avg	Ex-Fn	Mint
Rectangular or Square, 18K case, mvt. by E.W.C. Co. ...	$3,000	$4,000	$5,000
Rectangular, 40 diamond bezel, E.W.C. Co..............	4,000	5,000	6,000
Rectangular, 40 diamond bezel, E.W.C. Co., 18K band...	4,500	5,500	6,500
Square, 15J, by Le Coultre, white gold, diamond bezel ...	3,000	3,400	4,000
Tank, 18K case	1,000	1,100	1,200

Certina Round, 19mm, 17 jewels.

Certina Round, 19mm, 25 jewels, self wind.

CERTINA
SWISS

Style or Grade — Description	Avg	Ex-Fn	Mint
Round & Square, 27J, Town & Co. Caliber 25-651	$85	$100	$150
Round, 25J, alarm, date, autowind, sweep sec.	85	95	125
Round, 16J, sweep sec., ca. 1955, GF	50	65	85
Round, 'EA," chronograph, 3 reg., tachometer, 1950, stainless	150	175	225

CHOPARD
SWISS

Style or Grade — Description	Avg	Ex-Fn	Mint
Round, autowind, day-date-month & moonphase, 18K	$6,000	$6,500	$7,000
Round, autowind, day-date-month & leap year ind., 18K..	2,000	2,500	3,500
Ladies, round, diamond bezel, 18K case	1,000	1,200	1,500

CORNAVIN
SWISS

Style or Grade — Description	Avg	Ex-Fn	Mint
Round, 25J, decompression indicator, watertight	$200	$250	$325
Round, 21J, tachometer, 4 chapter rings, date, GF	100	125	165
Round, 17J, "Datocor," date, c. 1955	75	95	125

Cortebert, round, 15 jewels, "Sport day-date, moon phase, ca. 1950s.

CORTEBERT
SWISS

Style or Grade — Description	Avg	Ex-Fn	Mint
Rectangular, 16J, sweep sec., anti-magnetic, 14K	$200	$240	$300
Round, 21J, "Corteroter," stainless case	30	35	50
Round, 16J, day-date-month, moon phase, 18K	900	1,000	1,200
Round, 15J, "Sport," "Spirofix," c. 1950, stainless	40	45	60

CORUM
SWISS

Style or Grade — Description	Avg	Ex-Fn	Mint
Rectangular, 17J, "Golden Bridge," watch train in a straight line, all parts visible, presently made, 18K ...	$1,500	$1,700	$2,000
Rectangular, 16J, 18K case	600	700	850
Rectangular, gold ingot, 18K	1,200	1,300	1,500
Round, 16J, sweep sec., automatic, 18K	400	480	600
Round, $20 gold coin	1,800	2,000	2,500
Round, $10 gold coin	1,200	1,400	1,800

CYMA
By Tavannes
SWISS

MAN'S WRIST WATCH

Style or Grade — Description	Avg	Ex-Fn	Mint
Rectangular, 15J, enamel dial, 14K case	$195	$210	$245

Style or Grade—Description	Avg	Ex-Fn	Mint
Rectangular, 15J, "Sport," 2-tone dial, c. 1940, GF......	$40	$45	$60
Round, 17J, "Triplex," sweep sec., GF................	50	60	75
Round, 15J, early watertight, c. 1931, GF..............	75	100	135
Round, 15J, 18K....................................	250	300	350
Round, 15J, 14K....................................	195	210	245
Round, 15J, GF.....................................	55	65	85
Round, 15J, stainless	35	45	60
Round, 15J, silver "enamel dial"	125	150	225
Round, watersport, sweep sec..........................	20	30	45
Square or rectangular, 16J, 18K.......................	300	350	475
Square or Rectangular, 16J, silver or GF...............	95	115	135
Square, 15J, sweep sec. hand, 14K	150	165	200
Square, 15J, auto, watersport, stainless	40	45	60

Cyma Round, Swiss made, 12½ lignes.   **Cyma Rectangular**, 20mm, 15 jewels.

LADY'S WRIST WATCH

Style or Grade — Description	Avg	Ex-Fn	Mint
Round, 16J, c. 1925, GF.............................	$20	$30	$45
Round, 15J, GF.....................................	30	40	55
Round, 15J, stainless	20	25	35

DITESHEIM
SWISS

Style or Grade — Description	Avg	Ex-Fn	Mint
Rectangular, 16J, diamond dial, 18K, c. 1930............	$1,200	$1,300	$1,500
Rectangular, 16J, diamond dial, platinum case, c. 1930 ...	1,400	1,600	1,800
Lady's, tonneau, 50 small diamond bezel & case, platinum	600	800	1,000

DRIVA WATCH CO.
GENEVE

Grade or Name—Description	Avg	Ex-Fn	Mint
Rectangular, 15J, ¼ repeater, c. 1930s.................	$3,000	$3,500	$4,500
Rectangular, 17J, chronograph, c. 1930s, SS.............	500	700	900

DRIVA (continued)

Driva, quarter repeater, ca. 1930s, stainless steel case, 15 jewels, 1 gong, winding by bolt on the band.

DOXA
SWISS

Style or Grade — Description	Avg	Ex-Fn	Mint
Round, chronograph, moonphase, day-date-month,			
stainless	$400	$500	$600
Round, chronograph, 2 registers, stainless	100	110	125
Round, 17J, tacho-telemeter, c. 1955	150	185	225
Round, 17J, 14K	80	95	125
Round, 17J, GF......................................	20	25	45
Round, 17J, stainless	10	20	30
Round, 15J, chronograph, day-date-month, stainless......	200	250	300
Round, 15J, chronograph, 2 registers, GF	100	130	180
Round, 15J, autowind, date, c. 1960, 14K..............	90	110	140
Round, 15J, autowind, date, c. 1960, GF	30	40	55
Round, 15J, autowind, date, c. 1960, stainless	15	20	35
Round, 15J, sweep sec., autowind, 14K	80	100	130
Round, 15J, sweep sec., autowind, GF..................	15	20	30
Round, 15J, sweep sec., autowind, stainless	10	15	20
Round, 15J, c. 1948, 14K	70	80	100
Round, 15J, c. 1948, GF.............................	12	20	32
Round, 15J, c. 1948, stainless.........................	5	8	12
Square, date window, 14K............................	125	150	175
Square, date window, GF	50	60	70
Square, date window, stainless	25	30	40

Doxa Round, 18mm, 15 jewels   Doxa Tonneau, 18mm, 15 jewels   Doxa Rectangular, 18mm, 15 jewels

DUNHILL

Style or Grade — Description	Avg	Ex-Fn	Mint
Lighter with watch, 18K case	$500	$700	$1,000
Lighter with watch, silver	300	350	400

Ebel, square, 18k, applied gold numbers.　　　　Ebel, pocket/purse watch, slide open to wind.

EBEL
SWISS

Style or Grade — Description	Avg	Ex-Fn	Mint
Rectangular, pocket slide to open, day date, leather case ..	$200	$245	$300
Rectangular, pocket slide to open, leather case	135	150	185
Round, autowind, waterproof, rotating dial, stainless	400	500	650
Round, autowind, sweep sec., stainless..................	150	200	275
Square, 18K case & bracelet	1,000	1,200	1,500
Square, 18J, aux. sec., 1950, 18K	500	600	700

Eberhard & Co. Round Chronograph, 18 jewels, split second with 3 registers.

EBERHARD & CO.
SWISS

Style or Grade — Description	Avg	Ex-Fn	Mint
Round, 18J, split sec. chronograph, 3 registers, 18K	$2,800	$3,000	$3,500

EBERHARD & CO. (continued)

Eberhard, 17 jewels, tele-tachymetre, ca. 1930s.

Eberhard, chronograph, caliber 14.

Style or Grade—Description	Avg	Ex-Fn	Mint
Round, 17J, chronograph, 2 registers, 18K	$500	$600	$800
Round, 17J, chronograph, 2 registers, stainless	200	270	350
Round, 17J, spiral tachometer & telemeter, watertight, 18K	500	650	850
Round, 19J, chronograph, split sec., 3 reg., mid-'40s, GF.	1,000	1,500	2,000
17J, 18K case, time only	125	135	165

Ekegren, rectangular, jumping hour, minute hand.

Ekegren, rectangular, jumping hour, 18k, 18 jewels.

H. R. EKEGREN
GENEVE

Style or Grade — Description	Avg	Ex-Fn	Mint
Rectangular, 18J, jump hour, platinum case, 1920	$4,000	$5,000	$6,000

ELGIN WATCH CO.
U.S.A.

MAN'S WRIST WATCH

Style or Model — Description	Avg	Ex-Fn	Mint
B. W. Raymond, R.R. approved, 23J, 14K case	$175	$200	$250
B. W. Raymond, R.R. approved, 23J, gold filled	125	150	175
B. W. Raymond, R.R. approved, 23J, stainless	80	100	125
Lord Elgin, 21J, rectangular case, 14K.................	125	150	175

<table>
<tr><td>Elgin, rectangular, enamel bezel, ca. 1920s.</td><td>Elgin, B.W. Raymond, RR approved, 23 jewels.</td></tr>
</table>

Elgin, round, golf ball style, rotating hour.

Elgin, 6/0 size, orig. sold for $8.10.

Elgin, rectangular, 10/0 size, sold for $83.80.

Elgin, barrel, orig. sold for $42.90

Style or Grade—Description	Avg	Ex-Fn	Mint
Lord Elgin, 17J, rectangular case, 14K	$125	$150	$175
Lord Elgin, 17J, rectangular gold filled case	50	60	80
Lord Elgin, 21J, round 14K case	75	85	110
Lord Elgin, 21J, round gold filled case	30	35	45
Lord Elgin, 21J, round case 14K, diamond on dial (12) . . .	200	225	275
Lord Elgin, dome, digital, jump hr., YGF	100	145	195
Official Boy Scout on case, c. 1934	100	135	185
Doctor's Model, "duo dial," rectangular gold filled case . .	350	400	500
Rectangular, 14K case, diamond dial	200	250	300
Rectangular, gold filled case	40	55	65

ELGIN WATCH CO. (continued)

Style or Grade—Description	Avg	Ex-Fn	Mint
Rectangular, Shockmaster	$35	$40	$50
Tonneau, gold filled case............................	50	60	75
Round, gold filled case	20	25	35
Round, stainless steel case	10	15	25
Round, WWI, pierced top, 15J, sterling................	300	350	450
Round, WWI model, pierced top, 7J-11J, nickel	200	250	300
Round, rotating hour & min., golf ball shape, waterproof, GF	150	175	225
Square, gold filled case	40	50	60
Curvex, gold filled case, "1¾ inches" long	75	100	150
Digital Rectangular, triangle window, GF, 1940	250	300	350
Digital Round, triangle window, GF, 1940	150	200	250
Enamel Bezel, 14K	250	300	400
Enamel Bezel, 14K, presentation model, 18K	1,200	1,500	1,800
Round Enamel Bezel in blue, 1920	900	1,100	1,300

LADY'S WRIST WATCH

Style or Model — Description	Avg	Ex-Fn	Mint
Lady Elgin, small, 14K case, after 1940	$50	$60	$75
Lady Elgin, small, gold filled case, after 1940	12	15	25
Rectangular, small, 14K case, after 1940	40	45	60
Rectangular, gold filled case, after 1940................	20	25	45
Rectangular, 14K case w/small diamond	125	150	195
Rectangular, enamel deco design, WGF	100	125	150

ELGIN NATIONAL WATCH CO.
IDENTIFICATION OF MOVEMENTS
BY MODEL NUMBER

How to Identify Your Watch: Compare the movement of your watch with the illustrations in this section. Upon matching the movement exactly, the model number and size can be determined. While comparing, note the location of the balance, jewels, screws, gears and type of back plate (Full, ¾, Bridge) which will be clues in identifying the movement you have. Having determined the size and model number, you can now find your watch in the main price listing by name or number (which is engraved on the movement).

ELGIN WATCH CO. (continued)

Model 3, 3-0 size, three-quarter plate, open face, pendant set, first serial number 18,179,001, Grade 414, March, 1915.

Model 1, 5-0 size, three-quarter plate, hunting, pendant set, first serial number 14,699,001, Grade 380, Feb., 1910.

Model 2, 5-0 size, three-quarter plate, open face, pendant set, first serial number 17,890,001, Grade 399, Feb., 1914.

Model 2, 8-0 size, Grade 532, 539, sweep second.

Model 7, 8-0 size, Grades 554, 555, 556.

Model 20, 8-0 size, Grades 681, 682.

Model 1, 10-0 size, three-quarter plate, open face, pendant set, first serial number 8,752,001, Grade 255, Apr., 1902.

Model 2, 15-0 size, Grades 623, 624, 626.

15-0 Size, movement, Grades 670, 672, 673.

15-0 size, movement. Grade 674.

15-0 size, movement, Grades 557, 558, 559.

Model 2, 21-0 size, Grade 541, 533, 535.

Model 3, 21-0 size, Grade 547, sweep second.

Model 4, 21-0 size, Grades 617, 617L, 619, 619L.

Model 9, 21-0 size, Grades 650, 651.

Model 9, 21-0 size, Grades 655, 656.

Grade 607, self wind.

Grade 630, sweep second.

Grade 641, 642

Grade 643, self wind.

Grades 644, 645, self wind.

Grade 647, sweep second.

Grade 661

Grade 666, sweep second.

Grade 668, sweep second.

Grade 685

Grade 687

Grade 700

Grade 710

Grade 716

Enicar, round, 17 jewels, center seconds.

Enicar, round, 17 jewels, day-date, moon phase.

ENICAR
SWISS

Style or Grade — Description	Avg	Ex-Fn	Mint
Round, 17J, day date month, moon phase, GF	$125	$150	$200
Round, 17J, c. sec., watertight, SS	35	45	55
Tonneau, 15J, lady's GF case........................	15	20	30

ETERNA
SWISS

MAN'S WRIST WATCH

Style or Grade — Description	Avg	Ex-Fn	Mint
Rectangular, 17J, 14K case	$100	$125	$175
Rectangular, 17J, GF	50	60	70
Rectangular, 17J, stainless...........................	30	40	50
Rectangular, 15J, digital hour, min. & sec., 14K, c. 1935 .	1,100	1,200	1,500
Round, 21J, "Centenaire," autowind, sweep sec., date ...	150	165	200
Round, 19J, day window at 12, month at 6, date ring, 1945, 18K	200	300	450
Round, 17J, self wind, 14K case	95	110	155
Round, 17J, self wind, GF	35	40	55
Round, 17J, stainless	15	20	30
Round, 17J, self wind, date window, 18K case...........	175	200	225
Square, autowind, sweep sec., 18K, c. 1960	175	210	275

Eterna Round, 17 jewels, stem wind.

Eterna Round, caliber 1421, 17 jewels, self wind

ETERNA (continued)

Eterna, round, 19 jewels, 18k gold case, day-date-month, ca. 1945.

LADY'S WRIST WATCH

Style or Grade — Description	Avg	Ex-Fn	Mint
Rectangular, 15J, 14K case	$45	$50	$65
Rectangular, 15J, GF	25	30	40
Rectangular, 15J, stainless	10	15	20
Round, 15J, 14K case	35	40	45
Round, 15J, GF	20	25	30
Round, 15J, stainless	10	12	18
Tonneau, chronograph, 2 pushers, c. 1945	1,500	2,000	2,500

Eska, round, chronograph, triple date, moon phase.

Eska, round, 18k gold, multi-color enamel dial.

ESKA
KOCHER & CIE
SWISS

Style or Grade—Description	Avg	Ex-Fn	Mint
Round, 17J, cloisonne enamel dial in color, auto wind,18K	$500	$600	$700
Round, 17J, center sec., waterproof, 1955, 14K	100	150	225
Round, 17J, chronograph, triple date, 2 reg., GF	300	400	500
Square, 15J, chronograph, 18K, 1940s	400	500	600

Eska, square, chronograph, ca. 1940.

Evans, round, chronograph, 2 registers, ca. 1940.

EVANS
SWISS

Style or Grade—Description	Avg	Ex-Fn	Mint
Round, chronograph, 2 reg., 1940, 18K	$600	$700	$800

Exactus, round, day-date-month, moon phase, 3 registers, stainless steel case.

EXACTUS
SWISS

Style or Grade—Description	Avg	Ex-Fn	Mint
Round, 17J, chronograph, 3 reg., day date month, moon phase, SS	$350	$450	$550

EXCELSIOR PARK
SWISS

Style or Grade—Description	Avg	Ex-Fn	Mint
Round, chronograph, 2 reg., waterproof, SS	$200	$300	$400
Round, chronograph, 2 reg., GF	100	150	200

EXCELSIOR PARK (continued)

Excelsior, round, chronograph, gold filled.

Excelsior, round, chronograph, stainless steel

Excelsior, round, chronograph, waterproof.

Excelsior movement, chronograph, about 14 size.

FREY & CO., LTD.

Style or Grade — Description	Avg	Ex-Fn	Mint
Barrel, 15J, luminous dial, stainless	$15	$20	$35
Rectangular, 15J, stainless............................	10	20	30
Tonneau, 15J, luminous dial, GF	15	20	35
Ladies, curvex, 17J, rect. "baggette" style, GF	15	20	30

Frey & Co. Curvex, 17 jewels

Frey & Co. Barrel, 18mm, 15 jewels

Frey & Co. Tonneau, 15 jewels

GIRARD-PERREGAUX
SWISS

Style or Grade — Description	Avg	Ex-Fn	Mint
Cushion, 17J, date, sweep sec., GF.....................	$35	$45	$65

GIRARD-PERREGAUX (continued)

Girard-Perregaux, 9½ lignes, 17 jewels.

Girard-Perregaux Cushion, 17 jewels.

Girard-Perregaux, round, 39 jewels, auto-wind.

Girard-Perregaux, rec., 39 jewels, date, center sec.

Style or Grade—Description	Avg	Ex-Fn	Mint
Rectangular, 39J, center sec., date	$200	$250	$300
Rectangular, 17J, date window at 10 & 2, ca. 1945, 14K	500	550	600
Round, 17J, Deep Divers, stainless	45	60	85
Round, 17J, day-date, sweep second, GF	25	30	45
Round, 17J, chronograph, 3 registers, stainless	175	225	300
Round, 39J, auto wind, date, 1960, 18K	500	600	700
Round, 31J, chronometer, date, 18K	185	200	245
Round, 17J, Sea Hawk, GF	25	30	40
Round, 17J, Gyromatic, sweep sec., 14K	110	125	155
Round, 17J, Gyromatic, sweep sec., GF	30	40	60
Round, 17J, Gyromatic, sweep sec., stainless	25	30	45
Round, alarm, GF	100	125	150
Round, alarm, stainless	50	60	75
Round, chronograph, 3 reg., date, moon phase, caliber 7750, mvt. engraved, presently made, 18K	2,000	2,400	3,000
Tank, 17J, 14K	150	175	220
Lady's Square, 17J, 14K	40	50	85
Lady's Square, 17J, GF	25	30	40

Glycine, tonneau, 15 jewels

Glycine, rectangular, 18 jewels

GLYCINE
SWISS

Style or Grade—Description	Avg	Ex-Fn	Mint
Rectangular, 18J, round mvt., c. 1935, GF	$100	$110	$140
Round, 18J, large 18K case, tear drop lugs	250	290	350
Round, 18J, c. 1931, 14K	90	100	130
Lady's oval, 17J, art deco, platinum & diamond case & bracelet	2,000	2,200	2,500

Golay, rectangular, 18k & platinum, 18 jewels, ca. 1928.

GOLAY FILS
GENEVE

Style or Grade—Description	Avg	Ex-Fn	Mint
Rectangular, 18J, applied gold numbers, 1920, 18K	$1,500	$2,000	$2,500
Round, 32J, min. repeater, Adj.5P, 1920, 18K case	30,000	40,000	50,000
Lady's round, 32J, min. repeater, Adj.5P, 1920, 18K.....	40,000	50,000	60,000

Gruen, rectangular, double dial, ca. 1935.

Gruen, round, fancy lugs, 14k.

GRUEN
SWISS & U.S.A.
MAN'S WRIST WATCH

Style or Grade — Description	Avg	Ex-Fn	Mint
Chevrolet grill, 15J, c. 1920s, nickel case................	$400	$500	$650
Curvex, 14K case, 1½ inch long	325	350	400
Curvex, GF, 1¾ inch long	125	175	250
Curvex, with diamond on dial, 1¼ inch long, 14K case ...	375	450	500
Rectangular, duo dial (doctor), GF	550	600	700

GRUEN (continued)

Gruen, rectangular, Curvex, drivers watch.

Gruen, auto radiator, Curvex, 14k.

Gruen, rectangular, diamond dial, fancy lugs.

Gruen, rectangular, Curvex, fancy lugs.

Gruen, rectangular, Curvex style shown at top.

Gruen, tonneau, 14k, 19 jewels, ca. 1930.

Style or Grade—Description	Avg	Ex-Fn	Mint
Rectangular, verithin, stepped lugs, 14K	$300	$350	$425
Rectangular, curvex, 14K	300	350	425
Rectangular, 15J, duo dial, 1935, 14K	1,300	1,400	1,500
Rectangular, 15J, 14K case	150	175	200
Rectangular, 15J, GF	50	60	100
Rectangular, 17J, car driver's curvex, c. 1940s, 14K GF case	400	500	650
Rectangular, 17J, precision extra, c. 1935, 14K	150	175	200
Rectangular, 17J, fancy lugs, diamond dial, 14K	250	325	400
Rectangular, 21J, G#335R, 9 diamond dial, 14K case	350	400	475
Round, GF	25	30	55
Round, chronograph, GF	200	225	275
Round, rope style bezel, 14K white gold	200	250	300
Round, 17J, fancy lugs, 14K	250	300	350

Gruen, rectangular, very thin percision, fancy lugs.

Gruen, round, rope style bezel with diamonds.

Style or Grade—Description	Avg	Ex-Fn	Mint
Round, 17J, alarm, date, YGF	$70	$80	$95
Round, 17J, 24 hr. jump dial, 1-12 a.m. 13-24 p.m., YGF	125	150	175
Round, 17J, diver's watch, autowind, stainless	40	50	65
Round, 17J, Adj.5P, YGF	40	50	65
Round, 17J, G#435, 14K	100	130	150
Round, 17J, G#435, YGF	45	50	65
Square, 18J, heavy 14K case	175	225	275
Square, 17J, "Curvex," fancy lugs, 14K	300	350	425
Tank, 14K case	175	200	250
Tank, GF	50	75	100
Tonneau, 14K case	175	200	250
Tonneau, GF	70	80	90
Tonneau, Precision, flip top, hunter, 14K GF	400	500	650

LADY'S WRIST WATCH

Style or Grade—Description	Avg	Ex-Fn	Mint
Rectangular, platinum & sapphires	$200	$225	$250
Rectangular, platinum & small diamonds	175	200	250
Rectangular, small diamonds on case & 18K bracelet	300	450	600
Round or Square, GF	15	20	25

E. Gubelin, round, minute repeater, 18k, ca. 1956.

E. Gubelin movement, 29 jewels, minute repeater.

E. Gubelin, round, day-date, moon phase, ca. 1950.

E. Gubelin, round, ipso-matic, 25 jewels, 18k.

E. Gubelin, square, day-date, moon phase, 25 jewels.

E. Gubelin, rectangular, 18k, 18 jewels, ca. 1940.

E. Gubelin, tonneau, hunter style lid, ca. 1930s.

E. Gubelin, tonneau, 14k tu-tone, Curvex.

E. GUBELIN
SWISS
MAN'S WRIST WATCH

Style or Grade — Description	Avg	Ex-Fn	Mint
Cushion, min. repeater, by Audemars Piguet, 18K	$60,000	$70,000	$80,000
Cushion, 29J, min. repeater, by Audemars, 1910s, 18K ...	75,000	80,000	90,000
Hexagon, 17J, 14K band & case, 1930	2,500	3,000	3,500
Rectangular, 18J, 2-tone, digital, jump hour, min. hand, 14K...	5,500	6,500	7,000
Rectangular, 18J, hunting case, c. 1930s, 18K white case ..	3,000	4,000	5,000

E. GUBELIN (continued)

E. Gubelin, chronograph, 3 registers, ca. 1950s.

E. Gubelin, rectangular, jumping hour, ca. 1924.

Style or Grade—Description	Avg	Ex-Fn	Mint
Rectangular, 17J, curved, 1940, 18K	$4,500	$5,000	$5,500
Rectangular, 17J, mid-'30s, reverso case, by LeCoultre, 18K case	3,000	3,200	3,500
Rectangular, 18K case	450	550	700
Rectangular, with horizontal shutters & crown at 3 & 9, 14K case, c. 1930	8,000	9,000	10,000
Rectangular, 18K, perpetual calendar, day-date-month & moon phases	50,000	60,000	70,000
Round, GF	125	150	200
Round, self wind, center sec., date, 21J	300	325	375
Round, self wind, moon phases, day-date-month, 18K case	2,000	2,500	3,000
Round, chronograph, 3 registers, 18K case	700	800	1,000
Round, automatic, alarm, by Le Coultre, 18K	800	900	1,100
Round, 18K case & bracelet	2,000	2,500	3,000
Round, min. repeater, 18K case	28,000	30,000	40,000
Round, 29J, min. repeater, 1956, 18K band & case	40,000	50,000	60,000
Round, 29J, min. repeater, mid-'50s, by LeCoultre, 18K bracelet	30,000	40,000	50,000
Round, min. repeater, signed Patek Philippe, Geneve and Gubelin on dial, 18K case & bracelet by Gubelin, with c. 1955 papers, box & leather case	120,000	150,000	175,000
Round, 25J, Adj.5P, perpetual calendar, day-date-month and moon phases, split sec. chronograph, 2 registers, signed Patek Philippe, Geneve and Gubelin on dial, 18K case & Gubelin 18K bracelet, with papers, box, and leather case (3 examples made)	200,000	230,000	250,000
Round, 19J, triple date, moon phases, 1950s, 18K	5,000	6,000	7,000
Square, 18J, 2-tone, digital, jump hour, min. hand, 14K	3,800	4,200	4,800
Square, 25J, self wind, moon phase, day-date-month, 18K case and bracelet	3,000	4,000	4,500
Square, 18K case	295	395	600
Tonneau, 2-tone case, curvex	2,000	2,500	3,000

E. GUBELIN (continued)

LADY'S WRIST WATCH

Style or Grade — Description	Avg	Ex-Fn	Mint
Square or Round, 18K	$125	$135	$175
Square or Round, 18K case, diamonds on case	900	1,000	1,200

Guinand, chronograph, triple date, moon phase.

Guinand, chronograph, day-date, 3 registers.

C. L. GUINAND
SWISS

Size and Description	Avg	Ex-Fn	Mint
Round, chronograph, day date month, 3 reg., 18K case	$300	$350	$450
Round, chronograph, day date month, 3 reg., SS case	75	90	135
Round, chronograph, day date month, moon phase, 2 reg., 18K case	1,000	1,200	1,400
Round, chronograph, day date month, moon phase, 2 reg., SS	400	500	600

HAMILTON WATCH CO.
U.S.A.

MAN'S WRIST WATCH

Style or Model — Description	Avg	Ex-Fn	Mint
Cross Country, 18J, 5 hr. hands on center dial, 14K	$175	$200	$250
Doctor's Model, "duo dial," 17J, gold filled, Seckron	400	500	600

Flint Ridge, man's wrist watch, sports model with a protective spring cover, Grade 987, solid gold case, originally sold for $125.00. (Grade 979 sold for $150.00.)

Hamilton, Boulton, 19 jewels, 14k.

Hamilton, Judson, 19 jewels, tu-tone, gold filled.

Hamilton, Perry, Grade 987, gold filled.

Hamilton, Reagan, 17 jewels, 10k.

Hamilton, Sidney, 17 jewels, 10k.

Hamilton, Bagley, 17 jewels, 18k applied numbers.

Grade or Name—Description	Avg	Ex-Fn	Mint
Flintridge, 19J, 14K case w/pop up cover	$1,000	$1,100	$1,250
M#979, 19J, GJS, 14K Hamilton case	120	150	200
M#979, 19J, GJS, gold filled Hamilton case	60	70	85
M#982, 19J, GJS, Hamilton 18K gold case	250	350	450
M#982, 19J, GJS, Hamilton 14K gold case	125	175	250
M#982, 19J, GJS, Hamilton GF case	75	90	120
M#987, 17J, gold filled Hamilton case, sweep second	75	100	125
Barrel, Boulton, 19J, G–982, GF........................	60	80	100
Barrel, Judson, 19J, G#982, GF........................	60	80	100
Barrel, Perry, 17J, G#987, GF	60	80	100
Barrel, Reagan, 17J, G#987, GF	50	60	80
Barrel, Sidney, 17J, G#987, GF	60	80	100
Barrel, Webster, 17J, G#987, GF.......................	50	75	90
Cushion, 14K case, 17J	125	175	225
Cushion, 17J, gold filled case..........................	50	75	100
Cushion, 17J, G#987, engraved bezel, 14K, 1920	250	300	375

HAMILTON WATCH CO. (continued)

Hamilton, Martin, 17 jewels, 10k.

Hamilton, Russell, 17 jewels, gold filled.

Hamilton, Alan, 17 jewels, 10k.

Hamilton, Allison, 19 jewels, 14k

Hamilton, Brock, 19 jewels, Grade 982.

Hamilton, Cameron, 19 jewels, 14k.

Style or Grade—Description	Avg	Ex-Fn	Mint
Cushion, Bagley, 17J, G#987, GF	$50	$75	$100
Cushion, Martin, 17J, GF	50	60	80
Cushion, Russell, 17J, G#987, GF	50	75	100
Rectangular, 17J, hidden lugs, 14K	275	325	400
Rectangular, 17J, G#747, long lugs, 14K	200	225	275
Rectangular, 17J, rect. mvt. signed Illinois, GF	100	150	225
Rectangular, Alan, 17J, G#987, GF	60	80	100
Rectangular, Alliston, 19J, G#982, 14K	150	200	250
Rectangular, Andrews, 19J, G#401, 14K	140	175	200
Rectangular, Brandon, 17J, G#980, 10K GF	50	60	80
Rectangular, Brock, 19J, G#982, 14K	150	175	200
Rectangular, Cameron, 19J, G#982, 14K	150	175	200
Rectangular, Curvex, 19J, 14K case	250	300	400
Rectangular, Dodson, 17J, G#987, GF	$60	$80	$100
Rectangular, Dodson, 19J, G#982, GF	60	80	100
Rectangular, Donald, 19J, G#989, 14K	125	150	175
Rectangular, Dunham, 17J, G#987, GF	60	70	90
Rectangular, Dunkirk, 19J, G#982, 14K	150	200	225

Langdon   Dyson   Eric   Forbes

Hamilton, **Piping Rock**, Grade 979, ca. 1930.

Hamilton, **Coronado**, black enamel bezel.

Hamilton, fancy bezel, hinged back.

Hamilton, tonneau, blue enamel bezel, Grade 986.

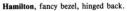

Style or Grade—Description	Avg	Ex-Fn	Mint
Rectangular, Dyson, GF	$50	$70	$90
Rectangular, Emerson, 17J, G#980, GF	75	100	125
Rectangular, Essex, 17J, G#980, GF	75	100	150
Rectangular, Forbes, GF	50	60	80
Rectangular, Foster, 19J, G#982, 14K.................	150	200	225
Rectangular, Gilman, 19J, G#982, 14K.................	200	250	300
Rectangular, Midas, 19J, G#982, 14K..................	150	200	250
Rectangular, Otis, 19J, G#982, Reverso style, 1940s, GF ..	1,200	1,400	1,600
Rectangular, Putman, G#987, 17J, 14K	125	150	175
Rectangular, Ross, 19J, G#982, GF....................	50	75	100

HAMILTON WATCH CO. (continued)

Hamilton, Otis, rectangular, Reverso, ca. 1945.

Hamilton, Dodson, rectangular, 17 jewels, gold filled.

Hamilton, Dunkirk, rectangular, 19 jewels, 14k

Hamilton, Emerson, rect., 17 jewels, gold filled.

Hamilton, Essex, rectangular, 17 jewels, Grade 980.

Hamilton, Midas, rectangular, hidden lugs.

Style or Grade—Description	Avg	Ex-Fn	Mint
Rectangular, Rutledge, 19J, G#982, Platinum	$450	$500	$550
Rectangular, Sutton, 19J, G#982, GF	60	75	95
Rectangular, Top Hat, 17J, G#982, 11 diamond dial, 14K .	900	1,000	1,200
Rectangular, Touraine, 19J, G#982, 14K	150	175	200
Rectangular, Whitman, 17J, G#980, GF................	60	70	90
Rectangular, Wilshire, 19J, G#982, GF	75	125	175
Rectangular, Yorktowne, 17J, G#980, GF	60	70	90
Round or Square case, 22J, 14K	125	140	160
Round, Army Issue, sweep sec. 24 hr. black dial, SS	40	50	75
Round, Endicott, 17J, G#987, GF.....................	50	60	80
Round, Langdon, 19J, G#982, GF	50	60	80
Round, Langdon, 17J, G#747, GF	50	60	80
Round, Lange, 17J, G#747, 14K	150	175	180
Round, Mystery, 22J, G#770, 14 diamond dial & bezel, 1955	300	400	500
Round, Neil, 17J, G#747, GF..........................	40	50	75
Round, Norde, 18J, G#748, 14K	150	175	180
Round, Nordon, 18J, G#748, GF	50	60	80
Round, Paige, 19J, G#982, GF	50	60	80
Round, Sentinel, 17J, G#987S, sweep second, hack set, GF	65	75	95

Hamilton, **Ross**, rectangular, 19 jewels, gold filled.

Hamilton, **Sutton**, rectangular, 19 jewels, gold filled.

Hamilton, **Touraine**, 19 jewels, 14k.

Hamilton, **Whitman**, rectangular, 17 jewels, gold filled.

Hamilton, **Yorktowne**, rect., 17 jewels, gold filled

Hamilton, **Wilshire**, rect., 19 jewels, gold filled.

Hamilton, **Seckron**, square, 17 jewels, doctors style.

Hamilton, **Winthrop**, rect., 17 jewels, 14k.

Style or Grade—Description	Avg	Ex-Fn	Mint
Round, Sentinel, 17J, GF	$50	$60	$70
Round, Spur, 19J, G-989, "Swirl Design," 14K	1,500	1,800	2,000
Round, Steeldon, 17J, G-747, SS	20	30	45
Round, Vandon, 17J, stainless	10	15	25
Round, selfwind, 23J, gold filled	40	50	60
Round, selfwind, 25J, gold filled case	40	50	60
Round, selfwind, 17J, 14K case	95	110	135
Round, Time Zone Dial (P.M.C.E.), 14K case	200	225	275
Round, 22J, small diamonds on bezel & dial, 14K	295	325	400
Round, 17J, small diamonds on dial, 14K	155	175	195

Hamilton, Linwood, rect., 19 jewels, gold filled.

Hamilton, Endicott, round, 17 jewels, gold filled.

Hamilton, Sentinel, round, sweep second.

Hamilton, Foster, rectangular, 19 jewels, 14k.

Hamilton, Brock, rectangular, 19 jewels, 14k.

Hamilton, Langley, tonneau, Grade 979.

Style or Grade—Description	Avg	Ex-Fn	Mint
Round, 17J, 14K case	$95	$125	$135
Round, 17J, gold filled case	40	50	60
Round, 17J, stainless steel	15	20	35
Square, 17J, 14K, diamond on dial	200	225	250
Square, 17J, 14K case	125	140	160
Square, 17J, gold filled case	50	60	75
Square, 17J, 2-tone dial, 14K	275	325	400
Square, Driver's watch, stem at 12:00, GF	200	250	300
Square, Eric, GF	50	60	80
Square, Glenn, 17J, G–747, diamonds on dial, 14K ....★	275	325	400
Square, Greenwich, 19J, G–987, GF	65	75	95
Square, Greenwich, 17J, G–987, GF	60	80	100
Square, Hastings, 17J, 14K	150	175	225
Square, Hastings, 17J, GF	60	80	100
Square, Norman, 19J, 14K	150	175	200
Square, Norman, 19J, GF	60	80	100

Hamilton, cushion, 17 jewels, ca. 1920.

Hamilton, rectangular, 17 jewels, long lugs.

Hamilton, rect. "Hamilton Illinois" on dial.

Hamilton, round, mystery dial with diamonds.

Hamilton, rectangular, Top Hat, diamond dial.

Hamilton, rectangular, hidden lugs, 14k.

Style or Grade—Description	Avg	Ex-Fn	Mint
Tonneau case, 17J, 14K case............................	$175	$200	$225
Tonneau case, 17J, gold filled case	50	60	80
Tonneau, 17J, G#986, blue enamel bezel	900	1,100	1,300
Tonneau, 17J, G#987, hinged back, 18K white gold	400	450	500
Tonneau, Coronado, G#979, 19J, barrel dial, 14K	700	850	1,100
Tonneau, Langley, 19J, G#979, 14K	150	175	225
Tonneau, Langley, 19J, #979, 14K	125	150	175
Tonneau, Perry, 17J, #987, GF	60	80	100
Tonneau, Piping Rock, 19J, G#979, round dial, 14K	1,000	1,200	1,400
Tonneau, Piping Rock, G#979, round dial, WGF	500	700	900
Tonneau, Webster, 17J, G#987, GF	60	80	100

Hamilton, Altair, gold filled.

Hamilton, Aquatel "B", gold filled.

Hamilton, Everest, gold filled.

Hamilton, Flight II, gold filled.

Hamilton, Converta, gold filled.

Hamilton, Meteor, gold filled.

Hamilton, Pacer, gold filled.

Hamilton, Polaris, 14k.

MAN'S ELECTRIC WRIST WATCH
500, 505 SERIES

Style or Grade—Description	Avg	Ex-Fn	Mint
Altair, center sec., 10K GF case	$175	$225	$275
Aquatel "B," center sec., 10K GF case	75	100	125
Converta II, center sec., 10K GF case	75	100	125
Everest, 10J, trapezoial, center sec., polished case, GF	75	85	125
Flight II, center sec., GF case	200	250	350
Flight II, center sec., 14K case	800	1,000	1,200
Gemini, cushion, center sec., 10K GF case	30	40	55

Hamilton, R.R. Special, stainless steel.

Hamilton, Sea-Lectric I, gold filled, water proof.

Hamilton, Saturn, 14k.

Hamilton, Savitar, 14k.

Hamilton, Sea-Lectric II, stainless steel.

Hamilton, Skip Jack, gold filled.

Hamilton, Summit, gold filled.

Hamilton, Taurus, gold filled.

Style or Grade—Description	Avg	Ex-Fn	Mint
Meteor, center sec., 10K GF case	$125	$150	$225
Nautilus, center sec., GF case	20	30	45
Nautilus, center sec., 14K	100	130	185
Pacer, triangular, center sec., GF case	200	250	300
Polaris, cente sec., 14K case	300	350	400
RR Special, center sec., 14K GF	125	150	200
RR Special, center sec., 10K GF case	40	50	65
RR Special, center sec., SS case	30	40	55
Saturn, center sec., 10K GF case	30	40	55
Saturn, center sec., 14K case	400	450	525
Savitar, center sec., 14K case	250	300	350

Hamilton, Ventura, ca. 1950s, 14k.

Hamilton, Spectra, water tight.

Hamilton, Vega, gold filled.

Hamilton, Titan II, gold filled.

Hamilton, Vantage, gold filled.

Hamilton, Victor II, gold filled.

Style or Grade—Description	Avg	Ex-Fn	Mint
Sea-Lectric I, watertight, center sec., GF case............	$125	$150	$200
Sea-Lectric II, watertight, center sec., GF case...........	35	45	65
Skip Jack, center sec., 10K GF case	30	40	55
Spectra, round, watertight, center sec., 14K case	300	350	450
Spectra II, square, center sec., 10K GF case	80	100	125
Summit, center sec., 14K GF	45	55	75
Summit II, center sec., 10K case	30	40	55
Taurus, center sec., 10K GF case......................	75	100	125
Titan, watertight, center sec., GF case	65	75	95
Titan II, watertight, center sec., GF	75	85	110
Titan III, watertight, center sec., 10K GF case	85	95	125
Vantage, center sec., 10K GF case.....................	100	125	150
Vega, center sec., 14K case	250	300	350
Vega, center sec., 10K YGF	100	125	150
Ventura, triangular, center sec., 14K case	1,000	1,200	1,400
Ventura, triangular, center sec., 6 diamond dial, 14K case.	900	1,000	1,200
Victor, square, center sec., 10K GF....................	100	125	150
Victor II, round, center sec., 10K GF..................	100	150	200
Electric, 6 to 12 diamonds on dial, center sec., 14K case ..	300	350	450

Style or Grade—Description	Avg	Ex-Fn	Mint
Electric, 6 to 12 diamonds on dial, center sec., GF case...	$175	$200	$250
Electric, 3 to 4 diamond dial, center sec., GF case	95	125	165
Electric, 20 to 40 diamond bezel, center sec., GF case	175	200	250
Electric, Model 500, 14K case.........................	95	115	140
Electric, Model 500, GF...............................	40	50	75
Electric, Model 500, 12 diamonds on dial	225	255	295
Electric, Model 500, triangular, GF....................	175	250	300
Electric, Model 500, triangular, 14K	800	900	1,000
Electric, Model 505, RR style dial, sweep sec., GF	65	75	95

Hamilton, Spur, enamel bezel.

Hamilton, Greenwich, Grade 987, gold filled.

Hamilton, Brandon, gold filled.

Hamilton, Steeldon, stainless steel.

Hamilton, Langdon, 10k gold filled.
Lange 14k Gold

Hamilton, Nordon, 10k gold filled
Norde 14k Gold

HAMILTON WATCH CO. (continued)

LADY'S WRIST WATCH

Style or Model — Description	Avg	Ex-Fn	Mint
Cushion, 14K case	$60	$70	$80
Cushion, gold filled	20	25	35
Cushion, stainless steel	10	15	22
Hunter style case, 100-120 diamonds on 14K case & bracelet	2,000	2,500	3,500
Locket or Wrist, convertible watch, 14K case	75	85	100
Locket or Wrist, convertible watch, gold filled	50	55	75
Rectangular or Square, 14K case	60	70	80
Rectangular or Square, gold filled	25	30	40
Rectangular or Square, stainless steel	15	20	28
Square or Cushion, 2 diamonds, 14K	60	70	80
Square or Cushion, 4 diamonds, 14K	70	80	90
Square or Cushion, 6 diamonds, 14K	80	90	100
Square or Cushion, 10 diamonds, 14K	100	110	125
Square or Cushion, 18 diamonds, 14K	200	245	295
Square or Cushion, 30 diamonds, 14K	335	385	495
Square or Cushion, 40 diamonds, 14K	600	685	800
Tonneau, 14K case	65	75	85
Tonneau, gold filled	20	25	35

Early leather wrist watch holder.   Early leather and gold wrist watch holder

Grade 986A, 6/0 size
Open face, ¼ plate movt., 17 jewels, double roller

Grade 987, 6/0 size
Hunting, ¼ plate movt., 17 jewels, double roller

Grade 987A, 6/0 size
Open face, ¼ plate movt., 17 jewels, double roller

Grade 987S, 6/0 size
Hunting, ¼ plate movt., 17 jewels, double roller

Grade 747, 8/0 size
Open face, ¼ plate movt., 17 jewels, double roller

Grade 980, 14/0 size
Open face, ¼ plate movt., 17 jewels, double roller

Grade 982, 14/0 size
Open face, ¼ plate movt., 19 jewels, double roller

Grade 982M, 14/0 size
Open face, ¼ plate movt., 19 jewels, double roller

Grade 989, 18/0 size
Open face, ¼ plate movt., 17 jewels, double roller

Grade 997, 20/0 size
Open face, ¼ plate movt., 17 jewels, double roller

Grade 721, 21/0 size
Open face, ¼ plate movt., 17 jewels, double roller

Grade 995, 21/0 size
Open face, ¼ plate movt., 17 jewels, double roller

Grade 911, 22/0 size
Open face, ¼ plate movt., 17 jewels, double roller

Grade 911M, 22/0 size
Open face, ¼ plate movt., 17 jewels, double roller

HAMILTON WATCH CO. (continued)

Grade 780, 21/0 size
17 jewels

Grade 770, 12/0 size
22 jewels

Grade 761, 21/0 size
22 jewels

Grade 757, 21/0 size
22 jewels

Grade 753, 12/0 size, 19 jewels
Grade 752, 12/0 size, 17 jewels

Grade 754, 12/0 size, 19 jewels
Grade 770, 12/0 size, 17 jewels

Grade 750 & 751, 21/0 size
17 jewels

Grade 748, 8/0 size
18 jewels

Grade 747, 8/0 size
17 jewels

HAMILTON WATCH CO. (continued)

Grade 735, 8/0 size
18 jewels

Grade 730, 8/0 size
17 jewels

Grade 679, 17 jewels
Grade 692, 694 - calendar

Grade 666 & 663, 17 jewels
Grade 668 - calendar

Grade 658, 661, 667, 17 jewels
Grade 665, 23J, **Grade 664**, 25J
Grade 662, 690 - calendar, 17J

Grade 623 & 624, 17 jewels

Grade 505, electric, 11 jewels

Man's wrist watch, cushion, 5/0 size.   Man's wrist watch, tonneau, 5/0 size

HAMPDEN WATCH CO.
U.S.A.
MAN'S WRIST WATCH

Style or Grade — Description	Avg	Ex-Fn	Mint
Cushion, 14K case	$125	$150	$175
Cushion, gold filled	50	60	70
Rectangular, 14K case	125	135	160
Rectangular, gold filled	40	50	60
Rectangular, stainless steel	10	15	25
Round, 14K case	70	80	90
Round, gold filled	30	35	45
Round, stainless steel	10	15	25
Tonneau, 14K case	125	150	175
Tonneau, gold filled	40	50	60
Upper Ten	15	20	28

LADY'S WRIST WATCH

Style or Grade — Description	Avg	Ex-Fn	Mint
Josephine, 9 lignes	$20	$25	$35
Lady Grace, 5½ lignes (Swiss)	20	25	35
Mary Jane, 9 lignes	20	25	35
Molly Stark Model or Diadem Model, gold filled	20	25	35

Harwood Self Wind Watch Co., 15 jewels, rim set by turning bezel clockwise. Harwood Self Wind Watch Co., 15 jewels, 18k, rim set.

HARWOOD SELF WIND WATCH CO.
ENGLAND & SWISS

Style or Grade — Description	Avg	Ex-Fn	Mint
Round, 15J, set hands by rotating bezel, self wind, 9K case	$350	$400	$450
Round, 15J, set hands by rotating bezel, self wind, GF ...	200	235	275
Round, 15J, set hands by rotating bezel, self wind, stainless	100	150	175
Round, 15J, set hands by rotating bezel, self wind, 14K ..	450	500	600
Tonneau, 15J, bezel set, 1920s, 18K white..............	1,200	1,400	1,600

HEBDOMAS
SWISS

Style or Grade — Description	Avg	Ex-Fn	Mint
Cushion, 7J, 8 day, by A. Schild......................	$250	$350	$450
Round, 7J, 8 day, Swiss	200	300	400
Round, 7J, 8 day, visible escapement	350	450	550

Helbros fancy rectangular ladies watch.   Helbros, 9½ lignes   Helbros, 12½ lignes

HELBROS
SWISS

Style or Grade — Description	Avg	Ex-Fn	Mint
Rectangular, 6J, YGF................................	$30	$40	$55
Square, 6J, YGF	25	30	45

HELBROS (continued)

Style or Grade—Description	Avg	Ex-Fn	Mint
Lady's Round, 17J, YGF	$10	$15	$25
Lady's Tonneau, 6J, YGF............................	15	20	30

HELVETIA
SWISS

Style or Grade—Description	Avg	Ex-Fn	Mint
Square, 17J, c. 1950s, SS............................	$30	$40	$55

Heuer Watch Co. chronograph, 17 jewels, c. 1945.

Heuer Watch Co., chronograph, 3 registers, triple date, moon phase

HEUER
SWISS

Style or Grade — Description	Avg	Ex-Fn	Mint
Round, 17J, "Carrera," chronograph, 3 reg., 1965.......	$300	$350	$425
Round, 17J, "Autavia," chronograph, 30 min., 12 hr. & 24 hr. counters, the 24 hr. counter on bezel	400	435	500
Round, 17J, day date month, selfwind, watertight, 18K...	100	120	155
Round, 17J, day date month, selfwind, watertight, SS	50	65	85
Round, 17J, chronograph, day date month, 18K case.....	600	800	1,000
Round, 17J, chronograph, day date month, SS case	100	150	200
Round, 17J, chronograph, day date month, moon phase, 18K case	1,000	1,200	1,500
Round, 17J, chronograph, day date month, moon phase, SS case	400	500	600
Round, 17J, chronograph, 2 reg., day date month, moon phase, 18K case	1,000	1,200	1,500

Heuer, round, day-date, moon phase.

Heuer, round, day-date-month.

Style or Grade—Description	Avg	Ex-Fn	Mint
Round, 17J, chronograph, 2 reg., day date month, moon phase, SS	$400	$500	$650
Round, 15J, chronograph, tele-tachometer, 18K	1,000	1,100	1,200
Round, "Skipper," chronograph, date & 15 min. reg., SS	200	250	300
Round, early chronograph, c. 1925, pusher on swivel horn at 6 o'clock, telemeter & tachometer, 18K	1,500	1,800	2,000
Tonneau, 17J, chronograph, 2 reg., c. 1945, 18K	3,000	3,500	4,000
Mareograph, chronograph, hr. reg., solar & lunar time & tides, 18K	600	700	800
Mareograph, chronograph, hr. reg., solar & lunar time & tides, 14K	500	600	700
Mareograph, chronograph, hr. reg., solar & lunar time & tides, 10K	400	450	500
Mareograph, chronograph, hr. reg., solar & lunar time & tides, SS	300	400	450

HUBER
MUNICH

Style or Grade — Description	Avg	Ex-Fn	Mint
Rectangular, 15J, by Movado, c. 1935, 14K	$400	$450	$555
Round, 16J, c. 1946, GF	90	110	140
Round, chronograph, caliber 13, c. 1935, 18K	600	800	1,000
Round, tacho-telemeter, 2 reg., caliber 71, c. 1945, 18K	600	800	1,000
Tonneau, 15J, "Nautica," early watertight, GF	150	185	250
Lady's, round, 15J, "Mimo," GF	20	30	45

E. HOWARD WATCH CO.
U.S.A.

Style or Grade—Description	Avg	Ex-Fn	Mint
Made for Howard by Hamilton, GF..................★	$350	$400	$475
Rectangular, curvex, GF	300	400	500

Illinois, **Beaubrummell**, 19 jewels, gold filled.

Illinois, **Chieftain**, 15 jewels, gold filled.

Illinois, **Champion**, 17 jewels, base metal.

Illinois, **Consul**, 19 jewels, 14k.

ILLINOIS WATCH CO.
U.S.A.

Style or Grade — Description	Avg	Ex-Fn	Mint
Tonneau, 14K case	$175	$225	$300
Tonneau, gold filled	75	100	125
Tonneau, stainless...................................	50	60	80
Tonneau, sec. bits at 9 o'clock, 14K case...............	200	250	350
Tonneau, sec. bits at 9 o'clock, gold filled	85	95	150
Tonneau, sec. bits at 9 o'clock, stainless	75	85	100
Square, 14K case	150	175	200
Square, gold filled..................................	85	100	125
Square, stainless	40	50	60
Rectangular, 14K case	175	225	300
Rectangular, gold filled	75	100	150
Rectangular, stainless	50	70	90
Rectangular, 17J, G#807, 14K, 1920	300	350	425
Illinois dial, Hamilton mvt., rectangular case	125	175	225

Illinois, **Major**, 17 jewels, gold filled.

Illinois, **Marquis**, 19 jewels, curved.

Illinois, **Mate**, 17 jewels, gold filled.

Illinois, **New Yorker**, 17 jewels, 14k.

Illinois, **Piccadilly**, 17 jewels, gold filled.

Illinois, **Pilot**, 17 jewels, gold filled.

Style or Grade—Description	Avg	Ex-Fn	Mint
Illinois dial, Hamilton mvt., round case................	$75	$100	$125
Military style, with black dial, gold filled	75	100	125
White dial, luminus hand & numbers	75	100	125
Ace, barrel, 17J, 3/0 size, GF	$75	$100	$125
Aviator, rectangular with cut corners, 17J, GF...........	75	100	125
Beau Brummell, tonneau, 19J, G#609, GF	100	125	150
Bostonian, square, 15J, link style bracelet, GF...........	75	85	100
Caprice, lady's handbag style covered in snake skin	75	85	100
Champion, cushion, 17J, GF	75	100	125
Chesterfield, rectangular, 17J, G#207, GF	100	125	150
Chieftain, barrel, 15J, G#605, GF	75	100	150

ILLINOIS WATCH CO. (continued)

Illinois, **Prince**, 17 jewels, gold filled.

Illinois, **Speedway**, 17 jewels, gold filled.

Illinois, **Jolly Roger**, 17 jewels, gold filled.

Illinois, rectangular, Grade 807, ca. 1920.

Illinois, rectangular, Grade 207, 12/0 size, 17 jewels.

Illinois, rectangular, 18/0 size, 1st, 2nd & 3rd model.

Style or Grade—Description	Avg	Ex-Fn	Mint
Consul, tonneau, 21J, G#601, 14K	$175	$225	$275
Consul, tonneau, 19J, G#609, 14K	150	175	200
Ensign, tonneau, 15J, G#605, GF	100	125	150
Jolly Rodger, cushion, 17J, 3/0 size, GF	100	125	170
Major, cushion, 17J, G#307, 3/0 size, GF	75	100	125
Marquis, tonneau, 19J, G#609, GF, curved	100	125	150
Marquis, tonneau, 17J, G#907 & 905, GF, curved	100	125	150
Mate, tonneau, 17J, 3/0 size, GF	75	100	125
New Yorker, square, 17J, G#607, 14K	200	250	300
Piccadilly, oval, 17J, G#607, GF	350	425	500
Pilot, octagonal, 17J, GF	75	85	100
Prince, tonneau, 17J, GF	75	100	125
Quarter Miler, barrel, 17J, 3/0 size, GF	75	85	100
Ritz, tonneau, 2-tone, GF	150	200	250
Speedway, tonneau, 17J, 3/0 size, GF	100	125	150
Tuxedo, rectangular, 17J, 14K	200	225	250
Whippet, barrel, 17J, 3/0 size, GF	100	125	150

LADY'S WRIST WATCH

Style of Grade — Description	Avg	Ex-Fn	Mint
Locket or Wrist Watch, convertible, 14K case	$75	$85	$95
Locket or Wrist Watch, convertible, gold filled	30	35	45
Locket or Wrist Watch, convertible, stainless	10	15	22
Rectangular, 14K case	60	70	90
Rectangular, gold filled	30	35	45
Square, gold filled.................................	25	30	40
Square, stainless	15	20	32
Oval dial, gold filled...............................	25	30	40
Oval dial, stainless	10	15	20
Purse style watch, with leather cover	60	70	80
Round, Illinois dial, Hamilton mvt., gold filled	15	20	30
Round, Illinois dial, Hamilton mvt., stainless	10	12	20

Ingersoll Military style with a pierced protective cover.

Ingersoll, 6/0 size, radiolite dial.

INGERSOLL
U.S.A.

Style or Grade—Description	Avg	Ex-Fn	Mint
Man's wrist watch, rectangular case	$5	$10	$15
Man's wrist watch, round case	5	10	15
Man's wrist watch, square case	5	10	15
Man's wrist watch, tonneau case	5	10	15
Man's or Lady's Radiolite...........................	10	15	25
Midget for lady	10	15	25
Military trench style with a pierced protective cover	45	50	85

E. INGRAHAM CO.
U.S.A.

Style or Grade—Description	Avg	Ex-Fn	Mint
Rectangular...	$5	$10	$15

Style or Grade—Description	Avg	Ex-Fn	Mint
Round	$5	$10	$15
Square	5	10	15
Tonneau	5	10	15
Wrist-O-Crat	10	15	25

International W. Co., tonneau, 17 jewels, ca. 1920.

International W. Co., tonneau, 18k, 17J, ca. 1925.

International W. Co., auto wind, waterproof, 18k.

International W. Co., center seconds, 18k.

International W. Co., square, 17 jewels, ca. 1940s.

International W. Co., center seconds, 21J, ca. 1950s.

INTERNATIONAL WATCH CO.
SWISS

MAN'S WRIST WATCH

Style or Grade—Description	Avg	Ex-Fn	Mint
Cushion, 15J, Brg. mvt., c. 1935, 14K	$450	$500	$575
Rectangular, 17J, 18K case	600	700	800

International W. Co., Royal Navy model, ca. 1950s. International W. Co., sweep second, 18k.

Style or Grade—Description	Avg	Ex-Fn	Mint
Round, 21J, autowind, sweep sec., stainless	$200	$250	$300
Round, 18J, large 18K case, tear drop lugs	500	550	625
Round, 18J, "Royal Navy," waterproof, 1950, SS	300	350	450
Round, 17J, 18K case................................	200	250	300
Round, 17J, sweep sec., stainless	125	140	200
Round, 17J, "Aquatimer," watertight, date, stainless.....	100	120	150
Round, 17J, center sec., 18K	500	550	625
Round, 17J, autowind, waterproof, date, 18K	1,000	1,100	1,300
Round, 15J, c. 1915, 18K	400	500	600
Round, 15J, c. 1946, GF	100	120	150
Round, chronograph, tachometer, 3 reg., date-date, caliber 7750, autowind, titanium case, presently made	1,000	1,200	1,500
Round, "Ocean 2000," auto, titanium case..............	500	600	800
Round, center sec., 18K..............................	600	700	800
Square, 21J, applied gold indexes, 1950, 18K	1,500	1,800	2,200
Square, 21J, stem wind, 18K case	400	500	600
Square, 17J, 18K case	200	250	300
Square, 17J, aux. sec., 1940, pink, 18K	1,200	1,400	1,700
Tonneau, 17J, c. 1920s, 18K case	1,500	1,700	2,000

LADY'S WRIST WATCH

Style or Grade — Description	Avg	Ex-Fn	Mint
Round, 18K case	$125	$145	$200
Round, small diamonds on bezel, 18K case	450	495	595

INTERNATIONAL WATCH CO.
MOVEMENT IDENTIFICATION

Caliber 51N

Caliber 51

Caliber 41

Caliber 93, Baguette

Caliber 92

Caliber 431

Caliber 91

Caliber 90

Caliber 96

Caliber 94

Caliber 84

Caliber 44

Caliber 85

Caliber 852
Calendar - 8521

Caliber 853
Calendar - 8531

Caliber 401

Caliber 60   Caliber 62   Caliber 61   Caliber 86

Caliber 75 & 76   Caliber 87   Caliber 89

Caliber 88   Caliber 70   Caliber 83

Caliber 64   Caliber 63   Caliber 64

Invicta, square, sweep second, 17 jewels.

Invicta, round, daty-date, waterproof.

Invicta, triple date, moon phases.

Invicta, day-date-month, center second.

Invicta, 17 jewels, waterproof.

Invicta, auto-wind, waterproof, 17 jewels.

INVICTA
Seeland, Inc.
SWISS

Style or Grade — Description	Avg	Ex-Fn	Mint
Rectangular, 15J, chronograph, min. register at 6 o'clock, a decimal register for seconds at 12 o'clock, 18K ★ ★ ★	$3,000	$4,000	$5,000

INVICTA (continued)

Style or Grade—Description	Avg	Ex-Fn	Mint
Round, chronograph, 2 register, 18K	$350	$400	$450
Round, 17J, chronograph, 2 register, stainless	110	130	165
Round, 17J, auto wind, c. sec., 18K case	100	120	140
Round, 17J, auto wind, c. sec., SS case	30	40	55
Round, 17J, c. sec., 18K case	125	150	175
Round, 17J, c. sec., SS case	25	30	45
Round, 17J, SS case	15	20	30
Square, 17J, center sec., 18K case	200	225	250
Square, 17J, center sec., SS case	75	100	125
Square, "Quadramatic," center sec., auto wind, c. 1950, 18K	185	195	235
17J, day date month, moon phase, auto wind, watertight, 18K	600	700	800
17J, day date month, moon phase, auto wind, watertight, SS	250	300	350
17J, day date month, auto wind, watertight, c. sec., 18K	150	200	225
17J, day date month, auto wind, watertight, c. sec., SS	60	70	85
17J, day date, auto wind, watertight, c. sec., 18K case	150	200	225
17J, day date, auto wind, watertight, c. sec., SS	45	50	65

JUNGHANS
SWISS

Style or Grade — Description	Avg	Ex-Fn	Mint
Round, 15J, sweep sec., stainless, c. 1960	$10	$15	$20
Round, 19J, tachometer chronograph, 2 registers, SS	150	175	225
Round, 21J, sweep sec., 36 hr., wind indicator	50	65	95
Round, "Minivox" alarm, c. 1955	75	85	100
Tonneau, 7J, stainless, c. 1940	35	45	60
Lady's round, 15J, stainless	10	12	15

Jules Jurgensen, tonneau, 31 jewels, 5 minute repeater, 18k gold, bezel with black champleve enamel, ca. 1906.

Jules Jurgensen, 15 jewels, jump hour, 18k, ca. 1930.

Jules Jurgensen, fancy lugs, 14k.

JULES JURGENSEN
SWISS
MAN'S WRIST WATCH

Style or Grade — Description	Avg	Ex-Fn	Mint
Rectangular, 18K case, 1950s	$250	$300	$350
Rectangular, 17J, fancy lugs, 14K	200	250	300
Rectangular, 15J, jump hr., revolving min., c. 1930s, 18K	3,000	3,500	4,000
Round, 18K case	175	200	250
Round, 17J, self wind, sweep sec., 18K	175	225	275
Round, ¼ repeater, 18K case..........................	15,000	18,000	20,000
Round, 17J, 4 diamonds at 12-3-6-9, 18K case	250	300	350
Round, 17J, auto wind, sweep sec., cal. date, 18K	150	175	200
Square, 18K case.....................................	200	225	275
Tank, 17J, 18K case, c. 1920s	500	600	700
Tonneau, 31J, Adj.7P, min. repeater, c. 1910, 18K case ..	15,000	17,000	20,000
Tonneau, 31J, 5 min. repeater, 18K, c. 1910.............	55,000	70,000	80,000

LADY'S WRIST WATCH

Style or Grade — Description	Avg	Ex-Fn	Mint
Rectangular, 18K case	$150	$175	$200
Rectangular, small diamonds on case, 18K	300	350	400

A. LANGE
GERMANY

Style or Grade—Description	Avg	Ex-Fn	Mint
World War II pilot's watch, black dial..................	$600	$800	$900
World War II skin diver's, straps to leg, oversize	1,500	1,800	2,000
World War II, rectangular	1,200	1,400	1,800

JEAN LASSALE
SWISS

Style or Grade—Description	Avg	Ex-Fn	Mint
9J, auto wind, caliber 2000, thin, c. 1978	$100	$125	$160

LAVINA
BY LeCOULTRE
SWISS

Style or Grade—Description	Avg	Ex-Fn	Mint
Rectangular, 17J, c. 1950s, 18K case...................	$100	$135	$165

Style or Grade—Description	Avg	Ex-Fn	Mint
Rectangular, 17J, ADJ, 1950, GF	$35	$45	$55
Round, 17J, c. 1950s, 18K case	95	125	155
Round, 17J, Glucydur bal., 1950, GF..................	35	45	55

Le Coultre, rectangular, duoplan, 15J, ca. 1940.

Le Coultre, rectangular, 17J, 14k, ca. 1950s.

Le Coultre, auto wind, 18k, ca. 1950s

Le Coultre, auto wind with power reserve indication.

Le Coultre, triple date, moon phase, ca. 1940s.

Le Coultre, triple date, moon phase, engraved bezel.

LE COULTRE & CO.
SWISS

MAN'S WRIST WATCH

Style or Grade — Description	Avg	Ex-Fn	Mint
Padlock shaped, 15J, duoplan movement, back wind, c. 1930, different color of gold cases, etc.	$1,000	$1,200	$1,500
Rectangular, 15J, Reverso case, 14K case, c. 1933	4,000	5,000	6,000
Rectangular, moon phase calendar, 14K.................	4,000	4,500	5,000
Rectangular, moon phase calendar, 18K.................	4,500	5,000	6,000
Rectangular, 18J, Reverso, fluted bezel, center sec., 1940, 18K...	6,500	7,000	7,500
Rectangular, 17J, Reverso standard, 1935, 18K	7,000	8,000	10,000

Le Coultre, Reverso, 17 jewels, ca. 1940s.

Le Coultre, Reverso, stainless steel, ca. 1930s.

Le Coultre, round, 18k, 17J, ca. 1960s.

Le Coultre, mystery watch, 17J, waterproof, ca. 1950s.

Le Coultre, astronomic with moon phases, ca. 1940s.

Le Coultre, alarm, 18k, 19J, ca. 1950s.

Style or Grade—Description	Avg	Ex-Fn	Mint
Rectangular, 17J, day date month, moon phase, c. 1940s, 18K case	$2,500	$2,700	$3,000
Rectangular, 17J, "Duoplan," 2 level mvt. for wind, 14K, c. 1940	1,000	1,100	1,200
Rectangular, 17J, moonphase, day-month-date on outer ring, GF	1,800	2,000	2,500
Rectangular, 17J, Glucidur bal., 1950, 14K	400	500	600
Rectangular, 15J, Adj.4P, "Reverso," SS	1,600	1,800	2,200
Round, 14K case	125	150	175
Round, 18K case	$150	$175	$250

Le Coultre, rectangular, 18k case & band.

Le Coultre, auto wind, 17J, 18k, ca. 1950s.

Le Coultre, chronograph, ca. 1950s.

Le Coultre, round, alarm, date, ca. 1950s.

Le Coultre, quartz, waterproof, ca. 1960s.

Le Coultre, triple date, moon phases, stainless steel.

Style or Grade—Description	Avg	Ex-Fn	Mint
Round, GF	$40	$50	$60
Round, moon phase, day-date-month, YGF	800	900	1,000
Round, 17J, wind indicator, self wind, GF	95	150	200
Round, "Memovox" alarm, GF	175	200	250
Round, "Memovox" alarm, date, GF	200	225	275
Round, 17J, Memovox, 21J, 1950, 18K	700	800	900
Round, alarm, 14K case..............................	400	500	600
Round, $20 gold piece	1,500	1,700	2,000
Round, moon phase calendar, 18K	2,500	3,000	3,200

LE COULTRE & CO. (continued)

Style or Grade—Description	Avg	Ex-Fn	Mint
Round, 19J, alarm, center sec., 18K, 1950	$300	$400	$600
Round, 17J, alarm, center sec., 10K GF, 1950	100	135	175
Round, 17J, chronograph, 3 reg., 1950, 18K	2,000	2,200	2,500
Round, 17J, chronograph, 2 reg., 1950s, 18K case	400	500	600
Round, 17J, day date month, moon phases, 10K GF	1,600	1,800	2,400
Round, 17J, auto wind with wind indicator, 14K.........	400	500	600
Round, 17J, auto wind, indicator at 9, 1950s, GF	200	250	300
Round, 17J, "Mysterious," 1960, 18K	1,000	1,200	1,500
Round, 17J, "Mysterious," waterproof, diamond dial, 1950, 14K	800	900	1,100
Round, 17J, "Mysterieuse," 3 diamond dial, 14K	900	1,000	1,100
Round, 15J, autowind, wind indicator	100	150	235
Round, 15J, 18K case & mesh band, c. 1965	500	550	600
Round, tachometer chronograph, 3 reg., 18K............	1,800	2,000	2,200
Square, 17J, cuff links, black dial, 14K	250	300	350
Tonneau, 13J, quartz, watertight, date, 1960s, 18K case ..	1,000	1,200	1,500
Travel Alarm with stand, demi hunter case	100	135	175

LADY'S WRIST WATCH

Style or Grade — Description	Avg	Ex-Fn	Mint
Rectangular, extra small mvt., 7mm, back wind, 18K case	$395	$445	$585
Rectangular, small diamonds on bezel	95	125	195
Round or Rectangular, GF	30	35	45

Leonidas, chronograph, day-date-month, 3 registers, stainless steel.

LEONIDAS
TAG-HEUER
SWISS

Style or Grade — Description	Avg	Ex-Fn	Mint
Round, chronograph, 2 reg., day-date-month, 18K	$300	$400	$500
Round, chronograph, day-date-month, moonphase, 18K ..	800	900	1,000
Round, 17J, day date month, moon phases, SS	150	200	250

LEONIDAS (continued)

Style or Grade—Description	Avg	Ex-Fn	Mint
Round, 17J, day date month, chronograph, 3 reg., SS	$400	$500	$600
round, 17J, SS......................................	30	40	50

LEMANIA
NOUVELLE LEMANIA
SWISS

Style or Grade—Description	Avg	Ex-Fn	Mint
Round, 17J, chronograph, 2 reg., 18K case..............	$600	$700	$800
Round, 17J, chronograph, 2 reg., SS	200	225	275

Le Phare, chronograph, 17J, 2 registers.   Le Phare, day-date-moon phases, 17J.

LE PHARE
SWISS

Style or Grade — Description	Avg	Ex-Fn	Mint
Rectangular, 17J, sector type, hour jumps back to 6, date	$500	$600	$800
Round, 17J, chronograph, 2 reg., 18K case..............	800	900	1,100
Round, 17J, chronograph, 2 reg., 14K case..............	600	700	900
Round, 17J, chronograph, 2 reg., SS case..............	125	135	165
Round, 17J, triple date, moon phases, GF	200	250	300
Round, tachometer, telemeter, 1 pusher, c. 1950, GF	300	350	400
Chronograph, 17J, 2 reg., GF & steel back..............	125	135	165

LIP
FRANCE

Style or Grade — Description	Avg	Ex-Fn	Mint
Rectangular, 1 min. tourbillon, the tourbillon can be seen from dial side which serves as a sec. hand, c. 1950 .... ★ ★ ★ ★	$60,000	$70,000	$85,000
Tonneau, 15J, 18K	500	600	700
Tonneau, 15J, GF....................................	90	125	185
Tonneau, 15J, stainless	65	95	145

Longines, 47mm, large Lindberg model.   Longines, small model Lindberg, ca. 1930.

Longines, flat square model, 14k.

Longines, mystery hand, 12 diamond dial.

Longines, duo-dial, hinged back, ca. 1930s.

Longines, rectangular, diamond dial, ca. 1935.

LONGINES
SWISS
MAN'S WRIST WATCH

Style or Grade — Description	Avg	Ex-Fn	Mint
Cushion, 17J, 14K case	$125	$150	$200
Cushion, 17J, GF	60	70	100
Rectangular, 17J, fancy lugs, 14K	350	400	475
Rectangular, 16J, duo-dial, GF	500	600	700
Rectangular, 15J, duo dial, 1930, 18K	2,000	2,200	2,500

LONGINES (continued)

Longines, rectangular, 17J, ca. 1930s.

Longines, rectangular, fancy lugs, 14k, 17J.

Longines, diamond dial, 14k, 17J.

Longines, round, 15J, 18k, ca. 1940s.

Style or Grade—Description	Avg	Ex-Fn	Mint
Rectangular, 18K case	$500	$550	$600
Rectangular, 14K case	200	225	250
Rectangular, GF	60	80	100
Rectangular, small diamonds on dial, 14K case	390	420	500
Rectangular, small diamonds on bezel, 14K case	395	435	525
Rectangular, doctor style dial, 18K case	1,200	1,500	2,000
Round, 16J, early watertight, stainless, c. 1940	40	50	65
Round, 17J, "Flagship" autowind, c. 1965	125	145	175
Round, 17J, G#232, 14K	130	155	180
Round, 17J, sweep sec., date, 18K case	200	250	300
Round, 17J, 18K case	150	175	225
Round, 17J, 14K case	125	150	175
Round, 17J, GF	20	27	35
Round, 17J, "Lindberg," 45mm, large model, movable bezel & center dial, 18K, c. 1937 .... ★ ★ ★ ★	25,000	30,000	35,000
Round, 17J, "Lindberg," 45mm, large model, movable bezel & center dial, silver	6,000	7,000	7,500
Round, 17J, "Lindberg," 45mm, large model, movable bezel & center dial, nickel	5,500	6,000	6,500
Round, 18J, chronograph, tachometer, 2 reg. 18K, c. 1926	1,200	1,400	1,600
Round, 19J, "Conquest" autowind, sweep second	120	135	165
Round, 25J, autowind, caliber 990, sweep second	40	50	65
Round, "Lindberg," small model, 18K case	3,000	4,000	5,000
Round, "Lindberg," small model, stainless	1,600	1,800	2,000

LONGINES (continued)

Style or Grade—Description	Avg	Ex-Fn	Mint
Round, "Nautical Miles," stainless steel	$200	$250	$300
Round, mystery style hands, 14K......................	400	500	600
Round, "Weems," large model, movable center dial, GF .	2,000	2,500	3,000
Round, "Weems," small model, movable bezel, 14K	500	600	700
Round, "Weems," small model, movable bezel, GF	250	275	300
Round, "Weems," small model, movable bezel, stainless .	200	250	275
Round, 1/5 sec. chronograph, 2 registers, 18K case.......	900	1,000	1,200
Round, 1/5 sec. chronograph, 2 registers, 14K case.......	800	900	1,000
Round, 1/5 sec. chronograph, 2 registers, GF	300	325	350
Square, 17J, flat, 14K	250	300	375
Tonneau, 17J, 14K case	175	200	250
Tonneau, 17J, GF	60	70	90

LADY'S WRIST WATCH

Style or Grade — Description	Avg	Ex-Fn	Mint
Round, small diamond on case & bezel, 14K case	$165	$250	$495
Round, plain, 18K case	80	85	95
Round, plain, 14K case	65	70	85
Round, plain, GF	15	20	28
Round, 17J, 6 diamond, 14K white gold	100	115	135

Mappin, duodial, 15 jewels, 9k gold, ca. 1930s.

MAPPIN
SWISS

Style or Grade—Description	Avg	Ex-Fn	Mint
Rectangular, 15J, duo dial, 9K case, 1930s	$1,500	$1,700	$2,000

MARS
SWISS

MAN'S WRIST WATCH

Style or Grade—Description	Avg	Ex-Fn	Mint
Rectangular, 15J, early auto wind, movement moves, c. 1934, flip top..................................	$400	$500	$600

Marvin, 26mm, 25 jewels, automatic wind, model 580.

MARVIN
SWISS

Style or Grade — Description	Avg	Ex-Fn	Mint
Square, 17J, chronograph, 2 reg., 18K, c. 1950	$1,500	$2,000	$2,500
Square, 17J, sweep sec., 14K, c. 1945...................	150	160	185
Lady's, Rectangular, digital, jump hour & minute........	150	200	250

MATHEY-TISSOT
SWISS
MAN'S WRIST WATCH

Style or Grade — Description	Avg	Ex-Fn	Mint
Round, 17J, chronograph, by Omega, 14K, c. 1933	$800	$850	$975
Round, 14K case	100	120	135
Round, $20 gold piece, hidden watch	1,100	1,200	1,600
Round, chronograph, 2 registers, 14K case	500	550	600
Round, self wind, chronograph, moon phase, day-date-month, 14K	1,000	1,400	1,600
Round, chronograph, 2 registers, moon phase, day-date-month, 18K	1,500	1,700	2,000
Square, 18K case.....................................	200	225	250

LADY'S WRIST WATCH

Style or Grade — Description	Avg	Ex-Fn	Mint
Round or Square, 14K case...........................	$55	$65	$80

Meylan, rectangular, 17J, 18k, ca. 1940s.

Meylan, tonneau, jump hour, ca. 1920s.

C. H. MEYLAN
SWISS

Style or Grade — Description	Avg	Ex-Fn	Mint
Rectangular, 17J, Adj.3P, hinged back, 18K.............	$600	$800	$1,000
Rectangular, 16J, digital jump hour, rotating min. hand, 14K..	2,000	2,500	3,000
Tonneau, 18J, jump hour, 1920, 18K	10,000	12,000	15,000

Mido Round, 17 jewels, automatic wind, sweep second hand.

Mido Round, 17 jewels, Chronograph with large 60 minute recorder.

MIDO
SWISS

Style or Grade — Description	Avg	Ex-Fn	Mint
Car radiator shaped, 15J, hinged back, 1940	$1,000	$1,200	$1,500
Rectangular, 15J, rotating disc for hands, 14K...........	800	1,000	1,200
Rectangular, 16J, "Direct-Time," 18K, c. 1935	500	585	695
Rectangular, 16J, time only, rose 14K	150	175	235
Round, 17J, "Multifort" caliber 917, 14K	100	130	200
Round, 17J, "Multicenterchron" tacho-telemeter, stainless	300	325	350
Round, 17J, chronograph, waterproof, SS...............	100	125	150
Lady's round, 15J, Adj.2P, silver, c. 1932	50	65	95

Mido, car radiator stype, novelty wrist watch, 15 jewels, ca. 1940s.

MILDIA
SWISS

Style or Grade—Description	Avg	Ex-Fn	Mint
Round, 17J, day date month, c. 1950s, SS	$45	$55	$65

Mimo, ladies baguette.

Mimo, rectangular, date, gold filled.

Mimo, jump hour, revolving minute & second.

Mimo, 8 day watch, ca. 1950s.

MIMO
SWISS

Style or Grade—Description	Avg	Ex-Fn	Mint
Rectangular, 15J, date, 1950, GF	$35	$45	$55
Rectangular, 15J, jump hour, 1950, GF	100	125	145
Rectangular, 15J, 8 days, 1950, GF	125	145	175
Lady's Rectangular, 15J, GF	10	15	20

Masonic Symbols, 17J, ca. 1950s.

Masonic Symbols, 17J, ca. 1950s.

MISCELLANEOUS WRIST WATCHES

Style or Grade—Description	Avg	Ex-Fn	Mint
Masonic, Swiss, quartz, multi-color symbols	$150	$200	$225
Rectangular, Swiss, jump hour, 9K	700	800	900
Rectangular, early auto wind, moving upper case, 1930s	600	700	800

MISCELLANEOUS WRIST WATCHES (continued)

Early auto wind, 17J, ca. 1930s.

Early auto wind, rock action wind, ca. 1930s.

Chronograph, 18J, 18k, ca. 1930s.

Chronograph, day-date-moon phase, 17J, ca. 1945.

Chronograph, 2 registers, tele-tachymetre.

Chronograph, 2 registers, split second, 17J, stainless.

Style or Grade—Description	Avg	Ex-Fn	Mint
Square, 17J, "Masonic," cervine, free Masonic symbols, 1945, silver	$750	$850	$1,000
Square, 17J, "Masonic," black dial, Masonic symbols, SS & GF	700	800	1,000
Square, 17J, "Masonic," circle on dial, Masonic symbols, SS	600	700	800

591

Minervia, minute repeater, repeats on 2 gongs.

Minervia, Sport, chronograph, 3 registers, 19J

Minervia, chronograph, 2 registers, 17J.

Minervia, center seconds, auto wind, 17J.

MINERVIA
SWISS

Style or Grade — Description	Avg	Ex-Fn	Mint
17J, chronograph, 3 reg., split sec., SS	$800	$900	$1,200
17J, chronograph, 3 reg., SS	150	200	250
17J, center sec., GF case, steel back	45	50	65
Round, 21J, min. repeater, 1930s	20,000	25,000	30,000
Round, 17J, chronograph, 2 reg., stainless	125	150	175
Round, 17J, chronograph, day-date-month	150	200	250
Round, 17J, tacho-telemeter, 2 reg., c. 1939	300	350	450
Round, 17J, min. repeater, 18K, c. 1925	20,000	22,000	25,000

MOVADO

Movado, day-date, 17J, 14k, ca. 1945.

Movado, day-date-month, 15J, ca. 1930s.

Movado Datograph, 15 jewels, ca. 1940s.

Movado Calendomatic, auto wind, waterproof, 18k.

Movado, round, 15J, 18k, ca. 1930s

Movado, rectangular, curved, polyplan, winds at 12 o'clock, ca. 1910.

MOVADO
SWISS

Style or Grade — Description	Avg	Ex-Fn	Mint
Calendermeto, moonphase calendar, open & close cover to wind, leather case	$400	$500	$600
Calendermeto, purse watch, moonphase calendar, open & close cover to wind, 14K	1,200	1,500	1,800
Curvex, 15J, "polyplan" wind at 12 o'clock, 46mm long, 18K, c. 1925	4,000	4,600	5,200

MOVADO (continued)

Style or Grade—Description	Avg	Ex-Fn	Mint
Ermeto, purse watch, open & close cover to wind, 14K case	$700	$900	$1,100
Ermeto, purse watch, open & close cover to wind, stainless	95	110	150
Hermetic pull apart, exotic skin cover	150	165	195
Rectangular, Curvex, wind at 12 o'clock, polyolan,			
c. 1910, 18K case................................	3,500	4,000	4,500
Rectangular, 15J, "Polyplan," 1910, 18K white..........	7,000	7,500	8,500
Round, GF...	25	30	35
Round, day window, 14K case	125	175	250
Round, day window, GF	50	60	75
Round, day window, stainless........................	40	50	60
Round, moon phase, chronograph, 2 registers, day-date-			
month, 18K	3,000	3,500	4,000
Round, day-date-month, 14K	600	700	800
Round, day-date-month, YGF	200	250	350
Round, day-date-month, stainless	175	200	250
Round, "Sub-Sea," sweep sec., date, stainless	70	80	95
Round, 13J, chronograph, 2 reg., 1940s, 18K case	1,500	2,000	2,500
Round, 15J, calendar day-date-month, moon phase, 18K..	1,800	2,200	2,500
Round, 15J, triple date, center sec., 1930, 18K...........	1,400	1,600	1,800
Round, 15J, center sec., 1930, 18K	1,000	1,200	1,500
Round, 15J, day date month, 1940s, 18K case	600	700	800
Round, 15J, center sec., time only, 1930s, 18K case	300	400	500
Round, 17J, triple date, 1950, 14K	1,200	1,400	1,600
Round, 17J, day date month, mid-'40s, 14K case	500	600	700
Round, 17J, tachometer, chronograph, 3 reg., stainess,			
c. 1950...	400	500	600
Round, 18J, triple date, 1940, 18K	1,600	1,800	2,200
Round, 28J, "Kingmatic," autowind, "Sub-Sea," 18K ...	225	300	375
Square, art deco, black dial, 18K case	350	400	500
Square, moon phases, calendar, "large"	3,500	4,000	4,500
Tonneau, 15J, "polyplan," winds at 12:00, 14K	3,500	4,000	4,500
Lady's, round, 15J, wind at 12:00, "Chronometer," 18K,			
c. 1915...	300	335	400

Movado Calendermeto, watch winds by opening and closing case, leather case.

MOVADO MOVEMENT IDENTIFICATION

Caliber 35   Caliber 65   Caliber 575   Caliber25, 27-Sweep Second

Caliber 28   Caliber 575, Ermeto-Baby   Caliber 578, Ermeto Calendine   579, Calendoplan Baby

Caliber 5   Caliber 15   Caliber 50SP   Caliber 105, 107-Center Second

Caliber 190   Caliber 375, 377-Center Second   Caliber 440, 443-Center Second

Caliber 510   Caliber 260M, 261   Caliber 150MN, 157-Sweep Second

MOVADO (continued)

Caliber 155, Calendermeto   Caliber 470, 477-Center Second   Caliber 473, 473SC-Calendar/Moon phase

Caliber 475, 475SC-Center Second   Caliber 225, 255M

Caliber 115   Caliber 118   Caliber 220, 220M

Caliber 221, 226   Caliber 223, 228   Caliber 224, 224A

Ulysse Nardin, split-second chronograph, ca. 1910.

Ulysse Nardin, chronograph, pulsations, ca. 1920s.

Ulysee Nardin, chronograph, 17 jewels, 18k, 1950s.

Ulysee Nardin, chronograph, 3 registers, ca. 1940s.

ULYSSE NARDIN
SWISS

Style or Grade — Description	Avg	Ex-Fn	Mint
Curvex, 14K case	$400	$500	$600
Rectangular, 18K case	225	250	300
Rectangular, 14K	200	225	250
Round, 13J, chronograph, 2 reg., 1940, 18K	2,000	2,500	3,000
Round, 17J, chronograph, 3 reg., c. 1940s, 18K case	1,000	1,100	1,300
Round, 17J, chronograph, medical, 2 reg., 1920, 18K	2,500	3,000	3,500
Round, 19J, split sec. chronograph, c. 1910s, silver	7,000	8,000	10,000
Round, 19J, chronograph, 2 registers, 18K, c. 1910	1,400	1,500	1,800
Round, 19J, chronograph, tachometer, 14K, c. 1910	1,200	1,400	1,600
Round, 25J, autowind, sweep sec., date, 14K	200	250	325
Round, 31J, chronograph, moon phases, calendar, 18K	2,000	2,200	2,500
Round, chronograph, 18K case, c. 1938	900	1,000	1,100
Round, pulse meter chronograph, 2 registers, 18K case	1,100	1,200	1,500
Round, 21J, self wind, date, 18K case	275	300	375
Round, self wind, 14K case	185	200	240
Round, self wind, GF	40	50	65

ULYSESS NARDIN (continued)

Style or Grade—Description	Avg	Ex-Fn	Mint
Round, $20 gold piece, hidden watch	$1,200	$1,400	$1,700
Square, 14K case	150	175	200
Square, 21J, chronometer, self wind, 14K case	175	200	275
Tank, 14K case	200	225	250
Tonneau, 14K case	180	195	225

LADY'S WRIST WATCH

Style or Grade — Description	Avg	Ex-Fn	Mint
Oval, 14K case	$100	$125	$175
Rectangular, 14K case	100	125	175
Round, 14K case	85	110	160
Round, GF	40	45	50
Square, 14K case	100	125	175
Tonneau, 14K case	100	125	175

National, day-date-month, 17 jewels, stainless.

National, square, 15 jewels, stainless

National, center second, waterproof, gold filled.

National, auto wind, waterproof, stainless.

NATIONAL
SWISS

Style or Grade—Description	Avg	Ex-Fn	Mint
Round, 17J, day date month, auto wind, GF & steel back	$65	$75	$85

NATIONAL (continued)

Style or Grade—Description	Avg	Ex-Fn	Mint
Round, 17J, watertight, auto wind, SS, 1952	$10	$15	$25
Square, 15J, GF, & steel back, 1952	15	20	25
Tonneau, 17J, c. sec., auto wind, watertight, GF & steel back	45	50	60

NEW ENGLAND WATCH CO.
U.S.A.

Style or Grade—Description	Avg	Ex-Fn	Mint
Alden	$8	$10	$15
Hale	8	10	15
New England model	5	7	10
Waterbury	15	18	25

Examples of **New Haven** wrist watches, 7 jewel movements usually found in base metal cases.

NEW HAVEN CLOCK & WATCH CO.
U.S.A.

Style or Grade — Description	Avg	Ex-Fn	Mint
Boy Scout, Tonneau case	$125	$150	$200
Tip Top	15	20	35
New Haven model, Tonneau case	15	20	35
New Haven model, rectangular	15	20	35
New Haven model, round case	10	15	20
New Haven model, square case	5	10	15

Example of a **New Haven** ladies wrist watch, 7 jewels in a base metal case.

NEW YORK STANDARD WATCH CO.
U.S.A.

Style or Grade — Description	Avg	Ex-Fn	Mint
Round case, gold filled	$10	$15	$25
Round case, base metal	5	7	12
Round case, "Crown" luminous dial & hands	10	15	20
Lady's wrist or pendant watch, GF....................	25	30	50

New York Standard Watch Co., Ladies wrist and pendant watch.

New York Standard Watch Co. man's wrist watch with a luminous dial and hands.

Omega Constellation, 17 jewels, auto wind with date.

Omega Electronic, F300, ca. 1950s.

OMEGA (continued)

Omega, cushion, 17 jewels, chronograph, ca. 1935.

Omega, square, 17 jewels, 18k, ca. 1950s.

Omega, triple date, moon phases, ca. 1950s.

Omega, rectangular, hidden winding stem, ca. 1930s.

Omega, flight master, chronograph, 3 registers.

Omega, Marine chronometer, mega quartz.

OMEGA
SWISS

Style or Grade — Description	Avg	Ex-Fn	Mint
17J, cosmic, day date month, moon phase, GF case	$300	$400	$600
17J, cosmic, day date month, moon phase, SS	300	350	450

OMEGA (continued)

Style or Grade—Description	Avg	Ex-Fn	Mint
Rectangular, 15J, hidden winding crown, 14K case	$2,000	$2,200	$2,500
Rectangular, 15J, slides apart to expose winding stem, 1930s, SS.	600	800	1,000
Rectangular, Mega, quartz, marine chronometer, SS.	300	400	500
Rectangular, 14K case	175	200	225
Rectangular, GF	60	70	80
Round, 17J, flightmaster, chronograph, 3 reg., c. 1960s, 18K case (only 12 made)	6,000	7,000	8,000
Round, 17J, Seamaster, calendar date, 1955, 18K	300	400	500
Round, 17J, autowind, 36 hr., wind indicator, center dial .	150	175	200
Round, 17J, caliber 321, tachymetre, "Seamaster," 3 reg., 2 pushers, 14K, c. 1945	850	900	1,000
Round, 17J, tachometer chronograph, "Uni-Compax," 14K.	800	850	1,000
Round, 20J, "Seamaster," autowind, sweep sec., date	85	95	110
Round, 20J, "Seamaster," autowind, sweep second	75	85	100
Round, quartz, "F300" + date, 1950, 18K band & case . .	1,400	1,600	1,900
Round, chronograph, caliber 28, 9-T, 1, 18K, c. 1933	1,000	1,100	1,250
Round, "Regulator," 2 dials, large sweep sec., 18K	700	850	1,000
Round, "Seamaster Professional," tachometer, 3 reg., 2 pushers, 1st watch worn on moon, 18K . . . . . ★ ★ ★	1,400	1,700	2,000
Round, "Speedmaster 125," tachometer, 2 reg., 24 hr. indicator, autowind, watertight, SS case.	250	300	400
Round, 14K case	100	125	150
Round, 18K case	175	200	250
Round, GF	20	25	35
Round, stainless steel	15	20	28
Round, ultra thin, 14K case	125	150	175
Round, Speed Master, Mark II, chronograph	200	225	250
Round, Speed Master, Professional, 3 registers, 18K.	1,200	1,400	1,700
Round, moon phases, day-date-month, 18K	1,200	1,600	2,000
Round, moon phases, day-date-month, 14K	900	1,200	1,600
Round, 17J, "Constellation" autowind, YGF.	75	100	150
Square, tachometer chronograph, "Uni-Compax," 18K . . .	2,000	2,500	3,000
Square, 14K case	150	175	220
Square, GF.	50	60	70
Square, moonphases, 3 dates, 18K, c. 1950.	2,500	3,000	3,500
Square, moonphases, 3 dates, 14K, c. 1950.	2,000	2,500	3,000
Tank, 14K case	175	200	275

LADY'S WRIST WATCH

Style or Grade — Description	Avg	Ex-Fn	Mint
Round, GF	$20	$25	$30

Orfina, triple date, center second, moon phases.

Orfina, triple date, moon phases, gold filled.

Orfina, day-date-month, stainless steel.

Orfina, date, 17 jewels, stainless steel.

ORFINA
SWISS

Style or Grade—Description	Avg	Ex-Fn	Mint
Round, 17J, day date month, moon phase, c. sec., GF ...	$150	$200	$250
Round, 17J, day date month, moon phase, GF case	100	110	135
Round, 17J, day date month, GF case	75	85	95
Round, 17J, days, steel	35	45	55
Round, 17J, SS case.................................	15	20	30

Oris Rectangular, 4 jewels. Oris Tonneau, 7 jewels. Oris Round, 15 jewels.

ORIS
SWISS

Style or Grade — Description	Avg	Ex-Fn	Mint
Man's, Round, 17J, auto, with wind indicator, c. 1956 ...	$100	$125	$175

Style or Grade—Description	Avg	Ex-Fn	Mint
Lady's, Round, 15J, sweep sec., autowind	$5	$8	$12

Perpetual Watch Co., 15 jewels. Note "L" shaped weight designed to wind watch automatically.

Perpetual Watch Co., diamond bezel, 15 jewels, ca. 1930.

PERPETUAL WATCH CO.
NEW YORK
1930

Style or Grade — Description	Avg	Ex-Fn	Mint
Rectangular case & mvt., by Frey, 15J, crown at 9 o'clock, 14K...	$400	$475	$700
Rectangular case & mvt., by Frey, 15J, crown at 9 o'clock, GF	175	200	250
Round, 15J, Harwood mvt., turn bezel to set hands, 14K case	400	450	550
Round, 15J, Harwood mvt., turn bezel to set hands, GF..	150	175	200
Lady's, Tonneau, 15J, by Frey, 1930, silver & diamonds..	600	700	800

P.P. & Co., asymmetric, 18 jewels, 18k, ca. 1960s.   P.P. & Co., rect., curvex, 18 jewels, 18k, ca. 1940s.

P.P. & Co., flared, serial number 975,435, ca. 1950s.   P.P. & Co., serial number 970,829, ca. 1947.

PATEK, PHILIPPE & CO. (continued)

P.P. & Co. split-second chronograph, triple date.

P.P. & Co., minute repeater finished by E. Gubelin.

P.P. & Co., auto wind, 18k, waterproof, ca. 1950s.

P.P. & Co., rect., serial number 837,118, ca. 1960s.

P.P. & Co., traveling man's watch, ca. 1963.

P.P. & Co., cushion, serial number 806,547, ca. 1920s.

PATEK, PHILIPPE & CO.
SWISS

Style or Grade — Description	Avg	Ex-Fn	Mint
Asymetric rectangular, 18J, the asymetric rectangular case leans over to one side, case dial & movement all signed, rare case design	$18,000	$22,000	$25,000

P.P. & Co., cushion, 18J, M. 12, ca. 1920.

P.P. & Co., cushion, M. 9¾, ca. 1910.

P.P. & Co., cushion, M. 9¼, ca. 1970s.

P.P. & Co., cushion, M. 9½, ca. 1980

P.P. & Co., Flared, M. 8, ca. 1945.

P.P. & Co., Flared, M. 8, ca. 1950.

Style or Grade — Description	Avg	Ex-Fn	Mint
Asymetric, Gilbert Albert model, 18J, M#8, c. 1960s, 18K case	$20,000	$22,000	$25,000
Curvex, 18K case	6,000	7,000	8,000
Curvex, larger size, 18K case	8,000	9,000	10,000
Cushion, 13J, quartz, date, center sec., 1960, 18K band and case	5,000	5,500	6,000
Cushion, 15J, split sec., chronograph, 2 reg. at 12 and 6, gyromax balance, 18K case, c. 1950	60,000	70,000	80,000
Cushion, 15J, early 1920s, 18K case, enamel dial	4,000	5,000	6,000
Cushion, 18J, M#12, Adj.5P, applied gold numbers, 1920s	4,000	4,500	5,000
Cushion, 18J, M#9¾, 1910s	3,000	3,500	4,000
Cushion, 18J, M#9¼, Adj.5P, 1970s	4,500	5,000	5,500
Cushion, 18J, M#9½, Adj.5P, 1980s, 18K	4,000	4,500	5,000
Flared, 15J, M#8, Adj.5P, 1945, 18K	8,000	10,000	12,000

PATEK, PHILIPPE & CO. (continued)

P.P. & Co., Flared, curvex, M. 9, ca. 1940s.

P.P. & Co., Flared, M. 9, ca. 1950s.

P.P. & Co., Flared, M. 8, ca. 1940.

P.P. & Co., Flared, M. 8. ca. 1950s.

P.P. & Co., Oval, quartz, ca. 1980s.

P.P. & Co., Oval, M. 10, ca. 1960s.

Style or Grade—Description	Avg	Ex-Fn	Mint
Flared, 18J, M#8, c. 1950, 18K case	$8,000	$9,000	$11,000
Flared, curvex, 18J, M#9, Adj.5P, c. 1940s, 18K case	8,000	10,000	12,000
Flared, 18J, enamel dial, gold applied, hour makers, rect. movt., 18K case, c. 1945	8,000	9,000	10,000
Flared, 18J, M#9, "Fausses-Cotes" decoration, 1950s, platinum	9,000	10,000	12,000
Flared, 18J, M#8, applied gold index, 1940, 18K	8,000	10,000	12,000
Flared, 18J, M#8, c. 1950s, 18K case	8,000	10,000	12,000
Oval, quartz, 18K band & case, 1980	4,000	4,500	5,000
Oval, 18J, M#10, Adj.5P, 1960, 18K	3,000	3,500	4,000
Oval, 18J, M#9¾, giromax bal., 1980s	3,000	3,500	4,000
Rectangular, 15J, "Chronometro Goldolo," 18K, c. early 1920s	8,000	9,000	10,000
Rectangular, 15J, M#12, hidden lugs, 1930, 18K	8,000	10,000	12,000

PATEK, PHILIPPE & CO. (continued)

P.P. & Co., Oval, M. 9¾, ca. 1980s.

P.P. & Co., rec., M. 12, hidden lugs, ca. 1930s.

P.P. & Co., rec., M. 12, ca. 1930s.

P.P. & Co., rec., M. 10, ca. 1920s.

P.P. & Co., rec., M. 9, starbrite steel.

P.P. & Co., rec., curvex, M. 10, ca. 1950s.

Style or Grade—Description	Avg	Ex-Fn	Mint
Rectangular, 15J, M#10, decorated enamel bezel, 1920, 18K	$7,000	$8,000	$10,000
Rectangular, 17J, M#9, Adj.5P, c. 1930s, starbrite steel case	2,000	2,500	3,000
Rectangular, 18J, platinum dial & case, day aperture at 10, date aperture at 12, month aperture at 2, barrel shaped movement, c. 1930	20,000	25,000	30,000
Rectangular, 18J, M#12, hidden lugs, 1930, 18K	5,000	5,500	6,000
Rectangular, 18J, M#10¾, fluted lugs, 18K	9,000	10,000	12,000
Rectangular, curved, 18J, M#10, Adj.5P, 1950, 18K	6,500	7,000	7,500
Rectangular, 18J, M#10, c. 1940s, fancy shaped 18K case	5,000	6,500	7,000
Rectangular, 18J, M#10, Adj.8P, c. 1920s, 18K case	7,500	8,000	8,500
Rectangular, 18J, M#9¾, made for Tiffany & Co., 1920, 18K	8,000	9,000	10,000
Rectangular, 18J, M#9¾, curvex, 1926, 18K	4,500	5,000	5,500

PATEK, PHILIPPE & CO. (continued)

P.P. & Co., rec., M. 10, fancy shape, ca. 1940s.

P.P. & Co., rec., M. 10, ca. 1920s.

P.P. & Co., rec., M. 9¾, ca. 1920s.

P.P. & Co., rec., curvex, M. 9¾, ca. 1926.

P.P. & Co., rec., M. 9½, ca. 1940s.

P.P. & Co., rec., M. 9, ca. 1960s.

P.P. & Co., rec., M. 9, 18k.

P.P. & Co., rec., M. 9, ca. 1940s.

Style or Grade—Description	Avg	Ex-Fn	Mint
Rectangular, 18J, M#9½, Adj.5P, c. 1940s, 18K case.....	$5,000	$5,500	$6,000
Rectangular, 18J, M#9, Adj.5P, 1960, 18K	6,000	6,500	7,000
Rectangular, 18J, M#9, Adj.5P, 18K	6,000	6,500	7,000
Rectangular, 18J, M#9, Adj.5P, gucidar bal., 1940, 18K ..	6,000	6,500	7,000
Rectangular, 18J, M#9, Adj.5P, 1940, 18K	3,000	3,500	4,000
Rectangular, 18J, M#9, aux. sec. dial, 1940, 18K.........	5,500	6,000	6,500

P.P. & Co., rec., M. 9, ca. 1940s.

P.P. & Co., rec., M. 9, ca. 1940s.

P.P. & Co., rec., M. 9, ca. 1940s.

P.P. & Co., rec., Top Hat, 18k band, ca. 1940s.

P.P. & Co., rec., M. 9, ca. 1950s.

P.P. & Co., rec., 18J, 18k, ca. 1950s.

P.P. & Co., rec., Reverso, M. 9, ca. 1930s.

P.P. & Co., rec., M. 9, platinum, ca. 1930s.

Style or Grade—Description	Avg	Ex-Fn	Mint
Rectangular, 18J, M#9, 1940, 18K	$5,500	$6,000	$6,500
Rectangular, Top Hat, 18J, M#9, massive band, c. 1940s, 18K	7,000	8,000	10,000
Rectangular, Reverso, 18J, M#9, Adj.5P, c. 1930s, 18K tu-tone gold case	15,000	20,000	25,000
Rectangular, 18J, M#9, 1950s, 18K	5,000	5,500	6,000

P.P. & Co., rec., M. 9, 18k case & band.

P.P. & Co., rec., M. 9, ca. 1920s.

P.P. & Co., rec., M. 9, ca. 1940s.

P.P. & Co., rec., M. 9, ca. 1940s.

P.P. & Co., rec., M. 9, ca. 1950.

P.P. & Co., rec., M. 8, hinged back, ca. 1920s.

P.P. & Co., rec., M. 8, ca. 1940s.

P.P. & Co., rec., M. 8, ca. 1940s.

Style or Grade—Description	Avg	Ex-Fn	Mint
Rectangular, 18J, M#9, Adj.8P, 1930, platinum..........	$6,500	$7,000	$7,500
Rectangular, 18J, M#9, curved case, band & case, 18K ...	14,000	16,000	18,000
Rectangular, 18J, M#9, Adj.8P, 1920s, 18K	6,000	7,000	8,000
Rectangular, 18J, M#9, glucidur bal., 1940s, 18K	5,000	5,500	6,000
Rectangular, 18J, M#9, Adj.5P, 1940, 18K	6,500	7,000	7,500
Rectangular, 18J, M#9, Adj.5P, 1950, 18K	9,000	10,000	12,000
Rectangular, 18J, M#8, hinged back, 1920, 18K..........	6,500	7,000	7,500

P.P. & Co., rec., M. 8, ca. 1940s.

P.P. & Co., rec., M. 8, curvex, ca. 1940s.

P.P. & Co., rec., M. 8, curvex, ca. 1940s.

P.P. & Co., rec., M. 8, dia. dial, platinum.

P.P. & Co., rec., M. 8, ca. 1945.

P.P. & Co., rec., top hat, M. 8, ca. 1940s.

P.P. & Co., rec., M. 8, ca. 1930s.

P.P. & Co., rec., M. 8, large lugs, ca. 1960s.

Style or Grade—Description	Avg	Ex-Fn	Mint
Rectangular, 18J, M#8, Adj.5P, 1940	$5,000	$5,500	$6,000
Rectangular, 18J, M#8, glucidur bal., 1940s, 18K	4,500	5,000	5,500
Rectangular, 18J, M#8, giromax bal., 1930, 18K	5,000	5,500	6,000
Rectangular, 18J, M#8, concave, 1940s, 18K	6,500	7,000	7,500
Rectangular, 18J, M#8, concave, 1930s, 18K	6,000	6,500	7,000
Rectangular, 18J, M#8, "11" dia. dial, 1936, platinum . . .	6,500	7,000	7,500
Rectangular, 18J, M#8, baton hands, 1945, 18K	5,500	6,000	6,500
Rectangular, top hat style case, 18J, M#8, Adj.5P,			
c. 1940s, 18K case	6,000	6,500	7,000

PATEK, PHILIPPE & CO. (continued)

P.P. & Co., rec., M. 8, fancy lugs.

P.P. & Co., rec., M. 8, platinum, ca. 1935.

P.P. & co., rec., M. 8, ca. 1945.

P.P. & Co., rec., M. 8, 18k.

P.P. & Co., rec., M. 7¾, dia. dial, ca. 1945.

P.P. & Co., rec., M. 7¾, applied gold numbers.

P.P. & Co., rec., M. 7¾, ca. 1945.

P.P. & Co., rec., M. 7¾, ca. 1950s.

Style or Grade—Description	Avg	Ex-Fn	Mint
Rectangular, 18J, M#8, Adj.5P, c. 1930s, 18K case.......	$7,500	$8,000	$8,500
Rectangular, 18J, M#8, large lugs, Adj.5P, c. 1960s, 18K .	7,000	7,500	8,000
Rectangular, 18J, M#8, Adj.5P, fancy superposed lugs, 18K case	5,000	6,000	7,000
Rectangular, 18J, M#8, Adj.5P, 1935, platinum..........	6,000	6,500	7,000
Rectangular, 18J, M#8, 1945, 18K......................	6,000	6,500	7,000
Rectangular, 18J, M#8, set with diamond on the lugs, 18K	5,500	6,000	6,500
Rectangular, 18J, M#7¾, 11 diamond dial, 1945.........	7,000	7,500	8,000
Rectangular, 18J, M#7¾, applied gold index, 18K	5,500	6,000	6,500

PATEK, PHILIPPE & CO. (continued)

P.P. & Co., rec., engraved bezel, ca. 1920.

P.P. & Co., rec., 18k, ca. 1940s.

P.P. & Co., rec., 18J, 18k, ca. 1940s.

P.P. & Co., rec., Reverso, serial number 823,401.

P.P. & Co., rec., 18J, 18k, Adj.8P.

P.P. & Co., rec., curvex, 18k, ca. 1926.

P.P. & Co., rec., 18k, M. 8, ca. 1943.

P.P. & Co., rec., 18J, 18k, ca. 1944.

Style or Grade—Description	Avg	Ex-Fn	Mint
Rectangular, 18J, M#7¾, "Fausses-Cotes" decoration, 1925, 18K	$6,000	$6,500	$7,000
Rectangular, 18J, M#7¾, giromax bal., 1950s, 18K	5,500	6,000	6,500
Rectangular, 18J, M#7¾, Adj.5P, c. 1940s, 18K case	5,500	6,000	6,500
Rectangular, 18J, platinum dial with 12 diamond hour markers, platinum case, c. 1955	5,000	6,000	7,500
Rectangular, 18J, M#7, diamond bezel & lapis-lazuli baguettes, 18K case	6,000	6,500	7,000

P.P. & Co., round, M. 12, ca. 1950s.

P.P. & Co., round, M. 12, ca. 1950s.

P.P. & Co., round, moon phase, triple date.

P.P. & Co., round, two time zones, two hands.

Style or Grade—Description	Avg	Ex-Fn	Mint
Rectangular, 18J, M#7, 1970s, dark blue dial, applied gold			
indexes, 18K case................................	$2,500	$2,800	$3,200
Rectangular, 18J, 18K rose gold case, c. 1940...........	5,000	6,000	7,000
Rectangular, 18J, hidden lugs, 18K 2-color gold case	7,000	8,000	9,000
Rectangular, 18J, curvex style, 18K gold case & bracelet ..	7,000	8,000	9,500
Rectangular, 18J, curvex long style, 11 diamonds on dial,			
platinum case, c. 1930s ....★★★	12,000	14,000	15,000
Rectangular, 18J, 18K hinged case, c. 1930s	6,000	7,000	8,000
Rectangular, 23J, "8 Jours" (8 day), 18K, c. 1920s ★★★	40,000	50,000	60,000
Rectangular, 18K case	3,000	3,500	4,000
Rectangular, rose gold 18K case........................	4,000	5,000	6,000
Rectangular, curvex style, offset lugs, 1940	4,500	5,000	5,500
Rectangular, 18J, Adj.5P, 18K Reverso case, c. 1930	15,000	20,000	25,000
Round, 15J, M#12, spade hands, 1910s, 18K	3,500	4,000	4,500
Round, 15J, early time only, Adj.5P, heavy 18K case,			
c. 1920s	2,500	2,800	3,200
Round, 16J, "Gondolo," 18K, c. early 1920s........★★	6,000	7,000	8,500
Round, 17J, M#12¾, anti-shock system, 1940, 18K	1,200	1,400	1,600
Round, 17J, M#10, Dauphine hands, 1920	2,000	2,500	3,000
Round, 18J, M#12, Adj.5P, auxiliary sec. dial, 1930, 18K .	2,500	3,000	3,500

P.P. & Co., round, M. 12, 18k, ca. 1940.

P.P. & Co., round, M. 12, 18k, ca. 1955.

P.P. & Co., round, M. 12, ca. 1950s.

P.P. & Co., round, M. 12, ca. 1950s.

P.P. & Co., round, M. 12, ca. 1950s.

P.P. & Co., round, center seconds, 18k, ca. 1950s.

Style or Grade—Description	Avg	Ex-Fn	Mint
Round, 18J, M#12, "Fausses-Cotes" decoration, 1950s ...	$1,600	$1,800	$2,000
Round, 18J, M#12, Adj.5P, anti-shock system, 1950, 18K.	2,000	2,200	2,500
Round, 18J, M#12, astronomic with moon phases, perpetual calendar, 18K	24,000	26,000	28,000
Round, 18J, M#12, 2 time zones, 2 buttons for turning each hr. hand, 18K	15,000	17,000	19,000
Round, 18J, M#12, Adj.5P, "Fausses-Cotes" decoration, 18K, 1940	4,000	4,500	5,000
Round, 18J, M#12, Glucidar bal., 1955, 18K	1,700	1,900	2,200

P.P. & Co., round, M. 12, ca. 1950.

P.P. & Co., round, M. 12, ca. 1945.

P.P. & Co., round, M. 12, ca. 1950.

P.P. & Co., round, Calatrava, M. 12, ca. 1940s.

P.P. & Co., round, Calatrava, M. 12, ca. 1940s.

P.P. & Co., round, world time, 41 cities, 18k.

Style or Grade—Description	Avg	Ex-Fn	Mint
Round, 18J, M#12, Adj.5P, 1950, 18K	$3,000	$3,500	$4,000
Round, 18J, M#12, Fausses-Cotes decoration, 1950.	1,700	1,900	2,100
Round, 18J, M#12, Fausses-Cotes decoration, 1950.	2,600	2,800	3,000
Round, 18J, M#12, Adj.5P, 1940s, 18K.	1,700	1,900	2,100
Round, 18J, M#12, aux. sec., 1950, 18K	2,600	2,800	3,000
Round, 18J, M#12, 1940, 18K	1,700	1,800	2,000
Round, 18J, M#12, gilt., "Calatrava," 1940, 18K	2,100	2,300	2,500
Round, 18J, M#12, Adj.5P, "Calatrava," 1940, 18K	2,200	2,400	2,600
Round, 18J, M#12, world time, 41 cities, 24 hr. dial, 18K.	40,000	45,000	50,000
Round, 18J, M#11¾, 1950s	1,500	1,700	1,900

P.P. & Co., round, M. 11¾, ca. 1950.

P.P. & Co., round, moon ph., triple date, ca. 1962.

P.P. & Co., round, triple date, moon phases, 18k.

P.P. & Co. mvt., serial number 888,149, ca. 1962.

P.P. & Co., round, triple date, moon ph., M. 11¾.

P.P. & Co., round, M. 11¾, water tight, ca. 1940.

Style or Grade—Description	Avg	Ex-Fn	Mint
Round, 18J, M#11¾, astronomic, manual wind, 1960, 18K	$25,000	$27,000	$30,000
Round, 18J, M#11¾, astronomic, moon phases, perpetual calendar, 1962	22,000	25,000	28,000
Round, 18J, M#11¾, Adj.5P, astronomic with moon phases, perpetual, 18K	20,000	22,000	25,000

P.P. & Co., round, M. 11½, water tight, ca. 1940.

P.P. & Co., round, m. 11½, Adj.5P, ca. 1940.

P.P. & Co., round, M. 11½, center sec., ca. 1960.

P.P. & Co., round, M. 11, ca. 1950.

P.P. & Co., round, M. 10, gold band, 18k.

P.P. & Co., round, M. 10, 18k, ca. 1950.

Style or Grade—Description	Avg	Ex-Fn	Mint
Round, 18J, M#11¾, watertight, 1940, 18K	$1,200	$1,400	$1,600
Round, 18J, M#11½, watertight, 1940, 18K	2,000	2,300	2,600
Round, 18J, M#11½, Adj.5P, 1940s, 18K	1,800	2,000	2,200
Round, 18J, M#11½, center sec., 1960, 18K	3,500	4,000	4,500
Round, 18J, M#11, straight line lever, 1950, 18K	1,600	1,800	2,000
Round, 18J, M#10, gold band & case, 18K	2,500	3,000	3,500
Round, 18J, M#10, applied gold index, 1950s, 18K	1,600	1,800	2,000
Round, 18J, M#10, watertight, 1950, 18K	2,300	2,500	2,700

P.P. & Co., round, M. 10, watertight, ca. 1950s.

P.P. & Co., round, M. 10, 18k, ca. 1950s.

P.P. & Co., round, M. 9¾, 18k, ca. 1950.

P.P. & Co., round, M. 9¾, center sec., ca. 1950s.

P.P. & Co., round, M. 9¾, Calatrava, ca. 1940.

P.P. & Co., round, 18J, 18k.

Style or Grade—Description	Avg	Ex-Fn	Mint
Round, 18J, M#10, watertight, 1950s, 18K	$2,500	$2,700	$2,900
Round, 18J, M#10, Adj.5P, champagne dial, c. 1970s, 18K case	4,000	4,500	5,000
Round, 18J, M#9¾, watertight, 1950, 18K	2,400	2,500	2,600
Round, 18J, M#9¾, center sec., 1950s, 18K	1,600	1,800	2,000
Round, 18J, M#9¾, "Calatrava," 1940, SS case.........	1,600	1,800	2,000
Round, 18J, watertight, 18K..........................	2,200	2,400	2,600

P.P. & Co., round, date-month, ca. 1945.

P.P. & Co., round, 20J, M. 12, 18k.

P.P. & Co., round, M. 11½, 20J, center sec.

P.P. & Co., round, 21J, 18k, ca. 1950s.

P.P. & Co., chronograph, ca. 1940s.

P.P. & Co., chronograph, triple date, moon phase.

Style or Grade—Description	Avg	Ex-Fn	Mint
Round, 18J, 18K case, waterproof......................	$1,800	$2,000	$2,500
Round, 18J, free sprung, 18K case	1,200	1,400	1,650
Round, 18J, minute repeater, 18K gold case & bracelet, slide repeat, dial has gold appied hour markers, monometal balance, c. 1960	80,000	100,000	125,000
Round, 18J, day & night, 24 hr. dial, world time, 41 cities listed, 2 crowns: 1 to set the 24 Hr, 41 cities & the other 24 hr., monometal balance, 18K case, c. 1950 ..	30,000	35,000	45,000

P.P. & Co., round, chronograph, M. 13, 18k.

P.P. & Co., round, chronograph, triple date, moon ph.

P.P. & Co., round, chronograph, 2 reg., ca. 1940.

P.P. & Co., round, chronograph, M. 13, 18k.

Style or Grade—Description	Avg	Ex-Fn	Mint
Round, 18J, colored world globe on dial, 41 cities listed on rotating bezel, day-night & 24 hr. & standard dial, 18K case, c. 1950	$35,000	$40,000	$50,000
Round, 18J, duo time zone two hr. hands with a thumb nail pusher to adjust extra hr. hand, 18K rose gold	10,000	12,000	15,000
Round, 18J, day-date-month & moonphase, 18K, c. 1960s	16,000	18,000	20,000
Round, 18J, watertight, stainless case, c. 1940s	1,000	1,200	1,500
Round, 18J, sweep sec. hand, 18K, c. 1935	2,000	2,500	3,200
Round, 18J, date, month, 1945, 18K	6,000	7,000	8,000
Round, 20J, "chronometer," Geneva Observatory on dial with 10 diamonds, second hand at 9 o'clock, Guillaume balance, very thick & heavy platinum case, c. mid 1950s ★ ★ ★	25,000	30,000	35,000
Round, 20J, M#12, Adj.5P, 18K	2,200	2,400	2,700
Round, 20J, M#11½, Adj.5P, center sec., 1940s	1,600	1,800	2,200
Round, 21J, M#275C, anti-shock, 1950, 18K	2,000	2,500	3,000
Round, 23J, M#13, chronograph, 2 reg., applied gold numbers, 1940	16,000	18,000	22,000

P.P. & Co., round, triple date, moon ph. ca. 1954.

P.P. & Co. movement, serial number 868,015, 23J.

P.P. & Co., round, chrono., 2 registers, ca. 1940s.

P.P. & Co., round, 30J, M. 12, gold rotor.

P.P. & Co., round, split-sec. chronograph, ca. 1958.

P.P. & Co. movement, 25J, serial number 868,984.

Style or Grade—Description	Avg	Ex-Fn	Mint
Round, 23J, M#13, chronograph, Adj.8P, day date moon phase, 1980, 18K	$65,000	$75,000	$80,000
Round, 23J, M#13, Adj.5P, glucidar bal., 1935, 18K	15,000	18,000	22,000
Round, 23J, M#13, chronograph, day date month, moon phase, Adj.8P, 2 reg., 18K	65,000	75,000	85,000
Round, 23J, M#13, Feuille hands, 2 reg., 1940s, SS	12,000	15,000	18,000
Round, 23J, M#13, chronograph, Adj.8P, 18K	22,000	24,000	27,000

PATEK, PHILIPPE & CO. (continued)

P.P. & Co., round, chrono., pulsometer, ca. 1965.

P.P. & Co., round, chrono., 2 registers, ca. 1943.

P.P. & Co., round, Calatrava, ca. 1950s.

P.P. & Co., round, Nautilus, 36J, ca. 1970s.

P.P. & Co., round, Nautilus, 36J, date.

P.P. & Co., round, diamond dial & bezel, ca. 1970s.

Style or Grade—Description	Avg	Ex-Fn	Mint
Round, 23J, M#13, Adj.8P, chronograph, astronomic, 1954, 18K	$65,000	$70,000	$75,000
Round, 23J, M#13, chronograph & pulsometer, Adj.8P, 1965, 18K	18,000	19,000	21,000

PATEK, PHILIPPE & CO. (continued)

P.P. & Co., round, self wind, 18k, ca. 1970s.

P.P. & Co., round, 36J, ca. 1970s.

P.P. & Co., round, World Time, map on dial.

P.P. & Co., round, 37J, self wind, 18k.

P.P. & Co., round, triple date, moon ph. watertight.

P.P. & Co. movement, 37J, caliber 27-460.

Style or Grade—Description	Avg	Ex-Fn	Mint
Round, 23J, M#12¾, chronograph, 2 reg., Adj.8P, 1943, 18K	$15,000	$20,000	$25,000
Round, 23J, chronograph, gold plated movement, 2 registers, monometal balance, 18K case, c. 1945	15,000	18,000	20,000
Round, 23J, chronograph, tachometer, watertight, monometal balance, SS case	10,000	12,000	14,000

PATEK, PHILIPPE & CO. (continued)

Style or Grade—Description	Avg	Ex-Fn	Mint
Round, 23J, chronograph & tachometer, 2 reg., platinum case & bracelet, c. early 1940s .... ★ ★ ★ ★	$60,000	$70,000	$80,000
Round, 23J, chronograph, 2 reg., Adj.8P, 1940s, 18K	16,000	18,000	22,000
Round, 25J, split sec. chronograph, silver dial, 2 reg., 18K case, c. 1945................................	60,000	70,000	80,000
Round, 25J, M#13, split sec. chronograph, 1955, 18K	60,000	65,000	70,000
Round, 29J, minute repeater, day-date-month-moonphase platinum case, 18K white gold bracelet, c. 1935	150,000	175,000	200,000
Round, 29J, minute repeater, 18K, c. 1950s	70,000	80,000	100,000
Round, 30J, M#12, "Calatrava," gold rotor, 1950s, 18K..	3,500	4,000	4,500
Round, 30J, M#10, "Calatrava," 18K	2,600	2,800	3,000
Round, 30J, watertight, 18K rotor, gyromax balance, 18K	2,000	2,200	2,600
Round, Nautilus, 36J, diamond dial, c. 1970s, 18K & steel case	6,000	6,500	7,000
Round, 36J, M#13, self wind, dia. dial & bezel, 1970s, 18K..	4,500	5,000	5,500
Round, 36J, M#13, self wind, Adj.5P, 1970, 18K	1,600	1,700	1,800
Round, Nautilus, 36J, M#7, date, 18K case & bracelet	10,000	12,000	16,000
Round, 36J, 52 diamonds on bezel, diamond hour markers on blue dial, gold mesh bracelet, all 18K	6,000	7,000	9,000
Round, thin mvt., 18K case, friction back...............	1,200	1,600	2,000
Round, 18K case & bracelet, all signed P.P.&Co.	2,000	3,000	4,000
Round, self wind with 18K rotor, 18K case, waterproof...	1,600	1,900	2,500
Round, gyromax balance, 18K case.....................	1,400	1,600	1,800
Round, 18K rotor, date window, 18K case, waterproof ...	2,500	3,000	3,500
Round, 23J, 18K rotor, 18K case, waterproof	1,800	2,000	2,500
Round, 30J, 18K rotor, gyromax balance, 18K case and bracelet all signed P.P.&Co., waterproof............	2,500	3,000	4,000
Round, 36J, free sprung, caliber 28-255, 18K case........	1,700	2,000	2,600
Round, 36J, M#12½, Adj.5P, 1970s...................	3,500	4,000	4,500
Round, 12 diamonds on bezel, 18K bracelet & case.......	3,000	3,500	4,000
Round, ¼ repeater, 18K case	30,000	40,000	50,000
Round, min. repeater, 18K case	70,000	80,000	90,000
Round, 23J, 2 registers, chronograph, pulse meter, 18K...	18,000	20,000	22,000
Round, split sec. chronograph, 2 registers, 18K case	50,000	60,000	70,000
Round, split sec. chronograph, 2 registers, day-date-month, perpetual, moonphase, 18K case	160,000	180,000	200,000
Round, World Time Zone, 41 cities, 24 hr. dial, color map on dial	60,000	70,000	85,000
Round, skeletonized, gyromax balance, free sprung, 18K..	10,000	12,000	15,000
Round, 37J, 18K rotor, perpetual calendar, moon phases, gyromax balance, free sprung, caliber 27-460Q, 1972, 18K case	20,000	22,000	25,000
Round, 37J, M#13, watertight, self wind, 18K	3,000	3,200	3,500
Round, 37J, M#12, Adj.5P, watertight, day date month, moon phase, 18K rotor & case, c. 1980s	20,000	24,000	29,000

PATEK, PHILIPPE & CO. (continued)

P.P. & Co., round, 18k gold band & case.

P.P. & Co., round, triple date, moon ph., 37J.

P.P. & Co., round, center sec., 18J, ca. 1952.

P.P. & Co., round, center sec., 18J, ca. 1950s.

P.P. & Co., round, 15J, 18k, ca. 1910.

P.P. & Co., round, man's ½ size, 18k, ca. 1920s.

Style or Grade—Description	Avg	Ex-Fn	Mint
Round, 37J, M#12, giromax bal., Adj.5P, 1950s, 18K case & band	$4,000	$5,000	$6,000
Round, 37J, M#12, astronomic, moon phases, perpetual calendar, self wind, 18K rotor, 1970, 18K	20,000	22,000	25,000
Round, 37J, M#11¾, astronomic, self wind, 1975, 18K ...	20,000	22,000	25,000

P.P. & Co., square, M. 12, ca. 1960s.   P.P. & Co., square, M. 12, ca. 1960s.

P.P. & Co., square, M. 10½, ca. 1950.   P.P. & Co., square, M. 10¼, ca. 1950.

P.P. & Co., square, M. 10, ca. 1940.   P.P. & Co., square, M. 10, ca. 1940.

Style or Grade—Description	Avg	Ex-Fn	Mint
Round, chronograph, 2 registers, moon phases, perpetual calendar, gyromax balance, 1965, 18K case, waterproof	$60,000	$65,000	$70,000
Round, chronograph, 2 registers, moon phases, perpetual calendar, gyromax balance, 1965, 18K case, not waterproof	55,000	60,000	65,000
Round, 18J, skeleton, 18K, c. 1970	6,000	7,000	8,000
Square, 37J, round mvt., 18K rotor, Adj.5P, white 18K	2,000	2,500	3,000
Square, 18J, M#12, 1960, 18K	3,000	3,500	4,500
Square, 18J, M#12, c. 1960s, 18K case	3,000	3,500	4,000
Square, 18J, M#10½, aux. sec., 1950, 18K	2,500	2,800	3,200
Square, 18J, M#10¼, giromax bal., 1950, 18K	1,500	1,600	1,800
Square, 18J, M#10, Fausses-Cotes, 1940, 18K	2,500	2,700	3,000

PATEK, PHILIPPE & CO. (continued)

P.P. & Co., square, 18k band & case, ca. 1950s.

P.P. & Co., square, M. 10, 18J, 18k.

P.P. & Co., square, M. 10, ca. 1950s.

P.P. & Co., square, M. 10, ca. 1950s.

P.P. & Co., square, M. 9¾, ca. 1948.

P.P. & Co., square, M. 9¾, ca. 1963.

P.P. & Co., square, M. 9¾, early 1910s.

P.P. & Co., square, M. 9½, ca. 1980.

Style or Grade—Description	Avg	Ex-Fn	Mint
Square, 18J, M#10, gyromax bal., 1940, 18K	$3,000	$3,500	$4,000
Square, 18J, M#10, sec. bits, 18K band, 1950s	4,500	5,000	6,000
Square, 18J, M#10, 18K	3,000	3,500	4,000

P.P. & Co., square, hidden lugs, gold & steel.

P.P. & Co., square, M. 7¾, ca. 1940s.

P.P. & Co., square, M. 7, ca. 1940s.

P.P. & Co., square, M. 6¼, ca. 1945.

P.P. & Co., tank, M. 9, ca. 1940.

P.P. & Co., tonneau, M. 10, ca. 1930.

Style or Grade—Description	Avg	Ex-Fn	Mint
Square, 18J, M#10, giromax bal., 1950s, 18K	$3,500	$4,000	$4,500
Square, 18J, M#10, glucidur bal., 1950, 18K	4,500	4,800	5,000
Square, 18J, M#9¾, c. 1948, 18K case	4,000	4,500	5,000
Square, 18J, M#9¾, Adj.5P, 1963, 18K	2,500	3,000	3,500
Square, 18J, M#9¾, early wrist watch, 1910s, 18K case & bracelet	5,000	6,000	7,000
Square, 18J, M#9½, 1980, 18K	5,000	5,500	6,000
Square, 18J, M#9, Adj.5P, hidden lugs, gold & steel	2,000	2,200	2,500
Square, 18J, M#7¾, c. 1940s, 18K case	2,500	3,000	3,500
Square, 18J, M#7, 1940s, 18K	2,800	3,000	3,200
Square, 18J, M#6¾, applied gold numbers, 1945, 18K	4,500	5,000	5,500
Square, 18J, sweep sec. hand, 18K, c. early 1920s	3,000	3,500	4,000
Square, 18J, onyx hour markers set in bezel, 18K, c. 1950s	7,000	8,000	9,000
Square, 18K case	1,800	2,000	2,500
Tank, 18J, M#9, "Fausses-Cotes" decoration, 1940, 18K .	6,000	6,500	7,000

P.P. & Co., tonneau, M. 9¾, ca. 1925.

P.P. & Co., tonneau, M. 9, cubist hands.

P.P. & Co., tonneau, M. 9, aux. sec. dial, ca. 1920s.

P.P. & Co., tonneau, M. 9, ca. 1910.

P.P. & Co., tonneau, split-sec. chrono., ca. 1924.

P.P. & Co., tonneau, min. repeater, platinum, ca. 1920s.

Style or Grade—Description	Avg	Ex-Fn	Mint
Tank, 18J, sec. dial at 9 o'clock, round mvt., 18K case, c. 1930	$3,000	$3,500	$4,000
Tank, engraved bezel, 1920, 18K	4,500	5,000	5,500
Tank, 18K case	2,800	3,000	3,200
Tonneau, 15J, M#10, mustached lever escapement, 1930, 18K	7,000	8,000	10,000
Tonneau, 15J, M#9¾, c. 1925, 18K case	6,000	6,500	7,000
Tonneau, 17J, M#9, cubist hands, 1930s	4,000	4,500	5,000
Tonneau, 17J, M#9, aux. sec. dial, 1920s, 18K	6,000	7,000	8,000
Tonneau, 18J, M#12, c. 1910s, curvex style, 18K case	10,000	12,000	14,000
Tonneau, 18J, M#12, center sec., watertight, Adj.5P, c. 1950s, 18K case	2,200	2,400	2,700

P.P. & Co., tonneau, Chronometro Gondolo.

P.P. & Co., round, 15J, 18k, early 1910s.

P.P. & Co., ladies rec., M. 7, ca. 1950s.

P.P. & Co., ladies rec., gold case & band, ca. 1940s.

P.P. & Co., ladies rec., M. 8, ca. 1950.

P.P. & Co., ladies rec., M. 8, ca. 1940.

Style or Grade—Description	Avg	Ex-Fn	Mint
Tonneau, 18J, M#9, gilt mvt., applied numbers, 1910s ...	$7,000	$7,500	$8,000
Tonneau, 29J, minute repeater, platinum dial & case, c. 1925	160,000	180,000	200,000
Tonneau, 32J, M#13½, split sec. chronograph, 2 reg., very thick, c. 1924, 18K case	35,000	40,000	45,000
Tonneau, minute repeater, platinum case, slide repeat, c. 1920s	100,000	125,000	150,000
Tonneau, "Chronometro Gondolo," hinged back, 1910s, 18K	12,000	14,000	16,000
Tonneau, 18K case	2,000	2,400	3,000
Barrel, day & month window, date & moonphase, enamel dial, 18K, c. 1925	70,000	80,000	100,000
Rectangular, 23J, tourbillon, 1 turn each 50 sec., rectangular mvt. by Bornard, 18K case, c. 1980 .... ★★★★	60,000	70,000	80,000
Round, 16J, (c. 1900 lady's pocket watch), 18K, mfg. 1945	1,600	1,800	2,000
Round, 23J, chronograph, 2 reg., 18K, c. 1965	12,000	14,000	15,000
Round, 27J, free sprung, 22K rotor, 18K case	2,200	2,600	2,800
Round, early calendar 1925, day-date-month & moon phase, enamel dial, sweep sec., 18K .... ★★★	30,000	40,000	50,000
Tank, day window at 10, date window at 12, day window at 2, moon phase at 6 o'clock, 18K, c. 1940 ... ★★★	60,000	70,000	80,000

PATEK, PHILIPPE & CO. (continued)

P.P. & Co., ladies rec., M. 5½, platinum.

P.P. & Co., ladies square. massive band, 18k.

P.P. & Co., ladies round, 5 min. repeater, ca. 1910s.

P.P. & P. ladies movement, serial number 174,603.

P.P. & Co., ladies round, 18k, 18J, ca. 1950s.

P.P. & Co., ladies, hidden dial, hinge lid set in dia.

Style or Grade—Description	Avg	Ex-Fn	Mint
Tonneau, 22J, minute repeater, 18K, c. 1925	$120,000	$125,000	$150,000

LADY'S WRIST WATCH

Style or Grade — Description	Avg	Ex-Fn	Mint
Rectangular, 18K case	$1,000	$1,200	$1,500
Rectangular, 18J, M#8, 18K band & case, 1940s	2,000	2,200	2,500
Rectangular, 18J, M#8, 1950, 18K......................	2,000	2,500	3,000
Rectangular, 18J, M#8, 1940, 18K......................	800	1,000	1,200
Rectangular, 18J, M#7, 1950s, 18K	2,000	2,500	3,000
Rectangular, M#5½, platinum with baguette diamonds ...	4,000	5,000	6,000
Round, 29J, 5 min. repeater, slide repeat, 1910s	75,000	80,000	90,000
Round, 31J, 5 min. repeater, platinum, c. 1920	70,000	80,000	100,000
Round, 18K case	800	900	1,000
Round, 18K case & bracelet	1,800	2,000	2,500
Round, small diamond on bezel, 18K case & bracelet	2,800	3,000	3,500
Square, 18J, M#7. Adj.8P, 1940, 18K	700	800	1,000
Square, 18J, M#5, massive band, 18K	3,500	4,000	5,000
Square, 18K case	800	1,000	1,200
Hidden dial, hinged lid, set in diamonds & band	12,000	14,000	16,000

PATEK, PHILIPPE
MOVEMENT IDENTIFICATION

Caliber 6¾, no. 60
S.no. 865000-869999
(1940-1955)

Caliber 7, no. 70
S.no. 943300-949999
(1940-1960)

Caliber 8, no. 80
S.no. 840000-849999
(1935-1960)

Caliber 8, no. 85
S.no. 850000-859999
(1935-1968)

Caliber 9, no. 90
S.no. 833150-839999
S.no. 970000-979999
(1940-1950)

Caliber 9, no. 90a
830000-833149
(1940-1950)

Caliber 10, no. 105
S.no. 900000-909999
(1940-1945)

Caliber 10, no. 110
S.no. 910000-919999
(1940-1950)

Caliber 10, no. 200
S.no. 740000-759999
(1952-1965)
S.no. 950000-959999
(1945-1955)

Caliber 23, no. 300
S.no. 780000-799999
(1955-1965)

Caliber 12, no. 600AT
S.no. 760000-779999
(1952-1960)

Caliber 12, no. 400
S.no. 720000-739999
(1950-1965)

PATEK, PHILIPPE & CO. (continued)

Caliber 12, no. 120
826900-829999 (1935-1940)

Caliber 12, no. 120A
92000-929999 (1940-1950)
960000-969999 (1946-1952)
938000-939999 (1952-1954)

Caliber 13, no. 130A　　**Caliber 13, no. 130B**　　**Caliber 13, no. 130C**
Chronograph, no. 862000-863995 (1940-1950); no. 867000-869999 (1950-1970)

Caliber 12-600 AT, S.no. 760,000-779,999 (1960-1970)

635

PERFINE
SWISS

Style or Grade—Description	Avg	Ex-Fn	Mint
Round, 17J, chronograph, tele. & tach., 2 reg., SS	$45	$55	$70

Piaget 20 dollar gold coin, flip top, ca. 1904.

Piaget, square, textured bezel, 18k, 18J.

PIAGET
SWISS
MAN'S WRIST WATCH

Style or Grade — Description	Avg	Ex-Fn	Mint
$10 gold piece, flip open case	$800	$900	$1,200
$20 gold piece, flip open case	1,200	1,400	2,000
Rectangular, 18K case	900	1,000	1,100
Rectangular, heavy 18K gold chain link bracelet	2,500	3,000	3,500
Round, 16J, thin model, 18K case, c. 1940	600	700	900
Round, 17J, 14K, c. 1955	600	700	850
Round, 30J, Grande Sonnerie min. repeater, 18K	15,000	20,000	25,000
Round, thin model, diamonds on bezel, 18K case	1,200	1,400	1,800
Round, "Polo," 18K, white & yellow gold case & bracelet	4,000	4,500	5,000
Square, 18K textured case	700	800	950

LADY'S WRIST WATCH

Style or Grade — Description	Avg	Ex-Fn	Mint
Round, small diamonds on bezel, 18K case	$785	$835	$1,000

TH. PICARD FILS
SWISS

Style or Grade — Description	Avg	Ex-Fn	Mint
Round, hectometre-tachometer, 2 reg., 14K, c. 1930	$600	$800	$1,000
Round, 17J, chronograph, SS, c. 1930	400	450	500

Pierce, auto wind, aux. sec., ca. 1948.   Pierce, chronograph, 2 registers, ca. 1948.

PIERCE
SWISS

Style or Grade — Description	Avg	Ex-Fn	Mint
Round, 15J, chronograph, 60 min. recorder	$30	$40	$65
Round, 17J, chronograph, telemeter, 2 reg., c. 1945	30	40	60
Round, 17J, chronograph, 2 reg., waterproof, GF	65	85	125
Round, 17J, GF case	30	40	55
Round, 17J, day date month, moon phase, c. sec., GF . . .	40	50	65
Round, 21J, alarm, "Duofon," c. 1960	20	30	40

Pontifa, chronograph, day-date-month, 3 registers, ca. 1948.

PONTIFA
SWISS

Style or Grade—Description	Avg	Ex-Fn	Mint
Round, 17J, chronograph, day date month, 3 reg., SS	$125	$135	$185
Round, 17J, chronograph, split sec., day date month, 3 reg., steel	600	700	800

Pronto, round, triple date, waterproof, auto wind.

PRONTO
SWISS

Style or Grade—Description	Avg	Ex-Fn	Mint
Round, 17J, chronograph, day date month, moon phase, steel	$350	$400	$450
Round, 17J, chronograph, day date month, steel	85	95	125
Round, 17J, center sec., steel	35	45	60

Pulsar, large, heavy 18k case with L.E.D. (light emitting diode) display case.

PULSAR

Style or Grade — Description	Avg	Ex-Fn	Mint
Cushion, large heavy, L.E.D. display, c. 1970, 18K	$400	$485	$600
Cushion, large heavy, L.E.D. display, c. 1970, 14K	375	445	550
Cushion, large heavy, L.E.D. display, c. 1970, YGF......	125	150	200
Cushion, large heavy, L.E.D. display, c. 1970, stainless ...	75	100	125

RECORD WATCH CO.
SWISS

Style or Grade — Description	Avg	Ex-Fn	Mint
Rectangular, 15J, GF, c. 1935	$50	$60	$75
Round, chronograph, day date month, moon phase, 2 reg., 18K case.................................	1,000	1,100	1,400

RECORD WATCH CO. (continued)

Record W. Co., chronograph, ca. 1940.   Record W. Co., round, day-date, moon ph., 1940s.

Style or Grade—Description	Avg	Ex-Fn	Mint
Round, chronograph, day date month, moon phase, 2 reg., 14K case	$800	$900	$1,200
Round, chronograph, day date month, moon phase, 2 reg., 10K case	500	600	700
Round, chronograph, day date month, moon phase, 2 reg., SS	400	500	600
Round, split sec. chronograph, 2 reg., tachom, c. 1940s, SS	1,000	1,200	1,500
Round, 32J, split sec. chronograph, 3 reg., moon phase, 18K case	3,000	4,000	5,000
Round, 20J, split sec., 2 reg., 1940, SS	1,200	1,400	1,700
Round, 17J, day date month, moon phase, 2 reg., 18K	1,000	1,100	1,400
Round, 17J, day date month, moon phase, 2 reg., 14K	800	900	1,200
Round, 17J, day date month, moon phase, 2 reg., SS	400	500	600
Round, 15J, triple date, moon phases, 18K	800	1,000	1,300

Recta rectangular, 15 jewels   Recta round, 15 jewels

RECTA
SWISS

Style or Grade — Description	Avg	Ex-Fn	Mint
Rectangular, 14J, curved incline style, 14K	$400	$480	$600

RECTA WATCH CO. (continued)

Style or Grade — Description	Avg	Ex-Fn	Mint
Rectangular, 15J, curved elongated, 14K	$300	$380	$500
Round, 17J, chronograph, 2 reg., 18K, c. 1945	650	750	900

ROAMER
SWISS

Style or Grade — Description	Avg	Ex-Fn	Mint
Rectangular, 17J, 14K, c. 1940.........................	$120	$130	$150
Round, 17J, date, stem wind, GF	35	45	60

ROCKFORD WATCH CO.
U.S.A.

Style or Grade—Description	Avg	Ex-Fn	Mint
Iroquois, 17J, chrome case	$125	$150	$175

RODANA

Style or Grade—Description	Avg	Ex-Fn	Mint
Round, 17J, center sec., auto wind, GF case	$20	$25	$32
Round, 17J, auto wind, SS case.......................	12	15	20
Ladies round, 15J, SS	5	6	8

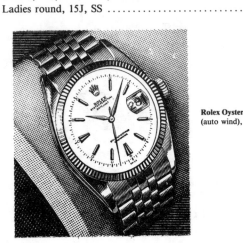

Rolex Oyster (water proof to depth of 16 feet, perpetual (auto wind), date just.

Rolex, chronograph, curved back, ca. 1940s.

Rolex, cushion, 17J, oyster, ca. 1934.

Rolex, cushion, graduated bezel, ca. 1928.

Rolex, oyster, ca. 1930s.

ROLEX
SWISS

Note: Quick Set (Q. Set) models date from 1981 up.

MAN'S WRIST WATCH

Style or Grade — Description	Avg	Ex-Fn	Mint
Cushion, 17J, chronograph, 2 reg., curved back, c. 1940s, 18K	$15,000	$18,000	$20,000
Cushion, 17J, oyster, perpetual, bubble back, stainless, c. 1934	450	550	600
Cushion, 15J, Adj.6P, oyster, c. 1928, 18K case	2,000	2,200	2,500
Cushion, 15J, Adj.6P, oyster, c. 1928, 14K case	1,400	1,600	1,800
Cushion, 15J, Adj.6P, oyster, c. 1928, 9K case	1,200	1,400	1,600
Cushion, 15J, Adj.6P, oyster, c. 1928, sterling silver	500	600	700
Cushion, 15J, Adj.6P, oyster, c. 1928, SS	350	400	500
Cushion, 15J, oyster, graduated bezel, c. 1928, 18K case	1,800	2,000	2,200
Cushion, 15J, oyster, graduated bezel, c. 1928, 14K case	1,400	1,500	1,700
Cushion, 15J, oyster, graduated bezel, c. 1928, 14K, steel back	1,200	1,300	1,400
Cushion, 15J, oyster, graduated bezel, c. 1928, 9K case	1,000	1,100	1,200

ROLEX (continued)

Rolex, cushion, oyster, center sec.

Rolex, octagonal, center sec., ca. 1930s.

Style or Grade—Description	Avg	Ex-Fn	Mint
Cushion, 15J, oyster, graduated bezel, c. 1928, sterling ...	$600	$700	$800
Cushion, 15J, oyster, graduated bezel, c. 1928, SS	350	450	600
Cushion, 15J, oyster, curved back, c. 1930s, 18K case	1,600	1,700	2,000
Cushion, 15J, oyster, curved back, c. 1930s, 14K, steel			
Cushion, 15J, oyster, stem wind, center sec., c. 1935, 18K case	1,500	1,800	2,200
Cushion, 15J, oyster, stem wind, center sec., c. 1935, 14K case	1,400	1,600	2,000
Cushion, 15J, oyster, stem wind, center sec., c. 1935, 9K case	1,200	1,300	1,400
Cushion, 15J, oyster, stem wind, center sec., c. 1935, SS .	500	550	600
back	1,400	1,500	1,800
Octagonal, 15J, oyster, stem wind, center sec., c. 1930s, 18K case	2,300	2,500	2,800
Octagonal, 15J, oyster, stem wind, center sec., c. 1930s, 14K case	1,400	1,500	1,700
Octagonal, 15J, oyster, stem wind, center sec., c. 1930s, 14K s. back....................................	1,200	1,300	1,400
Octagonal, 15J, oyster, stem wind, center sec., c. 1930s, 9K case	1,000	1,100	1,200
Octagonal, 15J, oyster, stem wind, center sec., c. 1930s, sterling...	600	700	·800
Octagonal, 15J, oyster, stem wind, center sec., c. 1930s, SS..	300	350	425
Octagonal, 15J, oyster, stem wind, c. 1930s, 18K case	2,000	2,100	2,200
Octagonal, 15J, oyster, stem wind, c. 1930s, 14K case	1,200	1,300	1,400
Octagonal, 15J, oyster, stem wind, c. 1930s, 9K case	1,000	1,100	1,200
Octagonal, 15J, oyster, stem wind, c. 1930s, sterling......	500	600	700
Octagonal, 15J, oyster, stem wind, c. 1930s, SS..........	250	300	400
Rectangular, 18J, Prince chronom., duo dial, c. 1930s, platinum	7,000	8,000	10,000
Rectangular, 18J, Prince chronom., duo dial, c. 1930s, 18K case	5,000	6,000	7,000

ROLEX (continued)

Rolex, rectangular, Prince duo dial, ca. 1930s.

Rolex, rectangular, Prince center sec., ca. 1930s.

Rolex, rectangular, black dial, tu-tone case.

Rolex, rectangular, duo dial, Adj.6P, 9k.

Rolex, rectangular, duo dial, curvex.

Rolex, rectangular, duo dial, ca. 1930s.

Style or Grade—Description	Avg	Ex-Fn	Mint
Rectangular, 18J, Prince chronom., duo dial, c. 1930s, 14K case	$4,000	$5,000	$6,000
Rectangular, 18J, Prince chronom., duo dial, c. 1930s, tu-tone 14K	5,000	6,000	7,000
Rectangular, 18J, Prince chronom., duo dial, c. 1930s, 9K case	3,000	3,500	4,000
Rectangular, 18J, Prince chronom., duo dial, c. 1930s, tu-tone GF	2,500	3,000	3,500
Rectangular, 18J, Prince chronom., duo dial, c. 1930s, GF case	1,500	1,600	1,750
Rectangular, 18J, Prince chronom., duo dial, c. 1930s, silver case	2,500	3,000	3,500
Rectangular, 18J, Prince chronom., duo dial, c. 1930s, SS	1,500	1,800	2,200
Rectangular, 18J, Prince, center sec., Adj.6P, c. 1930s, asymetric 18K case	8,000	9,000	10,000
Rectangular, 18J, Prince, black dial, tu-tone case, 18K, 1935	6,500	7,000	7,500
Rectangular, 18J, Adj.6P, curved back, 18K case & bracelet	5,000	6,000	7,000

ROLEX (continued)

Rolex, "Railway," fluted case, ca. 1930s.

Rolex, rectangular, prince, 18k case & band.

Rolex, duo dial, chronometer, ca. 1930s.

Rolex, rectangular, 17J, 14k, ca. 1938.

Style or Grade—Description	Avg	Ex-Fn	Mint
Rectangular, 17J, 14K case, c. 1960s....................	$800	$1,000	$1,200
Rectangular, 17J, GF	300	400	500
Rectangular, "Cellini," 19J, 18K case	900	1,000	1,100
Rectangular, "Cellini," 19J, diamonds on bezel, 18K.....	1,800	2,000	2,500
Rectangular, jump hour in window, platinum............	8,000	9,000	10,000
Rectangular, jump hour in window, 18K case............	7,000	8,000	9,000
Rectangular, jump hour in window, 14K case............	6,000	7,000	8,000
Rectangular, jump hour in window, GF.................	2,000	2,500	3,000
Rectangular, 17J, Railway Prince, c. 1930s, fluted case, 18K tu-tone......................................	9,000	10,000	12,000
Rectangular, 17J, Railway Prince, c. 1930s, fluted case, 18K cs..	5,000	6,000	7,000
Rectangular, 17J, Railway Prince, c. 1930s, fluted case, 14K tu-tone......................................	5,000	6,000	7,000
Rectangular, 17J, Railway Prince, c. 1930s, fluted case, 14K case	4,000	4,500	5,000
Rectangular, 17J, Railway Prince, c. 1930s, fluted case, 9K tu-tone.......................................	3,000	3,500	4,000
Rectangular, 17J, Railway Prince, c. 1930s, fluted case, 9K case	2,500	3,000	3,500
Rectangular, 17J, Railway Prince, c. 1930s, fluted case, SS	2,000	2,200	2,500
Rectangular, 17J, Prince, extra Adj.7P, asymetric dial, c. 1935, 18K case.................................	7,000	8,000	9,000
Rectangular, 17J, Prince, extra Adj.7P, asymetric dial, c. 1935, 14K case.................................	6,000	7,000	8,000
Rectangular, 17J, Prince, extra Adj.7P, asymetric dial, c. 1935, 9K case..................................	5,000	6,000	7,000

ROLEX (continued)

Rolex, rectangular, Prince, ca. 1935.

Rolex, rectangular, curved back, ca. 1940.

Rolex, jump-hour, duo dial, ca. 1930.

Rolex, jump-hour, duo dial, 15J, ca. 1930.

Rolex, tu-tone case, Adj.6P, ca. 1930.

Rolex, duo dial, Prince, 15J, ca. 1930s.

Style or Grade—Description	Avg	Ex-Fn	Mint
Rectangular, 17J, Prince, duo-dial, doctor style, platinum .	$5,000	$6,000	$7,000
Rectangular, 17J, Prince, duo-dial, doctor style, 18K gold.	4,500	5,000	6,000
Rectangular, 17J, Prince, duo-dial, doctor style, 14K gold.	4,000	4,500	5,000
Rectangular, 17J, Prince, duo-dial, doctor style, GF	1,500	1,800	2,000
Rectangular, 17J, M#7¾, Adj.7P, 1935, 14K	10,000	12,000	15,000
Rectangular, 17J, curved back, 1940, GF.	500	600	700
Rectangular, 15J, Prince Railway, Adj.6P, jump hr., c. 1930s, fluted tu-tone W&Y 18K case	10,000	12,000	13,500
Rectangular, 15J, Prince Railway, Adj.6P, jump hr., c. 1930s, fluted tu-tone W&Y 14K case	8,000	9,000	10,000
Rectangular, 15J, Prince Railway, Adj.6P, jump hr., c. 1930s, fluted 18K case	8,000	9,000	10,000
Rectangular, 15J, Prince Railway, Adj.6P, jump hr., c. 1930s, fluted 14K case	7,000	8,000	9,000
Rectangular, 15J, Prince Railway, Adj.6P, jump hr., c. 1930s, fluted 9K case	5,000	6,000	7,000

Rolex, duo dial, Prince, polished steel case.

Rolex, rectangular, Tudor quartz, 18k.

Style or Grade—Description	Avg	Ex-Fn	Mint
Rectangular, 15J, Prince Railway, Adj.6P, jump hr., c. 1930s, fluted SS case	$2,000	$2,500	$3,000
Rectangular, 15J, Prince chronom., duo dial, jump hr., platinum	11,000	12,000	13,000
Rectangular, 15J, Prince chronom., duo dial, jump hr., 18K case	10,000	11,000	12,000
Rectangular, 15J, Prince chronom., duo dial, jump hr. 14K case	8,000	9,000	10,000
Rectangular, 15J, Prince chronom., duo dial, jump hr., 9K case	5,000	6,000	7,000
Rectangular, 15J, Prince chronom., duo dial, jump hr., silver case	4,000	5,000	6,000
Rectangular, 15J, Prince chronom., duo dial, jump hr., GF case	2,800	3,000	3,500
Rectangular, 15J, Prince chronom., duo dial, jump hr., SS	2,500	2,800	3,000
Rectangular, 15J, Prince, Adj.6P, c. 1930, tu-tone 18K cs.	5,000	6,000	7,000
Rectangular, 15J, Prince, Adj.6P, c. 1930, tu-tone 14K cs.	4,000	5,000	6,000
Rectangular, 15J, Prince, Adj.6P, c. 1930, tu-tone 9K case	3,000	3,500	4,500
Rectangular, 15J, Prince, Adj.6P, duo-dial, 1930s, 9K case	1,400	1,600	1,800
Rectangular, 15J, Prince, c. 1930, black dial, 18K case ...	4,000	5,000	6,000
Rectangular, 15J, Prince, c. 1930, black dial, 14K case ...	3,000	4,000	5,000
Rectangular, 15J, Prince, c. 1930, black dial, 9K case	2,500	3,500	4,000
Rectangular, 15J, Prince, c. 1930, black dial, sterling silver	3,000	3,500	4,000
Rectangular, 15J, Prince, c. 1930, black dial, GF steel back	2,000	2,500	3,000
Rectangular, 15J, Prince, c. 1930, black dial, SS case.....	2,000	2,500	3,000
Rectangular, Tudor quartz, 18K & steel case............	200	250	300
Round, 26-30J, oyster, perpetual day date, 18K President bracelet & case..................................	4,000	5,000	6,000
Round, 26-30J, oyster, perpetual day date, 18K bark finish President bracelet & case	3,800	4,000	5,000
Round, 26-30J, oyster, perpetual date, Jubilee bracelet, 18K..	3,000	3,500	4,000
Round, 26-30J, oyster, perpetual date, Jubilee bracelet, 18K & SS	1,200	1,500	1,700
Round, 26-30J, oyster, perpetual date, Jubilee bracelet, 14K..	2,500	3,000	3,500

Rolex, President, bark finish, 18k gold.

Rolex, oyster, perpetual, day-just.

Rolex, 10 diamond dial, jubilee bracelet.

Rolex, 21J, date, center sec., ca. 1965.

Rolex, 21J, day-date, 10 diamond dial.

Rolex, 19J, center sec., ca. 1940s.

Style or Grade—Description	Avg	Ex-Fn	Mint
Round, 26-30J, oyster, perpetual date, Jubilee bracelet, 14K & SS	$600	$800	$1,000
Round, 26-30J, oyster, perpetual date, Jubilee bracelet, SS	200	300	600
Round, 26J, oyster perpetual, date, 10 diamond dial, 18K Jubilee bracelet & case........................	4,000	5,000	6,000
Round, 26J, oyster perpetual, date, 10 diamond dial, 14K Jubilee bracelet & case........................	3,500	4,000	5,000

ROLEX (continued)

Rolex, day-date, moon phase, waterproof, ca. 1950s.

Rolex, triple date, moon phase, 18k case & band.

Rolex, triple date, moon phase, large lugs.

Rolex, chronograph, 17J, 2 registers, ca. 1940s.

Style or Grade—Description	Avg	Ex-Fn	Mint
Round, 26J, oyster perpetual, date, 10 diamond dial, 14K Jubilee bracelet & case, gold & SS	$2,000	$2,500	$3,000
Round, 21J, oyster, perpetual, date, Adj.6P, 1965, 18K band & case	2,000	2,500	3,000
Round, 21J, oyster, perpetual, day date, Adj.6P, 18K band & case, 10 diamond dial, 1960	3,000	3,500	4,000
Round, 19J, oyster perpetual, center sec., c. 1940s, 18K ..	2,000	$2,300	2,600
Round, 19J, oyster perpetual, center sec., c. 1940s, 14K ..	1,800	2,000	2,200
Round, 19J, oyster perpetual, center sec., c. 1940s, 9K ...	1,500	1,600	1,800
Round, 19J, oyster perpetual, center sec., c. 1940s, SS....	500	600	700
Round, 19J, oyster perpetual, date, Adj.6P, c. 1948, 18K .	1,600	$1,800	2,000
Round, 19J, oyster perpetual, date, Adj.6P, c. 1948, 14K .	1,400	1,600	1,800
Round, 19J, oyster perpetual, date, Adj.6P, c. 1948, 14K steel	400	500	600
Round, 18J, Adj.7P, oyster perpetual, day date month, moon phases, c. 1950s, 18K case	8,000	10,000	12,000
Round, 18J, Adj.7P, oyster perpetual, day date month, moon phases, c. 1950s, 14K case	7,000	9,000	10,000
Round, 18J, Adj.7P, oyster perpetual, day date month, moon phases, c. 1950s, SS case	4,000	5,000	6,000

Rolex, chronograph, 3 registers, 18k, ca. 1950s.

Rolex, chronograph, pulsations, ca. 1960.

Rolex, chronograph, 3 registers, 17J, ca. 1940s.

Rolex, tachometer, 17J, 3 registers, ca. 1960s.

Rolex, chronograph, Daytona, waterproof, ca. 1950s.

Rolex, chronograph, Jubilee, ca. 1960s.

Style or Grade—Description	Avg	Ex-Fn	Mint
Round, 17J, chronograph, telemeter & tachometer, 2 reg., c. 1940, 18K case	$6,000	$7,000	$8,000
Round, 17J, chronograph, telemeter & tachometer, 2 reg., c. 1940, 14K case	5,000	6,000	7,000
Round, 17J, chronograph, telemeter & tachometer, 2 reg., c. 1940, 9K case	4,000	5,000	6,000

ROLEX (continued)

Rolex, Prince, Tudor, chronograph.

Rolex, Prince, quartz, Tudor, date.

Style or Grade—Description	Avg	Ex-Fn	Mint
Round, 17J, chronograph, telemeter & tachometer, 2 reg., c. 1940s, SS	$2,000	$2,200	$2,400
Round, 17J, chronograph, waterproof, 3 reg., c. 1950s, 18K case	8,000	10,000	12,000
Round, 17J, chronograph, waterproof, 3 reg., c. 1950s, 14K case	6,000	7,000	8,000
Round, 17J, chronograph, waterproof, 3 reg., c. 1950s, steel	2,000	3,000	4,000
Round, 17J, chronograph, 3 reg., day date month, c. 1940s, 18K	14,000	16,000	18,000
Round, 17J, chronograph, 3 reg., day date month, c. 1940s, 14K	12,000	14,000	16,000
Round, 17J, chronograph, 3 reg., day date month, c. 1940s, SS	5,000	6,000	7,000
Round, 17J, chronograph, 3 reg., SS	1,500	1,700	2,000
Round, Superlative Chronometer, Cosmograph, waterproof, 14k band & case	5,000	5,500	6,000
Round, 17J, Daytona, Cosmograph, 3 reg., c. 1960s, 18K.	5,000	6,000	7,000
Round, 17J, Daytona, Cosmograph, 3 reg., c. 1960s, 14K.	4,000	5,000	6,000
Round, 17J, Daytona, Cosmograph, 3 reg., c. 1960s, SS ..	1,200	1,400	1,600
Round, 17J, Daytona, Cosmograph, waterproof, 3 reg., 18K President gold band & case	8,000	8,500	9,000
Round, 17J, oyster, chronograph, Daytona, 3 reg., c. 1950s, 18K	4,000	5,000	6,000
Round, 17J, oyster, chronograph, Daytona, 3 reg., c. 1950s, 14K	3,000	4,000	5,000
Round, 17J, oyster, chronograph, Daytona, 3 reg., c. 1950s, steel	1,400	1,500	2,200
Round, thin model, 18K case	700	800	1,000
Round, thin, chronometer, 18K case	900	1,000	1,200
Round, oyster commander, black 24 hr. dial	350	400	500
Round, 15J, "Imperial Chronometer," oyster	200	250	300

Rolex, oyster, stainless steel case & band.

Rolex, oyster, date, mid-size, stainless case & band.

Rolex, auto wind, center. sec., ca. 1950s.

Rolex, oyster, perpetual, date, ca. 1940s.

Style or Grade—Description	Avg	Ex-Fn	Mint
Round, 17J, "Tudor," oyster prince, GF & SS	$100	$120	$170
Round, 17J, 'Tudor," sweep sec., stainless	100	125	160
Round, 17J, "Tudor," prince, date, oyster	125	135	170
Round, 17J, "Tudor," submariner, date, c. 1970	150	190	250
Round, 18J, standard model, 14K	600	800	1,000
Round, 18J, gold mesh bracelet, 14K case	1,000	1,200	1,700
Round, 19J, chronograph, tacho-telemeter, 2 reg., c. 1945, 14K...	6,000	7,000	8,000
Round, sweep second, 18K case	900	1,000	1,100
Round, sweep second, 14K case	800	900	1,000
Round, sweep second, GF	200	250	300
Round, precision, 14K case	700	800	900
Round, precision, moon phases, day-date-month, 18K case	10,000	12,000	14,000
Round, precision, moon phases, day-date-month, stainless	4,500	5,000	6,000
Round, chronograph, day-date-month, 3 reg., stainless ...	4,000	5,000	6,000
Round, chronometer, 18K case.........................	900	1,000	1,200
Round, chronometer, 14K case.........................	800	900	1,000
Round, chronometer, GF..............................	200	250	350
Round, "Speedking," sweep sec., c. 1935	200	250	300
Round, oyster, manual wind, 18K case.................	650	700	850

Rolex, oyster, date, 17J, ca. 1950.   Rolex, oyster, bubble back, ca. 1940s.

Rolex, oyster, center sec., 14k, ca. 1945.   Rolex, oyster, perpetual, ca. 1940.

Style or Grade—Description	Avg	Ex-Fn	Mint
Round, oyster, manual wind, 14K case..................	$600	$650	$825
Round, oyster, manual wind, 10K case..................	500	550	700
Round, oyster, manual wind, GF........................	200	250	350
Round, oyster, manual wind, stainless	200	250	300
Round, oyster, perpetual (bubble back), 18K case	2,500	3,000	3,200
Round, oyster, perpetual (bubble back), 14K case	2,200	2,500	2,800
Round, oyster, perpetual (bubble back), 10K case	1,500	1,800	2,000
Round, oyster, perpetual (bubble back), stainless.........	500	550	650
Round, oyster, perpetual (bubble back), stainless & gold ..	900	1,000	1,200
Round, oyster, perpetual, date just. (date only), 18K case .	1,500	1,700	2,000
Round, oyster, perpetual, date just. (date only), 14K case .	1,300	1,500	1,800
Round, oyster, perpetual, date just. (date only), 10K case .	750	950	1,100
Round, oyster, perpetual, date just. (date only), stainless & 18K gold, Q. Set Jubilee band	1,600	1,500	2,000
Round, oyster, perpetual, date just. (date only), stainless..	550	600	700
Round, oyster, perpetual, day, date, 18K bracelet, Jubilee clasp..	4,500	5,000	5,500
Round, oyster, perpetual, day, date, 18K bracelet, Jubilee clasp, 12 diamond dial	5,000	5,500	6,000
Round, oyster, perpetual, date, president, 18K bracelet with hidden clasp, 18K case, Q. Set	5,500	6,200	7,200

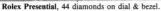

Rolex Presential, 44 diamonds on dial & bezel.　　Rolex, Luminor Paneral, ca. 1940s, military for diving.

Style or Grade—Description	Avg	Ex-Fn	Mint
Round, oyster, perpetual, day & date, 12 diamond dial, president, 18K bracelet with hidden clasp, 18K case, Q. Set	$6,000	$6,700	$7,700
Round, oyster, perpetual, day & date, 44 diamonds on bezel & 10 on dial, president, 18K bracelet with hidden clasp, 18K case	7,000	8,500	9,500
Round, oyster, perpetual, moon phases, day-date-month, sweep sec., waterproof, 18K case	20,000	23,000	25,000
Round, oyster, chronograph, 3 registers, 18K case	20,000	22,000	25,000
Round, oyster, chronograph, pulseometer, 2 reg., 18K case	18,000	20,000	22,000
Round, oyster, cosmograph, 3 reg., calibrated bezel, 14K .	4,500	5,000	6,000
Round, oyster, cosmograph, 3 reg., calibrated bezel, SS ..	1,200	1,400	1,600
Round, oyster, speedking, stainless steel case	250	300	350
Round, oyster, milgass, anti-magnetic, perpetual, stainless.	300	400	500
Round, oyster, perpetual, submariner, stainless	325	375	450
Round, oyster, perpetual, submariner, date, SS, Q. Set ...	800	900	1,000
Round, oyster, perpetual, explorer, stainless	450	500	600
Round, oyster, perpetual, explorer II, 24 hour bezel, stainless	500	550	650
Round, oyster, perpetual, sea dweller	800	900	1,000
Round, oyster, perpetual, GMT master, 17J, SS, old model	400	500	600
Round, oyster, perpetual, GMT master, 30J, 18K case	5,000	5,500	6,500
Round, oyster, perpetual, GMT master, 30J, SS, new style	700	800	900
Round, oyster, perpetual, "Superlative chronometer," SS .	350	400	450
Round, Tudor, Prince quartz, oyster, date, gold bezel & integral steel bracelet	400	500	600
Round, Tudor, Prince, oyster, date, chronograph, 3 reg.,SS	350	400	500
Round, Tudor, mini-sub, date	135	150	200
Round, Tudor, oyster, automatic	155	165	185
Round, 19J, "Cellini," 18K mesh band, 44 dwts total weight	1,000	1,250	1,400
Square, 17J, chronograph, 2 reg., tachometer, c. 1940s, 18K case	8,000	9,000	12,000
Square, 17J, ex. flat, stem wind, 1950s, 18K	2,200	2,400	2,700
Square, 17J, precision, c. 1940s, 18K case	1,200	1,400	1,600
Square, 17J, precision, c. 1940s, 14k case	1,000	1,200	1,400
Square, chronometer, perpetual, 18K case	1,800	2,000	2,500

ROLEX (continued)

Rolex, square, tachometer, ca. 1940s.

Rolex, square, extra flat, ca. 1950s.

Rolex, square, precision, 17J, ca. 1940s.

Rolex, square, auto wind, ca. 1945.

Rolex, hooded, bubble back, 26J.

Rolex, bubble back, 26J, ca. 1940s.

Style or Grade—Description	Avg	Ex-Fn	Mint
Square, precision, 14K case	$1,100	$1,200	$1,400
Tank, Rectangular, 2-tone YGF case, c. 1933	600	700	800
Tonneau, 26J, hooded lugs, c. 1950s, 18K case	5,000	5,500	6,200
Tonneau, 26J, hooded lugs, c. 1950s, 14K case	4,000	4,500	5,200
Tonneau, 26J, hooded lugs, c. 1950s, 14K steel back	3,000	3,500	4,200
Tonneau, 26J, hooded lugs, c. 1950s, 9K case	3,200	3,500	4,500
Tonneau, 26J, hooded lugs, c. 1950s, SS	1,500	1,700	2,000
Tonneau, 26J, oyster perpetual, 18K case	2,000	2,200	2,600
Tonneau, 26J, oyster perpetual, 14K case	1,800	2,000	2,400
Tonneau, 26J, oyster perpetual, 9K case	1,500	1,800	2,200
Tonneau, 26J, oyster perpetual, GF	1,000	1,100	1,200
Tonneau, 26J, oyster perpetual, SS	400	450	550

ROLEX (continued)

Rolex, tonneau, 26J, date, 14k.

Rolex, tonneau, stainless steel & gold.

Rolex, tonneau, graduated bezel, 18k.

Rolex, tonneau, 26J, steel back.

Rolex, tonneau, ¼ century club, ca. 1960s.

Rolex, tonneau, mercedes hands, ca. 1930s.

Style or Grade—Description	Avg	Ex-Fn	Mint
Tonneau, 26J, oyster perpetual date, 18K case	$1,800	$1,900	$2,000
Tonneau, 26J, oyster perpetual date, 14K case	1,400	1,500	1,600
Tonneau, 26J, oyster perpetual date, SS case	400	500	600
Tonneau, 26J, oyster perpetual, 18K case	1,600	1,700	1,800
Tonneau, 26J, oyster perpetual, 18K & steel back	700	800	900
Tonneau, 26J, oyster perpetual, 14K case	1,200	1,300	1,400
Tonneau, 26J, oyster perpetual, 14K & steel back	600	700	800
Tonneau, 26J, oyster perpetual, SS case.................	200	300	400
Tonneau, oyster perpetual, date, graduated bezel, 18K	1,400	1,600	1,800

Rolex, stars on dial, triple date, ca. 1945.

Rolex, day-date, moon phase, ca. 1945.

Rolex, tonneau, center sec., 18k, ca. 1945.

Rolex, tonneau, chronograph, day-date.

Rolex, man's small chronograph, ca. 1950.

Rolex, tonneau, oyster, quartz, day-date.

Style or Grade—Description	Avg	Ex-Fn	Mint
Tonneau, oyster perpetual, date, graduated bezel, 14K	$1,200	$1,300	$1,500
Tonneau, oyster perpetual, date, graduated bezel, SS	300	400	500
Tonneau, 25J, 1960s, ¼ century club, 14K case..........	3,000	3,500	4,000
Tonneau, 19J, tu-tone dial, mercedes hands, c. 1930s, 18K	2,800	3,000	3,500
Tonneau, 19J, tu-tone dial, mercedes hands, c. 1930s, 14K	2,200	2,400	2,600
Tonneau, 19J, tu-tone dial, mercedes hands, c. 1930s, 14K steel back	900	1,000	1,200
Tonneau, 19J, tu-tone dial, mercedes hands, c. 1930s, 9K case	1,500	1,600	1,800

ROLEX (continued)

Rolex, Benvenuto Cellini, 18k, diamonds.

Rolex, Benvenuto Cellini, thin model.

Rolex, Explorer II, stainless steel.

Rolex, GMT-Master II, oyster bracelet.

Rolex, Sea-Dweller 4000, date.

Rolex, Submariner, fliplock clasp bracelet.

Style or Grade—Description	Avg	Ex-Fn	Mint
Tonneau, 19J, tu-tone dial, mercedes hands, c. 1930s, GF.	$700	$750	$850
Tonneau, 19J, tu-tone dial, mercedes hands, c. 1930s, GF steel back	600	650	800
Tonneau, 19J, tu-tone dial, mercedes hands, c. 1930s, SS .	550	600	675
Tonneau, 18J, oyster perpetual, day date month, moon phases, star dial, 18K case........................	20,000	22,000	25,000

ROLEX (continued)

Style or Grade—Description	Avg	Ex-Fn	Mint
Tonneau, 18J, oyster perpetual, tri. date, moon phase, stem wind, 18K	$18,000	$20,000	$24,000
Tonneau, 18J, oyster, center sec., black dial, c. 1945, 18K	1,000	1,300	1,700
Tonneau, 18J, oyster, center sec., black dial, c. 1945, 14K	800	900	1,200
Tonneau, 18J, oyster, center sec., black dial, c. 1945, 9K	600	700	900
Tonneau, 18J, oyster, center sec., black dial, c. 1945, SS	200	300	450
Tonneau, 17J, oyster, chronograph, 3 reg., day date month, c. 1960s, 18K	18,000	20,000	24,000
Tonneau, 17J, oyster, chronograph, 3 reg., day date month, c. 1960s, 14K	16,000	18,000	20,000
Tonneau, 17J, oyster, chronograph, 3 reg., day date month, c. 1960s, SS	6,000	7,000	8,000
Tonneau, 17J, chronograph, 3 reg., snap back, day date month, c. 1960s, 18K	10,000	11,000	14,000
Tonneau, 17J, chronograph, 3 reg., snap back, day date month, c. 1960s, 14K	8,000	10,000	12,000
Tonneau, 17J, chronograph, 3 reg., snap back, day date month, c. 1960s, SS	3,000	4,000	5,000
Tonneau, 17J, chronograph, 2 reg., c. 1950s, heavy, 18K	8,000	9,000	10,000
Tonneau, 17J, chronograph, 2 reg., c. 1950s, heavy, 14k	7,000	8,000	9,000
Tonneau, oyster quartz, day date, 18K bracelet	2,000	2,500	3,000
Tonneau, oyster quartz, day date, 14K bracelet	1,800	2,000	2,800
Tonneau, oyster quartz, day date, diamond dial & bezel, 18K bracelet	2,500	3,000	4,000
Tonneau, oyster quartz, day date, diamond dial & bezel, 14K bracelet	2,000	2,500	3,200
Benvenuto Cellini, diamond bezel, diamond bracelet, 18K	13,000	14,000	15,000
Cellini, thin model, 18K case	1,500	1,600	1,700
Cellini, King Midas, geometric design, 18K bracelet & case	4,000	5,000	6,000
Explorer, oyster perpetual, SS case	200	250	300
Explorer II, oyster perpetual, date, SS case	300	400	500
GMT-Master, oyster perpetual, date, 18K case	2,000	2,500	3,000
GMT-Master, oyster perpetual, date, SS case	300	400	450
GMT-Master II, oyster perpetual, date, 18K case	2,000	2,500	3,000
GMT-Master II, oyster perpetual, date, SS case	300	400	500
Mid-size, oyster perpetual, date, 18K case	1,300	1,400	1,500
Mid-size, oyster perpetual, date, 14K case	1,200	1,300	1,400
Mid-size, oyster perpetual, date, SS case	300	400	500
Oyster, quartz, day date, pave diamond dial with sapphires, bezel, case & bracelet set with 107 diamonds, 8.06k total weight	90,000	95,000	100,000
Oyster, quartz, date, 18K case & bracelet	3,000	4,000	4,500
Round, diamond dial & super president bracelet all 18K	30,000	33,000	37,000
Sea-Dweller 4000, oyster perpetual, SS case	900	1,000	1,200
Submariner, 30J, oyster perpetual, date, 18K case	4,000	4,500	5,000
Submariner, 30J, oyster perpetual, date, 18K steel back	2,000	2,500	3,000

ROLEX (continued)

Rolex, bubble back, 26J.

Rolex, bubble back, 18J, ca. 1940.

Rolex, bubble back, graduated bezel, 26J.

Rolex, bubble back, graduated bezel, center sec.

Style or Grade—Description	Avg	Ex-Fn	Mint
Submariner, 30J, oyster perpetual, date, SS case	$400	$500	$600
Submariner, 30J, oyster perpetual, 18K case	3,000	3,500	4,000
Submariner, 30J, oyster perpetual, 14K case	1,500	2,000	2,500
Submariner, 30J, oyster perpetual, SS case	200	300	400

ROLEX OYSTER BUBBLE BACKS CASE & PERPETUAL (AUTO WIND)

Style or Grade—Description	Avg	Ex-Fn	Mint
Tonneau, 26J, center sec., c. 1942, 18K case.............	$3,000	$3,200	$3,500
Tonneau, 26J, center sec., c. 1942, 14K case.............	2,500	2,700	3,000
Tonneau, 26J, center sec., c. 1942, 9K case.............	1,800	2,000	2,300
Tonneau, 26J, center sec., c. 1942, SS	550	650	800
Tonneau, 26J, bubble back, c. 1940s, 18K case	2,500	3,000	3,500
Tonneau, 26J, bubble back, c. 1940s, 14K case	2,300	2,500	2,800
Tonneau, 26J, bubble back, c. 1940s, 14K steel back	1,600	1,800	2,000
Tonneau, 26J, bubble back, c. 1940s, 9K case	1,600	1,800	2,000
Tonneau, 26J, bubble back, c. 1940s, GF case	700	800	900
Tonneau, 26J, bubble back, c. 1940s, GF steel back	600	700	850
Tonneau, 26J, bubble back, c. 1940s, SS.................	500	600	750
Tonneau, 19J, center sec., c. 1940s, 18K case............	2,500	3,000	3,500
Tonneau, 19J, center sec., c. 1940s, 14K case............	2,300	2,500	2,800
Tonneau, 19J, center sec., c. 1940s, 14K steel back.......	1,600	1,800	2,000
Tonneau, 19J, center sec., c. 1940s, 9K case.............	1,600	1,800	2,000

ROLEX (continued)

Rolex, bubble back, 19J, center sec.

Rolex, bubble back, waterproof, ca. 1945.

Rolex, bubble back, Arabic & Roman nos.

Rolex, bubble back, 19J, stell & gold case.

Style or Grade—Description	Avg	Ex-Fn	Mint
Tonneau, 19J, center sec., c. 1940s, GF case	$700	$800	$900
Tonneau, 19J, center sec., c. 1940s, GF steel back	600	700	850
Tonneau, 19J, center sec., c. 1940s, SS case	500	600	750
Tonneau, 19J, Arabic & Roman numerals, c. 1940s, 18K .	2,500	3,000	3,800
Tonneau, 19J, Arabic & Roman numerals, c. 1940s, 14K .	2,200	2,500	3,200
Tonneau, 19J, Arabic & Roman numerals, c. 1940s, 14K steel back	900	1,000	1,200
Tonneau, 19J, Arabic & Roman numerals, c. 1940s, 9K cs.	1,500	1,700	2,000
Tonneau, 19J, Arabic & Roman numerals, c. 1940s, GF ..	800	900	1,000
Tonneau, 19J, Arabic & Roman numerals, c. 1940s, GF steel back	600	700	850
Tonneau, 19J, Arabic & Roman numerals, c. 1940s, SS...	500	550	650
Tonneau, 18J, oyster, perpetual, c. 1942, 18K case	2,600	2,700	3,000
Tonneau, 18J, oyster, perpetual, c. 1942, 14K case	2,000	2,200	2,400
Tonneau, 18J, oyster, perpetual, c. 1942, 9K case	1,400	1,600	1,800
Tonneau, 18J, oyster, perpetual, c. 1942, SS	500	600	750
Tonneau, 18J, center sec., mercedes hands, 18K case, pink	3,500	3,700	4,000
Tonneau, 18J, center sec., mercedes hands, 14K case	2,300	2,500	2,700
Tonneau, 18J, center sec., mercedes hands, 14K & steel bk.	1,600	1,800	2,000
Tonneau, 18J, center sec., mercedes hands, 9K case	1,600	1,800	2,000
Tonneau, 18J, center sec., mercedes hands, GF case	700	800	900
Tonneau, 18J, center sec., mercedes hands, GF & steel bk.	600	700	850
Tonneau, 18J, center sec., mercedes hands, SS case	500	600	750

ROLEX (continued)

Rolex, bubble back, 18J, ca. 1942.

Rolex, bubble back, mercedes hands, ca. 1940s.

Rolex, bubble back, black dial, ca. 1940s.

Rolex, bubble back, marked bezel, ca. 1940s.

Style or Grade—Description	Avg	Ex-Fn	Mint
Tonneau, 18J, center sec., mercedes hands, black dial, 18K	$2,500	$3,000	$3,500
Tonneau, 18J, center sec., mercedes hands, black dial, 14K	2,300	2,500	2,800
Tonneau, 18J, center sec., mercedes hands, black dial, 14K steel back	1,600	1,800	2,000
Tonneau, 18J, center sec., mercedes hands, black dial, 9K	1,600	1,800	2,000
Tonneau, 18J, center sec., mercedes hands, black dial, GF	700	800	900
Tonneau, 18J, center sec., mercedes hands, black dial, GF steel back	600	700	850
Tonneau, 18J, center sec., mercedes hands, black dial, SS.	500	600	750
Tonneau, 17J, center sec., mercedes hands, marked bezel, 18K case	3,000	3,200	3,500
Tonneau, 17J, center sec., mercedes hands, marked bezel, 14K case	2,300	2,500	2,800
Tonneau, 17J, center sec., mercedes hands, marked bezel, 14K steel back	1,600	1,800	2,000
Tonneau, 17J, center sec., mercedes hands, marked bezel, 9K case	1,600	1,800	2,000
Tonneau, 17J, center sec., mercedes hands, marked bezel, GF case	700	800	900
Tonneau, 17J, center sec., mercedes hands, GF steel back .	600	700	850
Tonneau, 17J, center sec., mercedes hands, SS case	500	600	750

ROLEX (continued)

Rolex, cushion, 15J, ca. 1928.

Rolex, round, date, jubilee bracelet.

Rolex, round, pleiade diamond dial.

Rolex, lady's dress watch, 14k, 2 diamonds.

LADY'S WRIST WATCH

Style or Grade — Description	Avg	Ex-Fn	Mint
Cushion, 15J, oyster, c. 1928, 18K case	$700	$800	$900
Cushion, 15J, oyster, c. 1928, 14K case	600	700	800
Cushion, 15J, oyster, c. 1928, 9K case	500	550	626
Cushion, 15J, oyster, c. 1928, sterling	400	450	550
Cushion, 15J, oyster, c. 1928, SS	200	250	325
Octagonal, lady's dress watch, 14K satin finish bracelet . . .	1,000	1,100	1,200
Round, 14K case	350	400	500
Round, oyster, 14K case	500	600	800
Round, oyster, stainless	150	200	250
Round, oyster, perpetual, date, 14K case	1,400	1,600	1,800
Round, oyster, perpetual, date, stainless	400	500	600
Round, oyster, perpetual, date, diamond dial, 14K case . . .	1,600	1,800	2,000
Round, oyster, perpetual, date, diamond on bezel, 18k band	4,000	4,500	5,000
Round, oyster, perpetual, date, diamond on bezel, 14k band	3,000	3,200	3,500
Round, oyster, perp., date, 40 dia. on bezel & dial, 18k band	5,000	6,000	6,500
Round, oyster, perpetual date, 18K & pleiade diamond dial	10,000	11,000	14,000
Round, oyster, perpetual date, 18K President bracelet	4,500	5,000	6,000
Round, oyster, perpetual date, 18K & steel Jubilee bracelet	1,200	1,600	2,000
Round, oyster, perpetual, 18K & steel Jubilee bracelet	600	700	1,200
Round, oyster, perpetual, SS oyster bracelet	300	400	500
Round, "Cellini" model, large diamonds on bezel, 18k band	1,000	1,100	1,200
Round, lady's dress, 14K, 2 full cut diamonds mes bracelet	2,000	2,500	3,000
Round, Tudor, quartz, date, 18K & steel	200	250	300
Square, 14K case	250	300	450
Tonneau, 14K case	300	350	500

ROLEX PERPETUAL WATCHES

OF Caliber Numbers
1030, 1035, 1036
1040, 1055, 1065

7007
7005
7018
7017
7026
7021
7000
7002
7015
7003
7012
7004
7013
7014
7010
7008
7016
6946

6955
6953
6954
6951
6950
6952
6957
6956
6958
6970
6970
6971
6903

ROLEX
GENÈVE - SUISSE
6960

6916
6915
6914
6913
6971
6930
6929
6932
6904
6907
6921
6910
6920
6922
6917

6967
6965
6968
6949
6948
6966
6959
6944
6945
6963
6964
6961
6962

663

ROLEX
MOVEMENT IDENTIFICATION

Ref. 90   Ref. 100   Ref. 150   Ref. 160   Ref. 161

(All without seconds)

Ref. 170   **Ref. 180**   **Ref. 200**   **Ref. 210**

without seconds without seconds without seconds sweep seconds

Ref. 250   **Ref. 270**   **Ref. 300**

without seconds without seconds ordinary seconds

Ref. 310   **Ref. 350**   **Ref. 360**

sweep second   jump hour   ordinary second

Ref. 400   **Ref. 420**   **Ref. 420**   **Ref. 500**

ordinary seconds ordinary seconds rotor   ordinary seconds

Ref. 510
sweep second

Ref. 520
sweep second

Ref. 520
rotor

Ref. 530
self wind, sweep sec.

Ref. 600
ordinary seconds

Ref. 620
ordinary seconds

Ref. 620
rotor

Ref. 630
self wind, sweep sec.

Ref. 700
ordinary seconds

Ref. 710
sweep seconds

Ref. 720
ordinary seconds

Ref. 720
rotor

Ref. 730
self wind, sweep sec.

Ref. 740
self wind, calendar, sweep sec.

Ref.800
ordinary seconds

Ref. 850
ordinary seconds

Ref. 72
chronograph, 3 registers

Ref. 23
chronograph, 2 registers

Above: Oyster style bracelet. **Below:** Presidential style band with hidden clasp.
Right: Jubilee style bracelet.

Rolls, made by Leon Hatot, S.A. Paris; early auto wind, c. 1920. The movement inside the case moves back and forth to wind.

Rolls, early auto wind, ca. 1930, according to patent Leon Hatot, made by Blancpain.

ROLLS
Rayville Watch Co.
SWISS

Style or Grade — Description	Avg	Ex-Fn	Mint
Rectangular, 16J, flip top, movement wind, c. 1930	$400	$500	$650
Square, 17J, self wind, Hatot Paten, 1930s, SS	400	500	650
Lady's rectangular, 16J, flip top, movement wind	300	345	400

ROSKOPH
SWISS

Style or Grade — Description	Avg	Ex-Fn	Mint
Round, large 41mm, c. 1920...........................	$35	$45	$55

Seiko round, 17 jewels.

SEIKO
JAPAN

Style or Grade — Description	Avg	Ex-Fn	Mint
Round, 17J, world time, autowind, date	$35	$45	$60
Round, 21J, chronograph, date, bezel rotates	40	60	65
Round, 21J, chronograph, tachometer, c. 1968	30	40	55

SINN
SWISS

Style or Grade—Description	Avg	Ex-Fn	Mint
Round, waterproof, chronograph, triple date, moon phase, 1950, 14K	$1,000	$1,200	$1,500

SOUTH BEND WATCH CO.
U.S.A.

Style or Grade—Description	Avg	Ex-Fn	Mint
Rectangular, 15J, 14K GF	$125	$150	$175
Round, 15J, 14K GF	125	150	175
Round, 6J, GF	65	75	90
Square, 15J, 14K GF	125	150	175
Lady's, 15J, GF	40	50	65

STOWA
GERMAN

Style or Grade — Description	Avg	Ex-Fn	Mint
Round, 15J, stainless, c. 1940	$45	$55	$70
Round, 15J, stainless, c. 1950	45	55	70

Tavannes, round, 15 jewels

Tavannes, tonneau, hour glass dial, curvex.

TAVANNES
SWISS

Style or Grade — Description	Avg	Ex-Fn	Mint
Round, 15J, stainless	$25	$30	$40
Round, 15J, "Ta-Cy" (Tavannes-Cyma W. Co.), GF	30	35	45
Tonneau, 15J, curvex style, 14K	300	350	425

SETH THOMAS
U.S.A.

Style or Grade—Description	Avg	Ex-Fn	Mint
Round, made in U.S.A., gold-filled	$25	$30	$45
Round, Swiss-made	5	7	10

Tiffany & Co., tonneau, movement by Patek, Philippe & Co., ca. 1910.

Tiffany & Co., rectangular, ca. 1935.

Tiffany & Co., minute repeater, automaton, 40mm.

Tiffany & Co., minute repeater, slide bolt to repeat.

TIFFANY & CO.
U.S.A. AND SWISS
MAN'S WRIST WATCH

Style or Grade — Description	Avg	Ex-Fn	Mint
Rectangular, 18J, by Patek, Philippe & Co., 1929, 18K ...	$4,500	$5,000	$5,500
Rectangular, 16J, by Touchon & Co., 14K	800	900	1,000
Rectangular, 18J, P.P. & Co. mvt., platinum	5,000	6,000	7,000
Rectangular, 18J, 18K case	800	1,000	1,200
Round, 17J, center sec., 1930s, 14K	500	600	700
Round, min. repeater, automaton, 18K, 40mm	3,000	4,000	5,000
Round, chronograph, 2 registers, moon phases, calendar, 18K case	3,000	3,500	4,000
Round, split sec. chronograph, 2 registers, moon phases, calendar, 18K case, by Patek, Philippe & Co	50,000	60,000	70,000
Square, 17J, 14K case	600	800	1,000

LADY'S WRIST WATCH

Style or Grade — Description	Avg	Ex-Fn	Mint
Square or Rectangular, 18K case	$350	$400	$500

Style or Grade—Description	Avg	Ex-Fn	Mint
Tonneau, 14K case	$325	$375	$475

Tissot, world time 24 hour dial, 24 cities.　　　　Tissot, chronograph, triple date, moon phases.

NOTE: Watches listed in this book are priced at the retail level, as complete watches having an original 14k gold-filled case, an original white enamel single sunk dial, and with the entire original movement in good working order with no repairs needed, unless otherwise noted.

TISSOT
SWISS

Style or Grade — Description	Avg	Ex-Fn	Mint
Round, 17J, world time, 24 cities, self wind, 24 hr. dial, 18K case	$2,500	$3,000	$3,500
Round, 17J, astronomic, moon ph., triple date, 1970, 18K	1,500	1,600	1,800
Round, 17J, world time zone, 24 hr., 24 cities, 1950, 18K .	2,500	3,000	3,500
Round, 17J, world time zone, 24 hr. 24 cities, 1950, 14K .	2,000	2,500	3,000
Round, 17J, world time zone, 24 hr. dial, 1950s, m. wind, 18K case	1,000	1,100	1,200
Round, 17J, chronograph by Omega, 18K, c. 1933	800	850	975
Round, autowind, day-date-month-moonphase, 18K	1,200	1,400	1,800
Round, self wind, 14K case...........................	125	150	175
Round, self wind, stainless	50	55	65
Round, chronograph, 3 registers, 14K case	600	700	800
Round, sea star, 2 registers, 14K case..................	450	550	650

TITUS

Style or Grade—Description	Avg	Ex-Fn	Mint
Round, 17J, chronograph, 2 reg., 18K case..............	$200	$250	$300
Round, 17J, chronograph, 2 reg., 14K case..............	175	200	225
Round, 17J, chronograph, 2 reg., SS case	85	95	135

Touchon, rectangular, jump hour, rotating minutes, ca. 1930s.

TOUCHON & CO.
SWISS

Style or Grade — Description	Avg	Ex-Fn	Mint
Rectangular, digital, jump hour, rotating minutes, 18K case	$4,000	$5,000	$7,000
Round, gold & enamel, 18K case, for Cartier	8,000	9,000	10,000
Square, large, bezel enameled, 18K, c. 1940	2,000	2,500	3,000
Tank, 14K case	400	500	600

Trebex, square, 15J, ca. 1940.

Trebex, round, 15J, ca. 1940.

TREBEX
LONDON

Style or Grade—Description	Avg	Ex-Fn	Mint
Round, 15J, aux. sec., 1950, GF	$10	$15	$20
Round, 15J, c. 1940s, GF case	5	6	10
Square, 15J, aux. sec., 1950, GF	10	15	20
Square, 15J, c. 1940s, GF case	5	6	10
Tonneau, 15J, c. 1940s, GF case	5	6	10
Lady's, 15J, 1950, GF	5	10	15

UNITAS
SWISS

Style or Grade—Description	Avg	Ex-Fn	Mint
Round, 17J, day date month, moon phase, SS	$125	$150	$200

671

Unitas, triple date, moon phase, ca. 1948.

Universal, round, triple date, moon phase.

Universal, aero compax, 4 registers, 17J.

Universal, tri-compax, moon phase, ca. 1940.

Universal, compax, massive case, ca. 1950.

Universal, aero compax, diff. meridian shown.

UNIVERSAL
SWISS

Style or Grade — Description	Avg	Ex-Fn	Mint
Cushion, 15J, quartz, day date, 1960, 18K	$400	$500	$600
Cushion, 15J, uniquartz, day date, c. sec., c. 1960s, 18K .	300	350	425

Universal, dato-compax, stainless steel, ca. 1950s.

Universal, reverso, "Cabriolet," ca. 1930.

Universal, triple date, moon phases, ca. 1940.

Universal, cushion, center sec., day-date, ca. 1960s.

Style or Grade—Description	Avg	Ex-Fn	Mint
Rectangular, 17J, 18K case	$300	$350	$450
Rectangular, 14K case	250	300	350
Rectangular, 15J, Reverso, "Cabriolet," 1930, SS	1,000	1,200	1,400
Rectangular, Reverso case, 18K	2,000	3,000	3,500
Round, moon phases, day & month, 2 registers, 14K case	1,600	1,800	2,000
Round, "aero" compax, 17J, dual time zone, 1940, 14K	1,600	1,800	2,200
Round, "aero" compax, 17J, 4 registers, 18K case	1,300	1,400	1,500
Round, "aero" compax, 17J, 4 registers, 14K case	1,100	1,200	1,400
Round, "aero" compax, 17J, 4 registers, stainless	500	600	650
Round, duo compax, 14K case	500	600	700
Round, duo compax, stainless	200	250	300
Round, 17J, day, date, month, moon phase, 14K bracelet	1,200	1,400	1,650
Round, 17J, tri-compax, day date month, moon ph., 18K	2,000	2,100	2,400
Round, 17J, tri compax, tachymeter, day-date-month, 3 registers, 18K case	1,700	1,900	2,200
Round, 17J, tri compax, tachymeter, day-date-month, 3 registers, 14K case	1,700	1,900	2,200
Round, 17J, tri compax, tachymeter, day-date-month, 3 registers, stainless	500	600	700
Round, 17J, compax, tach., fancy 18K case	1,800	2,000	2,300
Round, 17J, autowind, sweep sec., 18K, c. 1955	125	150	180
Round, 17J, autowind, sweep sec., 14K, c. 1955	115	130	160

Style or Grade—Description	Avg	Ex-Fn	Mint
Round, 17J, autowind, sweep sec., GF, c. 1955	$35	$45	$60
Round, 17J, autowind, sweep sec., stainless, c. 1955......	20	25	35
Round, 17J, center sec., mono date, 1950, GF...........	35	45	60
Round, 28J, "Polerouter," autowind, sweep sec., 18K....	185	225	300
Square, 17J, for Cartier, 1960, 18K	1,600	1,800	2,200

V&C, cushion, flat & thin, ca. 1960s.

V&C, flared, aux. seconds, platinum, ca. 1948.

V&C, flared, curvex, ca. 1940s.

V&C, flared, rect. movement, ca. 1948.

VACHERON & CONSTANTIN
SWISS
MAN'S WRIST WATCH

Style or Grade — Description	Avg	Ex-Fn	Mint
Cushion, day-date & moonphase, 18K, c. 1930..........	$20,000	$25,000	$30,000
Cushion, 17J, Adj.5P, flat & thin, 1960s, 18K	1,400	1,500	1,600
Flared, 17J, aux. sec., 1948, platinum	5,000	5,500	6,000
Flared, 17J, concave, 1940s, 18K......................	4,000	4,500	5,000
Flared, 17J, rect. movement, 1948, 18K................	3,000	3,500	4,000
Rectangular and also curvex, 18K case	3,000	3,500	4,000
Rectangular and also curvex, 14K case	2,000	2,500	3,600
Rectangular, 18K case	1,600	1,800	2,000
Rectangular, 14K case	1,000	1,200	1,500
Rectangular, big lugs, applied numbers, 1930s, 18K	2,500	2,800	3,200
Rectangular, 18J, Fausses-Cotes decoration, 1940, 18K ...	2,000	2,200	2,500
Rectangular, 17J, Fausses-Cotes decoration, 1946, 18K ...	3,000	3,500	4,000
Rectangular, 17J, black dial, 1947, 18K	3,500	4,000	4,500
Rectangular, 17J, aux. sec., 1940, 18K	2,800	3,000	3,300

V&C, rectangular, big lugs, applied numbers.

V&C, rectangular, 18J, 18k, ca. 1940.

V&C, rectangular, 17J, 18k, ca. 1946.

V&C, rectangular, 17J, black dial, ca. 1947.

V&C, rectangular, applied gold numbers.

V&C, rectangular, art deco bezel, ca. 1925.

V&C, single button chronograph, ca. 1910.

V&C, round, center sec., water tight, ca. 1950.

Style or Grade—Description	Avg	Ex-Fn	Mint
Rectangular, 17J, applied gold numbers, 1940, 18K	$1,300	$1,400	$1,600
Rectangular, 16J, flip top style, 14K, c. 1930	3,000	3,500	4,000
Rectangular, 16J, digital hour & min., 14K, c. 1935	5,000	6,000	7,000

V&C, round, triple date, ca. 1940.

V&C, round, triple date, 18k, ca. 1940.

V&C, self wind, 18k, ca. 1949.

V&C, round, applied gold numbers, ca. 1948.

V&C, triple date, moon phase, ca. 1940.

V&C, round, 17J, aux. seconds, ca. 1940.

Style or Grade—Description	Avg	Ex-Fn	Mint
Rectangular, 15J, art deco bezel, 1925, multi-color gold...	$4,500	$5,000	$5,500
Rectangular, 15J, mid-1920s, art deco multi-color gold case	2,000	2,500	3,000
Round, 15J, white enamel dial, 1910, 18K...............	6,000	6,500	7,000
Round, 15J, "T" style lugs, 18K, c. 1940s	1,600	1,800	2,000
Round, 17J, single button chronograph, 2 reg., 1910, 18K	25,000	30,000	35,000
Round, 17J, c. sec., graduated fancy bezel, 18K case	2,000	2,500	3,000
Round, 17J, center sec., watertight, 1950s, 18K	1,400	1,500	1,700
Round, 17J, 18K case.................................	1,,000	1,200	1,400

V&C, round, anti shock system, ca. 1940.

V&C, round, Glucidur bal., ca. 1950.

V&C, round, graduated bezel, ca. 1950.

V&C, triple date, moon phases, ca. 1945.

V&C, round, 18J, center sec., ca. 1940.

V&C, 19J chronograch, 2 registers, ca. 1950.

Style or Grade—Description	Avg	Ex-Fn	Mint
Round, 17J, 14K case................................	$700	$800	$1,000
Round, 17J, triple date, 1940, 18K	4,000	4,500	5,000
Round, 17J, self wind, 1949, 18K	1,400	1,500	1,700
Round, 17J, applied gold numbers, 1948, 18K	1,300	1,400	1,600
Round, 17J, astronomic, triple date, moon phases, 1940, 18K...	14,000	16,000	18,000
Round, 17J, aux. sec., 1940, 18K	1,200	1,400	1,600
Round, 17J, anti-shock system, 1940, 18K..............	1,500	1,700	2,000

VACHERON & CONSTANTIN (continued)

V&C, chronograph, 2 registers, ca. 1945.

V&C, minute repeater, 29J, ca. 1950.

V&C, round, 29J, watertight, ca. 1960.

V&C, round, 29J, center sec., auto wind, ca. 1950s.

V&C, round, center sec., date, auto wind.

V&C, round, 29J, auto wind, ca. 1940s.

Style or Grade—Description	Avg	Ex-Fn	Mint
Round, 17J, Glucidur bal., 1950, 18K	$1,500	$1,700	$2,000
Round, 17J, graduated bezel, 1950, 18K	3,000	3,500	4,500
Round, 17J, astronomic, moon ph., triple date, 1945, 18K	10,000	11,000	13,000
Round, 18J, center sec., 1940, 18K	1,200	1,400	1,600
Round, 19J, chronograph, 2 reg., 1950, 18K band & case .	14,000	16,000	18,000
Round, 19J, chronograph, 2 reg.,1945, 18K	10,000	12,000	15,000
Round, 29J, 1 min. repeater, 1950s, 18K case............	60,000	70,000	80,000

V&C, round, center sec., self wind, 18k.

V&C, chronograph, 2 registers, 18k.

V&C, square, 21J, center sec., ca. 1950.

V&C, square, 18J, black dial, ca. 1950.

Style or Grade—Description	Avg	Ex-Fn	Mint
Round, 29J, date, watertight, 1960, 18K	$1,600	$1,900	$2,200
Round, 29J, center sec., auto wind, 1950, 18K	1,500	1,600	1,800
Round, 29J, center sec., date, auto wind, 1950, 18K	2,000	2,200	2,500
Round, 29J, date, auto wind, 1940, 18K	1,700	1,900	2,300
Round, thin model, 18K bracelet & case	1,800	2,000	2,200
Round, "Obervation," inner dial has 360°, 18K	1,200	1,400	1,600
Round, "Royal," waterproof, stop/start, chronometer, 18K	1,400	1,600	1,800
Round, second center, self wind, 18K case	1,200	1,400	1,500
Round, second center, self wind, 14K case	800	900	1,000
Round, second center, self wind, date, gold rotor, 18K case	1,800	2,000	2,200
Round, second center, self wind, date, gold rotor, 14K case	1,400	1,600	1,800
Round, chronograph, telemeter, 2 registers, 18K case	8,000	9,000	10,000
Round, calendar, day-date-month on outer ring, 18K case	4,000	4,500	5,000
Round, moon phases, day-date-month, 18K case	8,000	9,000	10,000
Round, moon phases, day-date-month, 14K case	5,000	6,000	7,000
Round, 5 min. repeater, 18K case	35,000	40,000	45,000
Round, Mysterieuse, c. 1950, 18K	1,000	1,200	1,500
Round, "Trucchi," large 18K case	1,800	2,000	2,500
Square, 21J, center sec., 1950, 18K	3,500	3,700	4,000
Square, 18J, fancy lugs, 1940, 18K	3,000	3,500	4,000

V&C, triple date, moon phase, ca. 1947.

V&C, square, Glucidur bal., ca. 1950s.

V&C, square, 17J, aux. seconds, ca. 1950.

V&C, square, 17J, aux. seconds, ca. 1945.

V&C, square, applied gold numbers, ca. 1940.

V&C, square, 17J, baton hands, ca. 1950s.

Style or Grade—Description	Avg	Ex-Fn	Mint
Square, 18J, aux. sec., black dial, 1950, 18K	$2,500	$3,000	$3,500
Square, 17J, astronomic, moon ph., triple date, 1947, 18K	16,000	18,000	22,000
Square, 17J, day date month, moon ph., 1940s, 18K case .	10,000	12,000	15,000
Square, 17J, skeletonized, white gold with small diamonds	5,000	6,000	7,000
Square, 17J, GLucidur bal., 1950, 18K	2,200	2,400	2,700
Square, 17J, curved, triple date, moon ph., 1940s, 18K ...	16,000	18,000	22,000
Square, 17J, Glucidur bal., 1950, 18K	2,200	2,400	2,800
Square, 17J, applied gold index, 1940, 18K..............	2,800	3,200	3,500
Square, 17J, baton hands, 1950, 18K	1,600	1,800	2,200
Square, 17J, applied gold index, 1960, 18K..............	2,600	2,800	3,200
Square, 17J, aux. sec. dial, 1945, 18K	2,500	2,800	3,200
Square, 15J, shutters cover dial, 1955, 18K	5,000	6,000	7,000
Square, with shutters, crowns at 3 & 9 o'clock, 18K case..	7,000	8,000	10,000
Tank, date window at 12 o'clock, 18K, c. 1930	5,000	6,000	7,000

VACHERON & CONSTANTIN (continued)

V&C, square, with shutters, crowns at 3&9 o'clock

V&C, trapezoidal, 20J, Adj.5P, ca. 1970.

V&C, ladies square, 18k case and band, ca. 1960s.

V&C, ladies trapezoidal, 22J, ca. 1970.

Style or Grade—Description	Avg	Ex-Fn	Mint
Tank, day-date-month & moonphase, 18K, c. 1920	$10,000	$18,000	$20,000
Tonneau, 18J, Adj.5P, 1930, 18K	3,500	4,000	4,500
Trapezoidal, 20J, Adj.5P, 1970, 18K	2,000	2,500	3,000
Trapezoidal, 17J, c. 1940s, 18K case.................	4,000	5,000	6,000

LADY'S WRIST WATCH

Style or Grade — Description	Avg	Ex-Fn	Mint
Rectangular, with 34 small diamonds, platinum	$1,500	$2,000	$2,500
Square, 15J, 1960, 18K bracelet & case	1,600	1,800	2,200
Square, 18K case....................................	400	500	600
Square, 14K case....................................	300	325	425
Trapezoidal, 22J, angular balance, 1970, 18K............	1,800	2,200	2,600

Vulcain rectangular, 17 jewels.

Vulcain rectangular, 15 jewels.

VULCAIN
SWISS

Style or Grade — Description	Avg	Ex-Fn	Mint
Rectangular, 15J, sweep sec., GF......................	$8	$12	$20
Rectangular, 15J, sweep sec., 14K	90	100	120

VULCAIN (continued)

Style or Grade—Description	Avg	Ex-Fn	Mint
Round, 15J, alarm, "Cricket," stainless	$35	$45	$60
Round, 15J, alarm, "Cricket," GF	40	55	80
Round, 15J, alarm, "Cricket," 14K	120	135	175
Round, 15J, alarm, "Cricket," + date, 14K	125	140	185
Round, 15J, sweep sec., GF	8	12	20
Square, 15J, GF	3	5	10
Square, 15J, 14K	25	30	40

WESTCLOX
U.S.A.

Style or Grade—Description	Avg	Ex-Fn	Mint
Rectangular case	$10	$15	$20
Round case	8	12	15
Round, day & date	10	12	15
Round, luminous dial	10	12	15
Tonneau case	10	15	20

WHITE STAR
SWISS

Style or Grade—Description	Avg	Ex-Fn	Mint
Round, 17J, chronograph, 2 reg., waterproof, moon phases, triple date	$60	$80	$125
Round, 17J, day date, c. 1950s, SS	35	45	60

White Star, triple date, moon phase, ca. 1948.

Wig Wag, 15J, self wind by movt., ca. 1932

WIG WAG

Style of Grade — Description	Avg	Ex-Fn	Mint
Rectangular, 15J, "Universal Watch" on dial, 1932, chromium	$1,000	$1,200	$1,500
Rectangular, 15J, "Aster," flip top, stem at 9 o'clock, movement wind, c. 1930, stainless	400	500	600

Whittnauer, tonneau shaped movement.   **Whittnauer**, square, fancy lugs, black dial.

WITTNAUER
SWISS
MAN'S WRIST WATCH

Style or Grade — Description	Avg	Ex-Fn	Mint
Rectangular, 17J, SW, GF	$60	$70	$80
Rectangular, 17J, sector type, hour jumps back to 12, date	600	700	900
Round, 17J, auto wind, 14K...........................	100	120	140
Round, 17J, auto wind, YGF..........................	35	40	55
Round, 17J, auto wind, stainless	20	25	30
Round, 17J, chronograph, stainless....................	125	150	175
Round, 17J, auto wind, date, 14K.....................	120	130	150
Round, 17J, auto wind, date, YGF	40	50	70
Round, 17J, auto wind, date, stainless	25	30	35
Round, 17J, "2000," day-date, good until 2000 A.D., c. 1965...	125	135	185
Square, 17J, fancy lugs, black dial, 14K	250	300	375

LADY'S WRIST WATCH

Style or Grade — Description	Avg	Ex-Fn	Mint
Round, 17J, 14K case & mesh band, 10 DWTs total weight	$180	$200	$220

Wyler, face and movement, 17 jewels, early self wind watch. The watch winds by using the muscular movement of the wrist, back set.

WYLER
SWISS

Style or Grade — Description	Avg	Ex-Fn	Mint
Rectangular, 17J, back set, early autowind, c. 1932	$400	$500	$600
Round, 17J, Incaflex	$10	$15	$25
Round, 17J, Incaflex, day, date......................	20	30	45
Round, 17J, Skin Diver	10	15	25
Round, 17J, anti-magnetic, waterproof, stainless	25	35	55

Zenith oval.

Zenith, 9 lignes.

ZENITH
SWISS

Style or Grade — Description	Avg	Ex-Fn	Mint
Cushion, 15J, 18K, c. 1930...........................	$300	$350	$400
Round, 15J, chronograph, Telemere, spiral tachometer, 18K, c. 1930....................................	1,400	1,600	1,800
Round, 15J, chronograph, 2 register, 18K	500	600	700
Round, 15J, 18K, c. 1922	200	300	350
Round, 16J, 18K	180	225	285
Round, 17J, chronograph, 3 reg., 18K	600	800	1,100
Round, 18J, "Pilot," GF, c. 1955.....................	95	110	140
Round, 31J, chronograph & tachometer, 3 reg., date, autowind..	400	500	625
Round, early alarm, c. 1925	300	400	500
Round, "El Primero," day-date-month & moonphase, autowind, chronograph, 2 registers, 18K case	2,400	2,600	2,800
Round, "Espada," day-date-month, moonphase, auto-wind, chronograph, 2 registers, stainless case	450	580	750
Tonneau, 31J, astronomic, moon phases, triple date, auto wind, 18K	3,000	3,500	4,000
Tonneau, 15J, platinum, c. 1930	900	1,000	1,200
Tonneau, 15J, 18K, c. 1930	600	700	800
Tonneau, 15J, 14K, c. 1930	500	600	650
Tonneau, 15J, YGF, c. 1930..........................	50	75	100

Zenith, "El Primero," triple date, moon phase, ca. 1970.

Zodiac, self wind with reserve power gauge.

ZODIAC
SWISS

Style or Grade — Description	Avg	Ex-Fn	Mint
Rectangular, 17J, 14K case	$150	$170	$200
Round, 17J, 14K case................................	100	120	145
Round, 17J, sweep sec., GF	20	30	45
Round, sweep sec., 14K	110	125	160

WATCH TERMINOLOGY

ADJUSTED—Adjusted to compensate for temperature, positions, and isochronism.

ALARM WATCH—A watch that will give an audible sound at a pre-set time.

ANCHOR ESCAPEMENT—Also called the recoil escapement.

ANNEALING—Heating and cooling a metal slowly to relieve internal stress.

ANTI-MAGNETIC—Not affected by magnetic field.

Arbor

ARBOR—The mechanical axis of a moving part; on the balance it is called the "staff," on the lever it is called the arbor.

ASSAY—Analyzing a metal for its gold or silver content.

AUTOMATON—Animated mechanical objects and figures; actuated by the going, striking or repeating train.

AUXILIARY COMPENSATION—Additional temperature compensators found on marine chronometers.

Balance Cock

BALANCE COCK—The bridge that holds the upper jewels and the balance.

Balance Spring

BALANCE SPRING—Also called the hairspring; the spring governing the balance.

Balance Staff

BALANCE STAFF—The shaft of the balance wheel.

Balance Wheel

BALANCE WHEEL—A device shaped like a wheel that does for a watch what a pendulum does for a clock.

Banking Pins

BANKING PINS—The two pins which limit the angular motion of the pallet.

Bar Movement

BAR MOVEMENT—A type of movement employing about six bridges to hold the train.

Barrel

BARREL—Drum-shaped container that

houses the mainspring. A going barrel has teeth around the top or bottom and drives the gears.

BEAT—Refers to the tick or sound of a watch; about 1/5 of a second. The sound is produced by the escape wheel striking the pallets.

BEETLE HAND—Hour hand resembling a stag beetle; usually associated with the poker-type minute hand.

BELL METAL—Four parts copper and one part tin used for metal laps to get a high polish on steel.

BEZEL—The rim that covers the dial (face) and retains the crystal.

BI-METALLIC BALANCE—A balance designed to compensate for changes in temperature; made of a strip of brass and steel usually.

BISEAUTAGE—The grinding of a crystal to size it to fit a bezel.

BLIND MAN'S WATCH—A Braille watch; also known as a tact watch.

BLUING—By heating steel to about 540 degrees, the color will change to blue.

BOW—The ring that is looped at the pendant to which a chain or fob is attached.

BOX CHRONOMETER—A marine or other type chronometer in gimbals so the movement remains level.

BOX JOINTED CASE—A heavily hinged decorative case with a similated joint at the top under the pendant.

BREGUET KEY—A watch key permitting winding in one direction only.

BREGUET SPRING—A type of hairspring that improves timekeeping (see Overcoil).

BRIDGE—A metal bar which carries the pivot for the balance or other pivot-bearing gears.

BULL'S EYE CRYSTAL—Used on old watches; the center of the crystal was polished which achieved a bull's eye effect.

CALENDAR WATCH—A watch that shows the date, month and day.

CAP JEWEL—Also called the endstone, the flat jewel on which the staff rests.

CENTER WHEEL—The second wheel; the arbor for the minute hand; this wheel makes one revolution per hour.

CHAIN (Fusee)—Looks like a miniature bicycle chain connecting the barrel and fusee.

CHAMPLEVE—An area hollowed out and filled with enamel and then baked on.

CHRONOGRAPH—A movement that can be started and stopped to measure short time intervals and return to zero; also called a stop watch, but a stop watch does not keep the time of day.

CHRONOMETER ESCAPEMENT—A detent escapement used in marine chronometers.

CLICK—A name given to a part that permits the gear to move in one direction; a pawl and ratchet mechanism; a click can be heard as the watch is wound.

CLOCK WATCH—A watch that strikes the hour but not on demand.

CLOISONNE—Enamel set between strips of metal and baked onto the dial.

Club Tooth

CLUB TOOTH—Some escape wheels have a special design which increases the impulse plane; located at the very tip of the tooth of the escape wheel.

COARSE TRAIN—16,000 beats per hour.

COCK—the metal bar that carries the balance wheel; a bridge.

COMPENSATION BALANCE—A balance wheel designed to correct for temperature.

COMPLICATED WATCH—A watch with complicated works; other than just telling time, it may have a perpetual calendar, moon phases, equinoxes, up and down dial, repeater, musical chimes or alarms.

CONTRATE WHEEL—A wheel with its teeth at a right angle to plane of the wheel.

CONVERTIBLE—Made by Elgin; a means of converting from a hunting case to an open-face watch or vice-versa.

CRAZE (Crazing)—A minute crack in the glaze of enamel watch dials.

Crown   Crown Wheel

CROWN—A winding button.

CROWN WHEEL—The escape wheel of a verge escapement; looks like a crown.

Curb Pin

CURB PINS—The two pins that change the rate of a watch; these two pins, in effect, change the length of the hairspring.

CYLINDER ESCAPEMENT—A type of escapement used on some watches.

DAMASKEENING—The art of producing a design, pattern, or wavy appearance on a metal.

DEMI-HUNTER—A hunting case with the center designed to allow the position of the hands to be seen without opening the case.

DETENT ESCAPEMENT—A detached escapement. The balance is impulsed in one direction; used on watches to provide great accuracy; found on marine chronometers.

DIAL—the face of a watch. Some are enameled and hand-painted; some are made of gold or silver with diamonds for numbers, etc.

DISCHARGE PALLET JEWEL—The left jewel.

DOLLAR WATCH—Watches that sold for a dollar or close to a dollar ("the watch that made the dollar famous").

Double Roller

DOUBLE ROLLER—A watch with one impulse roller table and a safety roller, thus two rollers.

DRAW—The inclined position of the locking face of the pallet jewel; this causes the pallet to be drawn toward the escape wheel and the fork toward the banking pin where it is in position to receive the roller jewel.

DROP—The space between a tooth of the escape wheel and the pallet from which it has just escaped.

DUMB REPEATER—One that strikes the hour on the case or block rather than a bell or gong.

DUPLEX ESCAPEMENT—An escape wheel with two sets of teeth, one for locking and one for impulse.

EBAUCHE (i-bo-she)—A movement not completely finished or "in the grey;" in the rough; not detailed; a movement made up of two plates or bars with pillars, barrel and train, and assembly screws. These parts were roughly filed and did not include a dial, case, or escapement.

ECCENTRIC—Non-concentric; usually a cam.

ELECTRONIC WATCH—Newer type watch using quartz and electronics to produce a high degree of accuracy; accurate within a few seconds a month and accurate to within a minute a year.

ELINVAR—A hairspring made of a special alloy that does not vary at different temperatures and is not affected by magnetism: nickel, steel, chromium, manganese and tungsten.

Endshake

ENDSHAKE—The up and down play of an arbor between the plate and bridge or between the jewels.

END STONE—The jewel or cap at the end of the staff.

ENGRAVING—Cutting away to form a pattern.

EPHEMERIS TIME—The time calculated for the Earth to orbit around the sun.

ESCAPE WHEEL—The last wheel in a going train; works with the fork or lever and escapes one pulse at a time.

Fork

ESCAPEMENT—The device in a watch by which the motion of the train is checked and the energy of the mainspring communicated to the balance. The escapement includes the escape wheel, lever, and balance complete with hairspring.

FARMER'S WATCH—A large pocket watch with a verge escapement and a farm scene on the face or dial.

FIVE-MINUTE REPEATER—A watch that denotes the time every five minutes, and on the hour and half hour, by operating a slide.

FLINQUE—Enameling over hand engraving.

FLY BACK—The hand return back to zero on a timer.

FOB—A decorative short strap or chain.

Foliot

FOLIOT—A straight-armed balance with weights on each end used for regulation; found on the earliest clocks and watches.

FORK—The part of the lever that engages with the roller jewel.

FREE SPRUNG—A balance spring free from the influence of curb pins. Curb pins tend to destroy isochronism.

FULL PLATE—A plate (or disc) that covers the works and supports the wheel pivots. There is a top plate, a bottom plate, half plate, and ¾ plate. The top plate has the balance resting on it.

FUSEE—A spirally grooved, truncated cone used in some watches to equalize the power of the mainspring.

GENEVA STOP WORK—(See Maltese Cross)

GILT (or Gild)—To coat with gold leaf or a gold color.

GOING BARREL—The barrel houses the mainspring; as the spring uncoils, the barrel turns, and the teeth on the outside of the barrel turn the train of gears.

GOLD-FILLED—Sandwich-type metal: a layer of gold, a layer of base metal, another layer of gold—then the metals are soldered to each other to form a sandwich.

GOLD JEWEL SETTINGS—In high-grade watches the jewels were mounted in gold settings.

GREAT WHEEL—The main wheel of a fusee type watch.

HACK-WATCH—A watch with a balance that can be stopped to allow synchronization with another timepiece.

HAIRSPRING—The spring which vibrates the balance.

HALLMARK—The British silver or gold assay marker stamp. It gave the place (town), quality marks, maker's mark, and year.

HEART-PIECE—A heart-shaped cam which causes the hand on a chronograph to fly back to zero.

HELICAL HAIRSPRING—A cylindrical spring used in marine chronometers.

HOROLOGY (pronounced Haw-RAHL-uh-jee)—The study of timekeeping or the science of time.

HUNTER CASE—A pocket watch case with a covered face that must be opened to see the watch dial.

IMPULSE—The force transmitted by the escape wheel to the pallet by gliding over the angular or impulse face of the pallet jewel.

IMPULSE PIN (Ruby pin)—A pin on the balance which keeps the balance going (roller pin).

INCABLOC—A shock absorbing device which permits the endstone of the balance to "give" when the watch is subjected to an impact or jolt.

INDEX—A regulator that can alter the length of the hairspring through means of a lever that moves two curb pins.

ISOCHRONISM—"Isos" means equal; "chronos" means time—occurring at equal intervals of time. The balance should not vary in its swing. The watch will not run any faster one hour after it is wound than it will 24 hours later.

JEWEL—A bearing made of a ruby or other type jewel; the four types of jewels include: cap jewel, hole jewel, roller jewel or ruby pin, pallet jewel or stone.

KARRUSEL (Kar-oo-zell)—A style or type similar to a tourbillon; the escapement rotates its position in an effort to solve the error of positions.

KEY SET—Older watches that had to be set with a key.

KEY WIND—A key used on earlier watches to wind the watch (crank).

LEAVES—The teeth of the pinion gears.

LEVER ESCAPEMENT—Invented by Thomas Mudge in 1760.

Lever

LEVER SETTING—The lever used to set some watches.

LOCKING—Holding the escape wheel (lock) while the balance swings around.

MAINSPRING—A flat spring coiled or wound to supply power to the watch. If it were not for the mainspring the watch would not be portable. The unbreakable main is made of iron, nickel, chromium, cobalt, molybdenum, manganese, and beryllium. The non-magnetic mainspring was introduced in 1947.

MAIN WHEEL—The first driving wheel, part of the barrel.

MALTESE CROSS—The part of the stop works preventing the barrel from being overwound.

Marine Chronometer

MARINE CHRONOMETER—An accurate timepiece; has a dent escapement and sets in a box with gimbals which keep it in a right position; may have up and down dial.

MEAN TIME—Also equal hours; average mean solar time; the time shown by watches; hours shown by sundials vary in length. When time was averaged into equal hours, this was called mean time.

Meantime Screw

MEANTIME SCREWS—Balance screws used for timing, usually longer than other balance screws; when turned away from or toward the balance pin, they cause the balance vibrations to become faster or slower.

MICROMETRIC REGULATOR—A regulator used on railroad grade watches to adjust for gain or loss in a very precise way.

MICROSECOND—A millionth of a second.

MILLISECOND—A thousandth of a second.

MINUTE REPEATER—A watch that strikes or sounds the hours, quarter hours, and minutes on demand by moving a slide.

MOVEMENT—The works of a watch without the case or dial.

MUSICAL WATCH—A watch that plays a tune on demand or on the hour.

MULTI-GOLD—Different colors of gold—red, green, white, blue, pink, yellow, and purple.

NANOSECOND—One billionth of a second.

NATIONAL ASSOCIATION OF WATCH AND CLOCK COLLECTORS—Formed in 1943 to stimulate interest in the study and collecting of timepieces. Mailing address: N.A.W.C.C., P. O. Box 33, Columbia PA 17512.

NON-MAGNETIC—Resistant to magnetism; not affected by magnetic forces.

NUREMBERG EGG—Nickname for a German watch that was oval-shaped.

OIL SINK—A small well around a pivot which retains oil.

OVERBANKED—A lever escapement error; the roller jewel passes to the wrong side of the lever notch, causing one side of the

pallet to rest against the banking pin and the roller jewel to rest against the other side, thus locking the escapement and stopping the motion of the balance.

PAIR-CASE WATCH—An extra case around a watch—two cases, hence, a pair of cases. The outer case kept out the dust. The inner case could not be dustproof because it provided the access to winding the watch.

PALLET—The part of the lever that works with the escape wheel—jewelled pallet stones, entry pallet and exit pallet.

Parachute

PARACHUTE—An early shockproofing system designed to fit as a spring on the endstone of balance.

Pendant

PENDANT—The neck of the watch; attached to it is the bow (swing ring) and the crown.

PILLARS—The rods that hold the plates

694

apart. In old watches they were fancy.

Pinion

PINION—The large gear is called a wheel. The small solid gear is a pinion. The pinion is made of steel in some watches.

PLATE—A watch has a front and a back plate or top and bottom plate. The works are in between.

POISE—A term meaning "in balance;" to equalize the weight of the balance.

PONTILLAGE—The grinding of the center of a crystal to form a concave.

POSITION—As adjusted to five position; a watch may differ in its timekeeping accuracy as it lays in different positions. Due to the lack of isochronism, changes in the center of gravity, a watch can be adjusted to six positions: dial up, dial down, stem up, stem down, stem left, and stem right.

QUICK TRAIN—A watch with five beats per second or 18,000 per hour.

RACK LEVER ESCAPEMENT—Developed by Abbe de Hutefeuille in 1722 and by Petter Litherland in 1791; does not use a roller table, but a pinion.

Receiving Pallet

RECEIVING PALLET—Also called "R" stone; the first of two pallet jewels with which a tooth of the escape wheel comes into engagement.

REPEATER WATCH—A complicated pocket watch that repeats the time on demand with a sounding device.

REPOUSSE—A watch with a decorative design embossed on the case.

ROLLED GOLD—Thin layer of gold soldered to a base metal.

Table Roller

Safety Roller

Crescent
Roller Jewel
Horns
Fork Slot
Guard Pin

ROLLER JEWEL—The jewel seated in the roller table, which receives the impulse from the pallet fork.

ROLLER TABLE—The part of the balance in which the roller jewel is seated.

SAFETY PINION—A pinion in the center wheel designed to slip if the mainspring breaks; this protects the train from being stripped by the great force of the mainspring.

SAFETY ROLLER—The smaller of the two rollers in a double roller escapement.

SIDEREAL TIME—The time of rotation of the Earth as measured from the stars.

SIDE-WINDER—A mismatched case and movement; a term used for a hunting movement that has been placed in an open face case and winds at the 3 o'clock position. With an open face movement the pendant should be at the 12 o'clock position.

SILVEROID—A type of case composed of various metals.

SINGLE ROLLER—The safety roller and the roller jewel are one single table or roller.

SIZE—Systems used to size the movement to the case.

SKELETON WATCH—A watch made so the viewer can see the works. Plates are pierced and very decorative.

SKULL WATCH—A pendant watch that is hinged at the jaw to reveal a watch.

SLOW TRAIN—A watch with four beats per second or 14,000 per hour.

SNAILING—Ornamentation of the surface of metals by means of a circle design; sometimes called damaskeening.

SOLAR YEAR—365 days, 5 hours, 48 minutes, 49.7 seconds.

SPOTTING—Decoration used on a watch movement and barrels of movements.

SPRING RING—A circular tube housing a coiled type spring.

STACKFREED—Curved spring and cam to equalize the uneven pull of the mainspring.

STAFF—Name for the axle of the balance.

SUN DIAL—A device using a gnomon or style that casts a shadow over a graduated dial as the sun progresses, giving solar time.

SWIVEL—A hinged spring catch with a loop of metal that may be opened to insert a watch bow.

TOP PLATE—The metal plate in the back of a movement that houses the gears. This plate usually contains the name and serial number.

TORSION—A twisting force.

TOURBILLON—A watch with the escapement mounted on a platform which revolves once a minute. This is to compensate for various errors in positions. Also called a revolving carriage.

CENTER WHEEL AND PINION   THIRD WHEEL AND PINION   FOURTH WHEEL AND PINION   ESCAPE WHEEL AND PINION

TRAIN—A series of gears that form the works of a watch. The train is used for other functions such as chiming. The time train carries the power to the escapement.

TRIPLE CASE WATCH—An early watch with three cases.

UP AND DOWN DIAL—A dial that

shows how much of the mainspring is spent and how far up or down the mainspring is.

VERGE ESCAPEMENT—Early type of escapement with wheel that is shaped like a crown.

VIRGULE ESCAPEMENT—Early escapement introduced in the mid 1700s.

WATCH PAPER—A disc of paper with the name of the watchmaker or repairman printed on it; used as a form of advertising and found in pair-cased watches.

WIND INDICATOR—A dial that shows how much of the mainspring is spent.

WOLF TEETH—A winding wheel's teeth, so named because of their shape.

Cooksey Shugart   *Tom Engle*

ABOUT THE AUTHORS

Mr. Shugart, who compiled and published the highly successful first edition in 1980, has been joined with Mr. Engle, a widely known watch dealer and authority in the field. Each edition contains updated and revised information and prices, and has become the accepted standard reference work of the watch market.   Both authors have been avid pocket watch collectors for the past two decades, and both have been vitally interested in seeing a reliable and accurate pocket watch guide produced. "We see this book as an extension of the information we have been gathering for years and take great pride in sharing it with other fans who have a deep and abiding interest in the American pocket watch," the authors stated.

The authors have been long-time members of the National Association of Watch and Clock Collectors and have been students of horology for many years. Both have specialized in early American and Railroad-type American pocket watches.

The co-authors travel extensively throughout the country to regional meets and shows and keep an up-to-date pulse of the pocket watch market.

Because of the unique knowledge of the market these two co-authors possess, this volume should be considered one of the most authoritative pocket watch references on the market today.

Mr. Shugart resides in Cleveland, Tennessee, and Mr. Engle lives in Louisville, Kentucky.

ADVERTISE IN THE GUIDE

From the Renaissance…to the wristwatch
Experience and Expertise

PATEK PHILIPPE IN BRUSSELS, BELGIUM.

De Greef

24,26 Rue au Beurre,
1000 Brussels,
Belgium.

This watch costs in Belgium 150.000 B frs.
That means at the rate of 40 frs to One dollar: $3.750.
A tax of 33 per cent is included in that price. If exported you
will pay $2.820.

Do ask us for our catalogue, and let us quote our very
competitive prices, you will be surprised.

Telephone 2 511.95.98- Telefax 2 219.46.71.

International Head Office Geneva, Switzerland

Habsburg, Feldman S.A. · 202, route du Grand-Lancy · 1213 Onex/Geneva, Switzerland
Tel. (022) 57 25 30 · Telex 422 757 HFSA CH · Telefax (022) 576 498

Geneva City Location

Habsburg, Feldman · 1, rue du Mont-Blanc · 1201 Geneva

France

Habsburg, Feldman S.A.
Pascale Villiers le Moy
15, avenue Victor-Hugo
75116 Paris
Tel. (1) 4501 7855
Télex 620893
Fax (1) 45006950

Hong Kong

Habsburg, Feldman (HK) Ltd.
Swire House 14th Floor
11 Chater Rd.
Hong Kong
Tel. (5) 266934/8
Telex 65262

United Kingdom

Habsburg, Feldman Ltd.
John Lishawa - Crawley & Asquith
16 Savile Row
London W1X 1AE
Tel. (01) 4392755
Telex 917835 XUSPCE
Fax (01) 4392776

USA

Habsburg, Feldman Inc.
36 East 75th Street
New York, NY 10021
Tel. (212) 5704040
Telex 798271 HABSFELD NY
Fax (212) 5704624

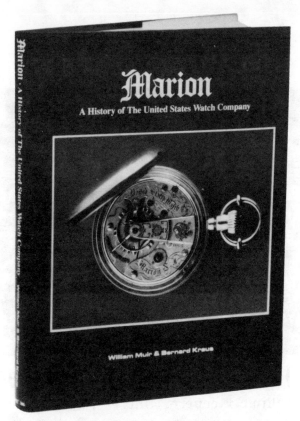

*Hardbound, 8¾" by 11¼", full color dust jack-
et, 256 B/W photos, 216 pages, detailed chronology, bibliography and index.*

The story behind the company that introduced "stemwinding" to
19th century America and built the watch labeled as the most expensive and finest made in this country, makes for that kind of absorbing reading found in a best selling novel.

The work includes a fascinating assortment of watch photos gathered over a period of 8 years from many private collections and notable museums plus the first statistically sound production estimates
for every watch made by the company.

Published as NAWCC Special Publication Number 1 in a limited
edition of 2000 copies, the retail price is $59.50. The NAWCC Mem-
ber price is $34.50. Because annual dues to join NAWCC are $25.00,
a new member can obtain BOTH the MARION book and NAWCC
membership benefits for the total price of $59.50. Order today!!

NAWCC, Inc., 514 Poplar Street, Columbia, PA 17512

Circa 1890 photo of the Lower Creede mining town courtesy Minerals Engineering Co.

The HOUSE OF COLLECTIBLES Series

☐ Please send me the following price guides—
☐ I would like the most current edition of the books listed below.

THE OFFICIAL PRICE GUIDES TO:

☐ 753-3	American Folk Art (ID) 1st Ed.	$14.95
☐ 199-3	American Silver & Silver Plate 5th Ed.	11.95
☐ 513-1	Antique Clocks 3rd Ed.	10.95
☐ 283-3	Antique & Modern Dolls 3rd Ed.	10.95
☐ 287-6	Antique & Modern Firearms 6th Ed.	11.95
☐ 755-X	Antiques & Collectibles 9th Ed.	11.95
☐ 289-2	Antique Jewelry 5th Ed.	11.95
☐ 362-7	Art Deco (ID) 1st Ed.	14.95
☐ 447-X	Arts and Crafts: American Decorative Arts, 1894–1923 (ID) 1st Ed.	12.95
☐ 539-5	Beer Cans & Collectibles 4th Ed.	7.95
☐ 521-2	Bottles Old & New 10th Ed.	10.95
☐ 532-8	Carnival Glass 2nd Ed.	10.95
☐ 295-7	Collectible Cameras 2nd Ed.	10.95
☐ 548-4	Collectibles of the '50s & '60s 1st Ed.	9.95
☐ 740-1	Collectible Toys 4th Ed.	10.95
☐ 531-X	Collector Cars 7th Ed.	12.95
☐ 538-7	Collector Handguns 4th Ed.	14.95
☐ 748-7	Collector Knives 9th Ed.	12.95
☐ 361-9	Collector Plates 5th Ed.	11.95
☐ 296-5	Collector Prints 7th Ed.	12.95
☐ 001-6	Depression Glass 2nd Ed.	9.95
☐ 589-1	Fine Art 1st Ed.	19.95
☐ 311-2	Glassware 3rd Ed.	10.95
☐ 243-4	Hummel Figurines & Plates 6th Ed.	10.95
☐ 523-9	Kitchen Collectibles 2nd Ed.	10.95
☐ 080-6	Memorabilia of Elvis Presley and The Beatles 1st Ed.	10.95
☐ 291-4	Military Collectibles 5th Ed.	11.95
☐ 525-5	Music Collectibles 6th Ed.	11.95
☐ 313-0	Old Books & Autographs 7th Ed.	11.95
☐ 298-1	Oriental Collectibles 3rd Ed.	11.95
☐ 761-4	Overstreet Comic Book 18th Ed.	12.95
☐ 522-0	Paperbacks & Magazines 1st Ed.	10.95
☐ 297-3	Paper Collectibles 5th Ed.	10.95
☐ 744-4	Political Memorabilia 1st Ed.	10.95
☐ 529-8	Pottery & Porcelain 6th Ed.	11.95
☐ 524-7	Radio, TV & Movie Memorabilia 3rd Ed.	11.95
☐ 081-4	Records 8th Ed.	16.95
☐ 763-0	Royal Doulton 6th Ed.	12.95
☐ 280-9	Science Fiction & Fantasy Collectibles 2nd Ed.	10.95
☐ 747-9	Sewing Collectibles 1st Ed.	8.95
☐ 358-9	Star Trek/Star Wars Collectibles 2nd Ed.	8.95
☐ 086-5	Watches 8th Ed.	12.95
☐ 248-5	Wicker 3rd Ed.	10.95

THE OFFICIAL:

☐ 760-6	Directory to U.S. Flea Markets 2nd Ed.	5.95
☐ 365-1	Encyclopedia of Antiques 1st Ed.	9.95
☐ 369-4	Guide to Buying and Selling Antiques 1st Ed.	9.95
☐ 414-3	Identification Guide to Early American Furniture 1st Ed.	9.95
☐ 413-5	Identification Guide to Glassware 1st Ed.	9.95

☐ 412-7	Identification Guide to Pottery & Porcelain 1st Ed.	$9.95
☐ 415-1	Identification Guide to Victorian Furniture 1st Ed.	9.95

THE OFFICIAL (SMALL SIZE) PRICE GUIDES TO:

☐ 309-0	Antiques & Flea Markets 4th Ed.	4.95
☐ 269-8	Antique Jewelry 3rd Ed.	4.95
☐ 085-7	Baseball Cards 8th Ed.	4.95
☐ 647-2	Bottles 3rd Ed.	4.95
☐ 544-1	Cars & Trucks 3rd Ed.	5.95
☐ 519-0	Collectible Americana 2nd Ed.	4.95
☐ 294-9	Collectible Records 3rd Ed.	4.95
☐ 306-6	Dolls 4th Ed.	4.95
☐ 762-2	Football Cards 8th Ed.	4.95
☐ 540-9	Glassware 3rd Ed.	4.95
☐ 526-3	Hummels 4th Ed.	4.95
☐ 279-5	Military Collectibles 3rd Ed.	4.95
☐ 764-9	Overstreet Comic Book Companion 2nd Ed.	4.95
☐ 278-7	Pocket Knives 3rd Ed.	4.95
☐ 527-1	Scouting Collectibles 4th Ed.	4.95
☐ 494-1	Star Trek/Star Wars Collectibles 3rd Ed.	3.95
☐ 088-1	Toys 5th Ed.	4.95

THE OFFICIAL BLACKBOOK PRICE GUIDES OF:

☐ 092-X	U.S. Coins 27th Ed.	4.95
☐ 095-4	U.S. Paper Money 21st Ed.	4.95
☐ 098-9	U.S. Postage Stamps 11th Ed.	4.95

THE OFFICIAL INVESTORS GUIDE TO BUYING & SELLING:

☐ 534-4	Gold, Silver & Diamonds 2nd Ed.	12.95
☐ 535-2	Gold Coins 2nd Ed.	12.95
☐ 536-0	Silver Coins 2nd Ed.	12.95
☐ 537-9	Silver Dollars 2nd Ed.	12.95

THE OFFICIAL NUMISMATIC GUIDE SERIES:

☐ 254-X	The Official Guide to Detecting Counterfeit Money 2nd Ed.	7.95
☐ 257-4	The Official Guide to Mint Errors 4th Ed.	7.95

SPECIAL INTEREST SERIES:

☐ 506-9	From Hearth to Cookstove 3rd Ed.	17.95
☐ 504-2	On Method Acting 8th Printing	6.95

TOTAL	

SEE REVERSE SIDE FOR ORDERING INSTRUCTIONS

━━━━━━━━━━━ **FOR IMMEDIATE DELIVERY** ━━━━━━━━━━━

VISA & MASTER CARD CUSTOMERS

ORDER TOLL FREE!
1-800-638-6460

This number is for orders only; it is not tied into the customer service or business office. Customers not using charge cards must use mail for ordering since payment is required with the order—sorry, no C.O.D.'s.

OR SEND ORDERS TO

THE HOUSE OF COLLECTIBLES
201 East 50th Street
New York, New York 10022

────── POSTAGE & HANDLING RATES ──────

First Book $1.00
Each Additional Copy or Title $0.50

Total from columns on order form. Quantity_____ $_____

☐ Check or money order enclosed $_____ (include postage and handling)

☐ Please charge $_____ to my: ☐ MASTERCARD ☐ VISA

Charge Card Customers Not Using Our Toll Free Number Please Fill Out The Information Below

Account No. _____ Expiration Date_____
                    (all digits)
Signature_____

NAME (please print)_____ PHONE_____

ADDRESS_____ APT. #_____

CITY_____ STATE_____ ZIP_____